A GENERAL

TREATISE ON STATUTES:

THEIR

RULES OF CONSTRUCTION,

AND THE PROPER BOUNDARIES OF LEGISLATION AND
OF JUDICIAL INTERPRETATION.

By Sir Fortunatus Dwarris, Knt.,
B. A., OXFORD, F. R. S., F. S. A.

WITH AMERICAN NOTES AND ADDITIONS,

AND WITH

NOTES AND MAXIMS OF CONSTITUTIONAL AND OF STATUTE CONSTRUCTION.

ALSO

A TREATISE ON CONSTITUTIONAL LIMITATIONS UPON THE
NATIONAL AND STATE LEGISLATIVE POWER;

WITH A CHAPTER ON

PARLIAMENTARY LAW AND PARLIAMENTARY PRIVILEGES.

BY PLATT POTTER, LL. D.,
ONE OF THE JUSTICES OF THE SUPREME COURT OF THE
STATE OF NEW YORK.

"*Optima est lex quæ minimum relinquit arbitrio judicis, optimus judex qui minimum sibi.*"
—Aphorism, 46, Bacon's Works, vol. vii, p. 148.

THE LAWBOOK EXCHANGE, LTD.
Clark, New Jersey

ISBN 9781584779391 (hardcover)
ISBN 9781616191757 (paperback)

Lawbook Exchange edition 2009, 2011

The quality of this reprint is equivalent to the quality of the original work.

THE LAWBOOK EXCHANGE, LTD.

33 Terminal Avenue
Clark, New Jersey 07066-1321

Please see our website for a selection of our other publications
and fine facsimile reprints of classic works of legal history:
www.lawbookexchange.com

Library of Congress Cataloging-in-Publication Data

Dwarris, Fortunatus, Sir, 1786-1860.
 A general treatise on statutes : their rules of construction, and the proper
boundaries of legislation and of judicial interpretation : with American notes
and additions, and with notes and maxims of constitutional and of statute
construction : also a treatise on constitutional limitations upon the national
and state legislative power ; with a chapter on parliamentary law and
parliamentary privileges / by Sir Fortunatus Dwarris [and] by Platt Potter.
    p. cm.
 Originally published: Albany, N.Y. : W. Gould & sons, 1871.
 ISBN-13: 978-1-58477-939-1 (cloth : alk. paper)
 ISBN-10: 1-58477-939-X (cloth : alk. paper)
 1. Statutes--United States. 2. Statutes--Great Britain. 3. Law--Interpretation
and construction. 4. Constitutional law--United States. 5. Parliamentary
practice--United States. I. Potter, Platt, 1800-1891. II. Title.
 KF425.D9 2009
 348.73'2--dc22

                                                                2008043997

Printed in the United States of America on acid-free paper

A GENERAL

TREATISE ON STATUTES:

THEIR

RULES OF CONSTRUCTION,

AND THE PROPER BOUNDARIES OF LEGISLATION AND
OF JUDICIAL INTERPRETATION.

BY SIR FORTUNATUS DWARRIS, KNT.,

B. A., OXFORD, F. R. S., F. S. A.

WITH AMERICAN NOTES AND ADDITIONS,

AND WITH

NOTES AND MAXIMS OF CONSTITUTIONAL AND OF STATUTE CONSTRUCTION.

ALSO

A TREATISE ON CONSTITUTIONAL LIMITATIONS UPON THE
NATIONAL AND STATE LEGISLATIVE POWER;

WITH A CHAPTER ON

PARLIAMENTARY LAW AND PARLIAMENTARY PRIVILEGES.

BY PLATT POTTER, LL. D.,

ONE OF THE JUSTICES OF THE SUPREME COURT OF THE
STATE OF NEW YORK.

"Optima est lex quæ minimum relinquit arbitrio judicis, optimus judex qui minimum sibi."
—Aphorism, 46, Bacon's Works, vol. vii, p. 148.

ALBANY:
WILLIAM GOULD & SON,
LAW BOOKSELLERS AND PUBLISHERS.
1871.

PREFACE.

THE republication of the Treatise of "Dwarris on Statutes," requires no apology. It is a standard work of the highest authority, acknowledged by all the courts of this country, as well as in England. It was out of print; could not be supplied at any price, though greatly demanded. No law library, can be regarded as complete, without it. Indeed, the student, who desires to possess a fair knowledge of the jurisprudence of the state and nation of which the statute law forms so striking and material a portion, will remain deficient in the necessary qualifications for an honorble profession, if found wanting in the proper knowledge which this work supplies, of the recognized parts and divisions of statutes, and of the different rules of construction and interpretation by which the different characters of statutes are governed. An applicant for admission to the bar of the state, or nation, should be debarred, who shall have advanced no further in the science of the law, than to suppose the rule of interpretation of all statutes was one uniform rule; that a *remedial* and a *penal* statute were to be construed alike; or who could not answer to the distinctions between, prospective and retrospective, public and private, enabling and disabling, enlarging and restraining, affirmative and negative statutes, and to the various other known divisions, as well as of the particular rules of construction applicable to each division; and, as applicable also to the various parts of the same statute; to the title; the preamble; the enacting part; the clauses; provisos and exceptions; and to the effect which each part bears upon the whole, and upon its construction. This treatise may therefore be regarded as elementary, and the necessary complement to the professional life of the lawyer.

This republication, has preserved all the original text of its author which has application to the division and construction of statutes, and has omitted only such portions of it, as relate exclusively to the institutions of Great Britain, their origin and history; the forms of summoning parliament; the composition of that body the degrees of nobility and the powers possessed respectively by each rank and order in that body.

In the volume here presented, the text of Dwarris will be found distinguished from that of the American author, by being in what is called solid printed matter without quotation marks; that of the American additions, by being in open leaded matter.

A republication of this work in America, would have failed of meeting public expectation had it omitted to add, to it, the American authority upon the same subject, or to notice such changes as our different theory of government, and the advance which general legal intelligence has made necessary. He has therefore added, by way of original text and commentary, as well as by notes, what he regards as the American law, in the enactment and construction of statutes.

Nor could a treatise upon American statutes, approach to any degree of practical use here, without contrasting the power of enacting statutes in this country with that of the mother country whose statutes, as well as common law, we have so extensively copied and adopted. To do this, it also became necessary to show the source and extent of the law making power in this country, and to introduce into the work, the effect of that new feature in legislative power, not known in England; of legislatures restrained and limited in their powers to enact laws by written constitutions, which, are the fundamental, superior and controlling authority. It also became necessary to show the effect of laws passed by legislatures, in cases where the legislatures have exceeded the constitutional limits.

The necessary distinction between statutes enacted by legislatures under restricted constitutional power, and those which are not, seemed to call for the American view of the statute construction, as distinguished from the English; and this has been attempted in this work. First, by a limited commentary upon the theory of American constitutional governments. Second, upon the limitations and restraints upon the legislative power; and, Third, upon the rights, immunities and privileges of the citizen, secured to him by these written constitutions, national and state.

These are divided into appropriate chapters, containing the rules recognized in American jurisprudence, for the protection, as well as the limitation of the constitutional securities of the citizen.

The limits of this work would not admit of an elaborate commentary upon the national constitution, like that of Justice Story, in two volumes; nor one extended enough to embrace an equally elaborate treatise upon thirty-six several and varying state constitutions, by showing the disparities between them, and the differences of state policy and jurisprudence under them respectively; but it is believed that the work is comprehensive enough, with the references it contains to judicial decisions and to standard legal treatises of established authority, to make it a convenient guide to the student who desires to extend his knowledge of constitutional law, and their limitations; to inspire him to seek the more elaborate and profound treatises upon the same subjects; and to present in a brief space, such elementary constitutional principles as are common to all the state governments, as well as to the national, in their protection to the citizen.

In doing this, the author has endeavored, as a general rule, to state established principles and adjudications, rather than his own opinions of the law; and he has not omitted to avail himself to some extent, of the views of those whom he regards as the ablest of jurists, commentators and authors that have presented their own views to the world. To Marshall, Kent, Story, and others, as jurists and authors; and including Smith, Sedgwick and Cooley as writers; to a greater or less extent upon the same subjects, he is indebted for many of his views contained in this work, which, in some respects, may be regarded as an abridgement of the more elaborate treatises; in other respects, while he has ventured to differ in some particulars from those authors, he has not done so without diffidence, nor without support, by reference to the opinions of others, whose authority he has cited to that end. Neither the subject of construction of statutes, nor that of constitutional power and limitations, has yet been exhausted by what has been written thereon. It is an extended field; and each day, through our courts, new views of construction, new rules of application, and new developments of constitutional power, or of restriction, are judicially promulgated; so that new questions are arising, which, if they do not absolutely demand new treatises on the same subject, will at least present temptations to other writers, to enter the same field.

There has also been added to this work, a chapter on parliamentary law, including parliamentary, or legislative privileges. We have no elementary, or other treatise upon, or applicable to that subject in this state, except a small compilation from Jefferson's manual and from the practice of legislative bodies, containing rules of proceeding in the legislature as to the order and government of the two houses, and the rights, privileges, and duties of the President of the senate, the Speaker of the house, and to the members of each house as among themselves, in the transaction of legislative duties, called "Croswell's Manual." As is claimed, and admitted, the common law of parliament, including the law of legislative privilege, in the state of New York, is almost identical with that of England, and has been, ever since the day of the statute of 13 Geo. 3, of which, the Revised Statutes of this state upon the same subject are substantially a transcript. He has therefore briefly but carefully compiled from the most authentic sources, the modern English common law of the two houses of parliament, which is believed to be the law in force here; so far as the same can be made applicable to our system. To demonstrate that modern English parliamentary law is now identical with that of this state, we have, in that chapter, shown the ancient, as well as the modern, and the repudiation of the former, subsequent to the day of the statutes which regulate it, and have cited as authority, the bold and independent adjudications of the judiciary, as well as parliament itself, against these ancient parliamentary assumptions.

If an apology is needful for the imperfections of this work, it may be stated that the whole labor has been performed, in such leisure hours during a period of less than two years, as he has been able to snatch from most pressing official duties, and even those hours, greatly interrupted by answering to the public demands. He cannot therefore hope to have escaped the commission of errors, nor to have avoided defects.

In the full belief, that the republication of the work of a standard author, will contribute to the diffusion of knowledge, and to public good; and in the hope that the other topics discussed, may contribute something to the same end, and, that even fair criticism, may discover in the work, sufficient of practical utility to justify its publication, is the ardent wish of the author.

SCHENECTADY, June, 1871.

CONTENTS.

TABLE OF CASES

REFERRED TO IN THIS VOLUME.

3

A GENERAL TREATISE ON STATUTES.

CHAPTER I.

INTRODUCTORY COMMENTARY.

OF THE DEFINITION OF STATUTES, ANCIENT AND MODERN. THEIR
ORIGIN, INCIDENTS, &c.

STATUTE LAWS, their definition, origin, manner of enactment,
forms, authentication, promulgation, force, interpretation, limitations, variety and incidents, are the subject of this work.[1]

History, as well as experience, has taught us, that in every civilized community, however high or low it may rank in the scale o
intelligence, there is an absolute necessity for the existence of a
power for the administration of justice. This necessity is so absolute and indispensable, that all social institutions, whatever may be
their object, seek to provide some recognized authority to admin-

NOTE 1.—While the design of this work is to present to the profession, an
American treatise on statutes and constitutional law, the labor assumed is greatly
relieved, and the performance of the duty, (it is believed) more satisfactorily discharged, by adopting, as far as it is practicable, a work of approved and standard authority, in all the courts of England and America, upon the subject of
statutes. There is, perhaps, no writer, in either country, whose work upon the
construction of statutes, has been more universally regarded by the courts and
bar, as authority, than the "Treatise upon Statutes, by Sir Fortunatis Dwarris,
Knt. B. A. of Oxford, F. R. S., F. S. A. of England." The text of this author, in that
part of his treatise, which has application to statutes generally, will be adopted
in this work. This will supply an almost importunate demand by the profession, for a republication in America, of that standard, and greatly desired work.
To this original of Dwarris, will be added by original text, and also by notes of
authority, such views of American law on the construction of statutes, as can be
brought within the scope of the work, with American authority upon Constitutional limitations, and legislative powers : and also, views of construction upon
such subjects of statute law as have no existence in England, or such as remain
untouched by the English author, with a chapter upon parliamentary law and the
law of parliamentary privilege.

5

ister justice. It requires uniform rules ; rules which shall be promulgated, and known by all the members of such social community. It becomes a necessity, which lies at the foundation of all civil society, otherwise, each individual of the community would attempt to administer justice for himself.

These uniform rules, so adopted by a community, are to a great extent, the rules of conduct by which its members are to be governed, and are therefore denominated its laws; and laws are regarded as the rules of right ; as the measure of justice between man and man ; and are generally found existing to a greater or less extent in an authentic form, either written or printed. But, in order to give binding force to laws, nothing is more certain than the indispensable necessity of *Government*. And it is equally undeniable, "that wherever and howsoever government is instituted, the people must cede to it some of their natural rights, in order to vest it with requisite powers." *a*

Government, implies the power of making laws. It is essential to the idea of a law, that it be attended with a sanction ; or in other words, a penalty or punishment for disobedience. If there be no penalty annexed to disobedience, the commands which pretend to be laws, will in fact amount to nothing more than advice or recommendation. This would not be government. Among the necessary powers of government, is that of legislation, which is the power in the government to make laws, not only, but to make the laws so made, the means of executing the legislative power.

"A law by the very meaning of the term, includes supremacy. It is a rule, which those by whom it is presented are bound to observe. This results from every political association. If individuals enter into a state of society, the laws of that society must be the supreme regulator of their conduct. If a number of political societies enter into a larger political society, the laws which the latter may enact pursuant to the powers entrusted to it by the terms of the compact, or constitution, must necessarily be supreme over the societies so united, and over the individuals of which they are composed. It would otherwise be a mere treaty, dependent upon the good faith of the parties, and not a govern-

a Federalist, Letter 2.

ment, which is only another word for political power and supremacy," a

The great aim and object then, of the political institution called government, is to provide for the safety and happiness of the society, and the individual members of which it is composed, and ustice is the end to be secured. It is government that secures the weaker against the violence and oppression of the stronger, and secures itself, by the possession of the power conferred by all.

When laws are made, and promulgated in their most authoritative form, namely, by legislation, they are then denominated statutes. Other authorities of law, are usages and customs; these are supposed to be based upon the precepts of natural right, and are also intended to be the measure of justice.

Statute law, by American definitions, is an act which is prescribed by the legislature, or supreme power of the State; it extends its binding force to all the citizens or subjects of that State. b

This definition, applies as well to the State in its national capacity, as to the several sovereign states, whose union compose the national body politic. These statutes, State and National, are equally the expressions in writing, of the sovereign or legislative will, known in ancient and elementary law books, as "*leges Scripta*," c or written laws, as distinguished from the "*leges non Scripta*," the unwritten or common law. The latter, owe their binding force to the principles of justice as declared by the courts, and to long usage and consent of the nation, or people. The former, to the positive command or declaration of the supreme power.

Statute law, in a republican form of government, is commonly applied to the acts of a legislative body, consisting of representatives chosen by the people. In monarchies, they are the written will of the sovereign power, whether expressed by absolute will of the king alone, or by a union of wills, of king, nobles and commons, when the commons act in a representative character. When expressed by the king alone, they are sometimes called *edicts, decrees, ordinances, rescripts, &c.*

a Federalist, No. 31.　　b 1 Kent Com. 447; 2d id. 456.
c 1 Black Com. 85.

Statutes are of both Divine,[2] and human origin; the former, having God, the latter man for their authority.

It is not within the scope or object of this work to discuss the question of the true origin of governments in either their ethical or political bearing; nor whether governments are based upon divine or human authority, but only assume that every duly organized government possesses the power to ordain and establish the laws by which its subjects shall be controlled; and confine this treatise chiefly to the subject of the written or statute laws.

The municipal laws of nations and of communities, are therefore, in their origin and intrinsic force, no other than the rules of being, given to man by God. But as the heavenly wisdom must flow through the impure channel of humanity, it is necessarily mingled with the provisions of human invention, and there must necessarily be some conflict with the primary perfection. Indeed, the divine rule itself, provides for human modifications. So that laws may be adapted to the particular circumstances, views, and wants of the subjects to whom, and to whose interests they are to be applied, and whether human modifications accord with the original right and perfection or not, they are alike *permitted* as laws; and become so essential to human association, that men cannot live in communities without them.

Human laws, which are intended to be an approach toward the perfection and majesty of the law of God, are entitled to a corresponding dignity and respect; they are entitled to the strongest affection; and should be enshrined in the hearts of a people who are the subjects of the government, and whose public sentiment they are supposed to express. They cannot be held in too high

NOTE 2.—" Because they had not executed my judgments; but had despised my *statutes;* and had polluted my Sabbaths, and their eyes were after their fathers idols. Wherefore I gave them *statutes,* also that were not good." Ezekiel 20, 24. If the wicked restore the pledge, give again that he had robbed, walk in the *statutes* of life without committing iniquity, he shall surely live, he shall not die. Ezekiel 33, 15. The *statutes* of the Lord are right, rejoicing the heart. Psalms 19, 9. Thou comest down also upon Mount Sinai, and speakest with them from Heaven, and gavest them right judgements, true laws, good *statutes* and commands; and madest known to them thy holy Sabbath, and commanded them precepts, *statutes* and laws by the hand of Moses thy servant, Nehemiah 9, 13, 14. See also Exodus 15, 26. Deut. 6, 17; 2 Kings 17, 15; 1 Chron. 29, 19; Micah 6, 16; Psalms 18, 22: Id. 119, 12, 16, 23, 26, 33, 54, 64, 68, 71, 117.

honor, or too jealously guarded and preserved, as the safeguard of all peace and security.

It is certain that no human authority can rightfully infringe or abrogate the smallest particle of natural or divine law ; and yet we cannot expect that all acts of legislators will, or can be, entirely good, or ethically perfect ; but if their goodness and binding quality in this respect, is to be determined by the subjects upon whom they are intended to operate, government, and subordination would cease ; there must, therefore, be magistrates clothed with the power to enjoin their authority.

When therefore, the supreme power of a community decrees anything which may even be injurious to one, or to a few of its subjects, it is their duty to acquiesce, and not to disturb the peace of society; attempt to subvert the constitution of their country, or to diminish the veneration for its laws, which would be bringing a greater evil upon the whole community.

This expresses what is generally understood to be the signification of law, to wit: "A rule of action dictated by some superior being."a It will therefore be our duty in this work to consider only human laws so dictated. Justinian, the great law-giver, reduced the principles of law to three general precepts. *First*, that we should live honestly. *Second*, that we should hurt nobody. And third, that we should render to every one his due. b This includes the whole doctrine of the law.

Statute law, is sometimes by law writers included in the more' general term, "Municipal Law," though this extends it to states or nations. But it is well defined by Blackstone, under the head of municipal law, as being "a rule of civil conduct prescribed by the supreme power in a state, commanding what is right, and prohibiting what is wrong."c Municipal law, in its technical meaning, also rests for its authority upon judicial decisions. d

But Chancellor Kent has given a more accurate definition of municipal law. He says: "It is composed of written, and unwritten, or of statute and common law. Statute law being the express written will of the legislature, rendered authentic by certain prescribed forms and solemnities."e Statute law becomes

a 1 Black, Com. 39.
b 2 Just. 1, 13.
c 1 Com. 44.
d 2 Kent's Com. 456.
e 1 Com. 447.

municipal, when its force is confined to a particular community, district or State.

It may be said, that a nations progress in morality, philosophy, letters, arts, science, trade and commerce, civilization and refinement, may be pretty accurately ascertained from their written, or statute laws. Their spirit, should, and doubtless does, enter into the language in which they are drawn. Just in proportion as these laws are grounded in natural justice, and speak a language, evincing moral and intellectual progress, they exalt and adorn the character of her people.

In our own, as in every system of jurisprudence, the statute law forms but a part of the law of the system; and it may be safely asserted, that no system of jurisprudence would be perfect, that should be confined to legislative enactments. It is not within the power of the human mind, or in any combination of minds, to foresee and provide rules beforehand, to regulate the conduct of men in every change and variety of circumstances and conditions, so that when individuals neglect, or violate rules thus prescribed, the departure from right, finds its exact description, and finds a recognized rule to be applied to it, which shall restore the legal relations of the parties.

Therefore it follows, that the laws of every community, consists of two elements. *First*, those rules of conduct which are introduced by the law making power in an express and positive form; which control the particular cases and circumstances to which they relate or describe, and which are called statutes, made by legislation; and *Second*, those precepts of natural right which are not superceded by statute law, and which, therefore, remain in full force as to all other circumstances and cases, and which forever continue in force as the measure of justice until superceded or changed by legislation; and while in force, controlled by the rudiments of legal science and the profoundest of human wisdom and experience, remain at all times the highest security and protection of the citizen.

Perhaps in no feature of a nation's character, more than in her written laws, is her moral and industrial character made manifest. They indicate the progress of her civilized development by their relative fitness and simplicity; and they afford materials for forming a judgment as to her lettered skill and intellective wisdom. Next to inspired revelation, the book which contains a nations laws, is most important. From this, the citizen learns the extent of his rights, and the nature of his political and social duties. In a country which has adopted it as one of its maxims, that "ignorance of law excuses nobody," it should be the aim of the lawmaker, that its statutes should be drawn in language clear and simple; that their meaning should be plain and unmistakable; and if ambiguity or doubt do seem to appear; its maxims and rules of interpretation should be formed in the soundest wisdom.

Of all the degrees of authority which man exercises over man, that of legislation is the most august and supreme. Statutes, generally, are made in affirmance of natural rights and duties, and are declarative of them. Sometimes, they are positive regulations for political reasons, for matters otherwise in themselves indifferent.a In an early stage of civil society, when laws were few and defective, and the execution of them feeble and precarious, much was necessarily left to the authority of the sovereign power; and this sovereign power was the king, who not only interpreted and administered the law, but explained and adopted it as a remedy to an existing case. Sometimes lords and prelates were called in, to aid in deliberation, when the king was overtasked, but all petitions for relief were then usually addressed to the king.

It was soon felt to be too much, "that the king should make, or even alter laws of his own mere pleasure, to suit his own private purposes."b It began first to be disputed, when the laws, or the alterations thereof, affected unfavorably the persons, or estates of the great barons, but it now excites no surprise, that in this rude age, the limits of executive, legislative and judicial authority were left undefined, as they were all alike combined in the person of the sovereign; and it is believed that it was the love of pomp and parade; a desire to increase his supports in this display; and to gratify this pride, that induced the sovereign to call these great chief barons into a council, or parliament. But the origin of parliaments is not a part of this work.

a 1 Smith's Com. Cha. 1 & 5.   b 1 Reeve's History of English Law, 85,

In an American treatise upon statutes, it will not be practically useful to devote much space in giving the origin, or in tracing the history and progress of the statute laws of England, though it is from that country that many of our statutes are borrowed; and it may indeed be conceded, that many of our wisest enactments are found to be nearly accurate transcripts of English statutes.

Though modern English writers now concur in defining their statutes to be "the written will of Parliament, composed of King, (Queen) Lords and Commons," it has been a question greatly mooted in history, as to the period of time when statutes, that are now expressly held to be such, were first passed in that country. The earliest statutes extant *in printed books*, are those of Henry III. *a.* During those of this reign, are *Magna Charta*, and *Charta de Foresta.*

. Before that period, what was sometimes called statutes, but more commonly known by the name of "*assise*," or "*constitutiones*," were mere ordinances of the king, who usually provided and ordained them. This was sometimes done by the advice of his council; sometimes the advice and consent of barons and dignified ecclesiastics were added; and in some instances, the consent of the whole commonalty was expressed. *b*

There is great diversity of opinion among English authors, and of course, much uncertainty as to the fact, as to the extent of the powers that were exercised at an early day by the Kings of England, with, or without the aid of parliament. Whether the lords, spiritual and temporal aided in framing statutes and ordinances, or were merely called in as councillors of the sovereign, is not quite certain. Ruffhead, in his preface to the English statutes, asserts, that down to the 23d of Edward the First, so little regard was paid to the authority of the commons, that their assent was not deemed essential to the passage of a law; and that Peers were considered merely counsellors; that the high authority of passing laws or ordinances was exercisd by the king, or by the king and his justices. Sir Edward Coke, is of opinion, that provisions made by two branches only, of the legislature, were *ordinances*, and not statutes; that *statutes* were designed for perma-

a Dwarris ch vii.   *b* Id.

nent law, and *ordinances* were merely temporary experiments, framed with a view to future and occasional amendment. *a*   But it appears, that in the second year of Henry the Fifth, the commons being dissatisfied with the limited influence allowed to them by the king, presented to him a strong memorial, then claiming, that it had ever been their freedom, that no statute or law should be made without their assent.   To this, it was answered by the king, "that the king, of his grace, especially granteth, that from henceforth, nothing be enacted to the petitions of his commons, contrary to their asking, whereby they should be bound without their assent; saving alway, our liege lord his prerogative, to grant and deny as he should please, such petitions." *b*

This petition of the commons, and the response of the king, was regarded as a complete change; and was claimed to be the first victory on the part of the commons.   Their power from thence, became an integral and indispensable part of the legislature, which they had long been laboring to establish, and which they now regarded as firmly consolidated and effectually secured against any future violations of their legislative rights.

When these councils became characterized by the name of parliament, it then became necessary to devise a plan for authenticating, preserving, and transmitting their decisions, or acts.   This was done by entering them upon what was called the rolls of parliament, which contained an account of all proceedings, legislative and judicial.   It was not until the reign of Edward III, that the constitutional principle was established, that the king and two houses of parliament in conjunction, were required in the enactment of statutes, and that they in conjunction, possessed exclusively the power of legislation.

After the commencement of the reign of Henry III, statutes began to be published in solemn form, with captions, which began: "Our Lord the King, etc., at his Parliament holden at, etc., by the advice and assent of the Lords, Spiritual and Temporal, and at the special request of the Commons of the realm being in the same Parliament, hath caused to be made divers statutes and ordinances," etc.

A reference, to this extent, to these English statutes and ordi-

a 4 Inst. 26.   *b* Dwarris, 37.

nances, seems to be necessary, in order to show what was their view of statutes; when our colonies first enacted laws, while yet subject to the British government; and also, at the time of our separation from them, and since; because the judicial interpretation given at that time by English law writers to statutes, was a part of the common law, which we also borrowed from that country, and then adopted as our own; and except in so far as we have wrought changes in this common law either by legislation or by finding it inapplicable to our changed form of government, and substituted changes more suited to the condition of a free people, we still follow in practice, the interpretations of those venerated sages of the English law whose writings we regard as standard authority.*

These law writers, and also distinguished jurists, inform us, that much of the common law which we so borrowed and adopted, is nothing else but ancient statutes and ordinances worn out by time; a that all our law began by the consent of the legislature; that many of those things that we take for the common law, were undoubtedly acts of parliament, though not now to be found of record. b

It would hardly be profitable in this work, nor within its design, to trace the antiquity of the statutes of other nations than that of England, for the reason that our early laws are in a large degree copied from those of that country, or adopted into our system.

The scholar, or curious student of the history of early legislation who desires further research into this branch of law-making power, is referred to the twelve tables of the Roman republic, to their frequent revisions of statute laws, and their forms of codification; especially as we have adopted into our jurisprudence some ideas derived from the civil law.

a Wilmot, ch. j. 2 Wils. R. 348.
b Hale's History of the Common Law, 66.

Note 3.—Where the English statutes are adopted into our own legislation, the known and settled construction of them, by the courts of law, is considered as silently incorporated into the acts; or is received with all the weight of authority. Pennoch v. Dialogue, 2 Peters, 2. It is proper, that the construction given to statutes in the country where they have been enacted, should follow the same statutes when adopted here. Cathcart v. Robinson, 5 Peters, 263.

The common law of England, as modified by positive enactment, together with the statute laws which were in force at the time of the emigration of the colonists, became in fact, the common law, rather than the common and statute law of the colony. The *statute* law of the mother country, therefore, when introduced into the colony of New York, by common consent, (because it was applicable to the colonists in their new situation and not by legislative enactment,) became the common law of the province.*a*

Such parts of the common law, as with acts of the legislature of the colony of New York, formed the law of the colony on the 19th of April, 1775, which have not been altered, continue the law of the State, subject to alteration by the legislature. Such parts as are repugnant to the constitution, are abrogated. Const. of N. Y. 1777 § 35; Const. of N. Y. of 1822, Art. 7, § 13; Const. of N. Y. 1846, Art. 1, § 17.

New statutes in America, became necessary at once, upon our separation from the mother country. The old customs and modes of business in England, were in many respects, unsuited to our new condition, and theory of government. But such of the English statutes as guarded and secured to the people at large, and to the individual, rights against the usurpations of power, were re-enacted here, with but slight changes. Among these, are the *habeas corpus*, the statute of frauds, the statute of wills, etc. The right of petition, and bill of rights were secured by the fundamental law, the written constitutions.

The best English definition of a *statute*, to be collected from approved authors, is "such acts as are made by the king's majesty, by and with the advice and consent of the lords spiritual and temporal, and commons in parliament assembled." This is the written will of parliament.

Our American statutes are made by like solemnities of form, and become the express written will of the legislature; and they are rendered authentic by prescribed constitutional and legal forms and requirements.

While it is true that our American legislatures, are in a great degree, modelled after the parliament of Great Britain; and, that the usages and customs of legislation here, are derived from the

a Bogardus v. Trinity church, 4 Paige, 498, 1 Mass. R, 60; 2 id. 534.

parliamentary, or common law of England; we are met at once
with a striking contrast, between the powers which may be exercised by an American legislature, and those which are exercised
by the British parliament.

" The authority of the English parliament, in the enactment of
laws has no bounds; it is transcendant. It is possessed of sovereign and uncontrollable power."   By the constitution of that
kingdom, this power, which is there despotic, runs without limit,
and rises above all control. The validity of an act of parliament
cannot be drawn in question by the judicial department." *a*

" It hath (says Sir Wm. Blackstone) sovereign and uncontrollable authority in the making, confirming, enlarging, restraining,
abrogating, repealing, reviving and expounding of laws, concerning matters of all possible denominations, ecclesiastical or temporal, civil, military, maritime or criminal. This being the place
where that absolute despotic power, which must in all governments reside somewhere, is entrusted by the constitution of these
kingdoms. All mischiefs and grievances, operations and remedies,
that transcend the ordinary course of the laws, are within the
reach of this extraordinary tribunal. It can regulate, or new
model the succession to the crown; as was done in the reign of
Henry VIII, and William III. It can alter the established religion of the land; as was done in a variety of instances in the
reign of Henry VIII, and his three children. It can change and
create afresh, even the constitution of the kingdom, and of the
parliaments themselves; as was done by the act of union, and
the several statutes for triennial and septennial elections. It can,
in short, do everything that is not naturally impossible; and therefore, some have not scrupled to call its power by a figure, rather
too bold; the omnipotence of parliament." *b*

Though they boast of a constitution, they have no written constitution. What is called the British constitution, consists of
the fundamentals of British polity, laid down in customs, precedents, decisions, and statutes. The common law in it, is a
far greater portion of it, even than the statutes of parliament.
Their constitution depends upon the caprice of parliament. It
can be changed by them; and it is changed by them from time to

a Dwarris   *b* 1 Black. Com. 161.

time to meet emergencies. They have actually, in several instances, changed by legislative acts, some of the most fundamental articles of government, and yet in no country, are the constitutional principles, of civil and political liberty, more discussed; and held to be sacred, than in Great Britain.

With us in America it is different. Such strong expressions of power, is entirely inapplicable to the idea of legislative authority in American States. This difference springs from the different theories upon which the two governments rest. In England, parliament is recognized as possessing the sovereign power of the country. The American legislature possesses but a portion of the sovereign power. The sovereignty is in the people; and the legislatures whom they create, can only discharge a trust, (guarded with restrictions, well defined) of which the people have made them the depository. When in a republican, or other form of government, it is asserted that the natural and necessary source of civil authority is in the people; it is intended that this is so, until the government has been formed; for before the formation of a government, it cannot be said the people have political rights. So that primarily, it may be asserted, that sovereignty resides in God himself, who is the source of all order, power, right, and authority. "By me kings reign, and princess decree justice;"*a* and St. Paul instructs us, that "there is no power but of God, that the powers that be, are ordained of God."*b* As therefore, the Deity himself, does not condescend, directly to administer the government of States; those upon whom the sovereignty rests, are His depositories of the civil power. "There is one law-giver."*c* It is in this qualified sense then, that we speak of human, or governmental sovereignty, and it is this sense that we say in our republican form of government, that the people are the source of power.

The national and State governments, all have constitutions reduced to writing. These constitutions emanate from the people, who are the original source of all political power. The people in their sovereign capacity, ordain and establish this fundamental law, which is paramount to the power of the legislature, and is the supreme law of the land. The powers of the legisla-

a 1 Proverbs 8, 15.   *b* 2 Romans 13, 1.   *c* 3 James 4, 12.

ture are derived from the constitution, and are subordinate to it. They are but one branch of the sovereignty, their acts depend upon, are limited by, and must be conformable to the constitution. Every act of the legislature repugnant to this written fundamental law, is absolutely void.

Notwithstanding the difference in power and effect, as we have shown, between the statutes passed by the English parliament, and those passed by the legislature of the American States, the law of interpretation of statutes in most respects, is in both countries, substantially in accord and harmony.

NOTE.—It is in regard to this harmony of views, and to the presentation of variances, wherever they are found to exist between the laws of the two countries, that much of this work will be devoted.

CHAPTER II.

GENERAL INTERPRETATION OF STATUTES. PUBLIC AND PRIVATE STATUTES. MANNER OF AUTHENTICATION OF STATUTES. DISTINCTION BETWEEN AMERICAN AND ENGLISH STATUTES. OF LEGISLATIVE POWER—ENGLISH AND AMERICAN. OF JUDICIAL POWER.

THE consideration, and the interpretation of American statutes, enacted under written constitutions which limit the legislative power, presents another, and a distinct branch of law for examination, not known to the law of England, and is not therefore, necessarily treated of by Dwarris and other English writers. *Particular* rules of interpretation, laid down by distinguished authors on municipal and civil law, as well in England as elsewhere, including American law, will be found in a subsequent chapter. Before proceeding to the general consideration of the different divisions and characteristics of statutes, a few *general* rules for their interpretation may not be inappropriate.

Professor Lieber in his work on "Legal and Political Hermeneuties,"*a* lays down this sound proposition; "that the very basis of all interpretation is, that no sentence or form of words can have more than one true sense." So that a statute enacted by the legislature, like the utterances of an individual, or of any other body of individuals, in the use of words, does so, to convey some certain meaning; and to find their precise meaning, is the whole object of interpretation. If words used, are so employed, that they are capable of two meanings, equally sensible, it amounts to such an absurdity, that it is equivalent to having no meaning at all. "Even if a man use words, from kindness or malice, in such a way that they may signify one or the other thing, according to the view of him to whom they are addressed, the utterer's meaning is not two-fold; his meaning is, simply, *not*

a Chap. 4, § 2.

to express his opinion." This principle of interpretation, may with equal propriety, be carried into a statute, where from its letter, such must be held to be its design.

In no case of human life in which we are called upon to act, to apply rules, or to understand what others say, can we dispense with common sense, and good faith; a but they are peculiarly requisite in interpretation, because its object is, to discover something that is doubtful, obscure, veiled; which, therefore, may admit of different explanations. If without common sense we may make even of strict syllogism, an instrument, apparently, to prove absurdities, how much more are those two ingredients of all honesty, necessary in interpretation. Common sense and good faith, are the leading and principal characteristics of all interpretation. The object must not be, to bend, twist, or shape the text until it can be forced into the mould of preconceived ideas; but simply and solely, to fix upon the true sense, whatever that may be.

Good faith in interpretation, means, that we conscientiously desire to arrive at truth; that we honestly use all means to do so; and that we strictly adhere to it; when known to us, it means, the shunning of subterfuges, quibbles and political shuffling; it means that we take words fairly as they were meant.

If good faith be not the guiding star to direct in the construc tion of solemn instruments, like constitutions and statutes, no human wisdom can devise an instrument of this character that may not be interpreted so as to effect any thing but that for which it was intended. We gain nothing by verbosity, or a minute enumeration of details; for the instrument, especially if it be a constitution, is to embrace all branches, and to hold good for many generations. If we attempt then to detail for every thing before hand, we only impede, fetter and obstruct. This has been fully proved by experience; if on the other hand the instrument contains only the great principles and general outlines of the power conferred, then faithless interpretation has free play. Constitutions are useful and indispensible for the clear understanding of citizens on the most important subjects affecting their rights; to give them a fair and intelligent knowledge of the all important elements of their rights to civil liberty; of the relation

a Liebers Political Ethics, vol. I, Book 1, chap. 6.

of the citizen to society in the aggregate, the State; and to furnish an independent judiciary a fulcrum, to rest its lever upon against laws hostile to that true relation of the individual to the State; laws, which might otherwise oppress him.

"It is not constitutions that make liberty. Liberty is not secured by a certain number of words written on parchment. The parchment, with its ink upon it, may be eaten by the worms; it may be torn to shreds by any daring hand; but if an independent judiciary shall pronounce the solemn expression of its true spirit, as the law of the nation, or of the State, the living words of their judicial interpretation, shall be perpetuated."a

Let all such judicial determinations bear the impress of good faith, with liberal views of construction in favor of civil liberty. "Let everything that is in favor of power be closely construed; everything in favor of the security of the citizen, and the protection of the individual, be liberally and comprehensively interpreted; for the simple reason, that power is power, and therefore able to take care of itself, as well as tending by its nature to increase, while the citizen may need protection."

For the same reason says Mr. Lieber,a ought we always to be ready to construe comprehensively, in favor of the independence of the judiciary, and against the executive, because, it is all important that the judiciary be independent, while it has none of those many influential means of the executive; no pageantry; no honors to bestow; no salaries to dispense; no army, navy, or grants of land at their disposal. It rests only on opinion, a mighty power indeed, in an honest and faithful administration of its department of the government. Hence it should be shielded."

All new laws, though penned with the greatest technical skill, and passed upon the fullest and most mature deliberation, are considered as more or less obscure and equivocal until their meaning be fixed and ascertained by a series of particular discussions and adjudications. Besides the obscurity arising from the complexity of the objects and the imperfection of human faculties; the medium through which the conceptions of men are conveyed to each other adds a fresh embarrassment, the use of words is to express ideas. Perspicuity, therefore, requires not

a Lieber's Political Hermeneutics, chap. 6, § 10.   b Id.

7

only that the ideas should be distinctly formed, but that they should be expressed by words distinctly and exclusively appropriated to them. But no language is so copious as to supply words and phrases for every complex idea, or so correct as not to include many, equivocally denoting different ideas. Hence it must happen; that however accurately objects may be discriminated in themselves; and however accurately the discrimination may be considered; the definition of them may be rendered inaccurate; by the inaccuracy of the terms in which it is delivered. And this unavoidable inaccuracy must be greater or less, according to the complexity and novelty of the objects defined. " When the Almighty himself condescends to address mankind in their own language, His meaning, luminous as it must be, is rendered dim and doubtful by the cloudy medium through which it is communicated."[a]

Here then are three sources of vague and incorrect definitions; indistinctness of the object, imperfection of the organ of conception, and inadequateness of the vehicle of ideas. Any one of these must produce a certain degree of obscurity.

No human wisdom can prepare a law in such a form, and in such simplicity of language, as that it shall meet every possible complex case that may afterward arise. Whatever skill and forethought the most profound of human law-makers may have called to his aid, it will be found that even such law-giver, though he may possess the highest of intellectual gifts, will not possess grasp of mind enough to draw up a constitution, or an enactment so perfect at the time it is drawn, that no doubtful case shall not afterwards arise as to its meaning. And as time wears on, and the wants and habits of society become changed, as they ever will change with the progressive march of intelligence, especially in a land enjoying the blessings of civil and religious freedom; the interpretations, suitable to a past age, will become more and more impracticable to the present, as to all new questions.

These are propositions so well confirmed by experience, that statesmen and lawyers now agree upon the wisdom of preparing such instruments with general outlines, in language clear and easily understood, rather than of attempting minute details, how-

a Federalist, No. 36.

ever elaborately extended; the tendency of which is found in experience to contract, and often to confuse the expression of intent. It is found to be far easier to obtain the intent of the legislator, when laws are brief and clear, and to rely upon good faith and common sense for their construction, than to be embarrassed at every step with details, which prevent the application of general principles, because the specific case has not been enumerated and singled out by the law-makers. It is, however, a well known maxim of jurisprudence, that the certainty of the law, is next in importance to its justice. By certainty of the law is meant, that it be well defined, known, and unchangeable, and also that its penalties fall with unerring certainty upon those who deserve them.

It has been shown that it is impossible to word laws in such a manner as to absolutely exclude all doubt, or to allow us to dispense with construction, even if they were worded with absolute (mathematical) precision, for the time for which they were made; because things and relations change, and because different interests conflict with each other. The very object of general laws, is to establish general rules beforehand; for if we would attempt to settle each case, according to the views, which, with the momentary interest it might itself suggest, we would establish at once the most insufferable tyranny or anarchy. This inherent generality, however, is likewise the reason why the application of laws require construction, since most cases occurring are of a complex character. It is in vain, therefore, to believe in the possibility of forming a code of laws absolutely distinct, like mathematical theories. All that true wisdom requires is to make laws as distinct and perfect as possible, following both the dictates of reason and the suggestions of experience, and carefully to establish rules of interpretation and construction, or legal hermeneutics.a

"Yet it is my settled conviction, that the clearest possible laws are an incalculable blessing to a community extending much farther than merely to the avoiding of unnecessary litigation, whilst obscure or unnecessarily intricate laws are a very curse to a nation, and serve to unite the lawyers into a compact, formidable and privileged class."b

a Lieber, chap. 6, sec. 7.   b Id.

Statutes admit of a variety of divisions, namely, public and private, declaratory and remedial, preceptive, prohibitive, permissive and penal, temporary and perpetual, affirmative and negative, prospective and retrospective, constitutional and unconstitutional.

In treating of the division of statutes, we shall omit that distinction which exists in England, but which has no application here, to wit, between *ancient* and *modern* statutes; those dating before and those after a certain period in English history.*a* American statutes that have not been repealed, or are not in some way abrogated, do not become impaired by mere lapse of time, but are all equally in force; and though here, as in England, we have acts known as *public*, and *private* acts, and also, as *local* and *personal* acts, unlike the English, our statutes are all printed and published.*b* Each of these divisions will be noticed in their appropriate place.

We might in this place refer to another division of statutes that exist here, which is unknown in England, to wit: statutes of the United States or federal government passed by Congress; statutes of the several States passed by the legislatures of the several States; and colonial statutes passed by the several colonial governments before their separation; to which it may perhaps be added, territorial acts, passed by the new territories before their admission in the Union as States. But this last division is of little practical importance, and calls for no special consideration.

The first division of statutes that I propose to notice, is that of general, or *public* acts, and such as are special or *private*.

A *public* act is a universal rule, that regards the whole community; and of this, courts of law are bound to take notice judicially, and *ex officio*, without the statute being particularly pleaded, or formerly set forth by the party who claims advantage under it.*c*   *Private* acts are those which concern only a particular

---

a The antiquarian or student who may be curious to learn the history of early ordinances of the King and his Council, is referred to the first volume of Dwarris which is chiefly devoted to such early history.

b Art. 6, Const. N. Y. of 1846, § 22; Const. U. S., art. 4, § 1; Statutes at Large, vol. 1; 122; vol. 9, 75.

c 1 Black. Com. 86. Com. Dig. tit. Parliament, R, 7.

species, thing, or person; of which the judges will not take notice without pleading them; as acts relating to any particular place; or to divers particular towns; or to one or divers particular counties; or to a college or university; etc.[1] It is sometimes difficult to draw the line between a public and private act, for statutes frequently relate to matters and things that are partly public and partly private. Generally speaking, statutes are public; and a private statute may rather be considered an exception to the general rule.a The most comprehensive, if not the most precise definition, is that given by Dwarris; "that public acts relate to the public at large, and private acts concern the particular interest or benefit of certain individuals, or of particular classes of men."

In a general act, there may be a private clause. b So, a statute which concerns the public revenue is a *public* statute, but some clauses therein, may, if they relate to private persons only, be *private*; for a statute may be public in one part, and private in another. c[2]

A general or public act, then, regards the whole community; special or private acts relate only to particular persons, or to private concerns. Public acts, the courts of justice are bound *ex officio* to notice, without their being formally set forth. Of private acts, the judges are not bound to take notice unless they be formally shown and pleaded. And this is the doctrine, though the private act should make void all proceedings to the contrary in such place. d

As the judges are bound to take notice of a general law, so it is their province to determine whether it be a statute or not, and whether public or private. 1t was held upon one e occasion that

a 1 Kent Com. 459.　　　　d Skin., 350.
b 4 Cowen. 79.　　　　　　e Lord Raym., 709.
c Dwarris.

NOTE 1.—The exceptions to this rule are in the State of Virginia. These private statutes need not be pleaded, yet they must be exhibited in court as documents. Even there, they will not be noticed judicially like public statutes. Le Grand v. Hamp. Sid. College, 5 Munf. R 324. And in Kentucky, the courts judicially notice private as well as public statutes, if printed without their being formally pleaded. Halbert v. Skyles, 1 Marsh. Ken. R 368. Farmers and Mechanics Bank v. Jervis, 1 Munroe, R. 4, 5.

NOTE 2.—Laws creating banks of issue, though not declaring themselves public, are public laws. Smith v. Strong, 2 Hill, 241; Bank of Utica v. Smedes, 3 Cowen 662.

the judges are not obliged to take notice of a statute of general
pardon, unless they are by such statute itself directed to do so ;a
for as a general pardon only relates to offenders, it is not a public
statute.   For it is added, it is by no means a consequence that
because a man is enabled to give such statute in evidence upon
the general issue, that the judges must take notice of it for any
other purpose.   But this appears to be a harsh construction, and
such as would scarcely be supported at the present day.   Accordingly, another case will be found, b decided about the same time,
in which a statute for the discharge of poor prisoners was relied
upon by the defendant, and an exception taken that it should have
been pleaded at large (being a private statute), as not extending
to all prisoners, but to such only as were in prison at a time mentioned in the act.   The court, however, construed it to be a public statute, holding that all the people of England might be interested as creditors; that, as a merciful act, it should have a favorable construction; and that poor prisoners ought not to be put
to the difficulty and expense of pleading it specially:—three
grounds, which were sound, merciful and just.

The probable grounds of the declared difference in the judicial
notice of statutes, public and private, may be (besides the solem-
nity and intrinsic authority of a public act of the legislature, and
the supposed greater notoriety of a matter of universal concern),
the extreme inconvenience of a contrary rule, and the difficulty
and uncertainty of which it would be productive.

The rule which we have given, however, without regard to the
supposed reasons for its adoption, depends on positive law, and
not on conjectural expediency.   Accordingly, the existence of a
public act must be tried by the judges, who are to inform themselves of this, in the best way they can.   A private act may be
put in issue and shall be tried by the record.³

---

a Ingram and Foot, 12 Mod. 613.   *b* Lord Raym. 120, Jones v. Axen.

NOTE 3.—A private act that confirms a land claim, is presumed to have been
passed with reference to the particular claims of the individuals who so claim to
be interested, and to the situation of the land embraced in the law at the time it
was passed; but such an act does not enlarge the parties rights as against adverse
claimants, nor conclude them.   Pollard's heirs v. Kibbe, 14 Pet. 353; Lanfear v.
Huntly, 4 Wall. 204.   Though an act confirming a deed given by an executrix on
a sale of land in order to pay the testators debts, will be held good as against the
heirs at law of the testator. Leland v. Wilkinson, 10 Pet. 294.

2. It has been held that where a statute makes it felony to steal the notes of a
particular bank, its act of incorporation thereby becomes a public statute,* U. S.
v. Porte, 1 Cranch. C. C. R. 369 ; and in Young v. Bank of Alexandria, 4 Cranch.
R. 388, an act of the State of Virginia, incorporating the Bank of Virginia was
declared a public act.

* What is a public act? 4 Pet. 166.

To both the general rules, that general or public acts are to be noticed judicially without pleading, and that special acts must be shown by pleading, there will be found in this country some other exceptions. Among these exceptions, are those that relate to the particular character of the statute, and among these, are the statutes of limitations, and the statute against usury. These are public and general statutes, yet the party who intends to avail himself of their benefits, must plead them, or he will not be permitted to give the defence arising under such statutes in evidence.

And though a cause of action appear in the declaration or complaint to have accrued upwards of six years before the commencement of the action, a defendant can only have the advantage of it by plea, or answer.*a*

But in pleading in a case which is to be governed by the principle of a statute of the mother country which became a part of the colonial common law, it is not necessary to refer to the statute; it is enough to plead the facts which bring the case within it as a part of the common law of the State.*b*

Acts of Parliament are, again, DECLARATORY of the old law, or introductory of new, or both, as by the addition of greater penalties, the destruction of particular customs, and the like. Declaratory, are necessarily in their terms, *affirmative* or *negative*. Both kinds of laws, those declared and affirmed, as well as those newly enacted, may be PENAL; the affirmance of the anterior law cannot properly be styled REMEDIAL. A subordinate division of REMEDIAL acts has been made into ENABLING and DISABLING—ENLARGING and RESTRAINING—statutes. Those against natural law and reason are said to be VOID.

It is proposed to examine the nature of each successively; the rules with regard to their construction will be more fitly considered at a future period.

a See 2 Chitty, Pl. 450 and notes; Puckle v. Moor, 1 Vents. 191; Lee v. Rodgers, 1 Lev. 110; Goold v. John, 2 Ld. Raym. 838; N. Y. Code, § § 74, 149, 150; Voorhees v. Voorhees, 24 Barb. 150; Sands v. St John, 36 Barb. 628.

b Bogardus v. Trinity Church, 2 Paige R 198.

3. A private act of incorporation is to be regarded as in the nature of a contract, and cannot effect the rights of individuals who do not assent to it; but their assent may be inferred from their acts, such as taking benefits under it. Beatly v. Knowler, 4 Pet. 166.

4. An act prescribing the boundaries of a county is a public act. Stephenson v. Doe, 8 Black. 508.

And first of DECLARATORY acts. These are made where the old
custom of the kingdom is almost fallen into disuse, or become
disputable, in which case the Parliament has thought proper, in
perpetuum rei testimonium, and for avoiding all doubts and difficulties, to declare what the common law is and ever hath been.
And such statutes are expressed affirmatively, or in negative terms.
A statute made in the affirmative, without any negative expressed
or implied, does not take away the common law. It follows, that
it does not effect any prescriptions or customs clashing with it,
which were before allowed; in other words, the common law continues to be construed as it was before the recognition by Parliament.

The next difference observable between public and private
statutes, is, that particular, as opposed to general acts, will not
bind *strangers;* though they should not contain any saving of
their rights. A general saving of the rights and interests of all
persons whatsoever, except those whose consent was given or purchased, and who were particularly named in the act, used to be
constantly added to all private bills; but it was held, that, even
if such saving were omitted, the act would bind none but the
parties. At present, it is usual *a* in preparing modern private
acts, to insert, *ex cautela*, a special saving clause, explaining how
far the rights of strangers are intended to be affected.

The reason of the rule is apparent, and the rule itself is founded
in wisdom and justice. Every person is considered as assenting
to a public act; *b* but it is a rule, that private acts of Parliament,
introduced only for the settlement of particular estates, ought to
be considered merely as common conveyances, and directed by
the same rules of law; and therefore they cannot be taken to
extend as a discharge of any person's right not mentioned in the
act. This, says the judicious and candid commentator on the
laws of the United States of America *c* is a safe and just rule,
and it was it was adopted by the English Courts in very early
times,*d* and does great credit to their liberality and spirit of
justice. It is supported by the opinion of Sir Matthew Hale, in
Lucy and Levington, *e* where he lays down the rule to be, that
"though every man be so far a party to a private act of Parliament as not to gainsay it, yet he is not so far a party as to give
up his interest." It is the great question in Barrington's case, 8
Rep.. "The matter of the act there directs it to be, between the
foresters and the proprietors of the soil; and therefore it shall
not extend to the commoners, to take away their common. Suppose a statute recites, that whereas there was a controversy concerning land between A. and B., and enacts, that A. shall enjoy

a See Hargrave and Butler's note to Co. Litt. 98.   *c* 1 Kent, 427.

b Per Lord Hardwicke, And. 40, 1 T. R. 93.   *e* 1 Ventris, 175.

d Bro. Parl. pl. 27; Barrington's case, 8 Rep. 138.

it, this would not bind the interest of third persons in that land, because they are not strictly parties to the act, but strangers; and it would be manifest injustice that the statute should affect them." This rule as to limiting the operation of private statutes, is adopted by the Courts of the United States of America.*a*

Another difference has prevailed in England with regard to offering these different statutes in evidence. The printed statute book has been at all times admitted as evidence of a *public* statute of Parliament, not as an authentic copy of the record itself, but as (so it is gravely said) hints of that which is supposed to be lodged in every man's mind already. *b* And now by the statute 41 Geo. 3 Ch. 90, § 9, made for the better and more effectual proof of the statute law, it has been enacted that the copies of the statutes of Great Britain and Ireland prior to the Union, printed by the printer duly authorized, shall be received as conclusive evidence of the several statutes in the courts of either kingdom. But as we have before stated, a *private* act may contain clauses of a public nature ; and *then*, the act, so far as those are concerned, is to be regarded as a public act.*c* The public are not generally considered as affected by the contents of a private act ; and facts recited in the preamble of a private act, is not proof of those facts as against a stranger, a third party, or the public.*s*

The regular proof of private acts of Parliament, is by an examined copy compared with the original in the Parliament office at Westminster.*d* But great inconvenience having been found to result from the necessity of such strict proof, a special clause has now, usually been inserted, providing that the act shall be deemed public, or providing that they should be printed by the King's printer, and that a copy so printed, shall be admitted as evidence of the act. In such cases, a copy purporting to be printed by the King's printer, will be admissible in evidence ; it is not necessary to prove that the act was printed at the King's printers.*e*

Where the copy of an act is incorrect, the court will be governed by the Parliament Roll.*f*

It should also be remarked, that there is a difference between proving private acts to a jury, and proving them on the issue of

a Kent's Comm. on American Law, vol. 1, 428.   *d* Phil. Ev. 306.

b Gilbert's Ev. 10.   *e* 2 Phil. Ev. 129, R. v. Shaw. 12, East. R. 479.

c R. v. Utterby, 2 Phil. Ev. 127.   *f* Rex v. Jeffrie, 1 Str. 446.

NOTE 5.—Every subject of a government is, in judgment of law, privy to the making of a public statute, and is supposed to know them. The passing of a public legislative act, is a public proceeding in all its stages, and when it is passed, it is in contemplation of law, the act of the whole body of the State. But recitals, even in a public act are not conclusive evidence of the facts therein stated. 2 Phil. ev. 272.

8

nul tiel record, which never goes to a jury; nothing less than an Exemplification under the Great Seal being sufficient in the latter case.

And so much for the division of statutes into public and private acts, with their respective incidents.

Statutes are either declaratory of the common law, or remedial of some defects therein.*a* Declaratory statutes are generally introductory of a new law; remedial statutes, are generally mentioned in contradistinction to penal statutes. In the construction of remedial statutes, three points are to be considered. 1st, the old law, 2d, the mischief, and 3d the remedy. That is, 1st, how the common law stood at the time of the making of the act; 2d, what the mischief was for which the common law did not provide, and 3d, what remedy the statute hath provided to cure this mischief. And it is the duty of Judges, so to construe the act, as to suppress the mischief, and advance the remedy.*b*

The authentication of our national statutes is now declared by an act of Congress, passed August 8, 1846, (Statutes at Large, Vol. 9, 75); by which it is enacted, that the laws and treaties of the United States, published by Little & Brown, shall be competent evidence of the several *public* and *private* acts of Congress, and the several treaties therein contained, in all the courts of law and equity, and of maritime jurisdiction, and in all the tribunals and public offices of the United States, and of the several States, without any further proof or authentication thereof.

By another act of congress, passed May 26, 1790, (1 Statutes at Large, Vol. 1, 122,) it is declared, that the acts of the legislatures of the several States shall be authenticated by having the seal of their respective States affixed thereto. Courts will presume that the person who affixed the seal had authority to do so.*c*

But these authentications, so far as they relate to the courts of the United States, refer only to *public* statutes. Private statutes, and laws, and special proceedings, are governed by a different rule. They are matters of fact, to be proved as such in the ordinary manner.*d*

An act of a State legislature, which contains a provision declaring it a public act, must be noticed by the courts of the United States without being specially pleaded,*e* otherwise not.

a 1 Black. Wm. 86, R. 22.   b Co. Litt. 11, 42.
c United States v. Amedy, 11 Wheat. 392 ; Same v. Johnson 4 Dallas, 412, 416.
d Leland v. Wilkinson, 6 Peters 617.
e Beatty v Knowler, 4 Pet. 152; Drawbridge Co. v. Shepherd, 20 How. 232.

Statutes and edicts of foreign countries must be produced in evidence.*a* If it does not appear that foreign laws in question were in *writing* as *public* edicts or statutes, they may be proved by parol.*b*

A copy of the Civil Code of France, presented to the Supreme Court of the United States with this endorsement : " *Le Garde des Sceaux de France a la Coeur Supreme Des Etats Unis,*" has been admited as evidence of the written laws of France.*c* The court held, that the endorsement was a sufficient authentication, inasmuch as it was given in reciprocation of a donation made by congress, to France, of the laws, resolutions and treaties of the United States.

In the State of New York, the Revised Statutes, *d* provide for the formalities of enacting laws by the legislature, the duty of the Secretary of State in certifying them, and indorsing on them the day of their passage, delivering such laws to the printer, and the time when it became a law ; and if certified by the presiding officers of the senate and assembly to have been passed by a vote of two-thirds of the members elected to each house, then the secretary shall add to his certificate the words, " *by a two-third vote,*" and which certificate is made presumptive evidence of such fact. If not so certified, the presumption is that the act was not passed by two-thirds of the legislature. Each volume of laws printed and published for the State shall contain the certificate of the Secretary of State, to the effect, that the said volume was printed under his direction. And all laws passed by the legislature, so certified, may be read in evidence from the volumes so printed under the directions of the Secretary of State.

By the provisions of the Code of Procedure of this State (§ 426), it is enacted, that printed copies in volumes of statutes, Code, or other written laws, and of the proclamations, edicts, decrees and ordinances by the executive power of any State or territory, or foreign government, when printed in books or publications purporting or proved to have been published by the authority thereof, or proved to be commonly admitted as evidence of the existing

a Robinson v. Cliffon, 2 Wash. C. C. R. 1. *c* Ennis v. Smith, 14 How. 401.
b Livingston v. Maryland Ins. Co. 6 Cranch. 674.
d 1 Revised Statutes, Marg. p. 157, 158.

law in the courts and judicial tribunals of such State, territory, or government, shall be admitted by the courts and officers of this State, on all occasions, as presumptive evidence of such laws, proclamations, edicts, decrees and ordinances.

A similar provision has been adopted by a large proportion of the States of the union. It will hardly be useful to go through with an examination of the enactments of the different States in this respect. It may suffice to say, that before these statutes of comity were passed, and in those States where no similar statute has yet been enacted, both public and private statutes at common law, could be proved by the seal of the State, or country whose law is thus sought to be proved. *a*

These mutual provisions of statute, on the part of the national and State legislatures, are supposed to arise from mutual interest and utility, as a kind of courtesy and comity between States, and from a sense of the great inconveniences that would result from a contrary doctrine. This inconvenience creates a kind of moral and reciprocal necessity between independent States, to do justice to others, that justice may be done to them in return. Especially does this seem to be demanded between sovereign States, between whom commerce has introduced frequent and intimate relations of extensive intercourse.*b* The intimate union of these States, as members of the same great political family, mutually dependent on each other in various ways; the deep and vital interests which bind them so closely together, all recognizing one common sovereign; would naturally create a greater degree of comity and friendship than is felt between foreign nations. Therefore, these provisions of statute comity between States. It is more than doubtful, however, whether the courts, independent of statute provisions, could declare or establish a common law comity between independent States.

The law-making power of the United States, and of the several States, (as in most other civilized governments,) is vested in the legislatures or representatives of the people, in the manner pre-

a Dougherty v. Snyder, 15 Searg & Rawle, 87 ; Story on Conft. of Laws, 530. A sworn copy is also admissible. Lincoln v. Battelle, 6 Wend. 482 ; 15 S. & R. 87.

b Blanchard v. Russel, 13 Mass. 4 ; Story on Confl. of L. § 25 ; Bank of Augusta v. Earle, 13 Peters, 519.

scribed by their fundamental law. This power of enacting laws, is sometimes called the sovereign power, but it is not, as we have seen, absolute sovereign power, in every sense or meaning of the word sovereignty, when applied to the authority of legislation under American written constitutions.[6] When applied to other States of the union in relation to each other; or to the national government in relation to foreign governments; so far as it concerns the question of independence, the legislative power may be called sovereign. So too under our improved system of government, limited by constitutional restrictions, when the legislature is acting upon subjects within its constitutional limits, it is possessed of power competent to regulate, control and direct the will of the whole and every subordinate member of the community; and in this respect it is believed it possesses absolute and unlimited power, incapable of being controlled.[7] Such an exercise of

NOTE 6.—Sovereignty, as applied to States, imports the supreme, absolute, uncontrollable power by which any State is governed.[*]

[*] 1 Black. Com. 49 ; 2 Dallas R. 471 ; Story on Const. § 207.

NOTE 7.—Courts are not at liberty to inquire into the proper exercise of power by the legislature, in a case where the latter have been acting within their constitutional limits. They are bound to presume that the legislatures have exercised the proper discretion. It is no part of the duty of the courts to enquire into the motives which actuated the legislature in the passage of a given act, though fraud and corruption be alleged. The courts have no right to impute to the legislature any other but public motives for their acts. In People v. Draper, 15 N. Y. R. 545, the court said, "We are not made judges of the motives of the legislature, and the court will not usurp the inquisitorial office of inquiry into the bona fides of that body in discharging its duties." See also, The Sudbury and Erie R. R. Co. v. Cooper, 33 Penn. St. R. 282 ; Ex parte Newmann, 9 Cal. 503.

Fraud, in procuring an act of the legislature, either by means of fraudulent representations, or by concealment from that body of material facts, whether the act be public or private, cannot be impeached in the courts. Englishbee v. Helmuth, 7 N. Y. Legal Obs. 186. Nor can the courts, for the purpose of impeaching a statute, go behind the records to enquire into the regularity of the proceedings of the legislature in passing an act. The People v. Develin, 33 N. Y. R. 269, and authorities cited.

NOTE 8.—If a law bear upon its face the requisite authentication, it is presumed to have been passed by the necessary constitutional majority. The vote by which it passed cannot be enquired into. Falconer v. Campbell, 2 McLean R. 195 ; White v. How, 3 id. 111.

NOTE 9.—If an act be constitutional, and clothed with the forms of law, the courts cannot inquire into the motives of the members of the legislature in passing it. Fletcher v. Peck, 6 Cranch. 87.

power, it has been held, is so conclusive, that though the legislature should, through misrepresentation or other cause, do injustice to an individual, there is no court or other power in the government, that can apply a remedy, or administer relief. *a*   Chancellor Kent, in his commentaries *b* notices this distinction between the British parliament and our own legislature.   He says, " the principle in the English government, that parliament is omnipotent, does not prevail in the United States ; though if there is no constitutional objection to a statute, it is, with us, as absolute and uncontrollable as laws flowing from the sovereign power under any other form of government."

The whole law-making power of the State is vested in the legislature, which is omnipotent, unless restricted by the express or implied provisions of the State or national constitutions, and where the power is so vested in the legislature, and unrestrained by the fundamental law, its unwise legislation affords no ground for the courts to nullify it.*c*   But their power is restrained, not only by the provisions of the State constitution, but by the powers granted by the people of the several States to the general government ; embodied in the federal constitution, which becomes the supreme power, within the scope and operation of the general government.   The latter government may exercise these powers in its appropriate departments, free and unobstructed by any State legislation or authority; and any interference by the State governments, tending to the interruption of the full legitimate exercise of the powers thus granted, is in conflict with a clause in the federal constitution which makes that constitution and the laws of the United States made in pursuance thereof, the supreme law of the land. *d*   The State legislatures, however, have power under their constitutions, to alter the common law of their States ;*e* but, no power to interfere with, or adjudicate upon claims of private persons or municipal corporations,*f* nor to pass any act impairing the obligation of contracts, or to interfere with the vested rights of individuals.*g*

a Nott & McCord's R. 401 ; 1 Bald. C. C. R. 74 ; Fletcher v. Peck, 6 Cranch. 171.
b 1 Kent Com. 488 ; Smith's Com. 262.
c People v. Denniston, 23 N. Y. 247 ; Bank of Chenango v. Brown, 26 N. Y. 467; Luke v. City of Brooklyn, 43 Barb. 54 ; Matter of Wilson, 4 City Hall Rec. 47.
d People v. Commissioners of Taxes, 2 Black. 620.   *e* 1 Code Rep. 49.
f Baldwin v. Mayor of N. Y. 42 Barb. 549. *g* Vrooman v. Jones, 5 How. Pr. R. 369.

The whole doctrine on this subject of legislation under the American system, is reduced to this; if the legislature pursue the authority delegated to them in passing statutes, their acts are valid and conclusively binding; if they transcend the bounds of that authority, their acts are invalid, and of no force. In the former case, they exercise the discretion vested in them by the people, to whom, (and not to the courts,) they are responsible for the faithful discharge of their trust. In the performance of this duty, the right to the exercise of their opinions on the questions of natural rights, is not subordinate to the judicial will; in the other case, if they violate the fundamental law, of which the courts may judge; the validity or invalidity of the act is to be determined by the judges.a

But the legislature of each sovereign State of the union, has also restrictions of its sovereign power imposed upon it, as has been stated, other than such as may be found in its own constitution. She is also a member of the American union, and that union has also a constitution, the supremacy of which all acknowledge, which imposes limits to the legislative powers of the several States, and which, none can claim a right to pass. b Besides conferring specified powers upon the national government, the constitution of the United States contains also certain prohibitions upon the action of the States, a portion of them designed to prevent encroachments upon the national authority, and another portion, to protect individual rights against possible abuse of State power. c

The people of the United States, in adopting that instrument, doubtless, had the object in view of shielding themselves and their property from the effect of sudden and violent acts, to which they might be exposed, arising from local or party feeling, that might affect legislative power in the several States. The constitution of the United States also contains what may be deemed a bill of rights for the people of each State. To this limited extent, the several States of the union, cannot be absolutely sovereign.

The theory of our political system is, that the ultimate sovereignty is in the people, from whom spring all legitimate authority.d

a Smith's Com. 267. c Const. U. S. Art. 1, § 10. Id. Art. 4.
b Marshall, Ch. J. 6 Cranch. 136. d Jameson on Const. Conventions, Ch. 8

They created the national constitution, and conferred upon it powers of sovereignty over certain subjects. Upon those subjects, it is supreme. They have also created State governments, upon which they conferred the remaining powers of sovereignty, so far as they allow them to be exercised at all. *a*

To this extent only, it seems to have been necessary in this place, to have examined the authority with which American legislatures are invested in the enactment of statutes; this being one of the special subjects of this work. We start then, with this conceded proposition; that the people, originally, were possessed of all legislative power; this power they committed to their respective State legislatures, in unlimited terms, except only as to such limitations as are imposed by the particular constitution of the State itself, and by the superior restrictions of the constitution of the United States. *b*

We cannot better express this idea of the powers and restrictions of the law-making power, than in the language of Denio, late Chief judge of the Court of Appeals of this State. He says, " The people, in framing the constitution, committed to the legislature the whole law-making powers of the State which they did not expressly or impliedly withhold. Plenary power in the legislature is the rule. A prohibition to exercise a particular power, is an exception. In inquiring, therefore, whether a given statute is constitutional, it is for those who question its validity to show that it is forbidden. I do not mean that the power must be expressly inhibited, for there are but few positive restraints upon the legislative power contained in the instrument. The first article lays down the ancient limitations which have always been considered essential in a constitutional government, whether monarchical or popular; and there are scattered through the instrument a few other provisions in restraint of legislative authority. But the affirmative prescriptions, and the general arrangements of the constitution, are far more fruitful of restraints upon the legislature. Every positive direction contains an implication against everything contrary to it, or, which would frustrate or disappoint the purpose of that provision. The frame of the government, the grant of legislative power itself; the organization of

a Cooley on Const. Lim. 8.   *b* Leggett v. Hunter, 19 N. Y. R, 463.

executive authority; the erection of the principle courts of justice; create implied limitations upon the law-making authority, as strong, as though a negative was expressed in each instance; but independently of these restraints, express or implied, every subject within the scope of civil government, is liable to be dealt with by the legislature. a

The question, whether a law is void for repugnancy to the constitution, is at all times a question of delicacy, which ought seldom, if ever, to be decided in the affirmative in a doubtful case. But a court, when impelled by duty, would be unworthy of its station, if it should be unmindful of the solemn obligations which that station imposes. But it is not upon slight implication and vague conjecture, that it is to be pronounced, that the legislature has transcended its power, and that its acts are to be deemed void. The opposition between the constitution and the law should be such, that the judge feels a clear and strong conviction of their incompatibility with each other.b But this branch of the subject will be discussed more at length hereafter.

It is not unusual for a legislative act to involve consequences which are not expressed in it; and it is the judicial power, which is an instrument employed by government, to determine how those consequences affect individuals, and how they are to be directed and controlled for the security of the agents who are called upon to execute the act. " Judicial power, as contradistinguished from the power of the laws, has no existence. Courts, of themselves, are mere instruments of the law, and of the government, and can will nothing. When they are said to exercise a discretion, it is a mere legal discretion; a discretion to be exercised in discerning the course prescribed by law; and when that is discerned, it is the duty of the court to follow it. Judicial power is never exercised for the purpose of giving effect to the will of the judge; always for the purpose of giving effect to the will of the legislature; or in other words to the will of the law." c

It would be a task which no law writer would undertake, to define what are the precise limits within which a legislature, in its discretion, is limited, when they keep within their constitu-

a People v. Draper, 15 N. Y. R. 543, 4.   b 6 Cranch. 128.
c Per Marshall, Ch. J., Osborn v. U. S. Bank, 9 Wheat. 366.

9

tional bounds. But every government should possess, and every constitutional government does possess, the means of protecting itself and its citizens, against encroachments, of even the legislative power, upon the other departments, and against violations of the fundamental law ; and this means, is the judicial power.

Every government must, in its essence, be unsafe, and unfit for a free people, where such a department as the judicial does not exist, with powers co-extensive with those of the legislative department. "What for instance, would avail restrictions upon the authority of State legislatures, without some constitutional mode of enforcing the observance of them? a No man familiar with the exercise of power, whose experience has taught him the frequency with which the legislature have overstepped the boundaries of their power, can do otherwise than admire the political wisdom of that system, which has provided a department, whose powers are co-extensive with that of the legislature, and whose duty it is to restrain and correct all infractions of the fundamental law." Where there is no judicial department to interpret, pronounce, and execute the law ; to decide controversies, and to enforce rights, the government must either perish by its own imbecility, or the other departments of government must usurp powers, for the purpose of commanding obedience, and this would be the destruction of liberty. b

"Laws, however wholesome or necessary, are frequently the object of temporary aversion, and sometimes of popular resistance." It requires that courts of justice should be able at all times to present a determined countenance against all licentious acts; to deal impartially and truly, according to law, between suitors of every description, or whether the cause, the question, or the party, be popular or unpopular." Nor is an independent judiciary less useful as a check upon the legislative power, which is sometimes disposed, from the force of party, or the temptations of interest, to make a sacrifice of constitutional rights ; and it is a wise and necessary principle of our government, that legislative acts are subject to the severe scrutiny, and impartial interpretation of the courts of justice, who are bound to regard the consti-

aFederalist, No. 80.   b 1 Kent's Com. 296.

tution as the paramount law, and the highest evidence of the will of the people." *a*

The power of interpreting laws, involves, necessarily, the function to ascertain, whether they are conformable to the constitution, or not; and if not so conformable, to declare them void and inoperative. As the constitution is the supreme law of the land, in a conflict between that and the laws, either of Congress, or of the States, it becomes the judiciary to follow that only, which is of paramount obligation. This results from the very theory of a republican constitution of government; for otherwise, the acts of the legislature and executive would, in effect, become supreme and uncontrolable, notwithstanding any prohibitions or limitations contained in the constitution; and usurpations of the most unequivocal and dangerous character might be assumed, without any remedy within the reach of the citizen. *b* The people would thus be at the mercy of their rulers in the State and national governments; and an omnipotence would practically exist, like that claimed for the British Parliament.

To the people at large, therefore, the institution of the judicial department is peculiarly valuable; and it ought to be eminently cherished by them. On its firm and independent structure, they may repose with safety, while they perceive in it a faculty, which is only set in motion when applied to; but which, when thus brought into action, must proceed with competent power, if required, to correct the error or subdue the oppression of the other branches of government.*c* But to insure a complete administration of public justice through this department, and to give permanency to the government, the judiciary should be so organized as to carry into complete effect, all the purposes of its establishment. It must possess wisdom, learning, integrity, independence and firmness. It must at once possess the power and the means to check usurpation, and enforce execution of its judgment.*d*

Hence it is, that there are but few men in society who will have sufficient skill, learning, firmness, and integrity, qualities all combined in one person, to qualify them for the stations of judges.

a Id. 294.   c Rawle, on the Const. ch. 21.
b Federalist, No. 78   d Story, on Const. § 1577.

CHAPTER III.

DIVISIONS OF STATUTES. DIFFERENCE IN CONSTRUCTION BETWEEN
AMERICAN AND FOREIGN COUNTRIES.

Acts of parliament are, it may be said, again, DECLARATORY of
the old law, or introductive of new, or both; as by the addition
of greater penalties, the destruction of particular customs, and the
like. Declaratory, are necessarily in their terms, *affirmative* or
negative. Both kinds of laws, those declared and affirmed, as well
as those newly enacted, may be PENAL; the affirmance of the anterior law cannot properly be styled REMEDIAL. A subordinate
division of REMEDIAL acts has been made into ENABLING and DIS-
ABLING—ENLARGING and RESTRAINING—statutes.

And first of DECLARATORY acts. These (*in England*) are made
where the old custom of the kingdom is almost fallen into disuse,
or become disputable, in which case the parliament has thought
proper, in *perpetuam rei testimonium*, and for avoiding all doubts
and difficulties, to declare what the common law is and ever hath
been. And such statutes are expressed affirmatively or in negative terms. A statute made in the affirmative, without any negative expressed or implied, does not take away the common law. *a*
It follows that it does not affect any prescriptions or customs
clashing with it which were before allowed; in other words, the
common law continues to be construed as it was before the recognition by parliament.[1]

a 2 Inst. 200; 1 Inst. 111, 115; Harg. & Butler's notes, Co. Litt. 115.

NOTE 1.—A declaratory statute, is sometimes intended to declare the meaning
and intent of a pre-existing statute. This kind of legislation is apt to create a
conflict between the proper functions of the legislative and–judicial departments
of the government; because such statutes are, necessarily, to a certain extent,
retrospective. It assumes the exercise of judicial power, in determining what the
law was before the declaratory statute was passed. In this they exceed their
power, and invade the domain of judicial authority. This kind of legislation,
sometimes happens after the courts in the due exercise of their legitimate authority, as interpreters of the law, have declared the meaning and intent of the statute to be otherwise than such as the new statute declares. Without referring to other
cases, a single instance may suffice. The legislature of New York, in 1853, passed
an act in relation to the liability of certain insurance companies to taxation, the
construction of which, was a question litigated and determined in the courts. In

The party may waive his benefit by such affirmative statute, and take his remedy by the common law,*a* which however does not mean that the statute is not binding, but that the party may take his election which to proceed upon. In like manner an affirmative statute does not repeal an affirmative statute; and if the substance be that both may stand together, they shall have a concurrent efficacy. But if the latter be contrary to the former, it amounts to a repeal of the former, for it is a general principle,

a Bro. Parl. Pl. 70; 1 Rep. 64; Cro. Eliz, 104,

1855, the legislature enacted a law declaring the intent of the act of 1853, to be different from the intent as declared by the courts ; such judicial decisions had been pronounced and were pending on appeal to the highest court, at the time of the enactment of the declaratory law. The Court of Appeals declared as follows : "All the judgments of the Supreme Court now under review, were rendered at the special term before the enactment of this statute. The cases since that time have been pending on appeal before the general term, and in this court ; and were so pending when the statute was enacted. As regards these cases, the mandate of the legislature, if it has any application, must be regarded as addressed to the appellate tribunals. We habitually look with great respect upon all acts of the legislature, and never refuse to give them effect, except where, upon the fullest consideration, we find that they conflict with the constitution. The act in question, considered as a persuasive argument for a particular construction of the statute of 1853, loses much of its weight from the consideration that the legislative bodies had been renewed in the interval between the two enactments, and that but a few of the members of the legislature of 1853 sat in that of 1855. But, if that were otherwise, we should feel constrained to rely upon the language of the statute which we are called upon to interpret, rather than any personal assurance as to the intention of its members. The acts of the legislature do not rest in any respect upon oral tradition. They are committed to *writing*, and it is by the *written* language that their sense is to be ascertained. As an authoritative mandate in favor of the construction claimed by the insurance company, we cannot accord to it any force whatever. In the division of power among the great departments of the government, the duty of expounding *written* laws, has been committed to the judiciary. The legislature has no judicial power ; and cannot upon any pretence, interpose its authority respecting questions of interpretation depending in the courts." People v. Board of Supervisors of New York, 16 N. Y. R. 431, 2 ; Dash v. Van Kleeck. 7 John. R. 477. Nor have the legislature the power to make the opinion of the Attorney General binding upon a contractor, as agent of the state prison, upon a contract previously made. Young v. Beardsley, 11 Paige, 93.

NOTE 2.—Nor would a statute declaratory of the common law, retroact upon past controversies, or reverse decisions which the courts in the exercise of their undoubted authority have made. Cooley on Const. Lim. 94. This would be a like exercise of judicial power, which if tolerated, might constitute the legislature a court of review in all cases where disappointed partisans could obtain a hearing, after being dissatisfied with the rulings of the court. Id.

that " *leges posteriores, priores contrarias abrogant.*"   But this is meant of a case where a statute by its matter necessarily implies a negative, for an act of parliament may be repealed by the express words of a subsequent statute, or by implication.

Next arises the consideration of those statutes which obtain the name of negative statutes, because they are penned in negative terms ; as the statute of Marlbridge, which is " *Non ideo puniatur Dominus per redemptionem ;*" and Magna Charta, " *Nullus capiatur aut imprisonetur.*"   And here, the rule prevails, that if a subsequent statute, contrary to a former, have negative words, it shall be a repeal of the former ; and a negative statute it is said too, so binds the common law, that a man cannot afterwards have recourse to the latter *a*.

The different operation of affirmative and negative statutes is thus illustrated : If a statute were to provide that it should be lawful for tenant in fee simple to make a lease for twenty-one years, and that such lease should be good ; this affirmative statute could not restrain him from making a lease for sixty years ; but the lease for more than twenty-one years would be good, because it was good by the common law, and to restrain him, it ought to have words negative ; as, that it *shall not* be lawful for

a Bro. Parl. pl. 72..

The legisla ure may within their legitimate powers, declare what the law shall be in future, but to declare what the law is, or has been, is the province of the judiciary.   See Greenhough v. Greenhough, 11 Penn. St. R. 494, and Reiser v. Tell Association, 39 id. 137.   In the latter case, the court say in relation to such a declaratory act, " It is the interpretation by one legislature of a written statute by another, and therefore an adjudication of private rights that have arisen under it.   And yet the former legislature said nothing like this, and nothing from which it can be inferred.   The legislature have no such authority over us, to change the laws of language.   If given language does not express a given meaning, they may give us other language that does ; but this will not change the meaning of former language.   In the very nature of language, this is impossible.   It is with, and by virtue of the new expressions, that we get the new meaning, and the meaning of the law is the law itself, and the law can be no older than the effectual expression of it.

NOTE 3.—A DECLARATORY law, founded upon a mistaken opinion of the legislature, though inoperative as to the past, may operate in the future.   P. M. Gen'l v. Early, 12 Wheat. 148.   A declaration of the legislature as to what they intended for the time in the past by a law, does not make the law what they intended it, if they are in error.   It only affects it in the future; the past law is to be determined by the judiciary; but it is the duty of the courts to give to a construing act its intended practical operation, as far as is possible.   Bassett v. U. S. Nott & Huntington R. 448.   In this country, where the legislative power is limited, declaratory laws. so far as they operate on vested rights, cannot change the rule of construction as to a pre-existing law.   Salters v. Tobias, 3 Paige, 388.

him to make a lease for above twenty-one years; or that a lease for more, *shall not be good.*[4]

Upon the rule itself, a nice, abstruse, and difficult question, and one much litigated, arises.

A man might have alleged a custom against the common law; if the statute be only declaratory of the common law, shall he not, in like manner, prescribe against the statute? Lord Coke remarks it as an important distinction between negative statutes of different kinds, that where they are only affirmative of the ancient, that is of the common law, there, a custom will equally prevail against the statute, as it before obtained against the common law. *a* Such negative statutes, according to him, cannot *extend* the common law, and no more effect is given to them than if the statutes were expressed in affirmative terms. If the statute be a mere affirmance, or declaration of the common law—whether the words used be affirmative or negative, can, it might be thought, substantially, make no difference. The one it is reasonably to be presumed, cannot have an operation more extended than the other. An affirmative statute, it is unqualifiedly laid down, does not take away a custom.*b* Thus, says Lord Coke, the statutes of Wills of 32 and 34 H. 8, do not take away a custom to devise lands, as it hath been often adjudged; so, a negative statute, in affirmation or declaration of the common law, may be prescribed against. "As the Statute of Magna Charta provideth that no leet shall be holden but twice in the year, yet a man may pre-scribe to hold it *oftener at other times;* for that the statute was but in affirmance of the common law." This instance of Lord Coke has been questioned, and seems liable to exception; it possibly may not be apt; but granting that it is doubtful, the objection applies to the fitness of the example, and not to the force of the rule. Another illustration is drawn by Lord Coke from the forest laws. "The statute of 34 E. 1, provideth that none shall cut down any trees of his own within a forest, without the view of the forester; but inasmuch as this act is in affirmance of the common law, a man may prescribe to cut down his woods within a forest without the view of the forester." This case also has been impeached, but still the reason and good sense of Lord Coke's distinction remains unimpaired. The pertinent inquiry still to be made is, whether the provision of the act be contrary to the former law? If not, the common law continues as in the case of affirmative statutes, to be construed as before its recognition, and the maxim *consuetudo privat communem legem* still

a 1 Inst. 115.   *b* 1 Inst. 111.

NOTE 4.—Where there are two *affirmative* statutes, such parts of the prior statute as may be incorporated into the subsequent statute, as consistent with it must be considered in force. Davies v. Fairbairn, 3 How. U. S. R. 636.

applies.* This is where the statute and the common law agree, where they differ, the rule is clear and certain. But a statute, it is apprehended, (and hence, perhaps, some confusion of ideas upon the subject,) may be at the same time declaratory of the ancient law and introductive of a new. While it affirms the common law, it may annihilate particular customs which were before allowed in derogation of that general law. The distinction, justly taken, is confined to such statutes as, though expressed in negative terms, are merely in affirmance of, or declaratory of, the common law. Cases in which the terms of the statute, fairly taken, import something more; enlarging—restraining—qualifying—or in anywise varying the law,—do not apply. But this view of the case, consonant as it is to reason, and not unsupported by authority,a cannot fearlessly be pronounced to be the law. It must be delivered as doubtful. It is the questionable doctrine of the latter cases,b that no prescription or custom is good against a negative statute, whether it be declaratory of the common law, or introductive of a new law; and this is the latest decision.

It is, as a maxim, generally true, that if an affirmative statute, which is introductive of a new law, direct a thing to be done *in a certain manner*, that thing shall not, even although there are no negative words, be done in any other manner.c But where the question was, whether an appointment of overseers made after the expiration of the time limited by the statute for such an appointment was valid? It was held to be so, for the statute (43 Eliz. ch. 4,) ought to receive a liberal construction; it was not in the power of the parish to compel the justices to make an appointment within the time. Although the statute be introductory of a new law, no negative ought to be implied.d

If a new power be given by an affirmative statute to a certain person, by the designation of that one person, although it be an affirmative statute, all other persons are in general excluded from the exercise of the power; since *expressio unius est exclusio alterius.* Thus, if an action founded upon a statute be directed to be brought before the justice of Glamorgan in his sessions, it cannot be brought before any other person, or in any other place.e So, by the Scotch law: "statutory provisions cannot be supplied by equipollents."f

But the designation of a certain person, to whom a new power is given, does not exclude another person who was by a precedent statute authorized to do it, from doing the same thing. g

a Harg. and Butl. Co. Litt. 115, (a) note 9. 2 Hawk. P. C. c. 10, s. 8.
b Lord Lovelace's case, 1 Jon. 271; 2 Bulstr. 36; Shower, 420.
c Hob. 298; Sid. 56; Stra. 1125; 2 T. R. 395.   d R. v. Sparrow, Bott. 11.
e 11 Rep. 59. Foster's case, id. 64.   f Alison's Practice Scotch Law.
g Foster's case, 11 Rep. 39.
* So the Spanish law holds that a custom being general and immemorial, may alter the anterior law. L. 6, Tit. 2 Partid. 1.

Laws declaratory in name, are often imperative in effect : legislative, like judicial interpretation being frequently deceptive, and establishing new law under guise of expounding the old. Acts to explain laws, are properly, acts of interpretation by legislative authority, or to borrow an expression from the writers on the Roman law, they are acts of *authentic* interpretation.*a*

Repeal acts, are revocations of former statutory laws, authorizing or permitting the parties, to whom the repeal extends, to forbear from acts, which they were before commanded to do. Hence, they are often named permissive laws; or more briefly *permissions.*[5]

Remedial acts are made from time to time, to supply the defects discovered in the anterior law, whether they arise from the general imperfection of all human laws; from change of time and circumstances; from mistakes and unadvised determinations, or from any other cause. And this being done, either by enlarging the ancient law when it was found too narrow, or restraining it where it was too luxuriant, occasioned the other subdivision into enlarging or restraining statutes.

A *remedial statute*, is one which supplies such defects, and abridges such superfluities in the common law as may have been discovered,*b* such as may arise either from the imperfection of all human laws, from change of time and circumstances, from mistakes, and unadvised determinations of unlearned (or even learned) judges, or from any other cause whatsoever;*c* and this being done either by enlarging the common law, where it was too narrow and circumscribed, or by restraining it where it was too lax and luxuriant, has occasioned another subordinate division of remedial acts into *enlarging* and *restraining* statutes. So, it seems, that a remedial statute may also have its application to, and effect upon other existing statutes, and gives the party injured a remedy; in other words; and for a more general definition, "it is a statute giving a party a mode of remedy for a wrong where he had none, or a different one before."*d*

Such a statute, it is universally held, is to be liberally construed, and that everything is to be done in advancement of the remedy

a Austin on Jurisprudence.   *b* 1 Black. Com. 86.
c Id.   *d* Chitt. Black. Com. note to p. 86.

NOTE 5.—Though the provisions of two acts be different, a general statute without negative words will not repeal a previous one, which is particular. Brown v County Commissioners, 9 Harris, Penn. 37.

that can be given consistently with any construction that can be put upon it.*a*

A *preceptive* statute, is one which commands certain, and it regulates the forms and acts which ought to accompany them.*b*

A *prohibitive* statute is one that forbids all actions which disturb the public repose, or injury to the rights of others, or crimes and misdemeanors; or when it forbids certain acts in relation to the transmission of estates, or the capacity of persons and other objects. *c*

A *permissive* statute, is one which allows certain actions or things to be done without commanding them, as for example— when it allows persons of a certain description, or indeed any person, to make a will.

A *penal* statute, is one which imposes a forfeiture or penalty for transgressing its provisions, or for doing a thing prohibited.

A *temporary* statute, is one which is limited in its duration at the time of its enactment. It continues in force until the time of its limitation has expired, unless sooner repealed.*d*

A *perpetual* statute, is one for the continuance of which there is no limited time, although it be not expressly declared to be so. If, however, a statute which does not in itself contain any limitation, is to be governed by another which is temporary only, the former will also be temporary and dependant upon its existence of the latter.*e*

An *affirmative* statute, is one which is enacted in affirmative terms. Such a statute does not take away the common law in relation to the same matter.*f*

A *negative* statute, is one expressed in negative terms, and so controls the common law, that it has no force in opposition to the statute.*g*

A *prospective* statute, is one which regulates the future, and is the only one which can be just, for no man can conform himself to the law which is yet unknown to him.*h*

a Johns v. Johns, 3 Dow. 15; Gillett v. Moody, 3 N. Y. 479; People v. Runkle, 9 John. R. 147.

b 1 Bouviers Inst. 48.
d Id.
f Jackson v. Bradt, 2 Caines R. 169.
h Bouvier's Inst. 49.

c Id.
e Bac. Abr. Statute D.
g Bac. Abr. Statute G.

A *retrospective* statute, is one which is made to operate upon some subject, contract, or crime, which existed before its enactment.

These laws are generally considered unjust, and are, to a certain extent, forbidden by that article of the constitution of the United States which prohibits the passage of *expost facto* laws, or laws impairing the obligation of contracts.

We shall have occasion hereafter, to notice the incidents of these several divisions or classes of statutes, when we come to treat of their power and effect, and the rules of construction by which they are governed.

A statute which gave bishops and other sole ecclesiastical corporations, (except parsons and vicars,) a power of leasing, which they did not possess before, viz., stat. 32 Hen. 8, c. 38, was an enabling statute. The stat. 13 Eliz. c. 10, which afterwards limited that power, is, on the contrary, a disabling statute.

Penal statutes are acts of Parliament, by which a forfeiture is inflicted for transgressing the provision therein contained.

A penal statute may also be a remedial law ;*a* and a statute may be penal in one part, and remedial in another part.*b*

Of no validity and VOID are, it is alleged : 1st, such acts as affect to bind future Parliaments ;*b* 2dly, such as are contrary to the laws of God and nature, and to right reason. But the latter doctrine is not admitted as excepting acts from construction, though it will decide their construction.

As to the former proposition it is clearly maintainable : Subsequent Parliaments cannot be restrained by the acts of former ones. It is only necessary to repeal the ordinance to destroy the prohibition ; and without a formal repeal, it seems that the act is *ipso facto* void. Some parts of *Magna Charta*, although it be expressly declared by the 42 Ed. 3, c. 2, that all statutes contrary thereto shall be void, have been repealed, and other parts have been altered by subsequent statutes ; yet such latter statutes, instead of being thus made void are said in Jenkin's Centuries, to have been constantly held to be in force.*c*

By construction, and that not always sound, things declared void by statute are often, it will be seen, only voidable at the

a 1 Wils. 126.   *b* Dougl. 702.   *c* Jenk. Cent. 2.

NOTE 6.—The principle cannot be controverted, that one legislature is competent to repeal any act which a former legislature was competent to pass. One legislature cannot abridge the powers of a succeeding one.* But if an act be done under a law a succeeding legislature cannot undo it. The past cannot be recalled by the most absolute power.

    * Marshall. Ch. J. 6 Cranch 135 ; Puffendorff, B. 1, Chap. 1, § 6.

election, or on the active motion of the party to be affected by them.

An act of Parliament shall not change the laws of nature,a for *jura naturae sunt immutabilia*, and they are *leges legem.* " *Nec vero per senatum aut per populum, solvi hoc lege possimus,*" says Cicero. " The law of nature stands as an eternal rule to all men," says Locke,* legislators as well as others, and the rules that they make for other men's actions must, as well as their own and other men's actions, be conformable to the will of God, of which *that* is a declaration. If a statute says that a man shall be a judge in his own cause, such a law being contrary to natural equity, shall be void. Such was the (at least intrepid,) opinion of Lord Chief Justice Hobart, in Day and Savage. Influenced by the same powerful sense of justice, Lord Coke, when Chief Justice, in Bonham's case,b unguardedly, perhaps, but fearlessly, declared, that where an act of Parliament is against common right or reason, or repugnant, or impossible to be performed, the common law shall control it, and adjudge it to be void. And Lord Holt, in the case of the City of Londonc and Wood, to the dismay of all mere lawyers, manfully expressed an opinion, that the observation of Lord Coke was not extravagant, but was a very reasonable and true saying. There is reason to believe that what Lord Coke said in his Reports upon this subject, is part of what King James alluded to, when he said that " in Coke's Reports were many dangerous conceits of his own, uttered for law, to the prejudice of the crown, parliament, and subjects." Lord Ellesmere, in his observations on Lord Coke's Reports, calls this passage "a paradox which derogateth much from the wisdom and power of Parliament, that when the three estates, King, Lords, and Commons, have spent their labor in making a law, three judges on the bench shall destroy and frustrate their pains, advancing the reason of a particular court above the judgment of all the realm. Besides, more temperately, did that reverend Chief Justice, Herle, *temp.* E. 3, deliver his opinion, 8 *E.* 3, cited by *Co. Rep.* 11, *f.* 98, when he said—some acts of Parliament are made against law and right; which they *that made them* perceiving, would not put them into execution; for it is *magis congruum* that acts of Parliament should be corrected by the same pen that drew them, than be dashed to pieces by the opinion of a few judges." So, Sir W. Blackstoned confines the rule of avoidance of unreasonable statutes, to any absurd consequences which arise out of them collaterally. The judges, he says, are in decency to conclude that *this* consequence was not foreseen by the Parliament, and only *quoad hoc* to disregard it.

a Hobart, 87,   c 12 Mod. 687.
b 8 Rep. 116.   d 1 Comm. 91.
* Lib. 2, C. 11, § 35, and see Hooker's Ecclesiastical Polity, 1, and Bishop Cumberland's *De Lege Naturae.*

If the Parliament will positively enact anything to be done which is unreasonable, he knows, he says of no power in the ordinary forms of the constitution that is vested with authority to control it.

But the advocate of natural, as opposed to positive or instituted law, may inquire what is intended by *contrary to reason?* Is not Lord Coke to be taken to mean, not merely capricious and without cause; absurd and even mischievous; but contrary to the law of nature, which we discover by the use of reason; to that light, distinct from revelation, by which we discern the boundaries of right and wrong? and then, our admirable commentator has himself, in another place, declared: "No human laws are of any validity if contrary to the laws of nature." An instance is found in the books, in which on the general doctrine that statutes contrary to common right and reason, &c., are void, and the position from Hobart being cited,*a* the judges observed, that they would not hold a statute to be void, unless it were clearly contrary to natural equity; adding with more of force perhaps, than of dignity, that they would *strain hard* rather than hold a statute to be void. Does it not follow as an irresistible inference, that if the statute *be* clearly contrary to natural equity,—if it impugn that original law which is coeval with our nature, and has God for its author, the judges, (according, at least, to the feelings of those presiding on that occasion,) *must*, with whatever reluctance —however averse to defeat a statute, their duty requires them— to declare it void! But say their enlightened opponents, to do this would be to set the judicial power above the legislative. Upon which two observations may be made: first, this argument seems to prove too much; for it applies as strongly to setting aside the collateral as the direct consequences of an act; and if the one take place, (barring the objection to the indecency of supposing it necessary,) why not the other: secondly, Lord Coke does not leave the decision to be governed "by the crooked cord of the discretion of the judges;" but it is to be "measured by the golden metwand of the law;"—he says it shall be controlled *by the common law.* To pronounce such a decision is, on the part of the judges, nothing more than to say, vast as is the power of an act of Parliament, there are some things which it cannot do. It can do no wrong; it cannot abrogate those living laws imprinted in our hearts from the commencement of our being. In the conceivable and barely possible case of a statute directing the commission of an offence against the law of nature, can there be a doubt that, in such instance, no human laws would be in any degree binding? or, what amounts to the same thing, that there exists a precedent and paramount obligation to disobey them? A statute cannot make it lawful to commit adultery with the wife

a 10 Mod. 115.

of B., for the law of God forbids it. Neither are positive laws, even in matters seemingly indifferent, any further binding than as they are agreeable to the laws of God and nature.a

On the other hand, it is said, that though the *principle* asserted above is undeniably true, yet the application of it, and the conclusion, are most dangerous.b It is certain that no human authority can rightfully infringe or abrogate the smallest particle of natural or divine law;* but we must distinguish, it is observed, between right and power, between moral fitness and political authority. It must not be entertained as a question of ethics, but of the bounds and limits of legislative power. All that can be done, it seems, is to follow the philosophical advice of Locke, who says, that if the magistrate shall enjoin anything unlawful to the conscience of a private person, such private person is to abstain from the action that he judges unlawful, and he is to undergo the punishment, which it is not unlawful for him to bear. The same *acquiescence in* the laws is enjoined in the admirable dialogue of Plato, entitled Crito.

The English lawyers adopt a more cautious and a very characteristic mode of proceeding. They do not inculcate implicit obedience to a law which leads to absurd consequences, or to an infraction of the natural or Divine law; neither do they proclaim the law itself, (which may be immoral, but cannot be illegal), of no validity, and null and void. They only hold it inapplicable, and declare that the particular case is "excepted out of the statute." A practical mode of dealing with cases where statutes collaterally give rise to absurd consequences, on the ground of such consequences being unforeseen, which cannot be denied to be reasonable.

The general and received doctrine certainly is, that an act of Parliament, of which the terms are explicit and the meaning plain, cannot be questioned, or its authority controlled, in any court of justice. Yet Sir Edward Coke, manfully, if not convincingly, defended his opinion before the council, and said : " If an act of Parliament, were to give to the lord of a manor, conusance of all pleas arising within his manor, yet he shall hold no plea whereunto himself is a party; for *iniquum est aliquem suœ rei, esse judicem.*" Now, Sir E. Coke had, in his Second Institute, put the same case, enlarged upon and illustrated it ; and successfully

a Fonbl. ch. 1, s. 3.   Jurisprudence, 36 and 48.—Bl. Com. vol. i.
b 1 Woodison's Lect.—do Elements of *ante.*

* Among the seven maxims or virtues essential to the written law of Spain, one is, "that its precepts ought to be respecting things *good, reasonable, just, and not opposed to the law of God,*" to attain its only object, justice, which is rooted virtue —*raigada virtud.—Ll.* 1 and 4, *Tit.* 1 *Patrid.* 1, *L.* 1, *Tit.* 1, *P.* 3 —So, the unwritten law, (*uso, costumbre, y fuero*) receiving its authority from the express or tacit consent of the supreme power, that consent cannot be supposed or presumed when the custom is opposed *to the law of God, to good reason ; to the law of the kingdom, and to natural law.—L.* 5, *Tit.* 2, *Patrid.* 1.—*L.* 8, *Tit.* 1, *Lib.* 2, *Recob.*

contended, that the case must be correctly *interpreted* to be exempted out of the provisions of the statute; that a contrary construction could not be within the meaning of the act. The law, therefore, was to be properly *construed* not to apply to such cases; but the law itself was not to be held void. See *post*, "Cases excepted out of statutes," *"Fit autem, non tollendo legis obligationem, sed declarando legum in certo casu, non applicare."a*

The principle as to the binding efficacy of statutes, does not prevail in the United States of America. There they hold, that as there is a written constitution, designating the powers and duties of the legislative, as well as of the other departments of the government, an act of the legislature may be void, as being against the constitution.*b* The judicial department, say they, is the proper power in the government to determine whether a statute, be or be not constitutional. The interpretation or construction of the constitution, is as much a judicial act, and requires the exercise of the same legal discretion as the interpretation or construction of a law. To contend that the courts of justice must obey the requisitions of an act of the legislature, when it appears to them to have been passed in violation of the constitution, would be to contend that the law was superior to the constitution, and that the judges had no right to look into the latter, and to regard it as the paramount law. It has accordingly become a settled principle in the legal policy of the United States, that it belongs to the judicial power, as a matter of right and of duty, to declare every act of the legislature made in violation of the constitution, or any provision of it, null and void.*c* But this question will be more appropriately examined in a future chapter.

So, also, in the United States. the rule is, that the courts cannot declare a legislative act void, because it conflicts with their opinion of natural rights, of policy, expediency, or justice.' The

---

a Grotius.   *b* Kent Com.

c 1 Kent Com. 318 ; Id. 330, 425, 6.

NOTE 7.—If Congress or a State legislature, pass a law, within the general scope of their constitutional power, the courts cannot pronounce it void, merely because in their judgment it is contrary to the principles of natural justice. Calder v. Bull 3 Dall. 399; Mingo v. Gilmour, 1 Car. L. Repos. 34 ; Albee v. May, 2 Paine, 74; Beale v. Woodhull, Pet. C. C. R. 2; Macomber v. Mayor of New York, 17, Abbott 35; People v. Huntington, 4 N. Y. Leg. Observ. 182.[8]

8.—"All the courts can do with odious statutes, is to chasten their hardness by construction. Such is the imperfection of the best human institutions, that, mould them as we may, a large discretion must be reposed somewhere. The safest, and in many cases the best security, is in the wisdom and integrity of public servants, and their identity with the people." Beebe v. S ate, 6 Ind. R. 528; Johnson v. Commonwealth, 1 Bibb. R. 603. "If the legislature should pass a law, in plain and unequivocal language, within the scope of their constitutional

courts are not guardians of the rights of the people of the State in these respects unless those rights are secured by some constitutional provision which comes within their judicial cognizance. The only remedy left to the people for unreasonable, unwise, or oppressive legislation, is by appeal to the justice and patriotism of the representatives of the people. If this appeal fails, the evil remains, until the people in their sovereign capacity correct it, by selecting more just and faithful representatives.*a*

We have no code of laws, supreme, and paramount to the legislative power, which defines the laws of nature, and by virtue of which, the courts can declare a legislative act void for its want of conformity to such natural law.*b* If it was in the power of the courts to declare a State law void, which conflicts with no constitutional provision on account of its supposed injustice, or oppressive operation, or its conflict with natural rights, the courts would become makers instead of expounders of the law. Their opinions would not be a judgment upon what was the pre-existing law, but upon what it is after they have amended or modified it so as to meet their ideas of reason, of justice, policy, or wise legislation. This could only be done by a direct usurpation of the legislative power, and a flagrant violation of judicial duty.*c*

There are, it is true, in our books of reports, various dicta, following the English rule, that acts, contrary to the principles of right and reason are void, *d* but they are not now followed as authority. In the highest court of the State of New York, in the case of Cochran v. Van Surlay, *e* it was declared in the leading opinion, "that it was only in express constitutional provisions,

a 1 Baldwin R. 74.   *b* Bennett v. Boggs, 1 Baldwin, 74.
c Smith's Com. 261.

d Regents of University v. Williams, 9 Gill. and Johnson 365; also, opinion of Chase J. in Calder v. Bull, 3 Dallas, 388 ; 1 Bay. 152. Goshen v. Stonnington, 4 Conn. 225.

e 20 Wend. 382.

powers, I know of no authority in this government to pronounce such an act void, merely because in the opinion of the judicial tribunals, it was contrary to the principles of natural justice; for this would be vesting in the court a latitudinarian authority which might be abused, and would necessarily lead to collisions between the legislative and judicial departments, dangerous to the well-being of society, or at least not in harmony with the structure of our ideas of natural government." Commonwealth v. McCloskey, 2 Rawle. R. 374.

limiting legislative power, and controling the temporary will of the majority by a permanent and paramount law settled by the deliberate wisdom of the nation, that a safe and solid ground for the authority of courts of justice could be found, to declare void any legislative enactment. Any assumption of authority beyond this, would be to place in the hands of the judiciary, powers too great and too undefined, either for its own security, or for the protection of private rights." In order to guard against so great an evil, it has been the policy of all the American States that have formed written constitutions since the revolution, and of the people of the United States when they framed the federal constitution, to define with precision, the objects of legislative power, and to restrain its exercise within marked and settled boundaries.

The ideas of natural justice, are not, and cannot be, regulated by a fixed standard. The ablest and purest men have differed, and ever will differ, on such a subject. The legislature possess, certainly an equal, if not a superior right, to the courts, to determine, by *their* opinion, what laws are consistent with the abstract principles of natural justice. That the necessity, and degree of necessity, for passing a law, not prohibited by the constitution, is a question of legislative discretion, and not of judicial cognizance, was held by Ch. J. Marshall, in McCulloch v. State of Maryland. *a* It is not a sufficient argument that this power may be abused by the legislature. It is an equally forcible argument to say the same thing as to the power of the courts. Such is the nature of all power. The abuse of power, is the tendency of all human institutions. We must be content to limit power where we can. Under our system of regulated power, as well as of regulated liberty; we must be content to repose in the confidence, that in our American government, we are as free from danger of abuse, as under any other form of government that ever did exist. *b*

Chief Justice Marshall, at an early day, expressed his views on this question, in an action between two individuals, claiming under an act of the legislature, in which action, corruption on the part

a 4 Wheat R. 316.   *b* Calder v. Bull, 3 Dall. 400.

Note 9.—The moral tendency and inexpediency of a statute is a question for the legislature, not for the court. Per Taney Ch. J. Brewer v. Blougher, 14. Pet. 198.

11

of the legislature was alleged, in the passage of the act. He said,a " This solemn question cannot be brought thus collaterally before the court. It would be indecent, in the extreme, upon a private contract between two individuals, to enter into an enquiry respecting the corruption of the sovereign power of a State. If the title be plainly deduced from a legislative act, which the legislature might constitutionally pass; if the act be clothed with all the requisite powers of a law; a court, sitting as a court of law, cannot sustain a suit brought by one individual against another, founded on the allegation that the act is a nullity, in consequence of the impure motives which influenced certain members of the legislature who passed the law."

The wisdom of man has never conceived of a government with power sufficient to its legitimate ends, and at the same time incapable of mischief. No political system can be made so perfect that its rulers will always hold it to the true course. In the very best, a great deal must be trusted to the discretion of those who administer it. In ours, the people have given larger powers to the legislature, and relied for the faithful execution of them, on the wisdom and honesty of that department, and on the direct accountability of the members to their constituents. There is no shadow of reason for supposing that the mere abuse of power was meant to be corrected by the judiciary.b

The soundest rule on this subject, it is believed, is, that the legislative departments of government are co-ordinate, and of equal dignity with the executive and the judicial departments; each is alike supreme in the exercise of its proper functions ; and cannot directly or indirectly, while acting within the limits of its authority, be subjected to the control or supervision of the other, without an unwarrantable assumption by that other, of power, which, by the constitution, is not conferred upon it.[10]

The American constitutions are supposed to apportion the powers of government between the three departments, executive,

a Fletcher v. Peck, 6 Cranch. 131.

b Sharpless v. Mayor, &c. 21 Penn. St. R. 162.

Note 10.—A prudent and discreet judge, is one that does not judge statutes to void because he considers them against common right and reason, but leaves Parliament to judge what is common right and reason. Dwarris, 481.

legislative, and judicial; but does not make either subordinate to the other when exercising the trust committed to it. The courts, it is true, may declare legislative enactments unconstitutional and void, in some cases,—not because they are against natural reason —nor because the judicial power is superior to the legislative; but because they are required to declare what the law is in the case before them. They are bound to enforce the constitution as the paramount law, whenever a legislative enactment comes in conflict with it.a Inasmuch as statutes are either enacted, interpreted, or enforced by one or the other of these three co-ordinate departments of the sovereign power, or by a union of all of them, a brief discussion of their respective powers, and the influence of each, in the control of government, here, may not be inappropriate.

In the establishment of our national and State governments, the highest evidence of wisdom, of patriotism, and statesmanship is manifest, in the policy of dividing the powers of the governments into the three departments, the executive, the legislative, and the judicial;·and, that their respective functions should be kept separate and distinct; and while they should be co-ordinate in rank and power, and all be acting in harmony, yet, within their respective spheres, each should be independent of the other, and be so organized, that, the proper exercise of their respective functions, in the powers of each, would be a conservative check upon the others, and so confine each in its action, to its legitimate sphere.[11]

While the equality and separate independence of these departments is to be implied in all these constitutions, several of the States made the grant of power to each, express; with a prohibition to each department, against the exercise of powers intended for the others. In Massachusetts, for instance, it was declared that, "in the government of this commonwealth, the legislative department shall never exercise the executive or judicial powers, or of either of them;

a Cooley, on Constitutional Limitation.

NOTE 11.—The legislative, executive, and judicial departments are co-ordinate in degree, to the extent of the powers delegated to each of them. Each in the exercise of its powers, is independent of the other, but all rightfully done by either, is binding upon the others. Dodge v. Woolsey, 18 How. U. S. R. 347.

the executive shall never exercise the legislative and judicial powers, or of either of them; the judicial shall never exercise the legislative and executive powers, or of either of them; to the end, that it may be a government of laws and not of men."a The same idea, in effect, is carried into other State constitutions.

Mr. Madison, one of the ablest and most distinguished of constitutional expounders, said, b " It is agreed on all sides that the powers properly belonging to one of the departments, ought not to be directly and completely administered by either of the other departments. It is equally evident that neither of them ought to possess, directly or indirectly, an overruling influence over the others, in the administration of their respective powers. It will not be denied, that power is of an encroaching nature, and that it ought to be effectually restrained, from passing the limits assigned to it."   .

Montesquieu, in his work on the Spirit of the Laws, says, c " When the legislative and executive powers are united in the same person, or in the same body of magistrates, there can be no liberty, because apprehensions may arise, lest the same monarch or senate should enact tyrannical laws, to execute them in a tyrannical manner.   Again, there is no liberty, if the judiciary power be not separated from the legislative and executive. Were it joined with the legislative, the life and liberty of the subject would be exposed to arbitrary control; for the judge would be the legislator. Were it joined to the executive power, the judge might behave with violence and oppression. There would be an end of everything, were the same man or the same body, whether of the nobles or of the people, to exercise these three powers, that of enacting laws, that of executing the public resolutions, and of trying the causes of individuals."

And Blackstone, who wrote his commentaries in regard to the laws of a monarchial government, says: d " In all tyrannical governments, the supreme magistracy, or the right of both making and enforcing laws, is vested in the same man, or in one and the same body of men; and where ever these two powers are united together, there can be no public liberty. The magistrate may

a Bill of Rights, Art. 30.　　　　b Federalist. No. 47.
c Book XI, Chap. 6.　　　　　　　d 1 Com. 146.

enact tyrannical laws and execute them in a tyrannical ma..ner, since he is possessed, in quality of dispenser of justice, with all the power, which he, as legislator, thinks proper to give himself. But when the legislative and executive authority are in distinct hands, the former will take care not to entrust the latter with so large a power, as may tend to the subversion of its own independence, and therewith of the liberty .of the subject." Again, he says: a " In the distinct and separate existence of the judicial power in a peculiar body of men, nominated indeed by, but not removable at the pleasure of the crown, consists one main preservation of the public liberty; which cannot long subsist in any State, unless the administration of common justice be in some degree separated from the legislative, and also the executive power. Were it joined with the legislative, the life, liberty, and property of the subject would be in the hands of arbitrary judges, whose decisions would then be regulated only by their opinions, and not by any fundamental principles of law ; which, though legislators may depart from, yet judges are bound to observe. Were it joined with the executive, this union might soon be an overbalance for the legislative."

But when we speak of the necessity of this division of power between these departments of government as indispensable to public liberty, it is not meant to affirm that they must be kept so separate and distinct as to have no common link of connection or dependence, in any sense whatever, but, that the whole power of these departments should not be exercised by the same hands which shall possess the whole power of either of the other departments ; and that such exercise of the whole, would subvert the principle of a free constitution. b

The line which separates the powers and functions of one department from the other, is not clearly expressed, or accurately defined ; the practical result, must be, the occasional invasions of the one upon the other, and a usurpation of functions which belong to the one, by the other. Minds of the ablest men will differ, as to the nature and extent of the prohibition. So long as these powers respectively, depend upon interpretation ; the different constitutions of the minds of men, more or less influenced

a Id. 269.   b Story on Const. § 525.

by interest, faction, an apparent necessity to meet a particular case, or a temporarily existing popular sentiment, the judgments and reasoning of men partake of some of the bias of public opinion. Practically, we know, that usurpations of power by one department upon another, have been assumed, and have had a temporary sympathy from popular favor. *a*

Mr. Story, says: "that in order to preserve in full vigor the constitutional barrier between each department when they are entirely separated, it is obviously indispensable, that each should possess, equally, and in the same degree, the means of self-protection. Now, in point of theory, this would be almost impracticable, if not impossible; and in point of fact, it is well known, that the means of self-protection in the different departments are immeasurably disproportionate. The judiciary, is incomparably the weakest of either, and must forever, in a considerable measure, be subjected to the legislative power. And the latter has, and must have, a controlling influence over the executive power, since it holds, at its own command, all the resources, by which a chief magistrate could make himself formidable. It possesses the power over the purse, and the property of the people. It can grant, or withhold supplies; it can levy, or withdraw taxes; it can unnerve the power of the sword by striking down the arm which wields it."*b*

"It is, without doubt," says DeLolme, a writer upon the English constitution, "absolutely necessary for securing the constitution of a State, to restrain the executive power. But, it is still more necessary to restrain the legislative. What the former can do by successive steps, (I mean subvert the laws,) and through a longer or shorter train of enterprises, the latter does, in a moment, as its bare will can give being to laws, so its bare will can also annihilate them; and if I may be permitted the expression, the legislative power can change the constitution, as God created the light. In order therefore, to insure stability to the constitution of a State, it is indispensably necessary to restrain the legislative authority."*c* He then proceeds to say, that he regards the division of the legislative power into two bodies, as an important aid in the restraining power.

a Federalist, No. 48.
c DeLolme's Book 2, ch. 3.   *b* Story, on Const. § 531

The truth is, says Judge Story, "that the legislative power is the great and overruling power in every free government. It has been remarked with equal power and sagacity, that the legislative power is everywhere extending the sphere of its activity, and drawing all power into its impetuous vortex."a And he adds, the opinion, that the founders of our government, were so impressed with dread of the royal prerogative, that they seemed not to have remembered the danger from legislative usurpations. The representatives of the people, will watch with jealousy every encroachment of the executive magistrate, for it entrenches upon their own authority. But who shall watch the encroachments of the representatives? Will they be as jealous of the exercise of power by themselves, as by others?" b In a representative republic, when the executive magistrate is carefully limited, both in the extent and duration of its power; and where the legislative power is exercised by an assembly which is inspired by a supposed influence over the people, with an intrepid confidence in its own strength; and which is sufficiently numerous to feel all the passions which actuate the multitude; yet so numerous, as to be incapable of pursuing the objects of its passions by means which reason prescribes; it is easy to see, that the tendency to the usurpation of power, is, if not constant, at least probable; and that it is against the enterprising ambition of this department, that the people may well indulge all their jealousy and exhaust all their precautions.c

There are many reasons which may be assigned for the engrossing influence of the legislative department. In the first place, its constitutional powers are more extensive, and less capable of being brought within precise limits, than those of either of the other departments.

The bounds of the executive authority are easily marked out, and defined. It reaches few objects, and those are known. It cannot transcend them, without being brought into contact with the other department. Laws may check, and bound, and restrain its exercise.

The same remarks apply with still greater force to the judiciary. Its jurisdiction is, or may be, bounded to a few objects or

a Story on Const. § 532.   b Id.

c See Federalist, Nos. 48 and 49.

persons; or however general and unlimited, its operations are necessarily confined to the mere administration of private and public justice. It cannot punish without law. It cannot create controversies to act upon. It can decide only the rights and cases as they are brought by others before it. It can do nothing of itself. It must do everything for others. It must obey the laws; and if it corruptly administer them, it is subjected to the power of impeachment.

On the other hand, the legislative power, except in a few cases of constitutional prohibition, is unlimited. It is forever varying its means and its ends. It governs the institutions, and laws, and public policy of the country. It regulates all its vast interests. It disposes of all of its property. Look but at the exercise but of two or three of its ordinary powers. It levies all taxes; it directs and appropriates all supplies; it gives the rules for the descent, distribution, and devises of all property held by individuals. It controls the sources and resources of wealth. It changes at its will the whole fabric of the laws. It moulds at its pleasure almost all the institutions, which give strength, and comfort, and dignity to society.a It is the direct visible representative of the people in all the changes of times and circumstances. It has the pride as well as the power of numbers. It is easily moved, and steadily moved by the strong impulses of popular feeling, and popular odium. It obeys, without reluctance, the wishes and the will of the majority of the body for the time being. The path to public favor lies open by such obedience; and it finds not only support, but impunity, in whatever measure the majority advises, even though they transcend the constitutional limits. It has no motive, therefore, to be jealous, or scrupulous, in its own use of power; and it finds its ambition stimulated, and its arm strengthened by the countenance and courage of numbers.

It has been supposed, that the right of appeal to the people to change the fundamental law, is an adequate protection to all the evils that such body may inflict. Judge Story doubts this, in the following language : " Whoever has been present in any assembly, convened for such a purpose, must have perceived the great diversities of opinion upon the most vital questions; and the extreme

a Story. § 534.

difficulty in bringing a majority to concur in the long-sighted wisdom of the soundest provisions. Temporary feelings and excitements, popular prejudices, an ardent love of theory, an enthusiastic temperament, inexperience, and ignorance, as well as preconceived opinions, operate wonderfully to blind the judgment, seduce the understanding.*a*

But, if the other two departments, the executive and judiciary, could make this appeal to the people, even then, in the opinion of Mr. Madison, they would not enjoy equal advantages on a trial. He says : *b* "the members of the executive and judiciary departments, are few in number, and can be personally known to a small part only, of the people. The judiciary, are removed too far from the people to share much in their prepossessions. The executive is generally the object of jealousy, and their administrations always liable to be discolored, and rendered unpopular. The members of the legislative department, on the other hand, are numerous. They are distributed and dwell among the people at large. Their connections of blood, of friendship, and of acquaintance, embrace a great proportion of the most influential part of society. The nature of their public trust implies a personal influence among the people. With these advantages, it can hardly be supposed that the adverse party would have an equal chance for a favorable issue. But the legislative party would not only be able to plead their cause most successfully with the people; they would probably be constituted themselves the judges. The same influence which had gained them an election into the legislature, would give them a seat in the convention. If this should not be the case with all, it would probably be the case with many, and pretty certainly with those leading characters on whom everything depends, in such bodies. The convention, in short, would be composed chiefly of men, who had been, who actually were, or who expected to be, members of the department whose conduct was arraigned. They would consequently be parties to the very question to be decided by them."

Not so, in any degree, is the case of the judiciary department. "It is never brought into contact with the people, by constant appeals and solicitations, and private intercourse which belongs

a Id. § 537. *b* Federalist, No. 48.

12

to the other departments of government. It is seen only in controversies, or in trials and punishments. Its rigid justice and impar-
tialities give it no claims to favor, however they may to respect.
It stands solitary and unsupported, except by that portion of
public opinion which is interested only in the strict administration
of justice. It can rarely secure the sympathy or zealous support
either of the executive or the legislature. If they are not, (as is
not unfrequently the case) jealous of its prerogatives, the constant
necessity of scrutinizing the acts of each, upon the application of
any private person, and the painful duty of pronouncing judgment that these are a departure from the law or constitution ; can
have no tendency to conciliate kindness, or nourish influence."

It may here be allowable, (and not without its use and practical advantage), to state shortly the division of statutes, according
to the foreign jurists ; with a brief sketch of their general nature
and distinctive qualities.

But it is necessary to premise, in order to guard against a misconception lying in the path of the English lawyer, that by
statutes the civilians mean, not the positive legislation, which in
England and America is known by the same name, viz. ; the acts
of Parliament and of other legislative bodies as contradistinguished from the common law ; but the whole municipal law of the
particular state, from whatever source arising a. Sometimes, the
word is used by civilians, in contradistinction to the Roman
Imperial Law, which they are accustomed to style, by way of
eminence, "The Common Law ;" since it constitutes the general
basis of the jurisprudence of all continental Europe, modified and
restrained by local customs and usages, and positive legislation.

Statutes are divided by civilians into personal, real and mixed.

Personal statutes are those which act upon the person directly
as their subject or object ; by fixing and determining its *state* either
universally or particularly ; without mentioning *things*, except with
reference to the *state* with which the *person* is affected. Of universal qualities, some take effect from birth, as *nobility b* legitimacy,
bastardy ; and these can only be affixed by the law of the domicil of
origin. Some take effect at a stated time after birth ; as the period
of majority, and the time when the civil capacity to contract commences. These are governed by the laws of the domicil of origin ;
each state being the most capable of judging from the physical
circumstances of climate and otherwise, at what time the faculties
of its subjects are to be considered morally and civilly perfect for
the purposes of society. Other qualities are universal, so far as

a Story on the Conflict of Laws, p. 10.   *b* Not in America.

the comity of nations extend, but take effect at an indeleminate time after birth, *as letters of nobility*, judgments or decrees of competent tribunals declaring any person an idiot, lunatic or bankrupt. The relation of marriage also seems of this nature as to its personal qualities, (the marital power,) however it may differ as to its consequences with respect to real property situate out of the territory where the act of marriage is celebrated. *a*

Thus an act done by a minor in regard to his property situate in the place of his domicil, without the consent of his guardian, is invalid there, and will be held invalid in every other place. So, if a married woman, who is disabled by the law of the place of her domicil from entering into any contract, or from transferring any property therein, without the consent of her husband, should make a contract or transfer property situate therein, the transaction will be held invalid, and a nullity in every other country. *b* " *Quando lex in personam dirigitur respicienda est ad leges illius civitatis, quæ personam habat subjectam.c* " *Qualitas personam, sicut umbra, sequitur.*"

But, as to acts done, rights acquired, and contracts made, by persons not declared incapable, in other countries, the *lex loci contractus* ought to prevail, and not the *lex loci domicilii*. And as the validity of the contract may depend upon the capacity of the contracting party, in regard to questions of minority and majority; competency or incomptency to marry; incapacities incident to coverture; guardianship, &c.; as a rule in other countries, the law of the domicil of birth or habitation is not generally to prevail, but the *lex loci contractus aut actus*. Such qualities as are last spoken of, can only be affixed by the sovereign or judge of the actual or real domicil. Great confusion and mischief, it is apparent, would arise, if the effects of judgments and decrees of idiocy, lunacy, &c., were not to be general and universal, and if the same person could be considered as capable to contract in one place, and incapable in another. Here, *d* therefore, one independent state will, by the comity of nations, and for the general convenience of mankind, give effect to the laws and judicial acts of another, so far as it can be done without prejudice to the fundamental principles of its own internal policy. *e*

Personal *particular* qualities, are those whereby a person generally incapable by his civil state, is rendered capable for some particular act; or a person generally capable by his civil state, is

a Modern statutes, in several of the states of this government, have changed this marital power. It is not proposed to review in this work, the variations from the common law which have been effected by such statutes in different states.

b Henry on Foreign Law, p. 4 ; Bullenois Pri. Genl. 6. .

c 1 Hertii Op. De Collis. Leg. § 4, art. 8, p. 123.

d Huber de jure civitatis, 1, 3, c. 10; Voet ad Pandectas, lib. 1, tit. 4, par. 2, n. 11

e Henry on Foreign Law, p. 2.

rendered incapable for some particular act.[12] Of the first class
is the statute 7 Anne, c. 19, enabling infant trustees to convey; of
the second is the act 1 Jac. 1, c. 15, s. 5, disabling persons subject
to the bankrupt laws from conveying or transferring their lands
to their children or others, except in a particular way.

If the object be of a personal nature, as to contract or become
security, the statute is purely *personal*, and the quality accompanies
the person everywhere. If the object be of a real nature, as to
alienate or settle lands, and the subject matter real property,
then the person is only affected with respect to this species of
property locally, and it is confined to the domicile; of which
dower in England is an example. Personal disqualifications, the
creatures of positive law, and especially such as are of a penal
nature are not generally regarded in other countries. Hence the
disqualifications arising from heresy, excommunication, popish
recusancy, &c., are not enforced in any country except in that in
which they originate. The acts of idiots, lunatics and married
women escaping into foreign countries, are not deemed obligatory
as regards property there, even if sanctioned by the foreign law
unless the law of their own country adopt such foreign law as a
rule to govern in such cases.

Real statutes, are those which affect directly *things* as their
object or motive, whether movable or immoveable, and independently of the personal state of him who is to exercise the acts of
ownership on them. According to this description, the statute of
22 & 23 C. 2, c. 10, regulating the distribution of the personal
property of intestates, is as much a real statute as that which
declares that no lands in England shall pass by a will not attested
by three witnesses. But there is nevertheless a marked difference
in the powers and operations of a real statute in these two cases.
With respect to immovable property, the law of the situation does
not defer by comity to the law of the actual domicile, which may,

NOTE 12.—Where the statute obliges an infant to indemnify the city, town or
county against the expense of supporting his illegitimate child, and makes it necessary for him to enter into a bond with sureties, for the purpose, as the only
means by which he can obtain a discharge from arrest; that provision, without
further words, gives the infant a legal capacity to make a binding obligation, and
his infancy is no defence to an action on the bond. People v. Moores, 4 Denio,
518; Baker v. Lovett, 6 Mass. 80, 4 Mass. 376, 1 Mason 83. Any disability created by the common law, is removed by the enactment of a statute. The competency of an infant to do all acts within the purview of such statute, is as complete
as that of a person of full age. And whenever a statute has authorized a contract
for the public service, which, from its nature and objects, is manifestly intended
to be performed by infants, such a contract must, in point of law, be deemed to be
for their benefit, and for the public benefit, so that when *bona fide* made, it is neither void nor voidable, but is strictly obligatory upon them.

perhaps, be content with two witnesses in the devise of lands ;*a
while a will made abroad, according to the law of the testator's
domicile, is allowed to pass personal, or even funded property in
England ;b and the statute of distributions gives way, with respect
to the personal property of intestates in England, to the laws of
the foreign domicile, in the case where a person dies intestate
abroad ;c and this by favor of the fiction of law that *mobilia
sequuntur personam.*

Whether a given statute be personal, real or mixed, and if
mixed, whether the personalty or realty prevail, is often a subject
of learned debate. The rules for distinguishing the several kinds,
and the application of those rules to the particular case, are often
keenly controverted among the civilians who seem to agree in
nothing but that the matter is full of difficulty and uncertainty.d

When the law of the domicile of the creditor and debtor differs
as to classing debts and rights, and rights of action, the law of the
debtor must prevail, in suits thereon, according to the maxims
actio sequitur forum rei, and *debita sequuntur personam debitoris.* It
is indeed a maxim, that debts and rights of action, *inhaerant ossibus creditoris,* attend the person of a creditor, but to recover them
he must follow the *forum rei,* and the person of the creditor. The
explanation of this seeming contradiction is, that personal actions
arising from debts or obligations, have two characters ; *active* as
they respect the right of the creditor, and *passive* as they regard
the obligation of the debtor. If the question regard the distribution of the creditors estate, the law of his domicil is to be observed ;
if the question be in what degree or proportion the representatives of the debtor should be charged with payments from his
effects, then it is of a passive nature, and the law of the domicile
of the debtor should be followed. The extent of the *vinculum
obligationes* of a contract, is regulated by the law of the place of
contract. A legal discharge of a debt in the country where it is
contracted, will operate as a discharge in all others. The place
where the bankrupt is arrested, taken in execution, or commits
an act of bankruptcy, or where the *concursos* of creditors, or *præ,*
and *concurrentiae,* are held in the proper place of distribution. All
other claimants must be drawn to the *locus concursus creditorum ;*
its law (*jus domicilii*) is binding, and the equitable doctrine of cession and discharge is now become a general principle acted upon

a Qy. *Voet, contra.*

b Thomas v. Walker, 2 Ves, 35, Fonblanque, vol, 2, 446; Henry on For. Law, 14.

c Lord Annandale's case before the House of Lords, 1828.

d Hertius de Collisione legem, § 4.

* Professor Voet, *Lib.* 1, *Tit.* 4, *part* 2, *sect.* 13, considers "*ad validitatem actus
cujusque, sufficere adhibitionem solemnitatum quos lex loci* IN QUO ACTUS GERITUR *præ-
scripserit observandas,*" and he assigns as a reason that *industria exquisitissima*
would be insufficient to acquire a knowledge of the laws of different countries.

in every country.a It is otherwise when the debt is contracted in a foreign country.b A foreign bankruptcy is no bar to the demand of a debt contracted in England; but by a decision not founded on any general principle, but upon the effect of the particular statute (54. Geo. 3 C. 137) a debt contracted in England by a trader residing in Scotland, is barred by a discharge under a sequestration, in like manner as debts contracted in Scotland.c

MIXED statutes affect both persons and things, and constitute a third class, which (after spending much time and profuse ink in unprofitable disputes) it was found absolutely necessary to admit; there being so many statutes which are not either purely personal or purely real. Whether a given statute be personal, real, or mixed; and if mixed, whether the personalty or realty prevail, is often a subject of learned debate. The rules for distinguishing the several kinds, and the application of those rules to the particular case, are often keenly controverted among the civilians, who seem to agree in nothing, but that the matter is full of difficulty and uncertainty. "In iis definiendes mirum est quam sudant doctores."d

In the case of the conflict of statutes, the following maxims seem to obtain :

Where the personal statutes of the domicil of origin or birth, and those of the actual domicil, are discrepant, the latter give way to the former, by comity, and for the reciprocal advantage of sovereigns, that each may preserve his authority over his own subjects. Thus the statute fixing the majority at twenty-one, habilitates the party in another domicil where the age of twenty-five is required.

When the domicil of origin gives a personal capacity, but that of the situation of the real property is different and prohibitory, the lex loci rei sitæ prevails.

But when statutes real, differ in degree, each has its effect pro tanto. If a man has possessions in different states, in one of which he is allowed by the law to dispose by will of a third, and in another only of a fifth, he may dispose of his properties severally, in conformity with each.

Marriage contracts are juris gentium.e Where there is a marriage contract, regulating the rights and properties of the parties, that will be held equally valid everywhere.f

a Hunter v. Potts, 4 T. R. 182 ; Sills and Warwick, 2 H. Black. R. 402 ; Ballantine and Golding, Cooke's Bankrupt Laws, 499.

b Smith v. Buchanan, 1 East. R. 16 ; Potter v. Brown, 5 East. 124, 2 H. Bl. 553, 8 T. R. 609 ; Lewis and Owen, 4, B. and A. 654.

c Sidaway v. Hay, 3 B. and C. 13.

d Hertius de Collisione legum, § 4.

e Scrimshire v. Scrimshire. 2 Hagg. Consist. Rep. p. 412.

f Story on Conflict of Laws, p. 159.

Where there is a change of domicil, the law of the actual domicil will govern the rights of the parties as to all future acquisitions.*a*

Where there is no express contract, the law of the matrimonial domicil will govern as to present,—and where there is no change of domicil,—as to future acquired property in that place; and as to personal property everywhere. As to immovable property, the *lex rei sitæ* will prevail.

Suppose a husband and wife, married in, and subjects of, England, should become permanently domiciled in France, would a will of the wife in France (which she could not make in England) in regard to her property in England, made in favor of her husband or others, be held valid in England? *b* Hertius, Paul Voet, John Voet, Burgundus, Rodenburg, Pothier and Merlin, hold that the law of the new domicil must, in all cases of a change of domicil, govern the capacities and rights of property of married women, as well as their obligations and duties; but the law of England is singularly reluctant to admit, by comity, any doctrine which is repugnant to the settled principles and policy of its own laws.

There is no doubt, that, where there is a change of domicil, the law of the actual domicil, and not of the matrimonial domicil, will govern future acquisitions of movable property, *c* provided always, that the law of the place do not prohibit such arrangements.*d* For though in general the law of the matrimonial domicil is to govern in relation to the incidents and effects of marriage, the doctrine must be received with many qualifications.

A marriage in France or Prussia may be dissolved for incompatibility of temper; but no divorce would be granted for such a cause in England, Scotland, or America. "If," said a learned Scotch judge,*e* " a man in this country (Scotland) were to confine his wife in a cage, or beat her with a rod of the thickness of the judge's finger; would it be any justification, in any court, to allege that these were powers which the laws of England conferred on a husband? and that he was entitled to exercise them because his marriage was celebrated in that country?"

"As to the constitution of marriage," says the same learned scotch judge, " as it is merely a personal consensual contract, it must be valid everywhere, if celebrated according to the *lex loci;* but with regard to the rights, duties and obligations thence arising, the law of the domicil must be looked to."

a Ibid
b Merlin. Repert. Testament, s. 1. 5, art. 1, p. 309.
c Stein's case, 1 Rose, Bank. Ca. Appx. 481; Henry on Foreign Law, 48; Burge Comm. on Col. and Foreign Law, pt. 1, c. 7, s. 18, p. 618.
d Huber, lib. 1, tit. 3, s. 2.
e Ferguson on Marriage and Divorce 399, per Lord Robinson.

The rule that a marriage which is valid where it is celebrated, is valid everywhere,[a] and if invalid there, is invalid everywhere, has three exceptions. First those marriages involving polygamy, and incest. Secondly, those publicly prohibited by the law of a country from motives of policy. Thirdly, those celebrated in foreign countries, by subjects entitling themselves under special circumstances to the benefits of the laws of their own country.

"The doctrine of the English courts in regard to the indissolubility of English marriages, celebrated in England, notwithstanding a subsequent divorce in a foreign country, affords," says Story, "a still more striking illustration; as, in its practical effects, it may render the issue of a second marriage illegitimate; so that a son, the issue of a second marriage in Scotland, may be legitimate there, and illegitimate in England; he may be a lawful Scotch peer, and yet lose the English estates which support his peerage."[b]

Marriages in foreign factories, in conquered places, in desert or barbarous countries,—at the embassador's hotel, by the resident chaplain, etc., are cases illustrating the third exception. But though the rule of international law certainly is, that between persons *sui juris*, marriage is to be decided by the law of the place where it is celebrated; in France, where parental restraints upon the marriage of minors are carried to the greatest extent, it is broadly laid down that the marriages of Frenchmen in foreign countries shall not be deemed valid, if the parties are not, by its own law, competent to contract, by reason of their being under parental power; that is, if they be under twenty-five years of age. Majority, in France, is now fixed at twenty-one, in all other cases, except for the sake of contracting marriage; when it is not attained until twenty-five.[c]

It was decided in *Lolly's* case, that a second marriage after a divorce in Scotland from a marriage originally celebrated in England between English subjects is void in England, although such divorce and second marriage would be good by the law of Scotland.[d] But in **Warrender v. Warrender**, it was held that the Courts of Scotland had a clear jurisdiction to decide a divorce between parties actually domiciled in Scotland, notwithstanding that the marriage was contracted in England; and that the House of Lords, sitting as a Court of Appeal, in a case coming from Scotland, were bound to administer the law of Scotland.[e]

[a] 1 Burge Com. on Col. & For. Law, ch. 5, § 3, p. 188.

[b] Story on Conflict of Laws, 108; citing Beazley v. Beazley, 3 Hagg. Ecc. R. 639.

[c] Code Civil, art. 148, 448.

[d] Lolly's Ca. 1 Russ. and Ryan, 236. Warrender v. Warrender, 8 Bligh. R. 891. And see 2 Clarke and Fin. R. 567, note. Macarthy v. De Caix, 2 Russ. and Mylne, 614.

[e] 8 Bligh, 891.

The doctrine in the English courts that the *lex loci contractus* shall not be permitted to prevail where it is *contra bonos mores*, or is repugnant to the settled principles and policy of our own laws, is supported in other instances. Where a question arose in the Court of King's Bench, whether a person born before marriage in Scotland, of Scotish parents, who afterwards intermarried there, and thereby became legitimate in Scotland, could inherit real property, as a legitimate heir in England, it was held by the Court, and afterwards confirmed in Error, that he could not.*a*

When the law of the domicil of the creditor and debtor, differs, as to classing debts and rights of action, the law of the domicil of the debtor must prevail in suits thereon, according to the maxims *actio sequitur forum rei* and *debita sequuntur personam debitoris.* It is, indeed, a maxim that debts and rights of action, *inhærent ossibus creditoris*, attend the person of a creditor; but to recover them, he must follow the *forum rei* and person of the debtor. The explanation of this seeming contradiction, is, that personal actions arising from debts or obligations have two characters, *active* as they respect the right of the creditor, and *passive* as they regard the obligation of the debtor. If the question regard the distribution of the creditor's estate, the law of his domicil is to be observed; if the question be in what degree or proportion the representatives of the debtor should be charged with payments from his effects, then it is of a passive nature, and the law of the domicil of the debtor should be followed.

The extent of the *vinculum obligationis* of a contract is regulated by the law of the *place* of contract.*b* The law of the place of contract, in the case of foreign contracts, is to govern, as to the nature, the obligation, and the interpretation of the contract; *locus contractus regit actum.* " This," said Lord Brougham, in delivering his judgment in Warrender v. Warrender, " is sometimes expressed; and I take leave to say, inaccurately expressed; by saying that there is a *comitas* shewn by the tribunals of one country towards the laws of the other country. Where the laws of one country consider the laws of another, in which any contract has been made, in construing its meaning or ascertaining its existence, they can hardly be said to act from courtesy, *comitas ;* for it is of the essence of the subject-matter to ascertain the meaning of the parties, and that they did solemnly bind themselves. Therefore the courts resort to the law of the country where the contract was made, not *ex comitate*, but *ex debito justitiæ.*" *c*

a Doe Dem. Birthwhistle v. Vardell, 5 B and Cres. 438 , S. C. 9 Bligh R. 32.

b 1 Emerig. Assur. ch. 4, s. 8, p. 122 ; Casaregis Disc. 179, Henry on Foreign Law, 139. And see Earl of Winchelsea v. Garetty, 2 Keane Rep. 298. Drummond v. Drummond, 6 Bro. P. R. 550.

c 8 Bligh R. 891.

13

A legal discharge of a debt in the country where it is contracted, will operate as a discharge in all others.*a* The place where the bankrupt is arrested, taken in execution, or commits an act of bankruptcy, or where the *concursos* of creditors, or *præ* and *concurrentiæ* are held, is the proper place of distribution. All other claimants must be drawn to the *locus concursos creditorum ; its* law (*jus domicilii*) is binding, and the equitable doctrine of cession and discharge, is now become a general principle acted upon in every country.*b*

It is otherwise *c* when the debt is contracted in a foreign country. A foreign bankruptcy is no bar to the demand of a debt contracted in England ; but by a decision not founded on any general principle, but upon the effect of the particular statute, 54 Geo. 3, c. 137, a debt contracted in England by a trader residing in Scotland, was deemed to be barred by a discharge under a sequestration, in like manner as debts contracted in Scotland.*d*

a Potter v. Brown, 5 East, 124.

b Hunter v. Potts, 4 Term Reports, Sills and Warwicke, 2 H. Bl. 402 ; Ballantine v. Golding, Cooke's Bankrupt Laws, 499.

c Smith v. Buchanan, 1 East, 6 ; Potter v. Brown, 5 East, 124 ; 2 H. Bl. 553, 8 T. R. 609 ; Lewis v. Owen, 4 B. & A. 654.

d Sidaway v. Hay, 3 B. & C. 13.

CHAPTER IV.

OF THE FORM OF STATUTES. THEIR PARTS. QUALITIES. AUTHO-
RITY AND RELATION.

A STATUTE, it has been already seen, is a written law, made by
the King, with the advice and consent of the two Houses of Parliament.[1] The mode of stating the enacting authority has varied
at different times.

The established form of a statute is, " BE IT ENACTED BY THE
KING'S MOST EXCELLENT MAJESTY, BY AND WITH THE ADVICE AND
CONSENT OF THE LORDS SPIRITUAL AND TEMPORAL, AND COMMONS IN
THIS PRESENT PARLIAMENT ASSEMBLED, THAT," &c.[2]

It is impossible to dissent from the doctrine of Lord Coke, that
acts of Parliament ought to be plainly and clearly, and not cun-
ningly and darkly, penned, especially in penal matters ; and the
rather when, (duly honoring the memory of Sir Thomas More,
and other victims of conscientious scruples,) we regard Lord
Coke's illustration of that maxim. "In times past," says that
great and honest lawyer, "I find that the Houses of Parliament

NOTE 1.—In America, it is, the written law of the people, made by their chosen
representatives, having the assent of the executive of the State, who is also
chosen by the people.

NOTE 2.—The enacting clause of a statute of congress, is thus expressed.
"Be it enacted by the Senate and House of Representatives in Congress assembled." In a New York statute, it is: "The people of the State of New York, represented in Senate and Assembly, do enact as follows." In other States of the
union, the form is substantially the same.

The constitutional requisites to the proper creation of a statute, in the National,
and in the several State legislatures, are in substance and effect, so nearly similar,
that it would be useless to do more than to give the outline of one.

By the constitution of the United States, (Art. 1,) the legislative power is vested
in the Senate and House of Representatives, but before any bill can become a
law, it must be presented to the President; if he approve he shall sign it; if not,
he shall return it with his objections, to the house in which it shall have originated; who shall enter such objections at large upon their journal, and proceed to
reconsider it. If after such reconsideration, two-thirds of that house shall agree
to pass the bill, it shall be sent, together with tne objections to the other house,
by which it shall also be reconsidered. If approved by two-thirds of that house,
it shall become a law.

have not been fairly dealt withal, but by cunning artifice of words, utterly deceived ; and that, too, in cases of the greatest moment, even in high treason.*a*

Lord Coke *b* commends some acts for being "shortly and artificially penned," and says, "it was the wisdom of ancient Parliaments to comprehend much matter in few words;" but this express recommendation (as it is) of brevity and compression, where the true legal effect, and real force and meaning of words, is duly understood, must not mislead. He *c* elsewhere pointedly says, "*abundans cautela non nocet*, and the ancient sages of the law did ever make things, as plain, and leave as little to construction, as might be."

The parts of statutes are—in a popular, though not legal, sense :
The Title; The Preamble ;
The Purview or Body of the Act;
Clauses; Provisos; Exceptions;
The date, or day of its receiving the royal assent.*

---

a 4 Inst. 42.   *b* 2 Inst. 306; id. 401.
c 2 Inst. 375.

NOTE 3.—By the constitution of the United States, Art. 1, Section 7, "every bill shall take effect as a law from the time it is approved by the President." This plain provision, as applicable to different cases, has had various interpretation. In Matthews v. Zanes, 7 Wheat. 164, it was declared that an act of Congress was operative from the date of its enactment, if no other time is fixed in the act. In such case the effect is prospective, and not retrospective. Matter of Richardson, 2 Story, C. C. R. 571. But it was held, in the Matter of Welman, in U. S. Dist. Court of Vermont, by Prentiss J., following the English decisions, that a statute which takes effect from, and after its passage, goes into operation the day on which it is approved, and has relation to the first moment of that day; 20 Vt. R. 653. This may be very well as a general rule, but it is a construction by mere fiction of law, and is not truth. By such a fiction, a law might relate back and take effect before it was actually signed by the President. A more sensible view was taken by Story J., in the "Matter of Richardson," supra. He said: "I am aware it has often been laid down, that in law there are no fractions of a day. But this doctrine is only true *sub modo*, and in a *limited sense*, where it will promote the right and justice of the case, *pro bono publico*. It is a mere legal fiction, and, therefore, like all other legal fictions, is never allowed to operate against the right and justice of the case. On the contrary, the very truth and facts in point of time, may always be averred and proved in furtherance of the right and justice of the case; and there may even be priority in an instant of time; or in other words, it may have a beginning and an end." Even in England, this rule of fiction was made to yield to the promotion of justice between parties, and, it was held that the fact could be alleged and proved to overturn this fiction. Roe v. Hersey, 3 Wils. R. 275. In illustration of the injustice of the fiction, the Court said: "Sometimes by a like fiction, the whole session of Parliament is considered as one day." All acts of Parliament of one session, are regarded as passed on the first day of the session.

The custom of prefixing titles to statutes did not begin till about the eleventh year of the reign of Henry VII, though particular instances may have occurred before that time.*a*

Common sense, and common justice, equally sustain the propriety of allowing fractions of a day, whenever it will promote the purposes of substantial justice. The time of the approval of an act, is a question of fact. The constitution declares *that* to be the time, when the law takes effect. This act of approval cannot look backward, and by relation, or fiction, make that a law at any antecedent period of the same day, which was not so before the approval. The constitution cannot be abrogated by construction. The law prescribes a rule for the future, not for the past. And this in a republican government, is a doctrine of vital importance to the security and protection of the citizen. This is in accordance with the spirit of another provision of the constitution, that no *expost facto law* shall be passed. Take the supposed case of filing a bankrupt petition on a certain day at noon, when the law was in full force ; and an act repealing the bankrupt law at eleven o'clock in the evening of the same day, or, the case of an act performed in the morning of a day, an act, that was innocent when performed, and a statute approved in the evening of the same day making such act an offence ; could the party performing the act be punished? clearly not. Here the law would regard the fractions of a day, and allow the fact to be alleged, and evidence to be given of the fact in furtherance of justice, and the matter of fact would overcome, even if the fiction stood against it.

In the State of New York, all fictions and presumptions of law on this subject, are changed by the Rev. Stat. (vol. 1, 157, § 12,) which provides that every law, unless a different time be prescribed therein, shall commence and take effect throughout the State, on, and not before the twentieth day after the day of its final "passage." In Mississippi, they have a *constitutional* provision, that no law of a general nature, unless otherwise provided for, shall be enforced, until sixty days after its passage, (Const. Art. VII, § 6.) In Michigan, by a like constitutional provision, no public act shall be in force, until ninety days from the end of the session of the legislature at which it was passed. (Const. Art. 4,

a Wiseman v. Cotten, Lord Raym. 77 ; Chance v. Adams, Hard. 324.

§ 20). In States where no constitutional or legal provision is made on the subject, the common law rule prevails; each State determining its own rule of interpretation. This is a question of great moment, inasmuch as the common law presumption, is:— "that every citizen knows the law, and according to the maxim— '*ignorantia legis neminem excusat.*'"

It is impossible that the citizens or subjects of an extensive and populous country, can obtain any accurate knowledge of the purport of an act on the day of its passage; and the doctrine, that the last act signed, is to prevail over, and to abrogate or nullify one duly enacted a few hours previous, is arbitrary, unreliable, and may be oppressive. These evils are obviated by the provisions of this, and other States above mentioned.

The title should properly distinguish the act, by such a name as expresses, in general terms, its main intent; and if not perpetual, its temporary duration.

The title of a statute, it has been *a* repeatedly held, is no part or parcel of the statute; for it is usually framed only by the clerk of that House in which the bill first passes, and is seldom read more than once.*b* In Wills v. Wilkins, Holt chief justice, said, "It is true that the title of an act of parliament, is no part of the law or enacting part, no more than the title of a book is part of a book; for the title is not the law, but the name or description given to it by the makers."*c*

a Barrington on Stat. 449, *notis;* 1 W. Bl. 85, R. v. Williams.
b 3 Rep. 33, Poulter's case.   *c* Wills v. Wilkins, 6 Mod. 62.

NOTE 4.—It is otherwise in American legislation; here the representatives prepare the whole statute, title, preamble, (if any,) and body of the statute.

Though the title of an act cannot control plain words in the body of the statute, yet, taken with other parts, it may assist in removing ambiguities. Where the intent is plain, nothing is left to construction; but where the mind labors to discover the design of the law-making power, everything which can aid this object, may be resorted to, and even the title of the act, in such case, may receive a due share of consideration. United States v. Fisher, 2 Cranch 386. The *intention* of the law-maker it has always been held, is the best guide in the construction of statutes. United States v. Palmer, 3 Wheat. 631. Williams v. Williams, 8 N. Y. R. 535.

In doubtful cases, the title of an act may serve to explain its general purport, and the inducement that led to its enactment, but even then it has little weight: Hadden v. Collector, 5 Wallace, 107, and when the title is at variance with its provisions, it is entitled to no consideration, though it may tend to explain a doubtful meaning of a part of it. id. It cannot be used to extend or restrain any positive provisions contained in the body of it. id. A law may be good, though it is in conflict with the title.

Being thus no part of the act, the title is said to afford "no legislative import." *a*

The mere title of an act is, therefore, a very insufficient and unsafe guide to assist us in ascertaining, even in the most general way, the scope and purport of the act; yet when the mind labors to discover the intention of the legislature, it naturally seizes upon every thing, even the title, from which aid may be derived. As an example of an act greatly "more spacious than its title," Lord Coke refers to the Statute of Uses, "which extends to jointures and dowers of women." The title to an act then, though no part of an act, is not to be wholly disregarded in putting a construction upon the statute. The object of the legislature is very often avowed in the title to an act, as well as in the preamble. But being no part of the act, in a legal sense, it would be preposterous to attempt to use it, in restraining or controling any provision of the act; it can only be used for the fact, of the makers having given the law a certain name; if that fact, can render any assistance in doubtful cases.

Titles, to legislative acts in the State of New York, and in several other of the States of the union, are matters of very great moment, in a constitutional view of the statute. By section 16 of article 3, of the constitution of New York of 1846, "no private or local bill which may be passed by the legislature, shall embrace more than one subject, *and that shall be expressed in the title.*" Acts passed by the legislature in violation of this provision, have been declared by the courts to be null and void. It was well said in an opinion in the supreme court of this State as follows: "Instances had occurred in which important enactments had been smuggled through the legislature, under the cover of some bill with a modest and unpretending title. To guard the legislature as well as the public, against this kind of imposition, the framers of the constitution adopted the above provision." "I am persuaded that such a provision (which was referred to in a statute) could only have made its way through the various forms of legislation, by clothing itself with the guise of a local measure, thus eluding the scrutiny which its own importance demands."*b* The act in question was an act entitled, "An act to enlarge the jurisdiction of the courts of general and special sessions of the peace, in and for the city and county of New York." The body of the act pro-

a 1 Ambler, 22.

b People v. McCoun, 3 Parker Crim. R. 299, 300; per Harris, J.

vided bringing convictions for capital offences before the Supreme Court and Court of Appeals of the State. This provision was declared to be void, because this general object was not expressed in the title. In another case, in the court of appeals, it was repeated, "that it was notorious, that the discrepancy between the headings, and the subjects of our laws was so frequent, that a constitutional provision was deemed necessary to guard against imposition upon a class of legislators, whose knowledge of bills was supposed to be gathered principally from the title."b "The purpose of this constitutional provision was, that neither the members of the legislature nor the public should be misled by the title."c So in another case, under the provisions of an act entitled "An act to amend and consolidate the several acts relating to the city of Rochester," was adjudged to be a local act; but among its provisions, was one, to increase the number of directors which the common council of the city of Rochester was entitled to elect, to compose the board of directors of the Rochester and Genesee Valley Railroad company. The court said, "No human ingenuity would ever discover *that* subject from the *title* of the bill." We are clearly of opinion that, in regard to the law in question in this case, the subject, or object, is not embraced in its *title*, and must therefore be held to have been passed in violation of this provision of the constitution.d

The same provisions in substance, are found contained in the constitutions of the following States: Ohio, Pennsylvania, Michigan, Minnesota, Maryland, Kansas, Kentucky, Nebraska, Louisiana, Texas, South Carolina, California, Alabama, Missouri, Iowa, Illinois, Indiana, Wisconsin, and New Jersey. The variations are slight and immaterial, some requiring the *object*, others—the *subject* of the act to be expressed in the title. Some declaring the whole enactment void, others—only so much thereof as is not so expressed.

The courts of these several States, with great uniformity have concurred in sustaining their constitutions, and in the condemna-

a Mayor, &c. v. Colgate, 2 Kern. 146.

b The Sun Mutual Ins. Co. v. The Mayor, &c. 8 N. Y. R. 253.

c People v. Hills, 35 N. Y. 452, 3 ; People v. O'Brien, 38 N. Y. R. 195 ; People, ex rel. Failing v. Com. of Highways, 53 Barb. 70; People v. Allen, N. Y. Trans.

tion of this vicious character of legislation, in violation of such provisions. The Supreme Court of Michigan say: "The history and purpose of this constitutional provision, are too well understood to require any elucidation at our hands. The practice of bringing together into one bill, subjects diverse in their nature, and having no necessary connection, with a view to combine in their favor, the advocates of all, and thus secure the passage of several measures, no one of which could succeed upon its own merits, was one both corruptive of the legislator, and dangerous to the State. It was scarcely more so, however, than another practice, also intended to be remedied by this provision, by which, through dexterous management, clauses were inserted in bills, of which the titles gave no intimation, and their passage secured through legislative bodies, whose members were not generally aware of their intention and effect. This clause was not designed to embarrass legislation by multiplying the number of bills, but it was intended to put an end to vicious legislation, which was little better than a fraud on the public, and to require, that in every case, the proposed measure should stand upon its own merits.*a* This is the substance of all judicial interpretation of this provision. It is not within the scope of this chapter to bring up in array, the great number of cases which have been held to be obnoxious or otherwise, to this constitutional provision; nor to show the effect upon the act in whole, or in part, where in a local act, more than one subject or object was embraced in the bill, though not expressed in the title. The provisions are variant in different constitutions, and the adjudications have been accordingly variant.'

a People v. Mahany, 13 Mich. R. 494.

NOTE 5.—In this State, in several recent cases, the courts have been strict, to sustain the integrity and spirit of this constitutional security. In an act of the legislature passed in 1851, chapter 389, entitled, "An act to amend and consolidate the several acts relating to the city of Rochester," was held first, to be a local act. In 1865, the legislature passed another act entitled, "An act to amend chapter 389, of the laws of 1851." By the former act, the common council of the city of Rochester were in a certain event authorized to choose four directors of the Rochester and Genessee Valley Railroad company. By the latter act, the said common council were authorized to choose seven directors in said company, instead of four. The title gave no intimation of such an object. It was held unconstitutional. People v. Hills, 35 N. Y. 449.

An act for the amendment of the charter of the city of New York was also held

14

In England, with a constitutional provision similar to our own, the Parliament, in avoiding the abuse above complained of, ran into an almost equal abuse by getting up bills, called hodge podge acts, in which all varieties of subjects of legislation was mixed up—in one act. The following is a specimen of the title to such an act passed in the 17 Geo. 11, ch. 40. "An act to continue the several laws therein mentioned, for preventing theft and rapine on the northern borders of England; for the more effectual punishing wicked and evil disposed persons going around in disguise, and doing injuries and violences to the persons and properties of his Majesty's subjects, and for the more speedy bringing the offenders to justice; for continuing two clauses; to prevent the cutting or breaking down the bank of any river or sea-bank; and to prevent the malicious cutting of hop-binds; and for the more effectual punishment of persons maliciously setting on fire any mine, pit, or delph of coal, or cannel coal; and of persons unlawfully hunting or taking any red or fallow deer in forests or chafes, or beating or wounding the keepers or other officers in forests, chafes, or parks; and for granting a liberty to carry sugars of the growth, produce, or manufacture of any of his Majesty's sugar colonies in America, from the said colonies directly to foreign ports, in ships built in Great Britain, and navigated according to law; and to explain two acts relating to the prosecution of offenders for embezzling naval stores, or stores of war; and to

to be a local act. In an act entitled, "An act to enable the board of supervisors of the city of New York to raise money by tax, for the use of the corporation of the city of New York, and in relation to the expenditure thereof, and to provide for the auditing and payment of unsettled claims against the city, and in relation to actions at law against said corporation." There was inserted a provision, amending the charter of the corporation, in relation to the term of office, and time of electing councilmen. This was held to be in violation of the constitution. People v. O'Brien, 38 N. Y. 193.

So, in an act, entitled "An act to regulate a highway in the town of Palatine," where the purview of the act, provided the reducing of the width of a particular highway, involving in effect, a donation of the land relinquished to the adjoining owner, it was held—that the object of the act was not stated in the title, and was unconstitutional. People v. Com. of Highways of Palatine, 53 Barb. 70; see also, Smith v. Mayor of New York, 34 How. Pr. R. 508; also, see cases not coming within the principle of this objection. People v. Stevens, 2 Abb. Pr. R. N. Y. 348; Matter of Tappen, 36 How. Pr. R. 390; Burnam v. Acton, 4 Abb. Pr. R. N. Y. 1; People v. McCann, 16 N. Y. 60.

prevent the retailing of wine within either of the Universities in that part of Great Britain called England, without license."

Taken in connection with what are acknowledged parts of the statute, (which it is not) the *title*, where the intent is not plain, may slightly assist in removing ambiguities, although it frequently alludes to the subject matter of the act, only in the most general or sweeping terms, and very often is not co-extensive with the provisions of the act.

The preamble to a statute usually contains the motives and inducements to the making of it; but it also has been held to be no part of the statute; or, rather, it is not an essential part, and is frequently omitted.[b]

A preamble is not only not essential, and often omitted, but it is, strictly speaking, without force in a legislative sense; being but a guide to, and not the vehicle of, the import of the statute.[a] And to what is it properly a guide, to the meaning of the enactment? No; but to the intentions of the framer, which is only the first stage on the road, in the construction of statutes.

"The influence of the preamble," says Story, in his Commentary on the constitution of the United States of America, "has a foundation in the exposition of every code of written law,—upon the universal principle of interpretation,—that the will and intention of the legislature is to be regarded and followed."

The preamble, is entitled to great consideration. It is, indeed that introductory statement *(procemium,)* to which both reason and authority point, for ascertaining the intention of the enactment.

"The preamble is properly referred to," says the American commentator, "when doubts or ambiguities arise upon the words of the enacting part. The preamble can never enlarge; it can-

[a] R. v Althoes, 8 Mod. 144; 6 Mod. 62; Wills and Wilkins, 6 Mod. 144.

NOTE e.—The preamble of an act, is the recital by way of introduction, or inducement to the enacting part, of the reasons upon which the enactment is founded. The preamble of a public statute recites the inconveniences which it proposes to remedy,—as that doubts exist as to what the law is,—or that some form of offence has been of frequent occurence, which it is necessary to punish with additional severity; or, the advantages which it proposes to effect; as in the New York Code; "whereas, it is expedient that the present forms of actions and pleadings in cases at common law should be abolished, that the distinction between legal and equitable remedies should no longer continue, and that an uniform course of proceedings in all cases should be established," therefore, etc. The reasons upon which a public statute is passed, are not generally of such a nature that they can be fully set forth with precision, and are too numerous to be recited, and they are, therefore, generally omitted. The preamble to a private statute, if used, should set forth the facts upon which it is founded. With us, in this country, in both public and private statutes, preambles are now omitted, as the general rule.

not confer any powers, *per se.* Its true office is to expound powers conferred, not substantially to create them."*a*

In doubtful cases, recourse may be had to the preamble, to discover the inducements the legislature had to the making of the statute; but where the terms of the enacting clause are clear and positive, the preamble cannot be resorted to.' Lord Coke considered the rehearsal or preamble, a key to open the understanding of the statute, and it is properly considered *b* a *good mean* for collecting the intent and showing the mischiefs which the makers of the act intended to remedy. The civilians say, *cessante legis proœmio, cessat et ipsa lex,* but English lawyers are aware how seldom, at least in the older statutes, the key will unlock the casket; how rarely the preamble is found to state the real occasion of the law, and the full views of the proposer of it. "It is nothing unusual in acts of Parliament," says Lawrence, J., in the case of the King and Marks, "for the enacting part to go beyond the preamble; the remedy often extends beyond the particular act or mischief which first suggested the necessity of the law." "Sometimes," it is well expressed by another reporter, "the legislature having a particular mischief in view, which was the primary object of the statute, merely state *that* in the preamble, and then go on in the body of the act, to provide a remedy for general mischiefs of the same nature, but of different species, neither expressed in the preamble, nor, perhaps, then in immediate contemplation." Indeed, Lord Coke's manner of expressing himself is very observable. Instead of saying that the preamble should control the enacting clauses, or of limiting precisely how far it should have that effect, which would have been attempting to mark a line, where, it is to be feared, one cannot be drawn, he cautiously says, that it is a good mean to find out the intention. In a late case, it was decided that a preamble may be important when the enactment which follows is capable of two senses. But, it is added, "though it may assist in construing ambiguous expressions, it cannot control clear ones."*c* Indeed, what sort of influence the preamble ought to have in expounding statutes, will be best explained by examples, at a future time, when the rules of

a Story's Com. Rules of interpretation of the Constitution, etc.

b 4 Inst. 330.   *c* The Salters Co. v. J., 3, 2 B. R. 109.

NOTE 7.—The preamble may be resorted to in aid of the construction of the enacting clause, if any ambiguity exists. Beard v. Rowan, 9 Peters, 301; Crespigny v. Witteboom, 4 T. R. 793; Sir Wm. Jones, 163; Barker v. Redding, Palmer 485; Bac. Abr. 380; Jackson v. Gilchrist, 15 John. R. 89, id. 116; Constantine v. Van Winkle, 6 Hill, 184; Clark v. Bynum, 3 McCord, 298; United States v. Webster, Davies R. 38; Blue v. McDuffie, Busbee Law, N. C. 131.

It is properly referred to, when doubts and ambiguities arise upon the words of the enacting part. It can never enlarge; it cannot confer any power *per se,* Its true office is to expound powers conferred; not to create them.

construction applicable to distinct parts of statutes are taken into consideration.

It will, perhaps, be found, that the rule is stated at once broadly, and with the greatest accuracy, by two of the judges, (Mr. Justice Buller, and Mr. Justice Grose,) in the case of Crespigny v. Wittenoom ;a that the preamble may be compared with the differen: clauses of the act, to collect the intention of the legislature ; a..d where the intention is apparent not to extend the act, the preamble may be used in restraint of the generality of the enacting clause, where it would be inconvenient if not restrained ; or it may be resorted to in explanation of the enacting clause, if it be doubtful.

Such is the whole extent of the influence of the title and preamble. Barrington has shewn in his observations on the statutes, by many instances, that a statute frequently recites that, which was not the real occasion of the law ; or states that doubts existed as to the law, when in fact none were entertained. The most common recital for the introduction of any new regulation, has been to set forth that doubts have arisen at the common law. Frequently these alleged doubts never existed at all ; and such preambles are supposed, therefore, to have much weakened the force of the common law, in several instances.

The preamble of an act of Parliament, reciting that certain outrages had been committed in particular parts of the kingdom, was adjudged by the court of King's Bench b to be admissible in evidence for the purpose of proving an introductory averment in an information for a libel, that outrages of that description had existed. Public acts of Parliament, it was said, are binding upon every subject ; the judges are bound to take judicial notice of their contents ; every subject is, in judgment of law, privy to the making of them, and supposed to know them ; the passing of an act of Parliament is a public proceeding in all its stages, and when the act is passed, it is, in contemplation of law, the act of the whole body of the kingdom. The court of King's Bench, for these reasons, were of opinion that the preamble in question had been properly admitted in evidence.

A preamble is often prefixed to a particular clause, whose tenor is to be guided by it.

The true meaning of the statute is generally and properly to be sought from the *purview, providing part, or body of the act.* The preamble of a statute is no more than a recital of *some* inconveniences which by no means excludes any other, for which a remedy is given by the enacting part of the statute. Great doubts have existed how far the preamble should control the enacting part of a statute ; but abundant cases have established that where the words in the enacting part are strong enough to take in the mischief intended to be prevented, *they* shall be extended for that purpose, though the preamble does not warrant it; in other words, the enacting part of the statute may extend the act beyond the preamble.

It will be found also, to be an established rule in the exposition of statutes, that the intention of the lawgiver is to be deduced from a view of the whole and of every part of the statute, taken and compared together. In construing acts of Parliament the courts are not to look only at the language of the preamble, or of any particular clause. If they find in the preamble, or in any particular clause, an expression not so large and extensive in its import as those used in other parts of the act, &c., it is their duty to give effect to the larger expressions.*a* Indeed a statute ought, upon the whole, to be so construed, that, if it can be prevented, no clause, sentence, or word, should be superfluous, void, or insignificant.*b*

But the general words in one clause of a statute may be restrained by the particular words in a subsequent clause of the same statute.*c* Where a general intention is expressed, and the act also expresses a particular intention incompatible with the general intention, the particular intention is to be considered in the nature of an exception.*d* While, if a particular thing be given or limited in the preceding parts of a statute, this shall not be taken away or altered by any subsequent general words of the same statute.*e* Indeed, where the intention of the legislature is not apparent to that purpose, the general words of another and later statute shall not repeal the particular provisions of a former one.*f* "It cannot be contended," says Lord Kenyon, "that a subsequent act of Parliament will not control the provisions of a prior statute, if it were intended to have that operation; but there are several cases in the books to show, that when the intention of the legislature was apparent that the subsequent act should not have such an operation, there, even though the words of such statute taken strictly and grammatically would repeal a former act, the courts of law, judging for the benefit of the subject, have held that they ought not to recieve such a construction.*g* And, if in the same act of Parliament, there be one clause which applies to a particular case, and another which is conceived in general terms, the former shall not restrain the signification of the latter.*h*

a Per Lord Tenterden, Doe *dem* Bywater and Brandling, 7 B. & C. 643.

b 1 Show. 108, R. v. Burchett, Hard. 344.

c R. v. Archbishop of Armagh, 8 Mod. 8.

d Churchill v. Crease, 5 Bing. 180; referred to in Terrington and Hargraves, Ib. 492, 3.

e Stanton v. The University of Oxford, 1 Jon. 26.

f Gregory's case, 6 Rep. 19 b.; Foster's case, 11 Rep. 68 b.

g Williams v. Pritchard, 4 T. R. 2, 4.   *h* 2 T. R. 164.

"Every word importing the plural number, shall extend and be applied to one person or thing, as well as to several persons and things; and every word importing the masculine gender only, shall extend and be applied to a female as well as to a male, &c."

Whether this arbitrary enlargement or contraction, of the ordinary meaning of words, has answered its intended purpose, is at the best, very doubtful. It must often be a question, whether the context *does* reasonably admit of the arbitrary construction of the words used. Amendments introduced on the sudden, will be often made by members of the legislature who are inexperienced, and little aware of the arbitrary change in the sense of ordinary terms. Definitions are not always found to render the meaning more clear; and they are sometimes, perhaps invidiously, suspected of being used to disguise the meaning. When a proposition is wanted which cannot be openly proposed, inquiry is censoriously said, to be oftentimes made, whether it cannot be concealed in a construction clause. In Courts of law, the interpretation clause is too often found to require an interpreter; and it may be questioned, whether it ever succeeds in giving an improved expression of the will of the lawgiver.

Interpretation clauses are by no means to be strictly construed, and convenience seems likely to lead to their being practically disregarded.'

NOTE 8.—A legislature cannot authoritatively interpret, or declare what the law is, or has been, but only what it shall be. It is the province of the court to declare the law of an existing statute. Ogden v. Blackledge, 2 Cranch 272; Ashley's case, 4 Pick. 23.

When the constitutional validity of a law is in controversy, and the law itself may be ambiguous in its import, that construction must be given to it which will sustain its validity, rather than the one which will render it inoperative and void. Rosevelt v. Goddard, 52 Barb. 533, 548; Ogden v. Saunders, 12 Wheat. 270.

The presumption is always in favor of the constitutionality of a law, and before declaring it void, the court must be satisfied that it violates the constitution, clearly, plainly, palpably. Speer v. School Directors, 50 Penn. St. R. 150; Brown v. Buzan, 24 Ind. 194. This, however, is only a presumption, and is not to be indulged to the extent of making all statutes constitutional, on the ground that we must presume the legislature intended to make all their acts effective, but only that the court, if possible, must give the statute such construction as will enable it to have effect, and to uphold it when not in conflict with the constitution. People v. Supervisors of Orange, 17 N. Y. 241. And this rule, I understand is the same whether applied to a part, or to the whole of a statute, when the whole is assailed; it is void only as to the excess of power. Nelson v. the People, 33 Ill. 390; McCullock v. State, 11 Ind. 424.

It is a curious, as well as an interesting study, to watch the progressive spirit of the periods, and to see how just in proportion, as the natural rights of man are understood, just in the same proportion are restraints imposed upon absolute and arbitrary acts of the government; and just in degree, as rights become

In Reg. v. Justices of Cambridgeshire; Reg. v. Justices of Shropshire, and Reg. v. Justices of Gloucestershire, Lord Denman said: "We cannot refrain from expressing a serious doubt whether interpretation clauses will not rather embarrass the courts in their decision, than afford that assistance which they contemplate. For the principles on which they are themselves to be interpreted, may become matter of controversy; and the application of them to particular cases may give rise to endless doubts.*a*

When for the purpose of a more than usually comprehensive enactment, it is deemed necessary to include the intended meaning of numerous words in the arbitrary import of one; or, that there should be numerous words bearing the same constructive import, that end should be attained by means of a schedule annexed to the act.

And notice should be taken of such schedule at this stage of the act in the following: "The word ———, shall be interpreted, as fully signifying its import, the meaning of each of the several words in schedule marked A, which is to this act annexed, as well in their singular as in their plural sense, etc." Schedules are dis-

---

a 7 A. and E. 480.

secured and protected, and as the science of true jurisprudence acquires form and certainty, just in the same degree does the law and its ministers rise in influence and importance. Look back to the day, when Justinian, the Emperor and great lawgiver of the Roman government, exercised all the powers of sovereignty, and made, modified and interpreted the law. In a rescript to his prefect, he uses this language: "We declare the imperial construction of laws, whether made on petition or in suits, or in any way whatever, to be absolute and final. Fcr, if the sovereign alone can make laws, he alone should interpret them; why else, when questions have arisen in controversies, have they been brought to us? and why, too, have judicial doubts reached our ears, if interpretation does not proceed from us alone? Who, indeed, is competent to solve the enigmas of the law, except he to whom the power of legislation is conceded? These absurd cavilings are, therefore, to cease, and the Emperor to be regarded as the only interpretor, as he is the only maker of laws." Cod. DeLegibus, Lib. 1, Tit. 14, § 12. Such was the language, that the master of the world of civil law, could, with impunity make use of. Where now, in christendom, is the monarch that dares to employ such language, or that dares to assume this despotic power?

It should be the pride of the citizen under the system of a free government, to compare his protections under a government of written constitutions, with the despotic power of the Roman Emperor over the people of his empire. Here, this power is distributed to three independent, co-ordinate departments; the law making power is exclusively confided to one, to the legislative department; which possesses no power to construe or enforce its own acts. Their construction is exclusively confided to the judiciary; and their enforcement to the executive. And the powers of each department so conferred and distributed, as that each acts as a check upon the other.

tinguishingly marked with different letters of the alphabet; and the different parts of the same schedule by means of different numbers. A. 1, B. 1, etc.

But the act of Parliament, and the schedule are sometimes. found to differ, and what will be the result of such discrepancy? "If there be any contradiction between the two, and they cannot be reconciled," then, said Lord Denman, "upon ordinary principles, the form, which is made to suit rather the generality of cases, than all cases, must give way."a "Words in schedules must be received as examples, not as overruling provisions," said Tindal, C. J.

The next clause in order, in those cases in which it is used, should be the repealing clause; showing what prior acts are totally repealed; "save so far as they repeal any other act or acts, or part or parts thereof; and what acts are partially repealed; and what statutes are recognized as being in full force, and as having immediate connection with the enactments of such former act.º

a Reg. v. Baines, 12 A. and E. 227.

NOTE 9.—Where a statute is intended to be repealed, its title is generally inserted in the repealing act; and therefore, the repeal of a statute is not to be inferred from a general and uncertain allusion to it in a repealing act. Chegary v. Jenkins, 3 Sand. Sup. C. R. 409.

A statute may be repealed by necessary implication, and without any express words; the leaning of the courts is against the doctrine, if it be possible to reconcile the two acts of the legislature together, though a statute may be repealed by the abrogation of a State constitution. A statute enacted under the constitution of this State, of 1821, prohibited the judges of appellate courts to take part in the decisions of causes determined by them, when sitting as the judges of any other court; this was held to be virtually repealed by the constitution of 1846, which abrogated the constitution of 1821. Pierce v. Delamatter, 1 N. Y. 17. So, too, if the latter part of a statute be repugnant to a former part of it, the latter part shall stand, and, so far as it is repugnant, be a repeal of the former part, because it was last agreed to by the legislature.

In 1828 the legislature of this State enacted a general statute in relation to repeals of particular acts, which was made a part of the Revised Statutes, and which contained also, general provisions as to the effect of statute repeals. So much of it as relates to that subject is transcribed, and is as follows :

§ 3. None of the statutes of England or Great Britain shall be considered as laws of this state ; nor shall they be deemed to have had any force or effect in this state, since the first day of May, in the year one thousand seven hundred and ighty-eight.

§ 4. No statute passed by the government of the late colony of New-York, shall be considered as a law of this state.

§ 5. The repeal of any statutory provision by this act, shall not affect any act done, or right accrued or established, or any proceeding, suit or prosecution had or commenced in any civil case, previous to the time when such repeal shall take effect ; but every such act, right and proceeding, shall remain as valid and effectual, as if the provision so repealed, had remained in force.

15

The praiseworthy object of this clause, is to point out that either *it* is the only statute of force upon the subject, by the repeal of all others; or to show what other statutes are to be considered in connection with it; so that the reader may be prepared with the auxiliary statutes at hand, before he enter on the consideration of the legislative details in the statute reciting them.

Where there are many statutes to be repealed, or otherwise mentioned, they should be arranged chronologically in a schedule, with a column showing the extent of the repeal; and they should be referred to in this part of an act.

The number of clauses in a statute, depends on the subject to be legislated upon. The remaining clauses in most general use, are, besides those already mentioned, a Saving clause; an Appeal clause; a clause showing to what places the operation of the act shall extend; a clause showing from what date, the operation of the act is to commence and how long it shall continue in force;

§ 6. No offence committed, and no penalty or forfeiture incurred previous to the time when any statutory provision shall be repealed, shall be affected by such repeal; except that where any punishment, forfeiture or penalty shall have been mitigated by the provisions of the Revised Statutes. such provisions shall apply to and control any judgment to be pronounced after the said statutes shall take effect, for any offence committed before that time.

§ 7. No prosecution for any offence, or for the recovery of any penalty or forfeiture, pending at the time at any statutory provision shall be repealed, shall be affected by such repeal : but the same shall proceed in all respects, as if such provision had not been repealed; except that all such proceedings had after the time when the Revised Statutes take effect. shall be conducted according to the provisions of the said statutes, and shall be in all respects subject to the said provisions.

§ 8. All statutes and parts of statutes which were repealed or abrogated by, or were repugnant to, any law hereby repealed, and which have not been re-enacted and consolidated in the Revised Statutes, shall continue to be so repealed, and shall be deemed abrogated.

§ 9. The repeal by this act, or any statute or part of a statute heretofore repealed, shall not be construed as a declaration or implication that such statute or part of a statute has been in force at any time subsequent to such first repeal.

§ 10. Where any statute not hereby repealed, refers to and adopts any statute or part of a statute which is herein repealed, the statute or part of a statute so referred to and adopted, shall not be deemed repealed by the provisions of this act, but shall be in force so far only as the same shall have been so adopted, and for no other purpose, and subject to the provisions of the two next sections.

§ 11. But if the statute or part of a statute so referred to and adopted, shall have been revised and consolidated in the Revised Statutes, all provisions contained therein repugnant to or inconsistent with those of the said Revised Statutes, shall be deemed repealed at the time specified in this act; and every such provision so referred to and adopted. which shall be modified by the Revised Statutes, shall be deemed to be so modified in respect to any use or purpose, for which such provision is herein declared to be in force, from and after the time when the Revised Statutes shall take effect.

§ 12. Where any statute or part of a statute, which is not hereby repealed, refers to and adopts any provision or rule of law which is abrogated or modified by the Revised Statutes, such provision or rule shall be deemed to be so abrogated or modified, as the case may be, as well in respect to such statute or part of a statute not repealed, as otherwise, from and after the time when the Revised Statutes shall take effect?

and lastly, the concluding clause of a public general act, the clause providing that the act may be altered and repealed in the same session of Parliament.

The defect of legislative language is found in its intricacy and complication; and in confounding the cases for facultative and mperative language, "*may*," and "*shall;*" and in the number of limitations, conditions and provisions interposed between the nominative case and its verb, or any other two dependent words. As a question of composition and interpretation, apart from parliamentary considerations, great inconvenience results from this accumulation of materials in one clause, from the constant combination of distinct enactments. Two or more distinct legal subjects are brought together in the same sentence, by means of the same *copula*. This always renders the meaning obscure, and causes the frequent necessity for the application of the interpretative process, *reddendi singula, singulis*.

It has not escaped the observation of lawgivers and jurists, of other nations as well as of our own, that owing to different interpretation put upon laws, expressed in the same general terms, much vexation and trouble arise. In fact, "the uncertainty of the law," which originates in a great measure, from the different interpretation to which one and the same law may be subject, has become proverbial. It has therefore, been the anxious desire of well disposed, and intelligent legislators in other countries, to avoid all interpretation, and consequent commentaries, by framing codes of law so exact, so perfect and complete, as to render interpretation superfluous. It was one of the great objects of the Prussian code, promulgated by Frederick the Great, as was therein declared, " to diminish legislation, and to make lawyers comparatively useless." As we are informed by Las Cases, Napoleon said that he, once entertained the idea that all principles of law might be reduced to a few concise forms, which ought to be combined according to fixed rules, similar to those of mathematics; and that thus, simplicity and certainty of law might be established. He soon, however, gave up this idea, when he came to discuss the various parts of the French Civil Code, with the other members of the committee appointed to draw up that work. In Bavaria, commentaries upon their penal code, were actually prohibited. The king's privy council under the sanction of the government, attempted, with true wisdom, to publish officially, the motives and explanations (something after the manner of the notes of the revisors of our statutes,) which were given in the course of the discussions in the council, for adopting the various laws. These motives, reasons, etc., were drawn up by them, reduced to a systematic whole, and published in three volumes, in 1813, 1814. But they did not find it equally wise to prohibit commentaries; for those who advised the king so to do, forgot, that as they felt bound, and attempted to explain the various provisions of the code, it would be found, that their own explanations, would carry along with them also, the necessity of being explained; and this, simply, because they were drawn up in human language. No code can possibly provide, by any attainable perfection and simplicity of language, for all specific cases, which most frequently consist of a combination of simple elements. Nearly every case is, in reality, a complex one, and because the various relations of men are forever changing, *a* and because the individuality of utterances, with expression of ideas, is dependent upon uniformity of mental endowments, as well as uniformity of culture, which are seldom, or never to be found. Interpretation never has been, it never can be dispensed with. It is a necessity that lies in the very nature of things, and will remain, so long as the character of the human mind is diversified, and language remains imperfect.

If it could be made to be generally recognized that the essentials of every law are simple; and that their direct expression is the perfection of law writing, the greatest defect of our statute law would cease. It is beyond a doubt, that the *casus legis* which can be described in a provision, or in a phrase interpolated into other matter by way of limitation, can be more easily expressed alone, and at the beginning of the enactment. It is equally beyond a doubt, that its proper place is, at the beginning, and that it is a misleading the reader to commence an enactment as if it were universal, and wind it up by a parenthetical qualification or proviso, which limits it to certain occasions only.*b*

After these general, but it is trusted not misplaced remarks

a Leibers Hermeneutics, ch. 2, § 12.

b It was proposed by a local act of Parliament to pave the town of Brighton and to manage its poor. The act was entitled, "To manage and pave the town of Brighton and the poor thereof."

upon the imperfect expression of the will of the lawgiver, it will be proper to proceed with the exact enumeration of the parts of a statute.

And first of the saving clause.

The purview of an act may be qualified or restrained by a saving in the statute.a   A saving in a statute, is only an exception of a special thing out of the general things mentioned in the statute.b But a saving clause in a statute, where it is directly repugnant to the purview or body of the act, and cannot stand without rendering the act inconsistent, and destructive of itself, is to be rejected.c But apart from a direct repugnacy, and short of a destructive saving, the general words in one clause of a statute may be restrained by the particular words in a subsequent part of the same statute.d

Where a general intention is expressed, and the act also expresses a particular intention incompatible with the general intention, the particular intention is to be considered in the nature of an exception.e   While, if a particular thing be given or limited in the preceding parts of a statute, this shall not be taken away or altered by any subsequent general words of the same statute.f Indeed, where the intention of the legislature is not apparent to that purpose, the general words of another and later statute shall not repeal the particular provisions of a former one.g   "It cannot be contended," said Lord Kenyon, that a subsequent act of Parliament will not control the provisions of a prior statute, if it were intended to have that operation ; but there are several cases in the books to shew, that when the intention of the legislature was apparent that the subsequent act should not have such an operation, there, even though the words of such statute taken strictly and grammatically would repeal a former act, the courts of law, judging for the benefit of the subject, have held that they ought not to receive such a construction."h   And if, in the same act of Parliament, there be one clause which applies to a particular case, and another which is conceived in general terms, the former shall not restrain the signification of the latter.i[10]

a 10 Mod. 155.

b Hollowell v. Corporation of Bridgewater. 2 And. R. 192.

c Plowd. 565.   d Rex v. Archbishop of Armagh, 8 Mod. 8.

e Churchill v. Crease, 5 Bing. 180; referred to in Terrington and Hargraves ib. 492–3.

f Stanton v. the University of Oxford, 1 Jon. 26.

g Gregory's case, 6 Rep. 10 b; Foster's case, 11 Rep. 00 b.

h Williams v. Pritchard, 4 T. R. 2, 4.   i 2 T. R. 164.

NOTE 10.—A saving clause in an act of Congress, saving State laws then in force, does not confine or validate such State law. If such State law contains a provision impairing the obligation of contracts, the act of congress merely leaves

A proviso is something engrafted upon a preceding enactment, *a* and is legitimately used, for the purpose of taking special cases out of the general enactments, and providing specially for them. In its abuse, it contains all unconnected matters; and disposes of whatever is incapable of combination with the rest of any clause. It was held by all the Barons of the Exchequer, in the case of the Attorney-General v. The Governor and Company of the Chelsea Waterworks, *b* that where the proviso of an act of Parliament was directly repugnant to the purview of it, the proviso should stand and be held a repeal of the purview, because it was said, it speaks the last intention of the lawgiver. It was compared to a will, in which the latter part, if inconsistent with the former, supersedes and revokes it. It has been remarked *c* upon this case in Fitzgibbon, that a *proviso* repugnant to the purview, renders it equally nugatory and void as a repugnant *saving clause;* and it is difficult to see why the act should be destroyed by the one, and not by the other; or why the proviso and the saving clause, when inconsistent with the body of the act, should not both of them be equally rejected. The distinction in the effect and operation of a saving clause and of a proviso in a statute, will be found in the books, laid down as positive, and without qualification ; but the reason of the distinction, is certainly not very apparent.[11]

a 9 B. & C. 835.   *b* Fitzg. 195; Bacon, Ab. tit. Statute.
c Kent's Comm. on American Law, vol, 1, p. 430.

them by such saving clause, to operate so far as constitutionally they may. Sturges v. Crowninshield, 4 Wheat. 122. A saving clause in a statute is to be rejected when it is directly repugnant to the purview or body of the act, and could not stand, without rendering the act inconsistent and destructive of itself. 1 Kent Com. 462; Plowd. 565, 8 Taunt. 13, 18.

The purview of an act may be qualified or restrained by a saving clause contained in it. This clause is only an exemption of some *special* thing, out of the *general* things mentioned in the act; but a saving clause therein which is directly repugnant to the purview of the act, and cannot stand without rendering the act inconsistent and destructive of itself, is to be rejected. Milton v. Elliot, 8 Taunt. 13. This, however, is not the rule as regards provisos.

NOTE 11.—The office of a proviso, generally, is either to except something from the enacting clause, to restrain its generality, or to exclude some possible ground of misinterpretation of it, as extending to cases not intended by the legislature to be brought within its purview. Minis v. United States, 15 Peters, 423; Wyman v. Southard, 10 Wheat. 1–30.

A proviso in a statute, is to be strictly construed; it takes no case out of the enacting clause which is not fairly within the terms of the proviso. U. S. v. Dickson, 15 Pet. 141. The office of a proviso, generally is, either to except something from the enacting clause, to qualify or restrain its generality, or to exclude some possible ground of misinterpretation of its extending to cases not

There is a known distinction in the law between an exception in the purview of the act and a proviso. If there be an exception in the enacting clause of a statute, it must be negatived in pleading; a separate proviso need not; *c* and that, although it is found in the same section of the act, if it be not referred to, and engrafted on, the enacting clause.*d* "The rule is," said Mr. Justice Ashurst, in Spiers v. Parker, "that any man who will bring an action for a penalty on an act of Parliament, must show himself entitled under the enacting clause; but if there be a subsequent exemption, that is a matter of defence, and the other party must show it, to exempt himself from the penalty." Mr. Justice Buller said, "I do not know any case for a penalty on a statute where there is an exception in the enacting clause, that the plaintiff must not show that the party whom he sues, is not within it." So, in a crimnal case, Lord Mansfield said, "what comes by way of proviso in a statute, must be insisted on for the purposes of defence by the party accused; but where exceptions are in the enacting part of the law, it must in the indictment charge that the defendant is not within any of them."*a*[12]

a 1 T. R. 141; 8 T. R. 542.   *b* 1 B. and A. 94.
c Fost. 430, 1 East R. 664; Burr R. 148, East. P. C. 167.

intended to be brought within its purview. Minis v. U. S. 15 Pet. 423; Huydkaper v. Burrus, 1 Wash. C. C. R. 119.

If a proviso in a statute, be directly contrary to the purview of the statute, the proviso is good, and not the purview. Townsend v. Brown, 4 Zabrish, (N J.) 80; Rex v. Justices of Middlesex, 2 B. and Adol. 818. But contra,—"a proviso repugnant to the purview of the statute, renders it equally nugatory and void, as a repugnant saving clause; and it is difficult to see why the act should be destroyed by the one, and not by the other, or why the proviso and the saving clause when inconsistent with the body of the act, should not both of them be equally rejected." 1 Kent Com. 463. And it is a settled rule, that where there is a *proviso* to a grant which is repugnant to the grant itself, the grant shall be good, and the proviso only void. Mason v. Boom Co. 3 Wall. Jr. C. C. R. A proviso is a limitation or exception, to the authority conferred, the effect of which is to declare, that the one shall not operate, or the other be exercised, unless in the case provided: Voorhees v. Bank of United States, 10 Peters, 471.

So it seems, that a saving clause in a statute *in the form of a proviso*, restricting in certain cases the operation of the general language of the enacting clause, was not void, though the proviso be repugnant to the general language of the enacting clause. The true principle undoubtedly is, that the sound interpretation and meaning of the statute, on a view of the enacting clause and proviso, taken and construed together, is to prevail. If the principle object of the act can be accomplished and stand, under the restriction of the saving clause or proviso, the same is not to be held void for repugnancy. 1 Kent Com. 463, note a; Savings Bank v. Makin, 23 Maine R. 360.

NOTE 12.—It may be as well here, to notice the distinction between a proviso and an exception contained in the purview of an act, although the exception is a

By the statute, 33 Geo. 3, c. 13, the indorsement by that act directed to be made by the clerk of the Parliaments, on every act of Parliament, of the day, month, and year, when the same shall have passed, and shall have received the royal assent, shall be taken to be A PART OF SUCH ACT, &c.

Such are the *parts* of a statute ; the next chapter will be a consideration of its qualities and incidents.

question that relates chiefly to pleading. An *exception* in the statute, must be negatived in pleading, but a proviso need not, and this seems to be upon the ground that an exemption is matter of defence which a party must show, to exempt himself from the liability or penalty. Spiers v. Parker, 1 Tenn. R. 141. So, too it has been held, in case of an exception, the plaintiff who sues, must show that the party whom he sues, does not come within it. 1 Kent Com. 463; People v. Toynbee, 11 How Pr. R. 333; 1 Chitt. Cr. L. 284.

CHAPTER V.

OF THE QUALITIES, INCIDENTS, AND GENERAL RULES AND MAXIMS OF INTERPRETATION OF STATUTES.

AMONG all civilized nations, we have always seen, formed by the side of the sanctuary of the laws, and under the controling guidance of judicial and legislative wisdom, a fund of maxims, rules, and decisions of doctrine, which have been sifted by the constant practice, and the collision, consequent upon judicial debates. These rules and maxims have been incessantly increasing the store of wisdom and knowledge thus acquired, until they have become the supplement of legislation in the establishment of law, and are regarded as the highest attainment towards the perfection of human reason, in the exposition of law.

The judicial power established to declare and apply the laws, needs, and is greatly aided, by such a fund of rules and maxims. These maxims apply equally to all men. They regard men in the aggregate, never as individuals. They are rules as proper to be known to the legislator, as to the magistrate, though their duties are variant. The science of the legislator, and his consequent duty, consists in searching in each case for principles most favorable to the common welfare; that of the judge, is to put these principles in action; to extend them by a wise and thoughtful application to private assumptions; and to study the spirit of the law, when perhaps, the letter destroys.

Perhaps no wiser man than Lord Bacon, ever graced the legal profession. In the exercise of his wisdom, he left a collection of legal maxims for study, to those who should come after him. His reasons for making the collection are so profound, it may be of advantage for all to study them. We have adopted his reasons. He says: "having, from the beginning, come to the study of the laws of this realm, with a mind and desire no less that the same laws should be the better by my industry, than that myself

16

should be the better by the knowledge of them; I do not find
that, without the help of authority, I can in any kind, confer so
profitable an addition unto that science, as by the collecting the
rules and grounds dispersed throughout the body of the same
laws. For hereby, no small light will be given. In new cases,
such wherein there is no direct authority, to sound into the true
conceit of the law, by depth of reason. In cases wherein the
authorities do square and vary, to confirm the law, and make it
received one way. And in cases where the law is cleared by
authority; yet, nevertheless, to see more profoundly into the reasons of such judgments and ruled cases, and thereby to make
more use of them for the decision of other cases, more doubtful.
So that the uncertainty of the law, which is the principle and
most just challenge that is made to the laws of our nation at
this time, will, by this new strength laid to the foundation, somewhat the more settle, and be corrected. Neither will the use
hereof be only in the deciding of doubts, and helping soundness
of judgment, but further, in gracing of argument,—in correcting
unprofitable subtlety,—and in reducing the same to a more sound
and substantial sense of law; in reclaiming vulgar errors, and
generally, in the amendment, in some measure, of the very nature
and complexion of the whole law."

DWARRIS' MAXIMS.

I. "An act of Parliament" (says Dwarris) binds all persons,
but such as are specially saved by it. "As if," says Sir R. Anderson, "a person be tenant in tail, and it is enacted that he shall
have his land to him and his heirs, he has the fee and the tail is
determined." Such is the example given; and it is to be hoped,
it illustrates the rule; but then follows another case, of a statute,
"taking his land from A. and giving it to B." *simpliciter ;* the land
goes from A. *et touts ses droits queux il avet devant,* sount extinct,
sinon que sont save especialment par les provises en le act."a
II. A statute which gives corporal punishment does not bind
an infant: *contra* of other statutes, if they do not except infants.b
III. Every statute made against an injury, gives a remedy by
action, expressly or impliedly.c
IV. An act of Parliament cannot alter by reason of time; but
the common law may, since *cessante ratione cessat lex.*d

a And. 148, pl. 82.   c 2 Inst. 55.
b Doctr & Student, lib. 2 fol. 113.   d Str. 190.

V. When statutes are made, there are some things which are exempted and *fore-prized* out of the provisions thereof, by the law of reason, though not expressly mentioned: thus, things for necessity's sake, or to prevent a failure of justice, are excepted out of statutes.*a*

VI. Whenever an act gives any thing generally and without any special intention declared, or rationally to be inferred, it gives it always subject to the general control and order of the common law"*b*

VII. Whenever a statute gives or provides any thing, the common law provides all necessary remedies and requisites. *c*

VIII. In statutes, incidents are always supplied by intendments; in other words, whenever a power is given by a statute, every thing necessary to the making of it effectual, is given by implication; for the maxim is *Quando lex aliquid concedit, concedere videtur et id, per quod devenitur ad illud. d*

The statute of Gloucester, C. 5. giving an action of waste against tenant for life and tenant for years, doth impliedly give authority to him in the reversion, by himself or by another, to enter, to see if any waste be done.

If an action of waste should now be given by a statute against tenant in tail after possibility extinct, treble damages would, although not mentioned, be recoverable, *e* for such damages are recoverable under a former statute, by which an action of waste is given; and wherever an old action is given in a new case, all that before appertained to the action is likewise given.

IX. *Quando aliquid prohibetur, prohibetur et omne, per quod devenitur ad illud.*

X. Wherever the provision of a statute is general, every thing which is necessary to make such provision effectual, is supplied by the common law.*f*

XI. If an offence be made felony by a statute, such statute does by necessary consequence, subject the offender, to the like attainder and forfeiture, and does require the like constuction as to those who shall be accounted accessaries before or after the fact, and to all other intents and purposes, as a felony at the common law does. *g*

XII. Misprision of felony is as well incidental to a felony created by a statute, as to one at the common law.

XIII. *Lex uno ore omnes alloquitur ; h* a maxim which does not require illustration, but which Lord Coke says is the pride of the English law; and it is pre-eminently so, of the written law; which lays down one clear and certain rule for all descriptions of per-

a Plow. Comm. 13 b.; 2 Inst. 118.   *b* Show. 455.
c The Protector v. Ashfield, Hard. 62.   *d* 2 Inst. 306 ; 12 Rep. 130, 131.
e Bro. Wast. pl. 68.   *f* 2 Inst. 48.
g 1 Inst. 235; 2 Inst· 222, Bac. Abridg. tit. Statute.   *h* 2 Inst. 184.

sons, and is both known and invariable. For, the written and statute law, being of old duly and formally promulgated to the people, could never be what Lord Bacon says of Henry VII's laws, " as a *nemo scit ;*" and of these rules of conduct, no judge, producing a manuscript decision of some former sage of the law, an unreported case, can say : "Lo! I have the law in my side-pocket !" *e*

XIV. *Nemo punitur sine injuria, facto, seu defalto.*

The statute of Gloucester provided, that in the case of a disseisor aliening lands and not being able to satisfy the damages, they, to whose hands the tenements shall come, shall be charged with the damages, &c. Now, if the tenant cometh to the land by act of law which he cannot withstand, and where there is no act or default in him, he shall not be charged. As if the disseisor alien to A. and his heirs, and A. dieth without heir, the law (that there may be a tenant to the *præcipe*) casts the land upon the lord. In this case, if the lord doth not take any profits of the land, in a writ brought against him for the land, the lord may plead the special matter, and so discharge himself from the damages ; for albeit he be a tenant of the land, yet is he no tenant (against his will) within the meaning of this law, because there is no wrong or default in him.*a*

XV. *Actus legis nemini est damnosus :*—An act for enlarging the term granted to a patentee for the enjoyment of his patent, provided that in each case the power, privilege, or authority granted by the letters patent should become vested in more than five persons or their representatives, at any one time, otherwise than by devise or succession, all liberties, privileges, &c., should cease. The patentees having become bankrupts, it was held that this clause applied only to an assignment by act of the party, and not to an assignment or transfer by operation of law.*b*

XVI. *Absoluta sententia expositore non indiget* : " this is the case," says Lord Coke, *c* "where the words are plain without any scruple, and absolute without any saving."

XVII. *Expressio eorum quæ tacite insunt, nihil operatur :* as where an advowson descending to divers coparceners, they do make composition to present by turns ; being no more than the law doth appoint. St. West'mr. 2, c. 5.*d*

XVIII. *Quæcunque intra rationem legis inveniuntur, inira ipsam legem, esse judicantur.*

XIX. So, *Lex beneficialis rei consimili remedium præstat ;* maxims too obvious in their application to need any enforcement.

---

a 3 Inst. 47, 49, 50; 1 Hawk. c. 41, § 4.　　*b* Watkins on Conveyancing.

c 2 Inst.

d Bloxam and another, assignees, v. Elsee, 6 B. and C. 169.

e 2 Inst. 533.　　　　　　　　*f* 2 Inst. 365.

The qualities, and incidents of statutes, as stated in the foregoing nineteen rules by Mr. Dwarris, which give their nature, parts, and properties, with incidental rules of interpretation, may be appropriately followed by the rules of interpretation of other distinguished writers on the same subject. Grotius, Puffendorf, Vattel, Rutherford, and Domat, have each devoted a chapter to this subject of interpretation; the doctrine and manifest equity and justice of which, have obtained general approbation, and are cited by commentators and distinguished jurists, as being wise and well established; rules, containing a combination of profound reasoning, with perspicuous and logical arrangement.

By *interpretation*, we speak of a necessity arising from the imperfection of language as a medium of expressing the intention. Interpretation, is the life of what would otherwise be the dead letter. Necessity, therefore, demands rules or laws of interpretation. These rules are fixed principles, deduced from right reason and rational equity, and are adopted by universal consent of nations, states, and lawgivers. In all treaties, conventions, and statutes, inasmuch as language is the instrument or medium of expressing the intent; circumstances, not the time forseen, give rise to different views, and sometimes to apparent contradictions, arising from the language of the same instrument. This creates a necessity for interpretation. Sometimes the language of a treaty, statute, or compact is obscure, sometimes the words are ambiguous, sometimes they express the meaning so imperfectly as either to fall short of expressing the true intention, or as not to express the whole of it, or else exceed the intention and express more than was designed. Both the end and the means of interpretation, will distinguish it from *criticism*. The end which criticism aims at, is to find out what are the words of the instrument or writer; whether for instance, it is forged or genuine; whether material parts have been added, or omitted, erased or altered. The end interpretation aims at, is to find out the intent of the statute, instrument, or writer; to clear up the meaning of words if they are obscure; to ascertain their sense if they are ambiguous; and to determine the design where the words express it imperfectly. We must not confound the two. The *interpretor's* work does not begin till the critic's is ended.*a*

a Rutherford's Inst. 402.

We make the following *extracts*, being forty-five maxims, from Vattel, which he applies as well to treaties and statutes, as to other compacts. He says:

"It is necessary to establish rules founded on reason, and authorized by the law of nature, capable of diffusing light over what is obscure, of determining what is uncertain, and, of frustrating the attempts of a contracting power void of good faith; beginning with maxims of justice and equity."

1. "The first general maxim of interpretation is, that it is not permitted to interpret what has no need of interpretation. When an act is conceived in clear and precise terms; when the sense is manifest, and leads to nothing absurd; there can be no reason to refuse the sense which this treaty naturally presents. To go elsewhere in search of conjectures, in order to restrain or extinguish it, is to endeavor to elude it."[1]

2. "If he who can, and ought to have explained himself clearly and plainly, and has not done it, it is worse for him; he cannot be allowed to introduce subsequent restrictions which he has not expressed."

3. "Neither the one or the other of the interested parties or contracting powers, has a right to interpret the act for himself."

4. "On every occasion when a person has, and ought to have shown his intention, we take it for true against him what he has sufficintly declared. In order to know the true sense of the contract, attention ought principally to be paid to the words of him who promises, for he *voluntarily* binds himself by his words. If the words of him who accepts the conditions, relate to the words of him who offers them, we ought to regulate ourselves by the latter."

5. "It is a question to know what the contracting powers have agreed upon, in order to determine precisely on any particular occasion, what has been promised and accepted; not only what one of the parties has had the intention to promise; but also what the other has reasonably and sincerely thought to be promised,

---

NOTE 1.—This maxim or rule has been adopted in this State, in the adjudications of the courts. Jackson v. Lewis, 17 John. 477 ; Waterford and Whitehall Turnpike Co. v. People, 9 Barb. 170 ; People v. N. Y. Cent. R. R. Co. 13 N. Y. R. 80.

and upon which he must have regulated his acceptance. The interpretation of every act, and of every treaty ought to be made according to certain rules, proper to determine the sense of them, such as the parties concerned must naturally have understood when the act was prepared and accepted."

6. "Since the lawful interpretation, ought to tend only to the discovery of the thoughts of the author; as soon as we meet with any obscurity, we should seek for what was probably in the thoughts of those who drew it up, and to interpret it accordingly. This is the general rule of all interpretations. It particularly serves to fix the sense of certain expressions, the signification of which is not sufficiently determined."

7. "The contracting powers are obliged to express themselves in such a manner, as that they mutually understand each other. This is manifest from the nature even of the act. Those who contracted concurred in the same will; they agreed to desire the same thing; and how could they agree, if they did not understand it perfectly."

8. "In interpretation, we ought not to deviate from the common use of the language, at least if we have not very strong reasons for it. In all human affairs, where there is a want of certainty, we ought to follow probability."

9. "Languages vary incessantly, and the signification and force of words change with time; therefore, when an ancient act is to be interpreted, we should know the common use of terms at the time when it was written; and this is known by carefully comparing with each other, an act of the same date, and cotemporary writers."

10. "Words, are only designed to express the thoughts; thus, the true signification of an expression in common use, is the true idea which custom has affixed to that expression."

11. "Technical terms, or terms proper to the arts and sciences, ought commonly to be interpreted according to the definition given of them by the masters of the art, or persons versed in the knowledge of the art or science to which the term belongs."

12. "Interpretation should only tend to the discovery of the will of the contracting power. We should then attribute to each term, the sense which he who speaks had probably in his mind."

13. "We ought always to give to expressions, the sense most suitable to the subject, or to the matter to which they relate."

14. "If any one of those expressions that have many different significations, are found more than once in the same piece, we cannot make it a law, to take it every where in the same signification."

15. "Every interpretation that leads to an absurdity, ought to be rejected."

16. "The interpretation which renders a treaty (or statute) null and void, cannot be admitted; it is an absurdity to suppose that after it is reduced to terms, it means nothing. It ought to be interpreted in such a manner, as that it may have effect, and not to be found vain and illusive."

17. "If he who has expressed himself in an obscure or equivocal manner, has spoken elsewhere more clearly on the same subject, he is the best interpretor of himself. We ought to interpret his obscure or vague expressions in such a manner, that they may agree with those terms that are clear and without ambiguity which he has used elsewhere, either in the same treaty or some other of the like kind."

18. "The connection and train of the discourse, is another source of interpretation. We ought to consider the discourse together, and in order perfectly to conceive of the sense of it, and to give to each expression not so much signification as it may receive in itself alone, as that it ought to have from the thread and spirit of the discourse."

19. "The interpretation ought to be made in such a manner, that all the parts appear consonant to each other; that what follows, with what went before; unless it manifestly appear that by the last clauses something is changed that went before."

20. "The reason of the law or treaty, that is, the motive which led to making of it, is one of the most certain means of establishing the true sense; and great attention ought to be paid to it whenever it is required to explain an obscure, equivocal, and undetermined point, or to make an application of them to a particular case. As soon as we certainly know the reason, which alone has determined the will of him who speaks, we ought to interpret his words, and to apply them in a manner suitable to that reason alone."

21. "We ought to be so much the more circumspect in this kind of interpretation, as frequently several motives concur to determine the will of him who speaks, in a law, or promise. It is possible, that he was influenced only by the union of all these motives, or each taken apart might have been sufficient to determine him. In the first case, if we are very certain that the legislature, or powers that formed the laws or the contract, had only in consideration one of many motives and many reasons taken together, the interpretation and application ought to be made in a manner agreeable to all these united reasons; and none of them ought to be neglected. But in the second case, when it is evident that each of the reasons that have concurred to determine the will, was sufficient to produce that effect, so that the author of the piece would, for each of these reasons taken separately, have done the same, as for them altogether, his words ought to be interpreted and applied in such a manner as they may agree with these reasons separately taken."

22. "When the sufficient, and only reason of a disposition, either of a law or a promise is very certain, and well known, we understand this disposition in the case where the same reason is applicable, though it is not comprehended within the signification of the terms. This is what is called extensive interpretation. We ought to apply rather to the spirit, than to the letter."

23. "To violate the *spirit* of the law, by pretending to respect the letter, is a fraud no less criminal than an open violation of it. It is not less contrary to the intention of the legislature, and only shows a more artful and more deliberate malice."

24. "When a case arises in which it would be too prejudicial to any one to take a law or promise awarding to the rigor of the terms, a restrictive interpretation is also then used, and we except the case, agreeably to the intention of the legislature, or of him who made the promise."

25. "If the subject, or matter treated of, will not allow that the terms of a disposition should be taken in their full extent, we should limit the sense according as the subject requires."

26. "If it be certain and manifest that the consideration of the present state of things was one of the reasons which occasioned the promise; that the promise has been made in consideration,

or in consequence of that state of things, it depends on the preservation of things in the same state."

27. "In unforseen cases, we should rather follow intention than words, and interpret the act as the party himself would have interpreted it, had he been present, or conformably to what he would have done if he had forseen the thing that happened."

28. "When things which enter into the reason of a law are considered, not as actually existing, but only as possible; or when the fear of an event, is the reason of the law, we can only except those cases where it is shown that the event is really impossible."

29. "Everything that contains a penalty is odious with respect to laws; in case of doubt, the judge ought to be inclined to the merciful side; and that it is indisputably better to suffer a guilty man to escape, than to punish one who is innocent."

30. "What tends to render an act null and without effect, either in the whole or in part, and consequently everything that introduces any change already agreed upon; is odious."

31. "When the subject relates to things favorable, we ought to give the terms all the extent they are capable of in common use; and if a term has many significations, the most extensive ought to be preferred; for equity ought to be the rule of all men wherever a perfect right is not exactly determined and known with precision. When the legislature have not expressed their will in terms that are precise and perfectly determinable, it is to be presumed that they desire what is most equitable."

32. "In things favorable, the *terms* of art ought to be taken in the fullest extent they are capable of; not only according to common use, but also as technical terms, if he who speaks understands the art as to which those terms belong, or if he conducts himself by the advice of men who understand that art."

33. "But we ought not from the single reason that a thing is favorable, to take the terms in an improper signification; this is only allowable to be done, to avoid absurdity, injustice, or the nullity of the act."

34. "Though a thing appears favorable when viewed in one particular light, yet if the propriety of the terms, in their full

extent, lead to absurdity or injustice, their signification ought to be limited according to the rules above given."

35. "If there flows neither absurdity or injustice from the strict propriety of the terms, but a manifest equity, or a great common utility requires a restriction, we ought to adhere to the most limited sense which the proper signification can admit, even in an affair that appears favorable in its own nature."

36. "In all cases, where what is only permitted, is found incompatible with what is prescribed, the latter has the advantage."

37. "The law or treaty which permits, ought to yield to the law or treaty which forbids."

38. "Everything being otherwise equal, the law or treaty which ordains, yields to the law or treaty which forbids."

39. "If opposition is found between two affirmative laws or treaties, concluded between the same persons or States, the last date is to be preferred to the more ancient."

40. "Of two laws or conventions, in all other things equal, we ought to prefer that which is the least general, and which approaches nearest to the affair to which it relates."

41. "What will suffer no delay, ought to be preferred to what may be done at another time."

42. "When two duties are found incompatible, the most considerable, and that which comprehends the higher degree of honesty and utility, merits the preference."

43. "If we cannot acquit ourselves at the same time of two things, promised to the same person, he is to choose, which, we ought to accomplish."

44. "Since the strongest obligation has the advantage over the weaker, if it happen that a treaty confirmed with an oath comes in opposition to a treaty that is not sworn to, everything else being equal, the first has the advantage."

45. "All other things being equal, what is imposed under a penalty, has the advantage of what is not enforced by one; and what bears a greater penalty, over what bears a less."

In these rules as copied, we have omitted the author's illustrations and examples. We have also intentionally omitted such of his rules of interpretation as are not in harmony with the spirit of a republican form of government, and which seem to be in conflict with the rules of Story, Kent, and other distinguished American commentators upon written constitutions, established by the people. He adds: "all these rules, ought to be combined together; and the interpretation made in such a manner, that it may be accommodated to all, so far as they are applicable to the case. When these rules appear opposite, they reciprocally balance and limit each other according to their strength and importance, and according as they more particularly belong to the case in question."

PUFFENDORF'S RULES.

Puffendorf has also given in his treatise on the law of nature and of nations, a set of rules for the interpretation of laws, (some of which he copies from Grotius.) A few of which that have some application, we copy. He says:

"The true end and design of interpretation, is, to gather the intent from the most probable signs, which are of two sorts; words and conjectures."

"As for *words*, the rule is,—unless there be reasonable objections against it, they are to be understood in their proper and most known signification; not so much according to grammar, as to the general use of them."

"As for terms of art, which are above the reach of the common people, the rule is, that they be taken according to the definition of the learned in each art."

"When a single *word* or *sentence* is capable of several significations; conjectures are necessary to find out the true. Both these cases rhetoricians call *ambiguous*. But logicians are more nice, who, if the variety of significations lies in a *word*, call it equivocal; if in a sentence, ambiguous."

"When we meet with a seeming repugnancy in the terms, conjectures are necessary to work out the genuine sense, by reconciling it if possible, to those terms that seem to be repugnant. But if there be a clear, evident repugnancy, the latter vacates the former. This rule applies to the making of laws, wills, and contracts."

"The effects and consequence, do very often point out the genuine meaning of words. If by taking them literally, they bear none, or a very absurd signification, to avoid such an inconvenience, we must a little deviate from the received sense of them."

" It gives great light to the interpretation of obscure passages, to compare them with others that have some affinity with them ; or to compare them with what goes before or follows in the context."

" Where laws are really repugnant, the judges should embrace that which is clear, in preference to that which is obscure."

" That which helps us most in the discovery of the true meaning of the law, is the *reason* of it, or the cause which moved the legislator to enact it. This ought not to be confounded with the *mind* of the law; for that is nothing but the genuine meaning of it; for the finding out of which, we call in the reason of it to our assistance."

" In promises and facts, as also in privileges, some things are *favorable*, some odious, and others of a *mixed* nature."

GROTIUS' RULES.

The following rules we take from Grotius :

" In cases that are not *odious*, words are to be understood according to the full propriety of popular use; and if in popular use there be several significations of the same word, the largest is to be taken; as the masculine may be taken for the common gender."

" In a matter of favor, if he that speaks be learned in the law, or speaks by the advice of those that are, his words are to be taken in the most comprehensive signification, so as not only to import as much as they do in common use, but to include that signification also which is used among lawyers."

" On the other hand, words shall be taken in a stricter sense than the propriety requires, if otherwise, injustice or an absurdity would follow."

" If it be not absolutely necessary to avoid injustice, to take the words in a stricter sense than their propriety demands, yet if there be a manifest advantage in such a restriction, we ought to stop at the narrowest limits of their proper signification, unless circumstances direct otherwise."

"In an odious matter, a figurative speech may be admitted to avoid a grievance."

"Sometimes the meaning of words are to be restrained, and although general terms be made use of, yet they ought to be taken with some exception or limitation; either, 1st, because of some original defect in the will of the speaker; or 2d, because of some accident which happens inconsistent with his design."

"1st. An original defect is in the will. First, When an absurdity proceeds from it, for no man in his wits can be supposed to will absurdities. Secondly, The will is supposed to be originally defective, when the reason ceases which alone fully and efficaciously moved the will."

"That which is only permitted, gives place to that which is commanded; for permission includes a liberty, but a command carries along with it necessity of acting."

"That which ought to be done at this present time, is preferable to that which may be done at any other time."

"An affirmative precept gives way to a negative."

"In covenants and laws that are in other respects equal, that which is particular and applicable to the present case, takes the place of that which is general."

"When two duties happen to interfere at the same point of time, that which is the more honest and profitable, is to be preferred."

"When two covenants, one upon oath, the other not, cannot both be performed together, the former ought to take place of the latter, unless the latter was added as an exception and limitation to the other."

· "An obligation imperfectly mutual, gives place to one that is perfectly mutual, and binding on both sides."

"The law of generosity, gives place to the law of gratitude; *cateris paribus*."

"Where laws are made by subordinate powers; that of the inferior, yields to that of the superior if both cannot be obeyed. Thus we ought to obey God rather than man."

"The more noble, useful or necessary the matter of one law is than that of another, the greater weight ought the law to have with us."

We have also selected from Rutherford's lectures or institutes, several rules of interpretation, omitting such as are copied from Grotius and Puffendorf, and such as relate only to the interpretation of contracts. He says p. 104.

" The way to ascer ain our claims as they arise from promises, contracts, or wills, and our obligations as they arise from instituted laws, is to collect the meaning and intention of the promisor, contractor, testator, or lawmaker, from some outward signs or marks. The collecting of such intention, from such signs or marks, is called interpretation."

" Words are the common signs that mankind make use of to declare their intention to one another; and when the words of a man express his meaning plainly, distinctly, and perfectly, we have no occasion to have recourse to any other means of interpretation."

" Interpretation consists in finding out, or collecting, the intention of a speaker or of a writer either from his words, or from other conjectures or from both. It may therefore be divided into three sorts, according to the different means that it makes use of for obtaining its end. These three sorts of interpretation are *literal*, *rational* and *mixed*."

" Where we collect the intention from the clear and plain words of the law, or of the writer, this is *literal* interpretation."

" Where words do not express the intention perfectly, but either exceed or fall short of it, so that we are to collect it from probable or rational conjectures, this is rational interpretation."

" Where words, though they do express the intention when rightly understood, are in themselves of doubtful meaning, and we are forced to have recourse to like conjectures to find out in what sense they were used, this is mixed interpretation; it is partly literal and partly rational. We collect the intention from the words indeed, but not without the help of other conjectures."

" Where the words of a contract, or of a will, or of a law, may be so strained as to admit of a sense, which, though it does not hurt the grammar, and is not inconsistent with the letter, is such a sense as common usage will not justify; we can scarcely call these words ambiguous. For words are then only to be looked upon as ambiguous, when they will admit of two or more senses, either of which is equally agreeable to common usage."

"The ambiguity of a writing, whether it is a law, a will or a contract, depends sometimes upon the doubtful sense of a single word; sometimes upon the doubtful construction of a sentence; and sometimes upon a comparison of one part of the same writing with another, or of the writing which is before us with some other writing which came from the same hand."

"When words or expressions are of doubtful meaning, the first rule in mixed interpretation is, to give them such a sense as is agreeable to the subject matter, of which the writer is treating. For we are sure on the one hand, that this subject matter was in his mind, and can on the other hand, have no reason for thinking that he intended anything which is different from it, and much less, that he intended anything which is inconsistent with it."

"The second rule in mixed interpretation is, to give all doubtful words or expressions that sense which makes them produce some effect; this effect, must in general be a reasonable one; and it must likewise, be the same that the lawmaker, or testator, or contractor intended to produce."

"There are numberless *circumstances* of laws, wills and contracts, which may help to ascertain their meaning, where use has been made of ambiguous words or expressions. These are divided into two sorts; into such as are connected with the instrument in origin only; and such as are connected with it in place as well as origin. To these two sorts, we may add a third; for there are some circumstances which seem to be connected with a law, contract, or will, rather in time, than either in origin, or in place."

"When the words of a law, contract or will are capable of two or more senses, so that the meaning of the writer is left doubtful; what has been spoken or written by the same lawmaker, testator or contractor upon some other occasion, is a *circumstance* of the doubtful writing."

"When we explain a doubtful part of the law, will, or contract, by the help of some other part of it, the clause which we make use of for this purpose, is a *circumstance* which is connected with the clause to be explained in place, as well as in origin; as they both came from the same hand, so they are both found together in the same writing."

"Cotemporary practice, is a circumstance which is connected with a law in time, and not only in time but in place too; for it consists in what was usually done in the place where the law was made, at or near the time of making it."

DOMAT'S RULES.

Domat's rules of law and of interpretation are appropriately selected to follow those of the preceding authors. We do not copy them in full, but extract such portions of them, as will be found useful in this connection, from Vol. 1, Cushing's edition, beginning at page 108. He says:

"Laws ought to be written to the end that the writing may fix the sense of the law, and determine the mind to conceive a just idea of that which is established by the law, and that it be not left free for every one to frame the law as he himself is pleased to understand it. We may, therefore, distinguish two ideas, which the words *law* and *rule* form in our minds. One, is the idea of what we concieve to be just, without making any reflection on the terms of the law; the other is the idea of the terms of the law; and according to this second idea, we give the name of rule or law, to the *expression of the lawgiver.*"

"Laws are of two sorts; one is of those which flow from the law of nature and equity, and the other is of such as derive their origin from the positive law, which is otherwise called human and arbitrary laws, because they have been established by men."

"The rules of the law of nature, are those which God himself hath established, and which He communicates to mankind by the light of reason. These are the laws which have in them a justice that cannot be changed; which is the same at all times, and in all places; and whether they are set down in writing or not, no human authority can abolish them, or make any alteration in them."

"Arbitrary rules, are all those that have been established by men, and which are such, that without offending natural equity, they may either prescribe one thing, or a thing quite different."

"All laws ought either to be known, or at least laid open to

18

the knowledge of all the world, in such a manner, that no one may
with impunity, offend against them, under pretence of ignorance.
Thus, the natural law being truth that is unchangeable; the
knowledge of which is essential to reason, nobody can pretend
ignorance of it, since they cannot say that they are destitute of
common reason, which makes this law known.   But arbitrary laws
have not their effect till the lawgiver has done all that is possible
to make them known; and this is done, by the ways that are
commonly practiced for the publication of these kinds of laws;
and after they are promulged in due from, it is presumed that
they are known to every body, and they oblige as well those who
pretend ignorance of them, as those who know them."

"The laws of nature being highly just, and their authority
always the same, they determine equally all that is to come, and
all that is past which remains undecided."

" Laws restrain and punish not only what is evidently contrary
to the sense of their words, but likewise everything that is directly
or indirectly against their intent, although it seem to have nothing
contrary to the terms of the laws, and also that everything that
is done in fraud of the law, and to elude it."

"If any case could happen that were not regulated by some
express and written law, it would have for a law, *the natural principles of equity;* which is the universal law that extends to everything."

" It happens in two sorts of cases, that it is necessary to interpret the laws.   One is when we find in a law some obscurity,
ambiguity, or other defect of expression; for in this case, it is
necessary to interpret the law in order to discover its true meaning.   And this kind of interpretation is limited to the expression,
that it may be known what the law says.   The other is, when it
happens that the sense of a law, how clear however it may appear
in the words, would lead us to false consequences, and to decisions that would be unjust, if the laws were indifferently applied
to everything that is contained within the expression.   For in
this case, the palpable injustice that would follow from this apparent sense, obliges us to discover by some kind of interpretation,
not what the law *says,* but what it *means;* and to judge by its

meaning, how far it ought to be extended, and what are the bounds that ought to be set to its sense."

"This principle of interpreting the laws by equity, does not only respect the laws of nature, but reaches likewise to arbitrary laws, they being all of them founded upon the laws of nature. If they are natural laws, we are to reconcile them by the extent and limits of their truth, if arbitrary, we are to fix their equity by the intention of the lawgiver."

"All rules, whether natural or arbitrary, have their use; such as is assigned to every one of them by universal justice, which is the spirit of them all. Thus the application of laws is to be made, by discerning what it is that this spirit demands; which, in natural law, is *equity;* in arbitrary laws, the intention of the law giver. It is in this discerning faculty, that the science of the law does chiefly consist."

"If a rule of natural justice being applied to a case that it seems to embrace, shows a result contrary to equity, we are bound to conclude that the rule has been improperly applied, and that the case should fall under some other law."

"If an arbitrary, or positive rule, is applied to a case which it apparently embraces, and the result is contrary to the intent of the legislator, the rule should not be applied to the case.

"But we must not consider as unjust and repugnant to equity, or the legislators intention, those decisions which appear rigorous and severe, when it is evident that rigor and severity, is the essential characteristic of the law in question; and that it could not be mitigated without impairing its effect; as for example, the law in regard to the formalities prescribed relating to the execution of wills; the severity and arbitrary character of the rule which annuls all wills where these formalities are neglected, is, in those cases an indispensable part of the law."

"If however, the severity of the law is not a necessary and indispensable part of it, but can be carried into effect by a milder interpretation and one more conformable to equity and natural justice; then this is to be preferred to the severe and strict construction."

"It follows from these rules, that the rule of interpretion is not fixed and invariable; that sometimes strictness, and sometimes a

milder and more equitable interpretation is to be followed. Rigor
becomes injustice when the law will bear an equitable interpretation, and rigor should be practiced when an equitable construction would defeat the law. This rigor or strictness is either an
unjust and odious severity, contrary to the spirit of the law, or,
it furnishes a just but inflexible rule. These two ideas are never
to be confounded; and the strict, or equitable construction ought
to be adhered to according to the rules here given."

" It is never a matter of indifference whether we apply a strict
or a liberal construction. In each case we are to enquire whether
the rule in question calls for a strict interpretation, or will bear
a liberal one; and then decide accordingly."

" Although the strictness of law appears at first sight opposed
to equity, it is nevertheless true that where it ought to be applied,
it is only on account of its inherent justice. What is equitable
cannot be contrary to justice; and so what is just cannot be contrary to equity."

" The obscurities, ambiguities, and other defects of expression
which may render the meaning of a law doubtful, and all other
difficulties in its construction and application should be resolved
by the natural sense of the language, according to the nature of
the subject, so as if possible at once to conform to the intent of
the legislator and to equity. This is to be arrived at by the different consideration of the nature of the law, its object, its connection with other laws, the exceptions to which it may be subject, and other similar considerations."

" To arrive at the meaning of a law, we are to weigh its terms
and examine its preamble, if there be one, in order to judge of
its provisions by its object and the whole context, and not to
limit its interpretation to what would appear different from its
intention, either in a single portion of the law or in a single
defective expression. We must prefer the evident meaning of
the whole law, to the inconsistent meaning of a defective expression."

" If in any law we find the omission of something essential to
it, or which is a necessary result of its provisions, and requisite
to give the law its full effect, we may supply what is wanting but

not expressed, and extend the law to what it was manifestly intended to embrace, but in its terms does not include."

"If the language of a law clearly expresses its meaning and intention, that intention must be carried out; but if the true sense of the law cannot be arrived at by the interpretation which may be made according to the rules here given, or the meaning be clear, and inconvenience appear to result, then we must have recourse to the sovereign to interpret, to declare, or to modify the law."

"If the provisions of a law are clear, but its object not understood, and in its application inconveniences appear to result, we are bound to presume that the law is useful and just; and its meaning and authority are to be preferred to mere abstract reasoning. Otherwise, many useful and well contrived rules would be overturned on grounds of alleged equity, or ingenious argument."

"Laws which favor what public utility, humanity, religion, freedom of intercourse, and other similar interests regard favorably, as well as those intended to favor particular individuals, ought to be interpreted with all the liberality to which these interests are justly entitled, in an equitable point of view, and ought not to be interpreted severely, nor be applied in a manner calculated to prejudice the persons intended to be favored."

"Laws which restrain natural liberty, as those which prohibit what is not of itself illicit, or which derogate otherwise from common right; laws fixing the punishment of crimes and offences, or penalties in matters of a civil nature which prescribe formalities that seem severe; those which permit parents to disinherit children; and others of a similar character; ought not to be so interpreted as to extend their provisions to cases which they do not embrace; and, on the contrary, they should receive all practical mitigation of equity and humanity."

"If any law or custom is established for particlar reasons contrary to other rules of common right, it ought not to be applied except to those cases for which it is expressly intended.

"The grants and gifts of sovereigns are to be favorably regarded, and to have that extension to which they are entitled from the natural presumption of princely liberality, provided however, that they are not to be so liberally construed as to injure other individuals."

"If the doubts or difficulties in regard to the interpretation of a law or a custom are solved by an old usage which has fixed the meanings, and which is supported by a uniform series of adjudications, we should adhere to the usage, which is the best interpreter of laws."

"In case any provinces or districts are without certain rules to decide difficulties in regard to matters which are there governed by usage; if these difficulties are not determined by natural justice, or by written law, but depend on custom and usage, we ought to adopt the principles which result from the customs and usages of the province or district."

"All laws necessarily bear with them all the powers or incidents necessary to fully carry out their intention. Thus, as the law permits boys to contract marriage at the age of fourteen, and girls at the age of twelve, it necessarily results from this law that those who marry, can, although infants, and not of full age, bind themselves in regard to the settlement, community of goods and the like."

"In laws which confer power, the greater authority implies the less. Thus those who possess their property have with still greater reason the right to sell it."

"In laws which *prohibit* acts, the lesser prohibition includes the greater. Those who are forbidden to manage or control their property, with stronger reason cannot alienate it."

"The implications arising from the two preceding sections, are to be restricted to subjects of the same nature as those to which the law applies according to those rules. Thus, the liberty that a minor adult enjoys, to make *a donatio causa mortis*, will not be extended so as to sustain a gift *inter vivos*."

"If a law grants an amnesty or pardon for past offences, it is to be understood as prohibiting similar acts in future."

"When a right comes to a person by reason of a law, this right is equally vested in him, whether he knows the fact or not; as a son is heir to his father, and owns the estate though he be ignorant of his father's death, and also ignorant of the law succession."

" Persons competent by law to act upon their rights, may waive the benefit or privilege created by law in their favor. But they cannot by renunciation or waiver effect the rights of third persons, nor can they waive or renounce in cases contrary to equity, good morals, or to any other law."

" No person by contract, testament, or otherwise, can hinder the effect of the law. Thus a testator cannot dispose of his estate to be controled or managed contrary to law."

" It is necessary to possess an ample knowledge of the rules of interpretation of laws in order to make the proper application of them."

AMERICAN RULES.

The following few rules and maxims of interpretation, may be regarded as general rules in the American standards. They have been selected from approved American authority, and this includes such of the English rules as have been adopted by our courts. They also include the rules of interpreting State laws by the national courts.

1. The interpretation by the United States courts within the jurisdiction of a State, of a local law, becomes a part of that law; as much so, as if it was incorporated in the body of it, by the legislature. If different interpretations are given in different States to a similar law, that law, in effect, becomes by interpretation, so far as it is a rule for action by the federal courts, a different law in one State, from what it is in the other.*a*

2. It is not permitted to interpret what has no need of interpretation. When an act is expressed in clear and precise terms; when the sense is manifest and leads to nothing absurd, there can be no reason not to adopt the sense which it naturally presents. To go elsewhere in search of conjectures in order to restrain or extinguish it, is to elude it.*b*

3. The popular, or received import of words, furnishes the general rule for the interpretation of statutes.*c*

a Christy v. Pridgion, 4 Wall. 196.

b Jackson v. Lewis, 17 John. 475; People v. N. Y. Cent. R. R. Co. 13 N. Y. R. 78; Waterford and Whitehall Turnpike Co. 9 Barb. 161; Vattel, B. 2 ch. 17, ◊ 263; United States v. Fisher, 2 Cranch, 358.

c Maillard v. Lawrence, 16 How. U. S. R. 251.

4. It is the duty of courts so to construe statutes as to meet the mischief and to advance the remedy, and not to violate fundamental principles.*a*

5. Where there is a discrepancy or disagreement between two statutes, such interpretation should be given, that both may, if possible, stand together.*b*

6. Statutes must be interpreted according to the intent and meaning, and not always according to the letter.*c*

7. The intention of the legislature may be found from the act itself; from other acts *in pari materia*; and sometimes from the cause or necessity of the statute, and wherever the intent can be discovered, it should be followed with reason and discretion, though such construction seem contrary to the letter of the statute; this is the rule where the words of the statute are obscure.*d*

8. A thing within the *intention*, is within the statute, though not within the letter; and a thing within the letter, is not within the statute, unless within the intention.*e*

9. Statutes should be interpreted according to the most natural and obvious import of their language, without resorting to subtle or forced construction for the purpose either of limiting or extending their operation. Courts cannot correct supposed errors, omissions or excesses, of the legislature.*f*

10. The office of interpretation is to bring the sense out of the words used, and not to bring a sense into them. *g*

11. The spirit of a law may be referred to in order to interpret words admitting of two meanings; but not to extend a law to a case not within its fair meaning.*h*

12. In the construction of a statute, every part of it must be viewed in connection with the whole, so as to make all its parts

a Hart v. Cleis, 8 John. R. 44.

b McCartee v. Orphan Asylum Society, 9 Cow. R. 437.

c People v. N. Y. Cent. R. R. Co. 13 N. Y. R. 81; Leavitt v. Blatchford, 5 Barb. 13, Plowd. 205; Holmes v. Carley, 31 N. Y. R. 289, 290; Brown v. Barry, 3 Dall. 365, 1 Pet. 46, 2 id. 627.

d 1 Kent Com. 462, Bac. Abr. Lit. Statute J. 5, 10.

e People v. Utica Ins. Co. 15 John. 380–1; Jackson v. Collins, 3 Cow. 89, and authorities supra.

f Waller v. Harris, 20 Wend. 561, 562; McCluskey v. Cromwill, 11 N. Y. 601-2.

g Lieber's Polit. Hermeneutics, 87; 11 N. Y. R. supra 601-2.

h Beebe v. Griffing, 14 N. Y. R. 244.

harmonize if practicable, and give a sensible and intelligent effect to each. It is not to be presumed that the legislature intended any part of a statute to be without meaning. *a*

13. Every legislative act must have reasonable construction. *b*

14. That which is implied in a statute, is as much a part of it as what is expressed. *c*

15. The presumption must always be in favor of the validity of laws, unless the contrary is clearly demonstrated. *d*

16. Statutes are to be construed to operate prospectively, unless a retrospective effect be clearly intended. *e*

17. All statutes in *pari materia* are to be read and construed together, as if they formed parts of the same statute, and were enacted at the same time. *f*

18. Statutes are to be interpreted with reference to the principles of the common law in force at the time of their passage, except when the statute itself, or the courts have otherwise determined, and this rule is the same in courts of equity as of law. *g*

19. Whether courts are interpreting an agreement between parties, a statute, or a constitution, the thing to seek, is, *the thought which it expresses.* To ascertain this, the first resort in all cases is to the natural signification of the words employed, in the order and grammatical arrangement in which they stand. If thus regarded, the words embody a definite meaning, which involves no absurdity, and no contradiction between different parts of the same writing; then that meaning apparent upon the face of the instrument, is the one which *alone* we are at liberty to say was intended to be conveyed. In such case there is no room for con-

a Ogden v. Strong, 2 Paine R, 584 ; 1 Kent Com. 162 ; People v. Draper, 15 N. Y. 532.

b Famurn v. Black Comal. 1 Sum. 46.

c U. S. v. Babbitt, 1 Black. 61 ; Gelpecke v. City of Dubuque, 1 Wall. 221.

d Cooper v. Telfair, 4 Cranch. 167.

e Jackson v. Van Zandt, 12 Johns. 176 ; Hackley v. Sprague, 10 Wend. 116 , People v. Supervisors of Columbia, id. 365 ; Snyder v. Snyder, 3 Barb. 621 ; Harvey v. Tyler, 2 Wall. 347 ; Blanchard v. Sprague, 3 Sum. 535.

f 1 Kent Com. 463 ; Smith's Com. § 639 ; 9 Barb. 161 ; Rogers v. Bradshaw, 20 John, 735 ; McCartee v. Orphan Asylum, 9 Cow. 437 ; Rexford v. Knight, 15 Barb. 627.

g Rice v. M. & N. W. Railroad Co. 1 Blatch· 359 ; Talbot v. Simpson, Peters C C. R. 188 ; Van Horne v. Dorrance, 2 Dallas, 316 ; How v. Peckham, 6 How. Pr R. 229.

struction. That which the words declare, is the meaning of the instrument; and neither the courts nor the legislature have a right to add to, or take away from that meaning.a

20. In the enactment of statutes, the rule of interpretation is, in respect to the intention of the legislature, that where the language is explicit, the courts are bound to seek for the intention in the words of the act itself, and they are not at liberty to suppose or to hold, that the legislature intended anything different from what their language imports.b

21. Statutes, by the authority of which a citizen may be deprived of his estate, must have the strictest construction, and the power conferred must be executed precisely as it is given, and any departure from it will vitiate the proceeding, and this is so whether it be in the exercise of a public or private authority, whether it be ministerial or judicial.c

a Newell v. the People, 7 N. Y. 99; McCluchey v. Cromwell, 11 N. Y. 593.

b Supervisors of Niagara v. the People, 7 Hill, 513.

c Sherwood v. Reade, 7 Hill 431; Striker v. Kelly, 2 Denio 323; Sheup v. Spier, 4 Hill 76; Downing v. Ruger, 21 Wend. 178; Powell v. Tuttle, 3 N. Y. 396.

CHAPTER VI.

OF THE EXCEPTIONS TO GENERAL RULES OF CONSTRUCTION, AND THE MANNER OF PLEADING OR TAKING ADVANTAGE OF PARTICULAR STATUTES. REPEAL OF STATUTES AND ITS EFFECTS, AND ACCIDENTS.

THE rules and maxims in the preceding chapter as to the general interpretation of statutes, as will be seen, have been selected from the books of the most approved authors, and the adjudications of courts and jurists upon that branch of law. They embrace all that can be regarded as needful on that subject. The law in regard to the interpretation of contracts, wills, covenants, and other facts, by the writers on those subjects, is not brought within the scope of this treatise, except in so far as their interpretation is identical with that of statutes. The rules of construction applicable to special cases, and to distinct parts of statutes with judicial exposition, selected from American and other authority as to the effect of the title, preamble, clauses, and provisos in statutes; with the meaning of particular words and expressions therein, will be found in a subsequent chapter; as will also the interpretation of written constitutions by the soundest of American writers.

The nature, parts, and properties of a statute having been thus considered, the next inquiry is, what are its accidents; how can it be pleaded, or in what way taken advantage of ?

In an action founded on a statute, the plaintiff ought a to aver every fact necessary to inform the court that his case is within the statute, concluding in general with an express reference to the statute. A public statute it is never advisable to set forth, since by reciting the act and concluding *contra formam statuti*, the risk of a fatal variance is incurred.

If part of a statute be public, and the residue thereof private, there is no necessity that the part which is public should be recited in pleading.b

a And. 62; Lut. 1089.
b 10 Rep. 57, the Chancellor of Oxford's case, Hob. 227, Sid. 24.

If a private statute be pleaded, it must be recited, and *nul tiel record* may be replied; but if the exemplification of a private statute under the great seal be pleaded, *nul tiel record* cannot be replied. *a*[1]

In pleading a statute it is not necessary to recite the title or the preamble. The title, said Lord Holt, is no more a part of the law than a title of a book is part of the book, and there is, for that reason, no necessity to recite it; but if a party do take upon him to recite the title of a statute, he thereby ties himself to an act so entitled, and if he cannot produce it, he is gone.*b*

We have said in a previous chapter that certain statutes, such as the statute of limitations, and the statutes to prevent usury, though public statutes, are required to be set up in pleading by the party who desires to interpose them as defences, and heretofore in practice, the courts have been disposed to look upon such defences with disfavor, especially in cases of latches, on the ground that such defences are inequitable and immoral. This is, with more modern views, believed to be a mistaken policy for the judiciary. The policy of the government, is for the legislature to direct; that of the duty of the judiciary is, to give full effect to the legislative will; and every effort by them to throw discredit on statutory provisions as unjust, as inexpedient, and is but to arrogate to themselves a censorship over the law-making power which our constitutions have nowhere entrusted to them. " All laws emanate from the same supreme power; and while they remain on the statute books are all entitled to equal respect and obedience." *a*[2]

a The Prince's case, 8 Rep. 28, Hale's H. C. L. 16.   *b* 6 Mod. 62.
c Sedgwick on Const. Law, 1u9.

NOTE 1.—The objection, that a statute was not constitutionally passed, in order to be available, must be set up in an answer by way of defence. Darlington v. Mayor, &c., of New York, 31 N. Y. 164, 2 Robertson 274.

NOTE 2.—Statutes of limitation are now regarded favorably in all courts of justice. They are called " statutes of repose." Usually they are founded in a wise and salutary policy, and promote the ends of justice. Lessee of Parish v. Ferris, 2 Black. 606 ; Tolson v. Kage, 2 Brod. & Bing. 217 ; Lewis v. Marshall, 5 Peters, 470. They are entitled to the same respect as other statutes and ought not to receive unfavorable construction or to be explained away. Bell v. Morrison, 1 Peters, 360 ; Willison v. Watkins, 3 Pet. 54 ; McCleny v. Silliman, id. 270. They rest upon sound policy and tend to the peace and welfare of society. They are often a very meritorious defence. Tracy v. Suydam, 30 Barb. 117. No one who has reflected upon the subject, and whose observation and experience qualify him to judge, but will sanction and applaud the wisdom and policy of a statute, the

A misrecital of the day on which the parliament was holden, or of the session, (as of the 29th of Eliz., when the session commenced the 28th Eliz.,) *a* or of the place of making the statute, or a repugnancy in reciting the day of its making, will be fatal ; so, if any material part be omitted or misrecited. *b* But trifling variations which do not alter the sense of the material parts of the statute would not, it is apprehended, now, be considered fatal. *c* It is no fault in the recital of a statute to omit altogether the day on which the parliament was holden ; for the judges are bound to take notice of the commencement of a session, and it is a safer course to omit it, to avoid the risk of a misrecital. If a mistake be made in reciting even a material part of a public statute, the defect, it seems, will not be fatal, unless the indictment conclude " against the form of the said statute ;" *d* for if it conclude " against the form of the statute in such case made and provided," the misrecital will be rejected as surplusage, and the court will give judgment upon that statute which warrants it. But where an indictment is founded upon a private statute, such a defect will not be cured by a general conclusion. *e* In civil actions, misrecitals of a private statute can only be taken advantage of by plea of *nul tiel record*, or, in assumpsit, under the general issue ; *f* while the time or place of holding the parliament being misstated, is ground of demurrer. *g* In pleading upon statutes, it has already been stated, that where there is an exception in the enacting clause, the plaintiff must show that the defendant is not within the exception ; but if there be an exception in a subsequent clause, that is matter of defence, and the other party must show it, to exempt himself from the penalty. *h* When a temporary

a 2 M. & S. 124 ; 2 Bingham, 255.

b Lord Raym. 382 ; Cro. Eliz. 186 ; Cro. Car. 522.

c 2 Haw. C. 25, s. 109.　　　　　　*d* Lord Raym. 210 ; Lutw. 140.

e 2 Haw. c. 25, s. 104 ; 2 Hale, 173.　　*f* Lord Raym. 381.

g Cow. 174.　　　　　　　　　　*h* 1 Term. Rep. 144.

object and obvious tendency of which is to promote the peace and good order of society, by quieting possessions and estates, and avoiding litigation. La Frombois v. Jackson, 8 Cow. 615, 616, per Viele, Senator.

We are not warranted in applying a different rule to the defence of *usury*, from that which we would hold applicable in other cases. It is a defence allowed and provided by law. The defendant (in that case) did not claim any indulgence from the court, but simply asked for the indulgence of those rules which the legislature has provided for all cases indiscriminately, whether the party invoking their exercise was seeking to visit his adversary with a forfeiture or not. The law has not made any distinction between such defences, and those where no forfeiture is involved ; and the court can make none. If the sense of the legislature is plainly expressed, the court has no judgment to pass upon the policy of its provisions. Catlin v. Gunter, 11 N. Y. 375, per Johnson, J. Bates v. Voorhees, 7 How. Pr. R. 235.

statute which has expired, is continued by taking notice of the latter. *a*

If one statute have prohibited the subsequent statute, it is sufficient to plead the former without doing of an act, and another be afterwards made which inflicts a forfeiture on the person who shall do the act ; the person who sues for the forfeiture must plead both statutes. *b*

No person is obliged to recite in pleading, any more of the statute than the clause which makes for himself, subject to the rule before stated, that if any proviso or exception is parcel of the clause which is pleaded, the exception must not be omitted, or it would be a misrecital of the clause. But, if one party have only pleaded such part of a statute as it was for his interest to plead, the other party may plead any other part of the statute. *c*

An act of Parliament sometimes directs the manner in which a defendant shall be entitled to take advantage of the enactment, as by pleading the statute in bar ; in such cases the party must pursue the remedy pointed out, or if he do not avail himself of it at the proper time, and in the manner and form prescribed, he cannot take advantage of it afterwards.*d*

If a statute in any case direct, what shall be pleaded, the plea must be in the words of the statute, and all indictments upon penal statutes must, it has been said, strictly pursue the statute ; that is, when properly understood, every indictment must contain all the circumstances necessary to constitute the crime ; and those circumstances must be stated positively, "without any periphrasis or intendment." But unless where technical words have been long established to be necessary in the description of particular offences, (and Lord Kenyon said he was not inclined to multiply the instances,) it is sufficient that the substance of the offence be charged with certainty, and by positive allegations contained in some (and it matters not in what) parts of the indictment brought within the words and meaning of the act. Thus it has been held sufficient to aver pretences to be false without charging that the defendant falsely pretended. *e*

The authority of a statute may be considered with reference to its extent, duration, and sanction.

1. It is the highest authority which this kingdom acknowledges upon earth.*f* It has power to bind every subject in the land, and the dominions thereunto belonging ; nay, even the King himself if particularly named therein. It can discharge a person from his allegiance, and restore him to a state of nature. *g* It can make his estate to cease in the same manner as if the party pos-

a Stra. 1066.   b Plowd. 206, Bac. Abr. title statute 1.

c Cro. Jac. 240 ; L. Raym. 120 ; 11 Mod. 207 ; 2 Hale 170.

d Taylor v. Blair, 3 Tenn. R. 452.   e The King v. Airey, 2 East, 20.

f 1 Bl. Com. 185.   g 12 Mod. Rep 88; The City of London v. Wood.

sessing it were dead; as is done by the 21 H. 8, c. 13, which declares, that if a person accept a second benefice, the first shall be void, in the same manner as if the incumbent had died.*a* It can dissolve a marriage, and enable the adulteress to intermarry with her paramour.*b* It can enable a man to have, or be, an heir, who could not otherwise have, or be, an heir.*c* An estate tail may be limited by a statute without a donor: and the validity of such a limitation is not to be measured by the rules of the common law; for the statute can control the rules of of the common law.*d* · It can do no wrong; but " it may do several things that *look pretty odd*," (Lord Holt's expression;) it can make Malta in Europe, and can make a woman a mayor, or a justice of the peace.*e*

It is the rule that the King shall not be restrained of a liberty or a right he had before, by the general words of an act of Parliament, if the King is not named in the act.' But if the statute be intended to give a remedy against a wrong,*f* to prevent fraud, *g* tortious usurpations, or the decay of religion, the King, though not named, shall be bound by it. So, the King, though not specially named, is bound by acts for the advancement of religion or of learning, or for providing for the poor; as by the act 10 Car. for uniting livings in Ireland. So the general words of the statutes which tend to perform the will of the founder or donor, shall bind the King, *h* although he be not named.*i* These instances, which are adduced in the books as exceptions to the rule, certainly open the door to great latitude of construction, and leave the rights of the Crown very unsettled in such matters. Yet the authorities which support the doctrine are mostly taken from times in which the prerogative was highly favored. They are collected in the case of Willion v. Berkley.*j* It was there held, by the Court of Common Pleas, that the King was bound by the *Stat. de donis.*

It was said in the Magdalen College case,*k* that where the King has any prerogative, estate, right, title, or interest; that by the general words of an act of Parliament, he shall not be barred of them. In later instances the claim is only asserted, that the King shall not be divested of any of his prerogatives but by plain and express words for that purpose, though all his other

a 6 Rep. 48; Mildmay's case.	*b* 12 Mod. *supra.*
c 1 Lev. 75.	*d* 1 Jon. 105; Raym. 355.
e 2 Jon. 12.	*f* 2 Inst. 681.
g 5 Rep. 14. (b.)	*h* Str. 516.
i 11 Rep. 73.	*j* Plowden, 239, 244.
k 11 Rep. 74.	

NOTE 3.—A similar rule of construction is found in this country. It has been held that the general words of a statute, do not include the government or effect its rights, unless such intention be clear and indisputable, upon the face of the act. United States v. Hewes, Crabbe. R. 307.

rights are no more favored in law than the rights of his subjects.*a*
The sensible conclusion seems to be, that in such cases he may
be precluded of such inferior claims as might belong indifferently
to the King or to a subject (as the title to an advowson or to a
landed estate,) but not stripped of any part of his ancient prerogative, nor of those rights which are incommunicable, and are
appropriated to him as essential to his regal capacity.*b*

In a modern case, arising upon the "act for the more effectual
administration of justice in England and Wales," the court said,
"In an act of Parliament, passed expressly for the further
advancement of justice, and in its particular enactments using
terms so comprehensive as to include all cases brought up by
writ of error, we think there is neither authority nor principle for
implying the exception of criminal cases, upon the ground that
the King, as the public prosecutor, is not expressly mentioned in
the act."

If an act speak of the King generally and indefinitely, naming
him in his politic capacity, it extends to all his successors; and
to a Queen, if the crown descend to a female. *c*

A statute beginning "*Rex perpendens*," &c; so, a statute saying,
"the King commandeth that no man shall disturb any electors to
make free election," are instances where the King, being named,
is bound. *d*

And though it is said that the King shall not be bound by a
statute (whether affirmative or negative) which does not expressly
name him,*e* yet if there be equivalent words, or if the prerogative be included by necessary implication, it would seem to admit
a different construction. Thus the stat. 7 H. 4, c. 4, provided
that *protection* should not lie for a warden of a prison, in debt
brought against him upon an escape.. "See," it is said, "that
this is a statute which *shall* bind the King; for none can grant
protection but the King only, and therefore that the statute says
that the protection shall not lie, is as much as to say, that the
King shall not dispense with the statute; *quod nota*."

Statutes often affect matters of subsequent creation,*f* in like
manner as an immemorial custom will embrace matters arising
within the time of legal memory.*g*

Reliefs of dignities are provided for by *Magna Charta*; dignities subsequently created, have been held to be within that provision.

Some statutes are temporary, others are perpetual. Every statute, for the continuance of which no time is limited, is perpetual,
although it be not expressly declared to be so. A temporary

a Rex. v. Archbishop of Armagh, 8 Mod. 8.　*b* 1 Woodis, 31.
c 12 Rep. 110.
e Br. Parl. pl. 6; Cro. C. 526; Ascough's case, 2 Hawk. Pl. C. 411, c. 42, § 3.
f Br. Parl. 30, cites 39 H. 6, 39.
d 2 Inst. 31.
g 12 Mod. 485.

statute continues in force (unless it be sooner repealed) until the time for which it is made expires; a perpetual one until it is repealed.

Acts of parliament altering other acts in force in the colonies, (of Great Britain) are considered as themselves applying there.

If an act be penal and temporary by the terms or nature of it, the party offending must be prosecuted and punished before the act expires. Although the offence should have been committed before the expiration of the act, the party cannot be punished after it has expired, unless a particular provision be made by law for the purpose. On this account, a temporary statute is sometimes a made to continue in force, after it has ceased to operate substantially, for the purpose of supporting prosecutions against those who have violated it during the term assigned for its continuance.

If a statute be temporary, and limited to a given number of years, and before the expiration of the time it be made perpetual by another act, it was formerly a question, under which statute offences were to be laid to have been committed. In the case of the College of Physicians it was laid down, that if a statute, which was to have continuance only for seven years, have been afterwards, by another statute, made perpetual, only the latter statute is to be considered in force. But this decision was erroneous, and contrary both to former b and to latter adjudications; which sufficiently establish, that if a statute be permitted even to expire, and afterwards be revived by another statute, proceedings ought to be referred to the first act, the law deriving its force from the first statute. "When a statute is continued," said Lord Hardwicke, in Rex v. Morgan, c "every person is estopped to say that it is not in force." And the Court of King's Bench, in Shipman v. Henbest, d held that the statute of 21 Jac. 1, c. 4, extends to statutes made since, which revive statutes made before it; in other words, that if an expired statute be afterwards revived by another statute, the law derives its force from the first act, which is to be considered as in operation by means of this revival. If, however, a temporary act be revived after it has expired, without a special provision reaching to the intermediate time, the intermediate time is lost. No proceedings can be pursued under a repealed statute, though commenced before the repeal, unless by special exception.e

Statutes of the realm, (*quœ edicta et statuta sunt,*) are the declared will of the supreme power in the state, which, unless they are repugnant to the laws of God, all subjects are bound to obey.

a 29 Geo. 3, c. 64 ; 33 Geo. 3, c. 66 ; 34 Geo. 3, c. 80, &c.

b Cro. Eliz. 750.   c Strange, 1066.

d 4 Term Rep. 109 ; *ex parte* Dryden, 5 T. R. 418.

e Miller's case, 3 Wils. 420 ; S. C. 1, W. Black. 451.

Created by an exercise of the highest authority which the constitution of this country acknowledges, they cannot be dispensed with, altered, amended, suspended or repealed, but by the same authority of parliament by which they were made. For it is a maxim of law, that it is *conveniens naturali œqitati unumquodque dissolvi eo ligamine, quo ligatum est.*

An act of parliament cannot be repealed by *non user. a* The Scotch lawyers hold, that a statute loses its force by desuetude, if it hath not been put in execution for sixty years. Other writers have extended this term to a century, and make a distinction between statutes half obsolete, and those *in viridi observantia.*

An act of Parliament* may be repealed by the express words of a subsequent statute, or by necessary irresistible implication. But an act, according to the positive rules of both Houses of Parliament, cannot be altered or repealed in the same session of Parliament in which it was passed, unless there be a clause inserted, expressly reserving a power to do so.

If a subsequent statute, contrary to a former act, have negative words, it shall be a repeal of the former act.

Every affirmative statute is a repeal of a precedent affirmative statute, where its matter necessarily implies a negative ; but only so far as it is clearly and indisputably contradictory and contrary to the former act " in the very matter " *(Foster's* case ;) and the repugnancy such, that the two acts cannot be reconciled ; for then " *leges posteriores, priores contrarias · abrogant.*" The leaning of the courts is so strong against repealing the positive provisions of a former statute by construction, as almost to establish the doctrine of "no repeal by implication." But this goes beyond the limits of *Foster's* case, that " such repeal is not to be favored ;" and, in a recent case, Lord Denman said, "while we hold that a positive enactment is not to be restrained by inference, we must also act on the maxim, ' *leges posteriores priores contrarias abrogant,*' whenever it comes in operation."*b* ⁴

a 2 T. R. 275.

b 2 Q. B. Rep. Reg. v. Inhabitants of St. Edmund's, Salisbury, p. 84.

* The following are the observations of the framers of the Code Napoleon:— " *Les lois conservent leur effet, tant qu'elles ne sont point abrogees par d'autres lois, ou qu'elles ne sont point tombees en desuetude. Si nous n'avons pas formellement autorise le mode d'abrogation par la desuetude ou le non-usage, c'est qu'il eut peut-etre ete dangereux de le faire. Mais peut-on, se dissimuler l'influence ee l'utilite de ce concert indelibere, de cette puissance invisible, par laquelle, sans secousse et sans commotion, les peuples se font justice des mauvaises lois, et qui semblent proteger la societe conire les surprises faites au legislateur, et le legislateur contre lui meme.*"—Discours preliminaire du premier projet du Code Civil.

It is elsewhere, in the same admirable dissertation, philosophically observed, " *Les codes de peuples se font avec le temps ; mais, a proprement parler, on ne les fai' pas.*"

NOTE 4.—The American authorities are substantially to the same effect. A statute can be repealed, only by an express provision of a subsequent law, or by

" If two inconsistent acts be passed at different times, the last,'' said the Master of the Rolls, " is to be obeyed, and if obedience cannot be observed without derogating from the first, it is the first which must give way. Every act of Parliament must be considered with reference to the state of the law subsisting when it came into operation, and when it is to be applied; it cannot otherwise be rationally construed. Every act is made, either for the purpose of making a change in the law, or for the purpose of better declaring the law, and its operation is not to be impeded by the mere fact that it is inconsistent with some previous enactment."a[5]

a The Dean of Ely v. Bliss, 5 Beav. 582.

necessary implication. To repeal a statute by implication, there must be such a positive repugnancy between the provisions of the new law and the old, that they cannot stand together, or be consistently reconciled. Cool v. Smith, 1 Black. 459; Wood v. U. S. 16 Pet. 342, 10 Barr. R. 448; Hartford v. United States, 8 Cranch, 109; Brown v. County Commissioners, 21 Penn. 37; Street v. Commonwealth, 6 Watts and Serj. 209; Bowen v. Lease, 5 Hill, 221; Williams v. Potter, 2 Barb. 316; People v. Deming. 1 Hilt. 271. In McCool v. Smith, 1 Black. U. S. R. 470, Justice Swayne said, " a repeal by implication is not favored; the leaning of the courts is against the doctrine, if it be possible to reconcile the two acts of the legislature together." Where a late statute, is absolutely repugnant to a former one, only in part, it repeals the former only so far as the repugnancy extends, and leaves all the remainder in force. Van Rensselaer v. Snyder, 9 Barb. 308, and cases supra.

NOTE 5.—The more natural, if not necessary inference in all such cases is, that the legislature intend the new law to be auxiliary to, and in aid, of the purposes of the old law. There should be therefore, a manifest and total repugnancy in the provisions of a new law to lead to the conclusion that the latter law abrogated, and was designed to abrogate the former. There are cases however, where, though the latter statute be not repugnant to a former one, and no express provision in the latter repealing the former, if the latter prescribe the *only* rules which shall govern, it repeals the former one in all those respects in which it differs from the latter as to the governing rule. Daviess v. Fairborn, 3 How. U. S R. 636. If the latter statute is upon the same subject matter with the former, and introduces some new qualification or modification, so that it is impossible both should be in force, then the latter repeals the former, but if it be possible that both can stand, by construction, the question resolves itself into an inquiry, what was the intention of the legislature? Did it mean to repeal, or take away the former law, or was the new statute intended to be merely cumulative? U. S. v. Case of Hair Pencils, 1 Paine, 400.

A repealing statute, is a total abrogation of the law repealed, but rights acquired, and which became perfect under the law before its repeal, are not affected by the repeal. Prusseaux v. Welch, 2 Western Law Monthly, 209.

A repealing act, and another act passed at the same session, suspending the effect of the repealing act for a limited period, leaves the former law in force

It is a general rule that subsequent statutes, which add accumulative penalties, and institute new methods of proceeding, do not repeal former penalties and methods of proceeding ordained by preceding statutes, without negative words. Nor hath a latter act of parliament ever been construed to repeal a prior act, unless there be a contrariety or repugnancy in them, or, at least, some notice taken of the former act, so as to indicate an intention in the lawgiver to repeal it. Neither is a bare recital in a statute without a clause of repeal, sufficient to repeal the positive provisions of a former statute. *a*   The law does not favor a repeal by implication, unless the repugnance be quite plain; and such

a Dore & Grey, 2 T. R. 365.

during the period the repealing act is suspended. This was held in relation to statutes of the state of Virginia ; that state having adopted the British rule of construction, that all statutes passed at the same session, take effect from the first day of the session ; so that both statutes are to be regarded as parts of the same act. Brown v. Barry, 3 Dallas, 367.

Where a statute is repealed by a subsequent one, and a third act is then passed declaring the first not to have been repealed by the second ; the third is inoperative as to all cases occurring before its passage. Ogden v. Blackledge, 2 Cranch. 194.

In the state of Ohio, the repeal of a repealing act does not revive the original statute ; nor does the repeal of a prohibitory act, make a valid contract entered into in violation of the act repealed. Milne v. Huber, 3 McLean, 212.

A subsequent act making a different provision on the same subject, is not to be construed as an explanatory act, but an implied repeal of the former, if the latter act be incompatible with the former. Dash v. Van Kleeck, 7 John. 497 ; Columbian Manufac. Co. v. Vanderpool, 4 Cow. 556 ; Livingston v. Harris, 11 Wend. 329.

If the latter part of a statute is repugnant to the former part, it shall stand, and so far as it is repugnant, shall operate as a repeal of the former part. So if there are two statutes on the same subject which are repugnant, the latest operates as a repeal of the first, so far as the repugnancy extends, but no farther. The latest expression of the legislative will must prevail. Harrington v. Trustees of Rochester, 10 Wend. 550 ; Bac. Abr. tit. statutes D ; Bowen v. Lease, 5 Hill, 225, and note; Williams v. Potter, 2 Barb. 316; People v. Deming, 1 Hilton 271; Van Rensselaer v. Snyder, 9 Barb. 302.

Repeals by implication, are not favored in law, and are never allowed but in cases where inconsistency and repugnancy are plain and unavoidable. Cases last, supra, and Wallace v. Bassett, 41 Barb. 92.

In a criminal case, where the judgment was pending for review upon a writ of error, and between the rendition of the judgment, and the hearing upon the writ, the statute upon which the judgment was rendered, was repealed, it was held that the judgment should be reversed, notwithstanding the judgment was correct upon the law when it was pronounced, on the ground that the repeal of the law imposing the penalty. though it took place after conviction, arrested the judgment, on the ground, that there was *then* no law that authorized the execu-

repeal carrying with it a reflection on the wisdom of former parliaments, it has ever been confined to repealing as little as possible of the preceding statutes. *a* Although, then, two acts of parliament are seemingly repugnant, yet if there be no clause of *non obstante* in the latter, they shall, if possible, have such construction, that the latter may not be a repeal of the former by implication. The same view has been taken where powers under several acts are such as may well subsist together. *b* A subsequent act, too, which can be reconciled with a former act, shall not be a repeal of it, though there be negative words; as the 1 & 2 Ph. & M. c. 10, that all trials for treason shall be according to the course of the common law, and not otherwise, does not take away 35 H. 8, c. 2, for trial of treason beyond sea. *c*

a 11 Rep. 63; Dyer, 347. *b* 15 East. 377.
c Forster's case, 11 Rep. 63.

tion of the judgment. In a civil case it would it seems be otherwise. Hartung v. the People, 22 N. Y. R. 95; Sanchez v. the People, id. 155.

The repeal of a statute creating an offence before trial for such offence, is a bar to a conviction. Cook v. Board of Police, 16 Abbott, Pr. R. 473, S. C. 40, Barb. 626.

Where some of the provisions of a statute are void for unconstitutionality, a general repealing clause in such statute which repeals all provisions of law in conflict with it, does not repeal provisions which conflict only with that part which is void. Harbeck v. Mayor, &c. 10 Bosw. 366.

When a new statute covers the whole subject matter of an old one, and adds offences and prescribes different penalties from those enumerated in the old law, it is, by necessary implication, a repeal of the former statute. Norris v. Croker, 13 How. U. S. R. 429.

The suspension of an act, cannot be construed to be a repeal of it. Brown v. Barry, 3 Dall. 365, note 15. All legislative acts are repealable. The most injurious consequences would be the result of a contrary doctrine. Bloomer v. Stolly, 5 McLean, 161; Kellogg v. Oshkosh, 14 Wis. 623.

Where a perfect right of action has accrued on a contract which is authorized by a statute, neither the contract, nor a suit pending for its enforcement will be affected by a repeal of the statute. Pacific Mail Steam Co. v. Jolliffe, 2 Wallace, 450. This is based upon the reason that there was a vested right independent of the statute. But it is otherwise in a case where a party is prosecuting for a penalty. A party has no vested right in a penalty until after judgment obtained. The legislature may discharge a defendant by repealing the law. Norris v. Crocker, 13 How. 429. And a prosecution for an offence punishable by fine and imprisonment, is barred by a repeal of the act creating it; and a saving clause in the repealing act, *excepting suits for "penalties and forfeitures"* does not reach the case. U. S. v. Mann, 1 Gallison, 177. So too, an indictment cannot be sustained under a statute which has been repealed without a saving clause. U. S. v. Passamore, 4 Dallas, 372. So it was held by Ch. J. Marshall in the case of the "Irresistable" 7 Wheat. 552, that an offence against a temporary act, cannot be

When there is a difference in the whole purview of two statutes, apparently relating to the same subject, the former remains in force. *a*

It has been held, however, that clauses which limit in any way the right of the crown, must be considered as repealed by subsequent statutes, unless expressly re-enacted. *b*

It has been before seen, that by a decision of the Court of Exchequer, if the latter part of the statute be repugnant to the former part thereof, it shall stand, and so far as it is repugnant, be a repeal of the former part; because it was last agreed to by the makers of the statute. *c*

On every act professing to repeal, or interfere with, the provisions of a former law, it is a question of construction, whether it operate as a total, or partial, or temporary repeal. The word "repeal" is not to be taken in an absolute, if it appear upon the whole act to be used in a limited, sense. *d* Where several acts of parliament upon the same subject had been totally repealed, and

a Rex v. Downes, 3 T. R. 569.   *b* Atty. Gen. v. Newman, 1 Price, 438.
c Fitzgib. 195.   *d* Rex v. Rogers, 10 East. 573.

punished after the expiration of the act, unless there be a particular provision made by law for the purpose.

A repealing act, like other acts, only takes effect from its approval by the President, or Governor. All prior proceedings on the same day are valid, and the precise time of executive approval it seems, may be inquired into as a question of fact. Richardson's case, 2 Story R. 571; Aukrim's case, 3 McLean, 571. The contrary of this, however, was held in Welman's case, 20 Vt. R. 653, and in the case of Howes, 21 Vt. 619. I think sound reason, and the highest demands of justice, are against the Vermont rule.

Where a statute imposes a penalty for an act done, injurious to the rights of others, such penalty to be recovered by the party aggrieved, the penalty is in the nature of a satisfaction to him, as well as a punishment to the offender. In such case the plaintiff has acquired a vested right to the penalty, as soon as the offence is committed; and a general repeal of the statute after action brought does not affect that right. President, &c., of London v. Harrison, 9 Barn. and Cres. 524; Company of Cutlers v. Ruslin, Skinner R. 365; Palmer v. Conly, 4 Denio, 374–5.

The repeal of a statute does not take away the plaintiff's cause of action under it for damages for an injury to his property. Vandekar v. Rensselaer & Sar. R. R. Co. 13 Barb. 390.

Where a right to damages has vested, under a statute, its repeal, attempting to destroy that right, is void, it is beyond the scope of legislative power. People v. Supervisors of Westchester Co. 4 Barb. 64.

Where a statute creating an offence is repealed, it is a bar to a subsequent action, for an offence committed before the repeal. Howard v. State, 5 Ind. (Porter) 183. The right to recover a penalty is lost by a repeal of the act, unless saved in the repealing act. Id. 535; Heald v. State, 36 Maine, 62.

others repealed in part, it was held that it must have been the clear intention of the legislature that only the part of an act particularly pointed out, should be repealed. *a*

If a statute, before perpetual, be continued by an affirmative statute for a limited time, this does not amount to a repeal thereof at the end of that time. *b* But *e contra* where a statute professes to repeal absolutely a prior law, and substitutes other provisions on the same subject, which are limited to continue only till a certain time, the prior law does not revive after the repealing statute is spent, unless the intention of the legislature to that effect is expressed. *c*

Where one statute is repealed by another statute, acts done in the meantime, while it was in force, shall endure and stand, and be good and effectual; but not so, it has been said (*quære tamen*) if the former act be declared *null* and void. *d*

By the repeal of a repealing statute, (the new law containing nothing in it that manifests the intention of the legislature that the former act shall continue repealed), the original statute is revived; but if a statute be repealed by several acts, a repeal of one act or two, and not of all, does not revive the first statute. *e* If a repealing statute, and part of the original statute, be repealed by a subsequent act, the residue of the original statute is revived.*f* If an act of parliament be revived, all acts explanatory of that so revived, are revived also. *g*

Where the words are, that " no statute, not expressly mentioned, shall be revived ;" but, by the repeal of the repealing statute, a statute is revived, which mentions another to be in force, this shall also operate as a revivor of the last-mentioned statute ; as was the case with the stat. 21 Hen. 8, of pluralities, mentioned to be in force by the stat. 25 Hen. 8, c. 21, which, was revived by the stat. 1 Eliz. 1, though that act says that no statute repealed by 1 & 2 Ph. & M. stat. 22, shall be in force, if it be not specially revived. *h* '

a Camden v. Anderson, 6 T. R. 723.   b Raym. 397.
c Warren v. Windle, 3 East. 205.   d Jenk. Cent. 283, pl. 6.
e The Bishop's case, 12 Rep. 7 ; Tattle v. Grimwood, 4 Bing. 496.
f 9 B & C. 354.   g 2 Burr. 747.   h 1 Vent. 22.

NOTE 6.—Where a statute reviving a statute which has been repealed, is itself repealed, the statute which was revived stands as it did before the revival. Calvert v. Makepeace, 1 Smith, (Ind.) 86.

NOTE 7.—Congress may make the revival of an act dependent upon a future event, and direct that event to be made known by proclamation. 7 Cranch, R. 382. Id 570.

When a statute is revived by a subsequent act, it is revived precisely in the form and with the effect which it had when it expired. Peck v. Pease, 5 McLean R. 486, and though there be an interval between the expired act, and the act reviving it, the rights of parties under the original act are preserved, unless the rights of third parties have intervened during the interval. Stevens v. McCargo, 9 Wheat. 502.

When an act of parliament is repealed, it must . be considered (except as to transactions past and closed,) as if it had never existed. The stat. 5 Geo. 4, c. 98, repealed all former bankrupt acts. That was repealed by 6 Geo. 4, c. 16, which repeal had the effect of setting up the old acts from the 2d of May, 1825, when the 6 Geo. 4, c. 16, passed, until the 1st of September, 1825, when the last mentioned act came into operation ; but they then ceased to exist, and the powers given by them were extinguished, the legislature having made no provision for issuing commissions after the 6 Geo. 4 took effect, upon acts of bankruptcy previously committed. "We are to look," said Lord Tenterden, a "at the stat. 6 Geo. 4, c. 16, as if it were the first that had ever been passed upon the subject of bankruptcy." So, in a criminal case, b an act, from its passing, repealed a former act, which ousted clergy from a certain offence, and imposed a new penalty on the same offence from and after its passing. It was held that an offence committed before the passing of the new act, but not tried till after, was not liable to be punished under either of these statutes. For the former act was repealed ; and as to the latter, the provisions cannot be retrospective, unless declared to be so by express words ; either by an enumeration of the cases in which the act is to have a retrospective operation, or by words which can have no meaning unless such construction is adopted. c

If an act be to have continuance for three years, and from thence to the end of the next session of parliament, it shall continue to the end of a session which begins after the three years, though a session within three years continue several months after the three years.

As every statute made against an injury, mischief or grievance, impliedly gives a remedy, the party injured, if no remedy be expressly given, may have an action upon the statute. d If a penalty be given by a statute, but no action for the recovery thereof be given, an action of debt will lie for the penalty. e [8]

a Surtees v. Ellison, 9 B. & C. 752; and see Maggs v. Hunt, 4 Bing. 212; Kay v. Gordon, 6 Bing. 582.

b Rex v, Mackenzie, R. & R. C. C. 429.

c Churchill v. Crease, 5 Bing. 178; Torrington v. Hargraves, id. 492.

d 2 Inst. 53; 10 Rep. 75.   e Poph. 175.

Note 8.—In the Revised Statutes of this State, Vol. 2, 480, § 1, it is provided, that where a pecuniary penalty or forfeiture is specially granted by law to any person injured or aggrieved by the act or omission of another, the same may be sued for in an action of debt or assumpsit. Under this statute it has been held, that in the absence of any provision to the contrary, the party injured or aggrieved by such act, may bring an action in his own name ; the implication of law is that the right so to sue is thereby given to the party so injured. Thompson v. Howe, 46 Barb. 287; Conly v. Palmer, 2 Comst. 182. The penalty when recovered is in the nature of satisfaction for the wrong done.

When a statute commands or prohibits a thing of public concern, the person guilty of disobedience to the statute, besides being answerable in an action to the party injured, is likewise liable to be indicted for the disobedience. *a* Wherever a statute forbids the doing of a thing, the doing it wilfully, although without any corrupt motive, is indictable. *b* If a statute enjoin an act to be done without pointing out any mode of punishment, an indictment will lie for disobeying the injunction of the legislature. *c* Thus where a statute commands a matter of public convenience, as the repairing of the common streets of a town, an offender against such statute is punishable, not only at the suit of the party grieved, but also by way of indictment for his contempt of the statute, unless such method of proceeding do manifestly appear to be excluded by it.

But if the thing commanded or prohibited by a statute can only be prejudicial to one or two persons, as if it be to repair the banks of a river, from want of having done which the ground of a certain person has been overflowed, no indictment lies ; the remedy being by an action upon the case. *d* So, if a statute, although it extend to all persons, chiefly concerns disputes of a private nature, as those between landlords and tenants relating to distresses, an offence against the statute is not indictable. *e*

If a statute inflicts a penalty for doing an act, the penalty implies a prohibition, and the thing is unlawful, though there be no prohibitory words in the statute. This rule applies to the case of a statute inflicting a penalty for making a particular contract, as a simoniacal or usurious contract, *f* in which it has been held that the contract was void under the statute, though there was a penalty imposed for making it. A question has been made, whether, where a statute creating a new offence, gives a penalty, and directs how it shall be recovered, the offence can be punished in any other way than that directed by the statute. *g* Upon which, the proper inquiry to be made is, 1st, Was the doing of the thing, for which the penalty is inflicted, lawful or unlawful before the passing of the act ? 2dly, Is there a general prohibitory clause in such statute, or no ?

When the statute, making the new offence, is not prohibitory, but only inflicts the forfeiture and specifies the remedy, an indictment will not lie. *h* The true rule was laid down by Lord Mansfield in the case of the King v. Robinson, *i* that where the offence was punishable before the statute prescribing a particular method of punishing it, then such particular remedy is cumulative, and does

a Cro, Eliz. 635; 2 Inst. 131, 163. *b* R. v. Saintsbury, 4 T. R. 457.
c R. v. Davis, Say. 133. *d* Sid. 209.
e 1 Hod. 71. *f* Per Lord Holt, Carth. 251; Skin. 222.
g Castle's Case, Cro. Jac. 643. *h* R. v. Wright, 1 Burr. 543.
i 2 Burr. 805; R. v. Boyell, 2 Burr. 832; Cown. 524, 656.

not take away the common law punishment, and either remedy may be pursued. Thus in Beckford and Hood, the question was, whether the right of property being vested in authors for certain periods, the common law remedy for a violation of it, attaches within the times limited by the act of parliament, there being certain penalties affixed for transgressing the law? "But it has been argued," said Lord Kenyon, "that as the statute, *a* in the same clause that enacts the right, has prescribed a particular remedy, that *that* and no other can be resorted to. And if such appeared to have been the intention of the legislature, I should have subscribed to it, however inadequate it might be thought. But their meaning in creating the penalties in the latter part of the clause in question, certainly was to give an accumulative remedy ; nothing could be more incomplete as a remedy than those penalties alone," &c.

This doctrine was recognized in a modern case : "The general rule of law and construction undoubtedly is, that where an act of parliament does not create a duty or offence, but only adds a remedy in respect of a duty or offence which existed before, it is to be construed as cumulative ; but this rule must in all cases be applied with due attention to the language of each act of parliament." *b*

But where the statute only enacts, that the doing any act not punishable *before*, shall for the future be punishable in such and such a particular manner ; there the particular method prescribed by the act must be specifically pursued, and not the common law method of proceeding. The mention of one method of proceeding, impliedly excludes that of indictment.

"It is in the general true," say the books, "that no statute is to have a retrospect beyond the time of its commencement ;" for the rule and law of parliament is, that *nova constitutio futuris, formam debet imponere, non præteritis.* And not only is it the doctrine of the English law that a statute is not to have a retrospective effect, but it is also founded on the principles of general jurisprudence.* A retroactive statute would partake in its character of the mischiefs of an *ex post facto* law, as to all cases of crimes and penalties ; and in matters relating to contracts or property, would violate every sound principle.' Before the day

---

a 7 T. R. 620; 6 East. 327.   *b* Per Tindal, C. J. 8 Bing. 394.

* "*En general, les lois n'unt point d'effet retroactif. Le principe est incontestible,*" &c, Discours Preliminaire du premier Projec du Code Civil.

ARTICLE 2—TITRE PRELIMINAIRE DE LA PUBLICATION DES LOIS : *La loi ne dispose que pour l'avenir; elle n'a point d'effet retroactif.*"

NOTE 9.—The American authorities are quite uniform on the retroactive effect of statutes. The general rule is, that no statute, however positive in its terms, is to be construed as designed to interfere with existing contracts, rights of action or suits, and especially vested rights, unless the intention that it shall so operate

on which the statute of frauds took effect (the 24th day of June, 1697), a verbal promise was made to give or bequeath a sum of money in consideration of marriage. *a* On an action against the executors, the question made, upon a special verdict, was, whether this promise, not being in writing, was within the 29 Car. 2, c. 3 ? By the court: "It cannot be presumed that the statute was to have a retrospect, so as to take away a right of action which the plaintiff was entitled to before the time of its commencement." And the court put the case of a will executed without the formalities required, which they said, would be valid, if made before the act, although the testator survived the passing of the act. In the case of Ashburnham and Bradshaw, a devise to charitable uses was made by a will dated in 1734. The testator lived till July, 1736, a month after the Mortmain Act had passed; and, upon a case, the judges certified that the devise was good; *b* notwithstanding the statute.

a Gilmore v, Shuter, 2 Lev, 227; S, C, 2 Mod, 210: 1 Vent, 330.
b 2 Atk, 36,

is expressly declared, and courts will apply new statutes only to future cases, unless there is something in the very nature of the case, or in the language of the new provision, which shows that they were intended to have a retroactive operation. And although the words of the statute are broad enough in their literal extent to comprehend existing cases, they must yet be construed as applicable only to cases that may thereafter arise, unless a contrary intention is unequivocally expressed therein. Wood v. Oakley, 11 Paige, 403; Butler v. Palmer 1 Hill, 325; Johnson v. Burrell, 2 Hill, 238; Dash v. Van Kleeck. 7 John. 499; Berley v. Rampacher, 5 Duer, 183; Calkins v. Calkins, 3 Barb. 806; Sackett v. Andross, 5 Hill 334; Vedder v. Alkenbrack, 6 Barb. 328; People v. Supervisors of Columbia Co. 10 Wend. 362; Van Rensselaer v. Livingston, 12 id. 490. Indeed some of the cases have gone even farther than this, and hold, that where vested rights are in question, that even express words in a statute giving in terms a retroactive effect to an enactment, cannot work that effect. In the case of Warren Manufacturing Co. v. The Etna Insurance Co. in the United States Circuit Court of Connecticut, Thompson, J., in an opinion reported in 2 Paines C. C. R. 517, says, in relation to a law purporting to have a retrospective operation, "But the law in question although it purports upon its face to have a retrospective operation, cannot be considered as having such effect and operation. It is a sound, general principle, that no statute ought to have a retrospective effect. It is the general rule that a statute takes effect from its date, when no time is fixed ; and it cannot upon sound principles be admitted, that a statute shall, by any fiction or relation, have any effect before it was actually passed. A retroactive statute partakes, in its character of the mischiefs of an *ex post facto* law, and when applied to contracts or property, would be equally unjust and unsound in principle as *ex post facto* laws when applied to crimes and penalties." The rule of interpretation by which that construction of a statute is to be avoided, which gives it a retrospective operation, has little or no application in construing the organic law. Matter of Oliver Lee & Co. Bank, 21 N. Y. 9. In the case of Jarvis v. Jarvis, 3 Edw. Ch. 466, the Vice

The question whether a retrospective act has any binding force, involves the question of legislative power. We have before said that the legislation of a state possesses all legislative power not prohibited by the constitution. But, by all known rules of interpretation, the general rule as to their power, by its very nature, is prospective. They are invested with the power to enact laws. Laws are rules of civil conduct, prescribed for, and, attaching themselves to the future actions of men. They must from necessity, and from their nature, be prospective; otherwise they cannot be rules of civil conduct. Laws cannot attach themselves to conduct antecedent to the creation of the rules themselves. This would be a thing impossible; for, at the time the particular transaction took place, there being no rule, a law subsequently passed, was not, and from the nature of the case, could not have

Chancellor approved of the rule laid down in the case last cited. Chancellor Kent, in 1 Com. 455, says, "a retrospective statute, affecting and changing vested rights, is very generally considered, in this country, as founded on unconstitutional principles, and consequently inoperative and void." "But this doctrine is not understood to apply to remedial statutes, which may be of a retrospective nature, provided they do not impair contracts, or disturb absolute vested rights already existing, and in furtherance of the remedy, by curing defects, and adding to the means of enforcing existing obligations. Such statutes have been held valid when clearly just and reasonable, and conducive to the general welfare."

In the constitution of the State of New Hampshire, part 1, § 23, it is declared, "Retrospective laws are highly injurious, oppressive and unjust. No such laws should, therefore, be made, either for the decision of civil cases or the punishment of offences." See Woart v. Winnich, 3 N. H. R. 473, and Dow v. Norris, 4 N. H. R. 16.

It is within the power of the legislature to pass an act which suspends the remedy upon the contract, provided it does not impair the ultimate liability. Stocking v. Hunt, 3 Denio, 274; Wolfkill v. Mason, 6 Abb. Pr. R. 221; Sullivan v. Brewster, 1 E. D. Smith, 681; Miller v. Moore, id. 639. And when the object of a statute is to correct an abuse, it is *remedial*, and the intent of the legislature may be gathered from cotemporaneous circumstances; and these should govern in case of ambiguity. Fairchild v. Gwynn, 16 Abbot Pr. R. 31. But even remedial statutes are to be deemed prospective in their operation, and are not to be applied to proceedings pending at the time of their enactment, unless a contrary intent appears. Trist v. Cabenas, 18 Abb. Pr. 143. See Litch v. Brotherson, 25 How. Pr. R. 416, and cases there cited.

The act exempting certain property from levy by execution, to satisfy debts contracted before its passage, is an *ex post facto* law, and is in conflict with the constitution of the United States. Morse v. Gould, 11 N. Y. R. 281; (overruling Danks v. Quackenbush, 1 id. 129); Rue v. Alter. 5 Denio 119.

been, an existing rule governing such a transaction; it would not then be, in that case, a rule of civil conduct. The conduct of the past must stand acquitted or condemned; be lawful or unlawful when judged by rules which had existence, at the time the transaction took place. It would be monstrous, were it otherwise. The future alone, can be called upon to observe the dictates of new rules. It has been justly said, "To establish a rule by which a person should be required to shape his *past* conduct, would be to legislate an *absurdity*; to grant what would be an utter impossibility." *a*

"But retrospective laws are not only inconsistent with the idea of a law as a rule of civil conduct, but they are in many instances, only the exercise of powers which are in their nature strictly *judicial*, instead of legislative. Such laws, when they are only such, look not upon the future, but upon the past: or in other

a Smith's Com 291.

Where an amendment of a statute is made by declaring it shall be amended so as to read in a given way, the amendment has no retroactive force; the new provision is to be understood as taking effect at the time the amended act would otherwise become the law. Ely v. Holton, 15 N. Y. R. 595.

The Supreme Court of the United States, I think, have drawn a distinction, which may be regarded as the rule both in England and this country, (except in States that have adopted a constitutional provision prohibitory of such laws,) which is as follows: "Retrospective laws, which do not impair the obligation of contracts, or partake of the character of *ex post facto* laws, are not condemned or forbidden by any part of the constitution of the United States." Satterlee v. Mathewson, 2 Peters, 380.

For the adjudications upon this subject, in other States, which are in harmony with the cases above cited, see: In Pennsylvania, McCabe v. Emerson, 6 Har. Penn, 111.

In Maine, Proprietors of Kennebec Purchase v. Laboree and others, 2 Green R. 275; Oriental Bank v. Freese, 18 Maine, 109; Austen v. Stevens, 24 id. 520; Webster v. Cooper, 14 How. U. S. R. 504.

In Vermont, Wires v. Farr, 25 Vermont 41.

In Connecticut, Plumb v. Lawyer, 21 Conn. 351.

In Massachusetts, Walter v. Bacon, 8 Mass. 468; Davison v. Johonnot, 7 Met. 389; Patterson v. Philbrook, 9 Mass. 151; Locke v. Dane, id. 360; Calder v. Bull, 3 Dall. 391.

In Mississippi, Boyd v. Barrenger, 23 Miss. 270; Garrett v. Beaumont, 24 id. 377; Murray v. Gibson, 15 How. U. S. R. 431.

In Ohio, Trustees of Cuyahoga v. McKaughey, 22 Ohio St. R. 152, and cases there cited.

But in drawing the precise line between cases that interfere with vested rights,

words, pronounce judgment upon acts done antecedent to their adoption; and in this respect, assume a judicial power, as contradistinguished from what is strictly *legislative* power. They assume to give character to facts which they did not possess at the time they took place, and then to judge of them in the new character thus legislatively created for them; to settle in some instances, old rights depending on laws as they existed before the act was passed, by new principles created and applied by the retrospective act having no existence antecedent to the time of its passage, which then, and not till then, sprang into being.'

But it is not intended to lay down the proposition that the legislature cannot under any circumstances pass a mere remedial

and cases that do not, the authorities are abundant, and not entirely in harmony; some of the States having constitutional provisions and regulations in this respect, and others not, and it is not deemed to be within the scope of this work, to review the adjudication, and give the various reasons which have controlled the courts in this regard.

It is, however, a fair conclusion from the view of all the cases, to hold and say, that the legislatures of the several States, have power, except where prohibited by the local constitutions, to enact retrospective statutes in certain cases; and it belongs to the courts to determine, whether such acts come within the spirit of the constitution which limits the legislative power, and whether a retroactive effect of such statute, interferes with vested rights. That all doubtful provisions of legislative enactment are for the judiciary to expound and to interpret, is no longer an open question.

A good illustration of this question arose directly, in this State, upon the statutes of 1848 and 1849, for the more effectual protection of the property of married women, which declared that the real and personal property of any female then married, should be her sole and separate property. A legacy had been bequeathed to a married woman, and the testator had died before the passing of those statutes, but the legacy had not been reduced to possession before that act took effect. The question presented was, to whom this legacy belonged, whether to the husband, or the wife. Denio, J. said, "The application of this statute to this case, would be a violation of the constitution of this State, which declares, "that no person shall be deprived of life, liberty or *property* without due process of law." (Const. Art. 1, § 6.) Before the act of 1848 took effect the husband had a right to this legacy, subject to certain contingencies which had not happened. By the terms of that act this legacy belonged to the wife, and it was held that the legislature had not the constitutional right to deprive the husband of this legacy. Westervelt v. Gregg, 12 N. Y. 202.

This case perhaps, as well as any other, expresses the spirit of the multitude of adjudications in which it is held that a statute a cannot have retroaction upon vested rights.

Every statute which takes away or impairs a vested right, required under pre-act, which in its effect, or by way of definition, may have a retroactive operation by way of relation to past events. Such acts of legislation as we have stated, when limited within the appropriate sphere, may, undoubtedly, be within the legislative power, and such acts have received judicial sanction.

It is sometimes difficult to distinguish, if really there be any distinction, between retrospective, and *ex post facto* laws, except that the constitution expressly prohibits the latter, and if the former are not inhibited, it is because there is a hair splitting difference, most difficult to define. In a general, literal sense, an *ex post facto* law, is one passed in regard to an act, after the act is done; but in its most comprehensive definition, it includes all retrospective laws, or laws governing or controlling past transactions, whether they are of a civil or criminal nature. Laws, however, which mitigate the character or punishment of a crime already committed, though retrospective, may not fall within the prohibition of the constitution, for they are in favor of the citizen. Ex post facto laws, it is held, relate only to penal and criminial proceedings, and not to civil proceedings which affect private rights retrospectively.*a* This is claimed to be the distinction. So that by this distinction, all acts legalizing past proceedings; all acts of relief, or pardon, or indemnity; all acts that mitigate the malignity of an offence, or modify the rigor of the criminal law, though retrospective; are not in the constitutional sense *ex post facto.*

a Dash v. Van Kleek, 7 John. 477.

vious laws, is retrospective and objectionable on that ground. Davis v. O'Farrell, 4 Greene (Iowa) 168.

An act releasing a portion of the duties on prize goods captured by private armed vessels, was held not to apply to captures previous to its passage, though the condemnation took place subsequently. Prince v. U. S. 2 Gall. 204. So a statute concerning the effect of wills upon after acquired lands, was held not to apply to a will previously executed, the testator having died subsequently. Carrol v. Carrol, 16 Howard, 275.

A statute limiting suits on foreign judgments, was held not to apply to judgments recovered before its passage. Murray v. Gibson, 15 How. 421.

A statute making valid a certificate of a proof of a deed, after a decree rendered in a court of equity, is void; it cannot change the then existing rights of the parties. Garrett v. Stockton, 7 Humph. 84.

Although the remedy of a party to a contract may be modified by subsequent statutes, yet a statute which takes away all remedy impairs its obligation. Bruce v. Schuyler, 4 Gilm. 221.

Justice Chase divides *ex post facto* laws into four classes. *a* 1st. Every law that makes an action done before the passing of a law, and which was innocent when done criminal, and punishes the action. 2d, Every law that aggravates a crime, or that makes it greater than it was when committed. 3d, Every law that changes the punishment, and inflicts a greater punishment than the law annexed to the crime when committed. 4th, Every law that alters the legal rules of evidence, and receives less or different testimony than the law required at the time of the commission of the offence in order to convict the offender.

The provisions of the second article of the new constitution of Missouri, which forbid any priest or clergyman from teaching or preaching, unless he shall first take "the oath of loyalty" declaring that he has never been in armed hostility to the United States &c, &c, that he has never by act or word manifested his adherence to the cause of the enemies of the United States, or his desire for their triumph; or his sympathy with those engaged in rebellion; that he has never come into or left the state for the purpose of avoiding enrolment or draft into the military service; was held, to be in effect a bill of attainder, and *ex post facto* law. *b* So too, the act of congress of 2d July, 1862, providing that after its passage no person should be admitted to the bar of the Supreme Court of the United States, or, after a certain day specified, to the bar of any circuit or district court, or of the court of claims, as an attorney or counsellor, without having first taken the oath prescribed in said act, declaring that the deponent has never voluntarily borne arms against the United States since he has been a citizen thereof; that he has not given aid, &c., to persons engaged in armed hostility thereto; or sought to exercise any office in hostility thereto, or yielding a voluntary support to any pretended government within, and hostile to the United States, &c, is within the prohibition of the constitution against bills of attainder, and *ex post facto*. *c*

But the following cases, which are put in books, may certainly happen in practice: A man may covenant *not* to do an act which is lawful, and a statute may be afterwards made which compels

---

a Calder v. Bull, 3 Dall. 386.   *b* Cummings v. Missouri 4 Wall. 277.
c Exparte, Garland, id. 333.

him to do the act : or, a man may covenant to *do* an act which is lawful, and by a statute made afterwards, he may be forbidden to do the act ; in both these cases it has been said, the statute repeals (or rescinds) the covenant. *a* But this doctrine has been impugned in a latter case, where it was held that the sense of the words of a statute passed subsequently, ought not to be strained, so as to avoid the contract ; to the benefit whereof some person was entitled, at the time the statute was made. *b* And in an action for a penalty, where the defendant had paid the duties under a new act discharging the penalty on such payment by a given day, Lord Mansfield said : "Here is a right vested, and it is not to be imagined that the Legislature could by general words take it away ; they certainly meant future actions." *c*

But these cases (actual or suppositious) do not apply, where, in order to prevent the mischief there contemplated, the statute gives due notice that the law shall not have any operation till after a definite and extended period, and time is given to bring their actions previously to its coming into operation. On this ground Fowler and Chatterton was decided. There the plaintiff sued in Hilary term, 1829, on a debt accrued six years before : held that the 9 Geo. 4, c. 14, which came into operation on January 1, 1829, precluded him from recovering on an oral promise to pay the debt made by defendant in Febuary, 1828 ; *d* because the operation of that act was postponed to give persons time to bring their actions.

The rule formerly was, that when the commencement of an act was not directed to be from any particular time, it took effect from the first day of the session in which the act was passed ; which might be weeks, if not months, before the act received the royal sanction, or even before the bill was brought into parliament. This was an extraordinary instance of the doctrine of relation working gross injustice, as well as being full of absurdity. Yet the rule was plainly declared as early as the time of Henry VI, *e* and uniformly adhered to, though the consequence of it, was sometimes, to render an act murder, which would not have been so without such relation. *f* The case of the Attorney General v. Panter is a strong instance of the application of this rigorous and unjust rule of the common law, even at so late a period as the year 1772. An act for laying a duty on the exportation of rice, *thereafter to be exported*, received the royal assent on the 29th of June, 1767, and on the 10th of June of that year, the defendants had exported rice. After the act passed, a duty was demanded upon the prior exportation, and it was adjudged, in the Irish Court of Exchequer, to be payable. The cause was carried by appeal to the British House of Lords, on the ground of the palpable injus-

---

a Salk. 198.

c 4 Burr, 2460.

e 33 H. 6, 18 ; Bro. 33.

b Lord Raymond, 1352.

d 6 Bing. 258.

f 1 Lev. 91.

22

tice of punishing the party for an act innocent and lawful when it was done; but the decree was affirmed upon the opinion of the twelve judges, that the statute by legal relation commenced from the first day of the session. *a* So, in the case of Latless v. Homes,*b* the judges held that they could not take notice of the great hardship of the case. The rule, indeed, was so firmly settled, and sanctioned by so many decisions, as to require the interference of the legislature to control it. Accordingly the stat. 33 Geo. 3, c. 13, enacts, that the clerk of the parliament shall endorse on every act the time it receives the royal assent, which shall be the date of its commencement, where no other is provided; thus abolishing the ancient rule, as liable to produce manifest injustice, *c* and substituting another rule designed to prevent the mischief that a statute should, by any fiction, or relation, have any effect before it was actually passed.

Although in an act of parliament, it is expressly enacted that it shall commence and take effect from a day named, yet if the royal assent be not obtained until a day subsequent, the provisions of a particular section, in its terms prospective, do not take effect till subsequent day. *d* In Rex v. Justices of Middlesex, *e* two acts of parliament which passed during the same session, and were to come into operation on the same day, were repugnant to each other, and the question was which was to take effect. (The case of the Attorney General v. The Chelsea Water Works company was cited from 2 Dwarris on Statutes, 675,) Lord Tenterden said, "We are of opinion that the act which last received the royal assent must prevail. Our decision is conformable with the doctrine laid down in the case cited. There it was resolved, that where the proviso of an act of parliament is directly repugnant to the provision of it, the proviso shall stand, and be held a repeal of the purview, as it speaks the last intention of the makers. At the time that resolution was come to, it was not possible to know which of the two acts, passed in the same session, received the royal assent first; for there was then no endorsement on the roll, of the day on which bills received the royal assent; and all acts passed in the same session, were considered as having received the royal assent on the same day, and were referred to the first day of the session. Now, however, it is known on what day each bill receives the royal assent by the provisions of stat. 33, Geo. 3, ch. 13.

There is nevertheless some, and that not inconsiderable hardship in the rule as it now stands; for a statute is to operate from the very day it passes, if the law itself does not appoint the time.

a Attorney General v. Panter, 6 Bro. A. C. 553.   *b* 4 T. R. 660.

c Words of preamble to 33 Geo. 3, c. 13.

d Barn v. Cavallo, (in error) 4 Nev. & M. 893.

e 2 B & A. 818, 2 Bing, N, D, 682.

It is impossible, in the distant parts of the United Kingdom, to
have notice of the existence of the law, until some time after it
has passed ; and in America in the wide spread dominion of the
United States, where the same rule is adopted, this inconvenience
is strongly felt. *a* It would be no more than reasonable, that the
statute should not be deemed to operate upon the persons and
property of individuals, or impose pains and penalties for acts
done in contravention of it, till such time had elapsed as would
enable the party, with proper diligence, to ascertain the existence
of a law, of which there is now no formal promulgation or publication,* on the principle of—" *Le mode progressif, calcule en raison
des distances.*" The Code Napoleon, after much discussion and
an enlightened consideration of the whole question, adopted the
true rule : It declared that laws were binding from the moment
their promulgation could be known : and that the promulgation
should be considered as known in the department of the consular
(afterwards imperial) residence one day after that promulgation,
and in each of the departments of the French Empire, after the
expiration of the same space of time, augmented by as many days
as there were distances of twenty leagues between the seat of government and the place.—*See Conference du Code Civil, Titre Prelim-
enaire : de la publication, des effets and de l'applieation des lois en
general.* This *projet* was three times revised and essentially altered, the first Consul taking an active and intelligent part in the
deliberations. On the *Redaction communique au Tribunat,* the
following were some of the " *Observations du* TRIBUNAT :" *Cet article donne lieu a la discussion des differents modes de publication des
lois, pour choiser celui que doit etre prefere. Le section se prononce
pour le mode progressif calcule en raison des distances. Le mode
progressif est fonde sur la nature : il faut rendre la loi executoire au
moment ou on la connait, &c—pp.* 19, 20.

To illustrate the inconsistency of our doctrine and practice : A
prisoner was indicted for maliciously shooting; the offence was
within a few weeks after the 39 Geo. 4, c. 37, passed, and before
notice of it could have reached the place where the offence was
committed. The judges thought the prisoner could not have been
tried if that statute had not passed, and as he could not know of

a R. v. Bailey, R. and R. C. C. 1; 1 Russ. C. and M. 109.

* " *Les lois ne peuvent obliger sans etre connues ; nous nous sommes occupes de la
forme de leur promulgation. Elles ne peuvent etre notifiees a chaque individu. On est
force de se contenter d'une publicite relative, qui, si elle ne peut produire a temps dans
chaque citoyen la connoisance de la loi a laquelle il doit se conformer, suffit au moins pour
prevenir tout arbitraire sur le moment ou la loi doit etre executee.*"—Discours preliminaire
du premier projet du Code Civil, p, 30,

In Spain, the written law, " that is, the reading (*legenda*) in which there exists
(*yace*) written instruction and chastisement," is not obligatory, unless published
by proclamation or edict; then it is universally binding, because all are bound to
know or study it.—L. 4, title 1, part 1; 1, 12, t 2, lib. 3, *Nov. Rec.*

that act, although strictly it did not excuse him, they thought it right that he should have a pardon. *a*

Such is still the operation of the new *law*, a later fact, a circumstance of matter subsequent, the law does not allow to extend or amplify an offence, " though laid together with the beginning, it should seem to draw it to a higher nature." *Œstimatio præteriti delicti ex postremo facto nunquam crescit.* " The law," says Bacon, " construeth neither penal laws nor penal facts by intendment, so as to be aggravated by matter subsequent; but considereth the offence in degree, as it standeth at the time when it is committeth.[10]   Therefore, if a man deliver goods to one to keep, and after retain the same person into his service, who afterwards goeth away with his goods, this is no felony by the statute 21 H. 8, because he was no servant at that time." *b*

An act of parliament made to correct an error by omission in a former statute of the same session, relates back to the time when the first act passed, and the two must be taken together, as if they were one and the same act, and the first must be read as containing in itself, in words, the amendment supplied by the last ; therefore, goods *exported* before the second act passed, but only *shipped on board* before the first passed, were held liable to duties subsequently imposed on the *exportation* of goods.   A case certainly of extreme hardship ; and admitted by the then Chief Baron, *c* to resemble the Attorney General v. Panter, which, he added, notwithstanding its hardship, is certainly good law. *d* But then it should be remembered that the provoking injustice of the former case occasioned that law, however " good," to be altered. The relation in bankruptcy has been greatly curtailed in its extent and operation ; *e* the relation of statutes, though restrained by the 33 Geo. 3, c. 13, is still capable of working extensive mischief and injustice.   The mischief, however, is greatly obviated, as was before observed, where the statute provides that the law shall not have any operation till after a definite and extended period ; as was the case with the stat. 9 Geo. 4, c. 14, commonly called Lord Tenterden's act, and the stat. 1 Wm. 4, c. 70, for the more effectual administration of justice in England and Wales.

a Bacon's Maxims, 39, 40.   *b* Thompson, C. B.
c Atty General v. Pougett, 2 Price 381.   *d* Eden's Bankrupt Law, 260.
e Fowler v. Chatterton, 6 Bing. 203.

NOTE 10.—A statute which imposes a punishment for acts specified, which were not, or may not have been punishable when the acts were committed, and for all acts that add new punishment is within the constitutional inhibition against the passage of *ex post facto* laws.   Matter of A. H. Garland, 32 How. U. S. R. 241. So also, a law which makes an act punishable in a manner in which it was not punishable when committed, or which increases the original punishment, is *ex post facto* and void.   Shepherd v. The People, 25 N. Y. 406.

By stat. 48 Geo. 4, c. 136, where any bill shall be introduced into any session of parliament, for the continuance of any act which would expire in such session, and such act shall have expired before the bill for continuing the same shall have received the royal assent, such continuing act shall be deemed to have effect from the date of the expiration of the act intended to be continued, except it shall be otherwise provided in such continuing act. But nothing therein contained shall extend to affect such person with any punishment, penalty, or forfeiture, by reason of anything done contrary to the provisions of the act continued, between the expiration of the same, and the date at which that continuing the same shall receive the royal assent.

CHAPTER VII.

GENERAL, QUALIFIED AND PARTICULAR RULES RELATING TO THE CONSTRUCTION OF STATUTES.

HAVING enumerated the various kinds of acts of Parliament and distributed them according to the most received and most satisfactory division of statutes,—having investigated minutely their nature, form, parts, qualities, authority, and relation,—it is next proposed to consider the rules for their interpretation.

The rules of exposition as to grants and pleadings, that "*Verba fortius accipiuntur contra proferentem ;*" "*Verba aliquid operari debent :*" "*Verba cum effectu sunt accipienda :' Divinatio non interpretatio est, quæ omnino recedit a litera,*" &c., are rules which have no place at all a in acts of Parliament, which are not *words of parties ;* neither in devises and wills, upon several reasons. Words of parties in deeds or grants are taken most strongly against the contractor, because men are supposed sufficiently careful not to prejudice their own interests by the too extensive meaning of their words. Acts of Parliament are not within the reason of the rules. The case is the same with some of the reasons for those maxims which obtain with respect to wills. It is said that the last will of a party is to be favorably construed, because the testator is *inops consilii*. "This we cannot say of the legislature," obserbed Lord Tenterden, (when lamenting that the last bankrupt act should have been framed with so little attention to the consequences of of some of its provisions,) "but we may say that it is '*magnas inter opes inops.'" b*

The construction of a statute indeed, like the operation of a devise, depends upon the apparent intention of the maker, to be collected either from the particular provision or the general context ; acts of Parliament and wills ought to be alike construed, according to the intentions of the parties that make them ; so far, instead of a dissimilarity, there is a resemblance.

The rules before mentioned being rules of some strictness and rigour, are qualified by other rules of more equity and humanity ; as that "*Verba generalia restringuntur ad habilitatem personæ vel, ad aptitudinem rei ;*" "*Verba ita sunt intelligenda ut res magnus valeat quam pereat :*" "*Ea est accipienda interpretatio, quæ vitio careat :*" (*i. e.* which does not intend a wrong,) and these latter and more

---

a Bacon's Maxims, 51.   *b* 9 B. & C 758.

benignant rules of construction seem to admit a more extended application. "For all words," says Lord Bacon, "whether they be in deeds or statutes, or otherwise, if they be general, and not express or precise, shall be restrained unto the fitness of the matter or person." As in the statute of wrecks, the provision that goods wrecked, if any live domestic creature remains in a vessel, shall be preserved to the use of the owner who shall make his claim within the space of a year, doth not extend to fresh victuals or perishable commodities; for, "in these and like cases, general words may be taken to a foreign intent, but never to an unreasonable, or impertinent, or repugnant intent."[a]

No doubt certain fundamental rules founded upon the universal principles of criticism, and the grammatical sense and meaning of words, must be alike, applicable to the exposition of deeds, grants and other written instruments, and to the construction of wills and statutes.

But the philosophical inquirer into the theory of laws, may, it has been contended, ascend still higher, and extend his views beyond the most comprehensive canons of verbal criticism. "It is not the words of the law," says the ancient Plowden, "but the internal sense of it, that makes the law: the letter of the law is the body; the sense and reason of the law is the soul."[b] Every statute ought to be expounded, not according to the letter, but according to the meaning: *qui hæret in litera, hæret in cortice.*"[c] The enlarged interpretation of a law, will penetrate the soul and spirit of a law, and reach the intent and meaning of a legislator.

Is it then, a *lex legum,* a general rule; an universal maxim; that in all cases, the design and intent of the framer, when it can be indisputably ascertained, shall prevail: *quod verba intentioni inservire debent?* If such be the case, as a maxim of universal jurisprudence it will be of constant application; it will extend, under partial modifications, to the interpretation of all instruments; wills, deeds and grants, equally with the construction of statutes. The subject deserves a brief and compendious examination, and will repay inquiry; for if ascertained to be well founded, it establishes a principle; it ascends to causes; "*et plenius et melius. est petere fontes, quam sectari rivulos.*" If the doctrine be unsound, it ought to be exploded; if it be only partially true, it should be qualified; and its just limits require to be discovered, defined, and distinguished.

It may be advanced then, as a proposition, more guarded than the alleged governing maxim—"the intention shall prevail;" that effect ought to be given to the intention of the parties to instruments, or to the object, spirit, and meaning of an enactment.

To take first, the case of a will. The intention of a testator, it

a Bacon's Maxims. p 52. b Eyston v. Studd, Plowd.
c 11 Rep. 73.

is always held, is to be the only guide in the interpretation of his will; and that intention when it can be ascertained, must prevail. Where the words used in a will were "all my personal estate," but it was clear the testator meant to give the real property over which he had an absolute personal power of disposition, the freehold has passed by that misdescription. *a* So, where it clearly appeared a testator's intention to bequeath his leaseholds and mere chattel interests, under the description of his "real estates;" such intention was carried into effect. *b* Nay, where the intention of a testator is clear and obvious, it has been held that it will control the legal operation even of technical words.

E contra, where the words of a will, aided by evidence of the material facts of the case, are insufficient to determine the testator's meaning, the will will be void for uncertainty. *c*

In the construction of deeds also, although *there* greater regularity and strictness are required, such exposition should, if possible, be made, as is most agreeable to the intention of the grantor. "The words," said Chief Justice Wills, "are not the principal things in a deed, but the intent and design of the grantor. These are the rules laid down by Plowden, Coke, and Hale; and the law commends the *astutia* of the judges, in construing the words in such a manner as shall best answer the intent." *d* "Those judges," it is said in the Earl of Clanricarde's case, "are exceedingly commended, who are curious, and almost subtle, to invent reasons and means, to make acts according to the just intent of the parties." *e*

So, in the construction of instruments in general, if the meaning can be collected, the courts will give full effect to the intentions of the parties. And any words by which the intention of the parties can appear, are held sufficient, however incorrect and ungrammatically expressed, if the meaning be clear. Thus, where a note had the words: "I promise not to pay," the court held it be a promisory note. *f* Where the condition, of the bond, was made void upon certain terms by the words of the condition, the court held that they must be taken in the same sense, as if the condition had been, that the bond itself should be void. *g* Where in a bargain and sale, the words "hath granted" were found without a nominative case, the court supplied the grantor, and this holding was affirmed in the House of Lords. *h* In a

a 11 East, 246; 16 East, 221; 6 Ad. & E. 167; id. 180.

b 1 Mylne & K. 571; 2 Russ. & M. 546.

c Wigram's Application of Extrinsic Evidence to the Interpretation of Wills, Proposition 6, p. 83.

d In Donne v. Parkhurst, 3 Atk. 136.

e Hob. 277.

g 2 Saund. 78.

f Bayley on Bills, p. 6.

h 10 Mod. 40.

recent case, the court supplied after the word "thousand," the immensely material word "pounds." *a*

E. contra, the courts have constantly rejected clauses, of which they were unable to ascertain the meaning. *b*   In Doe dem Wyndham v. Carew, Lord Denman said, " The court is not bound to find out a meaning for a proviso framed as this is." *c*   This is, where the words are insensible, and the purpose cannot be collected.   Where the real intention can be ascertained from the context, every intendment is made to give it effect.

As regards contracts, the Digest says, " *In conventionibus, contrahentium voluntas, potius quam verba, spectari placuit.*" *d*   "There are certain general rules of interpretation," says Story, treating of the conflict of laws, "recognized by all nations ; which form the basis of all reasonings on the subject of contracts.   The object is to ascertain the real intention of the parties in their stipulations ; and when these are silent or ambiguous, to ascertain what is the true sense of the words used, and what ought to be implied, in order to give them their true force and effect." *e*

If the full and entire intention of the parties does not appear from the words of the contract, and if the contract can be interpreted by any custom or usage of the place where it is made (custom of the country) that course is to be adopted : " *Sequamur quod in regione, in qua actum est, frequentur.*" *f*   The same where it can be construed by the usage of trade. *g*   Indeed " *in contractibus tacite veniunt ea, quæ sunt moris et consuetudinis* " *h*   Thus if a tenant is, by custom, to have the outgoing or waygoing crop, he will be entitled to it, although not expressed in the lease. *i* And if a lease be entirely silent as to the time of the tenant's quitting the premises, the custom of the country will fix it. *j*

It is in order to discover the intention, and then, upon the pratical notion, that all writings tacitly refer to the existing circumstances under which they are made, that courts of law admit evidence of particular customs and usages in aid of the interpretation of written instruments, whether ancient or modern, whenever from the nature of the case a knowledge of such customs and usages is necessary to a right understanding of the instrument *k*.   The law, it is said, is not so unreasonable as to deny to the reader of any instrument the same light which the writer enjoyed. *l*

a 8 B. & C. 568.   *b* 4 M. & S. 265.

c 2 Q. B. Rep. 317.   *d* Dig. Lib. 50, tit. 16, 1 219

e Story on Conflict of Laws, 226.   *f* Dig. Lib. 50, tit. 17, l. 34.

g Spicer v. Cooper, 1 Q. B. Rep. 428.

h Pothier Oblig., n. 95, Merlin Repertorie Convention, 67.

i Wigglesworth v. Dallison, Dougl. Rep. 201, 207.

j Webb. v. Plomer, 2 B. & A. 746.   *k* 1 Phill. on Evidence, 558.

l Wigram, Prop. 5, pp. 62, 74.

It is on the same ground, that, in construing a will, it must always be remembered, that the words of a testator, like those of every other person, tacitly refer to the circumstances, by which at the time of expressing himself, he his surrounded. Hence it is, that, for the purpose of determining the object of a testator's bounty, or the subject of disposition, or the quantity of interest intended to be given by the will, a court may inquire into every material fact relating to the person who claims to be interested under the will, and to the property which is claimed as the subject of disposition, and to the circumstances of the testator, and of his family and affairs But still the object and governing principle is to discover the intention, with all aids.

A court is bound to apply itself with all diligence and attention to find the meaning of a testator, if it can possibly be found, however difficult and obscure. But if, after every effort to find that meaning, it becomes impossible to solve the difficulty and dispel the obscurity ; if no judicial certainty can be obtained of his real meaning, then the court is not to supply a meaning by conjecture, or to adopt an arbitrary meaning for the purpose of giving some effect to unmeaning and ambiguous clauses *a*. In the words of Wigram, V. C., in his admirable work on *Extrinsic Evidence*, "the court is not to allow conjectural interpretation to usurp the place of judicial exposition." These remarks are cited to establish and to illustrate the general rules of construction, for they will be found equally applicable to the interpretation of statutes.

" In applying rules for interpreting statutes to questions on the effect of an enactment, we can never, says Vatell, safely lose sight of its object. That must be the truest exposition of a law, which best harmonises with its design, its objects, and its general structure." *b*

To a qualified extent, and with certain restrictions as to the use of astuteness and the exercise of invention, (which had better not be applied to acts of Parliament) the observations before cited as to the construction of deeds and wills, hold good in the construction of statutes. There, also, the great object of the rules and maxims of interpretation is to discover the true intention of the law ; and whenever that intention can be indubitably ascertained from allowed signs and by admitted means, courts are bound to give it effect, whatever may be their opinion of its wisdom or policy. "Whatever doubts I may have in my own breast," said Lord Mansfield, in the case of Pray v. Edie, *c* " with respect to the policy and expediency of this law, yet as long as it continues in force, I am bound to see it executed according to its meaning ; and however I may think that this is not a commendable defence

a Per Lord Abinger, C. B. 1 C., M. & R.

b Vatell, Bk. 2, ch. 17, § 285.   *c* 1 T. R. 313.

in the underwriter, yet that is a matter for his consideration, and not for mine. Let us consider, what are the mischiefs intended to be remedied, and the provisions of the act for remedying them."

The real intention, too, when collected with certainty, will always, in statutes, prevail over the literal sense of terms. For " every statute ought to be expounded, not according to the letter but according to the meaning." *a* When the stat. 18 Edw. 1, *quia emptores terrarum*, &c., says; Every man shall hold of the lord paramount *secundum quantitatem terræ*; this shall be construed according to the *value*, for so was the intent. *b* Hence, too, *son fait demesne* was interpreted *son tort demesne*; and *perdra la chose* hath ever been rendered *amittet locum. c*

" Whenever the intention which the makers of a statute entertained can be discovered by fit signs, it ought to be followed in its construction, in a course consonant to reason and discretion." What are to be the guides in such course will be considered hereafter, but it is proposed at present, to state and to illustrate the subordinate branches of the general rule.

A thing, which is within the object, spirit, and meaning, of a statute, is as much within the statute, as if it were within the letter. *d* [1]

a See *post*, Stat. Glouc. cap. 5.   *b* 11 Rep. 73.
c Pl. Com. 1057 b.   *d* Zouch and Stowell, Plow. 366 ; 10 Rep. 101.

NOTE 1.— In a previous chapter * we appended by way of notes, certain general maxims of interpretation, compiled from distinguished and acknowledged authors, and from American judicial authority. It is seen, that the present chapter also treats somewhat of general rules of interpretation, as well as such as are qualified and particular ; and as we did not in the previous notes exhaust the American view of construction, we propose to follow our author still further with our general rules, as well as such as are qualified and particular.

The best rule by which to arrive at the meaning and intention of a law, is to abide by the words which the lawmaker has used. U. S. v. Bright, Brightly, R. Q. same v. Warner, 5 McLean 178; Nicholson v. U. S. Devereaux C. C. R. 158. If from the view of the whole law, the intent is different from the whole literal import of some of its terms, the intent is to prevail. Brown v. Wright, 1 Green, 240.

Words, in a statute are never to be construed as unmeaning, and surplusage if a construction can be legitimately found which will give force to and preserve all the words in the act. Leversee v. Reynolds 13, Iowa 310 ; Hartford Bridge Co. v. Union Ferry, 29 Conn. 210.

Doubtful words, if not scientific or technical, are to be interpreted according to their familiar use and acceptation. The Fashion v. Ward 6 McLean 152. If they are found in a general statute they may be construed with reference to general usage ; and when a statute is applicable to a particular place only, such doubtful words may be interpreted by the usage at that place. Love v. Hinchley, 1 Abbott 436.

In the construction of a doubtful law the cotemperaneous construction of persons appointed to execute it, is entitled to great respect. Edward v. Darby, 12 Wheat. 210 ; U. S. v. The recorder, 1 Blatchford C. C. R. 218.

* Chap. 5.

By the 4 H. 7, c. 24, it is provided, that the right of a person, who was within the age of twenty-one years at the time of levying a fine, shall not be thereby bound; yet, if the disseissee die, leaving a wife with child, and the disseissor levy a fine, and afterwards the child be born, the child, although not within the letter of the statute, (because, as the age of a child begins only from its birth, it cannot be said to have been, at the time the fine was levied. *within the age of twenty-one years,)* is within the meaning; and his right shall be saved.

The words of 2 Westm. 2, c. 23, are *in casu quando vir amisit per defaltam tenementum quod fuit jus uxoris suæ, &c.* Only a loss by default of the husband is within the letter of the statute; but the construction has been, *a* that a woman shall have a right of *cui in vita*, although the loss was by default of both herself and husband; because, as she is presumed to have acted under the coercion of her husband, this case is within the intention of the makers of the statute.

The stat. 35 Geo. 3, c. 101, gave justices jurisdiction to suspend an order of removal made by them, on account of sickness, &c., of the pauper, "in case any poor person shall be brought before them." &c., the object of which remedial law would have been entirely frustrated by a literal construction of the words of it. The court, therefore, gave effect to the plain intention, by an undisguised departure from the strict letter of the act, and construed the words to mean "in case the question concerning the removal of any poor person shall be brought, &c." *b*

A thing which *is in* the letter of a statute, is not within the statute, unless it be within the intention of the makers. *c*

The statute of Marlbridge, c. 4, prohibits generally the driving of a distress taken in one county, into another. It has however been adjudged, that if land holden of a manor in one county, lie in another county, the lord may distrain upon the land, and drive the distress into the county where the manor lies; for as it would be inconvenient and a great loss to the lord, if he could not drive the distress to his manor, *d* this case, although within the letter, is not within the meaning of the statute. And this decision, further considered, will every way be supported, as agreeable to right reason. For the tenant, by doing suit and service to the manor, knows where the pound is, to give his beasts sustenance; and further knows where to have his replevy: so that this case is out of the mischief intended to be remedied.

The stat. Westm. 2, c. 12, gave damages to an appellee upon his acquittal; but if his life was never in jeopardy, (by reason of erroneous process or otherwise), held, that though this be within

a Plowden 57.   b Rexis Everdon 5 East., R. 101.
c Bac. Abr. tit. Statute 1.   d 2 Inst. 107.

the letter of the law, yet it is out of the meaning, and the defendant shall recover no damages. *a*

It will be remembered, that in a former part of this work, under the head of " Clauses how controlled by clauses," " Prior Acts by subsequent acts," the case of Williams and Pritchard was cited, to this effect; that where it is manifestly the intention of the legislature that a subsequent act of parliament shall not control the provisions of a former act, the subsequent act shall not have such operation, even though the words of it, taken strictly and grammatically, would repeal the former act. [2] In Bro. Tit. Parliament, 52, "where a statute is, that the merchant shall import bullion of two marks for every sack of wool exported; and then another statute was made that the merchant should not be charged except for the ancient custom, this does not repeal the first statute. (*Vide Causam,* 4 *E.* 4, 12.)" And the reason is, that though the words would have that operation *per se*, it clearly was not the intent of the legislature that the act should have that effect. The principal case itself, of Williams v. Pritchard, *b* decided that the land-tax act 27 Geo. 3, though the words were sufficiently large for the purpose, yet should not, (because it could not have been intended that it should) repeal the provisions of an act 7 Geo. 3, which exempted certain lands embanked from the Thames from land tax.

It thus manifestly appears, that in the interpretation of all instruments, whether wills, deeds, contracts and agreements, or statutes, a very great desire is felt, and constant endeavors used, to ascertain and to give effect to, the intention of their makers and framers. As applied to the construction of statutes, the doctrine is advisedly not enounced in the terms commonly employed, that "the intention must prevail." For over what, shall it be said the intention is to prevail? Over the declared sense of the legislature? The presumed meaning over the expressed sense! That is surely impossible. The rule will it is apprehended, be more correctly stated in the guarded terms :—That effect shall be given to the intention, whenever such intention can be indubitably ascertained by permitted legal means.

And what are the allowed means, the recognized signs, by which the interpreters of statutes are to explore the intentions of the legislature? Suppose it granted, that the primary object of construction is to ascertain the sense and intention of the law-

a 2 Inst. 386, citing 9 H, 5, 2.   *b* 4 T. R. 2.

NOTE 2.—An alteration in the phraseology, or the omission or addition of words in the revision of statutes, does not necessarily alter the construction of the act, or imply an intention to do so. Such intent, must be evident, or the change in language be palpable, before the courts will hold the construction to be changed, Crowell v. Crane, 7 Barb. 191.

maker, and the spirit and meaning of the law, it remains to ascertain how are the intention and meaning to be collected.

In the construction of a will, the first question asked is, What was the intention of the testator? The second must always be: Has he used proper language to carry his intentions into effect? The intention of a testator, is to be collected from the words employed by himself, in his will. No surmise or conjecture of any object which the testator may be supposed to have had in view, can be allowed to have any weight in the construction of his will; unless such object can be ascertained from the plain language of the will itself. And not only ought the courts to look to the words of the will alone, to determine the operation and effect of a devise, but they ought to disregard altogether the legal consequences which may follow their construction.

The judgment of a court, in expounding a will should be simply declaratory of what is *in* the instrument. *a* At the same time Courts of Law, though precluded from ascribing to a testator, any intention not expressed in his will, admit their obligation to give effect to every intention which the will, properly expounded, contains. The question in expounding a will, is not what the testator meant, as distinguished from what his words express, but simply, what is the meaning of the words.

In enforcement of this doctrine, Parke, B. said, in Doe dem. Gwillim: *b* "It is often extremely difficult to say what the actual intent of a testator was. The court is to ascertain, not what the testator actually intended, but what is the meaning of the words he has used. It must be often matter of mere conjecture what he actually meant to be done, but there can be no doubt, whatever, what is the meaning of the words he has used." The doctrine was admitted and extended by Lord Denman in Rickman v. Carstairs, in which case, the Chief Justice said, "The question in this and other cases of construction of written instruments is, not what was the intention of the parties, but what is the meaning of the words they have used." *c*

In the exposition of a statute, the intention of the Legislature may be discovered from different signs; but as a leading clue to construction to be made, it is to be collected from the words used. And while, as before stated it is a fundamental maxim that effect ought to be given to the intention and object of the framers, it must now be added, in order to give such rule its full signification; that it must be such an intention as the legislature have used fit words to express. "Although the spirit of an instrument," says Story, "is to be regarded no less than its letter, yet the spirit is to be collected from the letter. [3] It would be dan-

---

a Wigram's Examination of Rules as to Extrinsic Evidence, Introd. p. 9.
b 5 B & A. 129.
                                             c Ib. 663.

NOTE 3.—It is only in cases where the meaning of a statute is doubtful, that

gerous in the extreme to infer from extrinsic circumstances, that a case, for which the words expressly provide, shall be exempted from their operation, &c." *a*

To " try out the right intendment of a law," Lord Coke's usual course is, first to consider the true import of the words themselves, and then to refer to the old books and authors that wrote soon after the passing of the law. And this, he says, is *benedicta expositio;* a good and sound construction; when our ancient authors (text writers) and our year books (reports), together with constant experience (practice), do agree. *b* [4]

It is this view, and chiefly, if not solely, with the object of discovering, if possible, the intention of the legislators, that, when the words of an act are obscure or doubtful, considerable stress is laid upon the light in which it was received and held by the

a Story on the Conflict of Laws, Introd. Remarks, p. 10.
b 2 Inst. 11, 136, 181.

courts are authorized to indulge in conjectures as to the intention of the legislature, or to look to consequences in the construction of the law. When the meaning is plain and unambiguous the act must be carried into effect according to its language, or the courts would be assuming legislative authority;* and it is not for the court to say as to such clear language, that it embraces cases not described, because no reason is seen why they were not included. Scott v, Reid, 10 Pet. 524.

Note 4.—The best rule of interpretation to be adapted by the courts, is, to ascertain the meaning of the legislature from the words used in a statute, and the subject matter to which it relates, and to restrain its operation within narrower limits than its words import, if satisfied that the literal meaning would extend it to cases which the legislature never designed to include. Brewer v. Blougher, 14 Pet. 178. *

Note 5.—If by the words of a statute the *intention* of the legislature be improbable, the court must then giver it construction. The Hunter, Peters, C, C. R.

If, in a statute, there be a mistake apparent on its face, it may be corrected by other language in the act itself, and such mistake will not be fatal; nor will any misnomer of a person named in the act be fatal, if the person really intended can be collected from the terms of the act itself. Blanchard v. Sprague, 3 Sumner, 279. But where the descriptive words constitute the very essence of the act, unless the description be so clear and accurate as to refer to the particular object intended, and be incapable of being applied to any other, the mistake will be fatal. Id.

Statutes that are apparently in conflict, should be so construed that both may stand if possible. Johnson v. Byrd, Hempstead R. 434, and they are to be reconciled so far as they may be on any fair hypothesis, and validity given to each of them, if it can be, and is necessary to conform to usages under them, or to preserve titles to property undistributed. Beals v. Hale, 4 How U. S. R. 37.

The best, safest, and most reasonable, policy, in the American judicial departments, is, to adopt a liberal construction for statutes, and a strict construction of constitutional provisions.

* 2 Paine, 584.

contemporary members of the profession ; *"contemporanea expositio est fortissima in lege."* Great regard, says Lord Coke, " ought, in construing a statute, to be paid to the construction which the sages of the law, who lived about the time, or soon after it was made, put upon it ; because they were best able to judge of the intentions of the makers at the time when the law was made."

In the exposition of a statute then, the intention of a legislator may be discovered from different signs. As a primary rule it is to be collected from the words ; when the words are not explicit, it is to be gathered from the occasion and necessity of the law, the defect in the former law and the designed remedy ; being the causes which moved the legislature to enact it. But in arriving at a conclusion from these last mentioned premises, the greatest care and circumspection, and the exercise of the soundest judicial discretion, are required ; an attention, it will be seen, directed not only to the proper application of the rule, but to the reason upon which the rule is founded.

The rules by which the sages of the law, according to Plowden,*a* have ever been guided in searching for the intention of the Legislature, are maxims of sound interpretation, which have been accumulated by the experience, and ratified by the approbation of ages. The resolutions of the Barons of the Exchequer in Heydon's case were the following :— *b*

" For the sure and true interpretation of all statutes in general, be they penal or beneficial, restrictive or enlarging of the common law, four things are to be discerned and considered :—

" 1. What was the common law before the making of the act ?

" 2. What was the mischief and defect against which the common law did not provide ?

" 3. What remedy the parliament hath resolved and appointed to cure the disease of the commonwealth ?

" And 4thly, the true reason of the remedy. *ᶜ*

" It was then held to be the duty of the judges at all times, to make such construction as should suppress the mischief and advance the remedy ; putting down all subtle inventions and evasions for continuance of the mischief, *et pro privato commodo ;* and adding force and life to the cure and remedy, according to the true intent of the makers of the act, *pro bono publico."*

a Plowd. Rep. p. 205.   *b* 3 Rep. 7.

NOTE 6.—It is the duty of courts so to construe statutes, as to meet the mischief ; to advance the remedy, and not to violate fundamental principles. Hart v. Cleis, 8 John. 44.

In this State the rule is, to read statutes according to the most natural and obvious import of the language, without resorting to subtle and forced construction for the purpose of either limiting or extending their operation. Waller v. Harris, 20 Wend. 561–2.

Nor is this an antiquated doctrine: it is recognized and acted upon in modern cases. In Lyde v. Bernard, *a* Parke, B., said: "I admit that words may be construed in a sense different from their ordinary one when the context requires it, or when the act is intended to remedy some existing mischief, and such a construction is required to render the remedy effectual. For we must always construe an act so as to suppress the mischief and advance the remedy."

To guard against misconception, it becomes necessary to observe in this place, that the enlarged interpretation of statutes,—"to apply the remedy to the mischief;" said by Lord Coke "to have been ever the practice of the ancient sages of the law;" expounding a statute so as to give a right of action contrary to the letter of the enactment, is not now admitted; at least, it is said such principles of interpretation are applicable to old statues only, which were shortly worded; a topic treated hereafter.

First in importance, according to these able and experienced judges, is the consideration of what was the *rule* at the common law. "To know what the common law was, before the making of a statute, whereby it may be seen whether the statute be introductory of a new law, or only affirmative of the common law, is the very lock and key to set open the windows of the statute." *b*

Further, as a rule of exposition, statutes are to be construed in reference to the *principles* of the common law. For it is not to be presumed that the legislature intended to make any innovation upon the common law, further than the case absolutely required. The law rather infers that the act did *not* intend to make any alteration, *other* than what is specified, and *besides* what has been plainly pronounced; for if the parliament had had that design, it is naturally said, they would have expressed it. '

It was observed by the judges, in the case of Stowell and Zouch, that it was good for the expositors of a statute to approach as near as they could, to the *reason* of the common law. *c* The best interpretation of a statute, say other cases, is to construe it as near to the rule and reason of the common law as may be, and

a 1 M. & W. 113.   b 2 Inst. 301 ; 3 Rep. 31 ; 13 Hob. 83.
c Plowd. 365.

NOTE 7.—The same rule of interpretation is adopted by our courts, federal and state ; reference is had to the common law in force at the time of their passage. Mayo v. Wilson, 1 New Hamp. 55; How v. Peckham, 6 How. Pr. R. 229; Van Horne v. Dorrance, 2 Dall. 316; Rice v. M. & N. W. R. R. Co., 1 Blatch 359; Talbot v. Simpson, Peters C. C. R. 188.

Chancellor Kent says, "this has been the language of courts in every age, and when we consider the constant, vehement and exalted eulogy which the ancient sages bestowed upon the common law as the perfection of reason, and the best birthright and noblest inheritance of the subject, we cannot be surprised at the great sanction given to this rule of construction."

by the course, which *that* observes in other cases. *a* Such, indeed, has been the language of the courts in every age ; and when we consider the constant, vehement, and exalted eulogy which the ancient sages bestowed upon the common law, as "the perfection of reason," and the "best birthright and noblest inheritance of the subject," we cannot be surprised at the great sanction given to this rule of construction, and its careful observance. *b*

By the *stat. de donis* it was enacted, that a fine levied of entailed lands, "*ipso jurre sit nullus ;* " yet the construction was, that such fine should not be a nullity, but only a discontinuance ; because, at the common law, if a bishop, seised in right of his church, or a husband in right of his wife, had aliened by a fine, it was only a discontinuance. *c*

Though the assignee of tenant by courtesy or dower, is within the letter of the stat. of Gloucester, c. 5, for he holdeth in some manner for life, and the words are *ou en auter maner a terme de vie ;* yet no action of waste shall be brought by the heir against the assignee, but only against the tenant by courtesy or dower, these being the sole persons against whom it lay at the common law. *d*

When a statute alters the common law, the meaning shall not be strained beyond the words, except in cases of public utility, when the end of the act appears to be larger than the enacting words.

The stat. of Westmr. 1, c. 20, *de malefactoribus in parcis et vivariis*, shall not be extended to *forests*, because this act is in restraint of the common law.

If a statute make use of a word, the meaning of which is well known, and has certain definite sense at the common law, the word shall be expounded and received in the same sense in which it is understood at the common law. *e* Thus, the term "cottages" (which is used in stat. 31 Eliz. c. 7,) has the same signification there, as it had at the common law, and as is applied to it in Domesday Book. *f*

Secondly, The intention of the makers of a statute is sometimes to be discovered from the cause or necessity of making the act : hence, the direction to inquire into the *mischief* against which the common law had not provided. Thus, in Heydon's case, the common law was, that religious and ecclesiastical persons might have made leases for as many years as they pleased ; the *mischief* was, that when they perceived their houses would be dissolved, they made long and unreasonable leases. Before the first Marriage Act, 26 Geo. 2, c. 33, the mischief was, that

a 1 P. Wms. 252 ; 2 Inst. 148, 301 ; 1 Sand. 240.

b 1 Kent's Comm. on Laws of America, 434.

c 3 Rep. 83 ; the case of Fines, Hob. 97.   *d* 2 Inst. 300.

e 6 Mod. 143.   *f* 2 Inst. 736.

clandestine marriages, though illegal, not being vacated, but only punished by a committal to prison, which was found ridiculous and ineffectual, the practice still continued.

This cause and reason of the act (or, in other words, the mischief requiring a remedy) may either be collected from the statute itself, or discovered from circumstances extrinsic of the act, such as the state of the ancient law. To detect the mischief or defect in the former law which was the occasion of the act, recourse may be fairly and legitimately had to the title and the preamble; as these, from their custom of reciting the grievance, or part of it, may often serve to show the general scope and purport of the act, and the inducements which led to its enactment.

Thirdly, The remedy is to be gathered from the act itself. The *remedy* provided in the case before mentioned (Heydon's case,) was afforded by the stat. 31 Hen. 8, which provided "that all leases by any abbott, &c., or any other religious and ecclesiastical house, &c., of any land, whereof any estate or interest for life or years was then in being, should be utterly void."

And, fourthly, its *reason* was, that it was not necessary for them to make a new lease, so long as a former one had continuance, and therefore the intent of the act was to avoid doubling of estates, and to have but one single estate in being at a time. "For doubling of estates," says Lord Coke, "implies in itself deceit and private respect, to prevent the intention of the Parliament. If," (which was the question in that case) "the copyhold estate for two lives, and the lease for eighty years shall stand together, here will be doubling of estates *simul et semel*, which will be against the true meaning of Parliament." *a*

In the case also before stated for illustration, of the Marriage Act, the "remedy" was, that its enactments required the consent of the father, guardian, or mother to the marriage of persons who were under age, the marriage not being by banns. Illegitimate children being within the mischief and within the "reason" of the remedy, were held also, in R. v. Hodnett, *b* to be within the meaning of the act.

Again, as regards the reason of the law, it is a maxim that *Ubi lex est specialis et ratio ejus generalis, generaliter accipienda est:* thus the stat. 5 Hen. 4, that none be imprisoned by any *justice of the peace* but in the common gaol, to the end that they may have their trial at the next gaol delivery or sessions of the peace, has been thought to extend to *all* other judges and justices; for the same general reason applies in the case of all functionaries, upon whom it is equally incumbent to afford a prisoner speedy justice by due trial, without detaining him long in prison. *c* Here the reason of the rule is general, though the provision is special; it has therefore a general acceptation.

a Heydon's case, 3 Rep. 8.   *b* 1 T. R. 96; ib. 313.   *c* 2 Inst. 33.

The mischief, it has been already stated, may be discovered *aliunde*, that is to say, the former law may legitimately be regarded, and the title, preamble, and recitals referred to ; the remedy is to be collected from the act itself; and then the safe and established rule of construction is, that the intention of the law-giver and the meaning of the law, are to be discovered and deduced from a view of the *whole* and of every part of a statute taken and compared together.

It is the most natural and genuine exposition of a statute, to construe one part by another part of the same statute, for that best expresses the meaning of the makers ; and such construction is *ex visceribus actus.* a And this, CONSTRUCTION of itself imports ; *ex vi termini.* If, therefore, any part of a statute be intricate, obscure, or doubtful, the proper way to discover the intent, is to consider the other parts of the act ; for the words and meaning of one part of a statute frequently lead to the sense of another, b and in the construction of one part of a statute, every other part ought to be taken into consideration. s Thus, in the construction of cap. 9 of the statute of Gloucester, "*Purview est, que nul appeale soit abattu,*" &c.; this clause, taken by itself, is general ; and literally, as some have taken it, extendeth to *all* appeals, as of death, robbery, rape, felony, &c., but *ex antecedentibus et consequentibus fit optima interpretatio,* and all the antecedent clauses do concern the death of man (murder) ; it was therefore held, that the appeals of robbery, rape, felony, &c., are not within this act. c "In doubtful cases," said Trevor, C. J., "we may

a 1 Inst. 381.   b Stowell and Zouch, Plowd. 365.
c 2 Inst. 310.

NOTE 8.—In the construction of statutes one part must be construed by another ; to collect the legislative intention the whole must be inspected. The Stafford Justices, Brock. R. 162, and recourse may be had for this purpose to a proviso which has been repeated by a subsequent act. Bk. of Savings v. Collector, 3. Wall. 495.

Statutes are to be interpreted so as to give effect to all the words therein, if such interpretation be reasonable, and be neither repugnant to the provisions, nor inconsistent with the objects of the statute. U. S. v. Bassett. 2. Story R. 389. But it is otherwise if such an interpretation require the introduction of new provisions and clauses to render it sensible or practicable, ib. Every part of the statute must be viewed in connection with the whole, so as to make all its parts harmonious, if this be practicable ; and if it will admit of a construction which will give effect and operation to every part, it ought never to be construed, so as to draw after it unnecessary and superfluous provisions. Ogden v. Strong, 2 Paine 584. It is not to be presumed, that the legislature intended that any part of a statute should be without its proper meaning, force or effect, and when a state changes its constitution, all the laws continue in force not inconsistent with it. All laws repugnant to it are repealed by implication. Cass v. Dillon, 2 Ohio (N. S.) 607,

enlarge the construction of acts of parliament according to the reason and sense of the lawmakers expressed in other parts of the act, or guessed by considering the frame and design of the whole." *a*

It is another rule of interpretation, which is mentioned here, on account of its close affinity with the maxim last under consideration, th t one part of a statute must be so construed by another, that the whole may, if possible, stand; *ut res magis valeat quam pereat.* As, if land be vested in the king and his heirs by act of parliament, saving the right of A., and A. has at that time a lease of it for three years; here A. shall hold it for his term of three years, and afterwards it shall go to the king. For this interpretation furnishes matter for every clause of the statute to work and operate upon; *b* while, as has before been shown, *c* a saving totally repugnant to the body of the act, and which would render the statute nugatory, is rejected as void. Accordingly, it is a rule, that such exposition of a statute is to be favored, as hinders the statute from being eluded. *d*

Again, when words are capable of a twofold construction, whether in deeds or wills, or statutes; the rule is to adopt such an interpretation, *ut res magis va'eat quam pereat;* but "this," says Story, "is a rule of mere common sense."

As one part of a statute is properly called in, to help the construction of another part, and is fitly so expounded, as to support and give effect, if possible, to the whole; so is the comparison of one law with other laws made by the same legislature, or upon the same subject, or relating expressly to the same point, enjoined for the same reason, and attended with a like advantage. In applying the maxims of interpretation, the object is throughout, first, to ascertain by legitimate means; and next to carry into effect; the intentions of the framer. It is to be inferred, that a code of statutes relating to one subject, was governed by one spirit and policy, and was intended to be consistent and harmonious in its several parts and provisions. It is therefore an established *e* rule of law, that all acts *in pari materie* are to be taken together, as if they were one law; and they are directed to be compared in the construction of statutes, because they are considered as framed upon one system, and having one object in view. *'* If one statute prohibit the doing a thing, and another

a Archer and Bokenham, 11 Mod. 161.   *b* 1 Bl. Com. 89.
c Ante, p. 513.   *d* 2 Rol. 127.
e 4 T. R. 447; 5 T. R. 417; Earl of Ailesbury v. Patterson, Dougl. 30.

Note 9.— Several statutes that are *in pari materia* are to be construed as one statute, in explaining their meaning and import. Patterson v. Winn, 11 Wheat. 385; 6 The Harriet, 1 Story R. 251; U. S. v. Herves, Crabbe R. 307; Dubois v. McLean, 4. McLean R. 489, 3 Blatchford C. C. R. 325, and cotemporaneous, antecedent and subsequent statutes on the same subject matter may be examined and considered in construing the said act. Rodgers v. Bradshaw, 20 John 744; McCartee v. Orphan Asylum, 9 Cow, 507; Rexford v. Knight, 15 Barb. 642, 1 Kent Com. 463; Waterford & W. Turnpike Co. v. People, 9. Barb. 161.

statute be afterwards made, whereby a forfeiture is inflicted upon the person doing that thing, both are considered as one statute. *a* When an action founded upon one statute, is given by a subsequent statute in a new case, everything annexed to the action by the first statute is likewise given. *b* Indeed, the latter act may be considered as incorporated with the former.

The stamp acts are revenue laws, all made *in pari materie*, and to be taken together. Though they say, therefore, that an unstamped paper shall be void, yet they also make a provision to make it good; there being clauses in some of them to enable the party who has made a contract on unstamped paper, to get it stamped after it is made, on paying a certain penalty. So that if it be stamped at the time it is produced, it is sufficient. *c* [10]

And the rule, it is said, equally applies, though some of the statutes may have expired, or are not referred to, in the other acts. "It is a rule in the construction of statutes," said Lord Mansfield, *d* "that all which relates to the same subject, notwithstanding some of them may be expired or are not referred to, must be taken to be one system, and construed consistently;" and the practice has been so to do, in cases of bankruptcy, church leases, poor laws, and in other cases. Thus,—

The 13 Eliz. c. 10, concerning leases made by spiritual persons, being enlarged by the 14th Eliz. c. 11, although only the former of these statutes be recited in the 18 Eliz. c. 11, it has been holden, that the latter is virtually recited therein. *e*

In the same case it has been laid down, that there is such a connection betwixt all the statutes concerning leases made by ecclesiastical persons, that they are all to be taken into consideration in the construction of any one of them. The 32 Hen. 8. c. 28, is not recited in the 1 Eliz. c. 19, nor in the 13 Eliz. c. 10; yet a lease is not warranted by either of these statutes, unless it have the qualfications required by the 32 Hen. 8, c. 28.

The 22 and 23 Car. 2, c. 10, for the better settling of intestate's

a Stradling v. Morgan, Plow. 206.   *b* Bro. Waste, Pl. 68.
c Crossly v. Arkwright, 2 Term Rep. 609.
d Rex v. Loxdale and others, 1 Burr. 447, Bac. Abr. tit. Statutes, 1, 3.
e Bailey v. Murin, 1 Vent. 246.

NOTE 10.—Laws imposing duties, are not construed beyond the natural import of language, and they are never to be construed as imposing burthens upon citizens, upon doubtful interpretations. Adams v. Bancroft, 3 Ham. 384; U. S. v. Wigglesworth, 2 Story R. 369.

In construing laws relating to trade and commerce, the vocabulary of merchants is to be adopted in preference to that of mechanics. U. S. v. Sarchet, Gilp R. 273, and the word *import* is also to be used in its commercial sense. The Forester, Newberry R. 81. All mercantile terms used in a law are to be taken in the sense intended which is to be ascertained by laws in *pari materia*. U. S. v. Twenty-four Coils of Cordage, Baldwin R. 502.

estates, is continued, with some additional clauses, by the 1 Jac. 2, c. 17. It was holden by Lord Hardwicke, Chancellor, that for this reason the latter statute must be construed as if the former had been therein recited.*a*

Where acts are *in pari materie*, if the same word be used in both statutes, a distinction made in the one, is a legislative exposition of the sense in which it is to be understood in the other. *b* [11]

In the 1st sect. of stat. 53 Geo. 3, c. 159, upon which the case of Gale and Laurie depended the word "ship" only is used. But that act and the 7 Geo. 2, c. 15, and 26 Geo. 3, c. 86, are all *in pari materie*. "There can be no doubt," said Lord Tenderden, "that the first section of the act on which this question arises, is to be understood as if the words *with all her appurtenances* were used therein, supposing these words should make any difference in the sense." *c*

But as an act of Parliament, when repealed, "must be considered as if it had never existed," a doubt has been felt, how a subsequent statute can be taken to be incorporated with such act, not *in esse* or *fuisse*. And if an act, not a subsisting act, may be referred to, to assist in the construction of another act upon the same subject, yet how can an act, which is supposed to have never existed, be said to be *in pari materie* with any other act? It is a still broader proposition, that words can be used, borrowed from an act not subsisting; although for a collateral purpose it may be deemed competent to call in aid a repealed statute to assist in the construction of another statute.

To be sure, as a most profound and accurate judge has recently remarked: *d* "The courts do not deal in definitions." To stated facts, they apply the settled law in the particular case.

But it is different with the text writer. It is his province and duty to apply himself to the discovery and application of prin-

a Wallis v. Hodson, Barn. Chan. Rep. 276.
b King q. t. v. Smith, 4 T. R. 419,
c 5 B & C. 162.　　　　　　　　　　　*d* Maule, J., 7 Scott, N. C. 9 65.

NOTE 11—In the construction of a statute, the courts will look out of it to other statutes *in pari materia*, or statutes of a similar import, which may be regarded as one system in which the construction of any separate act may be aided by the examination of other provisions which compose the system. United States v. Collin, 3 Blatch. 325.

If in a subsequent clause of the same act, provisions are introduced which show the sense in which the legislature employed doubtful phrases previously used, that sense is to be adopted in construing those phrases.

Consequently, if a subsequent act on the same subject affords complete demonstration of the legislative sense of its own language, the rule already stated, requiring that the subsequent act should be incorporated into the prior or foregoing act, is a direction to guide the courts in expounding the provisions of a law.— Alexander v. Mayor, &c, 5 Cranch. 1.

ciples. Without analysis, or without generalization, he can be only a compiler of reported cases. However, as he is less practically occupied in dealing with facts, he often incurs the danger of falling into unnecessary refinement.

"It certainly appears strange," said Williams, J., in a late case, "that when an act of Parliament is *per se* abolished, it shall virtually have effect through another act." But, in that case, the former act was substantially re-enacted. *a* It does indeed seem to be the prevailing doctrine (and it is more rational in itself, than consistent with coeval maxims;) that, where one statute refers to another which is repealed, the words of the former act must still be considered as if introduced into the latter statute. "The objection arising from the repeal of the former statute," said Lord Denman , in Reg. v. Stock, "is not insisted on, and does not seem to be tenable." *b* In the case of Bussey v. Story, 4 B. & A. Parke, J., said : "This act of Parliament repeals those of 32 Geo. 3 and 41 Geo. 3, the provisions of which are only so far material, as they may aid in the construction of the enactments of the existing statute, &c." *c*

According then to the received doctrine, a repealed act " obliterated" from the judicial mind, and "considered as if it had never passed," *d* will often have more legal import a century later, from aiding the construction of subsequent statutes, than it ever possessed itself, while *in viridi observantia.* "This is shocking," * as said by Mansfield, C. J., of a certain construction on wills, "but it has been followed in a hundred cases."

Hitherto, it has been shown, that in the construction of statutes, effect ought to be given to the intention of the legislature and the object of an enactment; in like manner as in wills, deeds contracts and other written instruments, regard is constantly had to the just intent of the parties. But a necessary qualification has been annexed to that proposition; that the intention, to which such effect is to be given, must be such an intention and object, as the legislature have used fit words to express.

To a clear and logical consideration of the subject, next in order should follow the inquiry, how; in what sense; with what latitude, or under what restrictions, the words used are to be received and understood?

---

a Reg. v. Merionethshire, 6 Q. B. Rep. 343.   *b* 8 Ad. & Ellis, 405.
c Page 98.   *d* Expressions of Lord Tenterden, cited *ante.*

* The doctrine that shocked the Chief Justice of the Common Pleas, was this : —"That a remote reversion in fee of other lands, passed under a general devise" on the ground, that it was a forced construction to hold property to pass by a will which clearly was not at the time, in the contemplation of the testator. Morgan dem. Surman v. Surman, 1 Taunt. 292, speaking of Chester v. Chester, 3 P. Wms. 56. The doctrine in Chester v. Chester was, nevertheless, supported by Lords Thurlow and Eldon ; and when Sir W. Grant entertained a different opinion, his decision was afterwards reversed on appeal, 15 Ves. 396.

And lastly, after a full investigation what constitutes the competent or inefficient expression of the will of the lawgiver, the concluding proposition will be enounced; that effect cannot be given to an intention not expressed.

Subordinate to these principal divisions of the entire subject, will have to be discussed some particular topics; the letter of the law, (whether words are to be received in their popular or technical sense;) the context; the spirit of the act (whether statutes be in their nature remedial or penal;) the subject-matter and the provisions of acts.

And first of the language of an act; exploring the intention of the legislature, by the commonest and most natural of signs;—the words and the context. [12]

The words of a statute are to be taken in their ordinary and familiar signification and import, and regard is to be had to their general and proper use; for *jus et norma loquendi* is governed by usage; and the meaning of words, spoken or written, ought to be allowed as it has constantly been taken: *"loquendum est ut vulgus."a* But if the usage have been, to construe the words of a statute contrary to their obvious meaning by the vulgar tongue, and the common acceptation of terms, such usage is not to be regarded; it being rather, say the books, an oppression of those concerned (to force upon them a conventional meaning;) than a construction of the statute. *b* And though, where the words of a statute are doubtful, general usage may be called in to explain them, for *optimus legum interpres est consuetudo, c* usages that can control the words of an act of Parliament, must be universal, and not the usage of any particular place. *d*

And first, what language is to be regarded?

The intent of the legislature is not to be collected from any particular expression, but from a general view of the *whole* of an act of Parliament. *e*

a 4 Rep. 47.
b Vaughan, 169 ; Parker, 44.
c 2 Rep. 81.
d 1 T. R. 728.
e Per Best, C. J., 4 Bing. 196.

NOTE 12.—While it is the duty of courts in construing statutes, to give effect to the intent of the law making power, and to seek for that intent in every legitimate way, yet it is to be sought first of all in the words and language employed, and if the words are free from ambiguity, and express clearly the sense of the framers, there is no occasion to resort to other means of interpretation. Purdy v. The People, 4 Hill, 397, per Paige, Senator, id. 403; McClusky v. Cromwell, 11 N. Y. 601, 604; Waller v. Harris, 20 Wend. 561-2; Story const. § 392. The natural import of the words of any statute, according to the common use of them when applied to the subject-matter of the act, is to be considered as expressing the intention of the legislature, unless the intention so resulting from the ordinary import of the words be repugnant to sound acknowledged principles of national or state policy. Opinion of Sup. court, 7 Mass. 523-4.

25

In construing acts of Parliament, judges are to look at the language of the whole act, and if they find in any particular clause an expression, not so large and extensive in its import as those used in other parts of the act, and upon a view of the whole act, they can collect from the more large and extensive expressions used in other parts, the real intention of the legislature, it is their duty to give effect to the larger expressions. a   For, as has been before stated, the court is to give effect to every clause, section, and word, if an effect can be given to it.

As the construction is to be made upon the entire instrument, whole will, or complete statute, and not upon disjointed parts of it, consequently all its parts are to be compared, considered, and construed, with reference to each other :— [13]

Hence, general words may be restrained; hence, clauses may be controlled by clauses ; hence, if the same words occur in different parts of a statute or will, they must be taken to have been everywhere used in the same sense ; subject, perhaps, to the same qualification, in acts of Parliament, as in the case of a will; that the court may put a different construction upon the same words, when applied to different subject-matter, as was held by Lord Macclesfield, in Forth v. Chapman, where words were applied to different estates of realty and personalty. b   In Sheffield v. Lord Orrery, c and again in Southby v. Stonehouse, d Lord Hardwicke recognized the doctrine of Lord Macclesfield in Forth v. Chapman, that the same words may have different constructions to effectuate the intention of the party.

In the case of Porter v. Bradley, Lord Kenyon said : "It would be very strange, if words *had* a different meaning when applied to real and personal property. If such a distinction existed in the law, it certainly would not agree with the rule, "*lex plus laudatur, quando ratione probatur ;*" but it is not founded in law " e Again, in Roe. dem. Sheen v. Jeffery, Lord Kenyon made the same remark as in Porter v. Bradley, " That the very same words

a Per Lord Tenterden, 7 B. & C. 643.   c 3 Atk. 382.
b 1 P. Wms. 667 ; Forth v. Chapman.   d 2 Ves. Sen. 611.
e 3 T. R. 143.

NOTE 13.—It is an established rule in the exposition of statutes, that the intention of the lawgiver is to be deduced from a view of the whole and every part of a statute, taken and compared together. When the words of the statute are not explicit, the intention is to be collected from the context—from the occasion and necessity of the law—from the mischief felt—and the object and remedy in view; and the intention is to be taken or presumed, according to what is consonant to reason and good discretion. This was the rule laid down by Plowden, p. 10, 57, 205, 363, and by which Chancellor Kent says : "the sages of the laws have ever been guided in seeking for the intention of the legislature ;" and which he approves, " as maxims of sound interpretations, which have been accumulated by the experience, and ratified by the approbation of ages." 1 Kent Com. 462.

in the same clause in a will should receive one construction, as applied to one species of property, and another construction as applied to another, is not reconcileable with reason;" but he added, that if it had become a settled rule, it might be dangerous to overturn it. *a*

But in the case of Crooke v. De Vandes, *b* Lord Eldon remarks, that he had heard the case of Forth v. Chapman cited for years, and repeatedly by Lord Kenyon himself; and that he never knew it shaken. In Elton v. Eason, Sir William Grant, Master of the Rolls, thus begins his judgment: "There is no reason why the same words may not be differently construed, when they apply to different descriptions of property, governed by different rules. The case of Crooke v. De Vandes, in which the Lord Chancellor expresses his opinion very strongly in favor of the distinction in Forth v. Chapman, (and Lord Hardwicke has repeatedly recognised it,) appears to be just as strong as this." *c* And see Tenny dem. Agar v. Agar, *d* Dansey v. Griffiths, *e* Doe dem. Cadogan v. Ewart, *f*, Doe dem. Blesard v. Simpson, *g* and Lees v. Morley. *h*

But though words may be taken in a different sense in the same will or statute, when they apply to different descriptions of property, "it does not seem at all consistent with principle," said Lord Brougam in Doe dem. Winter v. Perratt, "that, in order to put a construction upon words, we should take some of them in a technical, and others in a popular sense, and even the same words in a popular sense to a certain extent, and a technical for the residue." So, Lord Cottenham observed in the same case: "It does not seem reasonable to adopt the strict legal sense as to part, and the popular sense as to any other part of the same description." *i*

In Reg. v. The Commissioners of the Poor Laws, Holborn Union, Lord Denman says, "We disclaim altogether the assumption of any right to assign different meanings to the same words in an act of parliament, on the ground of a supposed general intention in the act. We think it necessary to give a fair and reasonable construction to the language used by the legislature; but we are not to assume the unwarrantable liberty of varying that construction for the purpose of making the act consistent with any views of our own."

According to Vattel, it is by no means a correct rule of interpretation, to construe the same word in the same sense wherever it occurs in the same enactment. "It does not follow," he says, "either logically or grammatically, that, because a word occurs in one section with a definite sense, that therefore the same sense

a 7 T. R. 589.
c 19 Ves. 77.
e 4 M. & S. 61.
g 3 Scott, N, C. 774.
i 6 M. & G. 379.
b 9 Ves. 197.
d 12 East. 253.
f 7 A. & E. 657.
h 1 Youngs & Collier, 589.

is to be adopted in every other section in which it occurs. The framers of laws do not weigh only the force of single words, as philologists and critics, but of whole clauses and designated objects, as statesmen and practical reasoners. In common language the same word has often various meanings."a [14]

The peculiar sense in which a word is used in any section is to be determined by the context.

Words used in a consolidation act may have a different meaning from that of the same words when used in any of the acts comprehended. b [15]

If the words of a statute are plain, they must be strictly followed; but if they are ambiguous, the whole context must be looked to, for their explanation. c

The correct rule is to construe acts of parliament according to their grammatical and natural sense, unless the context show clearly that a different sense was intended. d

a Vattel, Bk. 2, ch. 17, § 285.

b Per Coleridge, J., in Reg. v. Justices of Kent, 2 Q. B. Rep. 692.

c Per Lord Abinger, 3 A. & E. 896.

d Per Parke, J., R. v. Ditcheatt, 9 B. & C. 186.

NOTE 14.—The statutes of one State or country, when they become the subject of adjudication in another, are to receive the same construction that is given to them in the courts of the former. Elmendorf v Ferry Co. 10 Wheat. 153; Smith v. Coudry, 1 How. 28.

NOTE 15.—In cases depending upon the statutes of one of the states, the federal courts follow the construction given to those statutes by the State court. Especially if the law relate to real property. Polk v. Wendal, 9 Cro. 87; Thatcher v. Powell, 6 Wheat. 119; McDowell v. Peyton, 10 Wheat, 454; Shelby v. Guy, 11 Wheat. 367; Bell v. Morrison, 1 Pet. 352; DeWolf v. Rabaud, id. 476; Daws v. Mason, ib. 503; Waring v. Jackson, ib. 570; Gardner v. Collins, 2 Pet. 58; Beach v. Viles, ib. 675; McCluny v. Silliman, 3 Pet. 270; Bk. of U. S, v. Daniel, 12 Pet. 33; Nesmith v. Sheldon, 7 How. 812; Suydam v. Williamson, 24 How. 427. And they follow this rule also as to the decisions of the highest courts of the states, whether it is founded upon the constitution of a statute, or on the unwritten law of the state. St. John v. Chew, 12 Wheat 153; Bk. of Hamilton v. Dudley, 2 Pet. 492; Henderson v. Griffin, 5 Pet. 151; Ross v. McClung, 6 Pet. 283; Green v. Neal, ib. 291; Livingston v. Moore, 7 Pet. 542; Brashear v. West. ib. 609; McCutchen v. Marshall, 8 Pet. 220; Murray v. Gibson, 15 How. 425; Beauregard v. N. Orleans; 18 How. 497; Sumner v. Hicks, 2 Blatch. 532; East Hartford v. E. Hartford Bridge Co., 10 How. 511, 541, 14 id. 489. And the federal courts will so hold, though it be not in accordance with their own opinion. McKeen v. Delaney, 5 Cranch. 22.

State laws are rules of decision in the federal courts, when they prescribe a law governing the right in litigation; but they do not govern as to the mode of proceedure. New England Screw Co. v. Bliven, 3 Blatch. C. C. 240; Campbell v. Claudius, Peters C. C. R. 484; Craig v. Brown, 3 Wash. C. C. R. 503; Beers v.

It is proper, first, to consider what is the meaning of the words used, in the largest ordinary sense, which, according to the common use of language belongs to them. *a* But where words are so general that they must receive some limitation in construction, and cannot be construed literally, what is the restriction that ought to be imposed upon them? This is to be learned from the context and from the general purview of the act. The object of all rules of construction being to ascertain the meaning of the language used, and it being unreasonable to impute to the legislature inconsistent intents upon the same general subject-matter, what it has clearly said in one part, must be the best evidence of what it has intended to say in another. The court must apply in such a case the same rules which it would use in construing the limitation of a deed; it must look to the whole context, and endeavor to give effect to the provisions, enlarging or restraining, if need be, for that purpose, the literal interpretation of any particular part. *b*

"The good expositor," says Lord Coke, "makes every sentence have its operation to suppress all the mischiefs; he gives effect to every word in the statute; he does not construe it so, that any thing should be vain and superfluous, nor yet makes exposition against express words, for *viperina est expositio quæ corrodit viscera textus, c* but so expounds it, that one part of the act may agree with the other, and all may stand together. For the best expositors of all acts of parliament, in all cases, are the acts of parliament themselves,—by construction and conferring all the parts of them together; " *Optima statui interpretatrix est (omnibus particulis ejustem inspectis,) ipsum statutum." d* All acts of parliament shall be taken by a reasonable construction to be collected out of the words of the acts themselves, according to the true intent and meaning of the makers." *e*

a Per Tindal, C. J., 5 M. & G. 80.   And see Maule, J., in Borradaile v. Hunter, 5 M. & G. 653.
b Per Coleridge, J., 6 A. & E. 7.
c 11 Rep. 34, citing 2 Bulstr. 179 ; 10 Rep. 105.
d Bonham's case, 8 Rep. 117.   *e* Case of Leases, 5 Rep. 6.

Haughton, 9 Pet. 329; Koory v. Merch. Bk., 16 Pet. 89; Kelsey v. Forsyth, 21 How. 85.

A state law which permits parties to be examined as witnesses in their own behalf, is a rule of decision, and as such, is obligatory upon the federal courts. Diblee v. Furniss, 4 Blatch. C. C. R.

State courts are bound by the decisions of the federal court in construing the constitution of the United States, its laws, and treaties of the Union. Elmendorf v. Taylor, 10 Wheat. 153.

The construction of a state law having been settled by a series of decisions of the highest state court, differently from a former decision of the federal court, the later construction of such law by the state court will be followed by the fed-

It is a safe method of interpreting statutes to give effect to the particular words of the enacting clauses. For when the legislature in the same sentence uses different words, the courts of law will presume that they were used in order to express different ideas. a So, if there be a material alteration in the language used in the different clauses, it is to be inferred, that the legislature knew how to use terms applicable to the subject-matter. "The several inditing and penning of the different branches," said the Judges in Edrick's case, "doth argue that the maker did intend a difference of the purview and remedies." b

  Again, when in several statutes *in pari materie*, the legislature is found sometimes inserting and sometimes omitting a clause of relation, it is to be presumed that their attention has been drawn to the point, and that the omission is designed. c

  If terms of art are used, they are to be taken in their technical sense. Thus, the expression "heirs of the body" conveys to

  a R. v. Bolton, 8 B. & C. 74.
  b 5 Rep. 119.
  c Moser v. Newman, 6 Bing. 561.

eral court. Green v. Neal, 6 Pet. 291; Suydam v. Williamson, 24 How. 427. But a circuit court of the United States, having adopted the construction of a state law placed upon it by the state court, its judgment will not be reversed because the state court subsequently overruled its own former decision. Morgan v. Centenices, 20 How. 1. Nor will the federal court alter its construction of a contract deliberately decided to be a valid one, because the state courts have since declared similar contracts to be invalid under the state constitution. Rowan v. Rumul, 5 How. 134.

  The federal courts are not bound by the construction placed upon a state law by the state courts, where the question is whether it be in violation of the constitution. Jefferson Br. Bk. v. Skelly, 1 Blatch. 436. Nor does the federal court hold itself bound by the construction of a will made by the state court, unless it arise from a settled rule of property. Lowe v. Vick, 3 How. 464.

  The decisions of the state courts as to the construction of contracts, or on questions of general commercial law, are not binding on the federal courts. Swift v. Tyson, 16 Pet. 1; Donnell v. Columbian Ins. Co., 2 Sum. 367; Thomas v. Hatch, 3 Sum. 367. Nor are the decisions of a state court, construing a deed by the rules of a common law, binding on the federal court. Foxcroft v. Mallett, 4 How. 353; Thomas v. Hatch, 3 Sum. 170.

  The constitution and laws of a state, so far as they are repugnant to the constitution and laws of the United States, are absolutely void. Cohens v. Virginia, 6 Wheat. 414.

  In cases of concurrent authority, when the laws of the United States and the laws of a separate state are in conflict, the state law must yield, but only so far as the conflict extends. Freeman v. Robinson, 7 Ind. 321.

  The state courts are bound by a decision of the supreme court of the United States, deciding that a state law is in violation of the constitution of the United States Gurovt v. Lafferty, 2 Gilman 383.

lawyers a precise idea, as comprising, in a legal sense, only certain lineal descendants.

It is a rule of construction, founded in reason and supported by many authorities, that words in a will, or statute, are to be construed according to their strict and proper acceptation, unless there be something to show that such a construction is not intended. Words of known legal import are to be considered as having been used in their technical sense, or according to their strict acceptation, unless there appear a manifest intention of using them in their popular sense. a Thus, an heir, properly and strictly, means a person whose ancestor is dead, *nemo est hœres viventis ;* but the familiar expressions, " heir to the throne," " heir to a title,"—" heir apparent,"—" heir presumptive,"—" prove," said Lord Cottenham, in Doe dem. Winter v. Perratt, " that the existence of a parent is quite consistent with the popular idea of heirship in the child ; and an heir apparent may take under the description of heir, if that be the sense in which the testator used the term." b

Words may be transposed in construction, c or words may be interposed, or read as if in a parenthesis ; d the word " or" may be read " and ;" and in the interpretation of both statutes and wills, " if " may be expounded " when ;" as in the rule on legacies borrowed from the civil law, where *cum* and *si* are precisely equivalent. 16

Words cannot be inserted ; " Every day," said Patteson, J., in a late case, " I see the necessity of not importing into statutes, words which are not to be found there. Such a mode of interpretation only gives occasion to endless difficulties." e In Lamond v. Eiffe, f Lord Denman said, " We are required to add some arbitrary words to the section, which would exclude us from acting in certain cases. We cannot introduce any such qualifications ; and I cannot help thinking that the introduction of quali-

a Poole v. Poole, 3 B. & P. 620, per Lord Alvanley. Jesson v. Wright, 2 Bligh, per Lord Redesdale.
b 6 M. & G. 379 ; 1 P. Wms. 229 ; 2 W. Bl. 1010.
c Stacey v. Nelson, 12 Mees. & W. 541.
d Davey v. Warren, 14 Mees. & W. 207.
e King v. Burrell, 12 A. & E. 468.   f 3 Q. B. Rep. 910.

NOTE 16—The word *or*, in its ordinary signification, corresponds to the word *and*, and equally to each if the sense of the statute requires it, but not to both. It has sometimes been construed to mean *and*, in order to give effect to a clause in a statute, will, or contract; but never to change a contract at pleasure. The inaccuracy of using *and* for *or*, requires that there should be strong reasons, in conformity with a clear intention. But *or* has been changed, or removed, and *and* substituted in its place. Douglass v. Eyre, Gilp. R. 149; Compare United States v. Hann, Amer. Law Reg. 663. But in a penal statute, it has been held that the word *and* cannot be substituted, and construed to mean *or*. United States v. Ten Cases of Shawls, 2 Paine. C. C. R. 166.

fying words in the interpretation of statutes is frequently a great reproach to the law. None of the distinctions suggested are contained in the plain words of the act ; and we cannot qualify them by any arbitrary introductions." So, in Everett and Mills, *a* Tindal, C. J., said, "It is the duty of all courts to confine themselves to the words of the legislature ; *nothing adding thereto, nothing diminishing.* We must not import into an act a condition or qualification which we do not find there."

The enabling statute, 11 Hen. 7, c. 12, entitled, "A Mean to Help and Speed Poor Persons in their suits," admits a plaintiff to sue in *forma pauperis.* It does not say he shall be admitted before he commences his suit, and therefore the court of common pleas (differing from Lord Abinger's inclination, rather than decision in the Exchequer,) "would not say it, when the act did not."*b*

It had been supposed, that, under stat. 5 Eliz. c. 4, s. 35, justices might not only order the discharge of an apprentice from his apprenticeship, but might also order a restitution of the premium or any part of it ; but in the case of R. v. Vandeleur, *c* the court (although reluctantly, on the ground that it would be an encouragement to masters to illtreat their apprentices) held, that the statute being silent, the order, directing a return of the premium, must be quashed. And the same was held in a modern case in the Court of Exchequer, East v. Pell. *d* "The court cannot insert or leave out words ;" R. v. Pereira. *e*

But in one case, In re Scott, upon the 9 Geo. 4, c. 32, the words "within three months after the determination of such petition," were qualified in construction, to mean *if such determination should take place, (expressio eorum quœ tacite insunt ;)* the court, in that case, modifying the language of the section, as a construction most consistent with the object of the legislature, and as giving effect to every enactment of the statute. *f*

For, the words of an act are, it is always said, to be modified by reference to the subject about which it is conversant. [17]

"In construing an act of parliament, the same rule of construction must be applied as in the construction of other writings ; and if the subject-matter to which an act of parliament applies, be such as to make a given construction of its clauses impossible or irrational, I cannot," said Wigram, V. C., *g* "for a moment, doubt the

---

a 4 Scott, N. C. 531.　　　　　*b* Brunel v. Wardle, 4 Scott, N C. 188.
c 1 Str. 69.　　　　　　　　　　*d* 4 M. & W. 665.
e 2 A. & E. 375.　　　　　　　　*f* 4 M. & W. 261.
g Salkeld v. Johnston, 1 Hare, 210.

NOTE 17.—The general rule, however, is, that words are to be received and interpreted according to their common or popular import, or their plain and actual meaning, and in such a way as to carry into effect, if possible, the whole of the statute. Maillard v. Lawrence, 16 How. U. S. R. 260–1; Wigg v. United States, Dev. 157, (Court of Claims 1855–6;) Chase v. Same, id. 158.

right, or the duty, of a court, to have regard to such subject-matter, as necessarily bearing upon the legal construction of the act. This is invariably done in the construction of wills and deeds; and the same principles are correctly applicable to the construction of an act of parliament."

In construing the words of an act of Parliament, and collecting from them the intentions of the legislature, the terms are always to be understood as having a regard to the subject-matter; for that, it is to be remembered, will always be in the eye of the framer of the law, and all his expressions directed to that end.[18] Thus the term "maintenance," is, in itself and abstractedly, equivocal; but when we find the statutes in which it occurs, *a* directed against the encouragement of litigation, and the upholding of parties to suits, we easily perceive what was designed to be prevented. The same with the terms, "evil procurers of dozens," upon which many fanciful interpretations might be put as of dozens of wine, &c.; yet in a statute relating to juries, there is no difficulty in understanding that the persons meant are "underhand instructors, and leaders of jurors returned." *Malveis procurers des douseins*, is "understood of such, as use to pack juries by nomination, or other practice." *b*

So, where the term "English money" is used in the statutes of employments, which relate to the circulation and employment of money with which "the stranger who brings merchandize into the realms of England, is to be paid and contented in hand, and to bestow the same money upon other merchandizes of England:" —the design and policy considered, it becomes clear, that what is intended, is all money current within England, although not coined in England. *c*

Other trades of skill and knowledge, besides those which are enumerated in the stat. 5 Eliz. c. 4, are held within it, if they were in use at the time; although the act being in restraint of the common law, is, in other respects, construed strictly.

".I think," said Maule, J., in Dewhurst, appellant, and Fielden,

a West. 1, c. 25; West. 2, c. 43; Artic. sup. Chartas, cap. 11.

b Articuli super Chartas, cap. x.; 2 Inst. 561.

c 2 Inst. 741.

NOTE 18.—Whenever any words of a statute are doubtful or obscure, the intention of the legislature is to be resorted to, in order to find the meaning of the words. The meaning of the legislature may be extended beyond the precise words used in the law, from the reason or motive upon which the legislature proceeded,—from the end in view,—or the purpose which was designed; the limitation of the rule being, that to extend the meaning to any case not included in the words, the case must be shown to come within the same reason upon which the lawmaker proceeded; and not only within a *like* reason. United States v. Freeman, 3 How. U. S. R. 565.

26

respondent, a "we should not in these appeals (registration cases), embarrass ourselves with the decisions on settlement cases. I also think it would be convenient that we should be spared discussions upon the tenement acts, which are not at all analogous to the reform and registration acts."

As regard must always be had to the subject-matter; so, in construing a statute, we must never lose sight of its object and intent. Provisions in acts of Parliament are to be expounded according to the ordinary sense of the words, unless such construction would lead to some unreasonable result, or be inconsistent with, or contrary to, the declared or implied intention of the framer of the law; in which case the grammatical sense of the words may be modified, restricted or extended, to meet the plain policy and purview of the act. But, in such case, the intent must be obvious, and must be collected from the words of the act. [19] "The court," said Coleridge, J., b "will not attempt to mould the language of an act for the sake of an apparent convenience, without the clearest evidence of a corresponding intention in the legislature." In another place, c the same learned judge observed: "If I thought the construction we are adopting put any force on the meaning of the act, I should be the last to concur in it; for the longer I sit here the more I feel the importance of seeking only the meaning of a statute according to a fair interpretation of the words, and acting upon that." Again: d "it is, in my opinion, so important for the court, in construing modern statutes to act upon the principle of giving full effect to their language, and of declining to mould that language, in order to meet either an alleged convenience or an alleged equity, upon doubtful evidence of intention, that nothing will induce me to withdraw a case

a Scott's New Cases, vol. 8, p. 1013 ; 7 M. & Gr. 187.

b 6 A. & E. p. 7.　　　　　　c Ibid.　　　　　　d Ibid.

NOTE 19.—The whole spirit, as well as the letter of a statute must be respected, and when the whole context of the law demonstrates a particular intent of the legislature to effect a certain object, some degree of implication may be called in to aid that intent. Dorousseau v. United States, 6 Cranch. 314, 323. But the statute is always to be so construed that it may have a reasonable effect, agreeably to the intent of the legislature, especially if the language is obscure. Gore v. Brazier, 3 Mass. 539, 540 ; opinion of Justices 22 Pick. 573. Richards v. Daggett, 4 Mass. 537 ; and it is always to be presumed that the legislature have intended the most reasonable and beneficial construction of their acts, if the words of the act are not precise and clear. Pearce v. Atwood, 13 Mass. 343, and such construction will be adopted as appears most reasonable, and best suited to accomplish the objects of the statute; and where any particular construction would lead to an absurd consequence, it will be presumed that some exception or qualification was intended by the legislature to avoid such conclusion. Commonwealth v. Kimball, 24 Pick. 370.

from the operation of a section, which is within its words, but clear and unambiguous evidence, but so to do is to fulfil the general intent of the statute, and also that to adhere to the literal interpretation, is to decide inconsistently with other and overruling provisions of the same statute."

It has been hitherto propounded, that words are to be taken in their ordinary sense; it now requires to be added: And not to be extended beyond it, to comprehend a case within the supposed meaning of the legislature. [20]

In interpreting the law, judges are to explore the intentions of the legislature; yet the construction to be put upon an act of parliament must be such as is warranted by, or at least not repugnant to, the words of the act. Where the object of the legislature is plain and unequivocal, courts ought, without violence to the words, to adopt such a construction as will best effectuate the intentions of the lawgiver. But they must not, in order to give

NOTE 20.—The words of a statute, if of common use, are to be taken in their natural, plain, obvious and ordinary signification; and it is an established rule in giving construction to a statute, first, to ascertain its intent. This may be determined from the language of the whole, and every part of the statute; and sometimes from the cause or necessity of making the statute. When ascertained, it should be followed with reason and discretion; though such construction may seem contrary to the letter of the statute, for it is the *intent* which often gives meaning to words otherwise obscure and doubtful. A thing which is within the intention of the makers of a statute, is as much within the statute as if it were within the letter; and a thing which is within the letter, is not within the statute, unless it be within the intention of the makers. Holmes v. Carley, 31 N. Y. R. 290; Chase v. N. Y. C. R. R. Co. 26 N. Y. 523. But all the provisions of the statute to this end, should be taken into consideration, and no interpretation should be given confined to a part of the statute, or to a separate section alone. Newell v. The People, 7 N. Y. R. 97.

A construction which is contrary to natural justice and equity, or which will be necessarily productive of practical inconvenience to the community, is to be rejected, unless the language of the lawgiver is so plain as not to admit of a different construction. To give a correct interpretation to the legislative will, where a statute was intended to remedy the injurious operation of a previous rule or principle of law, the court should place itself in the situation of the legislature which passed the statute; that is, to contemplate in the first place, the law as it previously existed, and the necessity and probable object of the change, and then give such construction to the language used by the lawmakers in providing the remedy, as to carry their intention into effect, so far as it can be ascertained from the terms of the statute itself. Opinion of Chan. Walworth in Court of Errors; Donaldson v. Wood, 22 Wend. 397.

Statutes tending to effect an object of great public utility, ought to receive the most liberal and benign interpretation, in accordance with the maxim *ut res magis valeat quam pereat.* Baring v. Erdman, Hazards Penn. Reg. The court in such

effect to what they may *suppose* to be the intention of the legislature, put upon the provisions of a statute a construction not supported by the words, though the consequence should be to defeat the object of the act. *a* Where the legislature has used words of a plain and definite import, it would be very dangerous to put upon them a construction which would amount to holding that the legislature did not mean what it has expressed. The fittest course in all cases where the intention of the legislature is brought into question, is to adhere to the words of the statute, construing them according to their natural import, in the order in which they stand in the act of parliament. *b* The most enlightened and experienced judges have for some time lamented the too frequent departure from the plain and obvious meaning of the words of the act of parliament by which a case is governed, and themselves hold it much the safer course to adhere to the words of the statute construed in their ordinary import, than to enter into any inquiry as to the supposed intention of the parties who framed the act. *c* They are not (as the most learned members of a learned body best know), to *presume* the intentions of the legislature, but to *collect them* from the words of the act of parliament; and they have nothing to do with the policy of the law. This is the true sense in which it is so often impressively repeated, that judges are not to construe statutes by equity, or views of policy, but to collect the sense of the legislature by a sound interpretation of its language, according to reason and grammatical correctness.

In the case of Green v. Wood, in the very latest number of the Queen's Bench Reports, *d* Lord Denman said: "We are bound to give to the acts of the legislature all possible meaning, which is consistent with the clear language used. But if we find language used which is incapable of a meaning, we cannot supply one. It is true that the words, as they stand, are useless, (a case, perhaps, not infrequent.) It is extremely probable that the alteration suggested would express what the legislature meant; but we, looking at the words, as judges, are no more justified to introduce

a Rex v. Stoke Damerel, 7 B. & C. 569.   *b* Rex v. Ramsgate, 6 B. & C. 712.
c Rex v. Inhabitants of Great Bentley, 10 B. & C. 527.
d 7 Q. B. Rep. 178.

case, will look into the object of passing the law, and if it can be discovered in its provisions, will not suffer it to be defeated. Russel v. Wheeler, Hemp. R. 3.

Where a limited jurisdiction is conferred by statutes, the construction ought to be strict as to the extent of jurisdiction; but liberal as to the mode of proceeding. Russel v. Wheeler, Hemp. R. 3.

Words intending to limit the powers of a corporation, cannot be construed to describe and so limit the rights of the public. Perine v. Ches. & Del. Canal Co., 9 How. 172.

A limitation of authority in a statute by a proviso, is a negation thereof. Commissioners v. Keith, 2 Barr. 218.

that meaning, than we should be if we added any other provisions. We can do no more than give such a meaning as the words authorize."

In Samuel v. Nettleship, a Patteson, J., said : "I cannot speculate as to the intentions of the legislature : the words appear to me to be quite plain."

The rule that words are to be taken in their ordinary sense, and not extended to comprehend cases within the supposed intention of the legislature, admits of some exceptions.

And first, in the case of ancient statutes ; which were accustomed, in the fewest words, to propound rules of the utmost possible generality. The rule and unbending character of these indiscriminate, general, rules of written law, constantly required mitigation. It received it through the medium of judicial construction. Pemberton, C. J., boasted that he had, since he was born, for his own share, made more law than King, Lords, and Commons. And, whatever may be said of judge-made law at present, when legislation is specific and diffuse, and aims at providing for every variety of case, there can be no doubt of the valuable improvements introduced by the judges at an earlier period of our history, when short statutory rules of universal operation, were found so harsh and unjust, as to make it indispensable for the judges, in such manner to modify and adjust the general rule, as to make it include particular cases—within the mischief, but perhaps opposed to the expressions of the law.[21] Speculative men complain of the unwritten law, and of the capriciousness and uncertainty of judge-made law; it may always be doubtful, whether more is not, necessarily, left to inference, under a rule of very extensive and remote generalities.

The extending a statute to advance the remedy contrary to the letter of an enactment, has been said, it will be remembered, to be applicable to old statutes only, which were shortly worded. In Gwynn v. Burrell, b Lord Brougham said: "The extreme conciseness of an ancient statute was the sole ground for the sort of legislative interpretation put upon the words." In another case, it was said, "Considering the concise language of statutes of an

a 3 Q. B. Rep. 188.   b 1 Scott, N. C. 810

NOTE 21.—The natural and obvious meaning should be taken, without resorting to subtle and forced construction. Courts cannot correct *supposed* errors, omissions or defects. The office of interpretation is to bring a sense out of the words and not to bring a sense into them. Though the spirit of a law may be referred to in order to interpret words admitting of two meanings ; but never to extend a law to a case not within its fair meanings. Beebe v. Griffin, 14 N. Y., 244 ; McCluskey v. Cromwell, 11 N. Y., 593. Statutes made relating to the administration of justice, are to receive liberal construction for the attainment of that important object. Mitchell v. Mitchell, 1 Gill. 66.

early period, it seems to be considered that they ought to receive an enlarged construction." *a* In Reg. v. Frost, *b* Lord Abinger said : " More than a hundred years ago, acts of Parliament were very short, and were to be applied to a variety of cases. It is said that we now construe acts of Parliament more literally than judges did formerly, and perhaps that is so. Now, they are very long (and variously elaborated and embellished, &c.), but still some of them, if construed literally, would lead to much absurdity."

So, in Patrick v. Stubbs, Lord Abinger said : " I never doubted that Lord Coke was right, when he says of the stat. Westminster 2, 'Here be five kinds of improvments expressed, and these five kinds are put for examples ; and besides these enumerated, there may be others, and yet it is not within the letter of the law.' And his observations apply to several ancient statutes, the framers of which were not so prolific of words as the authors of modern acts of Parliament. In the present day, in framing a statute the course is to employ all the rhetoric of conveyancers and special pleaders, and to provide for every case that suggests itself to the imagination of the person who draws the act. Formerly it was otherwise, and courts of law were left to interpret the meaning of the legislature." *c*

" Sometimes," says Lord Coke, " the makers of a statute put the strongest case, and by construction the lesser shall be included. In these cases they are put by way of example, and not as excluding other things of a similar nature. Thus, in the statute of Gloucester ; trespass, (as has been held by construction,) is put for debt, detinue, and covenant; so, county court for hundred court and court baron ; so, father for mother," &c. *d*

Sometimes things or places are named for excellency ; as London, of cities and burghs privileged ; Thames, of rivers, &c. This generality of expression induces an implication of other particulars not expressed.

At an earlier period, Lord Ellenborough thus expressed himself, speaking of an ancient statute : " *That*, it must be remembered, is a very ancient statute, passed at a period when no great precision of language prevailed. Where words are general and loose, they will admit of a more extended construction ; when they are precise, they exclude it." " In construing ancient statutes," said Lawrence, J., " attention is always to be paid to the language of the times." *e*

" Old acts of parliament," said Coleridge, J., in a case before cited, " are framed with generality and conciseness. In modern statutes, the legislature is careful to express all it intends, in so many words, that to go beyond their necessary implication is to

a Williams v. Wilcock, 6 A. & E. 335.   *b* 9 Carr. & P. 129.
c 9 M. & W. 830.   *d* Co. Comm., stat. Gloucester, c.11.
e 7 East, 134.

make, and not to interpret law." *a* In another case he says, " In a modern act, and one so full of words as this, the literal construction is the safe one." *b*

The second exception is, where there will be absurdity, inconvenience, and injustice, in giving effect to the plain words of the act. For words are to be construed " according to grammatical construction, avoiding absurdity." *c*

First, " the grammatical sense of the words used, should be adhered to ; but if that be contrary to, or inconsistent with, any declared purpose of the statute, or involve any inconsistency or absurdity, the grammatical sense must be modified so far as to avoid inconveniences. *d*

" No interpretation can be admitted which is inconsistent with the language of the act fairly understood, and considered with reference to the previous state of the law ; nor any which, although consistent with the words used, cannot give them some reasonable operation." *e*

In Perry v. Skinner, *f* Parke, B., said : " The rule by which we are to be guided, is to look at the precise words and to construe them in their ordinary sense, unless it would lead to any absurdity or manifest injustice ; and if it should, so to vary and modify them as to avoid *that* which certainly could not have been the intention of the legislature. We must put a reasonable construction upon their words."

The determination of the judges in Edrick's case, *g* is very deserving of attention. " And the Judges said : They ought not to make any construction against the express letter of the stat-ute ; for nothing can so express the meaning of the makers of an act, as their own direct words, for *index animi sermo.* And it would be dangerous to give scope to make a construction in any case against the express words, when the meaning of the makers doth not appear to the contrary, and when no inconvenience will thereupon follow ;" and therefore, in such cases, " *a verbis legis non est recidendum.*"—" *Divinatio est, non interpretatio, quœ omnino recedit a litera.*"

" The right rule of construction is to intend the legislature to have meant what they have actually expressed, unless some manifest incongruity would result from doing so, or unless the context clearly shows that such a construction would not be the right one." *h* [22]

a Gwynn v. Burrell, 2 Scott, N. C. 16.   *c* Per Parke, B.
b Reg. v. Rose, 6 Q. B. Rep. 157.   *e* Per Coleridge, J.
d Per Alderson, B ; Reg. v. Frost, 9 Carr. & P. 129.
f 2 M. & W. 471 ; and see Stocker v. Warner, 1 Q. B. Rep. 148.
g See Butler and Baker's case, 3 Rep. 27 ; Edrich's case, 5 Co. p. 118.
h Per Parke, J., R. v. Inhabitants of Banbury, 1 A. & E. 142.

NOTE 22.—When a statute is expressed in clear and precise terms, when the sense is manifest and leads to nothing absurd, there can be no reason to refuse

The first question to be asked, is, whether the words used in an act of parliament have a clear and intelligible sense and meaning? All acts of parliament are to be construed according to their exact meaning, if they have any which can be discovered; unless that construction would lead to some manifest absurdity. But where the meaning is ambiguous; where the clauses are confused and contradictory, and the words such as admit of two senses; the court will adopt that construction which will best carry the just and reasonable intention of the legislature into effect.

In Frost's case, the question was, whether the words, " at the same time," in the statute, meant *simul et semel*; at the same instant; or within the same interval of time. The delivery of the lists required, had, in point of fact, been made within the time required (ten days,) but not *uno flatu* with other instruments. It was contended, on the part of the crown, that the words admitting of two interpretations, that construction should be adopted which would best effectuate the intention of the legislature,— that a mere literal interpretation would lead to inconvenient consequences. On the other side, it was urged that there was no absurdity, to which the language could lead; and therefore that the court was bound to obey the plain language of the act. The judges were divided in opinion upon the point. *a*

" Where words conflict with each other," says Story, *b* " where the different clauses of an act bear upon each other, and would be inconsistent, unless the natural and common import of words be varied, construction becomes necessary, and a departure from the obvious meaning of words, is justifiable. But if, in any case, the plain meaning of a provision, not contradicted by any other provisions in the same instrument, is to be disregarded, because 'we believe the framers of that instrument, could not intend, what they say.; it must be one, where the absurdity and injustice of applying the provision to the case, would be so monstrous, that all mankind would, without hesitation, unite in rejecting the application."

a Reg. v. Frost, 9 Car. & P. 129.
b Story on the Conflict of Laws, Introd. Remarks, p. 10.

the sense which it naturally presents. To go elsewhere in search of conjecture in order to restrain or extinguish it, is to endeavor to elude it. Jackson v. Lewis 17 John 475 ; People v. N. Y. Cent. R. R. Co., 13 N. Y. 78. The great object of the maxims of interpretation is, to discover the true intention of the law ; and when that intention can be indubitably ascertained, and it be not a violation of constitutional right, the courts are bound to obey it, whatever may be their opinion of its wisdom or policy. 1 Kent. Com. 468.

It is only when a statute is ambiguous in its terms, that courts may rightfully exercise the power of controlling its language so as to give effect to what they may suppose to have been the intention of the lawmakers. Wood v. Adams, 35 N Hamp. R 36.

To effectuate the real intentions of the legislature, and to give a reasonable operation to the words they have used, it has thus, sometimes, become necessary, to put a construction, not strictly contrary to the words, but totally different to the mere literal construction of the clauses of an act of parliament. [23]

The statute of wrecks has been already referred to, and the provision that all goods are to be carefully kept for a year and a day, declared to be inapplicable to perishable commodities, which in popular language, will not keep a long time. Here, according to Bacon, the words are to be restrained *ad aptitudinem rei.*

The stat. 1 E. 2, *de frangentibus prisonam,* says, that a prisoner, who breaks prison, shall be guilty of felony; yet, if a prison be on fire, and a prisoner break it in order to save his life, he shall be excused. *a* He is not to be hanged, because he would not stay to be burnt.

The stat. 2 Geo. 3, c. 19, s. 1, enacts that "no person shall, upon any pretence whatsoever, take, kill, or have in his possession, any partridge, between the 12th day of February (altered by the 39 Geo. 3, c. 34, to the 1st of February), and the 1st day of September." The defendant (a qualified person) in the case of Simpson v. Unwin, *b* had some partridges in his possession, several days after February 1st. "Although this case," said Lord Tenderden, "may be within the literal meaning of the words taken by themselves, we must not give to them a construction, which will not only be contrary to the general intention of the legislature, but which will lead to this absurd consequence; that a party who might, at the last moment of the day on the 1st of February, lawfully kill a partridge, would be guilty of an offence by having the same partridge in his possession, at the earliest moment of the 2d." Per Patteson, J., "The statute must receive a reasonable construction; I think it would be absurd to say that a party who kills game within the time when he may lawfully do so, must consume it all upon the last day."

In Chapman v. Beecham, *c* Lord Denman said: "The objection on the words 'next ensuing,' cannot prevail; we cannot refer the words to the last antecedent, when by so doing, we turn the whole into nonsense." In Finch's Discourse of Law, book 1, chapter 1,

a Reniger v. Fogassa, Plow. 13. *b* 3 B. & A. 134.
c 3 Q. B. Rep. 733. R. v. Wright, 1 A. & E. 434.

Note 23.—Sometimes, when the words of a statute are obscure, the intention of the legislature is to be collected from the cause or necessity of the statute, and sometimes from other circumstances; and whenever it can be discovered, it ought to be followed with reason and discretion in the interpretation, although such interpretation seem contrary to the strict letter of the statute, for what is within the intention, is within the statute, and what seems to be within the letter, is not within the statute, unless it be within the intention. People v. Utica Ins. Co. 15 John. 358, 1 Kent. Com. 462.

it is said : " Words of construction must be referred to the last antecedent,—where the matter itself doth not hinder it." And this necessary qualification is illustrated by a striking case. In Guier's case, a an indictment for murder had the words : "John Guier husband to the said Emelin Guier of Hambridge aforesaid, in the county aforesaid, yeoman ;" and it was held that as "yeoman" must refer to John Guier, and not to Emelin Guier, the county also, related to the husband. 24

If sensible matter be alleged, insensible matter following, may be rejected. If there be no uncertainty in the case, a word may be referred to the only antecedent which can make sense of it. R. v. Wright. b And see Stracey v. Nelson, c that the relative need not be, of necessity, referred to all the antecedents ; and the judgment of Rolfe, B., that the relative may be referred to such antecedents only, as will give the clause a sensible and reasonable construction. d

"When words, per se, are repugnant and very absurd, what is necessary," it has been said, " may be supplied, by reasonable intendment and good construction." But it must be so supplied ex visceribus actus. A new term cannot be added to an act ; a new sense may.

But where a sense can be added, the addition must be a necessary implication from the words already used, in order to give them a sensible meaning and effect. It proceeds upon the ground, that the proposed addition is already necessarily contained, although not expressed, in the statute ; in which case it is not less cogent, because not expressed. For, as the intention is generally declared by words expressed and written, it also may be, by words necessarily implied, and therefore virtually written ; if implication be needed to render the construction sensible.

A statute 5 Geo. 2, c. 20, imposed a penalty on persons piloting ships " down the Thames." This was held by the court, not to extend to vessels, which, having performed their foreign voyages, are steered from one wharf to another on the river for the purpose of unloading their cargoes ; otherwise this absurdity would have followed, that no person would have been liable to a penalty for moving his vessel up the Thames without a pilot ; but he could not with impunity, move a yard down without a pilot. e

The stat. 29 Car. 2, c. 7, it was held, does not prohibit a baker baking dinners for his customers on a Sunday. Lord Kenyon said : " We should construe the statute so, that it may answer the

a 1 Dyer, 46 b.   b 1 A. & E. 448.
c 12 M. & W. 541.   d 10 M. & W. 728,
e R. v. Lamb, 5 T. R. 76; R. v. Neale, 8 T. R, 241.

NOTE 24.—Laws which create crimes, ought to be so explicit in themselves, or by reference to some known standard, that all may know what they prohibit. United States v. Sharp, Pet. C. C. R. 118.

purposes of public convenience, taking care at the same time that Sunday should not be profaned. The day will be better observed than if we adjudge this to be an offence. It falls within the reason of the exception." Ashurst, J.: "Though by this means, some few journeyman bakers are kept to work on a Sunday, it enables the rest of the community to attend public worship, which they could not have an opportunity of doing, if they had no means of having their dinners drest from home." *a*

The stat. 23 Geo. 3, c. 49, imposing a duty on such instruments, expressly says, that "no bill of exchange shall be received in evidence, unless it be first duly stamped." On an indictment for forging a bill of exchange, the objection was taken that it could not be received in evidence unless it were first duly stamped. All the judges held that it need not be stamped. It is not produced as a good instrument, but as a false one; and it is not competent to the person making such false instrument, to say on a criminal inquiry, that it is not good on another account. *b*

The stat. 5 & 6 Wm. 4, c. 50, s. 98, confers a power of certifying for the costs of a special jury, on the court before which an indictment shall be "preferred." The corresponding clause in a former act, 13 Geo. 3, c. 78, s. 65, said: "The court before which any such indictment shall be *tried*." Held by the court that the word "preferred," must be understood to mean "tried." Per Lord Denman : "If we were to decide against it, we should determine that the legislature have been guilty of a very extraordinary omission; for in a great majority of cases, the indictment is preferred before a different court from that by which it is tried. I am of opinion, therefore, that we may give to sect. 98 the construction contended for." Per Coleridge, J.: "The different construction, would in three cases out of four, take away altogether the effect of the clause." *c*

By the 2nd sect. of 3 & 4 Vict. c. 24, a judge's certificate, that an action was really brought "to try a right" must be given immediately after the verdict is delivered. The Court of Exchequer in the cases of Thompson v. Gibson, *d* and of Page v. Pearce, *e* have determined that the word "immediately" does not mean as soon as ever the verdict is delivered, but that the judge must necessarily have some little time for consideration ; and, therefore, that the word must mean, within a convenient time reasonably estimated. And a decision by Lord Hardwicke, and other authorities support this construction of the word "immediately." *f* But

a R. v. Younger, 5 T. R. 451.

b R. v. Hawkeswood, E. 23, Geo. 3; 1 Leach, 257; 2 East, P. C 955.

c R. v. Upper Papworth, 2 East, 413; Reg. v. Pembridge. 2 Law Journal, 1842, *contra*, Reg. v. Preston. 2 Dowl, P. C. 593,

d 8 M. & W. 288.   *e* Ib. 677.

f In strictness, "immediately" excludes all intermediate time and action, yet shall be construed "such convenient time as is reasonably requisite for doing a thing." R. v. Francis, Ca. temp. Hardw. 114. Pyms v. Mitford, 2 Leon. 77.

see the case of Grace v. Clinch. *a*   Where the judge had gone to another assize town, it might be too late to grant the certificate. In Shuttleworth v. Cocker, Maule, J., said : " It seems to be the intention of the act to exclude any impression being made upon the mind of the judge except what was produced at the trial ;" *b* and Lord Abinger said, in a later case, that he approved of, and was ready to adopt, this principle.   But in Page v. Pearce, the same Chief Baron said, " If acts of parliament could be construed literally, consistently with common sense and justice, undoubtedly they ought, and, if I could see upon this act of parliament, that it was the intention of the legislature, that not a single moment's interval should take place before the granting of the certificate, I should think myself bound to defer to that declared intention."

But where the intention of the framers of a law cannot be clearly seen, and where the meaning of the words used is obscure and doubtful, in such cases, it is said, the consequences of a particular exposition, may be considered in the construction.   The legislature did not mean the statute to be inoperative beyond all question ; its design is not to be defeated, if it can be helped ; *verba debent intelligi cum effectu.*   In construing a statute, if it be possible, no part of it, should be made void ; full sense and meaning must be given to every clause and provision.   So in a will, " one spells as it were," said Lord Kenyon, " every word to get at the intention."   But where the intention of a testator is, as is expressed in one of the old cases, " *cæca et sicca,* and senseless, and cannot be known," the courts find out for him, the very last intention he was likely to have entertained when he sat down to make a will, viz : that he meant to die intestate ; and the will is held void.

In the construction of a statute it is the office of an expositor to put such a sense upon the words, " that no innocent person shall receive any damage by a literal construction."   " Where a statute will bear two interpretations, one contrary to plain sense, the other agreeable to it, the latter shall prevail."   If words literally understood, bear only a very absurd signification, it is necessary to deviate a little from their primary sense ; and Blackstone admits, that if, out of acts of parliament, there arise, collaterally, any absurd consequences, manifestly contradictory to common reason, acts are, with regard to those collateral consequences only, held void.   Such cases, indeed, are excepted out of the statute by common sense, and the nonsensical words are said to be " controlled by the common law."

Again, " words are to be taken in a lawful and rightful sense ;" as where the words were, " Where no fine is levied in the " King's Court," they are to be understood, no fine levied by the husband and wife, which is lawful,—and not, no fine levied by the husband alone, which would work a wrong to the wife.

a 4 Q. B. Rep. 606.   *b* 1 M. & G. 840.

Where the meaning of a statute is doubtful the consequences, may be considered in the construction; but where the meaning is plain, no consequences it is said are to be regarded in the interpretation; for this would be assuming a legislative authority. *a* The consequences *are* to be considered; for the courts will not construe acts of parliament so as to admit of any absurd consequences. [25]

But it may be asked, how is this doctrine to be reconciled with the *dicta* frequently occuring in decided cases, that the judges are to expound the words of an act, according to their plain grammatical sense, without any regard to the consequences that may follow from their interpretation?

The answer is, that, *in* the act of construction, and during the period and gestation of interpretation, the consequences of any particular exposition, will be most unexceptionably, and properly, considered and weighed, for the sake of avoiding absurdity; but that after the court has arrived at a determinate conclusion, what is the fit construction that the meaning and context require them to put upon an act of parliament, the judges have nothing to do with the consequences of their decision. In Reg. v. The Justices of Lancashire, *b* Patteson, J., said, "I cannot tell what consequences may result from the construction which we must put upon the statute; but if mischievous, they must be remedied by the legislature." In Rhodes v. Smethurst, *c* Lord Abinger said, "A court of law ought not to be influenced or governed by any notions of hardship : cases may require legislative interference, but judges cannot modify the rules of law." In Hall v. Franklin, *d* Lord Abinger said, "We have been strongly pressed with the inconveniences that may result from the construction of the statute. We are not insensible to them; but the only proper effect of that argument, is to make the court cautious in forming its judgment; we cannot on that account put a forced construction upon the act of parliament."

Other difficulties present themselves not so easy of solution; and other discrepancies will be found to occur, much harder to be reconciled.

In treating of the construction of statutes by foreign jurists, a

---

a 10 Mod. 344.   *c* 4 Mee. & W. 63.
b 11 A. & E. 157.   *d* 3 M. & W. 259.

NOTE 25.—Where the words of a statute fixing the compensation of a public officer are loose and obscure, and admit of two interpretations, they should be construed in favor of the officer. U. S. v. Moore, 3 Story 87.

If the grant of a franchise admit of two interpretations, that is to be adopted which least restricts the public rights. Mills v. St. Clair Co., 8 How. 569; Perine v. Ches. & Del. Canal Co., 9 How. 172; Rice v. Min. & N. W. R. R. Co., 1 Blatch. 360.

passage was cited, containing the remark : " *mirum est in iis de finiendis, quam sudant doctores.*" *a*   And when the difficulties are considered, not only of making peace and atonement between the several disagreeing clauses and provisos in statutes, but also of reconciling apparently conflicting general principles, the observation will appear no less pertinent and just, as regards the interpretation of acts of parliament.   The great difficulty in the exposition of statutes, is the same, as is felt in the construction of wills.   In Counder v. Clark, Hobart, C. J., says, " We must pass between two main grounds, so as to offend neither ; one, that the devise must be taken according to the intention of the devisor ; the other, that the intention must be so expressed in the will written, that it may be certain to the court, and not against law." *b*

   The difficulties arising in the construction of statutes, may be illustrated by two recent cases (among many others), arising on the construction of the late statute of wills, 1 Vict. c. 26, ss. 3, 24 and 33.   Johnson v. Johnson, *c* and Winter v. Winter. *d*   The former decision, seems to have proceeded on the ground of a clear and plain intention, expressed *in*, and upon the face of the act. In the case of Winter v. Winter, Wigram, V. C., says, " Upon the face of the act itself, I certainly can find nothing to exclude the latter construction, in favor of the former ; and in the absence of anything upon the face of the act to fix the meaning of the words, I am bound, as well as I can, to fix that meaning, by considering the policy of the act, and the objects it was intended to accomplish."

   Consulting the text writers and the reporters, it will be discovered, that there are few subjects on which more contradictory maxims and doctrines have been ventilated; than upon the regard to be paid in construction, to the " policy of the act." [26]

   It is said in works of authority *e* to be a sound general principle in the exposition of statutes, that less regard is to be paid to the words that are used, than to the policy which dictates the act : The King v. Hale ; *f* The King v. The Mayor of Liverpool. *g* And see a case decided on the policy and provisions of the municipal corporation act.   Hine and Reynolds. *h*

   In the case of the The Inhabitants of St. Gregory, Taunton, J., said, speaking of the case of The King v. Hipswell : " The judg-

a Ante, p.
b Hob. 32.
e 1 B. & C. 123.
g c 1 A. & E. 176.

c 3 Hare Rep. p. 157.
d 5 Hare, 306.
f Cro. Car. 330; 3 Lev. 82.
h 2 Scott Rep. N. C. p. 419.

NOTE 26.—What is called the policy of the government, with reference to any particular legislation, is too unstable a ground upon which to rest the judgment of the court in the interpretation of statutes.   Hadden v. Collector, 5 Wall. 107.

   The courts are not bound by the construction placed upon a statute by one of the executive departments, though such construction is entitled to respect.   U. S. v. Dichron, 15 Pet. 161.

ment was rested by Mr. Justice Bayley, partly on the consideration of public policy; a very questionable and unsatisfactory
ground, because men's minds differ much on the nature and extent of public policy." Williams, J., added : "The ground of public policy, is a very unsafe one : it is best to adhere to the words
used in the act of parliament."

Deciding upon the policy of an act, was called by another
learned Judge (Burrough), "riding an unruly horse."

"Arguments," says Story, "drawn from impolicy or inconvenience, ought to have little weight. The only sound principle is to
declare *ita lex scripta est*, to follow and to obey. Nor if a principle
so just could be overlooked, could there be well found a more unsafe guide in practice, than mere policy and convenience. Men,
on such subjects complexionally differ from each other : the same
men differ from themselves at different times. The policy of one
age may ill suit the wishes or the policy of another. The law is
not to be subject to such fluctuations."*a*

It has been shown, that effect is to be given to the intentions of
the legislature, whenever the object of the framers of a law is expressed in apt terms, or can be clearly collected from the language
they have used. The language of acts has been adverted to, and
it has been seen that when technical terms are used, they are to
be taken in a technical sense; unless there be something in the
context to show that a different meaning was intended. In other
cases, words are to be taken in their ordinary sense, according to
grammatical construction; and not extended beyond it, to comprehend cases within the supposed meaning of the makers. To
this rule, there are two exceptions: 1st, in the case of ancient
statutes; and, 2ndly, where a literal construction, would lead to
absurdity and mischief.

It remains to illustrate the rule—that effect cannot be given to
an intention not expressed.

Of this rule there seem to be two branches. The first instance
that may be stated, is, where the legislature may have intended
to provide for a particular case, and yet not have carried its intention into effect. "We can only say of the legislature," said
Lord Ellenborough in Rex v. Shone, *quod voluit non dixit.*" *b* "If
the legislature intended more," said Lord Denman in Haworth v.
Ormerod, *c* "we can only say, that according to our opinion, they
have not expressed it."

Again, the subject may have been entirely overlooked by the
legislature.

A casus omissus can in no case be supplied by a court of law;
for that would be, to make laws. Judges are bound to take the
act of parliament as the legislature have made it. *d*

---

a Conflict of Laws, Story 17.   b 6 East, 518.
c 6 Q. B. Rep. 307.   d 1 T. R. 52.

In R. v. Powell, as to what owners of carts driven in London were liable to forfeiture, Ashurst, J., said, "The mischief which the legislature wished to remedy, is the improper behavior of persons driving carts in London, or the adjoining places. That mischief is as much to be apprehended when the owner lives at a distance as when he resides in London. However, the legislature confines the operation of the act to persons residing within prescribed limits, and as the defendant does not live within those limits he is not liable to the penalties of the act." *a*

"It is safer," said Mr. J. Ashurst, in a judgment on the game laws, "to adopt what the legislature have actually said, than to suppose what they meant to say. The heir apparent they have qualified, from a supposition that the esquire was so already. I cannot think it was their intention purposely to exclude the father, but in fact they have done it." *b*

In Brandling v. Barrington, Bayley, J., said, "I certainly think that the present case comes within the mischief intended to be remedied by the stat. 8 Ann c. 14, s. 1, and I should have been better satisfied if it could have been brought within the fair construction of the words of that enactment. But I think we should be attributing too comprehensive a meaning to the words of the statute." Holroyd, J., said, "This case does not appear to have been contemplated by the legislature, although it may perhaps be within the mischief which they intended to remedy by the 8 Ann. c. 14." *c*

The result is, that to bring a case within the statute, it should be not only within the mischief contemplated by the legislature, but also within the plain intelligible import of the words of the act of parliament.

In a late case on the municipal corporation act, Lord Denman said, "The legislature might have intended to give a concurrent jurisdiction to the county and borough sessions, however mischievous; or it might have intended to prevent the evils, but not carried its intention into effect; or the whole subject might have escaped attention. In any one of these cases, we should be bound to discover what the law is, and to declare it, without any regard to the consequences of its imperfection." *d*

So, if words go beyond the intention, it rests with the legislature to make an alteration. "Our decision," said Lord Tenterden in a late judgment, "may, perhaps in this particular case, operate to defeat the object of the statute; but it is better to abide by this consequence, than to put upon it a construction not warranted by the words of the act, in order to give effect to what we may suppose to be the intention of the legislature." *e* In another case, the same distinguished judge said, "The words may

a 4 T. R. 572.   *b* 1 T. R. 52.
c 6 B. & C. 475.   *d* Reg. v. Justices of Shropshire, 2 Q. B. Rep. 94.
e R. v. Barham, 8 B. & C. 104.

probably go beyond the intention, but if they do, it rests with the legislature to make an alteration; the duty of the court is only to construe and give effect to the provisions." *a*

An early instance of the courts giving effect to the provisions of an act, which probably went beyond the intention of the legislature, will be found in the construction put upon cap. 2 of the statute of Marlbridge; it was there enacted, that in certain cases, the distress being delivered up immediately, "*non puniatur dominus per redemptionem.*" "This branch," says Lord Coke, "is interpreted that the lord shall pay no fine, and therefore, since this act, by a consequent, (most probably not the design of the makers,) no action of trespass *vi et armis*, lieth against the lord in this case; for then, he should pay a fine." *b*

Although the intent of the legislature, is not to be collected from any particular expression, but from a general view of the *whole* of an act of parliament, *c* it is often material to attend to the collocation of words in a sentence.

When words are at the beginning of a sentence, they may govern the whole *d* as "*Nullus liber homo ;*"—"All widows ;"—"*Ensement et en meme le manere,*" &c. *e*

When words are at the end of a sentence, they may refer to the whole. *g* Thus the words, *per legem terræ*, in cap. 29 of Magna Charta, being towards the end of the chapter, have been always held to refer to all the precedent matter.

But if words are in the middle of a sentence, *f* and sensibly apply to a particular branch of it, can they be extended to that which follows? Agreeably to reason, and in grammatical construction, it should seem not; but as statutes are read without breaks and stops, it is not any time clear, that words belong to any particular branch of a sentence; it must be collected from the context, to what they relate; and they are often, as will be seen, to be read distributively—*reddendo singula singulis.*

An expression which has precedence in the order of the words, must be taken to have been used with reference to things or persons of a higher order, or superior rank. Thus where by the London tithe act, the houses of three classes of persons are exempt, to wit, the houses of great men, *(magnates)*, noblemen and noblewomen, (and it was no uncommon thing for the nobility to reside in the city in those days); Richards, chief baron, said, "I incline to think that the order of the words, (which is, by the rules of grammar a criterion of construction,) imports, that great men must mean persons superior in certain respects to noblemen and noblewomen, of which description there are certainly persons

a Notley v. Buck, 8 B. & C. 164.   *b* 2 Inst. 105.
c See *ante*, p. 573.   *d* 2 Inst. 45; id. 18.
e See post. Mag. Char. Merton. Glouc.   *f* 2 Inst. 50.
g 8 B. & C. 94.

in this country. This defendant, (the Dean of St. Paul's) is however, not one of either class of those privileged persons." *a*

Though used in their plan and ordinary sense, general words may be limited by the relative word " such," to a particular description of thing contained in a preceding section. *b* Thus, the 4th section of the stat. 3 Geo. 4, c. 39, which requires the defeasance to a warrant of attorney to be written on the paper or parchment on which the instrument itself is written, has been twice held to apply only to such warrants of attorney as fall within the former sections of the act, and which are void against the assignees of a bankrupt, and has been consequently held not to be void between the parties. *c* " Always in statutes, relation shall be made according to the matter precedent." *d*

Relative words in an act of parliament (words of reference in a subsequent statute) will make a thing pass as well as if it had been particularly expressed in the act itself; *e* *Verba illata inesse videntur*. Clauses of reference, incorporating provisions of former statutes, take effect as fully as if they had been repeated, and re-enacted in the body of the latter act, with relation thereto. " It is a sound rule of construction, but applicable," said Lord Denman in a recent case, " to modern as well as to ancient statutes, (perhaps indeed more so, from necessity, in consequence of the looseness of expression which now prevails;) that ' in the construction of general references in acts of parliament, such reference must be made only as will stand with reason and right.' " *f* " Where a provision is, in its original and natural application limited in respect to time and place, it is to give to general words of incorporation, a meaning contrary to reason, and it may be to justice, to hold that they apply to it." *g* A clause of reference in an excise statute was held to extend only to the general powers and provisions of that law, and not to every particular clause.

" The fair construction," said Ashurst, J., " to put upon the clause of reference in question, (which was a general clause), seems to be this :—that all the general powers and provisions given and made in acts *in pari materie*, shall be virtually incorporated in this, but that such provisions as are always considered as special provisions, shall not. The power of appealing from the judgment of the justices seems to be this kind, and does not attach without being expressly given. *h*

a The Warden of St. Paul's v. the Dean, 4 Price 65.

b R. v. Gwenop, 3 T. R. 135; R. v. Marks, 13 East 165; and for the effect of " such," 2 Inst. 111; 11 Rep. 33.

c Morris v. Mellor, 6 B. & C. 446. Holroyd, J. diss.; and Bennet v. Daniel, 10 B. & C.; Parke, J. diss.

d 6 Rep. 76 b. *f* 2 Inst. 287.

e Wheatley v. Thomas, Raym. 54. *g* 6 Q. B. Rep. 343.

h R. v. Justices of Surrey, 2 T. R. 504.

An instance of the ill effect of the incorporation of provisions by reference to another act, may be seen in Reg. v. The Recorder of Bath, *a* in which case Lord Denman says : " As it seems to us hardly possible to suppose it to have been the intention of the legislature, that an individual, interested and aggrieved should not have the power of questioning the validity of a vote at the sessions, we cannot avoid noticing with regret, that recourse should have been had to the method of giving an appeal by reference to another statute, instead of giving it plainly and directly by the statute itself." See also the Queen v. Stock, *b* that a right of appeal cannot be implied, but must be given by express words.

The rights of the crown can never be taken away by doubtful words, or ambiguous expressions, but only by express terms. Thus, a statute saying in general terms that the decision of the sessions shall be final, or that the proceedings shall not be removed by *certiorari,* or the like; will not take away the *certiorari* at the instance of the crown, unless there be some words in the act to show that the legislature intended that the crown should be barred. *c*

If a statute prohibit contraband goods under a penalty, a subsequent statute declaring goods contraband, will draw the penalty after it. *d*

Allusion was before made to the manner in which prior acts may be controlled (either enlarged or restrained) by subsequent acts. This doctrine may be further illustrated by the case of R. v. Gwenop. *e* The 22 Geo. 3, c. 44, was passed to protect soldiers, setting up trades, from incurring the penalties of the 5 Eliz. c. 4. The stat. 24 Geo. 3, c. 6, enlarging the privileges by the former act 22 Geo. 3, c. 44, declared that they should be irremovable during the time they exercised any trade.

It is generally to be taken that the legislature only meant to modify or repeal the provision of any former statute, in those cases where such its objects is expressly declared.

It is always to be presumed that the legislature, when it entertains an intention, will express it, and that too, in clear and explicit terms.

Affirmative words, it has been already seen, do not take away the common law,—a former custom,—or a former statute. So, general words do not take away a particular benefit or privilege; as the stat. West. 2. c. 18, which gives an *elegit*, does not take away the privilege an infant has that he shall not be sued during his nonage, if an eligit be against the heir of a conusor being an infant. *f*

a 9 A. & E. 877.
b 8 A. & E. 405.
c R. v. Allen, 15 East, 340. R. v. Inhab. of Cumberland, 6 T. R. 194; 3 B. & P. 354.
d 1 Price, 182.
e 3 T. R. 135.
f 2 Inst. 395.

Words of permission shall in certain cases be obligatory. Where a statute directs the doing of a thing for the sake of justice, the word *may* means the same as the word *shall*. The stat. 23 Hen. 6, c. 10, says the sheriff, &c., may take bail ; but the construction has been, that he shall be bound to take bail. So, if a statute says, that a thing *may* be done which is for the public benefit, it shall be construed that it must be done. Exception was taken to an indictment, (upon the stat. 14 Chas. 2, c. 12), against churchwardens and overseers, for not having made a rate to reimburse a constable, and it was urged, that the statute only puts it in their power, by the word *may*, to make such a rate, but does not require the doing it as a duty, for the omission of which they are punishable. The exception was not allowed ; and the court held that an indictment lies against them, if they refuse it. *a* [27]

Sometimes words and sections are governed and explained by conjoined words or clauses : *Noscitur a socio*. Where of words or clauses in conjunction, one has received a natural, or a technical,— a strict or enlarged interpretation, it is often contended that the others shall be taken in a like sense.

Where the words are general, and a statute is only declaratory of the common law, it shall extend to others, besides the persons or

a R. **v.** Flockwold Inclosure Commrs., 2 Chitty 251. R. v. Barlow, Salk. 609; Vern. 154.

NOTE 27.—With us, the word *may*, is sometimes a *permissive* and sometimes a *directory* word in the construction of a statute. *May*, in a statute, means *must*, whenever third persons or the public have an interest in having the act done which is authorized by such permissive language. Lucas v. Ensign, 4 N. Y. Leg. Ob. 142, N. Y. Com. Pleas. It may be construed to mean *shall*, when the public or individuals have a claim *de jure*, that the power shall be exercised. Newburgh Turnpike Co. v. Miller, 5 John Ch. 113; Malcolm v. Rodgers, 5 Cow. 188. But no general rule can be laid down on this subject, further than that such exposition ought to be adopted as shall carry into effect the true intent and object of the enactment. The ordinary meaning of the word, which is permissive, ought to be adopted, and must be presumed to be intended, unless it would manifestly defeat the object of the provision. Miner v. Mechanics' Bank, &c., 1 Pet. 64; N. Y. & Erie R. R. Co. v. Coburn, 6 How. Pr. R. 224; Buffalo Plank Road Co. v. Commissioners of Highways, 10 How. Pr. R. 239. In this last case it was held, that if the rights and interests are not concerned, or private persons have no lawful claim or interest in the exercise of the power, the word *may*, by which the power was conferred, should receive its ordinary meaning, and should be construed as conferring a discretionary power upon the officer or public body. See also Supervisors v. United States, 4 Wall. 435; City of Galena v. Army, 5 Wall. 705; Nave v. Nave, 7 Ind. 91; Livingston v. Lamin, 14 N. Y. R. 67; Hutson v. Mayor of New York, 9 N. Y. 169. The word *shall*, it has also been held, can be substituted for *may*, in the interpretation of a statute, when the good sense of the entire enactment requires the change. People v. Common Council of Brooklyn, 22 Barb. 404.

things named; *a* the stronger cases only are put, the weaker included :—thus where the king's bench only is mentioned, the provision was held to extend to the other principal courts. [28]

Sometimes, on the contrary, the expressions used are restrictive, and intended to exclude all things which are not enumerated—"*expressio unius est exclusio alterius.*" As exception strengthens the force of a law in cases not excepted, so, according to Lord Bacon, enumeration weakens it in cases not enumerated. Thus, coal-mines are rateable by the express words of the stat. 43 Eliz. c. 2; but it has been held, that, as other mines were known in the country when the statute passed, the mention of this inferior species of mine amounts to a tacit exemption or exclusion of all others, such as lead, tin, copper, iron or any other but coal mines. *b* Where certain specific things are taxed, or subjected to any charge, it seems probable that it was intended to exclude everything else, even of a similar nature; and *a fortiori*, all things different in *genus* and description, from those which are enumerated : as slate or lime quarries, where coal mines are named.

Where a general act of parliament confers immunities which expressly exempt certain persons from the effect and operation of its provisions, it excludes all exemptions to which the subject might have been before entitled at common law. The introduction of the exemption is necessarily exclusive of all other independent, extrinsic exceptions. *c* The maxim is clear, "*expressum facit cessare tacitum.*" *d* Affirmative specification excludes implication.

Statutes also are sometimes only directory what is to be done; at other times compulsory : that is, according to their provisions discretionary or imperative. The stat. 43 Eliz. c. 2, s. 5, enacted that male apprentices should be bound out by the parish till the age of twenty-four : yet a binding till twenty-one was held to confer a settlement; for the statute is only directory, and not compulsory in this respect. *e*

In Pearse v. Morrice, Taunton, J., said, "I understand the distinction between directory and imperative statutes to be that a

a 2 Inst. 256; Stat. West. 1, cap. 46.
b R. v. Cunningham, 5 East, 478.
c The Warden of St. Paul's v. The Dean, 4 Price, 78.
d 3 T. R. 442.   *e* R. v. Woolstanton, 1 Bott. 610.

NOTE 28.—Declaratory statutes are not common, or of much expediency in this country. They were resorted to in England to revive old customs, which had fallen into disuse, or which had become disputable; sometimes to resolve doubts or difficulties, and to declare what the common law is; and sometimes to explain doubts in regard to old or modern statutes, and in these respects, parliament assumed the judicial power of giving authentic interpretation. Such powers can only be exercised here by virtue of the legislative power, which is limited; and as we have already shown, (page   ), cannot act retroactively upon statutes which have had judicial interpretation from the courts, nor upon vested rights.

clause is directory, when the provisions contain mere matter of direction and nothing more; but not so, where they are followed by such words as are used here, viz : that anything done contrary to such provisions shall be null and void to all intents. These words give a direct, positive, and absolute prohibition. If they are not obligatory, I cannot conceive to myself, any words which can have a prohibitory force." *a* [29]

a 2 A. & E. 94.

NOTE 29.—The provisions of a law which are merely directory, are not to be construed into conditions precedent. Whitney v. Emmott, 1 Bald. 303. When the terms of a statute leave room for any administrative discretion to be exercised, it cannot be interpreted to be mandatory, or to be a condition precedent. But in a case where the salary of an officer is fixed by statute, which declares it to be a county charge, and that the supervisors shall audit and allow it as it becomes due, the statute is imperative, and the supervisors have no discretion. Morris v. The People, 3 Denio 381. A statute directing the mode of proceeding by public officers, is to be deemed directory, and a precise compliance is not to be deemed essential to the validity of the proceedings, unless so declared by statute. People v. Cook, 8 N. Y. 67. So too, the provisions of a law fixing the time for intermediate steps, after jurisdiction has been once acquired, are to be deemed directory, and a disregard of them does not avoid the proceedings. U. S. Trust Co. v. U. S. Fire Ins. Co., 18 N. Y. 199. Generally, the rule is, when a statute specifies the time within which a public officer is to perform an act regarding the rights and duties of others, it will be considered as directory merely, unless the nature of the act to be performed, or the language of the statute shows that the designation of time was intended as a limitation of power. People v. Allen, 6 Wend. 487; Jackson v. Young, 5 Cow. 269.

The statute which requires the officer before whom proceedings are had against an absconding, concealed, or non-resident debtor to make and file his report within twenty days after the appointment of trustees, and the latter to cause their appointment within thirty days, (2 R. S. 12, §§ 61, 68), is directory merely, and the omission to comply with these requirements within the prescribed time, will not vitiate the proceedings, or invalidate a conveyance of property made by the trustees. Wood v. Chapin, 13 N. Y. 509.

The provision in the statute limiting the time for a referee to make his report, &c., is merely directory. An extension of the period beyond a year, does not work a discontinuance of the proceedings. Matter of Empire City Bank, 18 N. Y. 200.

The statute (2 R. S. 369, § 38), which requires the sale of land under execution. where it consists of known lots or parcels, to be made separately and not in gross, is directory, and though a sale made in gross is voidable at the instance of the party aggrieved, it is not void. Cunningham v. Cassidy, 17 N. Y. 276.

A surrogate is required by 1 R. S. 447, § 10, on granting letters of administration, to take from the applicant a bond with two or more sureties; yet the omission to do so is not jurisdictional, and can be amended. Bloom v. Burdich, 1 Hill. 130.

The stat. 5 Eliz. c. 4, requires the binding of an apprentice to be for seven years; and the 41st clause avoids all indentures made otherwise than according to that law; yet it is established by decisions, that indentures for a less time are voidable only, as between the parties. a In the case before cited of Pearse v. Morrice, Lord Denman said: "It is extraordinary that there should be cases in

a R. v. St. Nicholas, in Ipswich, 1 Burr. S. C. 91.

Where, by a statute, deeds executed by commissioner of loans are required to be subscribed by two witnesses, and but one witness subscribed as such, but the deed was duly acknowledged, it was held good. Hatch v. Benton, 6 Barb. 37.

A provision of the statute (Code. § 289), that an execution against a married woman, shall direct the levy and collection of the amount against her from her separate property, and not otherwise, is directory merely. Thompson v. Sergeant, 15 Abbott. 452. And in general, where a statute requires an official act to be done by a given day, for a public purpose, it shall be construed as merely directory in regard to the time. Ex parte Heath, 3 Hill. 42.

The provision of the Code which requires a judge by whom a cause is tried without a jury, to file his decision, in writing within twenty days after the trial, is simply directory. Stewart v. Slater, 6 Duer. 84.

The provision of the city charter of New York, that every person appointed to office under the city government shall take the oath of office before the mayor, has been held to be merely directory; if it cannot be so taken, it may be administered by some other officer. Caniff v. The Mayor, &c., 4 E. D. Smith, 430.

A statute requiring the court to limit the time of the sentence of a convict, so that his imprisonment in the state prison shall expire between May and November, is merely directory; and a failure to comply with such requirement does not render the sentence void. Miller v. Finkle, 1 Parker Crim. R. 374.

This class of cases must not be confounded with those where a power or franchise has been created by statute which fixes or prescribes the mode of its exercise. In such cases, the power must be exercised in the mode pointed out in the act, and in no other, and those upon whom it is conferred, are confined strictly to the act creating it. Head v. Armory, The Providence Ins. Co., 2 Cranch. 127. In such cases, the act is the enabling statute; it creates all the power that is possessed, and all who act under it, must clothe their proceedings with all the solemnities prescribed by the power which the act demands. When a statute directs a person to do a thing in a certain time, without any negative words restraining him from doing it afterwards, the naming of the time will be considered as directory to him, and not a limitation of his authority. Pond v. Negus, 3 Mass. 232; People v. Peck, 11 Wend. 604; Ex parte Heath, &c., 3 Hill. 42; People v. Holley, 12 Wend. 486; Gale v. Mead, 2 Denio 232; The People v. Allen, 6 Wend. 486; People v. Dawson, 25 N. Y. 399; The People v. Cook, 14 Barb. 290, 2; Barnes v. Badger, 41 Barb. 98, 9.

A statute however, which declares "it shall be the duty of the supervisors, &c., to raise a certain sum of money by tax for the county buildings," is mandatory, and the courts can compel them to execute it. Caswell v. Allen, 7 John. 63.

The words shall or may, when used in a statute, are imperative only when the

which it has been held, that the words 'null and void,' should not have their usual meaning; but the word 'void' has certainly been construed as 'voidable' where the proviso was introduced in favor of the party who did not wish to avoid the instrument, &c." (" *Volenti non fit injuria.*) Per Patteson, J., "In R. v. Hipswell and R. v. Gravesend, the court has refused to carry that mode of construction further, and has given the words 'null and void,' their

public interests or rights are concerned. Malcolm v. Rodgers, 5 Cow. 188. And the rule is general, that where a duty is imposed upon officers by statute, whether by words, which are peremptory in themselves, or merely permissive, they have no discretion to refuse its performance as against a party having an absolute interest in it. Martin v. Mayor, &c., 1 Hill. 545.

And in all cases, in the courts, and especially in courts of inferior jurisdiction, where the authority to proceed is conferred by statute, and where the manner of obtaining jurisdiction is prescribed by the statute; and in all cases where one may be divested of his estate by a proceeding under statute authority, the mode of proceeding directed, is mandatory, and must be strictly complied with, or the proceeding will be utterly void. Corwin v. Merritt, 3 Barb. 341; Harrington v. The People, 6 Barb. 607; The People v. Common Council of Brooklyn, 22 Barb. 405; Bloom v. Burdick, 1 Hill, 130; People v. Schermerhorn, 19 Barb. 541; Ex parte Common Council of Albany, 3 Cow. 358; Barnard v. Vich, 21 Wend. 89; Brisbane v. Peabody, 3 How. Pr. R. 109; Rodgers v. Murray, 3 Paige 390; Atkins v. Kinnan, 20 Wend. 249; Sherwood v. Reade, 7 Hill. 431; Sharp v. Spier, 4 Hill. 76; Morse v. Williamson, 35 Barb. 472; Sherman v. Dodge, 6 John. Ch. 107; Denning v. Smith, 3 id. 331; Cohoes Co. v. Goss, 13 Barb. 138; Hubbell v. Weldon, Lalor 139. The true distinction is this: where the provision of the statute is the *essence* of the thing required to be done, and by which jurisdiction to do it is obtained, it is *mandatory;* otherwise when it relates to form and manner, and where an act is incident, or after jurisdiction has been obtained, it is *directory.* Marshall v. Langworthy, 6 Hill. 646; Striker v. Kelly, 7 Hill. 9.

There is a class of cases which hold, that whether a statute is to be regarded as *directory* or not, is made to depend upon the employment, or failing to employ negative words which import that an act shall be done in a particular manner or time, and not otherwise. Slayton v. Hulings, 7 Ind. 144; King v. Inhabitants of St. Gregory, 2 Ad. & El. 99. This rule does not appear to be universal. The use of negative words, is very often conclusive of an intent to impose a limitation, but their absence is by no means equally conclusive that the statute was not destined to be mandatory; this was held in District Township v. Dubuque, 7 Iowa 284. Lord Mansfield's rule is doubtless a better one, that whether the statute was mandatory or not, depended upon whether the thing directed to be done was the essence of the thing required. Rex v. Locksdale, 1 Burr. 447. This is doubtless the general New York rule, as to the duties of public officers. A statute directing the *mode* of proceeding, is directory, and not to be regarded as *essential* to the validity of the proceedings themselves, unless it be so declared in the statute. People v. Cook, 14 Barb. 290, S. C. 8 N. Y. 67. In other cases they are directory, when they relate to some immaterial matter where a compliance is

full effect." Per Williams, J., "No instance of that construction of 'void' as voidable, has been given except in settlement cases :" *(sed quære)* ; "and in these, I do not know why the obtaining of a settlement should not have been held to be 'an intent and purpose' within the meaning of the enactments then in question." See Governors of Bristol Poor v. Wait. *a* And in Reg. v. The Inhabitants of Fordham, *b* Coleridge, J., said, "I decline putting any construction upon the words 'of no force and validity.' Words as stringent as these, have been modified in many of the old cases; but I should be sorry to extend that mode of interpretation. But where the effect may be grammatically confined to the clause immediately preceding, and there is as good reason (so far as the language is concerned), for one interpretation as the other, one may fairly look at the consequences of each interpretation, in order to determine

a 1 A. & E. 164.   *b* 11 A. & B. 88.

matter of convenience rather than substance. People v. Schermerhorn, 19 Barb. 558. But when a power to affect property is conferred by statute upon those who have no personal interest in it, such power can be exercised only in the manner and under the circumstances specified ; the power must be strictly pursued, id. Strict compliance is necessary to confer jurisdiction, id. 559. This makes it mandatory.

A similar rule seems to have been adopted in the state of Michigan, in a case involving the validity of proceedings in the sale of lands for taxes, which is : "What the law requires to be done for the protection of the taxpayer is *mandatory*, and cannot be regarded as directory merely. Clark v. Crane, 5 Mich. 154. I understand the same rule prevails in Illinois; see Marsh v. Chestnut, 14 Ill. 223. In Massachusetts, Chief J. Shaw laid down the rule, in a case involving the legality of a tax under the provisions of a statute, as follows: "One rule is very plain and well settled, that all those measures which are intended for the security of the citizen; for securing an equality of taxation; and to enable every one to know with reasonable certainty, for what real and personal estate he is taxed, are conditions precedent; and if they are not observed, he is not legally taxed, and he may resist it in any of the modes authorized by law for contesting the validity of the tax. But many regulations are made by statute, designed for the information of assessors and officers, and intended to promote method, system and uniformity in the *modes* of proceeding, the compliance or noncompliance with which does in no respect affect the rights of taxpaying citizens. These may be considered as *directory*; officers may be liable to animadversion, perhaps to punishment, for not observing them, but yet their observance is not a condition precedent to the validity of the tax." Torry v. Milbury, 21 Pick. 67. In Wisconsin, the rule as to what are directory statutes, is this: "Where there is no substantial reason why the thing to be done might as well be done after the time prescribed as before; no presumption that allowing it to be so done, it may work an injury or wrong; nothing in the act itself, or in other acts relating to the same subject matter, indicating that the legislature did not intend that it should rather be done after the time prescribed, than not to be done at all; there the courts as-the choice. It is said that the whole rate shall be null and void if the form fail to satisfy any one of numerous requisites prescribed. But if you confine the clause of avoidance to the last requisite, the enactment becomes so reasonable and easy in practice, that one is glad to find the construction admissible." Per Lord Denman: "Perhaps, this discussion, and others on similar phrases, may induce the legislature to say on future occasions, in what respects they mean any particular provisions to be void, which they declare to be so, in general terms; and what consequences they intend, should result from this invalidity. In the absence of this, we have great difficulty in all such cases."

Yet, when a local statute enacted that certain guardians should have power to bind children apprentices, "provided such children be not bound for a longer term than until they shall have attained certain specified ages," it was held, that an indenture binding a boy for a longer term than that allowed by the act, was not absolutely void, but only voidable. *a* Per Lord Denman: "This is as mild a form of directing, and only directing, as can be." Taunton, J., thought "the enactment of a permissive nature, &c."

It will be seen hereafter under the head of penal statutes, and the strict rules of construction applied to such cases, that the words " utterly void," and "utterly null and void," have been restrained and cut down in other cases besides those relating to the settlement of the poor, to which Mr. J. Williams confined them in his observations in the case of Pearse v. Morrice before cited. True it is, that the most numerous instances of a wide and spirited departure from the words of the statute occur in this branch of the law; which as being directed by the constitution of the country to be administered by country gentlemen, ought to have been more entirely free from evasions of its letter, and nice and subtle distinctions.

The statute 43 of Elizabeth, c. 2, passed in 1601, never received a just construction, founded upon the words of the act, " as inhabi-

---

a R. v. The Inhabitants of St. Gregory, 2 A. & E. 99.

sume, that the intent was, that if not done within the time prescribed, it might be done afterwards. But when any of these reasons intervene, then the *limit* is established. State v. McLean, 9 Wis. 292.

In Illinois, it is held, that under a *directory* statute, a duty should be performed at the time specified, but may be valid if performed afterwards. Under a *peremptory* statute, the act must be performed at the time specified. Webster v. French, 12 Ill. 302.

And in general, it may be laid down as a rule, that when a statute directs certain proceedings to be done in a certain way, or at a certain time, and the form, or period, does not appear essential to the judicial mind, the law will be regarded as directory, and the proceedings under it will be held valid, though the command of the statute as to form and time has not been strictly obeyed; the time and manner not being the essence of the thing required to be done.

tant" and "occupier," till the year 1810, in the cases of Rex. v. Nicholson, and Williams v. Jones, *a* when the law upon this subject was for the first time settled. In the case of Rex v. The Mersey and Irwell Navigation Company, Parke, J., says, "Many of the early cases of rateability seem to have proceeded upon a disposition of the court, (pardonable, but perhaps not strictly correct,) to extend the operation of the statute of Elizabeth, so as to include as large a fund as possible in the rate." *b*

The stat. 3 Wm. and Mary, c. 11, s. 7, says that any unmarried person *not having child or children*, may gain a settlement by hiring and service for a year; and yet a widower, having children who have gained settlements in their own rights, has been deemed competent to gain a settlement. *c*

The stat. 8 and 9 Wm. 3, c. 70, declares, that no servant shall gain a settlement in any parish, "unless he shall continue and abide in the same service for one whole year." In the case of R. v. Clayhydon, Lord Kenyon said: "It is now too late to say that a constructive service pursuant to a hiring for a year will not confer a settlement, although I very much doubt whether a greater certainty on this subject would not have been obtained by attending strictly to the words of the act." And again in R. v. St. Mary Lambeth: —"If this point were not encumbered with decisions, and we were to revert to the words of the act of Parliament," &c. So in R. v. King Pyon's, Lord Ellenborough said, "I do not mean to disturb any of the cases which have been already decided, but I am not inclined to carry any of the decisions *further still from the plain words of the act.*"

The words, "poor person who shall be brought before any justice for the purpose of being removed," it was stated before, have been construed to mean "the question concerning the removal of any poor person;" being, says Lord Ellenborough, "the plain sense and spirit of the act, though somewhat straining upon words of it." *d* And Le Blanc, J. says, " a contrary construction would give effect to the letter by the repeal of the very object of the statute; though I cannot agree that every case, where a construction has been put upon a statute, in some instances directly contrary to the words of it, is a fit precedent to be followed by us." *e*

In the King v. The Justices of Leicester, the question arose, whether the stat. 54 Geo. 3, c. 84, was imperative. It was contended on one side, that before the 54 Geo. 3, for regulating the time of holding the Michealmas quarter sessions was passed, all the quarter sessions were holden under certain ancient statutes, which were deemed merely directory; and quarter sessions holden at other times than specified in the statutes, were always considered good.

a 12 East, 346.   *c* Anthony v. Cardigan, 2 Bott. 172.
b 9 B. & C. 111.   *d Ante*, p. 558.
e R. v. Everdon, 9 East, 101.

The stat. 54 Geo. 3, merely changed the time for holding the Michaelmas quarter sessions from the week after Michaelmas to the week after the 11th of October : it should therefore receive a construction similar to that which had been put upon the earlier statutes made in *pari materie*, viz. that it is directory only, and not imperative. To this it was answered :—That Stat. 54 Geo. 3, is imperative : That, admitting the former acts to have been directory, this statute seems to take away the discretionary power of the justices : for it appoints a new time instead of that formerly fixed. That, this must (if any language can) be considered imperative.

In giving judgment, Lord Tenterden said, "Looking at the earlier statutes upon this subject, we find that, by the 12 Rich. 2, c. 10, the justices are required to keep their sessions in every quarter of the year at least, but no particular days are specified. By the 2 Hen. 5, s. 1, c. 4, they shall make their sessions four times in the year, Michealmas, Epiphany, Easter, and the Translation of St. Thomas the Martyr, and oftener if need be. The modern statute merely substitutes the week after Michaelmas, &c. So long ago as the time of Lord Hale, the earlier statutes were considered directory :—'It is very plain,' Lord Hale says, 'that the quarter sessions are variously held in several counties, yet those are each of them good quarter sessions ; for these acts, especially that of 2 Hen. 5, are only directive and in the affirmative.' "It has been asked," proceeds Lord Tenterden. "what language will make a statute imperative, if the 54 Geo. 3, c. 84, be not so ? Negative words would have given it that effect, but those used are in the affirmative only." *a*

From these expressions the conclusion is sometimes drawn, that "negative words will make a statute imperative," which is incontestable ; adding "words in the affirmative are directory only." *b* But where affirmative words are peremptory, as that "the forms of proceedings set forth in the schedule annexed shall be used ;" Lord Kenyon observed, "I cannot say that these words are merely directory ;" and a material variance from the form prescribed was in that case held fatal, the justices not having pursued the authority of the statute. *c* [30]

Negative words will make a statute imperative ; and it is apprehended, affirmative *may*, if they are absolute, explicit, and peremp-

---

a R. v. Leicester, 7 B. & C. 12.   *c* Davison & Gill, 1 East, 64.
b Harrison's Index.

NOTE 30.—Affirmative words in a statute may be construed as a negative of what is not affirmed. Byron v. Sundburgh, 5 Texas R. 428.

Affirmatives in statutes that introduce new laws, imply a negative of all that is not in purview. So that a law directing a thing to be done in a certain manner, implies that it shall not be done in any other manner. U. S. v. Case of Han Penals, 1 Paine 406, Danes Abr. vol. 6, 591 to 593, and cases cited.

tory, and show that no discretion is intended to be given; and especially so, where jurisdiction is conferred.

And with regard to a form prescribed by the act, it should be observed that where a statute directs a particular mode of proceeding or gives a particular form, that form must be observed;—"*Non observata forma infertur adnullatio actus ;*" a *Ou recoverie est donc en especial case per estatut, il coveit que home aver touts voies accord al statut.*"b But, says Lord Mansfield in R. v. Loxdale, c "there is a known distinction between circumstances which are of the essence of a thing required to be done by an act of Parliament, and clauses merely directory. The precise time, in many cases, is not of the essence, while on the 43 Eliz. c. 2, nobody ever thought the number of overseers discretionary."

The 14th sect. of 4 Geo. 4, c. 75, (the Marriage Act,) points out the mode in which licenses are to be obtained, and the matters to be sworn to by the parties or one of them; and one of those matters, where either of the parties, not being a widower or widow, shall be under the age of twenty-one years, is, that the consent of the person or persons, whose consent to such marriage is required under the provisions of this act, has been obtained thereto. Then the 16th section specifies the persons who shall have power to consent; and proceeds:—"and such consent is hereby required for the marriage of such person so under age, unless there shall be no person authorized to give such consent." The language of this section, Lord Tenterden observes, is merely to *require* consent; it does not proceed to make the marriage void, if solemnized without consent. The 23d section enacts, *not* that the marriage shall be void, but that all the property accruing from the marriage shall be forfeited, and shall be secured for the benefit of the innocent party, on the issue of the marriage, &c., d and the act was held to be only directory.

"Where the superior courts have a jurisdiction, it can only be taken from them by the express words of an act of parliament, or by necessary implication." e But in 8 Bing. 394, Tindal, C. J., said, "Yet where the object and intent of the statute manifestly require it, words that appear to be permissive only, shall be construed as obligatory, and shall have the effect of ousting courts of their jurisdiction." In that case, on a full analysis of the statute in question, the courts thought the jurisdiction was taken away.

The words "it shall be lawful" are imperative, where, and only where, public duty requires the thing to be done. f

The words "shall and lawfully may," were held in Blewett v. Gordon, g as explained by the context, not to be obligatory; and see 10 Sim. 470.

a 2 Inst. 388.
b Stat. Gloucester, cap. 4.
e Per Ashurst, J., 4 T. R. 109.
g 1 Dowl. P. C., N. S.

c 1 Burr. 447.
d R. v. Birmingham, 8 B. & C. 20.
f See *ante*, p. 604.

The same words in Steward v. Graves *a* were held imperative, in accordance with the views of the framers of the act then under consideration, (7 Geo. 4, c. 66). But the acts under which the respective companies were consituted, were very different.

Words sometimes vary in their import, according to the subject to which they are applied. Hence it is often said they are to be understood in a certain sense, "*within the meaning of a particular act ;*" that is, they are to be construed with reference to the subject-matter to which they are there applied : so that the same words receive a different construction in different statutes.

In Staniland v. Hopkins, *b* Lord Abinger said, "The court is well aware of the difficulty of putting a construction free from doubt and perplexity on this act of parliament (the municipal corporation act) arising from the endeavour to frame by one act of parliament one universal charter for all municipal corporations and to combine with that object, all the principles of corporation law that are to be found in a long series of judicial decisions."

General words in an act of parliament are often, where the sense requires it, and in furtherance of the intention, to be taken distributely, "*reddendo singula singulis.*" They are thus applied to the subject-matter to which they appear by the context most properly to relate, and to which they are really most applicable. Thus the words "according to the provisions of the said act, and of this act," obviously import that the requisitions of two acts, (that act itself, and another act therein before-mentioned,) in their respective particulars are to be duly complied with ; as if the one under its circumstances require signature to an instrument only, and the other that it be under hand seal. *c*

Thus also, in the construction of the words, "for money or other good consideration paid or given" in the stat. 13 Eliz. c. 5, "paid" is referred to money, and "given" to "consideration." A man devised to "A. B. 100 sheep, ten bullocks, and 10*l.* payable quarterly ;" these words payable quarterly, have reference to the rent ; for ten bullocks per annum cannot be delivered quarterly.

In Reg. v. Cumberworth Half, *d* where the words were, "the feeding of a cow by and on the land." Patteson, J., said : "I think we must say '*reddendo singula singulis,*' that the feeding was to be 'on' the land while there was food on it, and by the owner of the land with hay, at other times."

In R. v. Faulkner, the words of an act were made to have a sensible construction, by being taken distributively. A power of com mitment for contempt is not to be vested by an inferential construction of an act of parliament, because, in a general clause, it invests a commissioner with the character of a judge of record. *e*

a 2 M. & G. 760.   *b* 9 M. & W. 195.

c 7 B. & C. 570.   *d* 2 Q. B. Rep. p. 49.

e 1 C., M. & R. 525.

Though a statute gives inaccurate names to things, if the court can discover its meaning, it will so expound it, as to give force to the intention of the legislature; thus it seems a statuable requisition of the "great seal of Great Britain" (used improperly, since the old great seal was, soon after the union with Ireland, destroyed in the presence of the Lord Chancellor), is substantially satisfied by the use of the great seal of the United Kingdom. a

So much for the text, or letter, which has largely engaged our attention. The sense and spirit of an act, however,—its scope and intention, are primarily to be regarded in the construction of statutes, and it matters not that the terms used by the legislature in delivering its commands, are not the most apt to express its meaning, provided the object be plain and intelligible, and expressed with sufficient distinctness, to enable the judge to collect it from any part of the act. The object once understood, judges are so to construe an act, as to suppress the mischief or advance the remedy. But yet the court is not at liberty, even for that purpose, to introduce or exclude words from any clause of a statute, but is bound to construe the words which the clause contains, with reference always to that which appears to be plainly and manifestly its object. b

A remedial act shall be so construed as most effectually to meet the beneficial end in view, and to prevent a failure of the remedy. As a general rule, a remedial statute ought to be construed liberally. Receiving an equitable, or rather a benignant, interpretation, the letter of the act will be sometimes enlarged, sometimes restrained, and sometimes it has been said, the construction made is contrary to the letter: which should be read—*ultra* the letter, and confined to ancient statutes. [31]

Thus, it is laid down, that a statute may be extended by construction, to *other cases* within the same mischief and occasion of the act, though not expressly within the words. The stat. 9 Rich. 2, c. 3, gives a writ of error to him in reversion, "if tenant for life, tenant by curtesy, &c., lose in a "*præcipe;*" resolved, that although the statute speaks only of reversions, yet remainders are also taken to be within the purview thereof. c

a R. v. Bullock, 1 Taunt. 80.   c Winchester's case, 3 Rep. 4.
b Bloxam & Elsce, 6 B. & C. 174.

NOTE 31.—In construing a remedial statute, which has for its end the promotion of important and beneficial public objects, a large construction is to be given, when it can be done without doing violence to its terms. Wolcott v. Pond, 19 Conn. 597.

This rule applies especially in statutes giving a right to appeal, which are to be liberally construed as in furtherance of justice. Pearson v. Lovejoy, 53 Barb. 407. So public statutes, in regard to public improvements. Hudler v. Golden, 36 N. Y. 446; Candee v. Heyward, 37 N. Y. 653.

The stat. of Marlbridge, cap. 29, gives a remedy to the successors of abbots, priors, &c., "*ad bona ecclesiæ repetenda.*" *Bona ecclesiæ suæ* are the words of the statute, upon which Lord Coke observes: "1st. If an obligation be taken from the predecessor, it is within this statute. 2d. The successor shall have, by the equity of this statute, an action of trespass for cutting down of trees, and carrying them away. Wherein it is to be observed, that acts that give remedy for wrongs done, shall be taken by equity." *a*

Everything that can, by the most beneficial interpretation, be comprehended under the word "goods" in its most enlarged sense, ought, in this case, to have been embraced by that act; but to include anything which could not, by the most indulgent acceptation, under any favorable circumstances, answer to the legal description of "goods,"* was, it is humbly conceived, to supply what the legislature had omitted, (whether designedly or otherwise), and therefore to make, and not interpret, law.

The same statute had provided before, (cap. 6), that "in feoffments to the heir, to defraud the lords of the fee of their wardships, no chief lord should leese (lose) his ward." The act was construed to extend equally to a grant, fine, recovery, lease and release, confirmation, or other conveyance. But then the words of the statute are *per hujusmodi fraudem nullus capitalis,* &c. By such fraud, *hujusmodi,* "that is," says Lord Coke, "such in mischief, or such in inconveniency; and therefore, all other fraudulent feoffments, tending to the same end, are within the statute, whatsoever colorable pretext they have." *b*

Such statutes, it is laid down, as give remedy which was not at common law, shall be taken by equity; as writ of entry *in casu proviso* is given by the stat. of Gloucester, cap. 6. And by the equity of the statute, a man shall have a writ of entry *in consimili casu. c* The words of the 13 Eliz. of fraudulent grants are, "Be it therefore declared, ordained, and enacted," &c.; and therefore like cases in *semblable* mischief shall be taken within the mischief of this act. But why?—by reason, it is added, of this word *(declared),* whereby it appears what the law was before the making of this act. *d* In Glover v. Cope, Lord Holt extended the 32 Hen. 8, c. 34, perhaps somewhat questionably, by equity. *e*

The reason why a case, not within the letter of a statute, is sometimes held by an equitable construction to be within the meaning of it, is, first, that the lawgiver could not set down every

a 2 Inst. 152.

c Bro. Parl. pl. 20; Kelw. 96 a, pl. 6.   *d* Co. Litt. 290 b.

e 3 Lev. 326; Show. 284.

b 2 Inst. 111.

---

* A *chose in action,* as an obligation, &c., is not within the stat. 21 Hen. 8, concerning larceny by servants in going away with, or embezzling their master's goods to the value of 40s. Bonds, indeed, are now liable to be taken in execution by statute, 1 & 2 Vict. c. 110, s. 12.

case in express terms; and, secondly, that a case within the mischief must have been intended to be within the remedy of an act. *a*

Plowden (after Aristotle) points it out as the best way to form a right judgment whether a case be within the equity of a statute, to suppose the lawmaker present, and that you have asked him the question, Did you intend to comprehend this case? Then you must give yourself such answer as you suppose he, being an upright and reasonable man, would have given. If this be,—"that he did mean to embrace it," you may safely hold the case to be within the equity of the statute; for while you do no more than he would have done, you do not act contrary to the statute, but in conformity thereto. *b*

But must not such a doctrine necessarily lead to speculations the most vague, and reasoning the most desultory; to the most arbitrary and the most conflicting decisions? Every judge is unfortunately in the case here supposed, to answer for himself, and not, as Cicero expresses it, "*habere in consilio legem.*" Is he not sure to make the answer favorable, whenever he inclines to think a case within the mischief? Such a notion surely, could only be supported, by admitting at once as a principle, (what *has been* broadly stated, speaking of old statutes which laid down general rules in the fewest words), that "judges have power over statute laws, to mould them to the truest and best use, according to reason and best convenience;" *c* as if the legislature had abdicated its functions, delegating all its powers and duties to the judges.

Much sounder, applied to acts of our own times, seems the doctrine of Jones, J., in the case of James and Finney, that "It is too general a ground, to put cases upon statutes, where things shall be taken by equity; but every statute stands upon its particular reason, upon consideration of the parts of the statute,—the mischief before, and what things are intended to be remedied by the same statute." *d* So, when a statute commences with a particular enumeration, no other thing shall be taken by equity. Unfortunately, many cases are extant as authorities, which are inconsistent with the juster views of the province and duties of judges at present entertained. Lord Tenderden observed: "There is always danger in giving effect to what is called the equity of a statute; it is much safer and better to rely on and abide by the plain words, although the legislature might have provided for other cases, had their attention been directed to them." *e* The legislature, as was once well observed by Mr. Justice Heath, "is always at hand," to supply deficiencies, or to correct mistakes.

Again, a remedial statute shall be extended by equity to other *persons* besides those expressly named. *f* The statute of *Circumspecte agatis*, &c., names only the bishop of Norwich, but has been

a 1 Inst. 24.　　　　　　　　　*b* Eyston v. Studd, Plow. 467.
c Sheffield & Ratcliffe, Hob. 346.　*d* Jones, 422, 423.
e 6 B & C. 475.　　　　　　　　*f* Porter's case, 1 Rep. 25.

always extended, by an equitable construction, to other bishops. Upon which doctrine the following observations were made in Platt's case: *a* "It is not unusual in acts of parliament, especially in the more ancient ones, to comprehend by construction a *generality*, where express mention is made only of a *particular;* the particular instances being taken only as examples of all that want redress in the kind, whereof the mention is made." Thus the act 1 Rich. 2, c. 12, orders that the warden of the Fleet shall not permit prisoners in execution to go out of the prison by bail or baston, yet it has been adjudged that this act extends to all gaolers. *b*

The remedy given by the 9 Ed. 3, c. 3, against executors, has been always extended, by an equitable construction, to administrators. And the ground is plain, that it reaches to all others in like degrees. Thus, where a statute gives action of waste against tenant for life or years,—by the equity of the statute, the action lies by tenant for half a year or less. *c* In the matter of Briant, clerk of the day rules in the king's bench prison, the court held, that though the clause requiring the residence of the marshal, did not in terms extend to the other officers, yet, considering the duties of those officers, in whom the public reposed a considerable confidence and trust, &c., &c., it was evident that the legislature intended to require the personal residence of these officers, and particularly of this person. *d*

Again, a remedial statute shall be construed by equity to extend to *other things* besides those expressly named. Uses were not within the stat. *de donis,* but "are taken within the equity;" *e* and in Chudleigh's case, Lord Coke furnishes numerous instances of acts made "against the fraud of uses," having been construed liberally and by equity, beyond the letter. *f*

A statute made *pro bono publico,* shall be construed in such manner that it may, as far as possible, attain the end proposed. *g* Therefore the New River water act was holden, although only the city of London be therein mentioned, to extend to places adjacent; because all statutes made for the convenience of the public, ought to have a liberal construction,—to be expounded largely, and not with restrictions. *h*

Again, it is, (somewhat too generally), laid down, that all statutes made to redress fraud, and to give a speedier remedy for right, being in advancement of justice, and beneficial to the public, shall for that reason be extended by equity. *i*

Again, a remedial statute will be extended by equity to other *places* than those mentioned within a statute. Thus, in a question

a Plow. 36.
c Eyston v. Studd, Plowd. 467.
e Corvet's case, 1 Rep. 88.
g Pierce and Hopper, Str. 253.
h New River Company v. Graves, 2 Vern. 431; Sty. 302.
i Wembish and Tallboys, Plow. 59.
b 2 Jo. 62, in Plummer and Whichcot.
d 5 T. R. 509.
f 1 Rep. 131.

as to the rightful custody of a ward, though it was found by the verdict that the ward in that case had in fact departed out of the house of her mother, yet in judgment of law it was held the mother still had the custody of her; such custody being inseparably annexed to the person of the mother, *jure naturæ. a* If one in execution makes his escape, and flies into another county, it may be argued that this shall be an escape, although he be taken on a fresh suit, because the sheriff cannot have the custody of him in another county, his authority not extending thither; but it was adjudged no escape. *b*

In like manner, statutes have been made to extend by construction to a *time* not mentioned; or to another time than what is mentioned, in the statute. The stat. Westm. 2, cap. 11, limits no time within which the accountant therein mentioned shall be imprisoned; yet it ought to be done *presently*, (27 H. 6, 8, a.) and the reason is given in Fogassa's case, that the generality of the time shall be restrained to the present time, for the benefit of him upon whom the pain may be inflicted. And a justice of the peace upon view of the force, ought to commit the offender *presently. c*

So, a remedial statute shall be extended to later provisions by subsequent statutes. It was before stated, and explained by instances, that statutes may extend to matters of subsequent creation; but it is also propounded and remains to be illustrated, that a subsequent statute may be, as the expressions vary, "taken within the meaning," or "holden within the equity," of former statutes. Thus, a devise to a woman, of land, for term of her life or in tail for her jointure and in satisfaction of dower, is a jointure within the act 27 Hen. 8, although land was not devisable till 32 Hen. 8. "And it is frequent in our books," says Lord Coke, "that an act made of late time, shall be taken within the equity of an act made long before. As the stat. of Marlbridge, which was made 52 Hen. 3, gave the wardship of the heir of the tenant who held by knight's service, notwithstanding a feoffment made by collusion; at which time and two hundred years more after; that is to say, till the 4 Hen. 7, c. 17, which gave the wardship of the heir of *cestuy que trust*, the heir of *cestuy que use*, was not in ward; and yet it is held in 27 Hen. 8, 9 a. b., that if *cestuy que use* after the stat. of 4 Hen. 7, makes a feoffment in fee by collusion to defraud the lord of his ward, it is taken within the equity of the stat. of Marlbridge." *d*

With a like-view, to promote the object of an act, the letter of a statute is sometimes *restrained* by an equitable construction; and it is held that a case out of the mischief intended to be remedied by a statute, shall be construed to be out of the purview, though it be within the words of the statute. *e* The words of the

a Ratcliff's case, 3 Rep. 39.
b Boyton's case, 3 Rep. 44.
c Plow. 45.
d Vernon's case, 4 Rep. 4.
e 2 Inst. 386.

statute lately quoted, of 2 Westm. c. 11, are general, that all bailiffs and receivers, who, in passing their accounts before auditors assigned, shall be found in arrear, may be committed to the next gaol : yet, if an infant bailiff or receiver be found in arrear, he shall not be committed, for he is not, by reason of his want of discretion, within the equity of the statute.*a*

If a law be made, that whoever does a certain act, shall be adjudged a felon, and suffer death, yet, if a madman do this, he shall be excused ; for, as the action is not to be imputed to him, but to an involuntary ignorance brought upon him by the hand of God, he is not within the reason of the law. *b*

"Though the words be general," says the ancient Plowden, "they are to be reduced to a particularity by exposition made according to the intent of the act. Those statutes which comprehend all things in the letter, the sages of the law have expounded to extend but to some things ; those which generally prohibit all people from doing such an act, they have interpreted to permit some persons to do it ; and those which include every person in the letter, they have adjudged to reach some persons only : all founded upon the intent ; collected, by considering the cause and necessity of the act, and comparing one part with another, and sometimes by foreign circumstamces."

Where particular words are followed by general ones, the latter are to be held as applying to persons and things of the same kind with those which precede. *c* The right of voting in cities and boroughs is conferred on the occupiers " of any house, warehouse, counting-house, shop, or other building ;" a cowhouse is within the act. The term building is not to be taken in its largest acceptation, but must be explained by the accompanying words. It would not include a wall or bridge, though they are " buildings ;" but it will, a cowhouse or a stable.*d* So, the large general words " other tenements and hereditaments," will have to be restrained to things *ejusdem generis* with those before specified. See the cases of Rex. v. The Manchester Water Works, *e* and R. v. Mosley, *f* where it was adjudged that the word "hereditaments" was to be construed with reference to the words previously used. Those words shewed, that the legislature in the act in question, referred to things of a corporal nature only.

Thus it appears, that the letter of a remedial statute may be enlarged or restrained by a liberal, or what is called an equitable construction, and there are also certain cases which are of necessity, by construction, *excepted out* of statutes. Such are cases out of the meaning of the law, and therefore not held to be within its operation, though included in the terms of it. It is principally

a Zouch and Stowell, Plow. 365.   b Eyston and Studd, Plow. 465.
c Sandiman v. Breach, 7 B. & C. 96; 6 A. & E. 729; 1 N. & P. 791.
d Whitmore v. Bedford, 5 M. & G. 13. e 3 D. & R. 20; 1 B. & C. 680.
f 3 D. & R. 335; 2 B. & C. 226.

with reference to such cases that, lastly, it is said, that a remedial statute shall be expounded "contrary to the words,' or "contrary to the general words," or merely "contrary to the text;" in all its shapes, a questionable doctrine,—in its stricter sense, quite inconsistent with the sounder principles of judicial interpretation, and requiring, it is apprehended, to be greatly modified, before it can be at all admitted as a rule of construction.

In the great case of the Posnati, Lord Ellesmere's rule was: "Words are to be taken and construed: 1. Sometimes by extension; 2, sometimes by restriction; 3, sometimes by implication; 4, sometimes a disjunctive for a copulative; 5, a copulative for a disjunctive; 6, the present tense for the future; 7, the future for the present; 8, sometimes by equity, out of the reach of the words; 9, sometimes words taken in a contrary sense; 10, sometimes figuratively; 11, and many other like constructions. And of all these, examples be infinite, as well in the civil, as common law."

"Now," says Petyt in his *Jus Parliamentarium*, "any one that reads this, will easily judge what the scope and consequences of the chancellor's rule may be. And he may as easily discern, how far it is capable of being improved, to baffle and elude any law whatsoever, and wrest it from its genuine and native sense to what you please."

The judges in Edrich's case declared, that it would be dangerous to give scope to make a construction in any case against the express words, but they added the qualifying words, "when the meaning of the makers doth not appear to the contrary, and when no inconvenience will thereupon follow." *a*

The true intent and meaning of a statute is no doubt always to be regarded; and to such purpose only, says one of the sages of the law, ought the words to be construed. *b* Constructions, both of statutes and of wills, are to be made according to the intent of the framers, and not by any strict or strained interpretations; *c* and sometimes acts of parliament are to be expounded differently in sex, name, number, person, occasion, degree, &c., from the letter, in order to preserve the intent. "All acts are to be taken by reasonable construction; and in doubtful cases, judges may enlarge or restrain the construction of acts of parliament, according to the sense of the law-makers." *d* For many times, things which are within the words of statutes, are not within the purview of them. Beneficial statutes, therefore, have always been taken and expounded by equity; *e* *ultra* the strict letter, but not, it is well and wisely said, *contra* the letter. In the language of Lord Bacon, before cited, words in a statute may be taken to a foreign, but never to an un-

a 5 Rep. 119.　　　　　　　*b* Williams and Berkely, Plow. C. 231.

c Butler and Baker's case, 3 Rep. 27.　*d* Per Trevor, J., 11 Mod. 161.

e Lord Buckhart's case, 37 & 38 Eliz.

reasonable or a repugnant intent. "A person ought not to think, if he have the letter on his side that he hath the law, in all cases," says the ancient Plowden; "words are only verberations of the air." "No statute shall be interpreted so as to be inconvenient and against reason."*a* "Words of a statute ought not to be expounded to destroy natural justice." *b*

For, there will be some things necessarily and in their nature, exempt from and excepted out of all statutes; dispensations allowed by law and reason, and prevailing over any form of words. Thus, for instance :—A man shall never be a judge in his own cause. Magna Charta, cap. 12, says, " *Assisæ non capiantur nisi in suis comitatibus;*" but if a man be disseised of a commote in the marshes of Wales,—that there be not a failure of justice,—notwithstanding this *negative* statute, the assize shall be taken in the county of Gloucester. For the lord marcher could not do justice in his own case; and if he should not have remedy in this case by the king's writ out of the chancery in England, he should have right, and no remedy by the law given for the wrong done unto him, which the law will not suffer. Therefore this case, of necessity, is by construction excepted out of the statute. *c*

So, for a like reason, the stat. of Westm. 1, cap. 3, which gives a re-disseisin to be tried *per primos juratores,* has been so construed, that where there was *no* first jury, it shall be tried by others; regarding it as an excepted case out of the meaning and purview of the act, though within the words. "For the statute," says Lord Coke, " albeit it be penal, shall not be so literally expounded, that, if it cannot be tried *per primos juratores,* it shall not be tried at all; for *verba intelligi debent cum effectu.* The case of there being no jurors at all in the former assize, was, it is plain, never contemplated, and the provision was not meant to apply to such a case ;—while justice is promoted by its taking effect upon the *alios,* whom the statute likewise speaks of." *d*

The case of a distress driven out of the county, where the manor is in another county, before cited, is another instance of beneficial construction, shewing that the statute does not extend to a case within the bare words, if it be clearly out of the true meaning of the statute; the purview not extending beyond the intent of the makers of the act. *e*

In Rex v. The Inhabitants of Cumberland, *f*— an indictment for not repairing a county bridge,—the question was, whether the *certiorari* were taken away from the prosecutor by the stat. 1 Ann. c. 18, s. 5; Lord Kenyon said : " The words of this act are very general : but if in their construction we were to read them in their full extent, it would introduce a solecism in the law; for

a 5 Rep. Cawdrie's case.   *b* Sty. 81.
c 2 Inst. 25.   *d* 2 Inst. 84.
e St. Marlbridge, c. 4, Inst. 107.   *f* 6 T. R. 154.

it must be remembered, that in these cases the defendants are the inhabitants of a county, and if the indictment cannot be removed by *certiorari*, and a suggestion entered on the record, ' that the inhabitants of this county are interested,' in order to have a trial elsewhere, the indictment must be tried by the very persons, who are the parties in the cause. If this were *res integra*, we should consider whether the extensive words of this statute ought not to be narrowed in their construction, in order to arrive at that point which is the object of all laws,—the attainment of justice. We should have been anxious, for reasons of substantial justice, to control the extensive operation of the general words of the statute of Ann."

In law, all cases cannot be foreseen or expressed ; the object of interpreting laws by what is called equity, is to supply as far as possible, this deficiency, by a recurrence to natural principles of justice. It is the same with cases excepted by reason and necessity, out of the prescribed rules.

There are other maxims of interpretation relating to this subject of expounding statutes by equity, deserving notice ; though such doctrines, founded sometimes upon principle or adjudged cases, sometimes also depend upon mere *dicta*, or very questionable authorities.

Thus, it is warrantably said, statutes which " give remedy for wrongs" shall be liberally construed or taken by equity. The statutes *de Eschaetoribus,—et Articuli super chartas, cap.* 19, for "restoring the mesne profits where a seisure had turned out unlawful," speak only of an *ouster le mayne;* yet being both beneficial laws, for restitution to be made to the party grieved, by equity they extend to liveries, *amoveas manus* upon petitions, and *monstrons de droit*, and by like equity to *ouster le maynes* upon traverses ; although traverses were not in use at the time of the making of these statutes." *a*

Again, statutes which " oust delay, and for expedition of justice" shall be benignly construed and are extended by equity. Thus, the stat. Westm. 2, c. 18, which gave an *elegit*, said, the " sheriff shall deliver ;" yet being a beneficial law, by equity it is extended to every other immediate officer to every other court of record. *b* So, in the stat. of Westm. 1, where " ancestor" is said ; predecessors is taken by equity ; *c* and again, where "tenant" is said, vouchee and tenant by receipt, (who are tenants *in law*,) have been included ; for acts of parliament made for suppression of falsehood practised for delay, as these false vouchers and assigns were, shall have a benign interpretation.

Where a contrary construction would lead to future disputes and constant litigation, it should be remembered, that " *boni judicis*

a 2 Inst. 572. *b* 2 Inst. 394, cap. 40.
c Cap. 42.

est causas litium dirimere."a　Thus, in a modern case, of Gale and Lawrie, Lord Tenterden said : "This construction (that—whatever is on board a vessel for the purposes of the voyage, belonging to the owner, constitutes a ship's appurtenances,) furnishes a plain and intelligible general rule; whereas, if it should be held that nothing is to be considered as part of the ship that is not necessary for her navigation or motion on the water, a door would be opened to many nice questions, and much discussion and cavil." *b*

No statute where the letter is ambiguous, shall be taken by equity, to maintain a mischief contrary to the letter and intent of the statute ; "but it shall be taken in the better intent, and largely, to toll and destroy the mischiefs and " inconveniences." This doctrine is illustrated by the case before mentioned, in which the stat. 1 & 2 Ph. & Mary, was held not to extend to treason committed out of the realm ; but such cases were to be triable as before. *c*

A statute which is to take away the common law ought never to have an equitable construction. See the stat. Westm. 2, cap. 35, abridging the *six* months in which proclamation should be made in a certain case, to three months. This branch restraining the common law, was held to extend only to the defendant in deed, and not to the defendant in law. *d*

A statute shall never have an equitable construction to overthrow an estate. *e* [32]

As regards the case of an inconvenience which rarely happens, opposed to mischiefs "*quæ frequentius accidunt*," there is some nicety ; and upon the construction of explanatory statutes, the authorities are painfully conflicting.

If the words of a statute do not reach to an inconvenience rarely happening, they shall not be extended to it by an equitable construction ; for the objects of statutes are mischiefs *quæ frequentius accidunt.* It is good reason in such case, and therefore sound construction, not to strain the words farther than they reach ; but the case is to be considered as a *casus omissus.* It was resolved by the judges in Sir George Curzon's case, upon the construction of the stat. 32 Hen. 8, giving power to dispose of two-thirds of a man's land, &c., "to and for the advancement of his wife, preferment of his children, and payment of his debts," &c., that, if there be grandfather, father, and divers sons, and the grandfather, in the life of the father, conveys his lands to any of the sons, it is out of the said act of 32 Hen. 8 ; for it is not common nor usual, *et ad*

a 2 Inst. 306.　　　　　　　　　b 5 B. & C. 162.
c Forster's case, 11 Rep. 78, *ante*, p. 552.　d 2 And. 149.
e 2 Inst. 442.

NOTE 32.—A statute giving a right to redeem land sold for taxes should receive a liberal construction. Dubors v. Hepburn, 1 Pet. 1. So also should a statute avoiding fraudulent conveyances. Bk. of U. S. v. Lee, 13 Pet. 107.

ca que frequentius accidunt, jura adaptantur, and the father ought to have the immediate care of his sons and issue. But if the father be dead, then the care of them belongs to the grandfather, and then, if he conveys any of his lands to any of the said sons, it is within the statute. *a*

But it is no reason, when the words of an act *do* sufficiently extend to an inconvenience rarely happening, that they should not extend to it, as well as if it had happened more frequently, because it happens but seldom. *b*

Statutes of explanation shall be construed only according to the words, and not by any manner of intendment; for it is incongruous, it is said, for an explanation to be explained. *c* An explanatory statute being a legislative exposition of the meaning of words used in a former statute, ought not to be extended by an equitable construction. For it was said by the court in the case of Butler and Baker, *d* "if any exposition should be made against the direct letter of the exposition made by parliament, there will be no end of expositions." When one act is made explanatory of another, the court cannot carry the explanation farther than is expressed in *that* act ; *e* it must be construed precisely, and no new interpretation can be made of it. *f*

E contra, this rule of exposition, that statutes of explanation shall always be taken literally, is peremptorily denied by Ch. J. Hobart. "For no statute law," he says, "should exclude all equity ; it is impossible that an act of parliament should provide for every inconvenience which happens ; equity must necessarily take place in the exposition of statutes." *g*

In the case of the Dean and Chapter of Norwich, it is said *arguendo,* and seems to be admitted by the court, *h* that statutes of explanation are always to be interpreted beneficially. The result seems to be that, on the one hand explanatory statutes shall not be extended by equity to new cases, and on the other, whilst the words are not to be strained beyond their fair import and meaning, they shall yet have such reasonable construction as will stand with the scope and intention of the makers.

Equitable construction has been frequently illustrated by the doctrines laid down in the case of the registry acts for giving priority to deeds and mortgages, according to the date of the registry. If a person claiming under a registered deed or mortgage had notice of the unregistered prior deed when he took his deed, and procured the registry of it, in order to defeat the prior deed, he shall not, it is held, prevail with his prior registry ; because that would

a 6 Rep. 77.　　　　　　　　　*b* Bole and Horton, Vaughan, 373.
c Cro. Car. 23; Plowd. 363.　　*d* 3 Rep. 31 a.
e Carth. 396.　　　　　　　　　*f* Jo. 35; Winch. 85.
g 2 Roll. Rep. 500; Winch. 123; Sir W. Jones, 39.
h 3 Rep. 75.

be to counteract the intent and policy of the statutes, which were made to prevent, and not to uphold frauds. [33]

That notice of a deed, even the most actual and direct, should ever have been admitted to supply the want of its registration, has been thought unwise and improper, and opposed to the policy of other countries. A more decisive opinion has been expressed, that the equity decisions dispensing with registry upon the ground of constructive notice, have led to many inconveniences, and much uncertainty and litigation. The greatest English lawyers have expressed their regret that either the registry act or the statute of frauds should have been broken in upon, and had their utility diminished, by construction.

The decisions upon the registry act, stat. 7 Ann. c. 20, s. 1, and upon the statute of enrolments, 27 Hen. 8, c. 16, [a] have proceeded upon the ground that statutes which were designed to prevent frauds, should never be used as a means to cover them. [b]

Upon the statute of frauds, the view taken was, that as it was made with a design to prevent uncertainty, perjury, and contrariety of evidence, either in marriage or any other treaties, the cases not liable to these inconveniences could not be within it. [c] But upon this statute (of frauds), there can be little doubt in the mind of any sound lawyer, that there are several decisions in which the courts, in their anxiety to defeat injustice, have a little stretched the language of the legislature. [d]

Upon the former subject (of registry), a case Doe dem. Robinson against Allsop, [e] came before the court of king's bench in 1821. In that case there were two assignments of the same lease,— of premises within the county of Middlesex, and that executed last, was registered first. The party claiming under the second assignment had full knowledge, when it was executed, of the prior execution of the first assignments. Abbott, C. J., said: "A court of law is now called upon for the first time, to put a construction on the words of this statute, by which it is enacted that every deed or conveyance that shall, after the 29th of September, 1709, be made and executed, shall be adjudged fraudulent and void, against any subsequent purchaser or mortgagee for valuable consideration, unless a memorial thereof be registered before the registering of the memorial of the deed or conveyance under which such subsequent purchaser or mortgagee shall claim. Now it is impossible that plainer words could be used; and I think, that, sitting in a

a Equ. Cases Abridged, 29.
b Cheval v. Nicholls, 1 Str. 664. Worsley v. Demattos, 1 Burr. 467. Le Neve v. Le Neve, 3 Atk. 646.
c Bac. Ab. Tit. Stat. 6.
d Knight v. Crockford, 1 Esp. 190. Lavagne v. Stanley, 3 Lev. 1.
e 5 B. & A. 142.

NOTE 33.—A statute shall never have an equitable construction in order to overthrow or divest an estate. Van Horne v. Dorrance, 2 Dallas 316.

court of law, we are bound to give effect to them, and that we cannot say, that this deed is not fraudulent, and void within the meaning of this act, because possibly it may turn out upon examination, that the defendant is entitled to some relief in equity. If there be any such ground, a court of equity may interfere, and this case shows clearly how inconvenient it would be, if this court were to enter into any equitable considerations. For here, it is clear, that the lessor of the plaintiff had, at all events, a lien on the instrument of conveyance. What effect that might have on a court of equity, I cannot say, but I think it, at least, is a fit matter for its consideration. We, however, in a court of law, must give effect to the words of the act."

Bayley, J.—"I think that we are bound, in a court of law, to give effect to the words of the statute. That seems to have been the opinion of the judges in the cases cited, although they thought that a court of equity would, in some cases, interfere to relieve the party. It is so laid down by Lord Hardwicke,a in Le Neve. v. Le Neve, and the words of Lord Mansfield, in Doe v. Routledge, are: —'Equity says, if the party knew of the unregistered deed, his registered deed shall not set it aside, because he has had that notice which the act of parliament intended he should have.' He, therefore, puts it as a case in which equity would interfere; and the circumstances of this case, show the propriety of our adhering to the words of the act; for I am by no means clear, that we should not work great injustice, if we were to decide in favor of the defendant."

This decision is in perfect accordance with the construction put upon the stat. 27 Eliz. c. 4, that voluntary conveyances are void against subsequent purchasers even with notice; and with those decisions at law, the courts of equity have not interfered; while in the case of the registry acts, equity has introduced a construction nearly, if not entirely, subversive of the objects of such latter statutes. In Gooch's case, b Wray, C. J., said: "If A. seised of land in fee, make a fraudulent conveyance, to the intent to deceive and defraud purchasers, against the statute of 27 Eliz. c. 4, and continues in possession, and is reputed as owner, B. enters into discourse with A. for the purchase of it, and by accident B. has notice and knowledge of this fraudulent conveyance, and, notwithstanding, concludes with A. and takes his assurance of him; in this case B. shall avoid the said fraudulent conveyance by the said act, nothwithstanding his notice; for the act has by express words made the fraudulent conveyance void as to a purchaser; and forasmuch as it is within the express purview of the act, it ought to be so taken and expounded in suppression of fraud."

And, according to the opinion of Lord Wray, it was unanimously agreed and resolved by the whole court of common pleas (Pasch.

a Cowp. 712.   b 5 Rep. 60.

3 Jacobi), in evidence to a jury in an *ejectione firmæ*, on a lease made by Standen to Howse plaintiff, against Bullock defendant, that where one Bullock had made a fraudulent conveyance of his land within the said act of 27 Eliz. to A. B. and C. and afterwards notwithstanding offered to sell the said land to Standen, and before assurance thereof made by Bullock, Standen had notice of the said fraudulent conveyance, and notwithsanding proceeded, and took his assurance of Bullock, that Standen should avoid by the same act, the said fraudulent conveyance; for the notice of the purchaser cannot make that good, which an act of parliament has made void as to him. "And true it is, '*quod non decipitur, qui scit se decipi.*' But in that case, the purchaser is not deceived; for the fraudulent conveyance, whereof he has notice, is void as to him, by the said act, and therefore shall not hurt him, nor is he, as to that, in any manner deceived."

Whatever doubts may be entertained of the propriety of extending the words of statutes by equitable construction, to embrace other cases,—conveyances,—times,—places,—persons,—and things, —besides those contained and expressly mentioned in the act, there can be no question that the words of a remedial statute are to be construed largely and beneficially, so as to suppress the mischief and advance the remedy.[34] "It is by no means unusual in construing a remedial statute," says a late case, "to extend the enacting words beyond their natural import and effect, in order to include cases within the same mischiefs." *a*

It is true with us, only of remedial statutes, what Cicero says of all laws: "*eas ex utilitate communi,—non ex scriptione, quæ in literis est, interpretari.*" Premising that this, and the opposite course followed with penal statutes, are only secondary rules, we proceed to illustrate the doctrine that remedial acts are to be liberally construed.

In the Magdalen College case, the question was, whether the queen was bound by the general words of the statute 13 Eliz. c. 10, avoiding "all leases, gifts, grants, feoffment, conveyances, or estates to be made, had, done, or suffered, by any master and fellow of a college to any person, or persons, bodies politic or corporate, other than for the term of twenty-one years, or three lives," &c. The master and fellows had granted certain premises by indenture to the queen, her heirs and successors for ever, with condition that she should, before a specified day, convey and assure the same to B. Spinola, a merchant of Genoa. "It was held that the queen *was* bound by the act. She is a person,—*(rex est persona mixta;)* and a body politic, (the case of the Duchy of Lan-

a 2 Y. & J, 196.

NOTE 34.—Statutes in derogation of the common law can not be extended by construction to embrace cases not fairly within the scope of the language used. Burnside v. Whitney, 21 N. Y. 148; Dwelly v. Dwelly, 46 Maine. 377.

caster.) The act being general, and made to suppress fraud, shall bind the queen, and the queen being included within the words, if she shall be exempt, it ought to be by construction of law ; and as this case is, the law will not make such construction, for reasons apparent in the act itself; *scilicet* the parliament have adjudged 'long leases made by colleges,' to be 'unreasonable,' and the law, which is the perfection of reason, will never expound the words of the act against reason. It was never seen, that an act made for the maintenance of réligion, advancement of learning, and exhibition of poor scholars, (and therefore to be favorably expounded) ; should be so construed, that a bye-way should be left, · by which the said great and dangerous mischief should be left open, and the necessary and profitable remedy be suppressed, and the queen made an instrument of injury and wrong."

Lord Coke adds, "that this act has been always construed beneficially to prevent all inventions and evasions against its true intention : that where the statute says—'masters and fellows of any college,' be the college incorporated by that name, or of 'warden and fellows,' or of 'provost, fellows, and students,' and be the college temporal, for the advancement of liberal arts and sciences, or merely ecclesiastical, or mixt : every ' such college is within the provision of this act, and the construction is the same with all manner of hospitals ; for this act has always had a benign and favorable construction." *a*

Penal statutes receive a strict interpretation. The general words of a penal statute shall be restrained, for the benefit of him against whom the penalty is inflicted. [35]

a 11 Rep. 67.

NOTE 35.—Penal statutes must be strictly construed, and never extended by implication. Andrews v. U. S., 2 Story 203; Strinson v. Pond, 2 Curt. 502; U. S. v. Ten Cases of Shawls, 2 Paine 162; Ferris v. Atwill, 1 Blatch. C. C. R. 151. The proper course is, in their construction, to search out and follow the true intent of the legislature, and to adopt that sense which harmonizes best with the context, and promotes in the fullest manner the apparent policy and objects of the legislature. U. S. v. Winn, 3 Sum. 209; The Enterprise, 1 Paine 32. They must bring the case within the definition of the law, but not so strictly as to exclude a case within its words in their ordinary acceptation. U. S. v. Wilson, Bald. R. 79. Nor so as to defeat the obvious intention of the legislature. American Fur Co. v. U. S., 2 Pet. 366; U. S. v. Willberger, 5 Wheat. 56; U. S. v. Morris, 14 Pet. 464. All its provisions must be taken together, and interpreted according to the import of the words, so as to give effect to its object and intent. The Harriet, 1 Story R. 251. And a further rule is, that an offender who is protected by its letter, cannot be deprived of its benefit on the ground that his case is not within its spirit. U. S. v. Ragsdale, Hemp. R. 497. Where there is such an ambiguity as to leave reasonable doubts of its meaning, the courts will not inflict the penalty. The Enterprise, 1 Paine 32. In such a statute, the word *and* cannot be

It is a maxim of the common law, that "*receditur a placitis juris, potius quam injuriœ et delicta maneant impunita,*" but this applies only to positive maxims, *placita juris* rather than *regulœ juris. a*

If the rule be one of the higher sort of maxims that are *regulœ rationales* and not *positivœ*, then the law will rather endure a particular offence to escape without punishment, than violate such a rule. Of this latter kind *(regulœ rationales)* is the rule that penal statutes shall not be taken by equity. Thus the stat. 1 Ed. 6, c. 12, having enacted that those who were convicted of stealing *horses* should not have the benefit of clergy, the judges conceived that this did not extend to him that should steal but one horse ; and therefore procured a new act for that purpose, in the following year.

Yet penal statutes are taken strictly and literally only in the point of defining and setting down the *crime* and the *punishment;* and not generally "in words that are but circumstances and conveyance in the putting of the case." Thus, upon the statute of Gloucester, that gives the action of waste against him that holds *pro termino vitœ vel annorum*, if a man holds but for a year he is

a Bacon's Maxims, 51.

construed to mean *or.* U. S. v. Ten Cases of Shawls, 2 Paine 162. Penal statutes are also local in their character, and there can be no recovery under them for offences, committed beyond the territorial jurisdiction of the state. 1 Philemore on International law 356; Ludlow v. Van Rensselaer, 1 John. 93; Van Schaick v. Edwards, 2 Caines 363. And in all cases under penal statutes, where there is a question of doubt, the party of whom the penalty is claimed, is entitled to the benefit of the doubt. Chase v. N. Y. Cent. R. R. Co., 26 N. Y. 523.

A statute which imposed a penalty upon any person who knowingly, &c., should aid or assist a tenant in removing goods," &c., it was held, by strict construction, to have contemplated physical aid or assistance, and that merely advising the removal, was not within the provisions of the act, nor was one who concealed a portion of the goods. Strong v. Stebbins, 5 Cow. 211; Palmer v. Conley, 4 Denio 375. So too under the same statute, where two persons concur, in the act of aiding, but one penalty attaches, and they may be sued jointly. Where the offence in its nature is one, the penalty will be held to be one, and several penalties cannot be imposed upon the several offenders. The true inquiry is, under a penal statute, can the single offence created, be committed by several persons. Ingersoll v. Skinner, 1 Denio 540. But if by the terms of the statute imposing a penalty, it provides a several penalty upon each person offending, a penalty may be recovered against each, and in such case, a joint action does not lie. Marsh v. Shute, 1 Denio 230. The better test is: What was the legislative intent? Although in general, offences are several, and each offender liable to a several punishment, yet, if by the terms of the statute the penalty is single, though several persons unite in the act prohibited, but one penalty can be recovered; this is sometimes by way of compensation to the individual injured by the offence. Palmer v. Conley, 2 N. Y. 182, S. C. 4 Denio 375.

within the statute; while if the law be, that for a certain offence a man shall lose his right hand, and the offender hath had his right hand before cut off in the wars, he shall not lose his left hand, but the crime shall rather pass without the punishment which the law assigned, than the letter of the law shall be extended.a

A penal law then, shall not be extended by equity; that is, things which do not come within the words, shall not be brought within it, by construction. The law of England does not allow of constructive offences, or of arbitrary punishments. No man incurs a penalty unless the act which subjects him to it, is clearly both within the spirit and the letter of the statute imposing such penalty. "If these rules are violated," said Best, C. J., in the case of Fletcher v. Lord Sondes, b "the fate of accused persons is decided by the arbitrary discretion of judges, and not by the express authority of the laws."

But, still, the intent is to be regarded; which is a primary rule, and that occasioned it to be said, that "equity knows no difference between penal laws and others." [36] The question is, does a case come within the meaning of the words? Thus, the enactment that made killing a master, treason, was held to include a mistress. c

If the statute 1 Ed. 6, had been, that he, that should steal one horse, should be ousted of his clergy, then there had been no question at all if a man had stolen more horses than one, but that he had been within the statute; for *omne majus continet in se minus. d*

Neither is it true, as it has been sometimes put, that the Court, in the exposition of penal statutes, are to *narrow* the construction. e "We are to look to the words in the first instance," said Buller, J., in R. v. Hodnett, f "and where they are plain, we are to decide on them. If they be doubtful, we have then to have recourse to the subject matter."

In construing penal statutes, we must not, by refining, defeat the obvious intention of the Legislature. Thus, on the Bribery Acts, to satisfy the term "procuring," it is necessary that the vote should be actually given: but as to "corrupting," that is not necessary; the corruption has been held complete, without the vote being given.g

By another restrictive rule of construing penal statutes, if general words follow an enumeration of particular cases, such general

a Bacon's Maxims, 58, 59.
c Hard. 208 ; Plowd. 86.
e Per Buller, J.
g 3 Burr. 1235.

b 3 Bing. 580.
d Bacon's Maxims, 59.
f 1 T. R. 96.

NOTE 36.—The same statute may be regarded as penal in one part or aspect, and demand strict construction, and in another part be remedial, and require a liberal interpretation. Fish v. Fisher, 2 John Cas. 89. Smith v. Moffat, 1 Barb. 65. Millend v. Lake, Ontario R. R. Co., 9 How. R. R. 238. Warner v. Hadner R. R. Co , 5 Barb. 454.

words are held to apply only to cases of the *same kind* as those which are expressly mentioned. By the 14 Geo. 2, c. 1, persons who should steal sheep, or any other cattle, were deprived of the benefit of clergy. The stealing of any cattle, whether commonable, or not commonable, seems to be embraced by these general words, " any other cattle," yet they were looked upon as too loose to create a capital offence. By the 15 Geo. 2, c. 34, the legislature declared that it was doubtful to what sort of cattle the former act extended besides sheep, and enacted and declared that the act was meant to extend to any bull, cow, ox, steer, bullock, heifer, calf and lamb, as well as sheep, and to no other cattle whatsoever. Until the Legislature distinctly specified what cattle were meant to be included, the judges felt that they could not apply the statute to any other cattle but sheep. The legislature by the last act says, that it was not to be extended to horses, pigs, or goats, although all these are cattle. *a* Yet horses are cattle within the Black Act, *b* and bulls are not cattle within 3 Geo. 4, c. 71. *c*

An instance of a statute penal upon particular persons, being taken *stricti juris*, was before mentioned in the statute *de malefactoribus in parcis*, not extending to those offending in forests. *d* So a curate of an augmented curacy (by Queen Anne's bounty) was held not to be liable to the penalties of the 21 Hen. 8, c. 13, for non-residence. *e* "If we had the power of Degislation," said Lord Kenyon in that case, " perhaps we should think it proper to extend the penalties created by the statute of Hen. 8, to all benefices with cure of souls ; but as it is our duty to expound, and not to make acts of parliament, we must not extend a penal law to other cases than those intended by the legislature, even though we think they come within the mischief intended to be remedied. The words of the statute of Hen. 8, are, 'Beneficed with any parsonage,' or 'vicarage ;' but this is neither a parsonage, nor a vicarage. For wise purposes, augmented curacies are made perpetual cures and benefices, by a subsequent statute, 1 Geo. 1, in order that such curates may be perpetual corporations ; but the act does not go on to say that they shall be considered as parsonages or vicarages ; if it had, the former law would have extended to them. These curates are still bound by the canon law to reside on their benefices ; but I do not think that they are liable to the penalties of the statute of Hen. 8, for non-residence."

By the stat. 2 Jas. 1, c. 22, searchers of leather, appointed under that act, are authorized to seize leather *insufficiently dried*, in order to carry it before other officers, called triers. They are liable to an action for seizing that which *is* sufficiently dried, though in their judgment it is not so, and though they are subject to a penalty for allowing leather which is insufficiently dried. The act of parlia-

a 3 Bing. 581.
b 2 W. Bl. 723
c Ex parte Hill, 3 C. & P. 225.

d Pl. Com. 124, a.
e Jenkinson v. Thomas, 4 T. R.

ment only authorizes the searchers to seize goods of a certain denomination; the goods in question in that case were not of that description. a[37]

Tumbling is not an entertainment of the stage disallowed within the words of 10 Geo. 2, c. 28. "This is a penal act of parliament, and we cannot," said Lord Kenyon, "extend it to entertainments that did not exist when the statute was made, though, perhaps, it is desirable that the prohibitions should be extended," &c. b

The stat. 9 Ann. c. 10, s. 40, inflicts a penalty on persons who wilfully open or detain letters after they have been delivered at the post-office. There are words at the end of the clause creating the forfeiture, which show that the legislature intended to restrain the operation of the general words, " no person, or persons," to those employed in the post-office; and it was held accordingly. c

When a good thing and a void thing, are put together in the same grant, the common law makes such a construction that the grant shall be good for that which is good, and void for that which is void. d But according to Hobart, e followed by Wilmot, J., in Collins v. Blantern, f where an instrument is void in part by the statute law, it is void for the whole. "The statute law is like a tyrant; where he comes he makes all void; but the common law is like a nursing father, makes only void that part where the fault is, and preserves the rest." Thus sheriffs' bonds are only autho- rized to be taken with a certain condition, and therefore if they are taken with any other condition, they are void in toto, and can- not stand good in part only. g

But this rule which is one of rigour, does not apply to different and independent covenants in the same instrument, which may be good in part, and bad in part. Thus, in Mowys v. Leake, h where a rector had granted an annuity out of his benefice, which was void by the statute 13 Eliz. c. 20, which says, "that all charg- ings of benefices with any person shall be utterly void," he was yet held liable upon his personal covenant to pay it, contained in the same deed, and Lord Ellenborough afterwards said: i "The case of Mowys and Leake is founded on admirable good sense and sound law: the court there held that it did not affect the personal covenant to pay the rent-charge, but only defeated the security of such rent-charge upon the living."

a Warne v. Varley, 6 T. R. 443.　　c Martin v. Ford, 5 T. R. 101.
b R. v. Handy, 6 T. R. 286.
d Per Hutton, J. Ley's Rep. 79.　　e Hob. Rep. 14.
f 2 Wils. 351.
g Per Lawrence, J., in Kerrison and Cole, 8 East, 231; and see Morgan and Others v. Horseman and Others, 3 Taunt. 241.
h 8 T. R. 411.　　　　　　　　　i Kerrison v. Cole, 8 East, 234.

Note 37.—A statute giving a penalty, implies a prohibition of that act rendered penal, and an act committed against it is consequently void, and amounts to no legal defence. Hallett v. Novion, 14 John. 273; Mitchell v. Smith, 1 Binn. 110.

And the court adopted the same construction in a later case upon the ship registry act, where a bill of sale transferred a ship by way of mortgage, without reciting the certificate of registry. The words of the act 26 Geo. 3, c. 60, s. 17, are, that "the bill, or other instrument of sale, shall be utterly null and void to all intents and purposes,"—if the certificate of registry be not truly recited therein. It was held that the object of the act was sufficiently answered by holding void so much of the instrument as was meant to convey the property in the ship, "that part of it only which operated as a bill of sale;" and that the mortgagor might be sued upon his personal covenant contained in the same instrument for the repayment of the money lent. For, to go further than to hold that the transfer shall be void, and to vacate the collateral covenant for the payment of the money lent, would be going beyond the reason and object of the legislature, in order to work injustice.

The stat. 5 Eliz. c. 4, s. 41, says, all indentures of apprenticeship made otherwise than is by that act directed, shall be "clearly void in law to all intents and purposes whatsoever." In an action for harboring an apprentice, as such, a it was contended that many cases have determined that the objection to the validity of the indentures for want of compliance with the requisites of the act, can only be taken by the parties themselves: upon which Mansfield, C. J., observed : "The words of the 41st section certainly at first startled one. Yet there have been many cases cited, b which say, that indentures which do not conform to the act shall be only voidable, and not void. If the word voidable were applied to adults, it would be extremely strange : with respect to infants, if applied to them, one can understand it. In all those cases the question arose with respect to the rights of infant apprentices ; but there has been no cases cited, where the doctrine that the contract is voidable, not void, is applied to the case of a master ; and it would be very wonderful if there were. But there is a ground, I think, which makes it impossible for the plaintiff to recover in this case, he not having complied with the provisions of this act, and contrary to the express provisions of the 26th section he being neither a householder, nor above the age of twenty-four ; for besides the words making it void to all intents and purposes, it is in the same section further provided, 'that every person that shall from thenceforth take, or newly retain an apprentice, contrary to the tenor and true meaning of that act, shall forfeit and lose for every apprentice so by him taken, the sum of 10l.;' so making it not only void, but unlawful." Hence it appears, that if it be doubtful whether a statute declaring an act, instrument, or

<hr>

a Gye v. Felton, 4 Taunt. 876.

b *Scil.* R. v. St. Nicholas Ipswich, 1 Bott. 525. Winchcourt v. Winchester, Hobb. 166. Barber v. Dennis, 1 Salk. 68. R. v. Evered, 1 Bott. 530.

contract void, make it voidable only, another clause in the same statute imposing a penalty on such act, instrument, or contract, is a clear test that it is *ipso facto* void.

A deed by which an annuity is granted, if it be not registered, will be absolutely void for want of enrolment. The stat. 17 Geo. 3, c. 26, s. 1, declared, that "all deeds whereby annuities are granted shall be null and void to all intents and purposes, unless a proper memorial thereof be registered according to the method prescribed by the act." In the case of Crosby v. Arkwright, *a* Buller, J., said: "In none of the numberless cases which have arisen upon this act, has it ever been doubted but that annuity deeds, not registered conformable to the statute, were void."

Statutes made for the advancement of trade and commerce, and to regulate the conduct of merchants, ought to be perfectly clear and intelligible to persons of their description. By the use of ambiguous clauses in laws of that sort, the legislature would be laying a snare for the subject; and a construction which conveys such an imputation ought never to be adopted. Judges, therefore, where clauses are obscure, will lean against forfeitures, leaving it to the legislature to correct the evil, if there be any. With this view, the ship registry acts, so far as they apply to defeat titles and to create forfeitures, are to be construed strictly, as penal, and not liberally, as remedial laws. *b*

In like manner, in the revenue laws, where clauses inflicting pains and penalties are ambiguously or obscurely worded, the interpretation is ever in favor of the subject; "for this plain reason," said Heath, J., in Hubbard and Johnston, "that the legislature is ever at hand to explain its own meaning, and to express more clearly what has been obscurely expressed." [38]

Whenever a statute gives a forfeiture or penalty against him, who wrongfully detains or dispossesses another of his duty or interest, in that case he that has the wrong shall have the forfeiture or penalty, and shall have an action therefore upon the statute, at the common law; and the king shall not have the forfeiture in that case. And so it was adjudged in the exchequer, upon conference with other judges, in an information for the treble value for not setting out tithes, in Iclington, in the county of Cambridge. *c*

If an act of parliament give a forfeiture for a collateral thing, the king shall have it; but where it is given in lieu of property and

---

a 2 T. R. 605. *b* Hubbard v. Johnston, 3 Taunt. 177.
c Co. Litt. 259 a.

NOTE 38.—Revenue laws which impose forfeitures for fraud, are not to be regarded as technically penal, so as to call for strict construction in favor of a defendant, but remedial, so as to effectuate the intent of the legislature. Cliquot's Champagne, 3 Wall. 115; Taylor v. U. S., 3 How. 197; U. S. v. Probasco, 11 Am: L. Reg. 419; U. S. v. Twenty-eight Casks of Wine, 7 Int. R. Rec. 4. Such laws are for the suppression of a public wrong, and to effect a public good.

interest, it shall go to the person injured. But where it is given for a crime, the king shall have the forfeiture, though he be not named. *a*

The words "shall forfeit," vests only a right or title and not the freehold, in deed, or in law, without an office to find the certainty of the land. *b* Where a statute gives a forfeiture "of all inheritances," it does not extend to an estate tail; but where it is "of all manner of inheritances," estates tail are comprehended. *c*

The stat. 8 Anne, c. 7, s. 17, imposing a penalty of treble the value on the importation of foreign goods prohibited to be imported into this country, extends to all such goods as have been, or may be, prohibited subsequently to that statute; as much as if they had been prohibited at the time of making that statute. *d*

If the penalty given by a statute is to be recovered in a court of record, this can only be recovered in one of the superior courts at Westminster; for being a penal law it ought to be construed strictly, and these are the courts in which the king's attorney general is supposed to attend. *e*

It was held in the case of Partridge v. Naylor, that if an *action* upon a statute giving a penalty, be brought against several defendants, only one penalty can be recovered. But where a conviction of two persons had taken place on a statute giving a forfeiture for deer stealing, and judgment was given that each defendant should pay the forfeiture; the conviction being removed, it was objected that there ought to be but one 30*l.* forfeited, and the last mentioned case was cited; *sed non allocatur*, for the words of the act are that they shall "respectively forfeit 30*l.*" And this penalty is not in the nature of a satisfaction to the party grieved, but a punishment of the offender; and crimes are several, though debts are joint : "which," said Powell, J., "distinguishes this from the case of Partridge v. Naylor." *f* The rule seems to be laid down with great clearness and good sense in the case of R. v. Clark, that where an offence created or made fraud by statute, is in its nature single, one single penalty only can be recovered, though several join in committing it; but if the offence be in its nature several, each offender is separately liable to the penalty. *g*

On the question whether two penalties can be incurred in the same day, the determinations have in like manner properly depended on the nature of the offence. The cases of Marriott v. Show *h* and R. v. Mathews, *i* in which it was held that only one

a Vin. Abr. Tit. Statute: Forfeiture.   *b* Pl. Com. 486.
c Jenk. 287, pl. 21; Hob. 354.   *d* Atty. Gen. v. Saggers, 1 Price 182
e R. v. Hymon, 7 T. R. 536.   Walwyn v. Smith, 1 Salk. 178; Cro. Eliz. 480
Noy. 62.
f The Queen v. King and Another, 1 Salk. 182.
g Cowp. 610.   *h* Com. 274.
i 10 Mod. 26, S. P. Hardman & Whitacre, Bull. N. P. 189.   R. v. Bleasdale, 4 T. R. 809.

penalty could be forfeited in one day, were upon the 5 Ann. c. 14, s. 4, for keeping or using greyhounds for the destruction of game, which was only a continuation of the same act. So in the case of Cripps v. Durden, on the 29 Car. 2, c. 7, for exercising a trade on Sunday, Lord Mansfield said: "There can be but one entire offence on one and the same day." That case was one continued exercising of the trade, one Sunday. But in the case of Brooke *qui tam* v. Milliken, on the 12 Geo. 2, c. 36, for selling books originally written and published here, and afterwards reprinted in another country and imported into this, the court held that where there had been two distinct acts of sale on the same day, this constituted two different offences, for which two penalties were recoverable. *a*

Immediately on filing an information, the right to the penalty vests in the informer, and therefore though the King may pardon the offence, so as to discharge his own share, he cannot deprive the informer of his. *b*

Where a statute (as Westm. 2, cap. 47,) says offenders shall be punished for the first trespass, in a given manner, (there, by burning their nets,) this ought to be by indictment at the suit of the King, and the punishment cannot be inflicted upon the delinquent, before, upon due conviction *secundum legem et consuetudinem Angliæ*, judgment is given. And where there are degrees of punishment inflicted in an increasing *ratio*, for the first, second, and third offences, there must be several convictions and judgments given upon legal proceeding for each offence, and an offender cannot be convicted of the third before he is convicted of the second, or of the second before he is convicted of the first. For though "*ex frequenti delicto augetur pœna*," yet *quod non apparet, non est*, in law; *et non apparet judicialiter, ante judicium. c*

It has been held that statutes that give costs are to be taken strictly, as being a kind of penalty. *d* And the authority of Cone and Bowles was recognized in another case by Lord Hardwicke, C. J., who stated it to be a settled rule that statutes which give costs are to be construed strictly. *e*

Costs are only due by act of Parliament, none being recoverable at common law; and the statute of Gloucester, which gives them, is only applicable to those cases where damages could be recovered before it passed. *f* Thus in sundry actions; in an action of waste against tenant for life or years,—in *quare impedit* (which was considered as a mere matter of spiritual concern,)—and in an action of debt for not setting out tithes (which could not be recovered in the temporal Courts before the reign of Ed. 6,) the party recovers no costs, because he had no right of action

a 3 T. R. 509. *b* Grosset v. Ogilvie (in error,) 5 Bro. P. C. 527.
c 2 Inst. 468, 478. *d* Cone and Bowles, 1 Salk. 205.
e R. v. Inhabitants of Glastonry, Rep. Temp. Hard. 357.
f Pilford's case, 10 Rep. 116; b.

before the statute of Gloucester. Lord Coke indeed, in his second *Institute*, lays down a rule apparently different from that in Pilford's case; for he says, "this clause (in the statute of Gloucester) doth extend to give costs where damages are given to any defendant or plaintiff by any statute made *after* this Parliament." In Witham and Hill, Lord C. J. Willes *a* was strongly inclined to overrule Pilford's case; but would not, though he thought it a very extraordinary one, because he considered the case before him distinguishable from it; and the constant endeavor has been, without contradicting that case, to take other cases out of the rule. The decision in subsequent cases has been said to depend entirely, upon whether the new statute *created* the damages. Wherever a party has sustained damage, and a new act gives another remedy, such a party may recover costs as well as damages. This is laid down by Lord Kenyon, as the correct rule, in Creswell and Hoghton. *b* There it was said, "where an act of Parliament imposes a duty, and any person is prejudiced by its non-performance, the party injured may recover damages and his costs." In the case of penalties, a distinction was taken *c* between those cases where the penalty is given to the party grieved, and those where it is given to a common informer. The Court said the instant the thing was done which occasioned the penalty, it was a debt at common law; and the action upon the statute for the penalty is similar to that upon a bond to recover a debt already due. So, it was established by a variety of cases, that where an action is given to the party grieved, (as in two cases against the hundred,) he is entitled to costs if he succeed, though he had no remedy before the statute of Gloucester, *d* except as by construction, he gets a *debt at common law*, and so damages. Being a duty to the party vested before action brought, he shall have costs; but in *tam quam* or other popular actions where the duty is not vested till the suit brought, and not a debt vested before, he shall not have costs. *e* In the College of Physicians v. Harrison, Lord Tenterden said, "Where a right is vested in a particular person or corporation, the withholding of that right, and thereby compelling the party to sue for it, is an injury for which damages may be recovered: and if damages, then costs will follow." *f* In that case, the defendant having succeeded, was consequently entitled to costs under the stat. 4 Jac. 1, cap. 3. Thus, though the distinction be fine in the case under the subsequent acts, is the doctrine supported and the authorities reconciled.

A justice of the peace, who has prosecuted a gaoler to conviction, for suffering a prisoner to escape, committed by him on a

a 2 Wils. 91.　　　　　　　　*b* 6 T. R. 355.
c In Ward and Snell, 1 H. Bl. 10.
d Grantham v. Theale, 3 Burr. 1723. Jackson v. Colesworth, 1 T. R. 71.
Woodgate and Knatchbull, 2 T. R. 254. Tyte v. Glowden, 7 T. R. 268.
e Per Holt, C. J., Skinner, 363.　　*f* 9 B. & C. 524.

charge of felony, is not entitled to the costs of the conviction under 5 W. and M. c. 11, s. 3, as being "a public officer prosecuting for the benefit of the public." a   Per Buller, J., "The Court has always put a strict construction on this act."

The stat. 7 Geo. 4, c. 74, s. 23, which provides for the allowance of costs to prosecutors and witnesses in certain cases of misdemeanor, does not apply where the indictment has been removed into the King's Bench by *certiorari*. b

Wherever a statute imposes terms, and prescribes a thing to be done within a certain time, the lapse of even a day is fatal, because no court can admit of any terms, but such as directly and precisely satisfy the law. c

In the construction of a penal statute, "near" is not equivalent to "next;" as where the expression "next market town" is used. d

Acts of Parliament which take away the trial by jury, or abridge the liberty of the subject, ought to receive the strictest construction. e

It is a well settled rule of law, that every charge upon the subject must be imposed by clear and unambiguous language. Acts of Parliament which impose a duty upon the public, will be critically construed with reference to the particular language in which they are expressed. When there is any ambiguity found, the construction must be in favour of the public ; because it is a general rule, that where the public are to be charged with a burden, the intention of the Legislature to impose that burden, must be explicitly and distinctly shown. [39] Hence a gift of an estate upon conditions, was held not "a sale" within the meaning of the 48 Geo. 3, c. 149, and that the conveyance was not subject to the *ad valorem* stamp duty. f

As to the Stamp Acts in general, Lord Tenterden observed in Tomkins v. Ashby : "Acts of Parliament imposing duties are so to be construed, as not to make any instrument liable to them, unless manifestly within the intention of the Legislature." g And see the rule laid down by Lord Ellenborough in Warrington v. Turbert. h

So, in the cases of tolls for repairing turnpike roads, where the toll was imposed on "the horses drawing a carriage," but persons

a R. v. Sharpness, 2 T. R. 47.
b R. v. Richards and Others, 8 B. & C. 420.
d 1 W. Bl. 20.
f Denn dem. Manifold v. Diamond, 4 B. &. C. 248.
g 6 B. & C. 541.

c 5 Bro· P. C. 438.

e Looker v. Halcome, 4 Bing. 184.

h 8 East, 242.

NOTE 39.—Upon sound principles of construction, a reference to a *term* used in a statute must be in its direct and primary sense, as expressly defined, and not in an assimilated interpretation, and this is more especially so when the express meaning will accomplish all that was designed by the framers of the law. Cruger v. Cruger, 5 Barb. 267.

repassing with the same, during the same day, were to be toll free; a second toll is payable in respect of a different carriage passing the same day with the same horses; *a* for the word "carriage" is introduced to limit the exemption, and you must otherwise, instead of giving effect to every word in an act of parliament, strike it out of the clause. But where the toll is imposed on the "carriage drawn by so many horses," it makes no difference in the exemption, whether drawn by the same or different horses. *b* And where the words of an exemption clause were, that "every person having paid the said tolls, shall pass and repass with the same horses, cattle, beasts, and carriages, toll free," &c., the court held that the same stage coach repassing with the same coachman, but with different horses and passengers, was not chargeable with the second toll. Bayley, J., said, "As a separate and distinct duty is previously imposed upon horses, upon cattle, upon calves, hogs, sheep, or lambs, which are properly denominated beasts, I think, *reddendo singula singulis,* that the exemption applies to every separate thing on which the toll was previously imposed. The fair construction of the clause is, that the word 'and' is not to be taken conjunctively, but disjunctively or distributively, and then the consequence will be, that if you return with the same horses, drawing the same carriage, you are to pay no toll; if you return with the same horses, mares, mules, or asses, laden or unladen, you are to pay no toll, &c.; and if you return with the same carriage, you are to pay no toll." *c*

In an action for dock dues, Lord Ellenborough said, "If the words will fairly admit of different meanings, it will be right to adopt that which is more favorable to the interest of the public, and against that of the company, because the company, in bargaining with the public, ought to take care to express distinctly what payments they are to receive, and because the public ought not to be charged, unless it be clear that it was so intended." *d*

In the Dock Company at Kingston upon Hull v. Browne, *e* Lord Tenterden said, "These rates are a tax upon the subject, and it is a general rule that a tax shall not be considered to be imposed without a plain declaration of the intent of the legislature to impose it."

In Parker v. The Great Western Railway Company, *f* Tindal, C. J., said: "Acts passed conferring great privileges upon companies, for which they profess to give the public certain advantages in return, should be construed strictly against the parties obtaining them, but liberally in favor of the public."

a Loaring v. Stone, 2 B. & C. 515.   *c* Waterhouse v. Kean, 4 B. & C. 200.
b Williams v. Sangar, 10 East, 66; and Gray v. Shilling, 2 B. & B. 30.
d Gildwit v. Gladstone, 11 East, 675.
e 2 B. & Ad. 58.   And see 1 B. & C. 424; 3 B. & A. 141; 6 Scott, N. R. 823; 2 M. & G. 175.
f L. J. 1844, C. P. 105.

Where, therefore, an act contained a clause authorizing a railway company, *a* to demand a rate not exceeding four-pence per ton per mile on all coals carried along the railway—and a subsequent clause, directed that for all coals shipped for exportation, a rate not exceeding one half-penny per ton per mile should be charged, it was held that the second clause was to be read as an exception ingrafted upon the first; and also that coals shipped for London, were coals shipped for exportation.

A power derogatory to private property, must be construed strictly, and not enlarged by intendment. *b* [40]

Private acts of parliament, conferring new and extraordinary powers of a special nature upon particular persons, affecting the property of individuals, or giving exemption from a general burden attaching by law upon all parties, should receive a strict interpretation. *c* Where particular powers are granted to a company, if they enter upon any man's land, they must clearly shew their authority; and if the words of the statute on which they rely are ambiguous, every presumption is to be made against the company, and in favor of private property. *d*

Where a local act empowered trustees to take and use lands for the purpose of making a road, making or tendering satisfaction to the owners or proprietors of private lands, a court of law would not confine the meaning of these words to the owners of the inheritance only, but considered them to extend to " all persons having any estate or interest in the land." *e*

The 70th and 71st sections of the London and Southampton railway act, provide for the crossing by the railway, of roads not being turnpike roads. By the 72d section, it is enacted that in all cases where the railway shall cross any turnpike road, such turnpike road shall be raised or sunk, by and at the expense of the company; the court of exchequer determined that a road on which toll-gates were by law erected, and tolls taken thereat, was a turnpike road within the meaning of the 72d section. *f*

A railway act provided that it should not be lawful for the railway company to make or establish any *public* station, yard, wharfs,

a Barrett v. The Stockton and Darlington R. C., 2 M. & G. 134; in error, 3 M. & G. 956.

b Lofft, 438.

c Rex v. Croker, Cowp. 26; 4 Mylne & C. 116.

d Scales and Pickering, 4 Bingham, 450; 2 Chit. 610; 2 Chit. 658.

e Lister v. Lobley, 6 Nev. & M. 340.

f Railway Co., 1 Railway Cases, 653.

NOTE 40.—Every statute derogatory of the rights of property, or that takes away the rights of a citizen, is to be strictly construed. Van Horne v. Dorrance, 2 Dall. 316. So also a statute in derogation of the common law. Brown v. Barry, 3 Dall. 367.

If a common law term be used in a statute, without defining it, it is to be understood in the sense of the English common law. McCool v. Smith, 1 Blatch. 459

&c., &c., upon the estate of G. without his consent. On demurrer, it was held that the word "public" did not necessarily override the whole sentences; and that if it did, then that, from the subsequent clauses, every convenience connected with the railway, must be considered as for the public use. a

Again it was held, that where parties under an act of parliament of a private nature seek to burden the property of others by subjecting it to a compulsory power, they must show unambiguous words in the statute. b In the Stourbridge Canal Company v. Wheeler, c Lord Tenterden said : "The canal having been made under the provisions of an act of parliament, the rights of the company are derived entirely from that act. This, like many other cases, is a bargain between a company of adventurers and the public, the terms of which are expressed in the statute ; and the rule of construction in all such cases is now fully understood to be this :—that any ambiguity in the terms of the contract, must operate against the adventurers and in favor of the public." "The powers," says Lord Cottenham in the cases before cited, of the Manchester and Leeds Railway Company, "given to these companies, are so large, and frequently so injurious to the interests of individuals, that I think it is the duty of every court, to keep them most strictly within their powers ; and if there be any reasonable doubt as to the extent of their powers, they must go elsewhere to get enlarged powers." d

In Lee v. Milner, Alderson, B., said : "The stipulations contained in acts of this sort are in the nature of conditions, and the legislature confers those privileges on such companies on the condition that they shall obey the different enactments contained in the different acts with reference to them." e

Private acts are to be regarded and construed as parliamentary contracts. In Blakemore v. The Glamorganshire Canal Company, (the leading case upon this subject,) Lord Eldon said, f "When I look upon these acts of parliament I regard them all in the light of contracts made by the legislature on behalf of every person interested in anything to be done under them. And I have no hesitation in asserting that, unless that principle be applied in construing statutes of that description, they become instruments of greater oppression than anything in the whole system of administration under our constitution. Such acts of parliament have

a Gordon v. The Cheltenham, &c., Railway Co., 5 Beav. 229.
b Webb v. The Manchester and Leeds Railway Co., 4 Mylne & C. 116; 1 Railway Cas. 576.
c 2 B. & A. 792.
d Webb v. The Manchester and Leeds Railway Co., 1 Railway Cas. 576. And see Lord Cottenham's judgment in Kemp v. The Brighton Railway Co., and his observations in Bell v. The Hull and Selby Railway Co., 1 Railway Cas. 495, 637.
e Lee v. Milner 2 Y. & E. 618. Pickford v. Grand Junction Railway Co., 10 M. & W. 400.
f 1 Myl. & R. 162.

now become extremely numerous, and from their number and operation, they so much affect individuals, that I apprehend those who come for them to parliament, do, in effect, undertake that they shall do and submit to, whatever the legislature empowers, and compels them to do, and that they shall do nothing else."

In a case between the same parties in the Exchequer Parke, B., said, "The deliberate opinions of Lord Eldon, Lord Lyndhurst, and Lord Wynford, have established that these acts of parliament constitute a contract or bargain between the public and the company."*a*

The principle so stated, was acted upon in R. v. Cumberworth by Lorn Tenterden and Patteson, J. *b* And in R. v. Edge Lane, Lord Denman said, "The remarks of Lord Eldon, considering his high authority and undoubted caution, have great weight. We also think, that where powers are entrusted by the legislature for an avowed and precise object, the pursuit and performance of that object should be rigidly watched." *c*

An act of parliament brought in on the petition of the corporation of London, is to be considered as a contract between the respective parties, notwithstanding it is (as many other acts of the same kind are) declared to be a public act." *d* "Whether an act is public or private," said Wigram, C., in the late case of Dawson v. Paver, *e* "does not depend upon any technical considerations, (such as having the clause that the act shall be deemed a public act,) but upon the nature and substance of the case." And see the same case as to mere general words in an act of this kind, binding the rights of strangers.

A statute which gives a new remedy, ought not, it is laid down, (but rather questionably, whilst expressed in such general terms,) to receive a liberal construction. What is doubtless meant, is a new remedy—by summary proceedings, or other deviations from our ancient constitution. *f*

A statute creating a new jurisdiction, ought to be construed strictly. *g* And the jurisdiction of the superior courts is not to be ousted but by express words or necessary implication. Tindal, C. J., in delivering his judgment in Crisp v. Banbury, *h* where the words were "that the matter shall be referred to the arbitration of," &c.; fully recognises this proposition.

There are several instances in which statutes giving a summary remedy before justices have been held not to exclude the right of action, but to be cumulative. *i* Yet where an act created penalties of 50*l.* and of 10*l.*, and enacted, that the former should be sued for in any of the courts at Westminster, and provided that

a 1 Cr., M. & R. 141. *b* 3 B. & Ad. 108.
c 4 A. & E. 723. *d* Prichard v. Heywood, 472.
e 5 Hare, 434. *f* Pool v. Neal, 2 Sid. 63.
g 10 Rep. 75 ; Stra. 258. *h* 8 Bingh 394.
j Holt N. P. C. 147, 3 E. & G. 1275.

it should and might be lawful for justices of the peace, &c., to hear and determine the latter, with a power to them to mitigate the penalties; it was held, that such proviso (clearly inserted for the benefit of the prosecuted) ousted the jurisdiction of the superior courts, as to the 10*l.* penalty.*a* In Timms v. Williams, 4 Q. B. R. 422, Lord Denman said, "As in the case of saving banks, so here (in the London Loan Society,) as it appears to me, the legislature has thought it useful to withhold the power of instituting expensive suits in the supreme courts, and to appoint a domestic *forum* to settle those small disputes which a society of this kind is likely to be engaged in."

It is a general rule in the interpretation of acts of parliament, that an enactment, the effect of which is to cut down, abridge, or restrain, any written instrument, shall have a limited construction. The enactment framed for such a purpose should be positive, and the words so clear and express, as to leave no doubt of the intention of the legislature. *b* The cases of Morris v. Mellor, and Bennett v. Daniel, as to the defeazance to a warrant of attorney, have been already noticed pp. 601, 602.

Statutes against frauds are a satisfactory exception to the rule, that penal statutes are to be taken strictly. There is no contradiction, except in terms, in holding, that where the offence is to be punished by setting aside a fraudulent transaction, or an instrument improperly obtained, the fullest effect shall be given to the provision framed to suppress the mischief,—whilst, where the offender is in danger of life or liberty, he must be brought strictly within the letter of the law. Statutes, therefore, against frauds, are always liberally and beneficially expounded. "Chancery will aid remedial laws," said Lord Keeper Wright, *c* though they are called penal; not by making them more penal, but *by letting them have their course.*" The statute of Marlbridge is a penal law, but yet, because it is of a beneficial nature, and for the public good comprehensively considered,—though the word in the act be "*faciant,*" it is extended to waste *omittendo,*—though the former term literally imports active waste.*d*

Though it is said, as has been lately shown, that where acts of parliament making a thing void, "it shall be void to all intents, and have a very violent relation;" *e* and though the stat. of 13 Eliz. c. 10, makes void certain leases by bishops "to all intents and purposes," yet such a lease is not void against the lessor himself. For, such rent reserved shall be good by the way of contract between the lessor and lessee, but is not incident to the reversion, and the lease is voidable by the successor.

---

a Oates v. Knight, 3 T. R. 442; 4 T. R. 100; 6 T. R. 242.
b Morris v. Mellor, 6 B. & C. 446; Bennett v. Daniel, 10 B. & C. 504.
c Ch. Prac. 215.
d 10 Mod. 282.
e 2 Jo. 19, citing 3 Hen. 7, 15; *et al.* Vin. Abr. tit. Stat. 139.

It was said by Horton, as early as 11 Hen. 4, that "a statute penal, as the statute of provisions, shall be taken *stricti juris;* but a statute made for common remedy for general mischief, may be taken by equity." *a* Thus the Riot Act and the Black Acts highly penal as are their provisions generally, are treated as re-medial acts in proceedings taken against the hundred.

Conformably to this doctrine, it is by no means unusual, in con-struing a semi-remedial statute (acting upon the offence and avoid-ing the transaction,) to extend the enacting words beyond their natural import and effect, in order to include other cases within the same mischief, and also within the apparent intention of the legislature. Thus, it was held, that the recitals in the disabling statute, 13 Eliz. c. 10, do not limit the force of the subsequent enactment to cases in which the mischief by the alienation is done to the personal interests of the successor of the alienor; for it is evident from the enactment, that the legislature intended to apply the prohibition to the case of persons who were seised either as mere trustees, or in a great measure as trustees, and among other persons, to the master or guardian of an hospital. *b* Indeed, it is largely held, that in the case of a remedial statute, "everything is to be done in advancement of the remedy that can be given, consistently with any construction that can be put upon it." *c*

But these last-mentioned terms are too general to convey any precise instruction. It will be more profitable, as resting upon more specified grounds, to examine carefully the deliberate opin-ions of deeply learned judges, upon an act framed with a partic-ular view to suppress frauds, (the 13 Eliz, c. 5,) and therefore an act, according to the rule under consideration, to be liberally and beneficially construed, to promote that end. It was held in the construction of this statute, that "the purchaser who shall avoid a precedent covenant made by fraud and covin, must be a pur-chaser for money or other valuable consideration; for, although it is said in the preamble, 'for money or other *good* consideration,' and likewise in the body of the act, 'or other *good* consideration,' yet these words are only to be intended of valuable consideration; and that appears by the clause which concerns those who had powers of revocation; for there it is said, 'for money or other good consideration paid or given,' and this word 'paid' is to be referred (*reddendo singula singulis*) to 'money,' and 'given' is to be referred to good consideration; so, the sense is,—for money paid, or other good consideration given, which words exclude all consid-erations of nature or blood, or the like. And this latter clause doth well expound these words mentioned before; for if consid-

---

a Br. Parl. pl. 13 ; citing 11 Hen. 4, 76.

b St. Peter's, York, Dean and Ch. v. Middeborough, 2 Y. & J. 196.

c Johnes v. Johnes, 3 Dow. 15. S. P. Acheson and Everitt, Cowp. 391.

eration of nature or blood should be good consideration within the proviso, the statute would serve for little or nothing, and no creditor would be sure of his debt."

So, "where one indicted for recusancy, and having the intent to flee beyond sea, made a gift, &c.," it was held within this act; "the words to defraud creditors and others of their" (inter alia) "forfeitures," extending to those "who had cause of action or suit," or "where anything shall by law be forfeit to the king or subject."

Again, in an obligation void by 5 Edw. 6, c. 16, was a lawful covenant for repayment of money in a certain case: held, that "if the addition of a lawful covenant should make the obligation of force, even as to that,—the statute would serve for little or no purpose;" for this cause it was adjudged that the obligation was utterly void. a

It should seem that a statute for the discharge of insolvent debtors ought to be construed strictly, quoad the cessio bonorum and the rights of creditors, because it gives away the property of the subject. "Let a statute be ever so charitable," said Holt, C. J., "If it give away the property of the subject, it ought to be construed strictly." b

It has been already stated, that a statute may be penal in one part, and remedial in another part. c There is no impropriety, it remains to be observed, in putting a strict construction on a penal clause, and a liberal construction on a remedial clause, in the same act of parliament. This has been done on the statutes which make it a felony to burn houses and other property, and give those who suffer from the felony, a remedy against the hundred. So, the 23d section of the stat. 11 Geo. 2, c. 19, authorizing the sheriff to grant replevins on taking bonds, in every replevin of a distress for rent, is remedial, and shall be construed liberally, though the 22d section is penal, and has been construed strictly. d

Statutes, though penal, have been "taken by intendment," to the end that they should not be illusory, but should take effect according to the express intention of the makers of the act. Thus, by the stat. 25 Edw. 3, the killing of a master is made treason, and it extends by construction as has been shown, to the mistress. e The stat. 3 Hen. 7, c. 1, is, that the wife or heir of him so slain, shall have the appeal; the heir of a woman who was murdered shall have the appeal; for apices juris non sunt jura. f

The letter of the law has now been largely treated, and its spirit copiously discussed, further it is indispensably necessary in the construction of statutes, to have regard to their provisions; to see of what they treat; the quid as well as the quo modo. For a

a Twyne's case, 3 Rep. 83.
c Dougl. 702.
e Poulter's case, 11 Rep. 34.

b 12 Mod. 513.
d Short v. Hubbard, 2 Bing. 355.
f 4 Rep. 4.

statute which treats of things or persons of an inferior rank cannot, by any gener l words, be extended to those of a superior. Thus, an old statute treating of " abbots, priors, hospitallers, &c.,"*a* and a later act speaking of "deans, prebendaries, parsons, vicars, and others having spiritual promotion," have been respectively held not to extend to bishops;—abbots and deans being the highest persons named, and bishops being of a still higher order. *b* So where, in 2 Westm. cap. 47, "for the protection of the salmon fishery in the Humber, Ouse, Trent, &c.," *Thamesis*—" *nobile illud flumen*" is not named ; though there be the general words " *et omnes aliæ aquæ in regno in quibus salmones capiuntur;*"—the Thames, therefore, is added by another act,—and in the first place. *c*

Yet, where in the *articuli cleri*, it was complained, (cap. ix.) " that the king's officers did some time take the *parson's* beasts in the king's highway ;" and the words were *animalia rectorum*, this law extended to abbots, priors, and the like. But this is not inconsistent with the received and familiar doctrine ; for the words *personæ ecclesiasticæ* afterwards occurring in the act, "parsons" were considered as being here named, for example.

But in the stat. of Marlbridge, cap. 19, a provision is made "touching essoigns in counties, hundreds, or in courts baron, or in other courts ;" and here, "although the act beginneth with inferior courts, contrary to rules, (as is known by common experience,) the general words *vel in aliis curiis* are interpreted to extend to the king's courts of record at Westminster, and other courts of record. And the cause is, for that otherwise, these general words should be void ; for it cannot, according to the general rule, extend to inferior courts, for none be more inferior or lower than these that be particularly named ; and so note a just exception out of the general rule." *d*

It is only repeated here, on account of its relation to the maxim under discussion, that where general words follow particular ones, the rule is to construe them as applicable to persons *ejusdem generis.* "Considering then," says Lord Tenterden, " in Sandiman v. Breach, *e* that in the 3 Car. 1, c. 1, (passed to prevent traveling on the Lord's day,) carriers of a certain description are mentioned, and that in the 29 Car. 2, c. 7, drovers, horse-coursers, waggoners and travelers of certain descriptions are specifically mentioned, we think that the words ' other person or persons,' cannot have been used in a sense large enough to include the owner and driver of a stage coach."

Such are the principal rules relating to the construction of statutes ; a few others may perhaps remain unnoticed, of minor

a Westm. 2, cap. 41.   *b* 2 Rep. 46.
c 2 Inst. 478.   *e* 7 B. & C. 100.
d 2 Inst. 136.

importance.* It is doubtless very desirable that statutes should be framed in such clear and precise terms, as to secure them from all ambiguity, and from all doubts and criticism as to their meaning. But it is to be feared, that, from the habits of legislators and the imperfections of language, such an event is quite hopeless, and the attempt impracticable. It is, unquestionably, often owing to the want of technical skill in the makers of the law, that statutes give rise to such distressing doubts, from the ambiguity that attends them. Great experience and learning are, however, it ought to be remembered, no less requisite for the interpretation, than for the preparation of laws. "It would be quite visionary," says the sensible and candid commentator on the laws of the United States of America, "to expect in any code of statute law, such precision of thought and perspicuity of language, as to preclude all uncertainty as to the meaning, and exempt the community from the evils of vexatious doubts and litigious interpretations. Various and discordant readings, glosses and commentaries, will inevitably arise in the progress of time, and perhaps as often from the want of skill and talent in those who comment, as in those who make the laws." *a*

a Kent's Comm. Vol, 1, 450.

* As that entries make good interpreters: "judicial precedents, and the right entries of pleas are good interpretations of statutes." *Dictum* per Lord Coke, 2 Inst. 380.

CHAPTER VIII.

PARTICULAR RULES OF CONSTRUCTION APPLICABLE TO DISTINCT
PARTS OF STATUTES: TITLE, PREAMBLE, CLAUSES, PROVISOS:
JUDICIAL OR AUTHORITATIVE EXPOSITION OF THE MEANING OF
PARTICULAR WORDS OR PASSAGES TO BE FOUND IN ACTS OF
PARLIAMENT.

THE comprehensive manner in which the several subjects of the
classification of statutes; the analysis of statutes and the rules
for their construction, have been treated in the preceding chapters, has necessarily anticipated much of what occurred to be said
on the subject of the particular rules of interpretation applicable
to distinct parts of acts of parliament. Examples may yet be
afforded of the degree of influence which the title or preamble
ought to exercise over the enacting clause, or one clause over another clause, or general words over special provisions in an act:
but as regards either leading principles or established maxims,
little curious or useful remains to be added. It is proposed, however, to proceed to a succinct statement, or brief recapitulation,
of the rules of exposition affecting the constituent parts of acts
of parliament.

The style and title, it will be remembered, is no parcel of the
act; but the object of an act is often avowed in the title, as well
as in the preamble. Yet though the title of an act may occasionally shed light on the former law and the contemplated changes,
it is really in itself, without legislative import.

The preamble states, with more or less accuracy, the object of
a law and the occasion of its making. Its first legitimate and unquestioned use, is to ascertain, what the cases are, to which the
act was intended to apply. It has never been disputed, that the
preamble to an act, may be properly used, to ascertain and fix the
subject-matter to which the enacting part is to be applied. a [1]

It is, at the same time, incontrovertible, that, if the enacting
words can be shown to go beyond the preamble, (and that they
may be justifiably carried beyond the preamble, there is no man-

a Fellowes v. Clay, 4 Q. B. R. 339. Salked v. Johnson, 1 Hare 196, and the
numerous cases there cited.

NOTE 1.—The reason why a preamble may be referred to, to determine the reason
and intent of the legislature when the language is ambiguous, is, that it states
the reasons and objects of the law. U. S. v. Webster, Davies 38. If the reasons
appear in any other equally solemn document it may also be resorted to. id.

34

ner of doubt; if the words be seen to embrace any other case within the mischief sought to be remedied,) effect must be given to such larger words. And a contrary construction is declared to be unfounded, mischievous and dangerous. *a*

The doctrine received with the greatest difficulty, and which occasioned the strongest controversy in Westminster Hall, is, the the proposition, that the preamble, may be sometimes used, to control and cut down the enacting part. This use of the preamble to an act of parliament, to restrain the operation of its enacting clauses in their application to cases within the act, formerly led to much difference of opinion, and is approached with great caution by modern judges. Lord Tenterden, in the case of Halton v. Cave warily pronounced the legal doctrine upon this subject in the following terms:—"The enacting words of an act of parliament, are not always to be limited by the words of the preamble, but must, in many instances go beyond it. Yet the words in the enacting part, must be confined to that, which is the plain object and general intention of the legislature in passing the act; and the preamble affords a good clue to discover what that object was." *b*

Perhaps, in the history of American jurisprudence and of American fundamental law, there is no single paragraph that possesses more profound significance, in the expression of the object and intent of the instrument, and of its framers, than that of the preamble to the federal-constitution. The highest judicial authority ever accords to it a significance becoming an instrument which was laying the deep foundations of a national government for American empire which should rest on the solid basis of the will of an intelligent and a free people; the highest original source of all legitimate earthly authority.

This preamble expresses the whole spirit of the instrument; and while it is never resorted to to enlarge the powers confided to the general government, or to any of its departments; and though it confers no power, *per se*, it has ever been referred to, and has been used for the purpose, as its true office would seem to be, to expound and express the nature, extent, and application of the powers conferred in the constitution itself.

Its whole history assures us, that this preamble was not adopted as a mere formulary; but as the most solemn promulgation of fundamental facts, vital to the character and future operations of

a Per Lord Denman, *ante*, p. 505, and per Lord Ellenborough in R. v. Marks, 504.
b 1 B. & A. 538.

a government of a great people. The design of the establishment of this constitution, is concisely and beautifully, but briefly expressed; and it comprehends six distinct objects. 1st, To form a more perfect union; 2d, To establish justice; 3d, To ensure domestic tranquility; 4th, To provide for the common defence; 5th, To promote the general welfare; 6th, To secure the blessings of liberty to themselves and their posterity. Here is found condensed, the reasons which have ever had their influence upon reflecting judicial minds in giving construction to this great fundamental law, the sheet anchor of our political hopes.

1. The first proposition to be advanced is, that the preamble cannot extend the enacting clause. In support of this doctrine, the case of Wilson v. Knabley may be cited. *a* In that case, Lord Ellenborough said, "I agree that the grievances recited in the preamble of the act, would have led one to suppose that the legislature meant to have given a larger remedy than the action of debt, against the devisee of land, to recover damages for a breach of covenant by the devisor. But for us to extend the words to the action of covenant, would be to legislate, and not to construe the acts of the legislature." Yet in a late case, the preamble was called in aid to give a meaning to a doubtful clause; where the particular writ (Elegit,) was not expressly named in the enacting clause. *b*

2. The preamble cannot restrain the enacting clauses, except where the words are ambiguous; or are not sufficiently large to embrace the case; or are so large, that convenience and the policy of the law, clearly require, that their generality shall be restrained. *c*

Lord Coke commends such construction of an act, as makes the purview agree with the preamble; but not such, it is said in the case of the King v. Althoes, *d* as may limit and confine the enacting part to the preamble.

It has, it should seem, been sometimes too broadly laid down, that the generality of the enacting clause *shall be* restrained and qualified by the preamble. In Copeman and Gallant, *e* it was said by Lord Cowper, that he could by no means adopt the notion that a preamble shall restrain the operation of an enacting clause; and he added, that if the preamble of the Coventry act had only recited the barbarity of slitting Coventry's nose, and the enacting clause had been general against the doing of anything whereby a man is disfigured or defaced, it might, agreeably to that notion, have been said, that cutting off the lip, or putting out an eye,

a 7 East, 128.   *b* Nash v. Allen, 4 Q. B. R. 784.
c Crespigny v. Wittenoon, 4 T. R. 193, and see *ante*, p. 508.
d 8 Mod. 144.   *e* 1 P. Wms. 320.

would hot have been within the meaning of this statute; because neither of these is mentioned in the preamble. In Ryall v. Rowles, a Parker, Ch. Baron, said: "It is laid down in 1 Jo. 163, and Palmer 485, upon the construction of the stat. 13 Eliz. that the preamble shall not restrain the enacting clause. But I take it to be agreed, that if the not restraining the generality of the enacting clause will be attended with an inconveniency, the preamble *shall* restrain it. In Copeman and Gallant, I must own that Lord Chancellor Cowper exploded the notion of the preamble's governing the enacting clause, and went upon another reason. I have great honor for Lord Cowper; but though I approve of the decree, I cannot subscribe to the reasons of it."

The opinion of Lord Cowper with respect to the operation of the preamble was equally disapproved of by Lord Hardwicke. In the same case of Ryall and Rowles, b the later chancellor said: "I shall not scruple to declare that I am strongly inclined to be of opinion with Lord Holt and my lord chief baron, that this clause is to be restrained by the preamble; and differ from Lord Cowper in the case of Copeman and Gallant."

The general purview of a statute is not, however, necessarily to be restrained by any words introductory to the enacting clauses. Larger and stronger words in the enactment part of a statute may extend it beyond the preamble. c If the enacting words are plain, and sufficiently comprehensive to embrace the mischief intended to be prevented, they shall extend to it, though the preamble does not warrant the construction.d In the case of R. v. St. Peter and St. Paul, in Bath, it was contended that the construction of the certificate act was to be restrained by the preamble. Lord Mansfield said: " Whatever might be the leading motive in passing that act, that statute authorizes the whole body of the poor, of whatever denomination, and with whatever object to leave their own, and to remove into any other parish; provided they can obtain the protection of a certificate. Contrary to the spirit and policy of the act, and not obliged by the letter, the court will not make an exception of a case which the act has not itself excepted." e

In R. v. Pierce, f Lord Ellenborough said: "It cannot by any means be regarded, as an universal rule that large and comprehensive words in the enacting clause of a statute are to be restrained by the preamble. In a vast number of acts of parliament, although a particular mischief is recited in the preamble, yet the legislative provisions extend far beyond the mischief recited. And whether the words shall be restrained or not, must depend on a fair exposition of the particular statute in each particular case, and not upon any universal rule of construction." In Freeman v.

---

a 1 Atk. 174.

c Cowp. 543. R. v. Marks, 3 East, 160.

e 1 Bott. 443.

b Id. 182.

d 3 Atk. 203.

f 3 M. & S. 66.

Lambert, a the same powerful chief justice said: "I confess, I am not for restraining the generality of the enacting clause by the preamble, without some reason for it." And Dampier, J., said: "I have always understood it as a standing rule in the construction of acts of parliament; that the enacting clause shall not be restrained by the preamble, if the enacting words are large enough to comprehend the case." In a late case of Hughes v. Done, b Lord Denman said: "To introduce, in the enacting part, an exception not there to be found, and which, if intended might have been so easily introduced and expressed, is we think to curtail and abridge the meaning of plain words in a manner which no rule of construction warrants."

But though the preamble cannot control the enacting part of a statute, which is expressed in clear and unambiguous terms, yet, if any doubt arise on the words of the enacting part, the preamble may be resorted to, to explain it. In truth, it then resolves itself into a question of intention; or in other words, recourse is had to the primary rules of interpretation. For the words being doubtful, the preamble is compared with the rest of the act, in order to collect the intention of the legislature, whether they meant it to extend to a case like that under consideration. The preamble of the stat. 22 Geo. 2, c. 44, which was confined to mariners and soldiers, recited that mariners and soldiers of different trades, and apprentices who had not served their times, were prohibited from setting up their trades in corporate towns, &c., either by reason of by-laws therein made or of the 5th Eliz. c. 4. To remedy this inconvenience it was enacted, that all such mariners and soldiers might set up their trades, in any town, notwithstanding these disabilities. The stat. 26 Geo. 3, c. 107, referring expressly to the former statute, says, that every person having served in the militia, may set up a trade "as freely and with the same provisions," &c. It was held clear on the meaning of the acts, which were made *in pari materie*, and *referring to the titles and preambles to discover the occasion and object* of making the laws, that they related to persons exercising trades, and not to common laborers, or husbandmen. c

The preamble of the annuity act recites "the pernicious practice of *raising money* by the sale of life annuities:" an annuity granted in consideration of the grantee's giving up his business to the grantor, was held not within the spirit or object of the act, which was intended as a check against hard bargains; the preamble stating as the occasion of the act, the mischiefs of granting annuities for small consideration by improvident persons. d

In Salkeld v. Johnson, e Wigram, V. C., said: "Courts of law have held that the mere subject-matter without any preamble, may safely be relied upon for restraining the operation of general

a 4 M. & S. 238.   b 1 Q. B. R. 301.
c R. v. Gwenop, 3 T. R. 135.   d Crespigny v. Wittenoon, 4 T. R. 791.
e 1 Hare, 196.

words. The stock-jobbing acts in terms are general, and would apply to transactions in foreign stock : a verbal construction which the courts have rejected, in favor of the obvious intention of the legislature to apply them only to British stocks." Henderson v. Bisc; *a* Wells v. Porter ; *b* Elsworth v. Cole. *c*

Clauses will sometimes be governed by provisions in another section of the act. A company were incorporated by statute and empowered to make a railway through certain districts. By sect. 5 of the act, they were directed to leave sufficient space for the public to pass, or to form new roads in lieu of any existing ones that might be injured by their railway. Section 70 empowered proprietors of lands, mines, &c., to make railways through their own lands and those of other persons consenting, and across and along any road or roads to communicate with the principal railway; and no reference was made to any former limitation of powers. It was nevertheless determined that the power in this clause was not absolutely given, but must be subject to the provisions of section 5, as to the condition of leaving space enough, independent of the railways, for the public to pass. *d*

A railway act empowered the company to make and maintain their railway over certain lands to a specified point. Section 4 enacted, that nothing in that statute should authorize the company to enter upon, take or damage any lands without the consent of the owner and occupier. Sections 16 and 17 empowered the company to contract with landowners for the purchase of land, and for grants of way-leave. Section 18 contained a clause of arbitration in case any person willing to grant or demise such way-leave, should not agree with the company as to terms. Section 43 enacted, that "in every case in which the said railway shall cross any other railway, the communication between them shall, if the company and the owners of such other railway do not agree about the same, be made in such manner as shall be directed by two engineers acting as arbitrators, and that the company shall make satisfaction (to be ascertained in the manner before pointed out) for temporary, permanent, or recurring injury, to be occasioned by such crossing." No regulation was made as to the manner in which, and times when, carriages on the first-mentioned railway should cross the other. The Court held that section 43 did not clearly introduce a compulsory power in the case where a railway was to be crossed, and, therefore. that the provision of section 4 must be taken to govern this clause, and make consent necessary. Although it should be impossible without so crossing, to carry the first-mentioned railway to the point specified in the act. *e*

a 3 Starkie, 158.   *b* 3 Bingh. N. C. 722.

c 2 M. & W. 31.   *d* Rex v. Morris, 1 B. & A. 441.

  e The Clarence Railway Co. v. The Great North of England Junction Railway Company, 4 Q. B. R. 46.

A local act provided (in sect. 159), that if the company formed under that act, wilfully entered upon and took possession of lands without consent and without having made a required payment or deposit, they should be liable to certain specified penalties : proviso, that the company should not be liable to the penalties, if they should *bona fide* and without collusion, have paid or deposited the compensation ; though not to the true owner. Held, by the court of exchequer, that the word "wilfully" does not override the whole of the 159th section ; but applies only to the first part of it. Held further, that the section did not apply in that case, the case not being within the mischief the legislature intended to guard against. That a penal section should be strictly construed : while a proviso which has the effect of saving parties from penal enactments, should be liberally construed.

"We are all of opinion," said Pollock, C. B., "that the section cannot be read precisely as it stands. We must give it some sensible construction ;" (it could not be read grammatically :) We ought so to read the 159th section as to bring the company in this instance within the protection of the proviso at the end of the section. *a*

"Upon all acts of parliament such construction should be made, as that one clause shall not frustate and destroy, but, on the contrary, shall explain and support, another." *b* In the case before cited, on the annuity act, *c* clauses and sections in one part of the act were made to illustrate obscure passages in another part. Thus the *third* and *fourth* clauses of the annuity act, 17 Geo. 3, c. 26 (requiring the consideration to be paid in money, or if paid in notes, and those notes afterwards not paid, empowering the court to order the annuity deeds to be cancelled,) were referred to by two of the judges, as showing the considerations contemplated by the act ; as was, with a like object, the *seventh* section, which prohibits brokers taking more than ten shillings for every 100*l.* actually paid ; while another judge held it apparent from the *whole* act, that it did not extend to a case like the one then before the court. "In cases," he said, "where money has been paid as the considerations, the courts order the money to be restored when they vacate the annuity deeds ; but the business, the relinquishment of which was the consideration of this annuity, we cannot order to be restored." In the case of R. v. Cartwright, *d* where the question was, whether a provision in an act were general, or related only to assaults on revenue officers, *qua* officers : Buller, J., said, the intention might be collected from other parts of the act. "It is fair to infer that the legislature meant to extend the indemnity in the first section to all those cases in which, by the subsequent clause

a Hutchinson v. The Manchester, Bury, and Rosseldale Railway Company, Easter Term, 1846.
b Hard. 344, pl. 1.   *c* Crespigney v. Wittenoom, 4 T. R. 791.
d 4 T. R. 490.

they gave the right of changing the venue." In this instance, and in many others, prior clauses are restrained by subsequent clauses in a statute.

But where a clause, which is separate and substantive, itself creates an offence, the court, it has been seen, may give judgment for that offence, as a misdemeanor, notwithstanding there be another section in the same statute, giving a specific punishment. *a*

In construing doubtful clauses in an act of parliament, it will often be a question whether a clause be a substantive independent clause, or only a qualification of an antecedent clause. Where a section is by way of proviso, it can only be considered as a clause dependent on a former clause, unless the manifest intention of the legislature require a different construction. ²

Upon obscure acts of parliament, or where the sections are numerous, involved, and intricate, it may be useful to begin the work of interpretation, by an endeavor to trace the method which the drawer of the act has observed in the distribution and arrangement of his subject.

A saving must be of a thing *in esse;* the nature of a saving is to preserve a former right, and not to give or create a new one. A saving, it has been seen, may restrain and qualify the purview, but was never allowed to overturn it. *b*

The effect of an exception introduced in the enacting clause, contradistinguished from the case where the exception is found in a subsequent clause, *c* viz: that every exception contained in the clause creating an offense must be negatived, but where the exception is introduced in a subsequent clause, it must come by way of defense on the part of the defendant, has been already noticed.

General words, it is established, may be qualified by subsequent clauses in the same statute ; but " a thing given in particular, shall not be tolled by general words." *d* ³ This is expressed in the un-

a R. v. Harris, 4 T. R. 202.   *b* 2 Inst. 32; Dav. 3, b. 4, in case of proxies.
c Rex. v. Jukes, 8 T. R. 542.
d Per Hutton, J., in Standon v. Univ. Oxon. Jo. 26.

NOTE 2.—The general system of legislation upon the subject-matter of a statute may be taken into view in order to aid the construction of a particular statute relating to the same subject. Fort v. Bench, 6 Barb. 74.

NOTE 3.—A statute applicable in terms to *particular* actions, cannot be applied by construction to other actions standing on the same reason. Jacob v. U. S., 1 Brock. 520.

If general words in a statute follow an enumeration of particular cases, they are held to apply only to cases of a like kind with those enumerated. U. S. v. Irvin, 5 McLean, 178.

But where *technical words* occur in a statute, they are to be taken in a technical sense, unless it appears that they were intended to be applied differently from their ordinary or legal acceptation. 1 Kent. Com. 462, Clark v. City of Utica, 18 Barb. 451. Thus, where a statute directed that a coroner should serve process

south maxim—*generalis clausula non porrigitur ad ea, quæ speciali-
ter sunt comprehensa. a* Not that this sentence is a whit more
barbarous in its language than many that have preceded it, of the
gems with which the text of this work has been studded and en-
riched. But unfortunately, as regards the effect of contrast, the
notion is adopted from the civilians; it being a maxim of the
Digest that, "*in toto jure, generi per speciem derogatur; et illud po-
tissimum habetur, quod ad speciem directum est.*" The meaning of
which is, that when the law descends to particulars, such more
special provisions must be understood as exceptions to any general rules laid down to the contrary ; and the general rules must
not *(vice versa)* be alleged in confutation of the special provisions. *b*
Conformably to this doctrine, it has been recently decided, as was
before shown, *c* that where a general intention is expressed in a
statute, and the act also expresses a particular intention, incompatible with the general intention, the particular intention is to be
considered in the nature of an exception. *d*

a 8 Rep. 118 *b.*   *b* Woodison's Elem. of Juris. 36.
c P. 514.   *d* Churchill v. Crease, 5 Bing. 180; ib. 492-3.

where the sheriff was *a party*, it was held that it must be technically a party ; that
being interested in the suit was not sufficient. Merchants Bank v. Cook, 4 Pick.
411. So in regard to the statute in regard to flowing lands, which declared that
the judgment should be *final,* it was held that these words were to be taken in a
technical sense. Snell v. Bridgewater, &c., Co., 24 Pick. 300. In regard to the
word *robbery* used in an act of congress, it was held that robbery was a technical
term, which was known, and its meaning fully ascertained by the common law, or
civil law, from the one or the other of which, it had been borrowed, and that it was
necessary to refer to those sources for its precise meaning. United States v.
Jones, 3 Wash. C. C. R. 209. The word *supercede*, was used in the militia act of
Massachusetts. The court said, the only way to ascertain the sense of the legislature in using the word, is to learn the military sense in which the word is commonly used; for in the enactment of laws, the terms of art or peculiar phrases are
made use of, it must be supposed that the legislature have in view the subject-
matter about which such terms or phrases are commonly employed. Ex parte
Hall, 1 Pick. 262.

Certain other words, used in statutes, have their meaning declared by the
statute in this state as for example under the general provisions concerning
crimes and their punishment. 2 Rev. Stat. 696, 7.

§ 30. The term "felony," when used in this act, or in any other statute, shall
be construed to mean an offence for which the offender, on conviction, shall be
liable by law to be punished by death, or by imprisonment in a state prison.

§ 31. Whenever the term "infamous crime," is used in any statute, it shall be
construed as including every offence punishable with death or by imprisonment
in a state prison, and no other.

§ 32. The terms "crime" or "offence," when used in this chapter, or in any
other statute, shall be construed to mean any offence for which any criminal punishment may by law be inflicted.

§ 33. The term "personal property," as used in this chapter, shall be construed to mean, goods, chattels, effects, evidences of rights in action, and all

Words and phrases, the meaning of which in a statute has been ascertained, are, when used in a subsequent statute, to be understood in the same sense. *a* ⁴ The legal effect of particular expressions (words or sentences), will therefore be considered with reference to—1st, the courts or judicatures designated by them; 2dly, the proceedings which may be had before those authorities; 3dly, the offences thereby either described or constituted; and 4thly, the punishments they direct, or allow, to be inflicted.

Where a statute directs a penalty to be recovered by action, bill, plaint, or information, in *any court of record*, the courts intended by the statute, *propter excellentiam*, are the four courts of record at Westminster. "As," says Lord Coke, *b* "if it be spoken of proof *(trial)* generally, although there are many proofs in law, yet it shall be intended of the best proof, and that is by jury; if it be spoken of the feast of St. Michael, where there are two feasts, it shall be intended of the most worthy and notorious feast. If

---

a Bac. Ab. tit. Statute I.   *b* Gregory's case, 6 Rep. 20.

written instruments by which any pecuniary obligation, or any right or title to property real or personal, shall be created, acknowledged, transferred, increased, defeated, discharged or diminished.

§ 34. The term "property," as used in this chapter, includes personal property as defined in the last section, and also every estate, interest and right in lands, tenements and hereditaments.

§ 35. Where the term "person" is used in this chapter, to designate the party whose property may be the subject of any offence, such term shall be construed to include the United States, this state, or any other state, government or country which may lawfully own any property within this state, and all public and private corporations, as well as individuals.

So in the statute called the "Code of Proceedure," in civil actions in this state, certain words are given a specified definition, as follows:

§ 462. The words "real property," as used in this act are co-extensive with lands, tenements and hereditaments.

§ 463. The words "personal property," as used in this act, include money, goods, chattels, things in action, and evidences of debt.

§ 464. The word "property," as used in this act, includes property real and personal.

§ 465. The word "district," as used in this act, signifies judicial district, except when otherwise specified.

§ 466. The word "clerk," as used in this act, signifies the clerk of the court where the action is pending, and in the supreme court, the clerk of the county mentioned in the title of the complaint, or in another county to which the court may have changed the place of trial, unless otherwise specified.

NOTE 4.—Where the terms of a statute which has received judicial construction, are used in a later statute, whether passed by the legislature of the same state or country, or by that of another; that construction is to be given to the later statute. Commonwealth v. Hartwell, 3 Gray. 450; Ruchmaboye v. Mottichmed, 32, Eng. L. & Eg. 84; Bogardus v. Trinity Church, 4 Sand. Ch. 633; Rigg v. Wilton, 13 Ill. 15; Adams v. Field, 21 Vt. 256. It is to be presumed in such case, that the legislature who passed the later statute, knew the judicial construction which had been placed on the former ones, and such construction becomes a part of the law.

speech be of J. S. generally, it shall be intended of the father or of the eldest son, for they are the most worthy. So, here it shall be intended of one of the superior courts at Westminster; for if the act is construed according to the letter, 'in any court of record;' then the court of oyer and terminer, gaol delivery, sewers, sheriff's tourn, leet, piepoudre, and others, will be within the act.

Then, it being left to the construction of the law, the rule is, '*quod verba equivoca et in dubio posita, intelliguntur in digniori et potentiori sensu.*'"

Another reason assigned is, that in popular actions or informations, "*tam pro domino rege, quam pro seipso,*" the suit shall be in such court where the king's attorney-general can attend. *a*

Where a statute speaks of indictments to be taken before justices of the peace, or " others having power to take indictments," it shall be understood only of other inferior courts, and not of the king's bench, or other courts at Westminster; *b* the rule being well established, as was ascertained in the last chapter, that where things of an inferior degree are first mentioned, those of a higher dignity shall not be included under general words.

Where an act of parliament gives authority to "one" person expressly, all others are excluded; *c* a special power is ever to be strictly pursued. *s*

a Gregory's case, 6 Rep. 19.   *b* 2 Rep. 46; 2 Hawk. c. 27, 124.
c 11 Rep. 59, 64.

NOTE 5.—Where a new right, or the means of acquiring it is given, and an adequate remedy for violating it is given in the same statute, the injured parties are confined to that remedy. Smith v. Lockwood, 13 Barb. 209; Thurston v. Prentice, 1 Mann. (Mich.) R. 193; Bassett v. Carlton, 32 Maine 553; Renwick v. Morris, 7 Hill. 575.

If a statute gives a remedy in the affirmative (without a negative express or implied), for a matter which was actionable at common law, this does not take away the common law remedy, but the party may still sue at common law as well as upon the statute. Crittenton v. Wilson, 5 Cow. 165; Jackson v. Bradt, 2 Caines. 169. But where a statute gives a new power, and at the same time provides the means of executing it, those who claim the power can execute it in no other way. Andover, &c., Turnpike Co. v. Gould, 6 Mass. 40; Franklin Glass Co. v. White, 14 id. 286. Where an inchoate right accrued under a statute, and by a subsequent revision of the statutes, the proceedings to perfect the right are regulated and prescribed;—such regulations must be pursued, or the party is remediless. People v. Livingston, 6 Wend. 526; People v. Phelps, id. 9. Where a statute which creates right, gives no remedy, a party may resort to the usual remedy. Dudley v. Mayhew, 3 N. Y. R. 9; Almy v. Harris, 5 John. 175. But if the statute confers the right, and prescribes an adequate remedy for protecting it, the party is confined to the statutory remedy, id. If the enforcing tribunal is specified, the designation forms a part of the remedy, and all others are excluded, id., and Miller v. Taylor, 4 Burr. 2322; Smith v. Lockwood, 13 Barb. 209.

Where an act of parliament gives power to " two justices finally to hear and determine an offence," it is necessarily supposed that they shall be together, or, which is the same thing, that they shall hold a special sessions for that purpose.   And the same construction obtains when they are to do any other judicial act, as to make an order of bastardy, or adjudge the settlement of a poor person. " For," as Dr. Burn says, " it is unknown to the laws of England, that two persons shall act as judges in the same cause, when at the same time one of them is in one part of the country, and the other in another." *a*

Generally, it is considered, that where a statute appoints a thing to be done " by one or more justices," without giving any appeal to the sessions, there the justices in sessions may do that thing ; but when an *appeal is given* to the sessions, the justices in sessions cannot proceed originally therein, because that method would take away the power of appealing.

The words, " general or quarter sessions" have received a judicial construction in R. v. The Justices of London, *b* and R. v. The Justices of Middlesex. *c*

" Sealed with the seal of the said court."   When the seal purports to be that of the court, the judges take notice that it is such ; and it is not necessary to prove the seal.   Doe dem. Duncan v. Edwards. *d*

That " it shall be lawful for the court to inquire into the title" under stat. 7 Wm. 4, and 1 Vict. c. 78, s. 24.   These words were construed to require the court to examine into the title.   Reg. v. Warwick. *e*

" Writs of error upon any judgment."   These words have been held to extend to judgments given in the court of king's bench upon error from the common pleas at Lancaster : *i. e.* to judgments on writs of error, as well as to original judgments, Nesbit v. Rishton. *f* [6]

" Prosecute with effect," see Morris v. Matthews, *g* " To make and prosecute such application" is satisfied by obtaining a rule *nisi*, whatever afterwards becomes of the rule, Haworth v. Ormerod. *h*

a Burn's Justice, Introduction, xxiv.	*b* 15 East, 639.
c 4 Q. B. R. 810.	*d* 9 A. & E. 554.
e 8 A. & E. 919.	*f* 9 A. & E. 431.
g 2 Q. B. R. 299.	
h 6 Q. B. R. 300.	

NOTE 6.—" Writ of error" is " a commission to judges of a superior court, by which they are authorized to examine the *record* upon which a judgment was given in an inferior court." Bacon Ab. Title " error;" Jac. L. Dict. " error;" Bouvier Dict. Title, " writ of error." It lies upon matter of law arising upon the face of the proceedings.

"Office:" A clerk to the justices holds an office, though not a chartered office, see Reg. v. Mayor of Carmarthen. *a*

"Proper officers;" see R. v. Walsh. *b*

"Expenses necessarily incurred." The expense of bringing offenders before the magistrates (including the fees of the justices' clerks) incurred in carrying into effect the stat. 5 & 6 Wm. 4, c. 71, are within these words. Reg. v. Mayor of Gloucester. *c*

Where a statute gives power to the justices to require any person "to take the oaths," or do any other thing, the law, by necessary implication, gives them power to issue their precept to convene the parties; "for when the law granteth anything to any one, *that* also is granted without which the thing itself cannot be, and it is against the office of the justices, and the authority given them by the law, that they shall go and seek the parties." *d*

Where a statute gives power to the justices of the peace, "to hear and determine an offence in a summary way," it is necessarily implied and supposed, as a part of natural justice, that the party be first cited by summons, and have opportunity to be heard, and answer for himself. *e*

In all cases, where justices may "take examinations," or other accusation or proof, though the statute doth not expressly set down that it shall be *upon oath*, yet it shall be intended, that it shall be upon oath. *f*

Where a statute appoints a conviction to be "on the oath of one witness," this ought not to be by the single oath of the informer; for if the same person shall be allowed to be both prosecutor and witness, it would induce profligate persons to commit perjury for the sake of the reward. *g*

Where an act of parliament empowers justices of the peace to "bind a person over," or to cause him to do a certain thing, and such person being in his presence, shall refuse to be bound or to do such thing; a power of commitment is said to be implied, and that the justice may commit him to the gaol, to remain there till he shall comply.

Where a statute limits a proceeding against a party to "six months;"—"a year," &c., after the act done; the day on which the

a 11 A. & E. 9.	*e* 1 Hawk. c. 64, s. 60.
b 1 A. & E. 485.	*f* Dalt. c. 115.
c 5 Q. B. R. 86.	*g* 2 Lord Raymond, 1545.
d 12 Rep. 131.	

NOTE 7.—"Office" is a public charge or employment, and the term seems to comprehend every charge or employment in which the *public* are interested." Matter of Wood, Hopk. 8, 2 Cow. 29 Note. Attorneys and counsellors, physicians, executors, guardians, &c., are not *public* officers. 20 John. 492. See People v Hayes, 7 How. Pr. R. 248.

act was done is to be reckoned in the six months, year, &c. *a*   R. v. Adderley; Castle v. Burditt. *b* [8]

"Three days at least," means three clear days. *c*

"One month or more" is a full month reckoned exclusively of the day of delivery of an attorney's bill, Blunt, Gent. v. Heslop. *d* [8]

"In or about a year," see Reg. v. St. Paul's Covent Garden. *e*

"Twenty-one days of, after, or from, the day of the execution," must be reckoned exclusively, see Williams v. Burgess and Walcott. *f*

"Parochial relief or other alms :" Alms applies only to such as are parochial, Reg. v. The Mayor of Lichfield. *g*

"Committed for trial at the assizes," Reg. v. Johnson. *h*

If an act of parliament say—an offender "shall be punished according to his demerit," these words import only that he shall be punished in the ordinary course of justice, by indictment. *i*

When a statute gives a "penalty to be recovered before justices of the peace," but prescribes no method of recovering it, the proper method is by indictment. *j*

Where a power is given "to inquire, hear, and determine," it always means according to the course of the common law, by a jury; and the proceedings must in such case be by indictment. *k*

"Heard and determined." See R. v. Justices of Warwickshire. *l*

"From any of the places aforesaid." To be read with reference to the immediate antecedents in the same section. Williams v. Newton. *m*

"Filed" held to be included in return of *non est inventus;* Hunter v. Caldwell. *n*

Though an indictment will not lie for an offence newly created by statute where another method of prosecution is appointed, yet

a 2 Dougl. 463.
b 3 T. R. 623.
c 4 B. & A. 522; 8 A. & E. 173; 12 A. & E. 472; 6 M. & W. 49.
d 8 A. & E. 577.
e 7 Q. B. Rep. 232.
f 12 A. & E. 638.
g 2 Q. B R. 693.
h 10 A. & E. 740.
i a 4 Inst. 171.
j Salk. 606.
k Per Lord Mansfield, MS. Rep. cited, Bac. Abridgment, tit. Stat. I, 2.
l 2 A. & E. 719.
m 14 M. & W. 747.
n Easter Term, 1847.

NOTE 8.—"A year," ordinarily means a calendar year, but the statute prescribing a year as the time during which a license to sell liquors shall be in force, means a license year, and it expires on the day named in the statute. The statute year is 365 days, in all written or verbal contracts; a half year is 182 days, and a quarter of a year 91 days. 1 Rev. Stat. 606, § 3.

NOTE 9.—A month in any statute, contract, or instrument, is a calendar month, unless otherwise expressed. 1 Rev. stat. 606, § 4. It was otherwise at common law, except in the case of bills and notes. A day consists of twenty-four hours, and commences and ends at midnight. Pulling v. People, 8 Barb. 386. And a statute forbidding an act to be done on a particular day, means the natural day of twenty-four hours, and not the solar day from sunrise to sunset, id.

if the statute give a recovery by action of debt, bill, plaint, information "*or otherwise*," it authorizes a proceeding by way of indictment. *a*

Every crime, the perpetrator of which is, by any statute, ordained to have judgment of "life or member," is a felony; although the word *felony* be not contained in the statute. *b*

But an offence shall never be made felony by the construction of any obscure or ambiguous words of a statute; and therefore if an offence be only prohibited "under pain of forfeiting body and goods," or of being "at the king's will for body, lands, and goods," it shall amount to no more than a misdemeanor. *c*

When a statute directs or appoints "commitment or imprisonment, but limits no *terminus a quo*, or time when it shall commence, it shall (for the benefit of him upon whom it is inflicted) be immediately, Foggassa's case, and Dr. Bonham's case. *d*

When a statute appoints "imprisonment," but limits no time, for its duration; the prisoner, in such case, must remain at the discretion of the court. *e*

Where an act of parliament gives power to the justice of the peace, to take order in any matter, "according to their discretions," this shall be understood according to the rules of reason, law, and justice, and not governed by private opinion. *f*

Where the amount of a security to be taken, is left in the *discretion* of any court, it will be good to follow precedents of former times; for "*discretio est discernere per legem, quod sit justum.*" *g*

"No *capias ad satisfaciendum* shall issue against a person "discharged under an insolvent act;" held to mean that a plaintiff who has a suit against the insolvent ought not to issue a *ca. sa.* not that, if issued, it shall be absolutely void, Ewart v. Jones. *h*

"Impound or otherwise secure," see Thomas v. Harris, *i* what will satisfy these words within 11 Geo. 2, c. 12.

Where an offence is cognizable "before a justice out of sessions," and the time and manner of punishment is not by law expressly limited, he may commit an offender to the house of correction, there to be kept to hard labor until the next general or quarter sessions, or until discharged by due course of law. *j*

It may be laid down as an invariable rule, that the law favors liberty, so that in the construction of a penal statute, where the interpretation is dubious, that sense must be pursued, *cæteris paribus*, which is more beneficial to the subject, or the party suffering. Thus, where an act directs that the justices shall commit an offender to prison for "twelve months," the justices may not alter the

a 2 Hawk. c. 25, s. 4.
b 1 Inst. 391; 2 Inst. 434; 3 Inst. 91.
c 1 Inst. 391; 3 Inst. 145; Hob. 270, 1 Hawk. c. 40, s. 2.
d Plow. Com. 17 b., and 8 Rep. 119.
e Dalt. 410.

f 5 Rep. 100; 8 Howell's State Trials, 55 *notis*.
g 2 Inst. 56, 298.
h 14 M. & W. 774.
i 1 Scott's N. C. 525.
j 17 Geo. 2, c. 5, s. 32.

words, and commit him for "a year;" for in this respect twelve months and one year are not the same; but the months must be computed at twenty-eight days to the month, and not as calendar months, unless it be so expressed in the act.

"Of" a place, imports dwelling; and is ordinarily, taken to mean that the party dwells at the place named; but in Reg. v. Toke, *a* Littledale, J., said, "I have great doubts, whether it is sufficiently averred that he dwells there."

"Expenses," this expression means actual disbursements, not allowances for loss of time, Jones v. Mayor of Carmarthen. *b*

"Payment" is not a technical word; it has been imported into law proceedings from the exchange and not from law treatises. It does not necessarily mean payment in satisfaction and discharge, but may be used in a popular sense. *c* [10]

Acts of parliament that speak of fines or ransoms "at the king's pleasure," are now always to be understood of the king in his courts, by his justices. *d*

An act inflicting a penalty for "a second offence," the indictment must recite the reord of the first conviction; and upon the evidence, the record of the first conviction must be proved. *e*

In all cases where a justice is required by an act of parliament, "to issue a warrant of distress for levying of any penalty inflicted, or any sum of money directed to be paid by such act;" it shall be lawful for such justice granting the warrant therein, to order and direct the goods distrained to be sold within a certain time to be limited in such warrant, so as such time be not less than four days, nor more than eight days, unless such penalty or sum of money, together with reasonable charges of taking and keeping the distress, be sooner paid. *f*

"By one broker or more." The use of the singular number is not sufficient to get rid of a positive provision for two appraisers in a prior statute, Allen v. Flicker and Another. *g*

"Final decree:" See Jones v. Reynolds. *h*

"Undue means:" Such are held to be:—Arbitrators carrying on examinations apart; whereas they ought to have been con-

---

a 8 A. & E. 232.

b 8 M. & W. 605.

c Maitland v. The Duke of Argyle, 6 M. & G. 40.

d 1 Hale, 375.

e 1 Hale, P. C. 686.

f 27 Geo. 2, c. 20.

g 10 A. & E. 640.

h 1 A. & E. 384.

NOTE 10.—It is otherwise held in this state. "Payment," in its legal import, means the full satisfaction of a debt by money, and it is only when the words used in connection with it plainly manifest a different intention, that the legal import of the term can be rejected. Manice v. Hudson R. Railroad Co., 3 Duer 441.

ducted by the arbritrators and umpire jointly in presence of the parties, Re Plews and Middleton. *a*

"Having upon view found." R. v. Milverton. *b*

" We having viewed, and, it appearing to us :" do not necessarily mean, that an order was made upon the view of the said justices, R. v. Marquis of Downshire ; *c* Reg. v. Jones. *d*

" Have adjudged :" is the same thing as saying that they adjudge. The words mean that the justices adjudge at that moment, R. v. Moulden ; *e* R. v. The Inhabitants of St. Nicholas, Leicester./

" Final port," what held, Moore v. Taylor. *g*

" No person shall maintain any action for, or recover any sum of money for spirituous liquors, unless contracted for at one time, to the amount of 20s." Where an unappropriated payment was made by the defendant, the plaintiff applied the payment to the items in his account charged for the spirits ; and sued for the residue. This was held no " action maintained" or "recovery" for the spirits within the terms of the act, Philpott v. Jones. *h*

" Artificers, calico-printers, handicraftsmen, miners, colliers, pitmen, potters, laborers, and others." Of these words in stat. 6 Geo. 3, c. 25, for " better regulating apprentices and persons working under contract," Lord Denman said : " Large as these words undoubtedly are, ' or other persons who shall contract with any persons whomsoever;' "—when we apply to them the ordinary rules for construing acts of parliament laid down by Dwarris on statutes, part 2, and acted upon in all times, we find ourselves compelled to say, that the ' other persons' are no , all persons whatever who enter into engagements to serve for stated periods, but persons only of the same description as those before enumerated. A justice, therefore, has no summary jurisdiction over a domestic servant," Kitchen v. Shaw. *i*

" Appeal against overseers' accounts to the next sessions :" means the next practicable sessions after the account has been deposited with the churchwardens and overseers for public inspection, Reg. v. Watts.*j*

"For the time being ; " see 8 Taunt. 691, for the meaning of these words in the case of parish officers, and 9 A. & E. 356, in the case of a company ; that the right to sue, did not remain in the officers after they had quitted office.

" Owner for the time being." By statute, an action against a shareholder for calls, was given against the " owner for the time being." Shares were sold after a call was made, but before it was payable. The court of Queen's bench held in the Birmingham

a 6 Q. B. R. 852.
b 5 A. & E. 841.
c 4 A. & E. 698.
d 12 A. & E. 686.
e 9 B. & C. 81.
f 3 A. & E. 85.
g 1 A. & E. 25.
h 2 A. & E. 44.
i 6 A. & E. 729.
j 7 A. & E. 461.

and Aylesbury company v. Thompson, *a* that the purchaser was not an owner for the time being. The common pleas have held, that until the deed is enrolled and entered, the company may compel the sellers to pay all the future calls. The London and Brighton railway company v. Fairclough. *b*

" Neglect : " What omission is equivalent to ; see King v. Burrell. *c*

" Treasurer for the time being : " means the officer and his successors. *d*

" Gross negligence," a misconstruction of a standing order, doubtful in its terms, is not such negligence as will disentitle a parliamentary agent to a remuneration for his labour. *e*

" Calls upon railway shares : " All calls upon railway shares, must be made with due observance of the requisites prescribed by the statute under which the company is formed. For what was deemed a sufficient compliance with the act in that particular case ; see the London and Brighton Railway Company v. Fairclough. *f*

" Levied and collected : " in 31 Geo. 1, c. 15, s. 3, the sheriff is entitled to poundage on the amount which comes to the hands of the Crown by means of the process. Where 800*l.* was levied, and the Crown accepted 500*l.* in satisfaction, the sheriff was entitled to poundage on 500*l.* only, R. v. Robinson. *g*

" By reason and colour of his office : " For the case of a sheriff taking more than the limited poundage on an eligit. See Nash v Allen. *h* [11]

" Executing : " Writs by sheriff. *i*   See Drew v. Lainson.   Colls v. Coates.

" Depending suits : " Unsatisfied judgments are pending suits, Howell v. Boven. *j*

" Satisfaction to the creditor " under the Insolvent Act, means pecuniary satisfaction, Kitching v. Croft. *k*

" Insolvency " is an inability in A. to pay his just debts, and does not import that he should have been discharged under the Insolvent Debtors' Act ; though the context may explain the words the other way : as in the Savings Bank Act, 3 & 4 Wm. 4, c. 14, where the words are " or become bankrupts or insolvents." *l* [12]

a 2 Railway Cas. 668.	*g* C., M. & R. 334.
b 2 M. & G. 674.	*h* 4 Q. B. R. 784.
c 12 A. & E. 460.	*i* 11 A. & E. 537, 826.
d 4 Q. B. R. 422.	*j* C. M. & R. 334.
e 4 M. & G. 124.	*k e* 12 A. & E. 586.
f 3 Scott, N. C. 68.	*l* C. M. & R.

NOTE 11.—Acts done *colore officii*, are the acts of an officer, which are of such a nature, that his office gives him no authority to do them. Seely v. Birdsall, 15 John 267. People v. Schuyler, 4 N. Y. 187.

NOTE 12.—A man is insolvent when his debts cannot be collected out of his property by legal process. Herrick v. Borst, 4 Hill 654. Insolvency and bank-

" Making or tendering satisfaction." These words do not im- ply that it is to be done before the mischief, but that they shall not do the act, without being liable to make compensation, Lister v. Hoxley and Another. *a*

" To the owners or promoters," includes lessees. *b*

" For anything done or omitted to be done in pursuance of the Act or in the execution of the power or authorities given by it." See Palmer v. The Grand Junction Railway Company; *c* Smith v. Shaw; *d* The Lancaster Canal Company v. Parneby; *e* Carpue v. The London and Brighton Railway Company. *f*

" Place of abode." Under the 24 Geo. 2 c. 44, s. 1, requiring a notice of action to justices to be indorsed with the name and place of abode of the attorney, the place of business was held a sufficient place of the attorney's abode, in Roberts v. Williams, *g* (*sed quære.*)

" Afore execution had " within stat. 3 Hen. 7, c. 10, means before obtaining the fruits of execution; satisfaction of the judgment, Newlands v. Holmes. *h*

" To pay the debt of another:" contemplates only promises made to the persons to whom another is liable; to the creditor and not to the debtor himself, Eastwood v. Kenyon. *i*

" Undertaking:" For the import of this term, see Pontet v. The Basingstoke Canal Company *j*; Myatt v. The St. Helen's Rail- way Company. *k* *

" Everybody politic, or corporate, and person or persons." These words extend to parishes, though they are neither bodies corporate or politic, or persons, Rex. v. Inhabitants of Barton *l*.

" Any offensive trade :" To use a house as a private lunatic

a 7 A. & E. 124.
b Id.
c i 4 M. & W. 749.
d 10 B. & C. 27.
e 11 A. & E. 230.
f 5 Q. B. R. 757.

g C., M. & R.
h 4 Q. B. R. 865.
i 11 A. & E. 438.
j 3 New Cas. 433.
k 2 Q. B. R. 364, N. Y. Code.
l 11 A. & E. 343.

* See definition in New York Code.

ruptcy are not synonymous terms. Mere insolvency never makes one a bank- rupt without the concurrence of some act tending to the injury of his creditors. Though insolvency is undoubtedly the larger term, and may include bank- ruptcy there is no necessary connection between the two. Sackett v. Andross, 5 Hill 344. Insolvency, in the abstract, means a general inability to pay ones debts ; an inability to fulfil ones obligations according to his undertaking ; a general inability to answer in the course of business, the liabilities existing and capable of being enforced. Not an absolute inability to pay ones debts at some future time, upon a settlement and winding up of all a trader's concerns ; but as not being in a condition to pay ones debts in the ordinary course, as persons car- rying on a trade usually do. Ferry v. Bank of Central N. Y., 15 How Pr. R. 451. Brower v. Harbeck, 9 N. Y. 594.

asylum, was held not to be a trade within these words, Doe dem. Wetherell v. Bird. *a*

"Use or exercise any trade or business whatsoever:" It was held, that keeping a school was a breach of convenant in this case, Doe dem. Bish v. Keeling. *b*

"Accepted the office:" The term accepted office, has a colloquial as well as a techincal meaning, Reg. v. Slatter. Whether he do accept or not, will be a legal inference from certain facts. *c*

"Introduced and established:" For the distinctions between them, see Gibson v. Kirk. *d*

"Wilfully waste or misapply:" Wilfully is connected with misapply, as well as with waste. The word "misapply," does not of itself import wastefulness, Carpenter v. Mason. *e*

"Incumbrance affecting the estate:" A sequestration at the suit of a creditor under which possession has been duly taken and the profits recovered, was held an incumbrance, &c., within the game qualification act, 18 Geo. 2, c. 20, s. 1, Pack v. Tarpley, Clerk. *f*

"Witness C. B., E. B., A. B." Held by a majority of the judges, not to be a good execution of a power, which required a will to be signed, sealed, and published in the presence of, and attested by witnesses, Doe dem. Spilsby v. Burdett. *g*

"Expenses incurred by the parochial fund:" A suit of clothes furnished to a poor boy on his being bound apprentice, was held not to be within these words of the statute, so as to cause the indenture to require the approval of two justices, Reg. v. The Inhabitants of Quainton. *h*

"Placing out or putting away," Reg. v. The Inhabitants of Wainfleet. *i*

"Placed, elected, or chosen." See Reg. v. Humphrey. *j*

"Inhabitants and occupiers." Reg. v. Inhabitants of Exminister. *k*

"Hereditaments." See Reg. v. Capell. *l* [13]

"Feoffments of lands or other hereditaments in England, "not otherwise charged 1 *l.* 15*s.*" A feoffment for the consideration of love and natural affection and 10*s.*, does not require two stamps of 1 *l.* 15*s.*. each. Per Lord Denman: "How can you make an

a 2 A. & E. 161.	*g* 9 A. & E. 936.
b 1 M. & S. 93.	*h* 1 A. & E. 133.
c 11 A. & E.	*i* 11 A. & E. 656.
d 1 Q. B. R. 855.	*j* 10 A. & E. 335.
e 12 A. & E. 630.	*k* 12 A. & E. 94.
f 9 A. & E. 468.	*l* 12 A. & E. 382.

NOTE 13.—Hereditaments is included in the definition of real property. Code N. Y. § 462. It is more comprehensive in meaning than "land," or "tenements," and includes whatever may be inherited, corporeal, or incorporeal. Canfield v. Ford, 28 Barb. 336.

ad valorem charge on natural love and affection?" Doe dem. Wheeler v. Wheeler. *a*

"Allowance" by a landlord for expenses or trouble, does not operate as a defalcation of the rent; but is collateral, Davies v Stacey and Parry. *b*

Upon an indictment or other criminal prosecution, no "damages" can be given to the party grieved; but it is every day's practice in the Court of King's Bench, to induce defendants to make satisfaction to the prosecutors, by intimating an inclination, on that account, to mitigate the fine due to the King. *c*

Where a statute generally prohibits any thing, the defendant may be prosecuted both by the king and the party grieved : for every contempt of a statute is indictable where no other punishment is limited; and the party grieved shall have his action for his private relief. *d* 14

"Miscellaneous words and sentences." The succeeding phrases it is impossible to reduce to any general heads; forming, as they obviously do, detached portions of sentences of a very miscellaneous nature.

"Absence :" See Reg. v. Perkin. *e*

The relative word "aforesaid," often refers and restricts, a clause, to the precedent purview. *f* Being a collective word, it may have reference, according to the intent, to two or three several matters, as to "every term named in an indenture ;" *g* unless "where it is impossible it can extend to other things, held in distinct rights and under different titles." *h*

The conjunction "and" couples sentences together, so that former adverbs refer to all the verbs subsequent; in this way preventing repetition and tautology. "And then and there gave the said Edward a mortal wound ;" on an objection that it was not stated that he gave it "feloniously, and of malice aforethought," the allegation was held sufficient, these words having been before mentioned. *i*

But "and" is relative as well as copulative. Where R. devised 100 sheep and 10 bullocks, and 10*l*. quarterly, the second "and" in the sentence disjoins and severs the rent from the sheep and

---

a 2 A. & E. 30.
b 12 A. & E. 510.
c 2 Hawk. c. 25, s. 3.
d 2 Inst. 163; 1 Hawk. c. 22, s. 5.
e 7 Q. B. R. 163.

f 10 Rep. 138; "Case on Sewers."
g 10 Rep. 107.
h 8 Rep. 47.
i 4 Rep. 40; "Case of Appeals and Indictments."

NOTE 14.—A like provision has been incorporated into the Revised Statutes of this state. 2 Rev. Stat. 696, § 54, (39), as follows: "Where the performance of any act is prohibited by any statute, and no penalty for the violation of such statute is imposed, either in the same section containing such prohibition, or in any other section of the statute, the doing of such act shall be deemed a misdemeanor."

bullocks; Sir Richard Pexhall's case. *a*   As in a case in the year books, where two were bound to stand to the abitrament of I. S. *de omnib' actionib' personalibus sectis et querelis; personalibus* shall be referred to all; but if the words were "*de omnibus actionibus personalibus, et sectis et querelis*," it shall be otherwise : for there the last *et* disjoins *querelis* from the whole first part of the sentence, and shall be taken generally without any reierence to *personalibus. b*

"And" is not always to be taken conjunctively. It is sometimes, in the fair and rational construction of a statute, to be read as if it were "or," and taken disjunctively and distributively. In Creswick v. Rokesby *c* and others, Dodderidge, J., said : "When the sense is the same they are all one, and the words conjunctive and disjunctive are to be taken *promiscue*." Thus, the conjunctive recited in a declaration, instead of the disjunctive, where the recital answers the sense of the statute, is sufficient; for the statute, notwithstanding the variance, is truly recited. So it is laid down in 2 Vent. 215. Nor according to the case of Halt v. Gaven, (Cro. Eliz. 307,) will the use of the word "and," instead of " or,"—hurt; if the word " or" in the statute has always been construed " and."

But where the statute uses the disjunctive " or," in which sense it is to be understood, and the plaintiff in his declaration mis-recites the statute and uses the word " and ;" the recital in the declaration, not answering the sense of the statute, all the authorities agree that the declaration is bad. Thus, by stat. 28 Eliz. c. 4, sheriffs are liable to a penalty for taking more than a certain sum on executions "upon the body, lands, goods, or chattels." A declaration on this act, in reciting the statute, stated it thus : " body, lands, goods, and chattels," and this was held to be a fatal variance. In arrest of judgment, Lord Kenyon said :—" The natural and obvious sense of the word, as mis-recited in the declaration, is to confine the provision of the statute to executions against all; but that is materially different from the words in the statute, which speaks distributively of writs against either of the objects of execution, and which inflicts a penalty on the sheriff for taking more than is allowed for executing any execution against either the body, lands, or chattels," &c. *d*

"Annual net value :"—See R. v. Inhabitants of Wistow. *e*

"All :"—"*qui omne dicit, nihil, excludit ; generale dictum* " *generaliter est intelligendum*." Therefore, where the Stat. of Merton, cap. 2, says *omnes viduœ*, and there are five kinds of dower, that chapter does extend to them all. *f*

a 8 Rep. 85.
b 9 E. 4, 43 b.
c 2 Bulstr. 47; 2 Hawk. c. 25, s. 102.   Waterhouse v. Kean, B. & C. 200.
d R. v. Marsack, 6 T. R. 771; R. v. Bland, 5 T. R. 370.
e 5 A. & E. 261.
f 2 Inst. 81.

"Any thing in this act to the contrary notwithstanding," is equivalent to saying that the act shall be no impediment to the measure, and precisely corresponds to the words in the second saving of the Stat. of Uses, 27 Hen. 8, c. 10, as if this act had not been made." Cheinie's case ; Sir Thomas Cecil's case. *a*

When a statute speaks of an "assignee," it is to be intended of such complete assignee, as has all the ceremonies and incidents requisite by the law to such character; not taking away any form or circumstance which the law requires. Therefore, assignee by fine shall not, under the 32 Hen. 8, c. 34, take advantage of a condition, without attornment. *b*

"At the time of the making" expounded to mean the same instant of the making *c*. "Forfeiture comes at the same instant that he dies." *d*

"Beneficial" and profitable are not convertible terms. A party holding a property, which is rateable, is not discharged, because he does it at a loss, R. v. Perrott *e*; Reg. v. Vange. *f* And for the distinction between profitable and beneficial, see Governors of Boston Poor v. Wait. *g*

"Boats, vessels, and other craft:" These words extend to steam boats, Tisdell v. Combe. *h*

"Convicted" has been often, according to many cases in the books, taken for attainted, and therefore extends to a judgment upon demurrer *i*; which in Foster's case was held to be a "conviction" within the stat. 23 Eliz.

A "college," to be such, in more than vulgar reputation, must have the "countenance of a legal commencement;" a lawful erection and foundation. And it should seem that no one can found or incorporate a college within this realm, or assign or license others to assign temporal livings to it, but only the king himself. And reputative colleges which had no lawful foundation, were held not to be given to the king by the stat. 1 Edw. 6, unless they had the countenance of the king's letters patent, or might have had a legal commencement but for some error or imperfection in the penning or proceedings. *j*

"Demised:" may well be taken for left to another or granted over to another; and whether the grant be by act in deed or by act in law. *k* [15]

a 7 Rep. p. 20.
b Mallory's case, 5 Rep. 112.
c Plowd. 188.
d Id. 258.
e 5 T. R. 393.
f 4 Q. B. R. 255.

g 5 A. & E. 8.
h 7 A. & E. 788.
i Dr. Foster's case, 11 Rep. 59.
j Adams and Lambert's case, 4 Rep. 108.
k Plowd. 103.

· Note 15.—The technical meaning of demise, is a lease for a term of years. Bouvier, Pit. 445. Voorhees and wife v. Presbyterian Church of Amsterdam, 5 How Pr R 71

An action is not properly said to be "depending" in any court, till the process is returned; but after an original writ is returned, then, it is said, it shall be considered pending, from the day of the *teste* of the writ. *a* The taxation of an attorney's bill, contemplated by the statute 2 Geo. 2, c. 23, s. 23, was evidently a taxation made upon the application of the client, before action brought; and where a judge's order for taxing it was not obtained till after, the courts of king's bench and common pleas formerly both held, that the defendant was not entitled to the costs of taxation, though more than one-sixth had been taken off by the master; yet the words of the section authorizing the court or judge to refer a bill to taxation are, "although no action or suit shall be then depending." *b*

Where the moiety of a penalty is given by statute to the treasurer of a "county, riding, or division," the word "division" does not apply to small districts, such as the Cinque Ports of Seaford in Sussex, but must be construed with reference to county and riding. and means something analogous to them. *c*

Where the authority emanates from a superior, "empowered" is imperative. In the case of a public duty such words not only authorize, they compel the exercise of the power, and performance of the duty. *d*

A "fit" person to execute an office, is he,—"*qui melius et sciat et possit, officium illud intendere.*" "This word *idoneus*," says Lord Coke, "is oftentimes in law attributed to those who have any office or function; and he is said in law to be *idoneus*, apt and fit to execute his office, who has three things,—honesty, knowledge and ability: honesty to execute it truly, without malice, affection, or partiality; knowledge to know what he ought duly to do; and ability, as well in estate as in body, that he may intend and execute his office, when need is, diligently, and not for impotency or poverty neglect it." If a coroner be "*senio confractus, aut morbo paralysis percussus, aut terras et tenementa in eodem comitatu non habet, &c.,*" so as to be "*minus idoneus ad officium illud exequendum, &c.,*" it is a good cause to remove him.

"Fixtures and fixed furniture:"—See Birch, Administrator of Vincent v. Dawson. *e* [16]

a 5 Rep. 47, 48, Cases of Pardons; 7 Rep. 30. "Discontinuance of process by death of the Queen."
b 4 Bing. 561; 8 B. & C. 635; 9 B. & C. 755.
c Evans q. t. v. Stephens, 4 T. R. 224, 459.   *e* 2 A. & E. 37.
d 5 T. R. 538; 5 T. R. 636; 7 A. & E. 925. R. v. St. Saviour's, Southwark.

NOTE 16.—Fixtures are chattels or articles of a personal value which have been affixed to the land. They must be permanently, habitually attached to it, or, must be component part of some erection, structure or machine attached to the freehold, without which, the erection, structure or machine would be imperfect and incomplete. Walker v. Sherman, 20 Wend, 656, Vanderpool v. Van Allen, 10 Barb. 162.

" Forthwith: "—Excludes intervention of delay. Reg. v. Robinson. *a* [17]

"From henceforth," " *de cœtero*," does not necessarily imply a new law; as may be seen upon the doubts arising on the Stat. Merton, cap. 2, *post*, chap. 11.

" Goods, materials, and provisions for the use of any workhouse : "—See Barber v. Watts. *b*

" Goods, wares, and merchandizes : "—Shares in a joint stock banking company, are not such within sec. 17 of the Statute of Frauds, Humble v. Mitchell. *c*

In Butler and Baker's case, as to the "power of a devisor to devise a manor," of divers notable reasons for the judgment, one was on the word "having." "If it be asked who can give and dispose by his last will in writing, &c.? the makers of the act (34 Hen. 8,) answer, *every person having manors ;* so that it is not said every person generally, but every person having, &c. And this word 'having' imports two things ; *scilicet*, ownership, and time of ownership, for he ought to have the land at the time of the making of his will, and the statute gives such person having, &c., authority to devise, &c. And Wray, Ch. J., in his argument, (which was the last that ever he made,) held, that this word imports, that 'the devisor ought to have the land, either at the time of the making of his will, or at the publication thereof, which amounts in law to a making'; "*d* or, at the time of the republication of the will by a codicil; which, when properly executed, caused the will to speak (as it is expressed) at the date of the codicil, as to the existing state of the property,—including the testator's intermediate acquisitions, as far as the fair and legal comprehension of the terms of the codicil would go. *e* And now stat. 1 Vict. c. 26, s. 24, makes all wills of realty as well as of personalty, speak from the death of the testator.

" Immediately," *maintenant*, applied to a descent of lands, (as where the stat. of 34 Hen. 8, speaks of " a descent immediately after the decease,") is as much as to say without any mean time, or mesne estate. He who is immediate heir, excludes all mesne heirs,—the same law, of an immediate tenant. A manor does not descent *immediately* where it is expectant on the refusal or disagreement of the widow; for, peradventure, she will not refuse in a year. Littleton says, that if a woman disseissoress take a husband, and hath issue, and dies, and afterwards the tenant by the curtesy dies, this dying seised shall not toll entry ; for the issue came not to his lands " immediately" after the death of his mother.

---

a See 3 A. & E. 284 ; 12 A. & E. 672.   *d* Butler and Baker's case, 3 Rep. 30.
b 1 A. & E. 514.   *e* Barnes and Crowe, 7 Ves. Jun. 486.
c 1. A. & E. 205.

NOTE 17.—Forthwith is construed to mean within twenty-four hours. Champlin v. Champlin, 5 Edw. ch. 328.

In other cases the word "immediately" has not received such a strict construction that a thing ought to be made *in ipso articulo temporis*, but is satisfied if it be made in convenient time. Thus, where a man is to make an obligation immediately after an award, he ought to have such time as the doing of the act requires, and then, of necessity, there ought to be a mean time between the award and the performance of the act. This was decided in 18 Ed. 4, c. 22, and affirmed for good law in Butler and Baker's case. *a*

"Immediately" cannot be satisfied, if an interval take place, Grace v. Church. *b*

"In or near the parish or division," in 43 Eliz. c. 2, is only directory. *c*

"In pursuance of this act." Reg. v. The Bristol and Exeter Railway Company. *d*

"Inland bill of exchange," is a bill drawn in, and payable in, Great Britain, Amner v. Clark. *e*

"In lieu :"—Where a fund provided by statute in lieu of other means of payment becomes the primary fund, Reg. v. St. Saviours', Southwark. *f*

"Instantly :"—This word has no definite meaning. Such words as *instanter* and *incontinenter* do not dispense with an allegation of time. Reg. v. Brownlow. *g*

"Interruption :"—An obstruction to the exercise of a *right;* not to the person, see Flight v. Thomas. *h*

"It was proposed :" indicates merely something in contemplation; a proposal, Reg. v. Brownlow. *i*

"Likewise," and "in like manner," so couple a clause or section by reference to a former clause or section, as to carry on its sense, and extend its operation. *j*

"Lands liable to rate :"—These words may extend to navigations, cuts, and canals, as well as to quays or wharfs, Reg. v. The Leeds and Liverpool Canal Companies. *k* Per Patteson, J., "They are not the less land for being covered with water." In the Regent's Canal Company, *l* the expression in the act was, "lands, whether covered with water or not."

"Liabilities" and "relative liabilities," in the parochial assessment acts, 6 & 7 Wm. 4, c. 96, s. 1. The court said this language was loose " and inartificial to a degree which rendered the discovery of a definite meaning, extremely difficult." Reg. v. Capel. *m*

"Manufacture :" What is a new manufacture within the stat.

a 3 Rep. 34.
b 4 Q. B. R. 610.
c R. v. Loxdale, 1 Burr. 447.
d 11 A. & E. 194.
e C., M. & R. 471.
f 7 A. & E. 425.

g 11 A. & E. 219.
h 11 A. & E. 701.
i 11 A. & E. 119.
j Stat. Gloucester, c. 2, *post*, cap. 11.
k 7 A. & E. 685.
l 6 B. & C. 720.

m 12 A. & E. 411.

21 Jac. 1, c. 3? That a new combination of materials previously in use, producing a new article, or a better article, or a cheaper article to the public, than that produced before, by the old method, is an invention or a manufacture intended by the statute, See Crane v. Price. *a*

"Materials for the repairs of the highway, and for the use of the inhabitants," were held not to be taken by the inhabitants for their private purposes, but only for repairs of roads. Rylatt v. Marfleet. *b*

"Merchandise :"—Stone not liable to duty upon merchandise, Fisher v. Lee. *c*

"Minister of a church :" See Reg. v. Mayor of Liverpool. *d*

"Non-cultivation" will not let in evidence of bad cultivation.

Whether "months" in an act of parliament mean lunar or calendar months, is a point, which, after frequent and solemn determinations upon it, is now taken to be so firmly settled that it should not be shaken. "I confess," said Lord Kenyon, in Lacon v. Hooper, "I wish that when the rule was first established it had been decided, that 'months' should be understood to mean calendar and not lunar months; but the contrary has been determined so long, and so frequently, that it ought not again to be brought into question. In the instance indeed, of a *quare impedit*, the computation of time is by calendar months, but that depend on the words of an act of parliament, *tempus semestre*. But for all other purposes, and in all acts of parliament where 'months' are spoken of without the word 'calendar,' and nothing is added from which a clear inference can be drawn that the legislature intended calendar months, it is understood to mean lunar months." *e*

When the stat. 31 Hen. 8, speaks of "dissolution—renouncing, —relinquishing,—giving up, forfeiture," &c., which are inferior means by which religious houses came to the king, the latter words or "by any other means come to the king," cannot be intended of an act of parliament, which is the highest manner of conveyance that can be; and therefore, the makers of the act would have put that, in the beginning and not in the end, after other inferior conveyances, if they had intended it to extend the act thereunto. But these words, "by any other means," are to be expounded by any other such inferior means. Archbishop of Canterbury's case. *f*

"Occupy," See R. v. Great Bentley, *g* Reg. v. The Inhabitants of St. Mary Kalendar. *h*

"Or "—is not always disjunctive. It is sometimes interpretative

a 4 M. & G. 603.
b 14 M. & W. 233.
c 12 A. & E. 522.
d 8 A. & E. 176.

e 6 T. R. 224.
f 2 Rep. 46.
g 10 B. & C. 520.
h 9 A. & E. 682.

or expository of the former word; "*balivam, vel jurisdictionem.*"
See stat. of Marlbridge. *a* [18]

"Other than:"—The sense of an exception. *b*

"Other person or persons:"—Persons of the same description
as those before enumerated.

In a proviso in 27 Hen. 8, the words are, "That if any wife
shall have any manors, lands, &c. unto her assured after marriage
for term of her life, *or otherwise* in jointure," &c., an estate in fee
simple was held to be within the express letter of the act, for
"otherwise" extends to all other estates conveyed to the wife not
mentioned before in the act, which are as, or more, beneficial to
the wife than the estates before mentioned. *c*

"Parish or place to which they belong:" For the construction
of these words as to repairs of chapels under 3 Geo. 4, c. 72, s.
20. See Craven v. Sanderson. *d*

"Parties grieved:" Whether the near relations of a person
whose body has been disinterred for dissection are "parties aggrieved" is doubtful, R. v. Toole. *e*

"Payments *bona fide* made" under the Bankrupt Act, 6 Geo. 4,
c. 16, see Bevan v. Venables. *f*

"Presently answer:" held in Plowden only presently become
debtor, not presently pay.

"Preferred:" before which indictment preferred, held not to
mean the court alone before which a bill is found, but that also to
which it is removed, R. v. Pembridge. *g*

Stat. Marlbridge, cap. 3. "*Non Ideo puniatur dominus per redemptionem.*" "Redemption" is fine: and *finis dicitur quia finem
litibus imponit;* the party redeems his offence for a sum of money,
which makes an end of his trangression and of his imprisonment
for it. *h*

Upon the stat. 27 Hen. 8, restraining tenants in tail from making unreasonable leases, much doubt arose what would satisfy the

a Post, cap. 11.	*e* 1 M. & R. 728.
b Plowd. 195.	*f* 3 New Cases, 400.
c Vernon's case, 4 Rep. 3.	*g* 7 Dowl. 1, 2 M. & Rob.
d See 7 A. & E. 880.	*h* Griesley's case, 8 Rep. 41.

NOTE 18.—"Or" in its ordinary signification, corresponds to either meaning,
one, or the other of the two; but not both. It is sometimes construed to mean
"and" when such construction has been necessary to give effect to a clause in a
will, or to some legislative provision, but never to change a contract at pleasure.
Indeed, it seems to be an inaccurate expression to say that "or" can ever mean
"and" It should rather be said, that for strong reasons, and in conformity with
clear intention, "or" has been changed, or removed, and "and" substituted in
its place. Douglas v. Egre. Gilp. 147, opinion of McLean J. in United States v.
Railroad Bridge Co. Am. Law Reg. old series, vol. 3, p. 613. "And" cannot be
construed to mean "or" in a penal statute, United States v. Ten cases of Shawls
2, Paine 162.

words "rendering the old and accustomed rent." If the ancient reservation were of the rent to be paid in gold, and the new reservation was to be paid in silver, it would not satisfy them. If a quarter of wheat was anciently reserved, and a new lease was made rendering eight bushels of wheat, this is all one in quality, value and nature; *et parum differunt quæ re concordant.* Joining two several farms (always before let for 20*l.* and 10*l.*,) in one demise, rendering 30*l.* entire rent out of both,—or letting parcel of a farm, rendering rent *pro rata*, were cases in which the lease was impeached, as being new rents and not the accustomed rent. But it was admitted in the case of two coparceners, that one might let her moiety, yielding the moiety of the accustomable rent; for it would be hard that the forwardness of her coparcener should prejudice her of the benefit of a fine which she might have, by making of a lease of her moiety. And this was different from the case of the lease of part with reservation of rent *pro rata*, which is his own act. &c., &c. *a*

"Revoking a submission :" The words of the stat. 3 and 4 Wm. 4, c. 42, s. 39, are not large enough to take away the power of revoking a submission to arbitration in case of a reference on the trial of an indictment: but apply only to civil actions, R. v. Bardell, 619.

"Separate and distinct dwelling house :" See Reg. v. The Great and Little Useworth, and N. Buddich. *b*

"Separate and distinct tenements." Reg. v. Ripon. *c*

"Stage wagons :" What carriages will satisfy these words, see Reg. v. Ruscoe. *d*

"Shipping for exportation :" These words are often used in a sense less extensive, than the exporting of commodities to foreign ports and places, and in the more restrained sense of carrying commodities from one port to another, within the kingdom. Barret v. Darlington Railway Company. *e*

"Subject to the laws and statutes now in force :" See R. v. Churchwardens of St. James Westminster. *f*

"Such :" The operation and effect of such, *hujusmodi*, has been before shown. Such in mischief and inconvenience.

"Such as have been heretofore usually rated :" These words refer not to legal rateability, but to rating in point of fact, and to the practice of rating in the particular parish not in the county generally. Reg. v. Rose. *g*

"Thereupon and thereby :" For the distinction between these terms, see Atkinson v. Raleigh. *h*

"Towards and unto :" See R. v. The Marchioness of Downshire. *i*

a Cases of leases, 5 Rep. 5.
b 5 A. & E. 361.
c See 7 Q. B. R. 225.
d 8 A. & E. 388..
e 2 M. & G. 134

f 5 A. & E 399.
g 6 Q. B. R. 153.
h 4 Q. B. R. 79.
i 5 A. & E. 232.

"Unless he shall have paid all such rates:" Payment of rates to entitle a person to be put on the burgess list of a borough under stat. 5 and 6 Wm. 4, c. 76, s. 9, must be a payment by the party's own act. Reg. v. The Mayor of Bridgnorth. *a*

"Undertaking:" The word is ambiguous. It may mean the speculation, or might be taken to include the land itself. *b*

"Unmarried:" in a will, "never having been married," Per Lord Alvanley in Maberly v. Strode. *c*

"Unmarried" by the legislature, 3 & 4 W. & M. c. 11, s. 7, 'not married at the time.' Bott's Poor Laws.

"Upon:" This word in most cases is used elliptically for upon condition of: as, "upon payment of costs:"—"Upon conviction of an offender."

"Upon" is sometimes used for after, within a reasonable time: Thus, "Roman Catholics may hold office upon taking certain oaths," 10 Geo. 4, c. 7, s. 14. "On admissions" in the case of copyholds.

"Upon"—construed "upon the occasion of," or "at the time of" admission. Reg. v. Humphery. *d*

"Usual covenants" does not mean universally inserted.

"With" taken to mean "and as incident thereto." The Durham and Sunderland Railway Company v. Walker. *e*

The words of the stat. of enrolments, 27 Hen. 8, c. 16, are "within six months after the date of the same writings indented:" upon which it was adjudged that if such writings have a date, the six months shall be accounted from the date; if they have no date then from the delivery; and the day is exclusive. And "from the date," and "from the day of the date," are of one sense, since in judgment of law the date includes the whole day of the date. If a lease is to begin from the day of the making, or from the day of the date, the day itself of the date is excluded. But where the demise is limited to begin from the making, and where it was worded "to have and to hold for three years from henceforth," the day of the delivery was taken inclusive, and the day itself held parcel of the demise. *f*

It has been held subsequently, that the words "from the day of the date" in a lease, mean either inclusive or exclusive, according to the subject-matter, and the court will construe them so as to effectuate the intention of the parties. *g*

"Wreck:" in stat. 3 & 4 Wm. 4, c. 52, s. 50, is not limited to goods forfeit after a year and a day under stat. Westminster 1. Barry v. Arnauld. *h*

The stat. 32 Hen. 8 c. 28, and 13 Eliz. c. 10, as to leases by

a 10 A. & E. 66.
b Doe dem. Myatt v. The St. Helen's Railway Company, 2 Q. B R. 374.
c 3 Ves. 450.
d See 10 A. & E. 335.

e See 2 Q. B. R. 966.
f Clayton's case, 5 Rep. 1.
g Pugh v. Leeds (Duke of) Cowp. 714.
h 10 Adel. & Ellis. 646.

spiritual persons, "whereupon the accustomed yearly rent or more shall be reserved," are *in pari materie,* and must be taken together. To render a lease valid under this statute, it must be made of land which had been previously let, or on which some rent had been reserved. *a*

A similar construction was put upon nearly the same words in a *power,* as may be seen in Doe. dem. Bartlett v. Rendle, 3 M. & S. 99. See also Fuller v. Abbott, 4 Taunt. 105.

" Year," and "yearly hiring." A year is the time wherein the sun goes round his compass through the twelve signs, viz: 365 days and about six hours. But in leap year the statute 24, Geo. 2, Ch. 25, enacts that the year shall consist of 366 ; so that in the case of Rex. v. Wormingall, *b* upon a question of yearly hiring, Lord Ellenborough said : "In those years which consist of 366 days, a hiring and service for a year, must be for that same number of days, in like manner as when the year was 365 days; it must have continuance during that number.

a Doe. d. Tennyson v. Yarborough, Lord; 7 Moore 258, **and** 1 Bing. 24.
b 6 M. & S. 350.

CHAPTER IX.

THE BOUNDARIES OF LEGISLATION AND OF JUDICIAL INTERPRETA-
TION SOUGHT TO BE ASCERTAINED : THE INSTANCES OF THE EXER-
CISE OF THIS BRANCH OF JUDICATURE IN OUR COURTS REVIEWED ;
OF LEGITIMATE CONSTRUCTION AND OF INTERPRETATIVE LEGISLA-
TION, IRRESPECTIVE OF CONSTITUTIONAL RESTRICTIONS.

"It is a remarkable fact, that in an enlightened age, and among
so many intelligent inquirers into the philosophy, both of history
and of law, so little attention should have been paid to the consideration of the important question,—What are the principles
upon which the jurisprudence of a country ought to proceed?
Certainty in the law, to a positive extent, is unfortunately unat-
tainable; immutability of laws, even if it were desirable (which it
surely is not) is still more impracticable. An extensive alteration
in the condition of the people,—a total change of circumstances,
must, at any time, induce some change of institutions, and render
absolutely necessary a sensible modification of the laws. Laws
must be accommodated—or laws will accommodate themselves—
to the growing necessities of mankind, and the varying state and
condition of human society. "Comment enchainer l'action du
temps? Comment s'opposer au cours des evenements, ou a la
pente insensible des mœurs? Comment connaitre et calculer d'a-
vance ce que l'experience seule peut nous reveler? La prevoyance
peut-elle jamais s'etendre a des objects que la pensee ne peut at-
teindre?—Les hommes ne se reposent jamais; ils agissent toujours; et ce mouvement, qui ne s'arrete pas, et dont les effets sont
diversement modifies par les circonstances, produit, a chaque instant, quelque combinaison nouvelle,—quelque nouveau fait,—quelque resultat nouveau." a [1]

The term "legislation," though ordinarily restricted, in its signification, to the act of making a law, or a code of laws, is some-

a Discours Preliminaire du premier projet du Code Civil, p. 20.

NOTE 1.—The following is believed to be a literal translation. "How arrest the
action of time? How oppose the course of events or the insensible change of
customs? How know and calculate in advance what experience alone can reveal
to us? Can foresight ever extend to objects which thought cannot attain? Men
never rest, they are ever active, and that movement which does not stop, and
whose efforts are diversely modified by circumstances, produces every moment
some new combination ; some new fact ; some new result."

times used to denote the whole body of a legislative act of whatever name or origin, and may not improperly be extended to embrace the entire map of what are denominated laws, taken attentively. It is in this latter sense that legislation is distinguished from jurisprudence. a

But it is not in the power of human intelligence whether combined in legislative bodies, or otherwise, to foresee and provide beforehand, for every combination of facts, or circumstances, which may occur in the infinite variety of human affairs. No human code; no body of legislators ever undertook to do this. No human wisdom could have accomplished such a task, if it had ever been undertaken. The lawmaker however desirous he may be to make his code complete, can only foresee and provide for classes of cases; and in doing this, he must rather be guided by the experience of the past, than by any faculty of discerning the future. b

There is accordingly, a large class of cases which are inevitably left unprovided for by every system of human legislation; and it becomes an interesting inquiry to determine how much has been actually settled by legislation, and the rules by which this fact is determined, and what are the rules of conduct, and what the measure of justice that applies to cases not included in the general provisions of legislation. The only answer that can be given to this latter inquiry is, that they are to be determined in each state or government, by what is called its jurisprudence, which is the administration of all the laws of the state including legislation. But jurisprudence, which consists in giving interpretation to, and in making application of statutes to particular cases, includes also the application of those precepts of natural right which have not been superceded by express legislation, and which therefore remain in full force as to all other circumstances and cases.

These precepts or principles of natural right, which are thus left unaffected by positive legislation, are those fundamental principles which are necessarily presupposed by every code, and by every act of legislation, general or special, while they are also rules to control legislation in the spirit of laws, determine when properly applied, what legal rights and duties have been violated,

a Cushing v. The Roman Law, § 27.   b Id. § 33.

and what ought to be done, in order that those whose legal relations are disturbed, may be placed, as near as may be, in the same situation in which they would have stood if the rules of right had been observed. This, equally with legislation, is a measure of justice. This is also jurisprudence. If a case is left wholly unprovided for by legislation or positive law, it is governed solely by the natural law ; if in part only, then partly by the natural, and partly by the positive law. The natural law thus becomes the complement of positive legislation, and supplies its deficiencies, in reference to all cases which are either wholly, or in part only, regulated by its provisions.

Principles of jurisprudence, as above described, become developed in two ways or forms. The first occurs when the question arises in the mind of an individual as to what the law requires him to do in a particular case. When this happens, the party either determines for himself what he ought to do, or he applies for information to some other person, who makes it a business, or profession, to consider and advise in such matters. The principles which are thus developed, gradually assume the character of usages, and become a part of the customary law. The second form in which jurisprudence technically so called is developed,— occurs in the administration of justice. The cases which are decided in this way, become precedents or authorities for similar and analogous cases subsequently occurring. a

Legislation being the establishment, beforehand, of those general principles by which civil conduct is to be regulated ; and jurisprudence, consisting of those principles which are developed in the application of the former to particular cases, it follows, that the latter will be more or less extensive, according as the former is more or less general or particular ; jurisprudence being the most extensive when the law is most general, and least extensive when the law goes furtherest into details and particulars. Legislation, though usually general, may nevertheless descend to minute details and particulars. When this is the case, it so far occupies the place which would otherwise be filled with jurisprudence Jurisprudence on the other hand supplying all that legislation leaves unprovided for in the administration of justice, and devel-

a Cushing on Jurisprudence, § 40.

oping principles which serve as rules of conduct for cases subsequently arising, so far stands in the place, and performs the functions of legislation. *a*

It will thus be seen to be a most difficult task to establish the precise boundary which separates legislation proper, from what is properly called jurisprudence, and to attribute to each the exact domain to which it is appropriately entitled. An examination of codes and systems would probably show, that the great outlines, embracing those institutions which are peculiar to each, and which, to a certain extent, are political in their character, have been the work of legislation; while those parts which have their foundation in natural justice, and are the same, or nearly so, among all nations of the same rank in civilization, and which chiefly affect the relations of the citizens to one another, have been the product of jurisprudence.

The great and essential difference between legislation and jurisprudence, that which separates one from the other distinctly, is the manner in which they respectively become established. The former takes the place where the law making power discovers occasion for it; and its provisions are framed prospectively for such classes of cases as the legislator thinks most likely to occur. The latter is only called into being when an actual case arises for its exercise, and is then adapted to the particular circumstances of that case. Legislation, when once established, becomes fixed and unalterable; and it receives no additions, but by subsequent legislation. Jurisprudence is constantly progressive, and continually enlarging and extending itself, as cases occur for its exercise, and adapting its principles to the social and political changes which are perpetually going on in society.

The French quotation, above cited by Mr. Dwarris, as also those which follow in this chapter, are a kind of preface to the code Napoleon. The importance of this code in the French system of jurisprudence for the time, and its value as continuing sound principles in the view of Mr. Dwarris, makes its history, perhaps, of interest to the student. The frequent revolutions in that country, based somewhat upon the oppressive institution of the state,—the privileges of the nobles,—of the church,—and a vicious financial system,—

a Id. 41.

seemed to have turned a portion of the popular fury against its legal
institutions; and these were rendered the more odious by the acts
of various assemblies, under different names, who exercised legislative power in a dictatorial and despotic manner. These new .
acts, by the new principles they asserted in effect, swept away all
the former principles of what was called the jurisprudence of the
state. '

About the year 1793, the celebrated lawyer Cambaceres, a native
of Montpelier, who had risen to the highest eminence in his profession, proposed a *code of laws*, conceived in the spirit of the age to
the then rulers, a body of men, who, it may be said, had cut their way
with the dagger and the sword, to first and simple principles. In
August of that year, he presented a draft of his code to the convention, entitled "Projet de Code Civile;" The work was too
great, and too profound, to be deliberated upon at so stormy a
moment, when the minds of the convention were too unsettled for
an undertaking so important as the settlement of a legal system
for the nation.

Two years later, in 1795, Cambaceres, then a member of the
council of Five Hundred, presented to this body an amended pro
ject of a code, which was ordered to be printed. Nothing decisive, however, was done by this convention towards the achieve-
ment of this great work.

· On the overthrow of the Directory, by the revolution of the 9th
November, 1799, the attention of the new consular government
was immediately turned to the subject of a code. Bonaparte
made it one matter of charge against the Directory, that they had
not achieved a work so loudly called for by the spirit of the age,
and the unsettled state of the jurisprudence of the country; and
especially the great interest which Cambaceres, their second Cousul,
had taken in his former efforts towards this end, and he (Cambaceres,) was then engaged by the first Consul to pursue the same
design. Accordingly, in the course of the first year of the Con-

NOTE 2.—The data upon which the following observations are made, and some
of its views adopted, are from a French author, (translated) entitled, "Les cinq
codes avec notes et traites pour servir a un cours complet de Droit Francais; a
l'usage des Etudiants en Droit, et de toutes les classes de citoyens cultives." Par
J. B. Liserf, Avocat aux conseils du Roi et a la cour de cassation, 8 vo., Paris, 1819,

sulate, a *third* project of a code, embracing the views of Cambaceres, was drawn up and presented to the government, by a commission of the council of Five Hundred, at the head of which was
Jacqueminot, who was afterwards a member of the Senate under
Napoleon.

Such was the condition of things, when Napoleon, by a consular
decree of the 12th August, 1800, ordered a commission to be instituted " to compare the order which had been followed in the
preparation of the *projects* for a civil code hitherto published, to
determine the plan, which the commission shall think best to
adapt, and to discuss the chief principles of civil legislation."
This commission consisted of Messrs Portalis, Trouchet, Rigot,
Premaneau and Malleville, and the Minister of Justice was added
to their number.

In the following year, 1801, these commissioners reported a
draft of a civil code, formed chiefly out of the materials of the
former projects. These were accompanied with a preliminary discourse on the principles by which they had been guided. This
discourse was entitled, " *Discours preliminaire du premier projet
du code civil*," and this is the authority from which Dwarris has
selected his French quotations.

This last mentioned draft of a code was, in the first instance
submitted to the court of Cassation, (of errors,) and the various
courts of appeal, and the reports of the judges of these courts
furnished the matter of some improvements in the draft, and it
was next submitted to the Council of State. In this body over
which Bonaparte, then first Consul, presided, every part of the proposed code was thoroughly discussed. After it had been discussed
in this manner, it was presented to the Tribunate, where it under-
went another discussion, and was returned to the Council of State,
as adopted, rejected, or amended.

In this way, five codes of law, were successively matured and
produced, viz : 1st. " *The Code Civile*," which was that called by
eminence " The Code Napoleon ;" 2d. " *The Code de Procedure
Civile*," by which the forms of actions and modes of proceedings,
from the tribunal of a justice of the peace up to the highest courts
in civil cases, were enacted ; 3d. " *The Code Penal*," or criminal
code ; 4th. " *The Code d'Instruction Criminelle*," or mode of pro-

ceeding in criminal actions; and, 5th. " *The Code de Commerce*," or code of law merchant. This whole body of law, comprising all these codes, was generally printed in one *duodecimo* volume.

We have dwelt more upon this history, and at greater length than might seem needful in this treatise, but we have seen already in our own state, the commencement of a system of codification already adopted, so far as regards the practice of the courts, and under a name that seems to have been borrowed from this French example, and with propositions, not yet adopted, borrowed from the same example, to extend to the whole system of *civil* and *criminal* jurisprudence of the state, by codification. It does not become us to say in advance, with what advantage to our own jurisprudence, if adopted.

It is said, by those who had the best opportunities of knowing, and pretty generally believed, that in no one prominent act of Napoleon's administration did he pride himself more, than in this code which bore his name. From the history which we have given of the manner in which it was drawn up and prepared; from the active part he took in commissioning the distinguished lawyers for that purpose;—from the fact that he presided over the body before whom it was so thoroughly discussed, and as we may believe from the active powers of his mind, he could well appreciate the points of such discussion;—and the fact that he honored the manuscript copy of this code with his imperial signature, we may perhaps, even at this day, judge somewhat as to the credit to which he was entitled, as the author of the Code Napoleon. His greatest admirers claim for him in this regard, to have been a second Justinian. This may be true, and still be an equivocal compliment; for history accords to Justinian about the same participation in the actual preparation of his great work called his Institutes, as to Napoleon in projecting his code. None will deny to either, the possession of imperial powers of mind; and none should detract from the credit of those great legal luminaries who prepared these codes for the consideration and adoption of their imperial masters. It is nevertheless true, that both Napoleon and Justinian rose to greatness in their respective empires, by other qualities of greatness, besides those which distinguished them as military chieftains.

But the Code Napoleon with its prefatory "*Discours Prelimin-aire*," became the statute law of France, and the jurisprudence of the countries dependent on French power. It was introduced in Holland,—in the Confederation of the Rhine,—in the kingdom of Westphalia,—in Bavaria,—in the kingdom of Italy,—in Naples,—in Spain,—and in various smaller states that were under the French influence. It was substantially founded on the principles of the civil law, the common basis of continental jurisprudence.

With all the merits of this French code, the downfall of the emperor was the signal for its disuse in the foreign dependencies of France ; but in that country itself, it was so strongly rooted in the confidence of the people as to sustain itself. By a royal ordinance of July 17, 1816, it is declared :

" We are too well convinced of the evils of a fluctuating legislation in a state, to think of a general revision of the five codes, which were in vigor in our kingdom, at the time that our constitutional charter-was granted. We reserve to ourselves, only to propose particular laws, in order to reform such things as admit of improvement; or in which time and experience shall have discovered imperfections. But although reforms of this kind can only be the work of time, and the fruit of long meditations, it is indispensable to suppress, from the present moment, those denominations, expressions and formulas in the different codes, which are not in harmony with the principles of our government, and which recall the recollection of times and circumstances, of which we would efface even the recollection."

In consequence of this decree, the various names and titles belonging to the imperial government, were erased, and the appropriate ones of the royal government, introduced in their stead. At various subsequent periods, laws have been enacted, considerably modifying, or wholly changing several important provisions of the " Code Napoleon."

This whole code was comprised in 2281 paragraphs, or sections, and numbered, like our own Code of Proceedure, for the greater facility of reference, but they are very brief and tersely written, and of about the average length of verses in the Bible. The work is divided into three books; each book into a certain number of titles ; and each title comprises one or more chapters. The preliminary title is used to effect an understanding and the application and interpretation of the provisions of every part of the code, and precedes the whole body of the work; therefore the significance of the quotations by our author, Dwarris.

Again, with the highest degree of certainty of which laws are susceptible, doubts will still arise upon the sense of enactments, or as to their application. In all cases where the legislature has not defined with perfect precision the exact nature of its provisions, some authority will be required to decide upon the meaning of the terms which it employs, or the cases to which its provisions shall extend.

In ancient times, cases of the first impression, and all matters presenting any serious doubt or difficulty, were usually "adjourned into parliament, to be resolved and decided there." a To this effect Bracton observes : " *Si aliqua nova et inconsueta emerserint, quæ nunquam prius evenerunt, et obscurum et difficile sit eorum judicium, tunc ponantur judicia in respectu usque ad Magnam Curiam, ut ibi per consilium curiæ terminetur.*" b For the high court of parliament met every year, " or oftener if need were," for the " maintenance and execution of the laws." c

In like manner it has been said in modern times, (and the sentiment has been before noticed with approbation,) parliament is always at hand to supply deficiencies and to correct mistakes. d

Is the legislature then to be interrogated, every time a doubt arises upon the construction of a statute, to decide particular disputes? Assuredly not. For would not this be endless? Would it not impair the usefulness, and derogate from the dignity of the judicature? Would it not give room for partiality and oppression? "Forcer le magistrat de recourir au legislateur, ce serait admettre le plus funeste des principes; ce serait renouveler parmi nous la desastreuse legislation des Rescrits. Car, losque le legislateur intervient pour prononcer sur des affaires nees et vivement agitees entre particuliers, il n'est pas plus a l'abri des surprises, que les tribunaux." And under such circumstances certainly : " On a moins a redouter l'arbitraire regle, timide et circonspect d'un magistrat qui pent etre reforme, et qui est soumis a l'action en forfaiture, que l'arbitraire absolu d'un pouvoir independant, qui n'est jamais responsable."

" Des lois intervenues sur des affaires privees seraient souvent suspectes de partialites, et toujours elles seraient retroactives et injustes pour ceux dont le litige aurait precede l'intervention de

a 2 Inst. 408.
b Bracton, lib. 1, ca. 2.
c 4 Edw. 3, ca. 14; 36 Edw. 3, ca. 20.
d *Ante*, p. 617, 641.

ces lois. De plus, le recours au legislateur entrainerait des lon-
gueurs fatales au justiciable," &c. *a* [a]

It follows, that the questions of construction before adverted to,
viz., the meaning of the terms employed by the legislature, and
the cases to which the provisions of the law are applicable, must
be left to the decision of the judges. If the judges of the inferior
courts are mistaken in their construction of a law, their decision
must be reviewed and corrected by the courts of superior jurisdiction. But by what maxims are the judges of both courts to be
guided in their expositions,—on what ground will their determinations rest? Are the courts to proceed upon established principles—to be governed by fixed rules; or, exercising a liberal discretion, to have recourse, in doubtful cases, to natural principles,
—to aid and to moderate the law according to equitable considerations,—to include in their deliberations those cases and circumstances which the legislator himself would have expressed, had he
foreseen them?

To an English lawyer, brought up with a sober veneration of
the wise maxim, (so consonant to the spirit of our constitution,
and so constantly to be traced pervading the whole body of our
jurisprudence,) that " *Optima est lex, quæ minimum relinquit arbitrio judicis; optimus judex, qui minimum sibi;*" *b* [b] the question would
seem to present little difficulty. An English judge, however, would
be in no slight degree astonished at finding it laid down as a
dogma of law, (as in the fourth article of the Titre preliminaire de
la publication des Lois :)—" Le juge qui refusera de juger, sous
pretexte du silence, de l'obscurite, ou de l'insuffisance de la loi,
pourra etre poursuivi comme coupable de deni de justice." *c* [c] On

a Discours Preliminaire, &c., p. 26.
b Aphorism, 46; Bacon's Works, vol. 7, p. 148.
c P. 26, Titre Preliminaire.

NOTE 3.—"To force the magistrate to appeal to the legislator, would be to admit the most fatal of principles; it would be to renew among us the disastrous
legislation of the Rescripts. For when the legislator interferes to decide on
matters arising, or warmly agitated among private individuals, he is no better
protected from surprises, than are the courts. We have less to fear from a controlled, timid, and circumspect decision of a magistrate who can be reformed, and
who is liable to forfeiture of his place, than from the absolute, or arbitrary decision of an independent power which is never responsible to any one.

Laws originating in private affairs, would be often suspected of partiality, and
they would always be retroactive and unjust to those whose suit would have preceded the intervention of those laws. Moreover, recourse to the legislator would
induce delays, fatal to the persons, amenable, &c."

NOTE 4.—"The Judge who should refuse to decide under the pretext of the
silence, the obscurity, or the insufficiency of the law, can be punished as guilty
of a refusal to render justice."

which law the following passage in the Discours Preliminaire *a*
may be considered as a commentary :—" Sur le fondement de la
maxime que les juges doivent obeir aux lois, et qu'il leur est defendu de les interpreter, les tribunaux, dans ces dernieres annees, ren-
renvoyaient par des referes les justiciables au pouvoir legislatif,
toutes les fois qu'ils manquaient de loi, ou que la loi existante
leur paraissait obscure.　Le tribunal de cassation a constamment
reprime cet abus, comme un deni de justice." [5]　From which important passage it is to be collected, that even among our enlightened neighbors, and at a very recent period, the boundaries of
legislation and of judicial interpretation were so vaguely defined,
and so imperfectly understood, that the Judges were constantly
either mistaking the principles, or erring in the application of
them.

The doctrine laid down in the fourth article of the *Titre Preliminaire*, before cited, will probably appear to the ordinary reader,
even in its present shape, not a little calculated to produce the
effect which the Consul Cambaceres denounced as the probable
result, before the adoption of an amendment suggested by him to
control it :—" peut faciliter les usurpations des tribunaux sur le
pouvoir legislatif." *b* [6]　The explanations, however, of this article,
which were afforded during the discussion of the *projet*, are highly valuable : *c*

Le Ministre de la Justice dit, " qu'il y a deux sortes d'interpretations, celle de legislation et celle de doctrine ; que cette derniere
appartient essentiellement aux tribunaux ; que la premiere est
celle qui leur est interdite ; que lorsqu'il est defendu aux juges
d'interpreter, il est evident que c'est de *l'interpretation legislative*
qu'il s'agit.　Il cite l'art. VII du titre 1er de l'ordonnance de 1667,
qui defend aux juges d'interpreter les ordonnances."

Le C. TRONCHET dit " que l'on a abuse, pour reduire les juges a
un etat purement passif, de la defense que leur avait faite l'assem-
blee constituante, d'interpreter des lois et de reglementer.　Cette
defense n'avait pour objet que d'empecher les tribunaux d'exercer
une partie de pouvoir legislatif, comme l'avaient fait les anciennes
cours, en fixant les sens des lois par des interpretations abstraites

a P. 25, Discours Preliminaire.
b Deuxieme redaction, seance de 14 therm. an IX.
c Titre Preliminaire, p. 28.

NOTE 5.—" On the basis of the maxim that Judges ought to obey the laws, and
that they are forbidden to interpret them, the courts of late years have referred
those amenable to justice, to the legislative power, whenever the laws were wanting, or when the existing law seemed to them obscure.　The superior court has
constantly repressed this abuse as a denial of justice."

NOTE 6.—" Can facilitate the usurpations of the courts over the legislative
power."

et generales, ou en les supleant par des arrets de reglement. Mais, pour eviter l'abus qu'on en a fait, il faut laisser au juge l'interpretation, sans laquelle il ne peut exercer son ministere. En effet, les contestations civiles portent sur les sens different que chacune des parties prete a la loi; ce n'est donc pae par une loi nouvelle, mais par l'opinion du juge, que la cause doit etre decidee. On craint que les juges n'en abusent pour juger contre le texte de la loi; s'ils se le permettaient, le tribunal de cassation aneantirait leurs jugements."

Le C. RÆDERER dit " que l'article IV donne trop de pouvoir au juge, en l'obligeant de prononcer meme dans le silence de la loi. Il appartient au juge djapplixuer la loi; il ne lui appartient pas de remplir les lacunes de la legislation, quand la loi garde un silence absolu."

Le C. PORTALIS repond " que le cours de la justice serait interrompu, s'il n'etait permis aux juges de prononcer que lorsque la loi a parle. Peu de causes sont susceptibles d'etre decidees d'apres une loi, d'apres un texte precis; c'est par les principes generaux, par la doctrine, par la science du droit, qu'on a toujours prononce sur la plupart des protestations." " En matiere criminelle le juge ne doit prononcer que lorsque la loi a qualifie de delit le fait qui est defere a la justice, et qu'elle y attache une peine; en matiere civile, au contraire, le juge ne peut se refuser a prononcer indistinctement sur toutes les causes qui lui sont presentees, parceque, s'il ne trouve pas dans la loi de regles pour decider, il doit recourir a l'equite naturelle. Ce serait trop multiplier les lois, que de les faire naitre des doutes des juges."a'

a Titre Preliminaire, p. 27.

NOTE 7.—The minister of justice says, "that there are two kinds of interpretations, that of legislation, and that of doctrine; that the latter belongs essentially to the courts; that the former is forbidden to them; that when the judges are forbidden to interpret, it is evident that it is the *Legislative Interpretation* that is meant. He quotes Article VII of the first act of the ordinance of 1667, which forbids the judges to interpret the ordinances. Trouchet says, that in order to reduce the judges to a state of purely passive, there has been an abuse of the prohibition put upon them by the Consituent Assembly, of interpreting the laws and making rulings. This prohibition had for its object only to prevent the courts from exercising a part of the legislative power, as the older courts had done, by fixing the sense of the laws by abstract and general interpretations, or by supplimenting them by rulings. But in order to prevent the abuse that has been made of it, one must leave to the judge the interpretation, without which, he cannot exercise his functions. In truth, civil disputes depend on the different sense that each of the parties gives to the law; it is not therefore by a new law, but by the opinion of the judge, that the case ought to be decided. It is feared that the judges may abuse this in order to decide against the text of the law; if they permitted themselves to do this, the superior courts would amend their decisions."

It is necessary to bear these explanations in mind, in perusing the following passages from the masterly discourse prefixed to these *Discussions sur le Code Civil;* and it is not less important to remember that in all civilized countries, except England, the United States of America, and ancient Rome, the jurisdiction of common law and of equity has been committed to the *same* courts, and that, by blending law and equity together, greater latitude is given to the judges in matters of property to modify the laws, in order to meet the purposes of justice in particular cases, than where the judges are bound by settled rules. With us, even in the courts of equity, which are supposed in some instances to admit of determinations according to conscience, and *arbitrium boni viri*, * but which really act upon settled principles, it has been a question with enlightened lawyers how far this most liberal description of equitable jurisdiction should be at any time permitted ; and whether courts of equity ought not to be, in all cases, governed by general rules. On the one hand it is admitted, that if this were the case the consequence would inevitably follow, that a judge would sometimes be bound to pronounce decrees which would be materially unjust ; since no rule can be equally just in the application to a whole class of cases, that are far from being the same in every circumstance. But on the other hand it has been thought, that even this dreadful evil should be tolerated, to avoid a greater—that of rendering judges arbitrary, and their decrees so fluctuating, that the public could never trust to them as a rule of conduct. *a*

The observations of Lord Hardwicke upon this subject, (of the establishment of general rules in our courts of equity,) are en-

Raederer says, "that Art. IV gives too much power to the judge, by obliging him to decide even in the silence of the law. It belongs to the judge to apply the law; it does not belong to him to fill the chasms of legislation when the law observes an absolute silence."

Portalis replies, "that the course of justice would be interrupted if it were only permitted to the judges to decide where the law has spoken. Few causes are susceptible of being decided according to precise law and text; the greater part of disputes have always been decided by general principles; by doctrine, and by the science of law. In criminal matters, the judge must only decide where the law has designated as a crime, the deed which is remanded, (or deferred), to justice, and when it attaches a penalty to it. In civil matters, on the contrary, the judge cannot refuse to pronounce indiscriminately on all the causes presented to him, because if there are in the law no rules by which to decide, he must have recourse to natural equity. To let the laws spring from the doubts of the judges, would be to multiply them unduly."

a Lord Kames' Principles of Equity.

* Story well explains the *arbitrium boni viri*, by the " *Vir bonus est quis ? Qui consulta patrum, qui leges juraque servat.*" Eq. J. vol. 1, p. 13. Courts of Equity are as much bound by precedents, as Courts of Law.

titled to great attention, and his remarks upon the subject of frauds seem quite conclusive upon that part of the subject. "Some general rules there ought to be, for otherwise the great inconvenience of *jus vagum et incertum* will follow; and yet the *Prœtor* must not be so absolutely and invariably bound by them, as the judges are by the rules of the common law. In the construction of trusts, which are one great head of equity jurisdiction, the rules are pretty well ascertained; so they are in cases of redemption of mortgages, which makes another great branch of that business. But as to relief against frauds, no invariable rules can be established. Fraud is infinite, and were a court of equity once to lay down rules how far they would go, and no further, in extending their relief against it, or to define strictly the species or evidence of it, the jurisdiction would be cramped, and perpetually eluded by new schemes, which the fertility of man's invention would contrive." *a*

In the same letter, but in the handling of a different topic, (which will be the subject of notice hereafter,) Lord Hardwicke expresses a decided feeling against a measure, the tendency of which would be to make the judges of the common law, law-makers in matters of property. Not so, *mutatis mutandis*, the French codifiers; by whom some contempt is indicated for the practical wisdom of those "qui osent prescrire imperieusement au legislateur la terrible tache de ne rien abandonner a la decision du juge." *s*

a Letter to Lord Kames; Lord Woodhouselee's Memoirs of the Life and Writings of Lord Kames; Parke's History of the Court of Chancery, Appendix, No. 4

NOTE 8.—"Who dare imperatively to prescribe to the legislator, the terrible task of abandoning nothing to the decision of the Judge." "Whatever we may do proceeds this same profound and analytic discourse, positive laws can never entirely take the place of natural reason in the affairs of life. The wants of society are so varied ; the intercourse of men is so active ; their interests are so multiplied, and their relations so extended, that it is impossible for the legislator to provide for every thing. In the very matters which especially engage his attention, there is a crowd of details which escape him, or which are too conflicting and too changing to become the subject of clearly expressed letter of the law."

A multitude of things is then necessarily left to the rules of custom ; to the discussion of learned men, or to the arbitrary decision of Judges.

The office to be performed by the law then, is to settle by broad views, the general maxims of law ; to establish principles, productive of uniform consequences; and not to descend into the details of the questions which may arise on every occasion.

It is the duty of the magistrate, and the lawyer, imbued with the general spirit of the laws, to direct its application.

Hence, among all civilized nations, we always see formed by the side of the sanctuary of the laws, and under the controlling guidance of the legislator, a

"Quoi que l'on fasse," proceeds the same profound and analytical discourse, a "les lois positives ne sauraient jamais entierement remplacer l'usage de la raison naturelle dans les affaires de la vie. Les besoins de la societe sont si varies, la communication des hommes est si active, leurs interets sont si multiplies et leurs rapports si etendus, qu'il est impossible au legislateur de pourvoir a tout. Dans les matieres meme qui fixent particulierement son attention, il est une foule de details qui lui echappent, ou qui sont trop contentieux et trop mobiles, pour pouvoir devenir l'objet d'un texte de loi."

"Une foule de choses sont donc necessairement abandonnes a l'empire de l'usage, a la discussion des hommes instruits, a l'arbitrage des juges."

"L'office de la loi est de fixer, par de grandes vues, les maximes generales de droit; d'etablir des principes feconds en consequences, et non de descendre dans le detail des questions qui peuvent naitre sur chaque matiere."

"C'est au magistrat et au jurisconsulte, penetres de l'esprit general des lois, a en diriger l'application."

"De la, chez toutes les nations policees, on voit toujours se former, a cote du sanctuaire des lois, et sous la surveillance du legislateur, un depot de maximes, de decisions, et de doctrine, qui s'epure journellement par la pratique et par le choc des debats judiciaires, qui s'accroit sans cesse de toutes les connaissances acquises, et qui a constamment ete regarde comme le vrai supplement de legislation."

"Il serait, sans doute, desirable que toutes les matieres pussent etre reglees par des lois."

"Mais a defaut de texte precis sur chaque matiere, un usage ancient, constant et bien etabli, une suite non interrompue de decisions semblables, une opinion et une maxime recue, tiennent lieu de loi. Quand on n'est derige par rien de ce qui est etabli ou connu, quand il s'agit d'un fait absolument nouveau, on remonte aux principes du droit naturel. Car, si la prevoyance des legislateurs est limitee, la nature est infinie; elle s'applique a tout ce qui peut interesser les hommes."

"Pour combattre l'authorite que nous reconnaissons dans les juges de statuer sur les choses qui ne sont pas determinees par les lois, on invoque le droit qu'a tout citoyen de n'etre juge que d'apres une loi anterieure et constante. Ce droit ne peut etre meconnu. Mais pour son application, il faut distinguer les matieres

a Discours Preliminaire, p. 20.

fund of maxims, of decisions and of doctrine, which is daily sifted by practice, and the collision of judicial debates, incessantly increasing by all the knowledge acquired, and which has constantly been regarded as the true supplement of legislation.

It would doubtless be desirable, that all cases should be decided by laws.

criminelles d'avec les matieres civiles," &c. "En matiere criminelle, ou il n'y a a qu'un texte formel et pre-existant qui puisse fon-
der l'action du juge, il faut des lois precises et point de jurisprudence. Il en est autrement en matiere civile : la, il faut une jurisprudence, parcequ'il est impossible de regler tous les objects civils
par des lois."
"Quand la loi est claire, il faut la suivre ; quand elle est obscure, il faut en approfondir les dispositions. Si l'on manque de
loi, il faut consulter l'usage ou l'equite. L'equite est le retour a
la loi naturelle, dans le silence, l'opposition, ou l'obscurite des lois
positives."

The tenor of these passages, (for the citation of which, from so
interesting a work, no apology is considered necessary to the intelligent reader,) may perhaps be thought, in some measure, to
confirm Bacon's sagacious opinion :—"*Apud nonnullos receptum
est, ut jurisdictio quæ decernit secundum equum et bonum, atque illa
altera quæ procedit secundum jus strictum, iisdem curiis deputentur ;
apud alios autem, ut diversis :—Omnino placet curiarum separatio.
Neque enim servabitur distinctio casuum, si fiat commixtio jurisdic-
tionum ; sed arbitrium legem tandem trahet.*" a Even as it is, when
the jurisdictions are separate, does not this effect appear to be
produced ; *arbitrium legem trahere?* how has the statute law been
dealt with?

Where so much is left to the discretion of the Judges, it is desirable to know whether any rules are prescribed for their government, and the guidance of that extensive discretion.

a De Aug. Scient. lib. 8, c. 3 aph. 45.

"But in default of a precise direction for every case, ancient customs constant and well established; an uninterrupted series of similar decisions; opinions, or received maxims, take the place of law. When we are directed by nothing
that is established or known ; when a case absolutely new occurs, we go back to
the principles of natural law. For if the foresight of the legislator is limited,
nature is infinite, and her rights apply to all that can interest men

"To contest the authority that we acknowlege in Judges of deciding things
that are not determined by the laws, we appeal to the right of every citizen of
being judged only in accordance with an anterior and fixed law. This claim
cannot be ignored. but for its application we must distinguish between civil and
criminal cases, etc."

"In criminal matters, where there is only a formal and pre-existing text which
can sustain the action of the Judge, precise laws are needed, and no jurisprudence. It is otherwise in civil matters ; there jurisprudence is needed, because
it is impossible to settle all civil cases by the laws."

"When the law is clear it must be followed ; when it is obscure, its intent
must be investigated. In the absence of law we must consult custom or equity.
Equity is the return to natural law in the silence ; in the opposition, or in the
obscurity of the positive laws."

The introductory discourse, so often already quoted, ouserves upon this head, and very judiciously : *a* " Il est trop heureux qu'il y ait des recueils, et une tradition suivie d'usages, de maximes, et de regles, pour que l'on soit, en quelque sorte, necessite a juger aujourd'hui, comme on a juge hier, et qu'il n'y ait d'autrss variations dans les jugements publics, que celle qui sont amenees par le progres des lumieres et par la force des circonstances." Again, and more emphatically : *b* " Le pouvoir judiciaire, etablie pour appliquer les lois, a besoin d'etre dirige dans cette application par certaines regles. Nous les avons tracees : elles sont telles, que la raison particuliere d'aucun homme ne puisse jamais prevaloir sur la loi, raison publique." [9]

Lastly, (and no longer mediately, but directly affecting the subject under consideration, viz., the boundaries of legislation and of judicial interpretation,) the same dissertation proceeds : " En effet, la loi statue sur tous : elle considere les hommes en masse, jamais comme particuliers ; elle ne doit point se meler des faits individuels, ni des litiges qui divisent les citoyens. S'il en etait autrement, il faudrait journellement faire de nouvelles lois : leur multitude etoufferait leur dignite et nuirait a leur observation. Le jurisconsulte serait sans fonctions, et le legislateur, entraine par les details, ne serait bientot plus que jurisconsulte. Les interets particuliers assiegeraient la puissance legislative ; ils la detourneraient, a chaque instant, de l'interet general de societe."

" Il y a une science pour les legislateurs, comme il y en a un pour les magistrats : et l'une ne ressemble pas a l'autre. La science du legislateur consiste a trouver dans chaque matiere les principes les plus favorables au bien commun : la science du magistrat est de mettre ces principes en action,—de les ramifier,—de les etendre, par une application sage et raisonee, aux hypotheses privees ; d'etudier l'esprit de la loi quand la lettre tue ; et de ne pas s'exposer au risque d'etre, tour a tour, esclave et rebelle, et de desobeir par esprit de servitude." *c* [10]

It cannot be denied, that these extracts given from the " *Dis-*

a Tit. Prel. p. 23.   *b* P. 31.   *c* P. 27.

NOTE 9.—" It is very fortunate that there are collections, and respected traditions of customs, maxims and rules, that we may in some manner be obliged to judge to day as we judged yesterday ; and that there are no other variations in public judgments, than those which are induced by the progress of knowledge and the force of circumstances."

" The judicial power established to apply the laws, needs to be directed in this application by *certain* rules ; we have marked them out ; they are such that the *private* judgment of no man, can ever prevail over *the* law ; over *public* judgment."

NOTE 10.—" In reality, the law decides equally in regard to all ; it considers men in the aggregate ; never as individuals ; it must not meddle with individual

cours Preliminaire du Premier Projet de Code Civil," [11] contain a very particular and even minute enumeration of the duties of the judge; but it may be thought to be still opon to inquiry, what are the functions of the legislator? The province of the legislator is shadowed out in the following passages, indistinctly indeed,— without relief, and in a manner wanting the bold and consistent aspect presented by the other part of the work.

"Il faut que le legislateur veille sur la jurisprudence; il peut etre eclaire par elle, et il peut de son cote la corriger ; mais il faut qu'il y en ait une."

" C'est a l'experience a combler successivement les vides que nous laissons."

" Les codes des peuples se font avec le temps ; mais a proprement parler, on ne les fait pas." *a* [12]

With us it has been shown to be the duty of the judges, where a case occurs which was not foreseen by the legislature, to declare it *casus omissus ;* or where the intention, if entertained, is not expressed, to say of the legislature, *quod voluit, non dixit ;* or where the case, though within the mischief, is not clearly within the meaning ; or where the words fall short of the intent,—or go beyond it ;—in every such case it is held the duty of the judge, in a land jealous of its liberties, to give effect to the expressed sense, or words, of the law, in the order in which they are found in the act and according to their fair and ordinary import and understanding.

As to deciding contrary to the plain words of an act of parliament,—as to holding that the legislature did not mean what it has

acts, nor with disputes that divide citizens. If it were otherwise, it would daily be necessary to make new laws ; their number would destroy their influence, and interfere with their observance. The lawyer would be without functions, and the legislator, involved in details, would soon be nothing more than the lawyer. Private interests would besiege legislative power; they would incessantly turn it aside from the general interest of society."

"There is a science for legislators, as there is one for magistrates, and the one does not resemble the other. The science of the legislator, consists in finding in each case the principles most favorable for the common welfare ; the science of the magistrate, is to put these principles in action,—to ramify them,—to extend them by a wise and thoughtful application to private assumptions ; to study the *spirit* of the law when the *letter* destroys, and not to expose himself to the risk of being by turns slave and rebel ; and to disobey in the spirit of servitude."

a P. 27.

NOTE 11.—" Introducting Discourse on the First Division of the Civil Code."

NOTE 12.—" The legislator must watch over jurisprudence ; he can be enlightened by it, and he can on his part correct it ; but there must be a jurisprudence. It devolves on experience successfully to fill the voids that it leaves. The codes of nations are said to be formed by time; but properly speaking they are not formed."

40

unequivocally expressed,—it may be observed that if with decided cases, the maxim of law be, (as it incontrovertibly is,) *stare decisis,* if the courts feel themselves bound by the positive authority of a solemn determination of the same question by former judges ; *a fortiori* ought they to be concluded, by the more positive authority of an act of parliament.

The duty of the judge is to adhere to the legal text, and not to travel out of what that expressly or impliedly contains. In the interpretation of the letter, if difficulties occur, he is to look to the spirit and object, and to be guided by the rules and the examples, which it has been a principal object of this work to collect, to compare, and to expound.

The legislator also, has his solemn duties. He is called upon, no doubt, to watch over both the jurisprudence and the judicature of his country ; to detect the deficiencies of the one, and to correct the excesses of the other. He is also to note his own miscalculations and failures, and to fill up the voids he has before left, as said by the French juris-consults. Where there has been an omission in an act,—or where his intention has been misconceived, and the remedy, in consequence, carried too far, or not given full effect to, he may supply *desiderata,* may state his own meaning with greater precision, and guard, for the future, against an application of the remedy more extensive than the intention. But—poor and limited would be his sphere, were it confined to these functions. The higher province and duty of the legislator is to exercise a *surveillance* over something more than the mere judicature of the country,—over the objects, as well as the administration, of the laws,—over the history of man and the progress of society. Silently but vigilantly is it incumbent upon him to watch the spirit of the age,—the growth of feelings,—the development of principles,—the changes of every kind produced by time,—the demand for different laws to protect newly-created species of property,—the instances in which society is found lamenting the want of a law adapted to existing circumstances,—the cases in which it is felt to be disturbed by laws utterly unsuitable,—the retention of antiquated forms—or the infliction of unprofitable severities.

These powers and duties, as explained by the English and French theories, are under a system where the legislative power is little short of absolute sovereign power. There, the powers of a judiciary, are truly, in degree, under the surveillance of the legislator. Under the American theory, the powers of the legislature, are limited by written constitutions, beyond the bound of which they may not pass, and it is conferred upon the courts of justice to declare all legislation void, which is in excess of the fundamental law. The complete independence of the courts of justice, is the essential and peculiar feature in our system. The limitations of legislative power, can be preserved in no other way than through the medium of the courts of justice. It is, and must be, the duty to declare void, all acts of the legislature which are contrary to the manifest tenor of the constitution. Without this, all the reservations of particular rights and privileges would amount to nothing.

It has been charged, by those whose minds are imbued with the idea of the perfection of the English and French systems of government, that this power of the courts in our system implies a superiority of the judiciary to the legislative power; that the power to declare an act void, must necessarily be superior to the power whose acts are declared void. Whatever may be the logic of this proposition, practically, there is no superiority of one co-ordinate department of the government over another.

We have shown in a subsequent chapter, a that the sovereign power of our governments, is distributed into three equal and co-ordinate departments of power; each distinct from, and independent of the other, each having power to act, only, within prescribed limits; and each, being sovereign while exercising its own powers within its proper sphere, but each limited in its power, by the constitution. It follows from this, that if the legislature pass an act contrary to the constitution, such act is void. It would be an imbecile and useless government, that did not possess the power to control its several departments in the exercise of a conferred and limited power. "To deny these propositions, would be to affirm, that the deputy is greater than his principal; and the servant above his master; that the representatives of the people are superior to the people themselves; that men acting by virtue of powers, may do, not only what their powers do not authorize, but what they forbid." b

By no provision of the constitution, are the legislature the constitutional judges of their own powers; they cannot set up their will, against the guaranteed rights of their constituents. It is far more reasonable to suppose, that the judicial power was intended to stand between the people and the legislature, in order to keep

a Chap. 10.   b Federalist Letter, 78.

the latter within the bounds assigned to them by the constitution. The interpretation of the laws, is the peculiar province of the courts. The constitution is, in fact, and must be, regarded by judges, as fundamental *law*. It therefore belongs to them, to ascertain its meaning, as well as of any particular act proceeding from a legislative body. If there should happen to be an irreconcilable variance between the constitution, and the statute, that which has the superior obligation and validity, ought to be preferred to the other ; the intention of the people, to the intention of their agents. *a*

Nor does this conclusion by any means suppose a superiority of the judicial to the legislative power. It only supposes that the power of the people is superior to both ; and that where the will of the legislature, declared in its statutes, stands in opposition to that of the people declared in the constitution, the judges ought to be governed by the latter, rather than by that which is not fundamental.

This exercise of judicial discretion in determining between two contradictory laws, is not an uncommon occurrence. Take the case of two statutes existing at one time, clashing in whole or in part with each other, and neither of them containing any repealing clause or expression. In such case, it is the conceded province of the court to determine their meaning and operation. So far as they can, by any fair construction be reconciled to each other, reason and law conspire to dictate that this should be done ; when that is impracticable, it becomes a matter of necessity, to give effect to one, in exclusion of the other. The rule which has obtained in the courts for determining their relative validity, is, that the last in order of time, shall be preferred to the first. But this is a mere rule of construction, not derived from any positive law, but from the nature and reason of the thing. It is a rule not enjoined upon the courts by legislative provision, but adopted by themselves, as consonant to truth and propriety, for the direction of their conduct as interpreters of the law.

It can be of no weight to say, that the courts, upon a pretense of repugnancy, may substitute their own pleasure, for the constitutional intentions of the legislature. This might as well happen in the case of two contradictory statutes ; or, it might as well as happen in every adjudication upon any single statute. The courts must declare the sense of the law; and if they should be disposed to exercise *will*, instead of *judgment*, the consequence would be equally the substitution of their pleasure, to that of the legislative body. The objection to the exercise of this power by the courts of justice upon this ground, if it would prove anything, would prove that there ought to be no judges, distinct from that body, or in other words, that the legislative body ought to possess also, judicial powers. *a* The powers, legislative and judicial, in the same hands, with no check or control other than their own will, might be pronounced the very best definition of tyrrany.

It is now comparatively rare that rules of universal and constant operation are laid down by statutes. In former times, a simple, general rule was enounced, with a corresponding simplicity of expression, and the praise of the ancient lawgiver was considered to be, in the words of Lord Coke, that "prudent antiquity included much matter in few words." *b* But such statute law could not maintain an unbending character. Its harshness would have been intolerable, if indiscriminating, general rules could not have been mitigated by judicial construction, in cases where they produced an unintended injury or oppression. In those times, the unquestionable use and advantage of interpretative legislation was, that it modified and adapted the law to special cases, and the sages of the law are accordingly and justly commended for the improvements they by these means effected in the institutions of the country.

No intelligent man will deny that, with us, the laws have, in a succession of ages, been gradually adapted to the free institutions of the country. Beyond all question, we are extensively indebted to the liberality of the judges, for much of the regulated freedom we at present enjoy.

Again, no reflecting man can fail to perceive that there has been the greater facility in making this adaptation, in so far as our laws were unwritten, or part-written, and therefore, in a certain sense, unascertained. So far, good has unquestionably resulted from our laws being in an unsettled state, and propounded in generalities. From not being more formally prescribed, the laws were less certain—from being less certain, they admitted of being rendered more complete.

It is the character of modern legislation, that it applies itself to particular cases, and classes of cases, and endeavors to adjust the law to their varieties, and to determine specifically every kind of right and every corresponding obligation. It is not easy to esti-

a Id. *b* 2 Inst. 306—id. 401.

mate the practical importance of specific legislation, in adjusting our law to the various interests of the community. But one of its effects has certainly been to put an end to verbal generalities in propounding the law, though the draftsman may not invariably succeed in his endeavor to supply its place with aptness and certainty of expression; and often indulges in too much verbiage. But *abundans cautela non nocet*, and to this period belongs the different praise of that wisdom "which aims to make things as plain, and to leave as little to construction as may be." *a*

Where the law was only part-written, it was left to the judges to adjust the law to special cases and to supply every deficiency by construction.

But, where the law *is* specifically prescribed and promulgated as the declared will of the supreme power in the state, the case is wholly different. Supposing the written law to require change or modification, it will hardly admit a question, whether such alteration is to be effected in a direct manner, by the superior power that originally created the law, or indirectly, by the subordinate authority employed to give it effect, and put it in operation; and if a doubt could exist upon the subject of the comparative competency and fitness of the legislature, and of the judicature of the country, to correct its laws, recourse should in preference be had to the legislature. For the legislature usually founds its regulations upon general principles; Courts of law—and of equity—frequently refine upon individual cases.

Their different functions have been thus illustrated. The lawgiver commands that housebreakers shall be hanged; the judge orders that for a specific burglary, a particular thief shall be hanged. The legislator determines a class and description of acts; and commands, with a like generality, that punishment shall follow. The judge orders a specific punishment, the consequence of a specific offence.

1st. Laws are made directly by statute, in the properly legislative way.

2ndly. Laws are made judicially, in the way of improper legislation.

Of this latter class, admitted and unexceptionable instances are —1. Laws fashioned by judicial decisions upon pre-existing customs; "*jus moribus constitutum.*" 2. Laws founded upon authority of learned writers and ancient sages of the law; "*jus prudentibus compositum.*" 3. Laws drawn from the natural law, founded on the law of God. 4. Laws of foreign original, fashioned on positive international law; the "*jus receptum.*"

The positive law made judicially, is equally binding with the law made in the properly legislative manner. Considered as moral rules turned into positive laws, customary laws are binding as

a 2 Inst. 375.

established by the state : established by the state directly, when the customs are promulged in its statutes; established by the state circuitously, when the customs are adopted by its tribunals. *a*

A portion of the sovereign power is tacitly delegated to the judge; though a subject, the judge is, in strictness, merely a minister. Since the state may reverse the rules which he makes, and yet permits him to enforce them by the power of the political community, its sovereign will "that his rules shall obtain as law," is clearly evinced by its conduct, though not by its express declaration. This is the explanation given, *b* why subject judges, who are properly ministers and administrators of the law, have commonly shared with the sovereigns in the business of making it.

But in a great variety of cases, as will be hereafter shown, the invasion by the judges, of the province of the legislature, has been quite unjustifiable. Yet, if in modern times, complaints be justly made of alterations in the laws effected by equitable interference, or by judicial usurpation, it is ascribable to the remisness of the legislature, which should long since have provided for a revision of our statute law.

The truth is, that the legislature, and not the courts, should be driven to comply with the necessities of mankind. But this, unfortunately, has not been the practice. When rules of law have been found to work injustice, they have been evaded, instead of being repealed. Obsolete or unsuitable laws, instead of being removed from the statute book, have been made to bend to modern usages and feelings. Instead of the legislature framing new provisions, as occasions has required, it has been left to able judges to invade its province, and to arrogate to themselves the lofty privilege of correcting abuses and introducing improvements. The rules are thus left in the breasts of the judges, instead of being put upon a right footing by legislative enactment.

Much of the evil just described, is no doubt attributable to the supineness of the legislature,—something to the narrowness of the rules of the common law,—but the principal share, to the want of a proper understanding at what point interpretation ought to end, and legislation should begin. *c* Let the discriminating reader look at Burke's eloquent panegyric upon Lord Mansfield, and then ask himself soberly—whether every improvement the orator ascribes to the Judge, however unquestionable meritorious, is not within the province, and ought not to have been effected by the intervention of the legislature? " He sought," it is said, " to effect the amelioration of the law, by making its liberality keep pace with justice, and the actual concerns of the world ; and not restricting the infinitely diversified conditions of men, and the rules of natural justice, within artificial circumscriptions, but conforming its principles to the growth of our commerce and our empire."

a Austin on Jurisprudence, 29.   *b* Id. *ad fin.*   *c* Butler's Reminis. voL 1.

It is not in the examination and solution of constitutional questions alone, that great abilities, and a thorough mastery of the
principles of government, are required of American legislators and
American jurists.   The ordinary course of legislation, in the state
and national councils, is full of intricate and perplexing duties,
and laborious research, if intelligently and appropriately performed.   It is not every man, that can make an animated address
at a popular meeting or run through the common places of party
declamation at a political caucus with fluent elocution and
steady pressure, who is qualified for a seat in the national, or in
the state legislatures, or, upon the judicial bench. *a*

All history and experience have taught us, that the great mass
of human calamities in our own period of experiment in government, as in all ages, has been the result of bad government; of a
capricious exercise of power; a fluctuating public policy; or a de-
grading tyranny in which a portion of its subjects have been held
in unequal bondage, through the means of a desolating ambition.
The besetting delusion in a popular form of government, especially when controlled by men unlearned, and unskilled in the
science of government, is, that its administration is a matter of ·
great simplicity; that its principles are clear, and that they, its
agents, are hardly liable to mistakes, and they easy satisfy themselves, that it is a satisfactory method of winning popular favor
by appeals which flatter popular prejudices; and that designs,
which they are thus enabled to accomplish by being sustained by
such evidence of approbation of their agency, is regarded as satisfactory evidence also of capacity.

But in truth, an intelligent and unprejudiced mind, ripe with
human experience, may safely assert, that just in proportion as a
government is free, and extended over a vast and populous
domain of diversified habits, manners, institutions, climates, employments, characters, passions, and even prejudices and propen-
sities, so in proportion the administration must be complicated.
Simplicity, belongs to governments only, where one will governs
all; where one mind directs, and all others obey; where few
arrangements are required, because no checks to power are allowed;
where law is not a science, but a mandate to be followed, and not

a Story on the Science of Government.

to be discussed; where it is not a rule for permanent action, but a capricious and arbitrary dictate of the hour. *a*

To fit a man for a legislator to enact laws in a sound system of free government, we may adopt the opinion of Lord Brougham. "It requires that he should read and inform himself upon political subjects; else they are the prey of every quack, of every imposter, every agitator, who may practice his trade in the country. If he do not read, if he does not learn, if he does not digest by discussion and reflection what he has read and learned; if he does not qualify himself to form opinions for himself, other men will form opinions for him; not according to the truth, and the interests of the people, but according to their own individual and selfish interest, which may, and most probably will be contrary to that of the people at large. The best security for a government like ours, (a free government,) and generally for the public peace, and public morals, is, that the whole community should be well informed upon its political as well as its other interests."

The principles of the constitution under which we live, and under which our legislators are called to act in the enactment of laws; the principles upon which the republics are founded; by which they are sustained, and by which they must be saved; the principles of public policy by which the national prosperity is secured, and national ruin averted; are not party credit, or party dogma's; but are principles inherent in, or fundamental to every citizen of the government. There are no secular blessings in human life of more inestimable value, than those derived from good government, where honest labor has its just reward, property its perfect security; domestic life undisturbed tranquility; and every citizen, without regard to rank, color or condition, an equal right to the enjoyment of liberty. These are rights secured by the constitution and made perfect by legislation.

As to the assumptions of jurisdiction by the court of chancery, it will be more satisfactory to rest upon the admissions of its ornament, as well as apologist, Lord Hardwicke; than to refer to the opinion of Mr. Humphreys, its less ardent admirer, that "its acts have been rather legislative than judicial." *b*

Whatever may be regarded as the distinct and certain origin of

a Id.   *b* Humphrey's Observations on the Laws of Real Property, &c,

the Court of Chancery in England, it was seldom resorted to, until
the passage of two noted statutes, the statutes of wills, and uses,
in the reign of Henry VIII, and after these, the statute of charitable uses, in the reign of Queen Elizabeth.   These, together, says
Mr. Justice Story, a "laid the foundation of that broad and comprehensive judicature, in which equity administers through its
searching interrogations addressed to the consciences of men, the
most beneficent and wholesome principles of justice.   The whole
modern structure of trusts, infinitely diversified as it is by marriage
settlements, terms to raise portions to pay debts, contingent and
springing appointments, resulting uses, and implied trusts, grew
out of this last named statute, and the constructions put upon it."

Under the guidance of Lord Bacon, the business of chancery
assumed a regular course ; and at the distance of two centuries,
his celebrated ordinances continue to be the pole star which
directed, and still directs the course of courts of equity.   At a
later day, the doctrines of the courts of equity attained a still
higher degree of perfection.   Lord Nottingham brought to that
branch of jurisprudence, a strong and cultivated mind, and pronounced his decrees after the most cautious and painstaking
study.   Lord Cowper, and Lord Talbot, pursued the same course
with the genuine spirit of jurists.   But, in England, it was reserved
for Lord Hardwicke, by his deep learning and extensive researches
and his powerful genius, to combine the scattered fragments into
a scientific system ; to define with a broader line the boundaries
between the departments of the common law and chancery ; and
to give certainty and vigor to the principles, as well as the jurisdiction, of the latter.   Henceforth, equity began to acquire the
same exactness as the common law.   At a still later period, we
have seen in the labors of Lord Eldon through a series of more
than twenty-five volumes of reports, a diligence, sagacity, caution
and force of judgment, which have seldom been equalled ; and
which gave dignity as well as finish to that great moral machinery
which administered the rules and doctrines of conscience *ex aequo
et bono.*"

But we may take pride in saying, that no higher degree of perfection in the system of equitable jurisprudence was ever attained

a Story's Progress of Jurisprudence.

in England, nor its administration conducted with a higher degree of credit for learning and research, than is to be found in the reported adjudications of Kent and Walworth, whose reported opinions and decrees are found moulded into a degree of moral beauty and perfection which their English predecessors have not surpassed, or been exceeded by the learned treatises upon equitable jurisprudence of Justice Story.

"New discoveries and inventions in commerce," says Lord Hardwicke, in a letter to Lord Kames before referred to, "have given birth to new species of contracts; and these have been followed by new contrivances to break and elude them, for which the ancient simplicity of the common law had adapted no remedies; and from this cause, courts of equity, which admit of a greater latitude, have, under the head *adjuvandi, vel supplendi juris civilis,* been obliged to accommodate the wants of mankind."

"Another source of the increase of business in the courts of equity has been, the multiplication and extension of trusts. New methods of settling and incumbering landed property have been suggested by the necessities, extravagance, or real occasions of mankind. But what is more than this, new species of property have been introduced, particularly by the establishment of the public funds, and various transferable stocks, that required to be modified and settled to answer the exigencies of families, to which the rules and methods of conveyancing would not ply or bend. Here the liberality of courts of equity has been forced to step in and lend her aid."

In comparing the present state of jurisprudence in this country, with that of a former day in England, we have much reason for congratulation. In arbitrary, and despotic governments, the laws rarely undergo any considerable changes through a long series of years. In free governments, and in those where the popular interests have obtained some representation or power, however limited, the case has been far otherwise. We can here trace a regular progress in the laws from year to year, and a gradual adaptation of them to the wants, employments, and improved condition of man under a free government, corresponding to their advancement with arts, in the sciences, in intelligence, and in the refinements and elegancies of life. As the citizen is made to feel his independence, dignity, and responsibility as a portion of the sovereign power; as civilization advances, and he becomes educated in the knowledge of his rights, and is called in to assist in the formation of the government of his choice; we find him engaging himself in adopting a system of fundamental law, in which, the judicial powers are separated from the executive and legislative authorities; and men are selected for judicial positions, whose sole duty it is, to administer justice, and correct abuses. "The punishment of crimes, at first arbitrary, is found gradually moulded into a system, and moderated in its severity; and property, which in other countries is inherited under a law of primogeniture, with a permanancy of tenure, becomes here, transmissable in equal portions to the descendants of those whose enterprise, or good fortune, has accumulated it." a

We know from the history of the times, that before the revolution, while our system of jurisprudence was substantially that of the mother country, our progress in the law was slow, though not slower, perhaps, than in other departments of science; the resources of the country were small, the population sparce and scattered, the business of the courts limited, the compensation for professional services moderate, and the judges not always selected from those learned in the law. Our colonial condition restrained our foreign commerce; the principal trade was to, or through the mother country, and our most important contracts began or ended there. While there were learned men in the profession, their number was small; and from the nature of the business which occupied the courts, the knowledge required for common use, was neither very ample, nor very difficult.

Since the war of independence, the progress of jurisprudence in this country has been most rapid, keeping equal pace with the progress of population, and to the advance in all the arts and knowledge that now characterize its people. With a union of thirty-six independent states, now, and two or more territories, now waiting for admission as states, in nearly all of which, the same common law, substantially is the acknowledged basis of their jurisprudence, and upon which, their statutes, part of their jurisprudence, are enacted; we find, notwithstanding the differences of habits, of climate, nationalities, peculiarities, local customs and judicial determinations, a far greater degree of uniformity in the law and its administration, than could have been expected. The

a Story on Jurisprudence.

task however, of administering justice for the causes above mentioned, in the state and national courts, owing to the somewhat complex system of national and state jurisdictions, is both laborious and perplexing, owing to the almost unavoidable consequence of their peculiar relations to each other,—and of course, one of the most common embarrasments, arises from the conflict of rival jurisdictions.

The most delicate, and at the same time, the proudest attribute of American jurisprudence, is the right of its judicial tribunals to decide questions of constitutional law.   In England, the legislative authority is practically omnipotent; the judicial power cannot reach them.   Here, says Judge Story, "the privilege of bringing every law to the test of the constitution, belongs to the humblest citizen, who owes no obedience to any legislative act which transcends the constitutional limits."   However much, at an earlier day, the sympathies of those learned in the English system, may have led them to question this doctrine, their views have been yielded, and at this day, the question is no longer mooted in the courts.   The wise and the learned, and the virtuous, are unanimous in sustaining the doctrine which the courts of justice have uniformly asserted; that the constitution, is not only the law for the legislature, but is the law, and the supreme law, which is to direct and control all judicial proceedings.

. "The discussion of constitutional questions," says judge Story, "throws a lustre round the bar, and gives dignity to its functions, which can rarely belong to the profession in any other country. Lawyers are here emphatically placed as sentinels upon the outposts of the constitution; and no nobler end can be proposed for their ambition or patriotism, than to stand as faithful guardians of the constitution, ready to defend its legitimate powers, and to stay the arm of legislative, executive or popular oppression.   If their eloquence can charm, when it vindicates the innocent and the suffering under private wrongs; if their learning and genius can, with almost superhuman witchery, unfold the mazes and intricacies by which the minute links of title are chained to the adamantine pillars of the law ;—how much more glory belongs to them, when this eloquence, this learning, and this genius, are employed in defence of their country ; when they breathe forth the purest spirit of morality and virtue in support of the rights of mankind; when they expound the lofty doctrines which sustain, and connect, and guide the destinies of nations; when they combat popular delusions at the expense of fame, and friendship, and political honors; when they triumph by arresting the progress of error and the march of power, and drive back the torrent that threatens destruction equally to public liberty and to private property; to all that delights us in private life, and all that gives grace and authority in public office."

" This is a subject, which cannot too deeply engage the most solemn reflections of the profession. Our danger lies in the facility, with which, under the popular cast of our institutions, honest but visionary legislators and artful leaders may approach to sap the foundations of our government. Other nations have the security against sudden changes, good or bad, in the habits of the people, or in the nature of their institutions. They have a monarchy gifted with high prerogatives; or a nobility graced with wealth and knowledge and hereditary honors; or a stubborn national spirit, proud of ancient institutions, and obstinate against all reforms. These are obstacles, which resist the progress even of salutary changes; and ages sometimes elapse before such reforms are introduced, and yet more ages before they are sanctioned by public reverence. The youthful vigor of our constitutions of government, and the strong encouragements, held out to free discussion, to new inquiries and experiments, expose us to the opposite inconvenience of too little regard for what is established, and too warm a zeal for untried theories. This is our weak point of defence; and it will always be assailed by those who pant for public favor, and hope for advancement in political struggles."

Under the pressure of temporary evils, or the misguided impulses of party, or plausible alarm for public liberty, it is not difficult to persuade ourselves, that what is established is wrong; that what bounds the popular wishes is oppressive; and that what is untried, will give permanent relief and safety. Frame constitutions of government with what wisdom and foresight we may, they must be imperfect, and leave something to discretion, and much to public virtue. It is in vain that we insert bills of rights in our constitutions, as checks upon legislative power, unless there be firmness in courts, in the hour of trial, to resist the fashionable opinions of the day. The judiciary in itself, has little power, except that of protection for others. It operates mainly by an appeal to the understandings of the wise and the good; and its chief support, is the integrity and independence of an enlightened bar.

While our judges remain fearless and firm in the discharge of their functions, corrupt and popular leaders at the bar cannot possess a wide range of oppression, but must stand rebuked in their career for power. But it requires no uncommon spirit of prophecy to foresee, that whenever the liberties of this country are to be destroyed, it will be when public opinion shall be lost in the integrity of the judiciary; when the conspiracy shall be bold enough to corrupt, and judges be found so wanting in character as to consent to be corrupted; then shall we see the courts of justice brought into public odium; and thus shall be seen removed, the last barriers between the people and despotism.

Thus it appears, that these objects, rendered necessary by a change of circumstances, have been effected by equitable interference,—that is, in truth, by judicial refinement, and not by the seasonable enactment of salutary laws. Instead of the encroachment upon the common law, of which Bacon was apprehensive, it seems that the Prætorian courts * overflowed their banks in an opposite direction, and, while sparing of injunctions, openly invaded the province of the Legislature. Upon a careful investigation of the course actually pursued, it will be found that, in general, inconvenient laws were set aside, and required changes were effected, by the use of technical fictions, and contrivances to evade inconsistent rules; and if there have been a lamentable want of politic institution, there has been thought to have been also, at times, some defect of judicial principle. Mr. Butler is decidedly of opinion, as regards the ascertaining and obtaining the proper boundary of interpretation and legislation, that the French courts of justice have shown greater moderation than our own, in the exercise of this important branch of judicature. a It certainly is a remarkable fact, that the jurisdiction or methods of proceeding in all our superior courts, will be discovered, on inquiry, to be founded in usurpation, and sustained by fiction.

a Reminis. vol. 1.

* "Maxime omnium interest certitudinis legum, ne curiæ prætoriæ intumescant et exundent in tantum, ut prætextu rigoris legum mitigandi, etiam rober et nervos iis incidant aut laxent, omnia trahendo ad arbitrium."—*Aphorism*, 43.

The jurisdiction of the court of King's Bench in civil actions, was notoriously acquired by contrivance, the court of common pleas having had, in former times, the exclusive cognizance of all suits merely civil, that is to say, which had nothing in the proceedings of a criminal nature, inasmuch as neither trespass nor violence were imputed to the defendant. But by a fiction of law, all persons alleged to be prisoners, in the custody of the Marshal of the Marshalsea, though not actually being so, were held, *as such*, liable to be sued in any personal action, by bill filed in the court of king's bench.

The court of common pleas always had a direct jurisdiction in civil suits; but "regularly," says Lord Coke, "the court cannot hold any common pleas in any action, real, personal, or mixed, but by writ out of the chancery, and returnable in this court, *a* (except by the privilege of its officers.)" Yet without setting out any original writ, the common *capias* proceeded upon the foundation of such supposed previous proceeding.

The peculiar jurisdiction of the court of exchequer at common law, related to matter concerning the king's revenue; "the effectual description of the jurisdiction of the court being," says Lord Coke, *b* "that it is for the profit of the king." Hence, it was early established, that any person being a debtor or accountant of the crown, might sue in the exchequer either at equity or at law, to obtain a right, the withholding of which rendered him less able to satisfy his debt to the crown.

It has been already seen, of what handles the court of chancery availed itself, and by what means it was enabled to assume a jurisdiction over real property, greatly more extensive than was ever possessed by the common law courts.

Upon the subject of legal fictions, (the instrument by which all these usurpations were affected,) the following judicious remarks were made by the intelligent persons appointed to inquire into the practice and proceedings of the superior courts of common law. The observations of the learned commissioners are so well founded, acute, and sensible, and so apt to the present purpose of this work, that no hesitation can be felt in citing and adopting them *verbatim*, as they occur in their first report. *c* "Our ancient institutions having been adapted to a rude and simple state of society, the courts, in later times, gradually became sensible of defects of jurisdiction and other inconveniences, to which the altered circumstances of the nation had naturally given rise. In some cases the remedy was supplied by legislative regulations; but where this was wanting, the judges were apt to resort to fiction, as an expedient for effecting indirectly, that which they had no authority to establish by law. But to whatever causes the invention or en-

a 4 Inst. 99.   *c* First Common Law Report, p. 82.
b 4 Inst. 112.

couragement of legal fictions may be assignable, we have no doubt that they have an injurious effect in the administration of justice, because they tend to bring the law itself into suspicion with the public, as an unsound and delusive system; while an impression of the ridiculous is also occasionally excited by them, of which the natural effect must be to degrade the science in some measure, in popular estimation."

The same observations apply to other cases :—to what has been termed the "clumsy" fiction of a lost grant in the case of an easement;—to judges presuming an act of parliament;—to directions to juries to presume the surrender of a term or something else absolutely contrary to the fact, in lieu of altering an inconvenient law by direct legislative enactment; *a* in short to all instances of ingenuity employed in contrivances to evade a law that requires to be altered.

It only remains to be stated, that there has not been any marked reciprocity of usurpation. The case of bills and attainder and bills of pains and penalties is the only familiar instance of the legislature quitting its proper province, and superseding the judicial functions.

a First Report of Real Property Commissioners.

42

CHAPTER X.

OF AMERICAN CONSTITUTIONAL POWER. ITS LIMITATIONS; ITS DIS-
TRIBUTION OF THE SOVEREIGN POWER TO THREE DEPART-
MENTS; THE INDEPENDENCE OF EACH DEPARTMENT OF THE
OTHER. THE FUNCTIONS OF EACH DEPARTMENT IN THE AD-
MINISTRATION OF THE LAW.

In the preceding chapter, was considered, the nature and extent of legislative power independent of any restriction, contained
in the written constitutions of the nation or state. In this, we
propose to show some of the limitations of legislative power; and
this seems to demand, that we show what constitutes the law-
making power in a free, republican form of government; and how
this power is organized under our system of written constitutions,
with its limitations and restrictions, into several departments; and
the separate powers and duties of each department.

This law making power, as our author has remarked, in all
civilized governments, is usually, vested in the sovereign power of
the state. By sovereign power, is usually meant, unlimited and
uncontrolled power. This, seems to have been the opinion of
almost all the ancient writers, that in whatever department of the
government this power was lodged, it was regarded as absolute,
and beyond control; that it must, absolutely, be possessed by
some one department of government; and that the person or power
in whom this sovereignty resides, is the supreme power in the
making and promulgation of laws; and this, is usually called the
legislative power. a

These opinions, however, are chiefly confined to, and are the
reasonings of the ethical and juridicial writers of Europe, among
whom no uniformity of opinion really exists. Burlimaqui says
"that this sovereign power is supreme and independent, and when
once established, it acknowledges no other upon earth superior or
equal to it." b "That among the essential parts of sovereignty, the

a Paley's Mor. Philos., 2 part 185.   b Prin. of Pol. Law, Pt. 1, Ch. 6.

first rank is given to the legislative power." *a* He however admits that God alone, by reason of His nature and perfections, has a natural, essential, and inherent right of giving laws to mankind, and of exercising an absolute sovereignity over them. *b* That human sovereigns are God's vicegerents on earth, which means, that, by the power lodged in their hands, and with which the people have invested them, they maintain, agreeably to the views of the Deity, both order and peace, and thus procure the felicity of mankind; and he quotes a passage from Cicero, to this purpose, viz: "Nothing is more agreeable to the Supreme Deity, that governs this universe, than civil societies lawfully established."

We do not propose in this work to fully discuss the diversities of theory upon the question of sovereignty, except in American governments; to show where this power resides; to trace it to its origin; to exhibit its power in the European governments as it is claimed by the various writers on this subject; or to compare their various theories for the purpose of drawing any conclusion therefrom. As it is understood to the ordinary mind, sovereignty is that public authority, which has no superior; it is the power to do any thing and every thing in a State, without being accountable to any one; to make laws and to execute them; it is that power which commands in organized civil society, and which orders and directs what each must do, to acquire its ends. With us, it is a union of all the powers of the state. Abstractedly considered, it belongs to the people, and resides, essentially in the body of the nation, but with us, the nation, by the people, now exercise this power by delegation. To the curious who may desire to investigate; to the student of history who may desire to make research; to the politician who may desire to learn and to compare the powers of different governments, and to the philosopher who seeks the profoundest sources of knowledge upon the science of governments, with all its incidents, we commend the theories of such juridicial writers as Grotius, Puffendorf, Burlimaqui, Coke, Blackstone, Domat, Locke, Burke, Christian, Wooddeson, and others of greater or less note.

It will be our object, to present in this treatise, the American idea of the powers of legislation; and to show how far the exercise

a Id. Pt. 3, Ch. 1.   *b* Id.

of sovereign authority is vested in our legislative bodies, only so far as is practically necessary to present the controlling force and authority of our own statutes.

Sovereignty, it is true, in our own, as well as in all other civilized governments imports the supreme, absolute, uncontrollable power by which any state is governed, *a* but sovereignty, in our republican form of government, is not vested alone in the law-making power.

It is not true therefore, in our form of government, as is laid down in the philosophy of Paley, that the sovereign power is necessarily lodged in one separate and distinct department of government where it remains absolute and uncontrolled; *b* nor according to the theory of Burlimaqui, that when its seat is ascertained, it possesses the power to judge in the last resort of whatever is susceptible of human direction which relates to the welfare and advantage of society; and that in this respect it acknowledges no superior or equal. These, and many others of the ancient writers upon this subject, based their opinions upon the assumption, that princes ruled by a right Divine, conferred by the immediate act of the Deity. But even this theory, has been exploded by the government of Great Britain, and most of the English writers now claim that the parliament of England, possesses the attribute o political, legal and moral omnipotence. *c*

By the theory of our government, the primary, as well as the ultimate sovereignty in human affairs, is in the people, from whom, all legitimate civil authority springs. This is applicable not only to the National, but to the State governments. In the international sense, the word *State*, is applicable only to the federal government, but as between the sovereign members of the American union, the word *Nation* is used as applying to the federal, and *State*,[1] as applicable to the several component members.

a Story on Const., § 207.   *b* Paley's Mor. Philos., Pt. 2, p. 185.
c 1 Black com. 160, 408; 8 Co. 118, Bac. Abr., stat. A.

NOTE 1.—In a republic, the sovereignty resides in the great body of the people, not as so many distinct individuals, but in their politic capacity. Penhallow v. Doane, 3 Dallas 93. The sovereignty of the United States, and of the several states, are distinct and independent of each other within their respective spheres of action; though both exist within the same territorial limits. Ableman v. Booth, 21, How. 506. They retain in severalty, a distinct but qualified sovereignty. Hubbard v. N. Railroad Co., 3 Blatch, C. C. 84.

When the people of the United States instituted civil government, they constituted it one federal nation. They declared in their preamble to the constitution, as follows: "We, the people of the United States, in order to form a more perfect union, establish justice, insure domestic tranquility, provide for the common defence, promote the common welfare, and secure the blessings of liberty to ourselves and our posterity, *Do ordain and establish* this Constitution of the United States of America."

The national government thus created by the voice of the people, became a national body politic and corporate, invested with supreme authority for national purposes, with power to exercise all such authority as was expressly or impliedly committed to its jurisdiction by the constitution.

It is the logical and necessary result, that the powers of a government established upon republican principles, and upon an express compact, like this, (if it may be called such,) that the extent and nature of its powers must be determined by the terms of the instrument itself. Within the conferred limits, the government must still be sovereign, and must exercise its sovereign power for national purposes, and must distribute to its various departments, their appropriate duties with power to exercise them.

"By this constitution of the United States, supreme legislative, judicial, and executive powers of the government are created, each distinct from, and independent of the other; each entrusted with a portion of the sovereign authority within the sphere of its prescribed duties and powers." *a*

"It must have sovereign authority, within the prescribed limits, to enact all laws necessary for the government of the society composing the nation;" and this power was therein conferred. *

By this analysis, we find this delegated authority thus conferred, distributed into three departments of power, and each independent of the other, viz: the *legislative*, the *judiciary*, and the *executive*.

The first, is the power to make new laws, and to correct, repeal

a Tiffany's American Theory, 62.

Note 2.—"All legislative powers herein granted shall be vested in a congress of the United States, which shall consist of a Senate and House of Representatives." Const. U. S., Art. 1, Sec. 1.

or abrogate the old. The second, is the power to apply the law to particular facts; to judge of differences which may arise among citizens or inhabitants of the state, and to punish crimes. This power is vested in courts of justice. The third, is the power to cause the laws to be executed. This power is exercised by a single individual as President, or Governor.

So too, "a government thus composed must have supreme authority to interpret and apply those laws to the rights of every individual and subject within its jurisdiction." This was also a provision of this fundamental law. [*]

" To be sovereign in its judicial department, there must exist no other or higher tribunal to which appeal can be taken to review its final judgments or decrees. A sovereign judiciary must possess the right of final interpretation and decision in applying the law." [a]

" To be sovereign in its executive department there must exist no other authority to stay the execution of its judgments and decrees." [*]

Thus it is seen, that while in its international character, the government of the United States stands equal in rank and equal in its powers of sovereignty to that of any other nation. Yet in the exercise of its powers, in behalf of and towards its own citizens, it is a limited government, deriving its existence and authority from the people, and entrusted by them with the exercise of such powers only, as are expressly granted, or given by necessary implication, in the constitution. And the people, in the constitution itself, reserve all powers not delegated to the United States by the constitution, nor prohibited by it, to the states respectively, or to the people. [*]

These departments of the sovereign power are still knit together by one common bond; all are disposed to act in harmony for the promotion of the great ends of the government, its security, its preservation, and the public good.

a Tiffany's Govt., § 111.

NOTE 3.—"The judicial power of the United States shall be vested in one supreme court, and in such inferior courts as congress may from time to time ordain and establish." Const. U. S., Art. 3, Sec. 1.

NOTE 4.—" The executive power shall be vested in a President of the United States, &c." Const. U. S., Art. 2.

NOTE 5.—Const. U. S., Art. 10.

The potential powers of a republican government which exercise their sovereignty, to wit: the legislative, the judiciary and the executive, are plainly discovered and easily distinguished, as are the division of duties conferred upon, and responsibilities assumed by each of these departments.

It is easy to discover in this organization, that it is one of the chief offices of sovereignty, to prescribe and declare to others, what they ought to perform, and what to omit; to establish general rules for the perpetual information and direction of all persons, in all points either of positive or of negative duty; to determine what each person should look to as his own, and what as another's; what is to be regarded as lawful or unlawful in the state; what is honest and what is dishonest; what degree of natural liberty each person retains, and what he has surrendered to governmental power, and after what manner each person is to exercise and regulate his own private rights, in order to secure the public good and public tranquility; this office is the legislative power.

Notwithstanding laws are thus prescribed, duties thus enjoined, and wrongs thus forbidden, as well in our own theory of government as in all others, it is still manifest that human nature is imperfect, and in many persons, greatly corrupted, so that experiment sadly informs us of the great want of reverence for prescribed laws. For which likewise, it is not enough to have a power to prescribe rules of conduct, and for the exercise of rights, and prohibition of wrongs, if it is invested with no further power. To secure therefore, the common natural rights of all men, as well as the observance of those particular laws which are enacted for the good of the whole people of a state, there must be added, not only the fear of punishment, but the power of inflicting what is feared; this is another of the objects of civil government. This power is the judiciary power, which is supposed to come to the aid of legislative. The office of this power is to hear and decide the causes of the people; to examine the conduct of the particular persons whose rights are affected by breaches of the prescribed laws; and to pronounce a proper sentence or judgment according to the prescribed rules, in case of breach or violation.

Still these powers and sovereignty, of prescribing laws and punishing its violations, would be inefficient for their designed objects, without another department of the same power; without officers to be appointed as co-ordinate magistrates to enquire into, pass upon, and settle all controversies and violations of law arising between the citizens and others, and between the public and the citizen; and whose duty it shall be to put the laws in execution; to compel such officers when once appointed to the performance of their duties; to call them to account on proper occasions for its non-performance; and also, in appropriate cases, to possess the powers of grace or pardon. This co-ordinate appointing and controlling power is called the executive power.

Thus distributing the powers of sovereignty into distinct councils, or bodies; it must necessarily follow, that each department exercising its appropriate functions and duties, must have conferred upon it, and must possess, all necessary power to compel the observance of those things of which it is given cognisance; for, to possess a right of declaring to others what they should do, or submit to, and yet be destitute of the power to enforce obedience to its order, would be to leave the department a helpless excrescence, and a vain pretence, destructive of the ends of its creation.

It is to be observed, in this connection, that the constitutions, national and state, having established these three separate departments, has also assigned to each, by true implication, distinct powers and duties; and from their distinct functions and the objects committed to them, there is also the necessary implication which has grown into a maxim that forbids each of them to encroach upon the powers and duties of either of the others. a   Each of these departments exercises its powers and functions upon objects which arise under, or are called into existence by the constitutions, laws, or of treaties. "These departments are co-ordinate in degree, to the extent of the powers delegated to each of them. Each in the exercise of its powers, is independent of the other, but all rightfully done by either, is binding upon the other. The constitution is supreme over all of them, because the people who ratified it, have made it so; consequently, any thing which may be done, and which is unauthorized by it, is unlawful." b

a Luther v. Borden 7 How. U. S. R. 1, 39.
b Dodge v. Woolsey 18 How. U. S. R. 347.

But when we speak of governments limited by written constitutions, we ought to enquire what is a constitution, in the American sense, of written constitutions? It may be well answered in the language of Justice Patterson, a of the supreme court of the United States : "It is the form of governments, delineated by the mighty hand of the people, in which certain first principles of fundamental laws are established." The constitution is certain, and fixed; it contains the permanent will of the people, and is the supreme law of the land; it is paramount to the power of the legislature, and can be revoked or altered only by the authority that made it. The life-giving principle, and the death-doing stroke, must proceed from the same hand. What are legislatures? Creatures of the constitution;—they owe their existence to the constitution;—they derive their powers from the constitution. It is their commission, and therefore all their acts must be conformable to it, or else they will be void. The constitution is the work, or will of the people themselves, in their original, sovereign, and unlimited capacity. Law, is the work, or will of the legislature in their derivative and subordinate capacity. The one is the work of the creator, the other of the creature. The constitution fixes limits to the exercise of legislative authority, and prescribes the orbit within which it must move. The constitution is the sun of the political system, around which all legislative, executive and judicial bodies must revolve ; and every act of the legislature repugnant to the constitution is absolutely void.

Notwithstanding the limitation of power under our system to the executive, as well as to the other departments of government, the existence of a government with sovereign power, is constitutionally established; and being established, none will deny the necessity of its possessing all needful energy to fulfil its legitimate functions. To the people, is committed the duty of the selection, as the safest depositories of this power. To their patriotism and judgment, must we look for a faithful exercise of the duties and privileges of choice. If this privilege is judiciously and discreetly exercised as the theory of the system has anticipated, the power will become vested in those, whose qualifications are best adapted to deliberation and wisdom, and best calculated to conciliate the

a Van Horne's Lessee v. Dorrance, 2 Dall. 308.

43

confidence of the people, and to secure their exalted privileges and highest secular interests. The qualities most befitting the executive magistrate, are judgment, decision, activity, energy, secrecy and despatch. His line of duties, are, in some particulars, defined by the constitution, but not all; some are defined by statute,—and some arise by necessary implication from the position. It is not within the objects of this work to treat of his essential duties. It is sufficient to say, that while acting within the sphere of his duties, he is entirely independent of the other departments.

We have elsewhere, discussed somewhat, the nature and extent of the powers and duties of the other departments.

The executive magistrate, whether it be President or Governor, forms an integral part of the legislative department, and possesses a qualified negative upon all laws. He possesses other executive powers, which, as they do not belong to the law making power, it does not come within the purpose of this work to enumerate or discuss. This negative power over the other branches of the legislative department, is a conservative power, and was intended in degree, to check the legislature, in the well known disposition of that body; as demonstrated in history and experience, from making encroachments upon the other departments, and gradually as uming to itself the exercise of executive and judicial power. *a* The apprehension of this disposition on the part of legislative bodies, was one of the main reasons for dividing the legislative body into two departments, of Senate and House of Representatives, *b* in the belief that the one might act in degree, as a restraint upon the other. Not only different individuals, but different bodies of individuals, will differ as to the extent of their own powers, and to the nature and extent of constitutional prohibitions; and generally, the most popular branch, are more easily moved by strong passions and excitement, under the temporary ascendency of some impetuous or popular leader, to act with less coolness and deliberation, to make encroachments upon the fundamental law, than the higher branch chosen from a more extended constituency.

a Story on Const., § 520.
b Federalist, Nos. 66, 67 and 68.

"One great object," says Chancellor Kent, "of the separation of the legislature into two houses, acting separately, and with co-ordinate powers, is to destroy the evil effects of sudden and strong excitement and of precipitate measures, springing from passion, caprice, prejudice, personal influence and party intrigue, which have been found by sad experience, to exercise a potent and dangerous sway in single assemblies. A hasty decision is not so likely to arrive to the solemnities of a law, when it is to be arrested in its course, and made to undergo the deliberation, and probably the jealous and critical revision, of another and a rival body of men, sitting in a different place, and under better advantages to avoid the prepossessions, and correct the errors of the other branch."

No portion of the political history of mankind is more full of instructive lessons on this subject, or contains more striking proof of faction, instability, and misery of states under the single dominion of an unchecked assembly, than that of the Italian Republics of the middle ages; and which arose in great numbers, and with dazzling but transient splendor, in the interval between the fall of the western and eastern empire of the Romans. They were all alike ill constituted, with a single, unbalanced assembly. They were alike miserable, and all ended in similar disgrace.

Notwithstanding the wisdom evinced in this distribution of power among the departments named, there is found, the omission to fix with precision, the lines which separate the duties and functions of the legislative, from the judicial. There is an inherent and practical difficulty, always, in confining power within proper boundaries, and especially is this the case, in the absence of express provisions in the fundamental law which confers the power, (if conferred at all,) by general terms. This is eminently true in regard to legislative and judicial duties under our system. All history and experience, shows the disposition of legislative bodies to disregard private rights, and to overstep the limits of that department of power. Nor is it without example, that the judiciary, whose duty it is so to declare, when laws are improperly and unconstitutionally enacted, have, in turn, acting in a spirit of jealousy at the encroachments of the legislature, sometimes, also, overstepped their own sphere of duty; but these have been infrequent, and less conflict has resulted, than perhaps under any other system that has ever been devised; so that with time,—experience,—free discussion,—an educated and intellectual bar,—and the freedom of the press,—it will doubtless be found the wisest, best, and most protective system to the citizen, that has ever been devised by human wisdom.

While it is clear to the apprehension of every student of our system of jurisprudence, and a point conceded by every jurist and statesman, that it was the clear intent, and a most leading feature and idea in the minds of the framers of our constitutions of the national and state governments, to separate and distribute the sovereign power of the governments between these three independent and co-ordinate departments; and though these constitutions have not in express terms defined or limited the powers of either, it is equally clear, that it was also the intent, that the executive should do no legislative act, the legislative no executive act, and that neither of these, should do a judicial act, nor the judiciary, an executive or legislative act. a

This view, makes it proper at this place to say a few words as to authority of the judiciary to declare legislative acts of no effect in certain cases.

When the constitution of the United States declared that the judicial power should extend to the cases therein specified, it did not define what was judicial power. It was doubtless regarded as unnecessary to enter into a detail of the specific powers of the judiciary. Courts did not originate in constitutions; they originated in the common law, and their powers were then as well established, and understood, as any other question. Their powers existed, and were known at common law. By adopting a judicial department, they, by implication, adopted their powers, and to whatever extent the constitution, or statutes enacted under it, conferred a new, or limited an existing power, the authority of the judiciary was so extended or restricted, as the case might be. Without such extension or restriction, the constitution and statutes are to be interpreted by the common law. So that, every court so duly constituted, with the constitutional declaration, that they shall possess judicial power in all cases of law and equity, it does,

a Sill v. Corning, 15 N. Y. R. 305; Cooley on Const. Lim. 174.

inherently, and necessarily possess all the incidental powers of a court as then known to exist at common law. All experience, as well as universal consent, has established this. If the courts possessed no powers but such as are declared in the constitution or statutes, they could not protect themselves from insult and outrage; they could not enforce obedience to their immediate orders; they could not imprison or otherwise punish for contempts committed in their presence ; they could not compel the attendance of witnesses, nor oblige them to testify when present ; they could not compel the attendance of jurors, nor punish them for improper conduct. These powers are not given by the constitution ; and wherever statutes have been enacted on these subjects, they are not grants of new power, but simply a regulation and limitation of the inherent or common law powers of the court. *a* It is then, the common law, from whence we derive all our definitions, terms, and ideas, which forms the substratum of our jurisprudence, and the interpretation of constitutional and legislative provisions. It is not possible to move a single step in any judicial proceeding, or to execute any part of our statutes, or of our constitutions, without having recourse to the common law. When a constitution secures a "trial by jury," it does not specify the number of which it shall consist, and in the absence of a statute regulating it, we look to the common law, to find it means twelve men. This is one of numerous illustrations that might be given. But where courts are created by written law, and their jurisdiction defined by written law, they cannot transcend that jurisdiction. *b*

To judge accurately of the constitutional intent as to the extent of powers conferred upon the judicial department in the absence of express specification of powers, we see such a department established, and as we have said, its powers at common law were well and fully understood, nor could we do such injustice to the wisdom and intention of the framers of those instruments as to suppose that they intended to create an equal co-ordinate department of governmental sovereignty that should be powerless when created. Experience, and contemporary practice, in the exercise of judicial power, confirms the idea, that the framers intended that there

a King of Spain v. Oliver, 2 Wash. C. C. R. 429.

b Exparte, Bollman & Swartout, 4 Cranch. 93.

should be a constitutional method of giving efficacy to constitutional provisions. What for instance, would avail restrictions upon legislative power, without some constitutional mode of enforcing the observance of them? The several states by the national constitution are prohibited from doing a variety of things; some of which, are incompatible with the interests of the union, others with the principles of good government. No sensible man will believe, that such prohibitions, would always be scrupulously regarded without the effectual power of the national or state judiciaries to restrain and correct the infractions of power. This judicial power, must possess a direct negative on unconstitutional laws, or the legislatures remain unrestrained, and humanly speaking, omnipotent.

While treating of the subject of courts, and their powers, it may be well to notice a distinction that exists between them as to the force and effect of judgments, as to their conclusiveness. There is one class of courts which are competent by their very constitution, to decide on their own jurisdiction, and to exercise it to final judgment without setting forth in their proceedings the facts and evidence upon which it was rendered. The record of such a court, is an absolute verity, not to be impugned by averment or proof to the contrary; there can be no judicial inspection behind the judgment, except by an appellate power, if there be one. The other class of courts, are inferior in rank; they are so constituted that their judgments can be looked through for the facts and evidence which are necessary to sustain them; their judgments and decisions are not evidence of themselves to show jurisdiction and its lawful exercise. Every requisite to show their jurisdiction must appear upon the face of their proceedings, or they are nullities. A perfect judgment of either class, concludes the subject in which it is rendered, and pronounces the law of that case. A judgment of court of record, whose jurisdiction is final,—is conclusive on all the world. It puts an end to all enquiry into the fact by deciding it. a

It is not within the purpose of this treatise, to enter upon a description of the various courts of the nation, and states, or to

a Grequous Lessee v. Astor 2 How. U. S. R. 341. Elliot v. Peirsol, 3 Peters 329 discuss the powers conferred upon them respect.vely; this is more appropriately the province of the writers of works of practice.

In this American theory of government, we see the exercise of the power of sovereignty, internally, among its own citizens, distributed between these three departments, viz: the executive, the legislative, and the judicial, each holding its appropriate check upon the other; each being sovereign in the exercise of the powers of its own department; each deriving its authority from the same source, the constitution; each limited in its powers by that instrument, and each equal and independent of the other department; but all combined, possess less or what is called the omnipotence of civil authority than the English parliament; because limited by the fundamental law, the written constitution.

Whenever, therefore, the officer of government is placed in the sphere, of either legislative, executive, or judicial departments, he is bound by his duty, and the solemn obligations of his oath, to support the constitutions of the state and nation, to uphold those fundamental instruments made by the people. Possessed of a portion of law-making or law-interpreting power, he is interdicted from exercising it in such a manner as to injure or impair the sources from which his authority is derived. If in the legislative department, he must be careful to commit no infractions of the constitution, by overstepping its limits of inhibition. If in the executive branch, he must carefully avoid every act which may have that injurious tendency. If in the judicial, he must fairly and patiently compare legislative acts with both constitutions, and honestly pronounce upon them as his judgment and conscience shall dictate, without regarding consequences. A due conformity to the oath of office of a judge, creates duties beyond those of passive obedience. It requires the active energies of the mind, to determine on the constitutionability of those laws, which may be brought before him in judgment; and in his decisions, he is bound to protect those paramount laws, which he has sworn to support. *a*

Every one can readily see, that judges may sometimes be thrown into a delicate situation by the exercise of this constitutional duty. They are subjected to the law-making power, by impeachment,

a Emerick v. Harris, 1 Birney 421.

and if that be wrongfully exerted, he must submit. In such case, he will still derive consolation from the integrity of his own mind, and the honest feeling, that he has discharged his duty with fidelity to the government. Posterity will sooner or later do him justice.

Having thus presented a brief, but definite view of the distribution of the powers of government, with the appropriate restrictions belonging to each, we shall not attempt to enter upon the vast field of inquiry as to the reasons which induced the framers of the constitution to adopt the provisions it contained. That inquiry, properly, belongs to political history. Our inquiry is, in regard to the source of the law-making power; what powers have been conferred to this end? how distributed, and to whom? and what powers each department may exercise? True, with these objects before us, we shall be called upon to state incidentally, why the judiciary should be separated from the other departments, and why, the others from it; why this system of checks and balances, making the system more complex, is indispensable to public liberty and protection? It is therefore sufficient here to say, that these provisions in the written constitutions of a free people, are the protection and preservation of the personal rights, the private property, and the public liberty of the whole people. Without accomplishing these ends, the government may, indeed, be called free, but it would be a mere mockery, and a shadow. "If" says Judge Story, "the person of any individual is not secure from assaults and injuries; if his reputation is not preserved from gross and malicious calumny; if he may not speak his own opinions with a manly frankness; if he may be imprisoned without just cause, and deprived of all freedom in his choice of occupations and pursuits; it will be idle to talk of his liberty to breathe the air, to bathe in the public stream or give utterance to articulate language. If the earnings of his industry may be appropriated, and his property may be taken away at the mere will of rulers, or the clamors of a mob, it can afford little consolation to him, that he has already derived happiness from the accumulation of wealth, or that he has the present pride of an ample inheritance; that his farm is not yet confiscated; his house has not yet ceased to be his castle; and his children are not yet reduced to beggary. If his public liberties, as a man and a citizen, his right to vote, his right to hold office, his right to worship God according to the dictates of his own conscience, his equality with all others, who are his fellow citizens; if these are at the mercy of the neighboring demagogue, or the popular idol of the day;—of what consequence is it to him that he is permitted to taste of sweets, which may be wantonly dashed from his lips at the next moment; or to possess privileges which are felt more in their loss, even, than in their possession? Life, liberty, and property stand upon equal grounds in the estimate of freemen; and one becomes almost worthless without the security of the others. How, then, are these rights to be established and preserved? The answer is, by the constitutions of government, wisely framed and vigilantly enforced; by laws and institutions, deliberately examined, and steadily administered by tribunals of justice above fear, and beyond reproach, whose duty it shall be to protect the weak against the strong, to guard the unwary against the cunning, and to punish the insolence of office, and the spirit of encroachment and wanton injury. It needs scarcely to be said, how much wisdom, talents, discretion and virtue, are indispensable for such great purposes.

We have taken upon ourselves, in our free form of government, the responsibility of accomplishing all these ends; the protection and preservation of personal rights, of property, and public liberty. We have chosen for ourselves, doubtless, the most complicated frame of republican government which was ever offered to the world. We have endeavored to reconcile the apparent anomaly of distinct sovereignties, each independent of the other in its own operations, and yet each in full action within the same territory. The national government, within the scope of its delegated powers, is, beyond all doubt, supreme and uncontrollable; and the state governments are, equally so, within the scope of their exclusive powers. But there is a vast variety of cases, in which the powers of each, are concurrent with those of the other; and it is almost impossible to ascertain with precision, where the lines of separation between them begin and end.

It is not within the scope of this work to treat of the superior wisdom of our own form of government, or to compare it with other forms; nor are the duties of the executive department of this, necessary here to be considered any further than it is necessarily

44

involved in its participation with the legislative, in the enactment of laws. It is with legislative enactments, and with the judicial construction or interpretation of such enactments, that this work is chiefly confined.

Besides this national government, there also exists at this time, thirty-six sovereign and independent states, component parts of the national government, besides several territories, inchoate states, which states between themselves, like the national government with other national governments, possess the powers of sovereignty; but as between themselves and their citizens, respectively, their powers are also limited, not only by written constitutions of their own, established by the people as the source of power, but have also other limitations and restrictions imposed upon them by the grants of power given by them, and the people thereof as members of the American nationality to the national government, the supremacy of which in certain particulars, imposes limits to the legislative powers of such several states; which limits, none have a right to pass. *a* Each state in its sovereign capacity of speaking, by its people having conceded a portion of its sovereignty to the establishment of the Union, the national constitution acts upon them, conjunctively, and separately, as it does upon its citizens. *b* •

These written constitutions, based upon the principles set forth in the declaration of independence, which is to be regarded as the

a Marshall, J. 6 Cranch. 136. *b* Dodge v. Woolsey, 18 How. 351.

NOTE 6.—The several states of the Union, form, for many, and for most important purposes, a single nation; and the federal government, in effecting the objects for which it was instituted, can, in those particulars, legitimately control all individuals or governments within the American territory. Cohens v. Virginia, 6 Wheat. 413–14. For all national purposes embraced by the federal constitution, the states, and the citizens thereof, are one, united under the same sovereign authority, and governed by the same laws; in all other respects, the states are necessarily foreign and independent of each other. Buckner v. Finley, 2 Pet. 590; Dodge v. Woolsey, 18 How. 350. The respective states are sovereign within their own limits, and foreign to each other regarding them as local governments. Bk. of U. S. v. Daniel, 12 Pet. 33. The Union was formed, by each of the states conceding portions of their equal sovereignties for all of them, and the United States constitution acts upon them conjunctively and separately, as it does also upon their citizens. Dodge v. Woolsey, 18 How. 351. And this union of the states is indissoluble by the act of any one, or of any portion of them.

interpreter of them, are the avowal, that in a republican form of government, all freemen, when they enter into organized society, are equal; that no man or set of men is entitled to exclusive privileges from the community; that absolute and arbitrary sovereign power over the lives, liberty or property of the citizen exists in no one department of the government, not even by a vote of a majority of the people; that all power is inherent in the people; that all free government, is founded on their authority, and instituted for their peace, safety, happiness, security and protection of property; that for the advancement of these ends, they continue to possess the inalienable and undefeasible right to alter, reform or abolish their existing government, and to establish another upon the same basis, and controlled by the same general principles; that all elections shall be free and equal, and full protection to be given against the abuse of its privileges; that no power for suspending the laws shall be exercised by any department, but in pursuance of established constitutional law.

In looking at these constitutional guaranties, while the citizen is secured and protected by them, he is not indebted to them, for these inherent and inalienable rights. Though they measure and limit the powers of the rulers, they do not measure the rights of the ruled. Constitutions are not the origin of society, or of private rights; it is not the fountain of law; or of power; "it is not the cause, but the consequence of personal and political freedom; it grants no right to the people, but is the creature of their power, the instrument of their convenience." Constitutions were designed for the protection of the people in the enjoyment of their rights, and in the powers which they possessed before the constitution was made; it is frame-work of the political government, and is necessarily based upon the pre-existing condition of laws, rights, habits, and modes of thought. There is nothing primitive in it; it is all derived from the source and fountain of power and right. "It presupposes an organized society; law, order, property, personal freedom, a love of political liberty, and enough of cultivated intelligence to know how to guard it against the encroachments of tyranny. A written constitution is in every instance, a limitation of the powers of the government in the hands of agents; for there never was a written republican constitution which delegated to functionaries all the latent powers which lie dormant in every nation, are boundless in extent, and incapable of definition." *a* " When therefore we are seeking for the true construction of a constitutional provision, we are constantly to bear in mind that its authors were not executing a delegated authority limited by other constitutional restraints, but are to look on them, as the founders of a state, intent only on establishing such principles as seemed best calculated to produce good government, and promote the public happiness, at the expense of any and all existing institutions which might stand in the way." *b*

The declaration of independence made the then thirteen colonies sovereign and independent states, thereby abolishing all English, and other foreign jurisdiction, and substituting a national government of their own creation. New states have since been added from time to time from territory under the national control, the precise position and actual power of which, it is not our purpose to discuss, except in so far as relates to the legislative power of enacting statute laws, and the judicial interpretation and construction thereof, with the limitations of legislative and judicial power affecting the same.

In order to prevent collisions of legislative or judicial authority between the national and state governments, which would otherwise be inevitable, as well as dangerous to the peace, harmony and stability of the Union under such a system, it was wisely provided in the constitution of the United States, that it, and the laws of the United States which should be made in pursuance thereof, should be the supreme law of the land, and the judges in every state should be bound thereby, anything in the constitution or laws of any state to the contrary notwithstanding. *c*

Besides this superiority of power in certain respects, conferred upon the national government by the terms of the national constitution itself, it also contains express prohibition of the exercise of state authority in certain specified particulars, to wit: " No state shall enter into any treaty, alliance or confederation; gran letters of marque and reprisal; coin money; emit bills of credit

a Cooley on Const. Lim. 37.
b Matter of the Oliver Lee Bank, 21 N. Y. 12.
c U. S. Const., Art. 6.

make any thing but gold and silver coin a tender in payment of debts ; pass any bill of attainder, or *ex post facto law,* or law impairing the obligation of contracts; or grant any title of nobility."

"No state shall without the consent of congress, lay any imports or duties on imports or exports, except what may be absolutely necessary for executing its inspection laws; and the net produce of all duties and imports laid by any state on imports or exports, shall be for the use of the treasury of the United States, and all such laws shall be subject to the revision and control of congress. No state shall, without the consent of congress, lay any duty of tonnage, keep troops or ships of war in time of peace, enter into any agreement or compact with another state, or with a foreign power, or engage in war, unless actually invaded, or in such imminent danger as will not admit of delay."

While, in the above enumerated particulars, the several states are made to yield to the federal government the exclusive superiority of authority; as a kind of compensation therefor, the constitution of national government contains a power of protection and guardianship over states, to prevent discrimination by the several states, against the citizens and public acts and proceedings of other states; among which are, that "full faith and credit shall be given in each state to the public acts, records, and judicial proceedings of every other state." a "The citizens of each state shall be entitled to all privileges and immunities of citizens in the several states." b "A person charged in any state with treason, felony, or other crime, who shall flee from justice, and be found in any other state, shall, on demand of the executive authority of the state from which he fled, be delivered up to be removed to the state having jurisdiction of the crime." c "The United States shall guarantee to every state in this Union a republican form of government, and shall protect each of them against invasion." d

Such are the express provisions of the federal constitution. There are also, certain implied powers, which, by judicial interpretation of the federal courts, are possessed by the general government, and which powers are prohibited to the states. All

a Const. U. S., Art. 4.   c Id.
b Id.   d Id.

powers in the federal constitution, which are necessarily implied, from the powers expressly granted, and which are necessary to carry the express powers into effect, are as much a part of the constitution, as its express powers ;—and such implied powers, are also as much prohibited to the states, *a* as if they had been expressly forbidden.

From this, it results, as was well expressed by Ch. J. Marshall in McCulloch v. State of Maryland, "that the government of the Union, though limited in its powers, is supreme within its sphere of action." " It is the government of all ; its powers are delegated by all ; it represents all, and acts for all. Though any one state may be willing to control its operations, no state is willing to allow others to control them. The nation, on those subjects upon which it can act, must necessarily bind its component parts."

This outline of powers, conferred upon the federal government becomes necessary to be presented for consideration, as they fall within the range of questions embraced in the design of this work ; inasmuch, as rules for the construction of the statutes passed by the national legislature, are, in degree, and to a limited extent, matters with which we shall deal.

The judicial powers and jurisdiction of the courts of the federal government, are, as we have seen in part, but not fully and specifically, enumerated in the constitution. Congress is left with the power to confer such jurisdiction, and to institute such proper courts and tribunals, inferior to the supreme court, *b* as shall secure the harmonious and efficient working, of a system of national jurisprudence under the constitution, not only, but in a class of cases, in the discretion of congress, to make the jurisdiction exclusive, or not, of state courts, *c* as policy may dictate. In still another class of cases, the states are permitted to legislate and give jurisdiction to state courts upon the same subjects, and such state laws remain valid, until the power of congress is exercised ; when the state laws will then become superceded, so far as they are in conflict with a law of congress on that subject. *d*

a McCulloch v. Maryland, 4 Wheat. 427; Weston v. City of Charleston, 2 Peters 467; Sturgis v. Crowninshield, 4 Wheat. 193.

b Const. U. S., Art. 1, § 8, and Art. 3, § 2.

c Martin v. Hunter's Lessees, 1 Wheat. 334.

d Sturgis v. Crowninshield, 4 Wheat. 122, 192-3.

The whole idea of the powers of the federal government, as contained in its constitution, is summed up in this : "It was ordained and established by the people of the United States for themselves, for their own government, and not for the government of the individual states. Each state established a constitution for itself, and in that constitution, provided such limitations and restrictions upon the powers of its particular government, as its judgment dictated. The people of the United States, framed such a government for themselves, as they supposed best adapted to their situation, and best calculated to promote their interests. The powers they conferred on this government, were to be exercised by itself ; and the limitations on power, if expressed in general terms, are naturally and necessarily applicable to the government created by the instrument. They are limitations of power granted in the instrument itself; not of distinct governments, framed by different persons, and for different purposes." *a*

Properly understood, there is no conflict of sovereignty or jurisdiction between the national and state governments. In one sense, both are sovereign, and yet as we have shown, in another sense, each is limited by its written constitution. The authority exercised by each state over matters within its jurisdiction, is sovereign and absolute. It has its origin also, in the people within its territorial limits who determine the extent and limitation of its power. It thus possesses all authority so conferred upon it, of legislative, judicial and executive power, and is competent to regulate, control and direct the will of the whole, and of every subordinate member of the state. '

<hr>

a Barron v. Mayor, &c., of Baltimore, 7 Peters 247.

NOTE 7.—The constitution of the United States is supreme over all the departments of government, and any thing which may be done, unauthorized by it, is unlawful. Dodge v. Woolsey, 18 How. 347. It is supreme over the people of the United States, aggregate, in their separate sovereignties, because they have excluded themselves from any direct or immediate agency in making amendments to it, ibid. The government of the Union is a government of the people; it emanates from them; its powers are granted by them; and are to be exercised directly on them, and for their benefit. McCulloch v. Maryland, 4 Wheat. 316. The constitution was made for the benefit of every citizen of the United States,— and there is no citizen, whatever his condition—or wherever he may be,—within the territory of the United States, who has not a right to its protection. U. S. v. More, 3 Cranch. 160. Therefore an act of congress passed in pursuance of clear

But while the several states of the Union are thus limited by their own written constitutions, and by the grant of power to the national government; yet in all matters where no question of national authority is involved, their sovereignty and power is so absolute, that the national courts hold themselves bound to accept and adopt the decisions of the state courts as correct expositions of their statutes and common law, and to follow their authority whenever the same question arises in the national courts. *a* Indeed it is so expressly enacted by an act of congress called the judiciary act of 1789.

It was competent to the people to invest the general government with all the powers which they might deem proper and necessary; to extend or restrain those powers according to their own good pleasure; and to give them a paramount and supreme authority. The people also had a right to prohibit to the states the exercise of any powers, which were, in their judgment, incompatible with the objects of the general compact; to make the powers of the state governments, in given cases, subordinate to those of the nation; or to reserve to themselves those sovereign authorities which they might not choose to delegate to either, and it must therefore be assumed they have done so. The constitution of the United States was not, necessarily, carved out of existing state sovereignties, nor a surrender of power already existing in state institutions. The powers of the states depend on their own constitutions, and the people of every state had a right to modify or restrain them, according to their own views of policy or principle. So on the other hand the sovereign powers vested in the state governments, by their respective constitutions, remain unaltered and unim-

a Sumner v. Hicks, 2 Black. 532; Jefferson Br. Bank v. Skelly, 1 Black. 436; McKeen v. DeLancy's Lessee, 5 Cranch. 29; Massingule v. Downs, 7 How. 767; Nesmith v. Sheldon, id. 812.

authority under the constitution, is the supreme law of the land. U. S. v. Hart, Pet. C. C. R. 390. And no state law can take away rights and privileges secured by the constitution and laws of the United States. U. S. v. Rathbone, 2 Paine 579. Where an unqualified power is granted to the general government, and the exercise of the same power by the state governments would be inconsistent with the express grants, such power vests exclusively in the general government. Golden v. Prince, 3 Wash. C. C. R. 313.

paired, except so far as they were granted to the government of the United States. *a*

The laws of the United States in their operation within the state governments are not to be considered as laws of a foreign government, but as laws operating upon and binding the same people as the government and laws of the several states. *b* °

a Martin v. Hunter, 1 Wheat. 324.   *b* Stearns v. United States, 2 Paine R. 300.

NOTE 8.—To prevent all conflict between the federal, and the state governments, it was wisely provided by an act of congress passed September 24, 1789, among other things as follows, § 34, " The laws of the several States, except when the constitution, treaties or statutes of the United States, shall otherwise require or provide, shall be regarded as rules of decision in trials at common law, in the courts of the United States in cases where they apply." This was but the expression of the spirit of the constitution, and would be but a reasonable common law construction, upon the national and State constitutions interpreted together.

The decisions of the state courts, concerning the title to lands, are to be treated as binding authorities in the courts of the United States. Rundle v. Delaware and Raritan Canal Co. 14 How. 93; Polk's Lessee v. Wendal, 9 Cr. 87; Thatcher v. Powell, 6 Wh. 119 ; Elmendorf v. Taylor, 10 Id. 152 ; Ross v. Barland, 1 Pet. 655; The Society for the Propogation of the Gospel v. Wheeler, 2 Gall. 138. The courts adopt the state decisions, because they settle the law applicable to the case; and the reasons assigned for this course apply as well to rules of construction growing out of the common law, as the statute law of the state, when applied to the title to lands. Sims v Irvine, 3 Dall. 425, 456; Waring v. Jackson, 1 Pet. 570; Davis v. Mason, Id. 503; Hamilton v. Dudley, Id. 2, Id. 492; Hinde v. Vallier, 5 Id· 398; Clarke v. Smith, 13 Id. 195 ; Wilcox v. Jackson, Id. 498; Amis v. Smith, 16 Id. 303; Fisher v. Haldeman, 20 How. 186; Miles v. Caldwell, 2 Wall. 35; Jackson v. Chew, 12 Wh. 167. The decisions of the state courts settling a rule of construction of devises of lands, is, therefore, within the law and binding on the federal courts. Ibid 153; Henderson v. Griffen, 5 Pet. 151; Smith v. Shriver, 14 Leg. Int. 172. So is a decision on the state law of descents. Gardner v. Collins, 2 Pet. 58. So is a decision of the question whether the statute of uses is a part of the common law of the state. Henderson v. Griffen, 5 Pet. 151. And so are decisions as to the lien of judgments on real estate. Massingill v. Downs, 7 How. 760; United States v. Morrison, 4 Pot. 124 ; Thompson v. Phillips, Bald. 246; Lombard v. Bayard, 1 Wall. Jr. 198. And in construing a statute of a state concerning lands, the supreme court adopts the construction settled in the state courts, though not in accordance with its own opinion. McKeen v. DeLancy's Lessee, 5 Cr. 22. The settled construction of a state statute by its supreme court, is considered as a part of its statute. Massingill v Downs, 7 How. 767; Nesmith v. Sheldon, Id. 812; Van Rensselaer v. Kearney, 11 Id. 297; Webster v. Cooper, 14 Id, 504; Green v. James, 2 Curt. C. C. 189 ; Woolsey v. Dodge, 6 McLean, 150; Thompson v. Phillips, Bald. 246; United States v. Mundel, 6 Call. 245.

This law adopts the acts of limitations of the several states, where no special provision has been made by congress, as rules of decision in the courts of the

45

A constitution then, is the fundamental law of the nation, or state, containing the principles upon which the government is founded, and regulating the division of the sovereign power into departments, directing to what persons each of these powers is to be confided, and the manner in which it is to be exercised; it is

United States, and the same effect is given to them as in the state courts. Mc-Cluny v. Silliman, 3 Pet. 270; Green v. Neal's Lessee, 6 Ibid. 291; Ross v. Duval, 13 Ibid. 45; Shelby v. Guy, 11 Wh. 361; Boyle v. Arledge, Hemp. 620. But not as against the federal government. United States v. Packus, 6 McLean, 443. It also includes the statutes of the several states which prescribe rules of evidence in civil cases. McNiel v. Holbrook, 12 Pet. 84; Hinde v. Vattier's Lessee, 5 Ibid. 398. But no state law made since 1789 can effect the rules of evidence in criminal cases in the federal courts. United States v. Reid, 12 How. 361.

The act of congress adopts the *local* laws of the several states as rules of decision, but it does not apply to the construction of contracts, or to questions of general commercial law. Swift v. Tyson, 16 Pet. 1; Watson v. Tarpley, 18 How. 520; Gloucester Insurance Co. v. Younger, 2 Curt. C. C. 322. Nor to the construction of private statutes. Williamson v. Berry, 8 How. 543. It applies only to the rights of persons and of property, and in those cases the state laws furnish rules of decision; but as to remedies and modes of proceeding, they are fixed by the act of 1792. Mayer v. Foulkrod, 4 W. C. C. 349; Campbell v. Claudius, Pet. C. C. 484; Lane v. Townsend, Ware. 288; Jones v. Vanzants, 4 McLean 606; Chicago City v. Robbins, 2 Black. 428. It relates to the rules for framing, not for executing the judgment. Wayman v. Southard, 10 Wh. 1; Parson v. Bedford, 3 Pet. 444; Keary v. Farmers' and Merchants' Bank, 16 Ibid. 89; Long v. Smith, Ibid. 65. It has nothing to do with the proceedings after judgment; it means only that the judgment shall be rendered according to the laws of the state. Reeside's Executrix v. United States, Dev. C. C. 99, 101. It is broad enough, however, to cover the rights of parties to costs. Hathaway v. Roach, 2 W. & M. 63.

The supreme court will adhere to its own decision upon the validity of a contract, notwithstanding subsequent state decisions declaring it unconstitutional. Rowan v. Runnels, 5 How. 134; Truly v. Wanzer, Ibid. 141; Sims v. Hundley, 6 Ibid. 1. But not in a case involving simply the construction of a state statute. Green v. Neal's Lessee, 6 Pet. 291; Woolsey v. Dodge, 6 McLean, 150.

A court of the United States cannot, by a rule, adopt the provisions of a state law, which is repugnant to, or incompatible with, a positive enactment of congress. Keary v. Farmers' and Merchants' Bank, 16 Pet. 89; Amis v. Smith, Ibid. 312; Massingill v. Downs, 7 How. 760.

It does not extend to cases in equity. United States v. Reid, 12 How. 363; Neves v. Scott, 13 Ibid. 268; McFarlane v. Griffith, 4 W. C. C. 585. Or in admiralty. The Independence, 2 Curt. C. C. 350. It means trials in a court of common law, when exercising that authority, as contrasted with the courts of admiralty and maritime or equity jurisdiction. United States v. Mundel, 6 Call. 258. The federal courts are governed in commercial and maritime cases, by the general and not by the local law. Mutual Safety Ins. Co. v. Cargo of the Brig George, Olcott, 89.

made by the authority of the people themselves, or by their delegates specially authorized; and it can be changed only by the like power. The legislature, which is only the creature of the constitution, cannot make any change in such fundamental law. *a* The constitution guarantees to every citizen, equal rights, protection and participation, direct or indirect, in the government. *b*

A learned commentator upon the constitution of the United States, says, "it is an original, written, federal and social compact, freely, voluntarily, and solemnly entered into by the several states, and ratified by the people thereof respectively; whereby the several states, and the people thereof respectively have bound themselves each to other, and to the federal government of the United States, and by which the federal government is bound to the several states, and to every citizen of the United States." *c* This is doubtless true of its character and its design, but not of the parties to the compact.

This view is not regarded as sound by the supreme court of the United States, so far as it is stated to be a *compact*, entered into by the states in their political capacity, as contradistinguished from the people thereof. The states never did, in fact, as states, ratify the constitution. They were not called upon by congress to do so, and were not contemplated, as essential to give validity to it. *d* "The convention which framed the constitution was indeed elected by the state legislatures. But the instrument when it came from their hands, was a mere proposal without obligation, or pretensions to it. It was reported to the then existing congress of the United States, with a request that it might be submitted to a convention of delegates, chosen in each state by the people thereof, under the recommendation of its legislature for their assent and ratification. This mode of proceeding was adopted; and by the convention, by congress, and by the state legislatures, the instrument was submitted to the people. They acted upon it in the only manner in which they can act safely, effectively, and wisely on such a subject, by assembling a convention. It is true, they assembled in their several states — and where else should they

a Bouvier's Inst. 9, 10.   *b* Wharton's Law Dict.
c Tucker's Black Com., Ap. note D., p. 140.
d Story on Const., § 362; McCulloch v. State of Maryland, 4 Wheat. 402 to 404

have assembled? No political dreamer was ever wild enough to think of breaking down the lines which separate the states, and of compounding the American people into one common mass. Of consequence when they act, they act in their states. But the measures they adopt, do not on that account cease to be the measures of the people themselves, or become the measures of the state governments. *a*

The several state constitutions are of like origin, but of more circumscribed jurisdiction, and in certain particulars, limited in the objects upon which they act. They are also original, written and social compacts, freely, voluntarily and solemnly entered into, between the people of the states respectively, and the respective state governments; and in which the people of the states, and the state governments respectively, have bound themselves to each other.

"The general and state governments, in this country, are a part of one and the same system, instituted by one and the same people, having one and the same general duty to perform for the people. Every national citizen is necessarily connected with business and interests of a domestic character; and there is but one class of institutions that can administer to his necessities, in respect to those subjects. That branch of internal administration, is by common consent, as well as by particular regulation, committed to the state administration." *b*

The state governments are as absolute in the exercise of their authority within the limits of their respective jurisdictions, as is the general government within its particular sphere; and every national citizen is as much interested in preserving intact, the state governments, as he is that of the general government; and of preventing encroachments of the one, upon the other. The national government is as much his own, as the state government. They are both created in the same manner, by the same authority, and for the same general purpose. They differ really, only, in the subjects, and extent of their jurisdiction.

It has happily thus far, been the disposition of both the national and state governments, in all their intercourse with each other in

a Per Ch. J. Marshall, 4 Wheat. 402-3.
b Tiffany's Theory, pp. 111, 112.

the administration of their respective governments, to avoid conflicts of authority between each other ; to bring the whole system into general harmonious action, and to establish and promote rules of comity, between the several states, and between the federal government and the several states, at least as fully as they exist between foreign states.   This disposition was manifested in the United States court, by a decided expression of the court to that effect. *a*   It has been supposed, says Ch. J. Taney, "that the rules of comity between foreign nations, do not apply to the states of this Union; that they extend to one another no other rights than those that are given by the constitution of the United States, and that the courts of the general government are not at liberty to presume, in the absence of all legislation on the subject, that a state has adopted the comity of nations towards the other states as a part of its jurisprudence ; or that it acknowledges any rights but those which are secured by the constitution of the United States.   The court think otherwise.   The intimate union of these states as members of the same great political family ;—the deep and vital interests which bind them so closely together ; should lead us, in the absence of proof to the contrary, to presume a greater degree of comity, friendship and kindness towards each other, than we could be authorized to presume between foreign nations.   And when, (as without doubt, must occasionally happen), the interest or policy of any state requires it to restrict the rule, it has but to declare its will, and the legal presumption is at once at an end.   But until this is done, upon what grounds could this court refuse to administer the law of international comity between these states ?   They are sovereign states ; and the history of the past, and the events which are daily occurring, furnish the strongest evidence that they have adopted towards each other the laws of comity in their fullest extent."

The foundation for a still stronger recognition of this comity, is laid in the federal constitution itself.   It contains a provision in regard to the laws of the states, and the proceedings of the judicial tribunals, which, though it gives them no extra territorial effect, has still a strong bearing upon the question of comity.   Article IV, § 1, declares, that, "Full faith and credit shall be given in

a Bank of Augusta v. Earle, 13 Peters, 590.

each state to the public acts, records and judicial proceedings of every other state; and that congress may, by general laws, pre-scribe the manner by which such acts, records and proceedings, shall be proved, and the effect thereof."

In pursuance of this power, the congress of the United States by an act of May 26, 1790, Ch. 38, provided the mode by which records, and judicial proceedings should be authenticated. Under these constitutional and statutory provisions, various decisions have been made, the general result of which is, that a judgment is conclusive in every other state, if a court of the particular state had jurisdiction, and would so hold it. *a* " But congress has never acted on the power in the constitution as to the public acts or laws of the states, any further than to declare that they shall be authen-ticated by having the seal of the respective states affixed thereto; nor is this method regarded as exclusive of any other which the states may adopt. And the states have differed as to the manner in which they shall be proved. In some cases, strict proof of them, as foreign laws, has been required; but the courts of other states, and the supreme court of the United States, influenced by the intimate and peculiar connection of the states, have shown a disposition to relax the usual rules of proof in this respect." *b* The authorities will be found in the note. *

a Mills v. Duryea, 7 Cranch. 481; Hampton v. McConnell, 3 Wheat. 234, 1 Kent's Com. 260.

b Sedgwick on Const. 78.

NOTE 9.—No other authentication of an act of the legislature is required, except the annexation of the seal of the state; it is presumed that the person who affixed the seal had competent authority to do so. United States v. Amedy, 11 Wh. 392; United States v. Johns, 4 Dall. 416; S. C. 1 W. C. C. 363. A printed pamphlet containing the laws of another state, is not admissible in evidence. Craig v. Brown, Pet. C. C. 352. In the courts of the District of Columbia, however, the statute book of one of the states, purporting to be published by authority of its legislature, and deposited in the department of state, under the act of congress requiring the secretary of state to obtain copies of the laws of the several states, is admissible evidence of the laws of such state. Commercial and Farmers' Bank of Baltimore v. Patterson, 2 Cr. C. C. 346 ; see Leeland v. Wilkinson, 6 Pet. 317. In the supreme court, the states of the confederacy are not regarded as foreign states whose laws and usages must be proved, but as domestic institutions, whose laws are to be noticed without pleading or proof ; and the state courts, in deter-mining questions subject to be reviewed in the supreme court of the United States, adopt the same rule, and will take notice of the local laws of a sister state

A valuable note of authorities upon pleading upon foreign judgments, and as to the distinctions between cases where jurisdiction may be enquired into, and otherwise, will be found on pages 260 and 261, 1 Kent Com.

in the same manner that the supreme court would do on a writ of error to their judgment. Baxley v. Linah, 4 Harris, 243, 250; Ohio v. Hinchman, 3 Casey, 479; Rogers v. Burns, Id. 526.

The judicial proceedings here referred to, are generally understood to be the proceedings of courts of general jurisdiction, and not those which are merely of municipal authority. 1 Greenl. Ev. § 505. And accordingly, it has been held, that the judgments of justices of the peace, were not within the meaning of these constitutional and statutory provisions. Snyder v. Wise, 10 Barr. 157; Warren v. Flagg, 2 Pick. 448 ; Robinson v. Prescott, 4 N. Hamp. 450 ; Mahurin v. Bickford, 6 Id. 167; Silver Lake Bank v. Harding, 5 Ohio, 545; Thomas v. Robinson, 3 Wend. 267. In Connecticut and Vermont, however, it is held, that if the justice is bound by law to keep a record of his proceedings, they are within the meaning of the act of congress. Bissell v. Edwards, 5 Day, 363; Starkweather v. Loomis, 2 Verm. 573 ; Blodget v. Jordan, 6 Id. 580 ; and see Scott v. Cleveland, 3 Monr. 62. But the proceedings of courts of chancery, and of probate, as well as of the courts of common law, may be thus proved. Scott v. Blanchard, 8 Martin, (N S) 303; Balfour v. Chew, 5 Id. 517; Johnson v. Rannels, 6 Id. 621; Ripple v. Ripple, 1 Rawle, 381; Craig v. Brown, Pet. C. C. 352; Hunt v. Lyle, 8 Yerg. 142; Barbour v. Watts, 2 A. K. Marsh, 290, 293. This clause is not restricted to the case of judgments. Hopkins v. Ludlow, Phila. R. 272.

This does not apply to the records of the courts of the United States. Mason's Administrators v. Lawrason, 1 Cr. C. C. 190. But though, in terms, it applies only to the state courts, the rule is equally applicable to those of the United States. Tooker v. Thompson, 3 McLean, 94. And a judgment of a court of the United States is admissible, when authenticated in the manner provided in this act. Buford v. Hickman, Hemp. 232.

It seems to be generally agreed, that this method of authentication is not exclusive of any other which the states may think proper to adopt. Kean v. Rice, 12 S. & R. 203, 208; The State v. Stade, 1 D. Chipm. 303 ; Raynham v. Canton, 3 Pick. 293; Biddis v. James, 6 Binn. 321; Ex parte Povall, 3 Leigh. 816; Pepoon v. Jenkins, 2 Johns. Cas, 129 ; Ellmore v. . ills, 1 Hayw. 359 ; Baker v. Field, 2 Yeates, 532; Ohio v. Hinchman, 3 Casey, 485.

The clerk who certifies the record must be the clerk of the same court, or of its successor; the certificate of his under-clerk, in his absence, or of the clerk of any other tribunal, office, or body, being held incompetent for this purpose. Sampson v. Overton, 4 Bibb. 409; Lothrop v. Blake, 3 Barr. 495; Donohoo v. Brannon, 1 Overt. 328; Schnertzell v. Young, 3 H. and McHen, 502. A surrogate acts as a clerk in certifying his proceedings, and as he also acts in the capacity of judge, he must certify as to the authentication. Catlin v. Underhill, 4 McLean, 199; Ohio v. Hinchman, 3 Casey, 484.

Whenever the court whose record is certified has no seal. this fact should appear, either in the certificate of the clerk, or in that of the judge. Craig v. Brown,

The direct result, or consequence of such an exercise of power by the states, is, that the laws of each state bind, directly, all

Pet. C. C. 353. The seal of the court must be annexed to the record itself; it is not enough that it is annexed to the judge's certificate. Turner v. Washington, 3 W. C. C. 126.

The certificate must be given by *the judge*, if there be but one; or if there b more than one, then by the chief justice, or presiding judge or magistrate of the court from whence the record comes; and he must possess that character at the time he gives the certificate. A certificate that he is the judge that presided at the time of trial, or that he is the senior judge of the courts of law in the state, is deemed insufficient. Lothrop v. Blake, 3 Barr. 495; Stephenson v. Bannister, 3 Bibb. 369; Kirkland v. Smith, 2 Martin (N S) 497. And so is the certificate of a judge styling himself "one of the judges" of the court. Stewart v. Gray, Hemp. 94; See Catlin v. Underhill, 4 McLean, 199; Erb v. Scott, 2 Harris, 22.

A record of another state is not admissible, if the certificate of the presiding magistrate omit to state, that the attestation of the clerk is in due form. Trigg v. Conway, Hemp. 538. The phrase "due form," means the form of attestation used in the state from whence the record comes. Craig v. Brown, Pet. C C. 354. And the certificate of the presiding judge being the evidence prescribed by law, that this form has been observed, is at once indispensable and conclusive. Ferguson v. Harwood, 7 Cr. 408; Tooker v. Thompson, 3 McLean, 93; Taylor v. Carpenter, 2 W. & M. 4. A certificate that the person whose name is signed to the attestation is clerk of the court, and that the signature is his own handwriting, is not in conformity with the provisions of the act. Craig v. Brown, Pet. C. C 352. Where, however, the record of a judgment of a state court is offered in evidence, in the circuit court, sitting within the same state, the certificate of the clerk and seal of the court is a sufficient authentication. Mewster v. Spalding, 6 McLean, 24.

A judgment of a state court has the same credit, validity, and effect, in every other court within the United States, which it had in the state where it was rendered; and whatever pleas would be good in a suit thereon, in such state, and none others, can be pleaded in any other court within the United States. Hampton v. McConnel, 3 Wh. 234; Mills v. Duryee, 7 Cr. 481; Westerwelt v. Lewis, 2 McLean, 511; Taylor v. Carpenter, 2 W. & M. 4; Warren Manufacturing Co. v. Etna Insurance Co., 2 Paine 502; Whitaker v. Bramson, Ibid. 209; Green v. Sarmiento, Pet. C. C. 74, s. c., 3 W. C. C. 17; Bryant v. Hunters, Ibid. 48; Field v. Gibbs, Pet. C. C. 157; Armstrong v. Carson's Executors, 2 Dall. 302; 2 Am. Leading Cases, 774. But although this act makes a judgment regularly recovered in another state, and duly authenticated, conclusive evidence of an established demand, as of the date of such judgment, it does not prevent the several states from enacting statutes of limitation, barring actions on such judgments in their courts. Bank of the State of Alabama v. Dalton, 9 How. 522; McElmoyle v. Cohen, 13 Pet. 312. Nor does it apply to a judgment recovered against a non-resident joint debtor, without notice to him; such a judgment is not entitled to any faith or credit out of the state in which it was rendered. D'Arcy v. Ketchum, 11 How. 165; Rogers v. Burns, 3 Casey, 525.

property, whether real or personal, within its territory; and all persons who are resident within it, whether natural born subjects or aliens, and also all contracts made and, acts done within it.

A state may, therefore, by statute, regulate the manner and circumstances under which property, whether real or personal, or in action, within it, shall be held transmitted, bequeathed, transferred or enforced ; the condition, capacity and state of all persons within it; the validity of contracts, and other acts done within it, the resulting rights and duties growing out of these contracts and acts, and the remedies and modes of administering justice in all cases calling for the interposition of its tribunals to protect, to vindicate, and to secure the wholesome agency of its own laws within its own domain. *a*

It is equally a necessary result of the independence, and distinct sovereignties of the several states, that neither their statutes, or other laws, have any inherent authority, nor are they entitled to any respect extra territorially, or beyond the jurisdiction that enacts them. But by a kind of courtesy or comity between states and nations, the principle is now generally received and adopted, that contracts are to be construed and interpreted according to the laws of the state in which they are made, unless from their tenor it is perceived, that they were entered into with a view to the laws of some other state. *b*

The grand boundary line which marks the obvious limits between the federal and state jurisdictions, is, that to the former is given jurisdiction in all matters arising under the political laws of the nation; and such as relate to its general concerns with foreign nations, or to the several states as members of the federal government. To the latter, is given jurisdiction of all matters of a civil nature between their citizens, or between their citizens and other persons, or such as properly belong to the head of municipal law, (with certain exceptions, to which we have before referred,) where, by special provision, contained in the federal constitution, either concurrent or exclusive jurisdiction is granted to the general government—and excepting also, all powers contained in the federal constitution which are expressly prohibited to the states, or which

a Story's Conflict of Laws, § 18.

Blanchard v. Russell, 18 Mass. R. 4; Bank of Augusta v. Earll, 13 Peters 589

46

can be exercised by them only with the consent, or under the control of congress; and powers which are prohibited to both the federal and state governments.

From these views it will be seen, and it logically and necessarily follows, that all other powers of government, compatible with the nature and principle of democratic governments, which are not prohibited by the bill of rights, or constitutions of the respective states, remain with such states or with the people thereof, and may be exercised by them, respectively in such manner, as their several laws and constitutions may permit or direct.

Subject to the limitations contained in the federal and state constitutions, the legislative power in the state of New York, (and it is believed to be the same in every other independent state), is not restricted in its power to enact laws, any more than is the British parliament. *a* In this respect the legislature is the direct representative of the people, and the depository of their power.

Statutes, or laws, under such a form of government, must therefore be made in conformity with the requirements of written constitutions. If the forms prescribed by the constitution have not been observed, or the power has not been delegated to the legislative body, the act is unconstitutional and void.

A *constitutional law*, is one made by the legislative power properly organized according to the requirements of the constitution. Such a statute, is binding upon all the people, citizens and others, who are within the territorial jurisdiction of the legislature, *b* and it is the duty of the executive department to see that such a law is faithfully executed.

An unconstitutional law, (if such can be called law,) is one made in contravention of the powers of the constitution, and for that reason it is absolutely void, because the constitution, which is the supreme and fundamental law of the land; — having greater force than any statute, *c* such a law, the executive is not bound to see enforced.

The courts possess the power, and it is their duty when a law is

a People v. Morrell, 21 Wend. 563; Butler v. Palmer, 1 Hill. 324; Bloodgood v. Mohawk & Hudson R. R. Co., 18 Wend. 9; Sill v. Village of Corning, 15 N. Y. R. 300; People v. Draper, id. 549.

c 1 Bowv. Inst. 47. *d* Id.

unconstitutional, to declare it to be so. They will however be careful not so to declare it, except the case be very clear. The determination of this question, is always a question of power, that is, whether the legislature in the particular case, in respect to the subject matter of the act; the manner in which its object is to be accomplished, and the mode of enacting it; has kept within the constitutional limits; and whether the law-makers have observed the constitutional conditions. *a* If these conditions and limitations have been observed by the law-making power, the courts will not enquire further; they will assume that the legislative discretion has been properly exercised. If the power to pass the law should depend upon extrinsic facts, the court will presume that such facts were before the legislature when the act was passed; nor will the courts ever enquire into the motives of the legislature where fraud and corruption are charged, and annul their action, or the statute, if the charge be proved true. *b*

In analogy to the system of Great Britain, and with the views of the omnipotent power of the English parliament, it was at an early day claimed by many, unfamiliar with the American theory of government; of written constitutions; and of a distribution of the sovereign power into departments; that the judicial department possessed no power to declare a statute void, even though its enactment was in conflict with express inhibitions of power contained in constitutions. These views were set at rest by the judicial power upon the earliest occasion.

Chief Justice Marshall, in giving his views on this subject, has done it so clearly, and so tersely, that to transcribe them, gives much better expression to the same ideas than we could give in our own language; we therefore copy them (with slight changes,) and adopt them. *c* He says, "The question, whether an act repugnant to written constitutions can become the law of the land, is a question deeply interesting to the people of the United States; but, happily, not of an intricacy proportioned to its interest. It seems necessary only to recognize certain principles, supposed to have been long and well established, to decide it."

That the people had an original right to establish, for their

a Cooley v. Const. Lim. 186, 7.   *b* People v. Draper, 15 New York, R. 545.
c Marbury v. Madison 1, Cranch. 68, 70.

future government, such principles, as, in their opinion, should most conduce to their own happiness, is the basis upon which the whole American fabric has been erected. The exercise of this original right is a very great exertion; nor can it, nor ought it to be frequently repeated. The principles, therefore so established, are deemed fundamental. And as the authority from which they proceed is supreme, and can seldom act, they are designed to be permanent.

This original and supreme will organizes the government, and assigns to different departments, their respective powers. It may either stop here; or establish certain limits not to be transcended by those departments.

The government of the United States, (and the government of the several states,) is of the latter description. The powers of the legislatures are defined and limited, and that those limits may not be mistaken or forgotten, the constitutions are written. To what purpose are powers *limited;* and to what purpose is that limitation committed to *writing;* if these limits may, at any time, be passed by those intended to be restrained? The distinction between a government with limited and unlimited powers is abolished, if those limits do not confine the persons on whom they are composed, and, if acts prohibited, and acts allowed, are of equal obligation. It is a proposition too plain to be contested, that the constitution controls any legislative act repugnant to it; or, that the legislature may alter the constitution by an ordinary act.

Between these alternatives there is no middle ground. The constitution is either a superior, paramount law, unchangeable by ordinary means, or it is on a level with ordinary acts, and is alterable when the legislature shall please to alter it. If the former part of the alternative be true, then a legislative act contrary to the constitution is not law; if the latter part be true, then written constitutions are absurd attempts, on the part of the people, to limit a power in its own nature illimitable.

Certainly, all those who have framed written constitutions, contemplate them as forming the fundamental and paramount law of the (state,) and consequently, the theory of every such government must be, that an act of the legislature repugnant to the constitution is void. This theory is essentially attached to a written constitution, and is consequently to be considered by courts as one of the fundamental principles of our society. It is not therefore to be lost sight of, in the further consideration of the subject.

If an act of the legislature, repugnant to the constitution, is void, does it notwithstanding its invalidity, bind the courts, and oblige them to give it effect? or, in other words, though it be not law, does it constitute a rule as operative as if it was a law? This would be to overthrow in fact, what was established in theory; and it would seem, at first view, an absurdity, too gross to be insisted on. It shall however, receive a more attentive consideration.

It is emphatically the duty and province of the judicial department to say what the law is. Those who apply the rule to particular cases, must of necessity expound and interpret that rule. If two laws conflict with each other, the courts must decide on the operation of each. So if a law be in opposition to the constitution; if both be the law, and the constitution apply to a particular case, so that the court must either decide that case, conformably to the law, disregarding the constitution, or conformably to the constitution, disregarding the law; the court must determine which of these conflicting rules governs the case. This is the very essence of judicial duty.

If then the courts are to regard the constitution; and the constitution is superior to any ordinary act of the legislature; the constitution, and not such ordinary act, must govern the case to which they both apply. Those who controvert the principle that the constitution is to be considered, in court, as a paramount law, are reduced to the necessity of maintaining that courts must close their eyes on the constitution, and see only the law.

This doctrine would subvert the very foundation of all written constitutions. It would declare that an act, which according to the principles and theory of our government, is entirely void, is yet, in practice, completely obligatory. It would declare, that if the legislature shall do what is expressly forbidden, such act, notwithstanding the express prohibition, is in reality effectual. It would be giving to the legislature, a practical and real omnipotence, with the same breath which professes to restrict their powers within narrow limits. It is prescribing limits, and declaring that those limits may be passed at pleasure; that it thus reduces to nothing, what we have deemed the greatest improvement on political institutions,—a written constitution, would, of itself, be sufficient in America, where written constitutions have been viewed with so much reverence, for rejecting the construction.

It has been regarded as curious, that in the absence of any express provision in the constitutions, or the statutes of the nation or states, that the judiciary should have assumed to exercise this extraordinary power, of checking the legislature in the exercise of their powers, to the extent of declaring statutes to be null and void when passed in violation of constitutional restrictions. But this has ever been regarded as an inherent power in the judicial department; a power that they have steadily, and sometimes vigorously exercised from the earliest days of the republics; and the exercise of the power, if not always conceded, has been universally acquiesed in as an admitted right. The judicial power of the government is conferred upon the courts. This includes all judicial power, and includes by implication, the power in question. By virtue of this power, the courts decide in all cases brought before them, what the true construction of a doubtful constitutional provision is, and when legislative acts are brought before them, they decide whether its provisions, or any of them, are infractions of the constitution. If their decision is, that the act is unconstitutional, it destroys its vitality, and puts an end to all proceedings under it.

The importance of this feature in our system, and its bearing on the character of the judicial department, is at once apparent. It limits the power of the legislature; it erects the judiciary at once, as was intended, into a co-ordinate department, and political authority in the government; it practically associates them with the law-making branch; it has had a very marked effect upon the character of the legal mind, and education of the country; and it has established in itself a degree of confidence and respect, to which the citizen looks as his best security. It has elevated the bar, by stimulating them to the highest professional efforts; and to persevering study and research; it has made judges themselves ambitious to master and declare the great principles of the government, and of American jurisprudence; and it has given a depth and breadth, and dignity, to discussions upon great legal and constitutional questions.

" The undisputed powers of the judiciary, are very great. They not only expound statutes, and mold and modify their own judgments, but they declare what is meant by the comity of nations, and apply the laws of foreign countries. The daily habits of business are under their control; new customs every day arising, stand or fall by their decisions ; and under the cover of the right to enforce public policy, and protect good morals, they excite a large and undefined authority over private conduct. To all this is added in America, the undisputed right to declare constitutional, law, and thus, in certain cases, to override the express will of the legislature itself. · These functions, are ample enough to gratify the most eager love of power; and to demand the exercise of the noblest intellect, and the application of the most vigorous industry." a

When a statute is adjudged to be unconstitutional, it is as if it had never been. Rights cannot be built up under it; contracts which depend upon it for their consideration are void; it constitutes a protection to no one who has acted under it, and no ·one can be punished for having refused obedience to it before the decision was made. And what is true of an act void in toto, is true also of any part of an act which is found to be unconstitutional, and which consequently, is to be regarded as having never, at any time, possessed any legal force. b So that nothing is law simply and solely because the legislature have declared it to be so, unless they have expressed their determination to that effect, by the mode pointed out by the instrument which invests them with the power, and under all the forms, which that instrument has rendered essential.

But in giving judicial construction to statutes, the courts ever keep in mind tho marked distinction that exists between statutes of the congress of the United States under the national constitution, and the statutes passed under the constitutions of the *several* states. The government of the United States, is one of *enumerated* powers; all its powers are specified;—they are either expressed in the constitution itself, or are necessarily to be implied from tho powers that are expressly conferred. And when these powers are

a Sedgwick on Const. Law 219.
b Cooley on Const. Lim. 188.

questioned, the only duty of the courts, is, to see whether the grant of specified power is broad enough to embrace the act. But statutes passed by state legislatures, under state constitutions, the courts will presume to be valid, for the reason that state legislatures have jurisdiction of all subjects on which its legislation is not *prohibited* by their own constitutions, or *limited* by the constitution of the United States. *a*

The rule of interpretation by which the two constitutions are distinguished, is just this; the constitution of the United States must have a strict construction ; state constitutions a liberal one. *b* All powers not granted to the Union are withheld, while the states, retain every attribute of sovereignty which is not taken away. By the constitution of the state of New York, "the legislative power of the state, is vested in the Senate and Assembly. This means of course, the *whole* legislative power," *c* because the words are general and unlimited. The people have thus parted with all the power of legislation, (which was originally in them,) except such as is prohibited. Where, therefore, the constitution is silent, and the legislature are guilty of no usurpation of power distributed to the other departments of the government, their power, humanly speaking, is omnipotent.

It is not therefore for courts to define, or set limits to the legislative power, nor can they hold a law to be void, which is not prohibited by the constitution because in their opinion, it violates the spirit of our institutions, or impairs any of those rights, which it is the object of a free government to protect ; nor can they declare it to be unconstitutional, because it is morally wrong and unjust. The constitution itself contains all the inhibitions that exist, against legislative action. If the courts can add to these, they *alter* this fundamental instrument, which they are not authorized to do, and themselves become aggressors, and violate both letter and spirit of that organic law, as grossly as the legislature could. *d* If

a Sill v. Village of Corning, 15 N. Y. R. 303; People v. Supervisors of Orange. 27 Barb. 593, 2 Park. Cr. R. 490; People v. N. Y. Cent. R. Co., 24 N. Y. 497, 504; Commonwealth v. Hartman, 17 Penn. St. R. 119; Kirby v. Shaw, 19 id. 260; Wiesler v. Hade, 52 id. 477.

b Commonwealth v. Hartman, 5 Harris, 119.

c People v. Toynbee, 2 Park. Cr. R. 510.

d Sharpless v. Mayor of Philadelphia, 9 Harris 161.

the courts can add to the things that are inhibited, they can also take away. If they can change at all, they can destroy entirely. They cannot supply what they may suppose is a *casus omissus* in the constitution, nor declare unconstitutional an act of the legislature which they conceive wrong, unjust, or oppressive.

Nothing then, is more important, in securing the harmonious workings of our system of free government, than that each of these three departments between whom the sovereign power is distributed, should, respectively, keep within its own legitimate sphere of action.

While the legislature cannot overstep the prescribed bounds of power contained in the constitution, the judicial power is also limited, and they are confined to the duty of ascertaining whether any given laws do violate the constitution. It is not for the judiciary or the executive departments to enquire whether the legislature has violated the genius of the government, or the general principles of liberty, or the rights of man, or whether these acts are wise or expedient,—but only whether the legislature has transcended the limits prescribed by the fundamental law. *a*

Upon the American theory of state governments, the legislature possess all legislative power not prohibited. Upon this theory, there is a vast field of undefined power, not reserved, given away or prohibited, in which the legislature can exercise full and uncontrolled dominion; their use of this great domain is limited only by their own discretion; the people have conferred on them the whole omnipotence of the British parliament, except in so far as it is limited by the prohibitions of the constitution itself, and by those powers which they had previously granted to be exercised by the federal constitution. True, these great powers so conferred by the people, are liable to be abused, and experience has taught the lesson, that they are abused; but this is inseparable from the nature of all human institutions. The wisdom of man has never conceived of a government with power sufficient to answer its legitimate ends, and at the same time incapable of mischief. *b*

a Weisler v. Hade, 52 Penn. St. R. 478; Sill v. Village of Corning, 15 N. Y. 303; People v. Supervisors of Orange, 27 Barb. 593 ; People v. Toynbee, 2 Park Crim. R. 533.

a Sharpless v. Mayor of Philadelphia, 9 Harris 161.

No political system can be made so perfect that those entrusted with power will not sometimes depart from the true course of rectitude. In the best, much must be trusted to the discretion of those to whom power is committed. So in ours, the people have confided large powers to the legislature, and must rely upon the wisdom and honesty of their representatives for a faithful execution of their duties; and the representative well knows, that he is directly accountable to his constituents for the manner in which he discharges his trusts, and that those constituents possess the power to correct the evil by dismissing him, or more properly, by refusal further to continue him in place.

In the practical workings of our system it is seen, and to be deplored, that from time to time, members of the legislature, not only forget their duties, but utterly disregard the obligations they owe to their constituency, nay, even recklessly trample upon the most sacred principles of right and justice; still, if they act within the scope of powers conferred upon them, and are not prohibited by the constitution, the judicial power cannot pronounce the act void, merely because in their judgment it is contrary to the principles of natural justice. *a* Nor is it certain that it would be wise to change the constitution for this cause, and confer upon judges the power of exercising a corrective against unwise, oppressive, or corrupt legislation. The power would still be left to the exercise of the judgment of fallible men, and it is not beyond the power of imagination, to conceive of judges, as corrupt as legislators.

But the question will be further discussed as to the legislative powers under state constitutions of the right to take private property for public use, when we come to treat of the right of *eminent domain*, and the extent of the taxing power.

a Calder v. Bull, 3 Dallas, R. 399. Satterlee v. Mattemore, 2 Peters, R. 380. Fletcher v. Peck, 6 Cranch. 87.

CHAPTER XI.

OF THE LIMITATION OF CONSTITUTIONAL POWER IN TAKING PRI-
VATE PROPERTY FOR PUBLIC USES, UNDER THE RIGHT OF
EMINENT DOMAIN.

WE have already shown the omnipotence of absolute legislative
power, when unrestrained by constitutional restrictions. Under
the sovereign power of every government, the right of taking private property for public use is one of its incidents. The necessity
for exercising this right, is to be determined by the legislative
power, subject to the constitutional permission, and its condition
of limitation.

The fifth article of the amendments to the federal constitution
prohibits private property from being taken for public use, without just compensation. This *condition*, is a right that pertains to,
secures, and may be claimed by every citizen of the United States.
This *right to take*, subject to this condition, has ever been held to
be one of the high prerogatives of sovereignty, when necessity
calls it into exercise for the public use, only, and it is thus limited
by the national constitution, and by the condition annexed, or
rendering to the citizen, a just compensation. The same condition
is imposed by the constitution of the state of New York, by section 6, article 1, of the constitution of 1846. In states where no
such condition is found in the constitution, it has been held to be
secured to the citizen by the principles of natural justice, *a* which
is ever the universal common law of mankind.

We find it declared by the highest court in this state, *b* notwithstanding the constitutional protection to private property, that
there are still two different and distinct principles upon which
private property may be justly taken, used, or destroyed for the
benefit of others. Both of these principles, are commonly compre-

a Bristol v. Newchester, 3 N. Hamp. R. 535; Jones v. Walker, 2 Paine, 688; De-
Varraigne v. Fox, 2 Blatch. 95.

b Stone v. Mayor of N. Y., 25. Wend. 173.

hended and confounded in the phrase of " taking or destroying private property for the public benefit." One of these principles is applied, when the property of an individual is taken by the authority of the state for the common use or benefit of the public; that is to say, either for the general use and benefit of the people of the state in its aggregate character, or else, of all such citizens, without distinction, as may happen to have occasion for the use of such property. Such as lands taken for a canal, or a road, are instances of such application.

Such, too in another and secondary form, is the taking of lands by a corporate company for a railroad, or turnpike, under state authority, where the company enjoying a public franchise, so far represents, and is a trustee for the public. And this is done solely by virtue of *that right of eminent domain*, whereby the whole property of individuals who compose the state, is held subject to the sovereign authority, to be used for the common advantage. It rests substantially upon the same foundation with the right of taxation.

Notwithstanding these safeguards in the constitution, it is and ever has been universally conceded, and at this day, cannot be justly disputed, that in our own government, (as really in every other civilized political government,) there inheres, necessarily, the right, and the *duty*, of guarding, securing, and continuing its own existence ; and of protecting and promoting the interests and welfare of the whole community at large. This power, and this duty, are to be exerted not only in the highest acts of sovereignty, and in the external relations of governments, but they reach and comprehend also, the interior polity and relations of social life, which should be regulated with reference to the advantage of the whole society. Among these powers of government, is that which is denominated *the eminent domain of the state*. This, as its name imports, is paramount to all *private* rights vested under the government, which last rights, are, by necessary implication, held in subordination to the power of eminent domain, and must yield in every instance to its proper exercise. *a*

It is a question not now controverted, that under every established form of government, the tenure of property is derived me-

a West River Bridge Co. v. Dix, 6 How. U. S. R. 531.

diately, or immediately from the sovereign power of the state, as a political body, organized in such mode, or exerted in such a way as the people have thought proper to ordain. It can rest on no other foundation; it can have no other guarantee. It is owing to this theory, only, that appeals can be made to the laws, either for the protection, or assertion of the rights of property. Upon any other hypothesis, the law of property would be simply the law of force. The instances of the exertion of this power, in some mode or other, from the very foundation of civil government, have been so numerous and familiar, that at this day, little doubt or question is seriously or intelligently made against it, and it seems to be as well conceded, that the power to exercise it remains with the state government, except when its exercise is demanded for national purposes; and, as is conceded, this power is not brought within the purview of the constitutional restriction. At all events, the power of appropriation of property to public uses, has never been held by any judicial tribunal as impairing the obligation of contracts between the state and its citizens in the sense of the constitution, nor, that this was a power granted to the general government.

The exercise of the right of eminent domain, by which individual property is taken for public use, is an inherent power of sovereignty, and is a necessity of government; were it not so, the will or caprice of an individual, might obstruct and defeat the most important enterprises for public or governmental improvements.

The constitution of neither the federal government, nor of the states, have altered this rule of the common law. The legislature of the state of New York have declared, that "the people of this state in their right of sovereignty, are deemed to possess the original and ultimate property in and to all lands within the jurisdiction of the state." a The right to take property for public use, therefore, is but the exercise of the power which was originally vested in the people in their collective capacity;—which they have retained over the property of individuals;—and which they can resume at any time when necessary for public use.

This right is complete without any action on the part of the state, in certain property in which it is supposed no interest had ever

a 1 Rev. Stat. 718, § 1, 4 Kent's Com. 3; Taylor v. Porter, 4 Hill. 145.

been acquired by individuals; such as the rights of navigation, in its lakes and other navigable waters; the rights of fishery in certain public waters; and the right of the state to precious metals which may be mined within its limits. It is seldom however, that it becomes necessary to speak of eminent domain, except in connection with those cases in which the government is necessitated to appropriate property against the will of the owners. The right itself is generally defined, as if it were restricted to such cases. It is said to be that superior right of property pertaining to the sovereignty, by which the private property acquired by its citizens under its protection, may be taken, or its use controlled for the public benefit without regard to the wishes of the owners. *a*

This right is supposed to have existed anterior to the constitution or statute; it is an acknowledged principle of the social compact, which is understood to have been assented to by the original members of it, that in public emergencies, the right of individuals over their property, must yield to the superior necessities of the state. The framers of our national and state constitutions, it is supposed, framed this protective clause from the principles laid down by the ancient writers of public law applicable to this subject. But except for the extreme right to resort to this power, the security of life, liberty and property, lies at the foundation of the social compact; and to say, that the grant of legislative power, includes in it the right to attack private property; is equivalent to saying, that the people have delegated to their servants the power of defeating one of the great ends for which the government was established.

This right, in a general sense, pertains to the state, rather than to the national government; though whenever the same reasons exist, on which the right rests, viz., the necessities of government, for the purpose of performing its ordinary and essential functions; perpetuating its existence; and controlling and regulating matters of a public nature for the benefit of its citizens in common; the national government possess the same inherent power to exercise the right of eminent domain, as an incident of government.

Private property taken for public use by right of eminent do-

a Cooley on Const. Lim. 524; Pollard's Lessees v. Hagan, 3 How. U. S. R. 223; People v. Mayor, &c., N. Y. 32, Barb. 112, 119.

.main, (unlike taking it by taxation,) is taken, not as the owners share of contribution to a public burthen, but as so much beyond his share ; a and it operates upon the individual, without reference to the amount or value exacted from any other individual, or class of individuals.

"This right of resumption of property for public use, may be exercised not only where the safety, but also where the interest, or even the expedience of the state is concerned, as where land is wanted for a.road, canal, or other public improvement." b " It belongs to the legislature to determine, whether the benefit to the public from an improvement, is of sufficient importance to justify the exercise of the right of eminent domain, in thus interfering with the private rights of individuals." In cases of public improvements, from which a benefit would result to the public, this right of *eminent domain* may be exercised, either directly by the agents of the government, or through the medium of corporate bodies, or by means of individual enterprise." c

But the sovereign power, has no right to take the property of one citizen and transfer it to another, even for a full compensation, where the public interest will not be promoted thereby; and an act of the legislature making such a transfer, would be a violation of the contract by which the land was granted by the government; and repugnant to the constitution. d

"It cannot be a rightful attribute of sovereignty in any government professing to be founded upon fixed laws, however despotic the form of the government might be, to take the property of one individual, and bestow it upon another.   The possession and exercise of such a power, would be incompatible with the nature and object of all government; for it being admitted that a chief end for which government is instituted, is, that every man may enjoy his own; it follows necessarily, that the rightful exertion of a power by the government, of taking arbitrarily from any man

a People v. Mayor of Brooklyn, 4 N. Y. 424.

b Beekman v. Saratoga & Schenectady R. R. Co., 3. Paige 73; Wager v. Troy Union R. R. Co., 25 N. Y. 530.

c Id; Williams v. N. Y. Cent. R. R. Co., 16 N. Y. R. 97; DeVarraigne v. Fox, 2 Blatch. 95.

d Varick v. Smith, 5 Paige, 137; Beekman v. Sar. & Schenectady R. R. Co., 3 Paige, 73.

what is his own, for the purpose of giving it to another, would subvert the foundation principle upon which the government was organized, and resolve the political community into its original cha-
otic elements," a even though compensation be made.

But it is no objection to the power conferred by the legislature
upon a corporation to take such property,—that it contributes
also to the emolument or advantage of such corporation, or to
that of individuals. b   But such a power should not be attempted
by the legislature, unless the benefit which is to result to the public is of paramount importance, in comparison with the individual
loss or inconvenience. c

There has been much controversy in the courts, imposing great
embarrassment on them, in settling the line of demarkation between a use that is public, and one that is strictly private ; no rule
can be laid down that will apply to all cases.

The great difficulty that attends the exercise of this right, is, in
determining the limits that rightfully bound it ; for while all admit
the right, no one succeeds in defining clearly the degree of necessity that justifies the exertion of it ; in fact, the attempt to establish a rule, would show that it was impracticable.   "It takes place
(say the writers upon natural law,) only in case of state necessity,
which ought not to have too great an extent, but should be tem-
pered as much as possible with the rules of equity. d

This right of eminent domain, is not of itself a power granted
by statute.   The scope of discussion proposed in this work, therefore, is, what limitations the constitution has imposed upon its exercise.

Whether or not the purpose for which private property is taken,
is a public use, must as a general rule, be left to the wisdom of the
legislature to determine. e   Some of the state governments by
their legislation, have gone much farther than others in the exercise of this power.   Its appropriate exercise by government, should
be confined to its own necessities, in furnishing facilities to its cit-

a Bloodgood v. M. & H. R. R. Co., 18 Wend. 56; Embury v. Connor, 3 N. Y.
511, 517; Taylor v. Porter, 4 Hill, 140.

b Heyward v. Mayor of New York. 7 N. Y. 314; Buffalo & N. Y. R. R. Co. v.
Brainard, 9 N. Y. 100; People v. Smith, 21 N. Y. 595.

c Id. 16.   d Burlimaque Prin. Law, 145.

e 2 Kent's Com. 340

izens, in regard to those matters of public needs. Convenience or welfare, which, on account of their peculiar character, and the difficulty of making provision for them otherwise, it is both proper and usual for the government to provide. a^1

This ground of public necessity rests upon the basis, that private property must yield and become subservient to the public welfare; and the power to take, may be exercised directly by the govern-

a Cooley on Const. Lim. 533.

Note 1.—The propriety of taking private property for a public use, is not a judicial question, but one of political sovereignty, to be determined by the legislature, either directly or by delegating the power to public agents, proceeding in such form and manner as it may prescribe. People ex rel Herrick v. Smith, 21 N. Y. 595, 598.

It was held by Judge McLean, in the supreme court of the United States, at Chambers, the report of which is found in Vol. 3, Law Reg., No. 3, Old Series, page 603, in the case of the United States v. The Railroad Bridge Co., that the right of eminent domain was in the state, and that they can authorize a railroad through the public lands of the United States located in such state. He said, p. 617, &c.: " A state in the discharge of its ordinary functions of sovereignty, has a right to provide for an intercourse between its citizens, commercial and otherwise, in every part of the state, by the establishment of easements, whether they be common roads, turnpikes, plank, or railroads. The kind of easement must depend upon the discretion of the legislature. And this power extends as well over the lands of the United States, as to those owned by individuals." "It is a power which belongs to the state, and the exercise of which is essential to the prosperity and advancement of the country."

An act of the legislature which authorizes a railroad corporation to use the streets of a city for laying the track of its road, is not taking of public property for local or private use, and is therefore constitutional. People v. Law, 34 Barb. 494. But where the adjacent proprietors have title to the centre of the street, subject to the public easement and rights in the street, it cannot be so taken except upon full compensation, they still possess rights which courts are bound to protect. People v. Law, 34 Barb. 494. The use of the street by the railroad is a new burthen, beyond the public easement, which cannot be imposed by legislative authority without compensation to the owners in fee. Wager v. The Troy Union R. R. Co., 25 N. Y. 526; Williams v. N. Y. Cent. R. R. Co., 16 N. Y. 97. But the use of streets in the city of New York, taken under the right of eminent domain, for city railroad purposes, under the authority of the act of the legislature, is not a taking of private property for public use in such a sense as to require compensation to be made to the owner of the adjacent lots. The fee of the streets in that city was acquired under an act of the legislature, 2 R. S. 209. Act of 1813. The city hold the fee of the streets in trust for public use, for all the people of the state, and not as corporate or municipal property. The trust being publici juris, it is under the unqualified control of the legislature. People v. Kerr, 27 N. Y. 188.

48

ment itself, or by the agents of government, individual or corporate whom the legislature may authorize for this purpose. *a* Among the purposes that have been declared public, is that of making public highways, turnpike and plankroads, railroads, and canals; of erecting and constructing wharves and basins; of establishing ferries; of draining swamps and marshes; of bringing water to cities, villages and towns; to raze houses to the ground; and to prevent the spreading of a conflagration.*b* This last case however is not by virtue of the right of eminent domain *c* but a regulation, or a right, growing out of the law of *inevitable necessity*, called the police power, belonging to every individual, not conferred by law, but tacitly excepted from all human codes. The right to appropriate private property to public uses, is to be regarded as lying dormant in the state, until legislative action is adopted, pointing out the occasions, the mode, conditions and agencies for its appropriation. It can then only be taken pursuant to law, but a legislative act declaring the necessity, is for this purpose, the law of the land, and no further adjudication or finding is essential. *d* The principle thus recognized, it has been held, is no violation of justice or sound policy, and in no degree tends to impair the obligation or infringe upon the sanctity of contracts. It rests upon the basis, that public convenience and necessity are of paramount importance and obligation, to which, when duly ascertained and declared by the sovereign authority, all minor considerations and private rights and interests must be held subordinate; otherwise great public improvements, rendered necessary by the increasing wants of society, in the development of civilization and the progress of the arts; might be prevented. The only true rule of policy, as well as of law, is, that a grant for one public purpose, must yield to another more urgent and important, and this can be effected without any infringement on constitutional rights of the subject. If in such cases, suitable and adequate provision is made by the legislature for the compensation of those whose property or franchise is injured or taken away, there is no violation of public faith or private right. *e*

a Beekman v. Saratoga and Schenectady RR. Co., 3 Paige, 72; Wilson v. The Black Bird Creek Marsh Co., 2 Pet. 251.

b 2 Kent's Com. 338.   *c* Russell v. Mayor of New York, 2 Denio, 461.

d Cooley on Const. Limit, 528.

e Central Bridge Corporation v. City of Lowell, 4 Gray, 481, 482.

But the property of individuals, cannot even be appropriated by the state, under this power, for the mere purposes of adding to the revenues of the state. The exercise of such a power for such a purpose, would be utterly destructive of individual right, and break down all the distinctions between *meum and tuum*, and annihilate them forever at the pleasure of the state. *a*

It is regarded as the duty of every government, as the wants of traffic and travel require facilities beyond those afforded by the common highways, or their own private ways, over which the public and individuals may pass with their own vehicles, or animals; to provide and establish a higher grade, and more improved character of thoroughfares for public use; and whether these are constructed and kept in repair by an assessment upon the citizen, by way of money or labor, by tolls on turnpikes and canals, or by fares on railroads, they are all equally projected for public use; the public at large are interested in their establishment, and the government have the right to appropriate private property to that end; and such right comes within this reserved power called the right of eminent domain.

The court of dernier resort in this state, seems to have settled the question of power under our constitution, as to the right of taking private property for public purposes, either directly by the state or otherwise; they have said, "that the regulation of all matters connected with the internal traffic and commerce of the state; the development of its wealth and resources; the advancement of its material interests; either by constructing of routes and means of communication and commerce between different parts of the state, by land or water, is clearly within the legislative power which, by the constitution, is vested in the senate and assembly. A restriction upon the legislature in respect of a matter which is properly the subject of legislation, will not be implied, but must be clearly expressed. It will not be presumed in the absence of a clearly expressed intent, that it was designed to cripple the power of the legislature in so important a part of its duties, as to deprive it of the power to develope the resources of the state, and attract within its limits the commerce and trade of other states by making available private enterprise, or by creating

a Buckingham v. Smith, 10 Ohio R. 296.

other facilities for travel and transportation ; or by any means which were accessible." a

This extraordinary power has been exercised to a much greater extent in some of the states than others, and this, creates such a diversity of views as to the extent of the power, that no line of demarkation can be laid down as a universal rule. By the law of the states of Massachusetts, Maine and Rhode Island, the estab- lishment of mills is regarded, as beneficial to the public, and mill owners and occupants, are authorized to overflow the lands of other persons, and to take such proceedings therefor, as are provided in the statutes ot those states ; b and the law of North Carolina is not materially, though somewhat different. c

The law in this respect, in Virginia, Kentucky, Missouri, Mis- sissippi, Alabama and Florida, are substantially alike. By these, a person owning the land on one side of a watercourse, who pro- poses to erect a water grist mill, or other machine or engine, use- ful to the public, may make application to the court, through which, by appraisement by a jury, he obtains the right to use the opposite bank—and the right to flow the lands of others, provided the flowing does not extend to a house, yard, &c., and not to create a public nuisance. The proceedings under the statutes being regular, immediately divests the title of the owner of the land and vests it in the commonwealth, in full and absolute dominion. d

The constitutional soundness of these statutes, has been greatly doubted in other states, but long acquiesence, and repeated judi- cial and legislative precedents, would seem now to put it out of the power of individuals, to test the soundness of the basis, upon which the governmental action has proceeded. e

An act of the legislature taking land in this state for public use, is not even unconstitutional, because the instrumentality employed

a The People v. N. Y. Cent. RR. Co, 24 N. Y. 497, 8; People v. Draper, 15 id. 545.

b The Boston & Roxbury Milldam Corporation v. Newman, 12 Pick. 467; French v. Braintree Manufac. Co., 23 id. 219; Rev. Laws of Mass., Ch. 116; Rev. Laws of Maine in Append. p. 9; Laws of Rhode Island (Ed. 1844) and Append. p. 15.

c See Gillette v Jones, 1 Dev. & Bat. R. 339, and the N. C. Statute therein re ferred to.

d Statute of Virginia in Append. p. 22; Statute of Kentucky of 1797, 1 Stat. Kentucky, 606; Laws of Indiana, 65, Rev. Code of 1831; Laws of Missouri, 587; Clay's Dig. of Laws of Alabama 376; Thompson's Dig. of Laws of Florida 401, &c.

e Matter of Townsend. 39, N. Y. 171.

for that purpose is a corporation created by the laws of another state; nor because such corporation derives a pecuniary benefit from the use of the lands so appropriated; nor because the lands appropriated, are to be used for the maintenance of a navigable canal which runs along the border of the state, but without its limits. If the use be in its nature public, the legislature are the sole judges of the question, whether the benefit to our citizens, or to the state is such, as to warrant the taking of private property therefor; and are also the sole judges of the question, what supervision or control over the use should be retained, in order to secure the contemplated benefits.

But it should be kept in mind however, that whenever in pursuance of law, the property of an individual is to be divested by these proceedings against his will, there must be a strict compliance with all the provisions of the laws, which are made for his protection and benefit. Those provisions must be regarded as in the nature of conditions precedent, which must not only be complied with before the right of the property owner is disturbed, but the party claiming authority under the adverse proceeding, must affirmatively show such compliance.

In the state of New York, the legislature have never, it is believed, attempted to exercise the right of eminent domain in favor of mills, " sites for steam engines, hotels, churches, and other like public conveniences," a and we do not therefore, deem it necessary to hazard an opinion, whether such a right would be sustained if granted; though the legislature have granted to municipalities, and districts, to take and appropriate for such uses, as for district school houses; to counties for their court houses and jails; and to cities for town halls, reservoirs of water, sewers, gas works, and other public works of like importance. In such cases the taking is public, the use is public; the benefits to accrue therefrom is public, as it is shared in a greater or less degree by the whole public. b

There is no species of property except money, or rights in action, that seem to be exempt from the power of government, to seize and appropriate it to public use under the right of eminent domain.

a Hay v. Cohoes Co. 3. Barb, 47.
b Cooley on Const Lim. 537 ; Nichols v. Bridgeport. 23 Com, 189.

Taking money under the right of *eminent domain,* when it must
be compensated in money afterwards, could be nothing more nor
less than a forced loan, which could only be justified as a last resort in a time of extreme peril, where neither the credit of the government, nor the power of taxation could be made available.
This would rather be a case, coming under no law, but that of an
overruling necessity. *a* The right to a franchise, is of no higher
order, and confers no more sacred title than the right to land,
and when the public necessities require it, the one as well as the
other may be taken for public purposes, on making suitable compensation ; nor does such an exercise of the rights of eminent domain, interfere with the inviolability of contracts, if such franchise
happens to be a grant. *b*

Lands for public ways, timber, stone and gravel to make and
improve or repair public ways and canals ; *c* a building that stands
in the way of a contemplated improvement ; or which for any
other reason it is necessary to take, remove or destroy for the
public good ; *d* streams of water, *e* corporate franchises, *f* and
generally it may be said, legal and equitable rights of every description, *g* may be so taken.

The legislature has power to authorize a corporation or individuals and their assigns in constructing and operating a railroad, " to run upon or intersect or use any portion" of the railroad
track of another company upon making due compensation therefor. *h* And where the legislature by an act authorize the construction of highways across railroad tracks, without compensation, they do not violate the constitutional provisions against
taking private property for public uses, or impair the obligation of
a contract. The title, which a railroad corporation acquires to
its own track, is qualified, as being taken for public use, and for

a Id 527.

b Richmond RR. Co v. Louisa RR. Co. 13 How, 71; West River Bridge v. Dix.
6 How, 507; Matter of Kerr. 42 Parb, 119.

c Wheelock v. Young, 4 Wend. 647; Lyon v. Jerome, 15 Wend. 569.

d Wells v. Somerset, 47 Maine R. 345. *e* Gardner v. Newburgh, 2 John.Ch. 162.
f Piscataqua Bridge v. N. Hampshire Bridge, 7 N. Hamp. R. 35.

g Cooley on Const. Lim. 526.

h Matter of Kerr, 42 Barb. 119, and' cases cited; Sixth Avenue R. R. Co. v.
Kerr, 45 Barb. 141.

the purpose of the incorporation, and is subject to the exercise by the legislature of all the powers to which the franchises of the corporation are subject. *a*

We have already said, the question of the necessity for the exercise of this power belongs to the government, and is only exercised when authorized by the legislative department, and over which the judicial power possesses no control. The question is always regarded as being one of political sovereignty in character.

We do not intend by this, to say, that the expression by the legislature that it is for the public interest in a particular case to exert the right of eminent domain, determines that question; that would be setting the legislative power above the constitution, but only to concede to the legislature the right to appropriate private property to public use.

When the public use is local and limited, the power is often conferred upon some local tribunal, or agent, and given to them to decide upon the necessity, and regulate the proceeding; and the omission to provide for a trial by jury in such case, is held to be no violation of constitutional right, *b* and the state is under no obligation to make provision for judicial contest upon that question; though this is often done, as in cases of laying out highways, &c.

The appropriation of private property for this purpose, must however, always be limited to the necessity of the case; and this question of necessity is one over which the judicial power has some control. No more of private property can be so appropriated than the proper tribunal shall adjudge to be necessary for the particular use for which the appropriation is made. When only a part of a man's lands are needed by the public, this will not justify the taking of the whole, even though it should be taken under the provisions of a statute of the legislature, authorizing the taking the whole. The moment the appropriation goes beyond the necessity of the case, it ceases to be justified by the principles which underlie the right of eminent domain. *c*

This question has caused much litigation in the courts, and was

a Albany Northern R. R. Co. v. Brownell, 24 N. Y. 345, 349.
b People v. Smith, 21 N. Y. R. 595.
c Cooley on Const. Lim. 540; Bennett v. Boyle, 40 Barb. 551.

left by the statutes of this state as unsettled, as to whom the power of exercising the discretion was vested; whether in the legislature, in the railroad or other corporation, or in the courts. This question has been very recently settled in this state in regard to railroads, by an amendment of the general statute concerning the formation of such companies, where new lands are required by an existing railroad company, and by a construction of that amended statute in the Court of Appeals *a* not yet reported.

Under an amendment of the general act of 1850, by the statute of 1854, existing railroad companies were authorized to acquire additional lands *for the purposes of such company*, as it would have in the location of a line of road in the first instance. By another amendment of this general statute, by the legislature of 1869, such railroad company, and such existing railroad company, were authorized to acquire such real estate, or such additional real estate, *for the purpose of its incorporation, or for the purpose of running or operating such road, or for any other purpose necessary to the operation of such railroads, &c.* In giving construction to this amended statute, the Court of Appeals, as appears from the syllabus of the case reported in the Law Journal, *b* laid down the following eight propositions, viz:

1. The right to take property for public use, is to be exercised by the legislative power, and this power can determine for what purposes private property can be taken, and when the necessity exists which calls for its appropriation,—and this power can be exerted through agents, whether individuals or corporations.

2. The legislature may therefore authorize a railroad corporation to take private property for the purpose of its incorporation, under a delegation of its power of eminent domain.

Under the general railroad act, this taking must be done through an application to the court, upon notice to persons interested, and a hearing and determination of the court thereupon.

3. Under the statute of 1869, extending the powers granted by the original act of 1850, the determination of the question of necessity, and extent of appropriation, is left with the court, and is not vested in the board of directors of the railroad company.

a Matter of the Application of the Rensselaer & Saratoga RR. Co. v. Davis.
b No. 57.

4. The legislature have the power to designate the particular premises which a railroad company may take for its uses, but this was not done by the statute of 1869, nor did it by that statute delegate to the railroad company, the power to determine the necessity for the appropriation of private property for corporate purposes.

5. The acquisition of lands for the purpose of speculation and sale, or to prevent interference by competing lines, or in aid of collateral enterprises remotely connected with the running of the road, though they may increase its revenue, are not such purposes as authorize the condemnation of private property.

6. The taking of private property for public use, is in derogation of private rights, and in hostility to the ordinary control of the citizen over his estate, and is not to be extended by implication. To authorize the taking of land under eminent domain, the express authority of the law must be shown.

7. The Rensselaer and Saratoga Railroad Company endeavored to take a quantity of land on the shore of Lake Champlain, for the building of docks to accommodate vessels bringing freight, and the construction of dwellings for its employees and officers. Held, under the circumstances, not necessary for corporate purposes.

8. The decision of the special term in such a matter, is a final adjudication of the question of the right of condemnation under the statute, and an appeal lies to the Court of Appeals from the decision of the general term thereupon.

A statute of this state, which enacted that in all cases where part only of a lot or parcel of land shall be required for laying out a street, if the commissioners deem it expedient to take the whole lot in the assessment, they shall have power to do so, and the part not wanted for the particular street or improvement, shall, upon the confirmation of the report, be vested in the corporation, who may appropriate the same to public uses, or sell the same in case of no such appropriation; was held to be unconstitutional, and assumed a power the legislature did not possess. *a*

The court in that case, held, " that the constitution by authorizing the appropriation of private property to *public use*, impliedly declares that for any other use, private property shall not be

a In the Matter of Albany Street, 11 Wend. 151.

49

taken from one, and applied to the private use of another. It is a violation of natural right, and if it is not in violation of the letter of the constitution, it is of its spirit, and cannot be supported. a

So, it is doubtless true, that while it belongs to the legislative department to determine and declare the propriety of the exercise of this power of the right of eminent domain, they cannot exercise it beyond the scope of the line of necessity, and an abuse of its exercise, can doubtless be controlled by the judicial power. The necessity upon which the exercise of legislative power depends, relates to the use, and the nature of the property. Should the legislature either by a direct exercise of the power, or through some subordinate agency, under a power conferred by them, abuse the authority, by using it irregularly, oppressively, or in bad faith, there can be no doubt of the power of the courts to furnish an effectual remedy against such acts. b

While it is conceded that the legislature have the power to determine *when* public uses require the assumption of private property—it is greatly doubted, nay, denied, that they can declare *that* to be a public use, that is not so; as in the case supposed by Chancellor Kent. c "If the legislature should take the property of A. and give it to B, such a law would be unconstitutional and void, even if the legislature should declare that to be a public use." Nor can it be a rule, that in all cases because the public interest in some degree will be promoted by such use, that it is therefore a public use. It can hardly be supposed that the implied constitutional permission to take private property stands upon a broader basis of right than such as existed by the principles of natural law.

Constitutional authority then, being not greater than that existing by natural law, and the legislative power being subordinate to the constitutional, the sacred right of private property is above the control of the legislative power, except in the cases of actual necessity for public use. This public use, is an inherent and inseparable quality, the character of which is not changed, merely, because the legislature choose so to denominate it. Legislative discretion must not be confounded with sovereignty; it is only one

a Id.   b Giezy v. C. W. & Z. R. R. Co., 4 Ohio R. (N. S.) 325.

c 2 Com. 340.

of three restricted organs of sovereignty, and inasmuch as sovereignty itself is prohibited from taking private property, except for public use, and upon due compensation, no subordinate power can do so.

The quantity of property that may be appropriated in any given case, is left, it is true, very indefinite, but there is no danger of permanent abuse, so long as the conservative power of the courts are left to protect such interests. It has been controverted in the courts, whether the power to take property by a railroad company under legislative authority, extends to an appropriation for depot, and station purposes, with grounds to receive and discharge freight, fuel and passengers ; but reason teaches that these are but the incidents to the main purpose, and are such indispensable appendages to the principal object, that the main object would be useless without it. *a*

We have thus far in this chapter, been treating of the reserved power in our constitution, and in every other sovereignty, to appropriate the private property of individuals, to public use. While it is conceded that this power exists, it exists only with a concomitant constitutional restriction, that it shall not be taken for public use without just compensation, *b* and with the further protection to the citizen, that when so taken, the compensation to be made therefor, when such compensation is not made by the state, shall be ascertained by a jury, or by not less than three commissioners appointed by a court of record, as shall be prescribed by law. *c*

This constitutional restriction in favor of the individual is so controlling, that the power to take his property cannot be exercised, unless the provision for compensation be made. This right of the individual is regarded as so sacred, that a court of equity will interpose by way of injunction to restrain action under a statute to take such property that makes no provision for compensation. *d* Such an act would be pronounced unconstitutional and void. *e*

a Rodgers v. Bradshaw, 20 John. 735.

b Const. of 1846, Art. 1, § 6.

c Id., Art. 1, § 7.

d Gardner v. Trustees of Newburgh, 2 John. Ch. 162.

e Perry v. Wilson, 7 Mass. R. 395; Stevens v. Middlesex Canal, 12 id. 466; Thatcher v. Dartmouth Bridge, 18 Pick. R. 501.

It seems however, that if the statute which authorizes the taking, in itself, provides a certain and adequate remedy for the payment of damages or compensation, that it is not absolutely necessary that the amount of compensation should be actually ascertained and paid before such property can be taken and appropriated to public use. *a*

The settled doctrine in this state, as far as it is expressed, is found in the case of Bloodgood against The Mohawk and Hudson Railroad Company, decided in its highest court, the court for the correction of errors; and reported in 18 Wend. R. pp. 9 to 77. The importance of the rule settled in this case, as the law of this state, will excuse a liberal citation from it. The plaintiff declared in *trespass quare clausum fregit*, alledging that the defendants, by their servants, entered his closes, with carriages, &c., and broke down, and destroyed his fences, and dug and subverted the soil, &c. The defendants justified under their act of incorporation by the legislature of the state, which authorized them by their agents, surveyors and engineers, to cause such examinations and surveys to be made, between certain points, (which included the line over the plaintiff's lands,) as should be necessary to determine the most advantageous route, place or places whereon to construct their railway; and made it lawful for the defendants to enter upon, and take possession, and use, all such lands and real estate as might be indispensable for the construction and maintenance of their railway, and the accommodations requisite and appertaining to them. Provided that all lands or real estate thus entered and taken possession of by the defendants, (which are not donations) should be purchased by the defendants of the owner or owners at a price to be mutually agreed upon betwixt them, *and* in case of disagreement of the price, it should be the duty of the governor of the state to appoint three commissioners, &c., to determine the damages, &c.; and then stating how the act provided for the manner of assessing and paying such damages, and further pleaded, that they entered the plaintiff's said closes, and for the purpose of causing such examinations and surveys to be made as might be necessary to determine the most advantageous route, &c., for said railroad, and for the purpose of taking possession of and using so much of such

a Rodgers v. Bradshaw, 20 John. 735, 744, 745.

closes as might be indispensable for the construction, &c., of their railway and accommodations requisite, and appertaining to them, and did then and there take possession for such purpose, which were the said supposed trespasses. To which answer there was a demurrer and joinder. Chancellor Walworth, who delivered the leading opinion of the court, laid down the law as follows: "It certainly was not the intention of the framers of the constitution to authorize the property of a citizen to be taken and actually appropriated to the public use, and thus to compel him to trust to the future justice of the legislature to provide him a compensation therefor. The compensation must be either ascertained and paid him before his property is thus appropriated, or an appropriate remedy must be provided, and upon an adequate fund, whereby he may obtain such compensation, through the medium of the courts of justice, if those whose duty it is to make such compensation refuse to do so." He adds, "In the ordinary case of lands taken for the making of highways, or for the use of the state canal, such a remedy is provided; and if the town, county, or state officers refuse to do their duty in ascertaining, raising or paying such compensation in the mode prescribed by law, the owner of the property has a remedy by mandamus to compel them to perform their duty. The public purse, or the property of the town or county upon which the assessment is to be made, may justly be considered an adequate fund. He has no such remedy, however, against the legislature to compel the passage of the necessary laws to ascertain the amount of compensation he is to receive, or the fund out of which he is to be paid." A very able, profound, abstract, and somewhat theoretical, but argumentative opinion was delivered in the case by Senator Albert H. Tracy, in which the whole doctrine relating to this subject, drawn as well from the natural rights of individuals, as from constitutional authority, and the extent of legislative power, was most learnedly discussed, the whole of which is worthy of being transcribed, and perpetuated in this, and every other work upon natural rights or constitutional limitations of legislative power, but its length forbids. No lawyer should omit to read it, who seeks to possess his mind with a knowledge of this branch of law.

At the close of the case, the court passed a resolution which may be quoted as the summary of the doctrine discussed in that case, and which remains the unimpaired and unshaken law of this state; which was in substance, "that the legislature of this state have the constitutional power to authorize the taking of private property for the purpose of making railroads or other public improvements of the like nature, whether such improvements be made by the state itself, or through the medium of a corporation, or joint stock company, on making ample provision for just compensation for the property taken to the owners thereof."

This provision for just compensation, it is seen, is the primary requisite to the appropriation of lands for public purposes under the right of eminent domain; and the courts have been quite uniform in holding, that this compensation must be pecuniary in its character, without allowances for supposed benefits to the proprietor, for in effect, it amounts to a power to compel the individual to convey, even against his will, when the public necessities require it. ' This is a right, which a magnanimous and just government will therefore never exercise without amply indemnifying the individual. *a*

This is doubtless the true rule, where the whole of a man's estate is taken, although he may own other estate in the vicinity which may be benefited by the public use; for the benefits or injuries which the owner receives or sustains to other property in common with the community generally, and which are not peculiar to him, and connected with his ownership, use, and enjoyment of the particular parcel of land, should be excluded altogether, as it would be unjust to compensate him for the one, or to charge him with the other, when no account is taken of such incidental benefits, and injuries with other citizens who receive or feel them equally with himself, but whose lands do not chance to be taken.

a Fletcher v. Peck, 6 Cranch. 145; Bradshaw v. Rodgers, 20 John. 104.

NOTE 2.—"The just compensation to the owner for taking his property for public uses without his consent, it has been held, means the actual value of the property in money, without any deduction for estimated profit or advantages accruing to the owner from the public use of his property. Speculative advantages or disadvantages, independent of the intrinsic value of the property from the improvement, are a matter of set off against each other, and do not affect the dry claim for the intrinsic value of the property taken." Jacob v. City of Louisville, 9 Dana, R. 114; Van Horne's Lessees v. Dorrance, 2 Dall. 315.

But where less than the whole lot or estate is taken, there is a class of cases that hold the rule to be in assessing the damages, to take into consideration how much the portion not taken is increased or diminished in value in consequence of the appropriation. *a* "The owner of the property is entitled to full compensation for the damages he sustains thereby; but if the taking of a part of his property for the public improvement is a benefit rather than an injury to him, he certainly has no equitable claim to damages." *b* If the same property that remains, will be more valuable when the improvement is made, than the whole of it was before, the owner will not sustain any damage, but will derive a benefit from it.

The time when this compensation must be made, is not fixed in the constitution of this state itself, nor in the federal constitution; but in some of the states, provision is made in their constitutions, that compensation must be made before the property is taken.

It has been held in this state, in effect, that no constitutional principle was violated by a statute that allowed private property to be entered upon temporarily, for the purpose of making a survey for a state appropriation, with a view of determining the proper location of a canal; and that for such a purpose, the state was not bound to make compensation, nor were its subordinate officers, who so entered, liable to an action of trespass. *a*

A distinction is found in the books, which seems to have been recognized, as settled, between property taken directly by the state, or a municipal corporation by state authority, and cases where it is taken by a private corporation, which, for this purpose, is clothed with the power to take, and regarded as a public agent, if the property is to be appropriated, for the benefit and profit of its members. If taken directly by the state, it is not essential to the validity of the law, that it should provide for making compensation *before* the actual appropriation; it is sufficient, if provision is made in the law, by which, the party can obtain certain com-

---

a Livingston v. The Mayor of New York, 8 Wend. 101; In the Matter of Furman Street. 17 Wend. 671; Parks v. Boston, 15 Pick. 205.

b Id., and McMasters v. Commonwealth, 3 Watts. (Penn.) R. 296.

a Bloodgood v. M. & H. RR. Co., 14 Wend. 51, & 18 Wend. 9; Gardner v. Newburgh, 2 John. Ch. 168.

pensation, and a proper tribunal is provided for determining it. *a* A very good reason obtains, why the rule should be different in cases where individuals, or private corporations, are authorized to take even for public purposes. The latter, might otherwise get possession, and despoil a party of his estate, and then prove irresponsible, by means of which the proprietor might loose his estate without means of redress, and thus the constitutional protection, become but a name and a mockery, to the spirit and intent of the constitution.

Chancellor Kent was of opinion, that in all such cases, the compensation, or offer of it, must precede, or be concurrent with the seizure and entry upon the private property taken under the authority of the state. *b* "That the government is bound in such cases, to provide some tribunal for the assessment of the compensation or indemnity, before which, each party may meet and discuss their claims on equal terms ; and that if the government proceed without taking these steps, their officers and agents may, and ought to be sustained by injunction." He granted an injunction in such case when acting as Chancellor, *c* and in support of his opinion, he cited the authorities of the profoundest writers upon the civil law, and the law of nature, and said, that this limitation of the power existed before it was incorporated into our own constitutions, was admitted by the soundest authorities; and adopted by all temperate and civilized governments, from a deep and universal sense of its justice. *d*

The distinction above referred to, shows, that the rule in this state, is not universal nor inflexible, inasmuch as it is neither a constitutional, or statute provision, that payment should precede, or accompany the appropriation, yet, we must concede, that such was, and is, the spirit of justice, and such, I think, was natural law before our constitution was adopted, which really, but incor-

a Bloodgood v. Mohawk & Hudson, RR. Co., 18 Wend. 9; Rodgers v. Bradshaw, 2 John, 744, 5; Calkin v. Baldwin, 6 Wend. 670; Rexford v. Knight. 11 N. Y. 313, 314; Lyon v. Jerome, 26 Wend. 497; People v. Hayden, 6 Hill, 359.

b 2 Com. 330, Note C.

c Gardner v. Village of Newburgh, 2 John, Ch. 162.

d Grotius (De Jur. B. & P. b. 8, Ch. 14, s. 7;) Puffendorf (De Jur. Nat. et Gent, b. 8, Ch. 5, s. 7;) Bynkershock, (Quaest Jur. Pub. b. 2, Ch. 15.) Code Napoleon, Art. 545.

porated into it, the law of nature. The constitutions of various of the states of the Union, have adopted it as fundamental law. *a*

Injuries done to property not appropriated, by the exertion of this power of resumption by the state, under the right of eminent domain, it is held, give no valid claim against the state, or its agents on account of the taking. It is perhaps as common, that estates adjoining, or in the vicinage of a public improvement, are injuriously affected as that they are benefited or increased in value. Unless the statute provides a relief in such case to the party, he is remediless. Every great public improvement, almost of necessity, more or less affects individual convenience and property, for the better or for the worse ; if for the worse, and the injury is consequential, or remote, it is to be borne, as a part of the price which the individual must pay, for the advantages of the social condition.*b* This is founded upon the principle, that the general good is to prevail over partial individual convenience. The loss is *damnum absque injuria*.

Upon the same principle; a statute passed to regulate the use of a navigable stream, which only incidentally affects the riparian owners, gives to the person so affected, no right to compensation, though if the stream is thereby diverted from its natural course, so that those entitled to its benefits are prevented from using it as before; such a deprivation of a right, is a taking, which entitles to compensation, notwithstanding the taking may be for the purpose of creating another and more valuable channel of navigation.*c* The owners of the land over which a stream flows, though they do not own the flowing water itself, yet have a property in the *use* of that water as it flows past them, for the purpose of producing mechanical power, or for any other of the purposes for which they can make it available, without depriving those below them on the stream, of the like use, or encroaching upon the rights of those

a Constitution of Indiana, Art. 21, § 1 ; Ohio, Art. 1, § 19 ; Kentucky, Art. 13 § 14 ; Oregon, Art. 1, § 19 ; Nevada, Art. 1, § 8 ; Mississippi, Art. 1, § 13 ; Minnesota, Art. 1, § 13 ; Kansas, Art. 12, § 4 ; Georgia, Art. 1, § 17 ; Florida, Art. 1, § 14.

b Lansing v. Smith, 8 Cow. 149; Troy & Boston RR. Co., v. Northern Turnpike Co., 16 Barb. 100.

c People v. Canal Appraisers, 13 Wend. 355 ; Billinger v. N. Y. Cent. RR. Co., 23 N. Y. 42.

above; and this property is equally protected, with that of a more tangible character. *a*

In another class of injuries, also, a party may sustain great and almost irreparable injury, where the law affords him no redress; such for instance as those resulting from the construction of public works, where, if an injury occurs in a case where the work was constructed upon a proper plan and without negligence, and if the injury is caused by accidental and extraordinary circumstances, the injured party is without remedy, and can demand no compensation; and this is so, even though the property was appropriated under the right of eminent domain. *b* But if in such case, however, there is want of reasonable care and skill in the construction of such work, and unnecessary damage is caused, it is not warranted by the right of eminent domain, and then, the corporation or its agents are responsible for it. Such damage however must be real, substantial and appreciable, and not merely theoretical or slight, or such as may be caused by an unusual or extraordinary swell of the waters. *c*

As it is competent for the state to declare the extent of the use to which private property is thus to be taken, whether for a temporary period, for an easement, or the entire fee, the amount of compensation will of course depend upon the character of the deprivation, and the extent of exclusion of use by the former owner, so that in all cases, where the complete fee is not taken, the original owner is vested with the remainder or reversion that is left, and whenever the public use ceases, or is discontinued, as a general rule, the estate reverts to the original proprietor, and he becomes restored to his complete and exclusive possession. The case of common highways, is within this class; there the public have a perpetual easement, but the fee, and the soil, is in the original owner or his assigns, and they may make any use of it which does not interfere with the public right of passage over it, and the public can use it for the usual purposes of a highway. *d* By special statutes however, in some of the cities, the fee of the

a Morgan v. King, 35 N. Y. 454; Cooley on Const. Lim. 557.

b Perry,v. City of Worcester, 6 Gray, 546–7, and cases cited; Sprague v. The **Same**, 15 Gray, 195.   *c* Id.

d Adams v. Rivers, 11 Barb. 390; Cooley on Const. Lim. 558.

streets is in the city absolutely; so in like cases, appropriations for alms-houses, canals, &c. *a*

The constitution of this state, though it authorizes the appropriation of private property to public uses, upon the condition of just compensation to the proprietor, has afforded to the individual owner, a still further protection against legislative abuse, and as a limitation upon the power to take. It declares that no member of this state shall be disfranchised or deprived of any of the rights or privileges secured to any of the citizens thereof, unless *by the law of the land*, or the judgment of his peers." *b*

It provides also, not only, that he shall receive a just compensation, but also that he shall not be deprived of his property " *without due process of law*," and, that in cases where the compensation is not made by the state, it shall be ascertained by a jury, or by not less than three commissioners appointed by a court of record, as shall be prescribed by law. *c*

What is " the law of the land," and "due process of law," had well defined common law meanings, before the adoption of this constitution, and must be regarded as but slightly qualified by the terms of the constitution itself.

Chancellor Kent says, the words, *by the law of the land*, as used originally in *Magna Charta* in reference to this subject, are understood to mean, " *due process of law*," *d* and, that the better and larger definition of *due process of law*, is, that it means law, in its regular course of administration. And it was held in the court of appeals of this state, *e* that these constitutional safeguards, in all cases, require a judicial investigation; not to be governed by a law specially enacted to take away and destroy existing rights, but confined to the question, whether under the pre-existing rule of conduct, the right in controversy has been lawfully acquired, and is lawfully possessed. So Lord Coke interprets, " *by the law of the land*," to mean, " by the due course and process of the law." *f*

a Heyward v. Mayor of New York, 7 N. Y. R. 314; Baker v. Johnson, 2 Hill, 348; Rexford v. Knight, 11 N. Y. R. 308; Munger v. Tonawanda R. R. Co., 4 N. Y. 010.

b Const. of N. Y. of 1846, Art. 1, § 1.

c Const. of N. Y. of 1846, Art. 1, § 7.　　　　*d* 2 Com. 13.

e Wyndham v. The People, 13 N. Y. R. 395.

f 2 Inst. 46.

And the courts of this state hold, that the words, " due process of law," import a judicial trial, and not a mere declaration of the legislative will by the passing of a law. *a*   It is therefore regarded as safe to say, "that without due process of law, that is, without judicial investigation, no act of legislation can deprive a man of his property, and that in all civil cases, an act of the legislature alone, is wholly inoperative to take from a man his property."

These provisions in substance, or in equivalent language, will be found in nearly .every state constitution.   They were rights that existed and attached to every citizen at common law, before the adoption of state constitutions; they can be traced back to *Magna Charta*, and were wrested from the king, as restraints upon the power of the crown.   They were imposed by the people as restraints upon the legislative power when they put forth their constitutions.

The concurrent adoption of these protective individual rights by nearly every state in the Union, and by the employment of nearly the same language, is evidence of the uniformity and extent of the construction we have given.[3]   The constitution of this state

a Taylor v. Porter, 4 Hill, 140; Embury v. Conner, 3 N. Y. R. 511; Westervel v. Gregg, 6 N. Y. R. 202.

NOTE 3.—The provision in the constitution of Alabama, is, "That in all the criminal prosecutions, the accused shall not be compelled to give evidence against himself, nor be deprived of life, liberty, or property, but *by due course of law*," Art 1. § 7.   *Arkansas*, "That no man shall be taken or imprisoned, or disseized of his freehold liberties, or privileges, or outlawed or exiled, or in any manner destroyed, or deprived of his life, liberty or property, but by the judgment of his peers, *or the law of the land*, Art 2. § 10.   *California*, like Alabama, except the words *process of law*, instead of course of law, Art 1, § 8.   *Connecticut*, same as Alabama, Art 1, § 9.   *Delaware*, substituting for the words, "course of law," "*the judgment of his peers or the law of the land*," Art. 1, §7.   *Florida*, "that no freeman shall be taken, imprisoned or disseized of his freehold liberties or privileges, or, outlawed or exiled, or in any manner destroyed, or deprived of his life, liberty or property, *but by the law of the land*," Art. 1, § 8.   *Georgia*, "No person shall be deprived of life, liberty, or property, *except by due process of law*," Art. 1, § 2.   *Illinois*, "That no freeman shall be imprisoned, or dissiezed of his freehold liberties or privileges, or outlawed or exiled, or in any manner deprived of life, liberty or property, *but by the judgment of his peers or the law of the land*," Art. 13, § 8.   *Iowa*, "No person shall be deprived of life, liberty or property, *without due process of law*,' Art. 1, § 9.   *Kentucky*, "Nor can he be deprived of his life, liberty or property, *unless by the judgment of his peers, or the law of the land*," Art. 13, § 12.   *Maine*, "Nor be deprived of his life, liberty, property or privileges, but by the judgment of his

of 1846, has some qualifying provisions, as to the tribunal or forum, in which, the value of these private interests taken for public use, shall be assessed. It has been claimed, that the right of trial by a common law jury of twelve men in all cases, is a constitutional right to the proprietor, of which he cannot be deprived, under the second section of the first article of the constitution of 1846, which declares, that "the trial by jury in all cases in which it has been heretofore used, shall remain inviolate forever."

This section, however, has had judicial construction by the court of appeals, in this state. *a* It was there held, that inasmuch, as for a period of twenty years preceding the adoption of that constitution, special juries had been drawn with reference to the apprais-

a Cruger v. The Hud. R. R. Co., 12 N. Y. 198.

peers, or the law of the land," Art. 1, § 6. *Maryland*, "That no man ought to be taken or imprisoned, or disseized of his freehold liberties or privileges, or outlawed or exiled, or in any manner destroyed or deprived of his life, liberty or property, *but by the judgment of his peers, or by the law of the land*," Declaration of Rights, § 23. *Massachusetts*, "No subject shall be arrested, imprisoned, despoiled, or deprived of his property, immunities or privileges, put out of the protection of the law, exiled or deprived of his life, liberty or estate, *but by the judgment of his peers, or the law of land*," Declaration of Rights, Art. 12. *Michigan*, "No person shall be deprived of life, liberty, or property, *without due process of law*," Art. 6 § 32. *Minnesota*, "No member of this state shall be disfranchised, or deprived of any of the rights or privileges secured to any citizen thereof, *unless by the law of the land, or the judgment of his peers*," Art. 1, § 2. *Mississippi*, "Nor can he be deprived of his liberty or property, *but by due course of law*," Art. 1, § 10. *Missouri*, same as Delaware, Art. 1, § 18. *Nevada*, "Nor be deprived of life, liberty or property, *without due process of law*, Art. 1, § 8. *New Hampshire*, same as Massachusetts, Bill of Rights, § 17. *North Carolina*, "That no freeman ought to be taken, imprisoned or disseized of his freehold liberties or privileges, or outlawed or exiled, or in any manner destroyed, or deprived of his life, liberty or property, *but by the law of the land*," Declaration of Rights, §12. *Pennsylvania*, like Delaware, Art. 9, § 9. *Rhode Island*, like Delaware, Art. 1, § 10. *South Carolina*, "No person shall be taken, imprisoned or dissiezed of his freehold liberties or privileges, or outlawed or exiled, or in any manner deprived of his life, liberty or property, *but by due process of law*," Art. 9, § 2. *Tennessee*, same as Florida, Art. 1, § 8. *Texas*, "No citizen of this state shall be deprived of life, liberty, property or privileges, outlawed, exiled, or in any manner disfranchised, *except by due course of law*," Art. § 16. *West Virginia*, "No person in time of peace shall be deprived of life, liberty or property, *without due process of law*," Art. 2, § 6. In the constitutions of the remaining states, it is believed, that the protective phrases are omitted, but that equivalent protection is afforded by the statutes and common law. *

* Cooley on Const. Lim. note to p. 351.

ment of damages in such cases, and that the term jury seemed to have been used in such proceedings as descriptive of the civil condition of the persons composing it, and by way of distinguishing between such a body of jurymen, and commissioners appointed by courts under other acts, to perform the same functions; they are called in such special acts sometimes as jurors, and sometimes as appraisers, or jury of appraisers, a majority of whom could make the certificate, of inquisition or appraisal, that the instances of such appraisal, prior the time of the convention who framed the constitution of 1840, was sufficient to establish the position, that the term *jury*, in those acts, did not necessarily import a tribunal consisting of twelve men acting only upon a unanimous determination, but on the contrary was used to describe a body of jurors, differing in numbers, and deciding by majorities, or otherwise, as the legislature in each instance directed.

The term *jury*, as used in those special statutes, it was held, was used in a sense in which it was known to the law, at the time of forming that constitution, as one of the modes of proceeding theretofore in use in taking private property. The other mode being that of appraisement by commissioners. These two modes had then been in use, and had been regarded as well calculated to secure both public and private rights. The term jury, therefore, when used in reference to the assessment of damages for taking private property, was not used in the common law, or the restricted meaning which belongs to it when used in reference to trials civil, or criminal; but in the broader sense which it had acquired in common use, under legislative acts. *a* This is the more obvious, from that other provision contained in the seventh section of the same article of this constitution before cited, that in such cases, the compensation "shall be ascertained by a jury, or by not less than three commissioners appointed by a court of record, as shall be prescribed by law."

This being the adjudication of the highest court of the state in giving construction to a statute of the legislature, and in effect giving judicial construction to the fundamental law made by the people themselves, and under which the legislature receive their authority to enact the law, we must regard this mode of ascer-

a Id. 200.

taining compensation, to be in accordance with the "law of the land," as secured to the citizen by the constitution; and this must also be, "by due process of law," "being a prosecution or suit instituted and conducted in the courts according to the prescribed forms and solemnities for determining the just compensation to be paid for private property taken for public use," under the authority conferred by the people upon the legislature, and in the constitution adopted by themselves, whereby they intended, not to destroy, but to secure the individual citizen from the arbitrary exercise of the powers of government, unrestrained by the established principles of private rights, and distributive justice.

It must be conceeded, that this conclusion has not been arrived at without its having received the most deliberate consideration of the courts, after years of struggle, and by a divided opinion. *a* There was a strong disposition, on the part of judges, to interpose the judicial department of the government as a barrier against aggressions of the other departments, and to hold that the citizen could only be secured in his property, by a judicial trial, and by a common law jury of twelve men, whose unanimous verdict should be had in the case.

But the wants of the public, stimulated by the progressive spirit of the age, upon the one hand, and the obstructions which a spirit of avarice, by individuals, interposed upon the other, rendered such a restriction impracticable, and it was seen, that it was the *remedy*, and not the *right*, which was really the question to be settled, and it was hardly doubtful that the forms of administering justice, and the duties and powers of courts in relation thereto, were incidents to a branch of the sovereign power, and that these must be subject to the legislative will. It therefore become necessary to constitute particular tribunals for the adjustment of such controversies, bringing the parties to submit themselves to the exercise of more summary remedies in this regard. There is no perceptible reason, why private rights may not be as well protected under the one system as the other, both being under the protection of judicial proceedings in the courts, and controlled by rules equally impartial in their application.

a See Cases of Hoke v. Henderson, 4 Dev. (Maryland R.) 1; Jones v. Perry, 10 Yerg. R. 59; Embury v. Conner, 3 N. Y. 511; Taylor v. Porter, 4 Hill, 140.

Besides, "*the right to a particular remedy is not a vested right.*" This is the general rule; and the exceptions are of those peculiar cases where the remedy is a part of the right itself. As a general rule, every state has complete control over the remedies which it shall afford to the parties in its courts. *a* When not restricted by the constitution, it may abolish one class of courts and create another, *b* and it may abolish old remedies, and substitute new. And any rule or regulation in regard to the remedy, which does not, under pretence of regulating it, impair the right itself, cannot be regarded as beyond the proper province of legislation. *c*

There must not be a confounding of the taxing power, under which property is taken for public use, with the right of eminent domain. The clause in the constitution of the United States that private property shall not be taken for public use without just compensation, applies to the right of eminent domain, and has no reference to property taken for taxes. *d*

This provision of the constitution is intended solely as a limitation on the exercise of power by the government of the United States, and is not applicable to the legislation of the states. *e* The constitution of the United States was ordained and established by the people of the United States, for themselves, for their own government, and not for the government of the individual states. Each state established a constitution for itself, and in that constitution, provided such limitations and restrictions on the powers of its particular government as its judgment dictated. Therefore, when the constitution of a state provides that private property shall not be taken for public uses, and the highest court of such state has sustained the validity of a law which violates this constitutional provision, the courts of the United States have nothing to do with it.

a Lord v. Chadbourn, 42 Maine R. 429; Rosier v. Hale, 10 Iowa 470; Holloway v. Sherman, 12 Iowa 282; McCormick v. Rusch, 15 Iowa 127; Rockwell v. Hubbell, 2 Doug. (Mich.) 197; Cusir v. Douglass, 3 Kansas 123; Smith v. Bryan, 34 Illinois 377.

b Foster v. Essex Bank, 16 Mass. 245, 272; Hampden v. Commissioners, &c., 6 Pick. 508; In Bank, 16 Ohio 354–5; Hepburn v. Curts, 7 Walts. 300.

c Cooley on Const. Limits, 361, 362.   *d* Howell v. City of Buffalo, 37 N.Y. 270.

e Barron v. Mayor of Baltimore, 7 Peters, 243; Withers v. Buckley, 20 How. U. S. R. 84.

Taking lands for widening of a street, with a restriction on adjoining land, which may be used for the purpose of extending court yards, is the taking for public use, and entitles the proprietors to an award of damages. In such case, dominion is asserted over the land by the public, to the extent of depriving the owner of his right to enjoy it for any other purpose than as a court yard. *a*

a Matter of Bushwick Avenue, 48 Barb. 9.

51

CHAPTER XII.

OF THE CONSTITUTIONAL AUTHORITY TO TAKE PRIVATE PROPERTY FOR PUBLIC PURPOSES UNDER THE TAXING POWER.

IN the preceding chapter we have taken a survey of the power to take private property for public uses under the right of eminent domain, notwithstanding the constitutional prohibitions contained in the federal and state constitutions. In this chapter we propose to take a brief view of, and to bestow a few considerations upon the nature, extent and power to take private property for public uses under the taxing power of the constitution itself, and of both the federal and state constitutions.

The right of acquiring and possessing property, and having it protected, is one of the natural, inherent, and inalienable rights of man. Men have a sense of property; it is necessary to their subsistence, and correspondent to their natural wants and desires; its security was one of the objects that induced them to unite in society. No man would become a member of community, in which he could not enjoy the fruits of his honest labor and industry. The preservation of property is one primary object of the social compact, and it is by the constitution made a fundamental law. But still, every person ought to contribute his proportion to the public burthens, to public purposes, and to the public exigencies, though no one can properly be called upon to surrender or sacrifice his whole property, real and personal, for the good of the community, without receiving a recompense in value. This would be laying a burthen upon an individual, which ought to be sustained by the society at large. Such an act, if attempted, would be monstrous legislation, and would shock all mankind. Nor can the legislature divest one citizen of his estate and vest it in another, with or without compensation. It is inconsistent with the principles of reason, justice, and moral rectitude; it is incompatible with the comfort, peace and happiness of mankind;—it is contrary to the principles of social alliance in every free government; and to the letter and spirit of the constitution. *a*

"The right of *taxation*, and the right of *eminent domain*, rest substantially upon the same foundation. Private property may be constitutionally taken for public use in two ways, that is to say, by *taxation*, and by right of *eminent domain*. These are rights which the people collectively retain over the property of individuals, to resume such portions of it as may be necessary for public use. Compensation is made, when private property is taken in either way. Money is property. Taxation takes it for public use; and the tax-payer receives, or is supposed to receive, his just compensation in the protection which government affords to his life, liberty and property; and in the increase of the value of his possessions, by the use to which government applies the money raised by the tax." *b*

When private property is taken by right of *eminent domain*, special compensation is made for the following reasons: It is not taken as the owner's share of contribution to a public burthen, but as so much beyond his share. Special compensation is therefore to be made in the latter case, because government is a debtor for the property so taken; but not when taken for taxes, because the payment of taxes is a duty, and creates no obligation to repay otherwise than in the proper application of the tax. *Taxation* operates upon a community, or upon a class of persons in a community, and by some rule of apportionment. The exercise of the right of *eminent domain*, operates upon an individual, and without reference to the amount, or value exacted from any other individual or class of individuals. Keeping these distinctions in mind, it will never be difficult to determine which of the two powers is exerted in any given case.

Having given the provisions of the national and state constitutions, relating to the protection of the private property of the citizen, in language broad, and clear, it is still seen, that these words of protection, cannot be taken in their strictest and most literal sense as against the necessities of the government itself; and these clauses, furnish a good illustration of the impossibility

a Van Horne's Lessee v. Dorrance, 2 Dallas, 310.

b People v. Mayor of Brooklyn, 4 N. Y. 422, 424.

of construing constitutional provisions in a spirit of literal strictness. When a tax is levied, "private property" is clearly taken
for public use, and taken without *direct* actual compensation ; the
compensation is in theory, and indirect, on account of supposed
benefits; as an equivalent for the property taken. If therefore
this was rigidly interpreted, it would at once arrest the operations
of any government to which it was applied. Such, however, is
not its construction. The restriction on taking private property
without compensation, does not apply to the power of taxation.
The powers of the state over property, embraces not only taxation,
but also other public purposes; eminent domain, police, public
health, public morals, and perhaps other public interests where
state exigencies demand its exercise. The legislative power,
being in this respect sovereign, in extraordinary emergencies, like
that of public safety, or defence, and to which power, individual
rights must be surrendered when the general welfare of the state
demands it.

Under the eighth section of article one, of the constitution of the
United States, congress is given power "to lay and collect taxes,
duties, imposts, and excises." This power to tax, is not an exclusive power in the national government ; the several states possess
the power for the regulation of their own internal policy—to preserve the public health, or peace, or to promote their own peculiar interests. *a*

Chief Justice Marshall has given this subject of the taxing power,
his especial consideration. *b* He says, "The power of legislature,
and consequently of taxation, operates on all the persons and
property, belonging to the body politic. This is an original principle, which has its foundation in society itself. It is granted by
all, for the benefit of all. It resides in government as a part of
itself, and need not be reserved when property of any description,
or the right to use it in any manner, is granted to individuals or
corporate bodies. However absolute the right of an individual
may be; it is still in the nature of that right, that it must bear a
portion of the public burthens; and that portion must be determined by the legislature. This vital power may be abused ; but

a Story on Const. § 447.

b Providence Bank v. Billings, 4 Peters, 562–3.

the constitution of the United States, was not intended to furnish the correction for every abuse of power which may be committed by the state governments. The interest, wisdom, and justice of the representative body, and its relation with its constituents, furnish the only security, where there is no express contract, against unjust and excessive taxation, as well as against unwise legislation generally."

In another case, he said, a "The power of taxing the people, and their property, is essential to the very existence of government, and may be legitimately exercised on the subjects to which it is applicable, to the utmost extent to which the government may choose to carry it. The only security against the abuse of this power, is found in the structure of the government itself. In imposing a tax, the legislature acts upon its constituents. This is, in general, a sufficient security against erroneous and oppressive taxation. The people of a state, therefore, give to their government a right of taxing themselves, and their property; and as the exigencies of government cannot be limited, they prescribe no limits to the exercise of this right, resting confidently on the interest of the legislator, and on the influence of the constituents over their representative, to guard them against its abuse." "And it is unfit for the judicial department, to enquire, what degree of taxation is the legitimate use, and what degree, may amount to an abuse of the power." b

One of the arguments against the exercise of this right, is, that the admitted power of taxation, may be so exercised under legislative authority, as greatly to impair the value of private property. This is doubtless, sometimes true; the power may be wisely or unwisely, justly or unjustly exercised; but, as a power, it rests upon the theory, that full compensation is received by the individual in the benefit conferred by the tax itself. The support of government, and other objects of public utility promoted by taxation, are supposed to return to the individual the value which has been taken from him as his share of the public burthen. This is neither depriving a man of his property in a constitutional sense, nor taking it for public use under the right of eminent domain. c It is

a McCulloch v. Maryland, 4 Wheat. 428.   b Id. 430.
c Wyndham v. The People, 13 N. Y. 404–405.

not sufficient that a law impairs the value of property, in ever so great a degree, because this destroys no right. It leaves to the owner unimpaired, his right to keep, to use, and to dispose of his property. It therefore does not deprive him of any right in it. The levying and collecting of taxes, is not within the meaning of the clause in the constitution, which provides that private property shall not be taken for public use, without just compensation. *a* Nor is a statute, which directs the expenses of street improvements to be assessed on those owners who are benefited thereby, rendered unconstitutional from the fact that the money thus assessed, was to reimburse the city for money advanced for that purpose. *b*

Applying these principles, to the powers of our own state constitution, which are recognized to be sound by the highest court in this state, it is held, *c* that taxation proceeds upon the principle of the maxim, that "he who receives the advantage ought to sustain the burthen." And it is added, "that the power of taxation, and of apportioning taxation, or of assigning to each individual his share of the burthen, is vested exclusively in the legislature, unless this power is limited or restrained by some constitutional provision. The power of taxing, and the power of apportioning taxation, are identical and inseperable. Taxes cannot be laid without apportionment; and the power of apportionment is therefore unlimited, unless it be restrained as a part of the power of taxation."

"There is not, and since the original organization of the state government, there has not been, any such constitutional limitation or restraint. The people have never ordained that taxation shall be general, so as to embrace all persons, or all taxable persons within the state, or within any district, or territorial division of the state; nor that it shall or shall not be, numerically equal, as in the case of a capitation tax; nor that it must be in the ratio of the value of each man's land, or of his goods, or of both combined, nor that a tax must be co-extensive with the district, or upon all the property in a district which has the character of, or is known to the law of a local sovereignty. Nor have they ordained or for-

a Howell v. City of Buffalo, 37 N. Y. 267.
b Id ; People v. Lawrence, 36 Barb, 177.
c People v. Mayor of Brooklyn, 4 N. Y. 425 to 432.

bidden that a tax shall be apportioned according to the benefit which each tax-payer is supposed to receive from the object on which the tax is expended. In all these particulars the power of taxation is unrestrained."

" The application of any one of these rules or principles of apportionment, to all cases, would be manifestly oppressive and unjust. Either, may be rightfully applied to the particular exigency to which it is best adapted."

Taxation is sometimes regulated by one of these principles, and sometimes by another; and very often it has been apportioned without reference to locality, or to the tax-payer's ability to contribute, or to any proportion between the burthen and the benefit. The excise laws, and taxes on carriages, and watches, are among the many examples of this description of taxation. Some taxes affect classes of inhabitants only. All duties on imported goods, are taxes on this class of consumers. The tax on one imported article, falls on a large class of consumers. While the tax on another, affects comparatively but a few individuals.

" The duty on one foreign commodity, is laid for the purpose of revenue mainly, without reference to the ability of its consumers to pay ; as in the case of the duty on salt. The duty on another, is laid for the purpose of encouraging domestic manufacturers of the same article ; thus compelling the consumer to pay a higher price to one man, than he otherwise could have bought the article for, from another. These discriminations may be impolitic, and in some cases unjust ; but if the power of taxation upon importations had not been transferred by the people of this state to the federal government, there could have been no pretence for declaring them to be unconstitutional in state legislation."

The taxing power may be concurrently exercised by the state and national governments, to a certain extent, but the national government has the power to withdraw from the exercise of state, the power of taxation as to such property as comes within the powers conferred upon the general government, and as to which, when exercised by the general government, their powers are exclusive and supreme. The right of taxation in the states, extends to all subjects over which its sovereign power extends ; and no further. The sovereignty of a state extends to everything which exists by its own authority, or is introduced by its permission; but it does not extend to those means which are employed by congress to carry into execution their constitutional powers. The power of state taxation, is to be measured by the extent of state sovereignty, and this leaves to a state the command of all its resources, and the unimpaired power of taxing the people, and property of the state. This principle relieves from conflicting sovereignty between the two powers. *a* For what purposes the state may exercise this power, will be shown hereafter.

"A property tax for the general purposes of the government, either of the state at large, or of a county, city, or other district, is regarded as a just and equitable tax. The reason is obvious. It apportions the burthen according to the benefit more nearly than any other inflexible rule of taxation. A rich man derives more benefit from taxation in the benefit and improvement of his property than a poor man, and ought therefore to pay more. But the amount of each man's benefit in the general taxation cannot be ascertained and estimated with any degree of certainty; and for that reason, a property rule is adopted instead of an estimate of benefits. In local taxation, however, for special purposes, the local benefits may, in many cases be seen, traced and estimated to a reasonable certainty. At least, this has been supposed and assumed to be true by the legislature, whose duty it is to prescribe the rules on which taxation is to be apportioned; and whose determination of this matter, being within the scope of its lawful power, is conclusive."

It had been held, in a case decided in the second judicial district in this state, *b* "that legitimate taxation was limited to the imposing of burdens or charges for a public purpose, equally upon the persons or property within a district known and recognized by law as possessing a local sovereignty for certain purposes, as a state, county, city, town, village, &c., excluding from the operation of taxing power all those cases in which the expenses of laying out public squares, and of opening or widening of streets, or other like improvements are charged upon certain persons or property in consequence of supposed benefits. And that a tax to be valid,

a 1 Kent's Com. 425.

b The People v. The Mayor of Brooklyn, 6 Barb. 209.

must be apportioned upon principles of just equality. And also, that this was a fundamental principle of free government, which, although not contained in the constitution, limits and controls the power of the legislature.

The case which enunciated this doctrine, was taken to the court of last resort in this state, where the doctrine was declared not only to be new, but dangerous. Said the Court of Appeals, *a* " this doctrine clothes the judicial tribunals with the power of trying the validity of a tax by a test, neither prescribed nor defined by the constitution. If by this test we may condemn an assessment apportioned according to the relation between burthen and benefit, we may, with far better reason, condemn a capitation tax, on the ground, that numerical equality, is not just equality ; or a general property tax for a local object, because it compels one portion of the community to pay more than their just share for the benefit of another portion. All discriminations in the taxation of property, and all exemptions from taxation on the grounds of public policy, would fall by the application of this test. If this doctrine prevails, it places the power of the courts above that of the legislature, in a matter affecting not only the vital interests, but the very existence of the government. It assumes that the apportionment of taxation is to be regulated by judicial, and not by legislative discretion. It obstructs the exercise of powers which belong to, and are inherent in the legislative department, and restrains the action of that branch of the government in cases in which the constitution has left it free to act."

The doctrine which was thus repudiated by the Court of Appeals, it seems originated in the state of Kentucky, under an especial, or peculiar clause in their state constitution, not found in ours. But the whole doctrine of the constitutionality of the power of assessment and taxation in this state, was thoroughly considered in our court of dernier resort, and the clear, elaborate and able opinion of Ruggles, J., adopted by the whole court, forms of itself, an exhaustive view of the subject, never since questioned, and makes of itself, a chapter on this subject worthy of being perpetuated as elementary law.

Various cases which were supposed to have been decided upon

a The People v. Mayor of Brooklyn, 4 N. Y. 429.

52

the contrary principle, were ably reviewed by the Court of Appeals, and the distinction either pointed out, or the dicta contained in them intimating a contrary doctrine overruled. And the court say, "There never was any just foundation for saying, that local taxation must necessarily be limited by, or co-extensive with any previously established district. It is undoubtedly wrong, that a few should be taxed for the benefit of the whole; and it is equally wrong, that the whole should be taxed for the benefit of the few. No one town ought to be taxed exclusively for the payment of county taxes; and no county should be taxed for the expenses incurred for the benefit of a single town. The same principle of justice requires, that where taxation for any local object benefits only a portion of a city or town, that portion only, should bear the burthen. There being no constitutional prohibition, the legislalature may create a district for that especial purpose, or they may tax a class of lands or persons benefited to be designated by the public agents, appointed for that purpose without reference to town, county, or district lines. *General* taxation, for such local objects, is manifestly unjust. It burthens those who are not benefited, and benefits those who are not burthened."

" This injustice has led to the substitution of street assessments, in the place of *general* taxation; and it seems impossible to deny, that in the theory of their apportionment, they are far more equitable than *general* taxation for the purpose they are designed for."

" The same principle of apportionment, has been applied to bridges, and turnpike roads. The money paid for their construction and maintenance is reimbursed by means of tolls. Tolls are delegated taxation; and this taxation is charged and apportioned upon those only, who derive a benefit from the original expenditure, and in proportion to that benefit. General taxation upon a town or county for the building of a bridge, is valid and lawful, but obviously unjust; and because, it compels one to pay for the benefit of another. Tolls are more equitable, because they equalize the burthen with the benefit."

" But this theory of apportioning taxation, is not confined in practice to street assessments and tolls on bridges and turnpike roads. The main revenues of the state, canal tolls, are regulated upon the same principle; and so far as the objection to street assessments applies to the principle of selecting those only who are benefited, and laying the burthen upon them in proportion to their respective advantages, it applies with equal force to tolls on bridges and turnpikes, and on the public canals. The difference is only in the mode in which each tax-payer's share of the burthen is ascertained."

"It has been said, that the benefits derived from the grading and paving of a street, are sometimes fanciful and imaginary, and always uncertain and incapable of being estimated with that exactness which is necessary for the purposes of justice to the individuals assessed. But this is a consideration to be addressed to the legislature, and not to the judicial authorities The courts cannot assume that this proposition is true in point of fact. The legislature has evidently acted on the belief that it is untrue."

"That mistakes may have happened,—that abuses may have been practiced—and that injustice may have been done, in making street assessments, it is not necessary to deny. Mistakes, abuses, and injustice, have often occurred in general taxation. These are not grounds upon which either system of supplying the public treasury, can be denounced as unconstitutional. If the systems are imperfect, they should be reformed by the legislature. If the street assessments are in their practical operation oppressive and unjust, the statutes which authorize them should be repealed. The remedy for unjust or unwise legislation, is not to be administered by the courts. It remains in the hands of the people; and is to be wrought out by means of a change in the representative body, if it cannot otherwise be obtained."

"The constitution has imposed upon the legislature the duty of restraining the power of municipal corporations in making assessments, and preventing abuses therein. a To assume that this duty has been, and will be neglected, is a denial of that reasonable confidence which one department of the government ought always to entertain towards the others. The danger of abuse which is supposed to exist in the making of street assessments, exists in a greater or less degree in every conceivable system of taxation according to value; and if the courts have authority to annul, any other tax assessed upon valuation on the same ground,

a Const. of 1846. Art. 8 § 9

it need not be said, that this would be a much more alarming power, than the unlimited right of taxation entrusted by the people to their representatives;"

" The difference between *general* taxation, and special assessments for local objects, requires that they should be distinguished by different names, although both derive their authority, from the taxing power. They have always been so distinguished, and it is therefore evident that the word *tax*, may be used in a contract, or in a statute, in a sense which would not include a street assessment, or any other local or special taxation within its meaning. Several cases have been found in which it has been adjudged to have been so used. But in no case, has it been adjudged, that street assessments are not made by virtue of the legislative taxing power. If there are expressions to the contrary, in some of the cases, it will be found that they are *dicta*; inapplicable to the point decided, or if applicable, that they were unnecessary to the decision, and not well considered.[1]

The line which distinguishes between the cases of taking private property for public purposes under the right of eminent domain; and that of the taxing power under the constitution, has been one of the most prolific sources of controversy and litigation in the courts. This is the natural result of an education of the masses of our people, who, under a system of a free government, which seems to confer upon the individual citizen absolute rights; a system which teaches them to look with jealousy upon the exercise of power, whenever it comes in conflict with the sole and absolute dominion of the citizen, over his own posessions.

But it is no longer a question of constitutional power, in this state, that the legislature can compel public burthens to be borne by the persons who ought to bear them; or who, in the judgment of the legislature ought to bear them, without, or even against the consent of such persons; and the legislature have the

NOTE 1.—Among the cases criticized as coming within the charge of dicta, in applicability, not necessary to the decision, or not well considered ; are, Matter of Mayor of New York, 11 John, 80 ; Bleecker v. Ballou, 3 Wend. 266 ; Sharp v. Spier, 4 Hill, 76. The following decisions are found to sustain the principles above laid down. Livingston v. Mayor of New York, 8 Wend. 85–101 ; Owners of Ground Assessed v. Mayor of Albany, 15 Wend. 376, as to taxing power; Thomas v. Leland, 24 Wend. 65 ; Striker v. Kelly, 7 Hill, 9–23.

power to authorize and direct a tax to be assessed, and levied, upon the property of such persons as in their judgment ought to bear the burthen to pay the expenses of any such public improvement, or supposed public benefit. The liability of the persons upon whom the expenses of improvement is cast, stands upon the same ground as all other liability to taxation. *a*

The legislature may designate any one to institute proceedings to acquire private property for public purposes, as where the commissioners of the Central Park in the city of New York, a recognized public body were authorized to institute such proceedings, the question whether such a body had, apart from this legislative power, a legal existence, was held to be immaterial. *b*

The legislature, even, possess the power to levy a tax upon the taxable property of a town, and appropriate the same to the payment of a claim, made by an individual against a town. Nor is it a valid objection to the exercise of such power, that the claim to satisfy which the tax was levied, was not recoverable by action against the town; *c* and the courts have no power to supervise or review the doings of the legislature in such cases. *d* It can thus recognize claims founded in equity and justice, in the largest sense of these terms, or in gratitude or charity. *e*

"It is well settled, that the authority to raise money by the exercise of the taxing power, is not in conflict with the constitutional provisions, protecting private property from seizure. The two principles co-exist in the constitution, and it is not difficult to distinguish between them. *f* This power is frequently resorted to for the purpose of promoting education, and carrying out the system of common schools. For such purposes in this state, the power has ceased to be questioned. It prevails and is exercised equally in other states. *g*

We are now treating of the constitutional power of this state. It is needless, as well as useless in this work to discuss it as a question of state policy, or as to the extent which this power

a Brewster v. City of Syracuse, 19 N. Y. 116–118.
b Matter of Central Park Extension, 19 Abbott, 56.
c The Town of Guilford v. Supervisors of Chenango Co. 13 N. Y. R. 143.
d Id. 148.   *e* Per Denio, J. Id. 149.
f Id. see Booth v. Town of Woodbury, 32 Conn. R. 118.
g Commonwealth v. Hartman, 17 Penn. 119.

ought to be exercised.   This work does not intend to discuss questions of political, or domestic policy.   Under the question of power,
it is now held, that the legislature of a state unless restrained by
its constitution can authorize a county, or a town to take stock in
a railroad or other public improvement ; to borrow money to pay
for the same ; and to levy a tax to repay the loan ; that this authority can be conferred in such a manner as to accomplish the
purpose, either with or without a popular vote; and when the
legislature have power to authorize the act, it can by retrospective
legislation, cure the evils arising from an irregular execution of
such power. a[1]

Whatever may be the interpretation of the legislative power
under constitutions of other states, in the state of New York, it
would seem to be settled, that where the fundamental law has not
limited, either in terms, or by necessary implication, the general
powers conferred upon the legislature, courts cannot declare a
limitation, under the notion of having discovered something in the
spirit of the constitution upon a subject which is not even mentioned. b

In relation to the taxing power, there is found no restriction in
the constitution upon the power of the legislature ; it is therefore
limited, only by their own discretion.   It possesses all the power

a The People v. Mitchell, 35 N. Y. 551-3; Wall, U. S. R. 327; Thompson v.
Lee County.

b People v. Fisher, 24 Wend. 220; Benson v. Mayor of Albany, 24 Barb. 248
Grant v. Courter, id. 237.

NOTE 2.—In the case of Sweet v. Hulburt, reported in 51 Barb. 312, the author
is found concuring in the decision of that case, which, in some respects, is in
conflict with the principles above laid down in this work. So far as it is in conflict, he desires to say, he failed to give that case all the consideration, that his
subsequent and better examination of the law has impressed upon his mind, and
though he concurred then, in the result, though not in all the reasonings, his
better judgment now is, that the case, upon the principle of the power of constitutional right of taxation, for the purposes in the act mentioned, was erroneously
decided. The word " *donated* " in the act in que tion, did not express the true
spirit of the act. Had the word " *contribute* " which was its spirit, instead of " *do-
nate*" which was its letter, been used, the spirit of the act would have been better
expressed, and no *legal* objec ion could have been raised against it. I think the
true rule is, that though a law, unjust in its operation, should be, o: s enact,
nevertheless, if not forbidden by the constitution, the remedy is not in an appeal
to the judiciary, but to the people, who must apply the corrective.

of legislation that was possessed by the British parliament, except
by the express or implied restrictions in the constitution itself. *a*
To determine an act of the legislature, with reference to taxation
for a public improvement or a public object, to be unconstitutional,
we must see the prohibition contained in the constitution itself, in
express terms, or by necessary implication from its terms.

"But there is a spirit existing among the people, and cases are
found, where the courts have been disposed to encourage this
spirit and hold, that a law, though not prohibited by the constitution, is void if it violates the spirit of our institutions or impairs
any of those rights which it is the object of a free government to
protect, and it is claimed that the courts can declare such an act
unconstitutional, if they deem it wrong or unjust," or, to borrow
the language of a modern case, *b* "in delegating to a Senate and
Assembly with the approval of the governor the power to make
laws, under certain limitations and restrictions, but without enumerating and defining those powers, the people did not, nor did they
intend to, invest that body with authority to make laws inconsistent with natural right." And also, *c* "There are certain vital
principles which will determine and overrule an apparent and
flagrant abuse of legislative power; as to authorize manifest injustice by positive law; or to take away that security for personal
liberty or private property, for the protection of which governments are instituted. An act of the legislature, contrary to the
first great principles of the social compact, cannot be considered
a rightful exercise of legislative authority."

This sounds well, and is well written, but is it sound in theory,
as constitutional law? Under what power of the constitution, are
the courts authorized to nullify a law of the legislature except for
its infraction of that instrument? If the legislature, under the
admitted authority of the taxing power, have been unjust or oppressive in the enactment of a law, has the right ever been heard
of, under our system; has the power ever been discovered in our
constitution, that clothes the judiciary with authority to declare

a See People v. Morrill, 21 Wend. 563; Butler v. Palmer, 1 Hill, 324; Bloodgood v. Mohawk & Hudson R. R. Co., 18 Wend. 9; Leggett v. Hunter. 19 N. Y.
R. 445, and cases cited; Sharpless v. Mayor of Philadelphia, 21 Penn. 148.

b Sweet v. Hulburt, 51 Barb. 318.   *c* Id. 317.

the law to be void, because it is unjust? It would be assuming a
right on the part of a court, to change the constitution;—to supply what they might conceive to be its defects; to interpolate into
it, whatever in their opinion ought to have been put there by its
framers. The constitution has expressed in terms of prohibition,
the things which the legislature may not do. If the judiciary
shall assume that there are certain other things that the legislation shall not do, and so declare it, do they not extend the list?
Do they not thereby alter that instrument? Do they not become
aggressors themselves? Do they not thus violate both the letter
and spirit of that organic law, even more than the legislature possibly could? If they can *add* to the reserved rights of the people,
they can take them away; if they can mend, they can mar; if
they can remove the landmarks that the people established for
their own protection, they can obliterate them; if they can change
the constitution in any particular, there is nothing but their own
will to prevent them from demolishing it entirely.

In a case, in the state of Pennsylvania a Chief Justice Black
held this language : he said, " The great powers given to the legislature are liable to be abused. But this is inseparable from the
nature of human institutions. The wisdom of man has never conceived of a government with power sufficient to answer its legitimate ends, and at the same time incapable of mischief. No political system can be made so perfect, that its rulers will always hold
it to the true course. In the very best, a great deal must be
trusted to the discretion of those who administer it. In ours, the
people have given larger powers to the legislature, and relied, for
the faithful execution of them, on the wisdom and honesty of that
department, and on the direct accountability of the members to
their constituents. There is no shadow of reason, for supposing
that the mere abuse of power was meant to be corrected by the
judiciary."

The leading and most prominent objection raised to the exercise
of the taxing power to favor railroad corporations, is on the ground,
that they are private corporations, and that such taxation, is, consequently, to be applied to a private purpose. If the premises of
this proposition were sound, such taxation would clearly be unau-

a Sharpless v. Mayor of Philadelphia, 21 Penn. St. R. 161, 2.

thorized and void. But the right of taxation depends upon the object for which the fund is raised, or the ultimate *use* to which it is to be applied, and not upon the character of the person or corporation whose agency is employed in applying it. It having been settled in this state that railroads organized under legislative authority are public improvements, and that the public have an advantage and interest in them; the public may also be taxed for this purpose, though it be done under the direction and agency of an individual or private corporation. *a*

It is believed to be a narrow view of governmental duty, to insist upon confining the state, to the performance of such duties only, as are necessary to sustain the existence of government; as for instance, to the administration of justice, the preservation of peace, and protection of individual interests; nor has it so confined itself. Schools, colleges, institutions of charity and benevolence, institutions for the promotion of arts and sciences, and other objects too numerous to mention, have not only been established, and their objects promoted by state policy, but taxes have been laid upon individuals by which, their private property has been so taken and appropriated. Canals, bridges, roads, and other means of passage and transportation from one part of the country to another for commercial purposes, have been constructed by the state at public expense from individual taxation, not only here, but by every civilized government; ancient or modern. If these are not public improvements, the law directing taxation for them is void. It has upon this assumption, therefore, been adopted as the policy of this state, enacted into law by its legislature, and sustained by judicial interpretation. It is held that the state may employ the agency of individuals or corporations to construct such works, and though the company may be private, the work they undertake, is for the public benefit, to do which, is within the power of the state, as well as the duty; and the state may therefore, delegate a sufficient share of the sovereign power by way of taxation and eminent domain, to enable such agents to perform the work. The power of taxation by the legislature is unrestrained by the constitution, except by a provision that through it, they cannot take private property for private purposes. The courts, hold those

a Bonaparte v. The Camden and Amboy RR. Co., 1 Baldwin R. 223.

purposes and objects to be public, which develop the physical resources, promote its commerce, and establish public benefactions
for the poor, the blind, or the insane.   These are clearly the purposes of a wise and humane government.   The theory of our government, then seems to be this; the people by their constitution
have invested the legislature with all legislative power, and this
includes the power of enacting laws for taxing themselves for public
purposes, and for the exigencies of government, and the only remedy
of the people for unjust legislation done within admitted bounds,
is to change their representatives, and thus correct the evil.

Taxation is always a delicate, a peculiarly flexible, and a most
indefinite power.   There are certain propositions, however, that
must be conceded, and they may be laid down as established.
First, that every citizen is equally bound to support the government, and aid in promoting its beneficent ends.   He must also
submit to the inherent power of sovereignty in the government to
exercise the right of eminent domain, limited only by the fundamental security that he receive just compensation for private
property taken for public benefit.   Second, that every citizen,
when called upon, should contribute in the form of taxation, direct,
or indirect, to burthens resulting from the administration of the
government and its laws, under which he claims protection.   The
taxpayers compensation, is in his reciprocal benefit.   Equality, is
the great object of the constitution, and should be of the laws;
but mathematical equality is practically impossible.   The history
of sustained taxation, in every form, always shows actual inequality.   A tax may be constitutionally imposed upon one class
of property only, and many may own no such property; or, it may
be specific, and therefore arbitrary, and will be also necessarily
unequal; or it may be on all property *ad valorem;* and even then
those owning no taxable property will contribute nothing, even
though they derive great personal benefit from the appropriation
of the taxes.   And in whatever form, or for whatever purpose,
taxes may be imposed, and however nearly they may seem to
approximate to equality, they will be found to be necessarily unequal when tested by the only rule or principle of taxation; which
is, an equal degree of benefit to each person in the use made of
the tax.   There is no human process by which a relative degree of

interest can be precisely graduated. It is undeniable, that all the citizens of one county, or a town, have not the same equal interest in a local improvement, such as a road, or a bridge, or a plank or railroad, but there is no method by which the exact interest of each can be ascertained; this exactness therefore, must in degree, be disregarded in taxing for the construction or repair of such improvements, and it is seen that not the local inhabitants alone, are benefited, the people of other localities, counties or towns, are also benefited by these improvements, and the whole public as well as the local citizen are benefited to the extent, that such improvements contribute to the social and commercial intercommunication between the citizens of the different localities; and yet, the taxes to construct or repair a highway or a bridge cannot be levied beyond the limits of the town or county within which the public improvement is made. Inequality of taxation is not therefore, unconstitutional. *a*

The legislative power in this state, under the constitution, has been so ably, faithfully, and fully, presented, and established by the highest court of the state, including in the principle, the taxing power, that an omission to copy their views, when discussing this subject would seem to be inexcusable.

Chief Justice Denio, in pronouncing the opinion of the court, said: *b* "In the first place, the people in framing the constitution, committed to the legislature the whole law-making power of the state, which they did not expressly or impliedly withhold. Plenary power in the legislature for all purposes of civil government, is the rule. A prohibition to exercise a particular power is the exception. In enquiring, therefore, whether a given statute is constitutional, it is for those who questions its validity to show that it is forbidden. I do not mean that the power must be expressly inhibited, for there are but few positive restraints upon the legislative power contained in the instrument. Every positive direction contains an implication against anything contrary to it, or which would frustrate or disappoint the purpose of that provision. The frame of the government; the grant of legislative power itself; the organization of the executive authority; the erection of the prin-

a County Judge of Shelby Co. v. Shelby RR. Co. **3 Kentucky R.**
b People v. Draper, 15 N. Y. 543.

cipal courts of justice; create implied limitations upon the law-making authority as strong as though a negative was expressed in each instance. But independently of these restraints, express or implied, every subject within the scope of civil government, is liable to be dealt with by the legislature. As it may act upon the state at large by laws affecting at once the whole country, and all the people, so it may in its discretion, and independently of any prohibition, expressly made or necessarily implied, make special laws relating to any separate district or section of the state. As a political society, the state has an interest in the repression of disorder, and the maintenance of peace and security in every locality within its limits; and if from exceptional causes, the public good requires that legislation, either permanent or temporary, be directed towards any particular locality, whether consisting of one county or several counties, it is within the discretion of the legislature to apply such legislation as in its judgment, the exigency of the case may require; *and it is the sole judge of the existence of such causes.* The representatives of the whole people, convened in the two branches of the legislature, are, (subject to the exceptions which have been mentioned,) the organs of the public will in every district or locality of the state. It follows, that it belongs to the legislature to arrange and distribute the administrative functions, committing such portions as it may deem suitable, to local jurisdictions, and retaining other portions to be exercised by officers appointed by the central power; and changing the arrangement from time to time, as convenience, the efficiency of administration and the public good may seem to require. If a particular act of legislation does not conflict with any of the limitations or restraints that have been referred to, it is not in the power of the courts to arrest its execution, however unwise its provisions may be, or whatever the motives may have been which led to its enactment. There is room for much bad legislation and misgovernment within the pale of the constitution; but when *this* happens, the remedy which the constitution provides, by the opportunity for frequent renewals of the legislative bodies, is far more efficacious than any which can be afforded by the judiciary." This extended extract, seems to be called for, to excuse the concurrence with a different view of legislative power, expressed in the case of Sweet v. Hulburt above referred to, a so far as it differs from this. This case coming from a higher source of authority must be controlling as the law of this state, and as being the settled interpretation of constitutional power in the legislative body. Nor does this case stand alone.

The Supreme Court of this state, whose unreversed and unquestioned adjudications we must now regard as the law of the state, have laid down the following propositions in regard to the taxing power of the legislature, as connected with the construction of public works, and especially as connected with taxation in aid of railroads, which will equally apply to other public improvements. b

First. That all the inherent power of the people for self government, not delegated to the general government, is reserved to, and belongs to the state.

Second. That of such reserved powers, the entire legislative power, is subject to no restrictions or limitations, except such as are contained in the state constitutions.

Third. That the taxing power belongs to the legislature, and is subject to no limits or restrictions outside of the United States and state constitutions.

Fourth. That the power to authorize the construction of works of internal improvement, and to provide for their construction by officers or agents of the state, rests with, and pertains to, the legislature, to be exercised within its exclusive discretion.

Fifth. That such works may be constructed by general taxation, and in case of local works, by local taxation; or the state may aid in their construction, by becoming a stockholder in private corporations; or authorize municipal corporations to become such stockholders for such purpose.

Sixth. That railroads are public works, and may be constructed by the state, or by corporations, and lands taken for their use are taken for the public use, and may be so taken on payment of a just compensation.

Seventh. That the legislature is the exclusive judge in respect as to what works are for the public benefit; in regard to the expediency of constructing such works; and as to the mode of their

a 51 Barb. 312.

b Clark v. City of Rochester. &c., 24 Barb. 489.

construction, whether by the state, or by private or municipal corporations, in whole or in part.

Eighth. That the legislature may authorize municipal corporations to subscribe to a stock of a railroad company, with the consent and approval of the majority of the corporators duly ascertained. [3]

Ninth. That the passage of a law authorizing such subscriptions to the stock of a private corporation, or to take *effect* upon the approval or assent of a municipal corporation by the vote of the corporators, is not a delegation of power to the corporation to pass a law, but is a legitimate case of conditional legislation, and is entirely within the discretion of the legislature.

In enforcing these propositions, a member of the court remarked, *a* "The constitution of the United States, and that of our own state, constitute the only restriction or limitation of the legislative power. It is, aside from these limitations, supreme, uncontrollable and omnipotent, in respect to all other matters and subjects. The taxing power, is one of the inherent powers of government, and belongs appropriately to the legislative department." Another eminent judge in the same case, remarked as follows: "It is not denied but that the state may provide by law, for the construction of a railroad through the agency of its own officers, taking all lands necessary for the purpose by virtue of its right of eminent domain; or delegate the power to build the road, and take the

a Id. 480.

NOTE 3.—Since the rule adopted in the above eighth proposition, the highest court of this state, and also the court of the United States, have given interpretation of constitutions, and the subject of legislative power of taxation for the construction of railroads, and have carried the rule beyond what is laid down in this proposition. In the case of The People v. Mitchell, 35 N. Y. 551, it was held that a county, or other municipal corporation, may subscribe for stock in a railroad or other public improvement if authorized so to do by the legislature; and that the legislature can authorize such municipal corporation to take stock therein; to borrow money to pay for the same; and to levy a tax to repay the loan. That this authority can be conferred in such a manner as to accomplish the purpose, either with, or without a popular vote; and when they have authorized the act upon the condition of receiving the popular vote, the legislature can by retrospective legislation, cure any evils arising from an irregular execution of the power. The same rule, and in terms similar and in almost identical language, has been held by the Supreme Court of the United States, in the case of Thompson v. Lee County, reported in 3d Wallace Reports, 327.

lands required for it, to a private corporation. Nor is it disputed that the state may, under its taxing power, charge the expense of such public improvement, made by itself, upon the citizens of a particular locality which may be supposed to be more immediately benefited by the improvement; nor is it controverted that a municipal corporation may be authorized by law, to make such public improvements as are required by the interests of its locality, and tax the citizens of the locality to defray the expense. The power of the state, to this extent, is unquestioned, and so well established by long exercise of it, and by judicial decisions, as to render a discussion of it unnecessary if not unprofitable."

" There is nothing more easy than to imagine a thousand tyrannical things which the legislature may do, if its members forget all their duties, disregard utterly all the obligations they owe to their constituents, and recklessly determine to trample upon right and justice. But to take away the power from the legislature because they may abuse it, and give to the judges the right of controlling it, would not be advancing a single step, since the judges can be *imagined* to be as corrupt and wicked as legislators."

" I am thoroughly convinced, that the words of the constitution furnish the only test to determine the validity of a statute; and that all arguments based on general principles, outside of the constitution, must be addressed to the people, not to the courts."

These propositions, and the conclusions drawn from them, seem to be the views upon which the New York courts have also proceeded in giving constitutional construction, and in establishing the law of this state. They are also sustained, by the construction given by the national and other state courts. '

NOTE 4.—A few of the cases favoring the New York constitution are as follows: Fletcher v. Peck, 6 Cranch. 87, where it was held, "If a state legislature shall pass a law within the general scope of their constitutional powers, the court cannot pronounce it to be void, merely because it is in their judgment, contrary to the principles of natural justice." The ideas of natural justice are regulated by no fixed standard; the ablest and purest men have differed upon the subject; and all the court in such an event could say, would be, that the legislature, (pos sessing an equal right of opinion,) had passed an act which, in the opinion of the judges, was contrary to abstract principles of right." In Golden v. Rice, 3 Wash. C. C. R., it was said, " that the state legislatures may make such laws as they see fit, unless inconsistent with the powers exclusively vested in the government of the United States, or by some article of the federal or state constitution." In

Bennet v. Boggs, 1 Bald. 74, it was said, "We may think, the powers conferred by the constitution of this state, too great or dangerous to the rights of the people, and that limitations are necessary; but we cannot affix them." "We cannot declare a legislative act void because it conflicts with our opinions of policy, expediency or justice." "The remedy for unwise and oppressive legislation within constitutional bounds, is by appeal to the justice and patriotism of the representatives of the people. If this fails, the people in their sovereign capacity can correct the evil; but courts cannot assume their rights."

In the Providence Bank Case v. Billings, 4 Peters, 514, 562, Chief Justice Marshall said, "The power of legislation, and consequently of taxation, operates on all persons and property belonging to the body politic. This is an original principle which has its foundation in society itself. It is granted by all, for the benefit of all. It resides in government as part of itself, and need not be reserved when property of any description, or the right to use it, in any manner is granted to individuals, or corporate bodies. However absolute the right of an individual may be, it is still in the nature of that right, that it must bear a portion of the public burthens, and that portion must be determined by the legislature." In Commonwealth v. McCloskey, 2 Rawle, 374, the court say, "If the legislature pass a law in plain, unequivocal, and explicit terms, within the general scope of their constitutional power, I know of no authority in this government, to pronounce such an act void, merely because in the opinion of the judicial tribunals it was contrary to the principles of natural justice; for this would be vesting in the court, a latitudinarian authority which might be abused, and would necessarily lead to collisions between the legislative and judicial departments, dangerous to the well being of society, or at least, not in harmony with the structure of our ideas of natural government." In Norris v. Clymer, 2 Barr. 285, the court said, "The constitution allows to the legislature, every power, which it does not positively prohibit." In Commonwealth v. McWilliams, 1 Jones, (Penn.) R. 71, the court said, "From the commencement of the government, our representative bodies have exerted the unchallenged power to lay taxes, mediately or immediately, for every purpose deemed by them legitimate. Among these purposes, the construction and maintenance of roads and highways, to meet the necessities, and to facilitate the commerce of the people, have ever been deemed of first importance. Without these, a commercial community could scarcely exist. Indeed, they are so essential to the progress of civilization and the cultivation of the arts of life, that the degree of refinement attained by a people, may, in some sort, be measured by their extent and condition." "No one has yet dreamed of doubting the validity of that power when applied in maintenance of the ordinary roads of the country."

In Commonwealth v. Hartman, 5 Harris, 119, the court say, "The legislature has jurisdiction on all subjects on which its legislation is not prohibited. In applying this principle to the present case," (an act to provide for the establishment of common schools,) "it is enough to say, that there is no syllable in the constitution which forbids the legislature to provide for a system of general education, in any way which they, in their own wisdom may think best. But it is argued, that for the purpose of promoting education, and carrying out the system of common schools, laws may be passed which will work intolerable wrong, and

produce grievous hardship. The answer to this is, that a decent respect for a
co-ordinate branch of the government, compels us to deny that any such danger
can ever exist. But if a law, unjust in its operation, and nevertheless not forbidden by the constitution, should be enacted, the remedy lies, not in an appeal
to the judiciary, but to the people, who must apply the corrective themselves;
they have not intrusted the power to us." In Wilson v. Mayor of New York, 4
E. D. Smith, 678-9, Woodruff, J., said, "The power of the state to tax all property within its limits, whether real or personal, cannot be denied." "In the apportionment of taxes, and the assigning to persons or to property the portion
which each shall contribute, to the public burthens, the legislature have the sole
and exclusive power, of determining what is just and equitable, and upon what
description of persons, and upon what property within the state and in what
ratio, the imposition shall be made." "The inquiry is, in this tribunal, not
what property might equitably be taxed, nor what property it is expedient to tax,"
&c. In the case of the Fire Department v. Noble, 3 E. D. Smith, 441, it was held
that a statute imposing a tax upon foreign insurance corporations for the benefit
of the fire department, as a condition to their right to take insurances, was not an
infraction of the constitution which forbids taking private property for public use
without just compensation; that a tax upon a particular business may be levied
for the benefit of a public charity, and may be paid directly to the persons having
the benefit thereof. A tax may be legally levied under a statute for that purpose
for losses sustained by default of a county treasurer. People v. Supervisors of
Livingston, 17 N. Y. 486. The legislature can apportion the public burthens
among all the tax-paying citizens of the state, or those of a particular section or
territorial division, and although a statute may be unconstitutional under which
public expenses are incurred. a tax may be properly levied to meet those expenses. People v. Haws, 34 Barb. 69. When the legislature determines that a
public improvement will be a benefit to the adjacent property, and that the expenses of making the same shall be paid by the owners of such adjacent property,
the courts have nothing to do with the correctness or incorrectness of the determination, but must assume the fact to be as the legislature declares it. The wisdom or justice of the taxation, is not a subject of judicial inquiry, nor is the purpose for which the tax is imposed. People v. Lawrence, 36 Barb. 177. Taxes
for bounties to volunteers; taxes upon the owners of dogs, are legal subjects. A
local tax upon lands adjacent to the Long Island Railroad Company, for the
benefit of that company, as a public improvement, was held to be a legitimate
exercise of the taxing power. Litchfield v. McOmber, 42 Barb. 288. An act to
tax the citizens of the locality of Utica, to pay the additional expense of terminating the Chenango canal at that place, instead of Whitesborough, was held a
proper exercise of the taxing power. Thomas v. Leland, 24 Wend. 65. And
finally, "The raising money for a local improvement is an exercise of the taxing
power, *inherent in the legislature;* and this power of taxation, implies a power to
apportion the tax (territorially) as the legislature shall see fit, and moreover, that
this power of apportionment has no limit, where there is no constitutional restraint; and that the constitutional inhibition against depriving a person of life,
liberty or property from being taken for public use without just compensation,
has no application to such a case." Matter of Trustees of the N. Y. P. E. Public

School, 31 N. Y. 582–3; Howell v. City of Buffalo, 37 N. Y. 267; People v. Smith, 21 N. Y. 595; People v. Law, 34 Barb. 494; Thomas v. Leland, 24 Wend. 65; Livingston v. Mayor of New York, 8 Wend. 85; Bank of Rome v. Village of Rome, 18 N. Y. 38; Grant v. Courter, 24 Barb. 232; The Cincinnati, &c., R. R. Co. v. Commissioners of Clinton Co., 21 Ohio, 77; City of Bridgeport v. Housatonic R. R. Co., 15 Conn. 475; People v. Lawrence, 36 Barb. 177; McCulloch v. Maryland, 4 Wheat. 316; and see United States v. The Railroad Bridge Company, 3 Law Register, Old Series, 617, Per McLean, J.

Opposed to this view, are found several recent decisions of the courts of some of the western states; among them those of Ch. J. Cooley, of the state of Michigan, in the case of the People ex rel The Detroit & Howell R. R. Co. v. The Township Board of Salem, in the supreme court of that state. Also, of Ch. J. Dixon, of the supreme court of Wisconsin, in the case of Whiting v. Sheboygan Railway Co., reported in American Law Register, Vol. 9, N. S. 156; Weeks v. The City of Milwaukie, 10 Wisconsin, 242. Also a case in Iowa, Hanson v. Vernon, reported in 27 Iowa R.; not yet come to hand, from a note of it, supposed to be to the same effect as those of Michigan and Wisconsin, which are conceded to be the ablest opinions opposed to the doctrine which we have shown to be the established law of New York.

It does not become us to deny, or controvert the soundness of views expressed in these opinions;—to question the wisdom of those states, in adopting a state policy in accordance with those judicial expressions. We do not claim for the state of New York a superior wisdom in the adoption of the entirely opposite view of policy, or in the construction given by the judiciary of the taxing power, under a somewhat different constitution, and as to what constitutes a public use of property, and the power of the legislature to declare it;—nor, whether the judicial department of other states may not possess the power to control the legislative department, and deny them the power to declare, whether their citizens, and which of them, shall bear the burthens of taxation, to pay the expenses, of so-called public improvements.

These are questions of state policy, as to which, each independent state, in its sovereign capacity, must determine for itself. The judicial department of each such state, are the interpreters of their own local constitutions and statutes, and we therefore assume, that their courts, have correctly enunciated in those opinions, the law which is to control the action of those states.

But inasmuch as the highest judicial authority of our own state, under our own local constitution, have given a different, and the opposite interpretation of our own constitution and statutes; and as the other departments of our own state government, have declared, adopted and practiced a different state policy, we claim that the citation of the decisions of other states which have given a different interpretation to the legislative power from that established in this state, (however wise such other rule might be as an original question to be settled) is calculated to mislead and confuse the profession, and the citizen whose private interest dictates the desire for a different construction. We may add to the cases above cited, as in degree, sustaining them. Griffith v. Indiana & Ohio R. R., 20 Ohio, 609, and dicta of Judge Patterson, 2 Dallas, 304, of Judge Chase in same and 3 Dallas, 388; and Sweet v. Hulburt, in the supreme court of this state, before referred to, and commented upon, not appealed to the court of dernier resort.

Did our limits permit, we should gladly transfer the able exposition of the law of constitutional interpretation, given in the opinions of the courts of these western states, to which we have referred in this work. It may be sufficient however, briefly to refer to the points of agreement and of departure, in the views of construction of the constitution of those states and our own.

1. They *agree* with us, that taxation for the purpose of taking the private property of one person, to bestow it upon another, is unconstitutional and void.

2. They agree with us, that the legislature do possess the power to grant the right to take private property for public purposes.

3. While they agree, that the legislature may grant the right to take property by the exercise of eminent domain, to a railroad corporation, and though they agree to the grant of power by the legislature to tax for *public* purposes, yet they hold, that a railroad corporation, whose road is constructed by itself, is exclusively private property, owned, controlled, and operated by a private corporation, for the benefits of its own members, and that it is for the judiciary, and not for the legislature to determine whether or not the purpose is a public one; that an act of the legislature declaring the purpose of such a railroad to be public, and authorizing taxation in its aid, is unconstitutional and void. In this, it is seen, the cases are in direct conflict with the New York authorities. People v. Lawrence, 36 Barb. 177; supra and other cases cited, where it is held that the power, wisdom, or justice of taxation upon persons benefited by such improvements, is not a subject of judicial inquiry, but belongs to the legislative department. This is the first great point of divergence.

It is no part of our purpose to compare the soundness of the opinions of the judiciary of one sovereign state with those of another. The difference in their local constitutions may be sufficient to account for the difference in results. The right of eminent domain and the taxing power are entirely different, the one from the other, in the method of exercising their respective powers, though each is called into use for public purposes. Nor is it any part of our design here to enquire into the reason, or to explain the apparent inconsistency in the proposition, that the legislative department do possess the authority and may declare the purpose of a railroad corporation to be *public*, so as to enable them to exercise the right of eminent domain in taking private property; but have no power to declare the purpose of the same project public, so as to authorize taxation upon the persons to be benefited by the construction of their road. The curious searcher for information on these points, will seek the explanation in the adjudications, as manifested in the able enunciation of the reasons contained in the opinions referred to, upon which these different sovereignties seem to have adopted as their respective state policies.

CHAPTER XIII.

OF THE CONSTITUTIONAL PROTECTION, THAT LIFE, LIBERTY, AND
PROPERTY BE NOT TAKEN WITHOUT DUE PROCESS OF LAW.

LIFE, liberty, and property of a citizen may be forfeited and
lost, *but not without due process of law.* This protection is contained in both the national and state constitutions. *a* It originated
in Magna Charta, *b* and constitutes one of its fundamental articles,
in which it is declared, that "no free man shall be taken, or
imprisoned, or dissiezed of his freehold, or liberties, or free customs, or be out-lawed, or exiled, or otherwise destroyed, nor will
we pass upon him nor condemn him, but by lawful judgment
of his peers, or by the law of the land." "The judgment of his
peers," was by the law of England, the trial of a man by a jury
of his equals, and in this country, means a trial by jury, who are
called the peers of the party accused. This question was briefly
and partially, but indirectly considered in a former chapter.

Our ancestors brought these privileges with them to America
as their birthright and inheritance, and as a part of the common
law, which then interposed its guardianship, and threw around
them on every side, its protection against the approaches of arbitrary power. These privileges, as rights, are now incorporated,
not only into all our constitutions state and national, but will be
found in all the statutes of the states made in subordination to
the fundamental law, recognizing and confirming these rights in
the citizen; and all statutes are void, and without effect, which are
found to be obnoxious to these solemnly secured privileges.

"That government can scarcely be deemed to be free, where
the rights of property are left solely dependent upon the will of a
legislative body, without any restraint. The fundamental maxims
of a free government seem to require, that the rights of personal

a Const. United States amendment 1, Art. 4; Const. New York, Art. 1, § 6.
b 9 Hen. III, ch. 29.

liberty and private property should be held sacred. At least no court of justice in this country would be warranted in assuming that the power to violate and disregard them, a power so repugnant to the common principles of justice and civil liberty, lurked under any general grant of legisiative authority, or, ought to be implied from any general expressions of the will of the people. The people ought not to be presumed to part with rights so vital to their security and well being, without very strong and direct expressions of such an intention." *a*

The term, right, in civil society, Chanceller Kent defines to be, *b* "that which any man is entitled to have, or to do, or to require from others within the limits prescribed by law." The absolute rights of individuals may be resolved into the right of personal security—the right of personal liberty—and the right to acquire and enjoy property. These rights have been justly considered and frequently declared, by the people of this country, to be natural, inherent, and unalienable. The effectual security and enjoyment of them depend upon the existence of civil liberty ; and that consists in being protected and governed by laws made, or assented to, by the representatives of the people, conducive to the general welfare."

Before the adoption of our American constitutions, the words "by the law of the land," had a well defined meaning at common law, and had been rendered, "due process of law." *c* Our constitutions adopt the very words of this common law definition, and mean undoubtedly by that, that to work a change of property from one private person to another, some proceeding must be had in a court of justice, or before magistrates ; at least that the legislature should have no power to deprive one of his property, and transfer it to another, by enacting a bargain between them, unless it be in the hands of the latter, a trust for public use." *d*

In a subsequent statute, passed in the reign of Edward III, Magna Charta in this respect, was itself changed. The clause, "but by the law of the land, or the judgment of his peers," was altered to read thus : without being brought to answer by due process of law."

a Wilkinson v. Leland, 3 Peters 657, Per Story J.   *b* 2 Com. 1.
c 2 Coke's, Inst. 50.   *d* Matter of John and Cherry street, 19 Wend. 676.

The words "*due process of law*," said Judge Bronson, *a* cannot mean less than a prosecution or suit instituted and conducted according to the prescribed forms and solemnities for ascertaining guilt, or determining the title to property. It will be seen thai the same measure of protection against legislative encroachment, is extended to life, liberty and property; and if the latter can be taken without forensic trial and judgment, there is no security for the others. If the legislature can take the property of A. and transfer it to B., they can take A. himself, and either shut him up in prison, or put him to death. But none of these things can be done by mere legislation. There must be "due process of law."

What then is due process of law? The definition given of this clause that has been more frequently quoted, or, perhaps adopted by the courts than any other, is that given by Mr. Webster, *b* who said : " By the law of the land, is most clearly intended the general law, which hears before it condemns, and proceeds upon inquiry, and renders judgment only after trial. The meaning is, that every citizen shall hold his life, liberty, property and immunities under the protection of general rules which govern society. Every thing which may pass under the form of legislative *enactment*, is *not* therefore the law of the land." " A construction that would do this, would render constitutional provisions of the highest importance, completely inoperative and void. It would tend directly to establish the union of all powers in the legislature. There would be no general permanent law for courts to administer, or for man to live under. The administration of justice would be an empty form, an idle ceremony. Judges would sit to execute legislative judgments and decrees ; not to declare the law, or to administer the justice of the country." *c*

To give this clause, therefore, any value, it must be understood to mean, that no person shall be deprived, by any form of l gislation, or governmental action, of either life, liberty, or property, except as a consequence of some judicial proceeding appropriately and legally conducted. It follows, that a law, which, by its own inherent force, extinguishes rights of property, or compels

a Taylor v. Porter, 4 Hill 147 ; Embury v. Conner, 3 N. Y. 517.

Dartmouth College case, 4 Wheat, 519, 581.

c Westervelt v. Gregg, 12 N. Y., 200.

their destruction, without any legal process whatever, comes directly in conflict with the constitution. a

One of the means attempted by which a citizen is sometimes to be deprived of his property, or of his personal liberty, are *ex post facto* laws, or laws retrospective in their nature. The New York Code of 1849, section 460, in form, authorized an appeal "in any suit in equity, pending in the Supreme Court on the first day of July 1847." Under this act, a party brought an appeal to the Court of Appeals from a final decree in equity, where the time previously allowed by law for appealing had expired, and the decree had been executed. It was held by Jewitt, J., b that this statute which contingently deprived a person of property, the right to which was perfect under prior laws, was within the prohibition of the constitution. The direct effect of this provision of the Code, if valid, was the granting of a new trial or hearing upon all the questions both of law and evidence arising in the case, after it had been lost by neglect of the complainant under the provision of law as it existed at the time the decree was made, and after it had become final upon the rights of the parties involved in the suit, and the defendant had acquired possession of the fruits of the litigation by due execution upon it. It was therefore held that the act was invalid as contrary to the clause in article 1 section 6, of the constitution of this state, which provides, that "*no person shall be deprived of life, liberty or property, without due process of law.*" It was in effect, annulling a complete and final decree by which property had been acquired and possessed. Contingently, it not only deprived such person of the property thus acquired, but compelled him to pay to his adversary, such sum of money, as the appellate court might determine he ought to pay. The money which had been adjudged to be paid by the decree, and received by the defendant under it, was his property in a legal sense, at the time of the passing the act, and though it did not absolutely deprive the party of the money decreed to him, contingently it had that effect.

So an act of congress passed in 1865, requiring attorneys and counsellors at law, to take an oath: *First.* That he had never voluntarily borne arms against the United States since he was a

a Wyndham v. The People, 13 N. Y. 434.
b Burch v. Newbury, 10 N. Y., 374

citizen thereof. *Second.* That he had not voluntarily given aid, counsel, countenance, or encouragement to persons engaged in armed hostility thereto. *Third.* That he has never sought, accepted, or attempted to exercise the functions of any office whatsoever under the authority, or pretended authority, in hostility to the United States. *Fourth.* That he has not yielded a voluntary support to any pretended government, authority, power or constitution within the United States, hostile, or inimical thereto;" was held to be in violation of the provisions of the constitution; not only as being *ex post facto* law, but also as against the inhibition against the passage of bills of *attainder. a* It was said, that this act operated as a legislative decree, judicial in its character, of perpetual exclusion against a class of citizens for past transactions; that an exclusion from any of the professions, or any of the ordinary avocations of life for past conduct, could be regarded in no other light than as a punishment for such conduct.

The trial by jury, especially in all criminal cases, is justly dear to the American people. It has always been an object of deep interest and solicitude, and every encroachment upon it has been watched with great jealousy. The right to such a trial, as is seen, is secured by being incorporated into the federal constitution, into the constitution of this state, and it is believed into the constitution of every state in the Union. It is said to have been one of the strong objections originally taken against the constitution of the United States, that there was the omission to provide for the right of trial by a jury in all civil cases. So strongly was this objection pressed, that its advocates, after the adoption of the original, were able to secure this right in a somewhat qualified sense by the seventh amendment made thereto, as proposed by congress, which afterwards received the assent of the people, and so established its importance, as a fundamental guaranty to what was regarded as the rights and liberties of the people. *b* The qualification however, was first, to cases where the value of the controversy exceeded twenty dollars, and second, the implication arising from the language "shall be preserved," as qualifying it to such cases of trial by jury as existed at common law at the time and prior to

a Matter of Garland, reported in 32 How. Pr. R. 241.

b Parsons v. Bedford, 3 Peters, 445.

the adoption of the constitution that is, the existing law was "*preserved.*" The same provision in effect is secured by our state constitution. "The trial by jury in all cases in which it has heretofore been used, shall *remain* inviolate forever." *a*

Beyond the reasons which might be advanced by jurists of the greatest experience as to the most judicious modes of trial in cases not criminal, there has ever existed in the minds of the mass of citizens, a tenacity of opinion in favor of the system of trial by jury; they insist upon it as one of the great bulwarks of civil and political liberty, and they are ever watching it with unceasing jealousy and solicitude. It is claimed, that the same reasons which secured a trial by jury in criminal cases; which was to protect against oppression and tyranny on the part of rulers; and from violence and vindictiveness on the part of the people, under circumstances of excitement and passion; demands a corresponding protection where their personal liberty, property, or character are involved; that at common law these rights came down to them as a fundamental right secured by *Magna Charta*, and is secured by the provision in our own fundamental law, that no man shall be arrested or imprisoned, or deprived of life, liberty or property except by the judgment of his peers, or by the law of the land. And this claim as to a class of actions, has been especially endorsed by our highest state court in a recent case, in which it was said, *b* The wisdom of the time-honored rule of the common law which refers questions of fact to the jurors, and questions of law to the judge, is not more conspicuous in any class of civil cases, than in those which involve questions of negligence. Cases of that nature frequently come before the courts, in which men of equal intelligence and judgment differ in their conclusions, simply because they differ in experience and habits, in temperament or mental organization. That *average* judgment which is the result of the deliberations of twelve men of ordinary sense and experience is recognized by our jury system as a juster standard than the judgment of one man, of equal experience and sense, in the determination of questions of fact, and it is especially valuable in the de-

a Murphy v. The People, 2 Cow. 816; Jackson v. The People, id. 819; Livingston v. Mayor, 8 Wend. 99; Colt v. Eves, 12 Conn. 251.

b Willis v. Long Island R. R. Co., 34 N. Y. 679.

cision of the question of negligence. On the trial of an issue of that nature, if there is any doubt, however slight, either as to what facts are established by the testimony, or as to the conclusion with respect to the fact of negligence that may be drawn legitimately from the circumstances proved by the average of men of common sense, ordinary experience, and fair intentions, the case should not be taken from the jury. It is only where the case is entirely clear upon the testimony; where there is no rational doubt, either as to the circumstances proved, or as to the conclusions of fact which may be properly drawn from them, that a judge is justified in deciding a question of negligence as matter of law. But this view is perhaps more a question of practice, than of construction, though it partakes of the spirit of the constitutional protection.

An unlimited power in a constitution creating a judicial department, and to constitute courts, includes in it, the power to prescribe a mode of trial; consequently, if nothing was said in the constitution on the subject of juries, the legislature would be at liberty either to adopt the system of trial by jury, or to let it alone. So far as criminal cases are concerned, in both the national and state constitutions, the question is settled by express injunction, but so far as regards civil cases, the national constitution was originally silent, and by the constitution of this state, the right of the legislature to direct, is qualified by limitation to cases in which it therefore had been used. It had been claimed that the specification in the national constitution of an obligation to try all criminal cases by jury, by the rules of construction, excluded the obligation to try civil causes in the same way, a though it did not abridge the power of the legislature to appoint that mode. This was amended afterwards, as has been stated, by the seventh amendment, with a qualification. The pretence therefore, either that it is the constitutional right of the citizen to have every case tried by a jury, or, that the right of trial in civil cases is denied by implication of the constitution, is without foundation.

It may therefore be stated, that jury trials are nowhere abolished, in national or state constitutions, and with equal certainty it may be stated, that in most of the civil controversies that arise between individuals, in which the great body of the people are

a Federalist, by Hamilton, No. 83.

likely to be interested, the trial by jury as an institution, will re main as heretofore, and in the situation in which it is placed by the state constitutions.

At the time of the adoption of these provisions in the national and state constitutions, throughout the Union, and in the several states, the common law was the basis of our jurisprudence, and was probably that of the new states since received into the Union. But it may as well be remarked here, that the provision in the United States constitution is only intended for proceedings under acts of congress, and does not apply to actions in state courts. *a*

The phrase " common law," found in this clause of the constitution of the United States, is used in contradistinction to "equity" and "admiralty " and " maritime" jurisprudence. The constitution had declared, in the third article, " that the judicial power shall extend to all cases in law and equity arising under that constitution, the laws of the United States, and treaties made or which shall be made under their authority, &c.," and to all cases of admiralty and maritime jurisdiction. It is well known that in civil cases, in courts of equity, and admiralty, juries do not intervene, and that courts of equity use the trial by jury only in extraordinary cases, to inform the conscience of the court. When therefore we find that this amendment requires that the right of trial by jury shall be preserved in suits at " common law " the natural conclusion is, that this distinction was present to the minds of the framers of the amendment. By common law, they meant what the constitution denominated in the third article, "law," not merely suits which the common law recognized among its old settled proceedings, but suits in which legal rights were to be ascertained and determined, in contradistinction to those, where equitable rights alone were recognized, and equitable remedies were administered; or where, as in the admiralty, a mixture of public law, and of maritime law, and equity, was often found in the same suit. Probably there were few, of any, states in the union, in which some new legal remedies differing from the old common law forms were not in use; but in which, however, the trial by jury intervened, and the general regulations in other respects, were according to the course of the common law. Pro-

a Colt v. Eves, supra; Livingston v. Moore, 7 Peters R. 551.

ceedings in case of partition, and of foreign and domestic attachments, might be cited as examples, variously adopted and modified.

In a just sense, then, the amendment may be well construed to
embrace all suits, which are not of equity and admiralty jurisdiction, whatever may be the peculiar form which they may assume
to settle legal rights.   And congress seems to have acted with reference to this exposition in the judiciary act of 1789, ch. 20, (which
was contemporaneous with the proposed amendment;) for in the
ninth section, it is provided, that, "the trial of issues of fact in
the district court in all causes, except civil causes of admiralty
and maritime jurisdiction, shall be by jury;" and in the twelfth
section it is provided, that "the trial of issues in fact in the circuit courts, shall in all suits, except those of equity and admiralty
and maritime jurisdiction, be by jury; and again in the thirteenth
section, it is provided, that "the trial of issues in fact in the
supreme court in all actions at law against citizens of the United
States, shall be by jury."

The same construction in effect was given to a similar constitutional provision in the state of Pennsylvania, in the following
words: "Trials by jury shall be as heretofore, and shall remain
inviolate."   At the time of the adoption of that constitution, justices had jurisdiction in actions not exceeding ten pounds.   The legislature of that state, by an act increased this jurisdiction to twenty
pounds, and imposed certain liabilities to courts, and to parties
in certain circumstances, who demanded trials by jury in that class
of cases.   This latter act was claimed to be unconstitutional.   The
court held, a that though the legislature could not constitutionally
impose any provisions substantially restrictive of the right of trial
by jury, they might give existence to new *forums*; and they might
modify the powers and jurisdiction of former courts, in such instances as are not interdicted by the constitution from which their
legitimate powers are derived; still, the sacred, inherent right of
every citizen, a trial by jury, must be preserved.   "It shall remain
inviolate as heretofore."

This provision, securing to the citizen his right and privileges,
unless deprived of them "by due process of law," was designed, says
Denio, J., b "To protect the citizen against all mere acts of power,

a Emerick v. Harris, 1 Binney, 424.   b Westervelt v. Gregg, 12 N. Y. 212.

whether flowing from the legislative or executive branches of the government. It does not of course touch the right of the state to appropriate private property to public use upon making due compensation, which is fully recognized in another part of the constitution; but no power in the state can legally confer upon one person or class of persons, the property of another person or class, without their consent, whatever motives of policy may exist in favor of such transfer." To give this clause, "due process of law," its true and proper value to the citizen, it must be made to mean, that no person shall be deprived, by any form of legislation, or governmental action, of either life, liberty, or property, except as the consequence of some judicial proceeding, appropriately conducted. It follows, that a law, which by its own inherent force extinguishes rights of property, or compels their extinction, without any legal process whatever, comes directly in conflict with the constitution. *a*

The meaning of this provision, then, according to its best interpretation by judicial authority, as well as history is, that no member of the state shall be disfranchised, or deprived of any of his rights or privileges, unless the matter shall be adjudged against him upon trial had according to the course of the common law; he is to be secured the benefit of those rules by which judicial trials are regulated, and to place those rules beyond the reach of legislative subversion. It is thus, that these rules are incorporated into the constitution itself, and made thereby a part of the paramount law. Trials, therefore, at least such as are criminal, are to be regulated and conducted in their essential features, not by statute but by common law. This is the constitutional guaranty. "These are but the rules which reason applies to the investigation of truth, and are of course, unchangeable." There has been in England, and in this country, a concurrence of opinion and holding, that all those fundamental rules of practice and evidence, which have generally been deemed essential to the due administration of justice, and which have been acted upon and enforced by all their common law courts for centuries, should be placed by the constitution beyond the reach of legislation." *b*

a Wyndham v. The People, 13 N. Y. 434.
b Id. 447.

So far as this provision includes the right of trial by jury in criminal cases, it is hardly necessary that it be further discussed. The express provisions in the fifth and sixth articles of the first amendment of the constitution of the United States, which contain the provision we have been examining, are all that need be said on that subject. The whole of which are as follows:

Article 5. "No person shall be held to answer for a capital or otherwise infamous crime, unless upon presentment or indictment of a grand jury, except in cases arising in the land or naval forces, or in the militia, when in actual service, in time of war, or public danger; nor shall any person be subject for the same offence, to be twice put in jeopardy of life or limb; nor shall be compelled in any criminal case, to be a witness against himself; nor be deprived of life, liberty, or property without due process of law; nor shall private property be taken for public use, without just compensation."

Article 6. "In all criminal prosecutions, the accused shall enjoy the right to a speedy and public trial, by an impartial jury, of the state and district wherein the crime shall have been committed; which district shall have been previously ascertained by law; and to be informed of the nature and cause of the accusation; to be confronted with the witnesses against him; to have compulsory process for obtaining witnesses in his favor; and to have the assistance of counsel for his defence."

The mode of trial it is seen, in all criminal actions, is a trial by a jury, and is surrounded by certain safeguards, which are made as well by the constitution as by statutes, a part of the system; and which government cannot dispense with. Among these, is, that the accused shall have a *speedy* trial. Though this is a positive injunction of the constitution, it is to have a reasonable construction in favor of the accused. If when charged with crime he is willing to proceed at once to trial, no delay on the part of the prosecution should be held reasonable, except that which is necessary to secure the attendance of witnesses; and this reasonableness, is a matter which it is the province of the court to control. If the government officer, acting under the responsibility of his official oath, represents the excuse of absent, or foreign witnesses, or witnesses who by reason of sickness, or other temporary infirinity, cannot be obtained at earliest possible day in court, it is with reason supposed to be the duty of the court, to grant some delay. So on the other hand, a judicious court, in view of the constitutional security in this respect intended for the accused; and in view of the immense power of oppression that may be brought by prosecuting officers. The courts will ever appreciate actual difficulties, and duly regard the rights of the accused, and especially, in cases where delay will result in keeping him in confinement.

In cases not capital, it seldom fails, that the accused can avoid confinement, by recognizance of bail; and here again, the constitution throws its protection around the accused, and commands that unreasonable bail shall not be required. This command, which the court is under the solemn obligation to obey, appeals to the sense of justice of the court or judge to regard, in fixing the amount of bail. No conscientious magistrate can, capriciously, allow this constitutional privilege of the accused to be set at naught.

So too, there is the further security to the accused, that the trial shall be *public*. By this it is not meant that every person who sees fit, shall in all cases be permitted to attend criminal trials, because there are many cases where, from the character of the charge, and the nature of the evidence by which it is to be supported, the motives to attend the trial on the part of portions of the community would be of the worst character, and where a regard to public morals and public decency, would demand the exclusion at least of the young from the hearing, and of witnessing the evidence of human depravity, which the trial must necessarily bring to light. The requirement of a public trial, is for the benefit of the accused, that the public may see that he is fairly dealt by and not unjustly condemned, and the presence of interested spectators may keep his triers keenly alive to a sense of their responsibility, and to the importance of their functions. This requirement is fairly met, if, without partiality or favoritism, a reasonable proportion of the public is suffered to be present, notwithstanding those persons whose presence could be of no service to the accused, and who would only be drawn thither by a prurient curiosity, are excluded altogether. *a*

a Cooley on Const. Lim. 312.

But a far more important requirement is, that the proceeding to establish guilt, shall not be inquisitorial, and the criminal shall not, in a criminal case, " be compelled to be a witness against himself," and in this state, as a still further protection to the accused, the legislature have provided by a statute, *a* " that in the trial of all indictments, complaints, and other proceedings against persons charged with the commission of crimes or offences; and in all proceedings in any and all courts, and before any and all officers and persons acting judicially; the person so charged, shall. at his own request, but not otherwise, be deemed a competent witness ; but the neglect or refusal of any such person to testify, shall not create any presumption against him." There is a still further security and protection to the accused upon his preliminary examination, which the statute directs shall not be on oath ; and before it is commenced, the accused shall be informed of the charge made against him ; and he shall be allowed a reasonable time to send for and advise with counsel ; and if he desires it, he may have his counsel present during his examination, and during the examination of the complainant and the witnesses on the part of the prosecution. *b* And it is made the duty of the examining magistrate to inform the accused of his privilege. to refuse to answer any question that may be put to him, *c* and in case he answers, the interrogatories put to him shall be reduced to writing by the magistrate, or under his direction, and they shall be read to the accused, who is entitled to correct and add to them until they are made conformable to what he declares is the truth before they are certified and signed by the magistrate. All these preliminary proceedings are connected with, and incident to the system of trial by jury.

But as we have seen, except in criminal cases, this constitutional guarantee is to be reasonably interpreted. It was not intended by this provision, as may be learned from its language, to tie up the hands of the legislature in every conceivable case, so that no matter can be judicially settled except by a jury trial, and, as will appear, it has been frequently decided, there are matters that come before courts, referees, and commissioners for adjudication, where

---

a Laws of N. Y. 1869, Chap. 678.
c Id., § 15.
b Rev. Stat. 708, § 14.

this provision of the constitution is not impaired, even though a jury trial, in the technical sense of the term, is not given.

"Due process of law," therefore, includes every process and proceeding which any of the guarantees of the national or state constitutions confer. The first article of the constitution of this state declares, that "no member of this state shall be disfranchised, or deprived of any of the rights or privileges secured to any citizen, *unless by the law of the land*, or, *the judgment of his peers*." And also by section two, that "the trial by jury in all cases in which it has heretofore been used, shall remain inviolate forever." Due process of law, not only includes these guarantees, but also as we have shown, includes the right to have the prosecution conducted according to the prescribed forms, as used in judicial proceedings.

Questions have arisen, both in criminal and civil proceedings in the courts of this state, as to what constituted a jury within the meaning of the constitution of this state, for the trial of criminal offences, below the grade of capital and infamous offences ; and also, for obtaining compensation in civil cases, for private property taken for public use.

It is conceded, that the jury referred to in the above constitutional provision, is a common law jury of twelve men, *a* but the explanatory words, "as heretofore used,"—means, as used prior to the adoption of that constitution. By article 7, § 2, of the constitution of 1821, the provision as to trial by jury was in substance the same, as in that of 1846 above cited. The statutes of the state previous to the adoption of the constitution of 1821, as well as subsequent, expressly authorized the trial of petit larceny, and offences not infamous in their character, under the degree of grand larceny without indictment, without a jury, where the accused neglected to give security to appear at the next court of general sessions. *b* And the first law authorizing a trial by jury in any case, in a court of special sessions, for such offences, was passed subsequent to the adoption of the constitution of 1846. *c*

The conflict that arose under these provisions, was, from the

a Wyndham v. The People, 13 N. Y. 484.

b 1 Greenleaf Laws, N. Y. 422, R. L. 1813, 504, 7.

c Duffy v. The People, 6 Hill, 78.

claim made, that in whatever court the person charged might be tried, he was entitled to have his guilt or innocence determined by a jury of twelve men. This was opposed, and finally held by the courts of this state, that under the constitution and statutes, persons charged with crimes not capital, or otherwise infamous, may be held to answer without being first indicted or presented by a grand jury, as the legislature should provide. *a* By an act of the legislature of 13th April, 1813, under the constitution of 1777, certain offences, viz., petit larceny, misdemeanor, breach of the peace or other minor offences, under the degree of grand larceny, were made triable by a court of special sessions, without any jury whatever. This act was modified by the legislature in 1824, so as to give the party accused the right to be tried by a jury of six men, *b* and these statutes were regarded as in force when the present constitution was adopted.

Trials for offences of this minor grade, had uniformly been authorized under these statutes, without a jury, and with a jury of six men ; and the highest courts had ratified the practice, and they also held, that it was in the power of the legislature to confer upon courts of special sessions, the right to try offences below the grade of felony without indictment and without a jury. *c* And though the Revised Statutes have modified still more these rights of trial before courts of special sessions, and made the right of trial to depend upon the condition, that the accused is unable to furnish bail to appear at a higher court, it is still in the power of the special sessions, in such case of failure of bail, to try him, whatever may be the desire or demand of the accused to be tried elsewhere. It is an entire question of power of the legislature, to confer this jurisdiction upon the courts to try such cases, with or without consent of the accused. They can grant or withold their consent to allow a jury; the granting it is a privilege.

But if a party be arrested for a statute misdemeanor, as for instance for a violation of the "act to suppress intemperance," and is brought before a justice of the peace and desires to have his case passed upon by a grand jury, and if indicted, to be tried by a jury of twelve men, and is able and willing to give bail for his

---

a The People v. Fisher, 20 Barb. 652.   *b* Sess. Laws, 1824, Ch. 238
c Duffy v. The People, 6 Hill. 78; Wyndham v. The People, 13 N. Y. 484

appearance before the next court of oyer and terminer or general sessions, he cannot be summarily tried by the justice, against the consent of the party so charged. *a* The state constitution provides, "that the trial by jury, in all cases in which it has been heretofore used, shall remain inviolate forever." *b* Under our statute laws existing at the time of the adoption of the constitution, a justice could hold a court of special sessions, and could try without a jury, if one should not be demanded ; or with a jury of six men, if one should be requested—persons charged with certain misdemeanors, who should elect to be thus tried, or persons who should fail to give the requisite security to appear at a court of oyer and terminer or general sessions, where they could not be tried without indictment, nor by any but a common law jury of twelve men. This privilege existed when the constitution was adopted, and was reserved in it to the citizen ; when therefore the party charged, demanded this privilege, and offered to comply with the condition, it left the justice without jurisdiction to proceed.

So too, as to this constitutional right of trial by jury, it can only be claimed where the subject is judicial in its character. The taking of private property for public purposes under the right of eminent domain, or under the taxing power, do not partake of this judicial character. They are both emanations of the law-making power. They are attributes of political sovereignty, for the exercise of which, the legislature is under no necessity to address itself to the courts. In appropriating the property of the citizen under these powers, for a public purpose, under legislative and constitutional authority, with a proper provision for compensation, the act of the legislature itself, is held to be " due process of law." *c* The constitution itself excepts these cases from the absolute right of a trial by jury, or being made subject to judicial contests, and prescribes the manner in which the compensation shall be ascertained. The constitution nowhere inhibits the exercise of this power by the legislature, or of their delegating the power to public officers, or to corporations established under legislative authority, to secure a judicious appraisal of property in order to carry on enterprises in which the public are interested.

a Hill v. The People, 20 N. Y. 369.   *b* Art. 1 § 2.
c People v. Smith, 21 N. Y. 598.

CHAPTER XIV.

OF THE POLICE POWER OF THE GOVERNMENT, UNDER STATE CON-
STITUTIONS, BY WHICH PRIVATE PROPERTY MAY BE TAKEN FOR
THE BENEFIT OF OTHERS.

BESIDES the methods of taking private property of the citizen
by right of eminent domain, and by the taxing power, there
exists another power by which private property may be taken, used
or destroyed for the benefit of others, and this is called the *police
power;* sometimes called the law of overruling necessity.

It is clear, that before the adoption of either our state or
national constitutions, it was well settled common law, as we find
both by the best elementary law writers, and by uniform adjudications in the courts, that in cases of actual necessity,—as that of
preventing the spread of fire,—the ravages of a pestilence, or any
other great calamity, the private property of any individual may be
lawfully taken, used or destroyed for the relief, protection, or safety
of the many, without subjecting the actors to personal responsibility.   In these cases, the rights of private property must be made
subservient to the public welfare.   The maxim of law is, that a
private mischief is to be endured, rather than a public inconvenience. " On this ground," says Chancellor Kent, *a* " rest the rights of
public necessity.   If a common highway be out of repair, a passenger may lawfully go through an adjoining enclosure.   So it is
lawful to raze houses to the ground to prevent the spreading of a
conflagration.   These are cases of urgent necessity, in which no
action lay at common law by the individual who sustained the injury ; but private property must in many other instances, yield to
the general interest." *b* [1]

a 2 Kent Com. 338.   *b* 1 Dall. U. S. 363.

NOTE 1.—Of this principle there are many striking illustrations besides those
stated. If a man be assaulted, he may fly through another's close. 5 Bac. Abr.
173. In time of war, bulwarks may be built on private ground. Dyer 8, Brook
Trespass. And as the safety of the people is a law above all others, it is lawful to
part affrayers in the house of another man. Keyl. 46, 20 Vin. Abr. f. 407, § 14;
Puffendorf lib. 2, Ch. 6, § 8.

This power to take private property by which the burthen falls upon the citizen, seems at first blush, to be so contrary to a sense of common justice, and falls so unequally and oppressively upon the individual, that it is most natural that we should search for a proper basis for its support. It is claimed that the protection of the citizen is found in the constitutions of both the state and nation which declare " that private property shall not be taken for public use without just compensation." But our highest courts have held, that this police power, or the law of overruling necessity, is not controlled by this constitutional limitation; *a* that such restriction in the constitution was not designed for, and should not be extended to such a case ; that this clause in the constitution has reference only to cases where the property of an individual is taken for some public benefit or advantage.ᵇ

a Russel v. The Mayor of New York, 2 Denio, 461, 483; Mayor of New York v. Lord, 17 Wend. 285; Stone v. Mayor of New York, 25 Wend. 157.

NOTE 2.—In an old case reported in 12 Co. 13, it was held, that even the king could not take the private property of the subject for making a wall about his own house, or a bridge to come to his house, for that, would not be for the public benefit. " But when the enemies come against the realm to the sea coast, it is lawful to come upon any land adjoining to the same coast, to make trenches or bulwarks for the defence of the realm, for every subject hath a benefit by it. And therefore by the common law every man may come upon any land for the defence of the realm, and in such case, and on such extremity, they may dig for gravel for the making of bulwarks, for this is for the public, and every one hath a benefit by it. And for the commonwealth, a man shall suffer damage; as for saving of a city, or town, a house shall be plucked down if the next be on fire;—and the suburbs of a city in time of war, for the common safety shall be plucked down; and a thing for the commonwealth, a man may do, without being liable to an action." In the case of Governor, &c., v. Meredith, 4 Tenn. 797, Buller, J., said, "There are many cases in which individuals sustain an injury for which the law gives no action; for instance, pulling down houses, or raising bulwarks for the preservation and defence of the king, done against the king's enemies." This is one of the cases to which the maxim applies " *Salus populi suprema est lex.*"

In Mouse's case, 12 Co. 63, Mouse brought an action in trespass, for the value of a hogshead of wine cast overboard of a barge. A ferryman from Gravesend to London with passengers, including the plaintiff and freight, a part of which was this cask of wine belonging to the plaintiff. While on the water, a great tempest happened, and a strong wind, so that the barge and all the passengers were in danger to be drowned, if this hogshead of wine and other ponderous things were not cast overboard for the safety of the lives of the passengers. It was resolved, *per totam curiam*, that in case of necessity for the saving of the lives of the passengers, it was lawful for the defendant, being a passenger, to cast the cask of the plaintiff out of the barge, with other things in it. "*Quod necessitas cogit, defendit.*"

The seventeenth section of the first article of the constitution of this state provides and declares, that such parts of the common law, &c., as did form the law of the colony of New York on the 19th day of April, 1775, &c., shall be and continue the law of this state, subject to such alterations as the legislature shall make concerning the same. But all such parts of the common law, &c., as are repugnant to this constitution were abrogated. This doctrine of overruling necessity, or police power, was the common law of this state at the time of the adoption of this state constitution of 1846. It was brought from England by our ancestors as a part of their system of common law; was adopted by the colonists as the law of the land; it is not clearly repugnant to the constitution; but being adopted by it, is in effect a part of it.

The common law, existing at the time of the adoption of our state constitution, was adopted by the constitution as a part of itself. At common law, public nuisances could be abated under the police power, or even by an individual who for such purpose became a part of the police power, even to the injury or destruction of private property invested in such subject of nuisance; and an act of the legislature conferring authority upon a municipal body, to remove, abate, suspend, alter, improve and purify, anything dangerous to life, or health, as a public nuisance, even to the destruction of such private property, is not within the prohibition of the constitution against taking private property without just compensation, nor in violation of that other provision, that the individual shall not be deprived of his property "without due process of law." Nor is the creating such municipal board with power to make by-laws concerning such police matters, a delegation of the legislative power, or trust, nor is it inhibited by the sixth article of the constitution, as the creation of a local court with judicial powers; for the reason, that the legislature, having power to create a sanitary board, within a specified district, possessing sanitary powers,—as a necessary result, they can confer upon such board the power to pass all needful rules and ordinances to carry out the purposes of such creation. *a*

And the same rule has become the settled policy of this state by its repeated statutes, and the adjudications thereon. "It is

a Coe v. Shultz, 47 Barb. 64; Cooper v. Shultz, 32 How. Pr. 107.

right that this police sanitary power should exist somewhere, though large and discretionary powers are conferred by the legislature. If the civil authorities were obliged to wait the slow progress of the prosecution, the evil arising from nuisances, and from pestilential diseases, would present an alarming condition of things. *a* Our statutes abound with laws of this character. The constitution of the state, is to be resorted to, not to see what powers are conferred upon the legislature, but what have been withheld by the people. The legislature can provide such agencies for the administration of the law, and the maintenance of public order, and especially in regard to the police, and of security to the life and the health of its citizens, as it shall judge suitable, where no prohibition, expressly made, or necessarily implied, is found in the constitution. *b* As the police and sanitary powers were possessed by municipal corporations at common law, it is believed, that without any legislation conferring the authority, they could regulate by proper ordinances and by-laws, the manner of carrying on any trade or business within the municipality so far as to prevent monopolies; the sale of unfit commodities; and insure proper conduct of those who practice it; prevent slaughter houses and the slaughtering of animals, tallow chandlers, and the like, within the walls, or certain limits of a city. *c*

Puffendorf informs us that this law of necessity is an exception to all human ordinances and constitutions, and that therefore it gives a right of doing many things otherwise forbidden. *d* Perhaps from this idea, originated the common expression, "that necessity knows no law." Be this as it may, it is certain, that even this law of necessity, is still subject to the law of reason, and subject to control. If in the exercise of this power, it should be so carelessly and negligently exercised, as to produce an injury, there can be no doubt, the persons exercising it would be held responsible, by that old and well established maxim of the common law, that a person using his own natural rights, is subjected to such a restricted exercise of them as not thereby to occasion injury to another. The exercise of this right of overrulling necessity is

a Van Wormer v. The Mayor of Albany, 15 Wend. 264.

b People v. Draper, 15 N. Y. 533.

c Willcock on Municipal Corporations, 141.   *d* B. 2, ch. 6.

also called the exercise of a natural right which belongs to every individual, not conferred by law, but tacitly excepted from human codes,*a* and is governed by the same rules and maxims of common law, but when duly and discreetly exercised for the relief, protection or safety of the many, no liability attaches to those who exercise it.

It may therefore be regarded as a settled principle, growing out of the nature of an organized society that every holder of property, however absolute and unqualified may be his title, holds it under the implied liability that his use of it shall not be injurious to the equal enjoyment of others having an equal right to the enjoyment of their property; nor injurious to the rights of the community. And as has been said, when treating of the right of eminent domain, all property of the state is derived, directly or indirectly, from the government, and held subject to those general regulations which are necessary to the common good and general welfare. Rights of property, like all other social and conventional rights, are subject to such reasonable limitations in their enjoyment, as shall prevent them from being injurious, and to such reasonable restraints and regulations established by law, as the legislature, under the governing and controlling power vested in them by the constitution, may think necessary and expedient.

All legislative power being vested in the legislature, except such as is therein prohibited, they possess, under that authority, all power to make, ordain and establish all manner of wholesome and reasonable laws, statutes and ordinances, either with penalties or without, not repugnant to the constitution as they shall judge to be for the good and welfare of the state, and of the citizens thereof.*b*

It may now be regarded as the law of this state, settled by its highest court, that there are cases, notwithstanding this constitutional protection, in which the property or rights of individuals may be justly sacrificed to the necessities of others, where neither the state, as a whole, nor the public, in a general sense of that term, may have any interest in such a sacrifice. This may be seen in the cases of imminent peril referred to, when the right of

a Russel v. Mayor, of N. Y., 2 Denio 474 ; Mayor of N. Y. v. Lord, 17 Wend. 297.
b Commonwealth v. Alger, 7 Cush. 53.

self defence, or the protection of life or property, authorizes the sacrifice of other and less valuable property. Among the instances, given by the court, by way of illustration, are the throwing overboard goods in a storm, and the pulling down of houses to prevent the spreading of a conflagration. *a*

This, says the court, is a natural right, arising from inevitable, and pressing necessity; when of two immediate evils, one *must* be chosen,—the *less*, is voluntarily inflicted, in order to avoid the greater. Under such circumstances, the general and natural law of all civilized nations, recognized and ratified by the express decisions of our common law, authorizes the destruction of property by any citizen, without his being subject to any right of recovery against him by the owner. The agent in such destruction, whether in protection of his own rights, or those of others which may be accidentally under his safeguard, acts from good motives and for a justifiable end; so that against him, the sufferer has no rightful claim. But the loser may have an equitable right of compensation against those who have benefited by his loss in the preservation of their property. In Marine losses of this nature the common law has been able to establish a just rule of compensation and assessment; and the same principle, so far as it is possible to apply it, would be equally equitable in similar losses by land.

But as to most of these cases, from the impossibility or extreme difficulty of ascertaining the parties benefited, or protected from loss, and of settling the average proportions of the loss between them, by any general rule, the sufferer is commonly left without legal remedy. Thus, those who, whether magistrates or private citizens, under the pressure of inevitable danger, and to prevent a greater calamity, find themselves compelled to destroy the effects of others, are not, and ought not to be adjudged trespassers, although they do not act for the state or for the public, but merely for the service of some few of their neighbors, or fellow citizens, and have thus inflicted involuntary injury upon some, to prevent a much greater calamity falling upon others. *b* This injustice however to individuals whose property is so destroyed, can be corrected, as it should be, by proper legislation.

a Stone v. Mayor, of N. Y. 25 Wend., 174.
b Id. 175 ; The Saltpetre case, 12 Coke 13.

We have no general statute in this state, regulating the exercise of this power, and but a local law for the city of New York. *a* This statute it was held, was a mere regulation of the common law right of any person to destroy property in the case of immediate and overwhelming necessity to prevent the ravages of fire or pestilence. "Statutes of this description merely appoint a municipal agent, to judge of the emergency, and direct the performance of acts which any individual might do at his peril, without any stat-- ute at all." *b* It will be more convenient in this chapter to call this power, *the police power.*

It was well said, in our highest court, *c* that "the police power, is of necessity, despotic in its character, commensurate with the sovereignty of the state; and individual rights of property beyond the express constitutional limits, must yield to its exercise. And in emergencies, it may be exercised to the destruction of property, without compensation to the owner, and even without the formality of an investigation. It is upon this principle that health and quarantine laws are established; that a building is blown up to arrest a conflagration in a populous town; that a public market is purged of infectious articles; that merchandize on ship board infested with pestilence, is cast into the deep, and public nuisances are abated. It is the public exigency, which demands the summary destruction, upon the maxim, that the safety of society is the paramount law. It is the application of the personal right or principle of self preservation to the body politic."

It was held in our Court of Chancery, *d* in 1835, and has never since been questioned, that the legislature are the sole judges as to the expediency of making police regulations interfering with the natural rights of our citizens, which regulations are not prohibited by the constitution.

We have been examining this question simply as a question of power. It is no purpose of this work to discuss the justice or equity of a constitutional or a statute provision. It might even be defended in most instances, upon the ground that it was not even

a 2 R. L. of 1813, p. 368.

b Per. Comstock J. in Wymhamer v. the People, 13 N. Y. 402.

c Id. 451.

d Varick v. Smith, 5 Paige, 160.

unjust to the individual. Take the case of a spreading conflagration. If the necessity is shown to be such, that the property itself would otherwise have been destroyed, the proprietor suffers no injustice by its police destruction, and the security of the many is promoted. As a question of power, it must be regarded in this state, to be settled, and founded upon principles which are above and beyond the reach of constitutional restriction. It is the plain and simple principle of preservation of life and property in cases of iminent hazard, by the sacrifice of that which is less valuable, and which, from the very exigency of the case, must be left to the decision and determination of the moment.

Blackstone defines this power of public *police* or *economy*, " as the due regulation and domestic order of the kingdom, whereby individuals of the state, like members of a well regulated and well governed family, are bound to conform their general behavior to the rules of propriety, good neighborhood, and good manners; and to be decent, industrious and inoffensive in their respective stations." *a* " This police power of the state," says Ch. J. Redfield, *b* extends to the protection of the lives, limbs, health, comfort, and quiet of all persons, and the protection of all property within the state. It must of course be within the range of legislative action, to define the mode and manner in which, every one may so use his own, as not to injure others. And it has been held that even the corporation of the city of New York, possessed a police power so to order the use of private property in the city, as to prevent its proving pernicious to the citizens generally." *c* " A contrary doctrine, would strike at the root of all police regulations. Every right, from an absolute ownership in property, down to a mere easement, is purchased and held subject to the restriction, that it shall be so exercised as not to injure others. Though at the time, it be remote and inoffensive, the purchaser is bound to know at his peril, that it may become otherwise, and that it must yield to laws and regulations and remedies for the suppression of nuisances." Corporations, enjoy the prerogatives of government to a prescribed extent. Among these, is the power to pass by laws, regulating the police power.

a 4 Black. Com. 162.   *b* Thorpe v. R. & B. R. R. Co., 27 Vt. R. 149.
c Stuyvesant v. Mayor of New York, 7 Cow. 604; Hart v. Mayor of Albany, 9 Wend. 593.

The subject of the police power of the state, has recently been a subject of interesting and of extended discussion, and the courts have, to a certain extent, settled some important propositions in relation thereto; among which are the following:

1. "It is within the constitutional authority of the legislature to establish new civil divisions of the state, embracing in the districts so created, several towns, cities or counties, or such portions thereof as may be deemed appropriate for the general purposes of civil administration."

2. "The organization for *police* purposes, of districts not co-terminus with others recognized by the constitution, is not inconsistent with the continuance of such antecedent civil divisions, for every general purpose prescribed in the organic law."

3. "The police powers, exercised in the towns, cities and counties, respectively, were vested in the local authorities by legislation, and not by irrevocable constitutional grant."

4. "The legislature has authority to arrange the distribution of these powers, as the public exigencies may require; apportioning them to local jurisdictions, to such extent as the law-making power deems appropriate, and committing the exercise of the residue, to officers appointed, as it may see fit."

5. "This is a continuing. legislative power, in virtue of which, from time to time, as occasion may require, jurisdiction committed to the towns, cities or counties, may be resumed and vested in other authorities appointed by the state governments."

6. "The state has an interest in the repression of disorder, and the maintenance of peace and security in every locality within its limits; and if, from exceptional cases, the public good requires that legislation, either permanent, or temporary, be directed towards any particular locality, whether consisting of one county or several counties, it is within the discretion of the legislature to apply such legislation, as, in its judgment, the exigency of the case may require; and it is the sole judge of the existence of such causes." *a*

These propositions were laid down in a case wherein the opinion of the court, the act was one, in which the ends it sought to attain, and the efficiency of the agencies it sought to organize, was

a People v. Shepherd, 36 N. Y. 286; People v. Draper, 15 N. Y. 544.

for the preservation of order ; the protection of person and property ; the detection and arrest of culprits ; and the punishment and prevention of crime.

It is a power, which like all other powers, may be abused. With this, however, and with hardships and injustice, we have nothing to do, in this work. The people, by their representatives, must guard these abuses as best they may. Nor is it needful to say, that this power is confined in its exercise, to the principle, that the use for which it is taken, is strictly, what is called public use ; nor attempt to draw a line that shall distinguish between public and private uses. The preservation of the life of a citizen, is a matter of public interest, much more, of many citizens. The arresting of a devastating fire, or plague or other calamity, is also a matter of public interest ; and yet, in the first instance, it might seem to affect only private individuals. It may be, that in the one case, an overwhelming necessity would require the taking of the life of another citizen which is also a matter of public interest ; and in the other case, the same necessity might require the destruction of private property. In the first case it is the sacrifice of one life, for the saving of many lives ; in the other the sacrifice of the property of one for the necessary protection of the property of many.

Looking at this power, then, as it seems to be a power conceded, by our own, and other states, whether it is exercised as it exists at common law, tolerated by the constitution, or as regulated by legislative enactments, not inhibited by the constitution, we may regard it as a settled principle, growing out of the nature of well-ordered civil society, that every holder of property, and rights of property, however absolute and unqualified may be his title, holds it under the implied liability that it may be so regulated that its use shall not be injurious to the equal enjoyment of others, having an equal right to the enjoyment of their property, nor injurious to the rights of the community. All property is to be regarded as held by the citizen subject to those general regulations which are necessary to the common good and general welfare. *a*

This power, however, differs from the right of eminent domain. The latter, is the right of government to take and appropriate private property to public use when the public exigency requires it ;

a Commonwealth v. Alger, 7 Cushing 85.

which can be done only on condition of providing a reasonable compensation therefor. This power, is *the police power*, which is subject to no such condition, "It is a power much easier to perceive and realize the existence of, and to learn its source, and the principle of its power, than to define its boundaries, or prescribe limits to its exercise. There are many cases where such a power is exercised by well-ordered governments, and where its fitness is so obvious that every reasonable mind will acknowledge its justice. Under this power are enacted statutes which prohibit the storage of powder within cities, and near to habitations and public highways; to restrain and regulate the erection of wooden buildings within cities and populous towns; to prohibit buildings from being used as hospitals for contagious diseases; for the preventing the carrying on of noxious or offensive trades; to prohibit the erection or raising of dams which may cause stagnant water to stand or spread over lands near inhabited towns, villages or cities, thereby causing noxious exhalations, injurious to health and dangerous to life. *a*

"The prohibition in such case, though it may greatly diminish the profits to the owner, it does not give him a right to compensation for its use. It is not such an appropriation to public use of private property as comes within the power of eminent domain, and the right of compensation to the proprietor. Doubtless the proprietor of a vacant lot in a city, might obtain a better percentage by way of rent, by erecting a wooden, than a brick or stone tenement. The owner of a warehouse could store his own powder with less expense of transportation in his city building, than in a place remote; a landlord might let his building for a small pox hospital or slaughter house for an increased rent. They are restrained by this power; not because the public take or use it for any benefit or profit to themselves, but because the use would be noxious, and contrary to the maxim "*Sic utere tuo, ut alienum non laedas.*" These are a few of the many and various cases, where this police power may be exercised. ²

a Id. 86; Hart v. Mayor, 9 Wend. 571 ; People v. Draper, 25 Barb. 374 ; Commonwealth v. Tewksbury, 11 Met. 55, 57 ; Baker v. City of Boston, 12 Pick. 184; Mayor, &c. v. Miln, 11 Peters 102, 132,

NOTE 3.—It is settled law that it is competent for the legislature to regulate the sale and disposition of liquors. Such is the effect of the "Act to regulate the sale

This police power, which, as has been said, is inherent in every government, and not restricted by our constitutions, can be brought into active exercise for the protection of the citizen by the sovereign power in all needful emergencies. Every sovereign state possesses within itself, absolute and unlimited legislative power, except so far as it is prohibited by the fundamental law. There is no arbiter in such case, beyond the state itself, to determine what legislation is just. Whatever therefore is so declared, by the ultimate power of a state, as there can be no appeal, must, in view of the law, be taken to be just and right. By the exercise of this police power, the legislature may protect the mass of citizens by the control of existing corporations, such for instance, as railroads, in protecting of the lives, limbs, health, comfort, and quiet of all persons, and the protection of their property, against aggres-

of intoxicating liquors within the Metropolitan District of the State of New York," passed April 14, 1866. Therefore, the third section of the act is not unconstitutional, as tending to divest the owner of his property without due compensation. In the Matter of James DeVaucene, 31 How. Pr. R. 289. Nor is the act of 1866, creating the Metropolitan Board of Health of New York, unconstitutional, as conferring upon the board the right to deprive a citizen of his liberty or property without due process of law. Cooper v. Schultz, 32 How. Pr. R. 107. This was an act entitled "An act to create a Metropolitan Sanitary District and Board of Health therein, for the preservation of life and health, and to prevent the spread of disease," and it gave large powers to carry out the objects expressed in its title. The government, it was held, clearly possessed the power itself, for the safety and health of its citizens; and they could delegate this power to a proper body of men. The abatement of a nuisance is not the appropriation of private property to private use without the judgment of one's peers. It is the suppression of a thing declared to be illegal by the laws of the land, and which may be destroyed by any citizen, if done in such a manner as to invade no law of property, or for the preservation of the peace, and when where the law invests a public body with the power to do such an act, in express terms, by no rule of construction can such a law be held to be unconstitutional. Weil v. Schultz, 33 How. Pr. R. 7. Though the digging of a ditch upon the lands of a private owner, under the authority of the legislature, for the purpose of draining such land, and that of an adjoining proprietor, is, it has been held, a taking of property within article one, sections six and seven, of the constitution of this state, of 1846, and the act of the legislature, professing to authorize such taking void, where it does not provide for the payment of a just compensation to be ascertained by a jury, or by commissioners appointed by a court of record. People v. Nearing, 27 N. Y. 306. The mode of assessing and of apportioning the compensation and expenses of executing the work, however. upon those benefited thereby, is wholly within the discretion of the legislature. Id.

sion, and against what may be declared negligence, in the management of such corporations.

The maxim, which has been quoted, "*Sic utere tuo est alienum non laedas,*" is one of universal application, and it must, of course, be within the range of legislative action, to define the mode and the manner in which every one, (which includes railroads,) may so use his own as not to injure others. *a* So far as railroads are concerned, this police power is two-fold. 1. The police of the roads, which, in the absence of legislative control, the corporations themselves exercise over their operatives, and to some extent, over all who do business with them, or upon their grounds, through general statutes. And, 2. By the general police power of the state, by which persons and property are subjected to all kinds of reasonable restraints and burthens, in order to secure the general comfort, health and prosperity of the state.

Of the perfect right and authority to do this, no serious question ever was, and upon acknowledged principles, never can be made. So far as natural persons are concerned, it has not been doubted, and no good reason is perceived, why it should be doubted in the case of artificial persons. Upon this principle, the legislature may require, even of existing, as well as all future railroad corporations, to maintain cattle guards at all crossings, and to erect and maintain fences and gates upon the sides of the road, and farm crossings; and to respond in damages for all cattle injured, or other damages for negligent omission of such structures; and this police power might doubtless be extended so as to include the supervision of track, tending switches, running upon the time of other trains, running a road with a single track, using improper rails, not using proper precaution by way of safety beams, in case of the breaking of axles, the number of brakemen upon a train, with reference to the number of cars, employing intemperate or incompetent engineers and servants, running beyond a given rate of speed, and all kindred and similar protections to any extent, may be the subject of legislation; most of which have been, and are now, subjects of judicial determination. *b* In the state of Connecticut,

a Thorp v..Rutland & Burlington R. R. Co., 27 Vt. R. 149.

b Thorp v. R. & B. R. R. Co., 27 Vt. 150; Hyeman v. West R. R. Corporation, 16 Barb. 353, S. C. 13 N. Y. 1.

the statute *a* requires the trains upon all their railroads, to come to a stand before passing a drawbridge, and not permit a train to pass a switch, unless there be a switchman standing at the junction with a white flag, &c. And in the state of Massachusetts, the same provision is made, (among other regulations,) before crossing another railroad. *b* All this, is by virtue of the police power of the state.

The legislature may, no doubt, prohibit railroads from carrying freight, if they deemed it prejudicial to the public interests ; and probably, might make them insurers of the lives of their passengers. The statutes giving relatives a right to recover damages when any person is killed, is one step in that direction, and has wrought an important change in the law in that regard.

So too, it is believed, that under this police power, the legislature might with perfect justice, if sound policy was thought to require it, make towns and counties severally responsible for damages, afterward arising, from robbery, or other crimes committed whereby its citizens, or others, should be subjected to loss of property. Indeed, statutes have been passed to this end, in this state, for the payment by counties, and cities, for real or personal property destroyed or injured in consequence of any mob or riot occurring in such county or city. *c* This is taking private property neither by right of eminent domain, or the taxing power.

In Massachusetts, towns are made liable to damages for loss of life or property by reason of their highways being out of repair. *d* And other states have enacted like statutes under the same police power. In Connecticut, *e* New Hampshire, *f* and Rhode Island, *g* similar enactments have been made by the legislature, and it is believed in other states, like statutes exist.

The statutes regulating division fences between the proprietors of adjoining lands, and requiring them to be of a given height and quality ;—restraining wild, or vicious domestic animals dangerous to persons or property, and to compensate the persons and owners of

a General Statutes, 201, §§ 540, 541.
b General Statutes, 362, § 93.
c Laws of N. Y. of 1855, Ch. 428; Stone v. Mayor, &c., 25 Wend. 181.
d General Statutes 247, §§ 21, 22.
e General Statutes 493, § 6.
f Compiled Statutes 149, § 1.   *g* Rev. St. 125, § 14.

property for injuries ;—to destroy noxious weeds ;—requiring railroads to ring a bell or blow a whistle in approaching and crossing highways and streets ; and creating liability to penalties for neglect of such requirements. All these, and numerous other enactments of the legislature coming fairly under the police power, are wise, and reasonable, and legal provisions, to protect the public against danger to their persons, or to loss of property ; indeed the instances and illustrations are too numerous to attempt a recital. Those given, will suffice to establish the power and character of them.

The limit to the exercise of the police power, can only be this : the regulation must have reference to the comfort—the safety—or the welfare of society ; it must not be in conflict with the provisions of the constitution. And in case of corporations, it must not, under mere pretense of regulation, take from them, any of the essential rights their charter confers. a This is not intended as a denial of the power of the legislature to alter, modify or repeal a charter in certain cases.

One of the most important of these illustrations of the police power under state constitutions, is that of regulations affecting commerce. Among these, quarantine regulations, and health laws of every description, will readily suggest themselves, and these are, or may be sometimes, carried to the extent of ordering the destruction of private property when infected with disease, or otherwise dangerous. b These regulations have not been questioned as to their authority. The right to pass inspection laws, and to levy duties, so far as may be necessary to render them effectual, is an express power by the constitution of the United States. c

The principle involved under this point, is well and quite fully expressed by the supreme court of this state, d in giving construction to a statute, conferring authority upon harbor masters, to regulate and station all ships and vessels lying in the East and North rivers, within the limits of the city of New York. It was said, "this statute was passed for the preservation of good order in the harbor. It appears to be a necessary police regulation, and

a Cooley on Const. Lim. 577.
b Cooley on Const. Lim. 584.
c Art. 1, section 10.
d Venderbitt v. Adams 7 Cow. R. 348 to 353.

not void, although it may interfere, in some measure, with individual rights. The harbor master had jurisdiction under the act over all private wharves. They were subject to all police regulations. The power exercised in this case is essentially necessary for the purpose of protecting all concerned. It is not,—in the legitimate sense of the term,—a violation of any right; but the exercise of a power indispensably necessary, where an extensive commerce is carried on." " Police regulations are legal and binding, because for the general benefit; and do not proceed to the length of impairing any right in the proper sense of that term." " The sovereign power in a community, therefore, may, and ought to prescribe the manner of exercising individual rights over property. It is for the better protection and enjoyment of that absolute dominion which the individual claims. The power rests on the implied right and duty of the supreme power to protect all by statutory regulations, so that on the whole, the benefit of all is promoted. Every regulation in a city may and does, in some sense, limit and restrict the absolute right that existed previously. But this is not considered as an injury. So far from it, the individual, as well as others, is supposed to be benefited. It may then be said, that such a power is incident to every well regulated society; and without which it could not well exist."

A case is then supposed, where the legislature should authorize the grant of a road through the wild lands of A. without his consent; a right that has been assumed and acted upon ever since we became an independent government. No compensation is allowed in such cases to the owner. Can he defeat the operation of such a law, by saying his private right is invaded? Such a law, (it is then said,) is constitutional and obligatory; because in many cases, necessary for the public benefit, and not deemed injurious to the individual whose land is taken. a

" The line of distinction between that which constitutes an interference with commerce, and that which is a police regulation, is sometimes, exceedingly dim and shadowy, and it is not to be wondered at, that learned jurists differ when endeavoring to classify the cases which arise." b

a See also case of the owners of the Brig Gray v. Owners of Ship John Fraser, 20 How. U. S. R. 187, 8. b Cooley on Lim. 586.

Congress, under the federal constitution, has the undoubted power to regulate commerce, and whenever it is pleased to exert its power upon the subjects so conferred, it is probable the state power is excluded and even where this power is not exercised by the general government, the state power is not always unlimited. This power was attempted by the state of Maryland, requiring all importers of foreign goods to take out a license, for which they should pay $50 to the state, and in case of neglect or refusal, to subject the importer to certain penalties and forfeitures. This question was brought into the federal court. *a* The act of the state legislature was held to be repugnant to that provision in the constitution of the United States, which empowers congress to regulate commerce with foreign nations, and among the several states, &c. That the authority given by congress to import, included the power to sell the thing imported. The Maryland act denied to the importer the right of using the privilege he had purchased of the United States, until he should have made another purchase of it from the state of Maryland. This was not such a police power as the state could exercise.

So too, in a case, in which the state of New York, attempted by its legislature to exercise this police power by imposing taxes upon alien passengers arriving at the port of New York, *b* it was held by the judges of the federal court *c* that this statute was in conflict with the provisions of the constitution of the United States. But in another case, quite difficult to distinguish from this, a statute of this state which required the master of every vessel arriving in the port of New York, from any foreign port, or from a port of any of the other of the states of the Union, to make a report in writing, containing the names, ages, and last legal settlement of every person who shall have been on board the vessel commanded by him during the voyage, &c., to be stated in the report under penalties prescribed in the act, was held to be within the police power of the state, and not in conflict with the provisions of the constitution of the United States. *d* It was also held, that

a Brown v. State of Maryland, 12 Wheat 419, 445.
b 1 Rev. Stat. 445.
c Smith v. Turner, 7 How. U. S. R. 283
d Mayor, &c., v. Miln, 11 Peters 102.

persons are not the subject of commerce, and not being imported goods, they do not fall within the reasoning founded upon the construction of a power given to congress, "to regulate commerce," and the prohibition of the states from imposing a duty on imported goods.

"A state has the same undeniable and unlimited jurisdiction over all persons and things within its territorial limits, as any foreign nation, when that jurisdiction is not surrendered to or restrained by the constitution of the United States. It is not only the right, but the bounden and solemn duty of a state, to advance the safety, happiness, and prosperity of its people, and to provide for its general welfare, by any and every act of legislation which it may deem to be conducive to these ends ; where the power over the particular subject or the manner of its exercise, are not surrendered or restrained by the constitution of the United States. All those powers which relate merely to municipal legislation, or which may more properly be called *internal police*, are not surrendered or restrained ; and consequently, in relation to these, the authority of a state is complete, unqualified, and exclusive."

" It is at all times difficult to define any subject with precision and accuracy. It is emphatically so in relation to a subject so diversified and various (if not conflicting) as this. It may, however, be said, that every law comes within the regulation of *police*, which concerns the welfare of the whole people of a state, or any individual within it, whether it relates to their rights or their duties ; whether it respects them as men, or as citizens of the state in their public or private relations ; whether it relates to persons or property, of the whole people of a state, or of any individual within it ; and whose operation is within the territorial limits of the state, and upon the persons and things within its jurisdiction." This may be exemplified by the right of every state to punish persons, who commit offences against its criminal laws within its territory.

So then, it must follow, that while a state is acting within the scope of its legitimate power, as to the end to be attained, it may use whatever means, being appropriate to the end, it may think fit, although such means may be the same, or so nearly the same, as scarcely to be distinguished from those adopted by congress acting under a different power; subject, only, to this limitation, that in the event of collision, the law of the state must yield to the law of congress.

The line which separates the regulations of commerce, from those of state police, is sometimes not so distinct as to prevent conflict of opinion; but fortunately for the public security, there is the conservative power of the judiciary to determine the right. One of the questions so approaching this line, is that of the inspection laws of the states, which are claimed to be regulations of commerce.

It was well said by the supreme court of the United States, a "that inspection laws may have a remote and considerable influence on commerce, will not be denied; but that a power to regulate commerce. is the source from which the right to pass them is derived, cannot be admitted. The object of inspection laws, is to improve the quality of articles produced by the labor of a country; to fit them for exportation; or, it may be, for domestic use. They act upon the subject before it becomes an article of foreign commerce, or of commerce among the states, and prepare it for that purpose. They form a portion of that immense mass of legislation, which embraces everything within the territory of a state, not surrendered to the general government: all of which can be most advantageously exercised by the states themselves. Inspection laws, quarantine laws, health laws of every description, as well as laws for regulating the internal commerce of a state, and those which respect turnpike roads, ferries, &c., are component parts of this mass."

"No direct general power over these objects is granted to congress; and consequently they remain to state legislation. If the legislative power of the Union can reach them, it must be for national purposes; it must be where the power is expressly given for a special purpose, or is clearly incidental to some power which is expressly given. It is obvious, that the government of the Union, in the exercise of its express powers, that, for example of "regulating commerce with foreign nations and among the states," may use means that may also be employed by a state, in the exercise of its acknowledged powers; that, for example, of regulating

a Gibbons v. Ogden, 9 Wheat. 203, 204, &c.

commerce within the state. If congress license vessels to sail from one port to another in the same state, the act is supposed to be, necessarily incidental to the power expressly granted to congress, and implies no claim of a direct power to regulate the purely internal commerce of a state, or to act directly on its system of police '

"So a state in passing laws on subjects acknowledged to be within its control, and with a view to those subjects shall adopt a measure of the same character with one which congress may adopt, it does not derive its authority from the particular power which has been granted, but from some other, which remains with the state, and may be executed by the same means."

"All experience shows, that the same measures, or measures scarcely distinguishable from each other, may flow from distinct powers; but this does not prove that the powers themselves are identical. Although the means used in their execution may sometimes approach each other so nearly as to be confounded, there are other situations, in which they are sufficiently distinct to establish their individuality."

"In our complex system, presenting the rare and difficult scheme of one general government, whose action extends over the whole, but which possesses only certain enumerated powers; and of numerous state governments which retain and exercise all powers not delegated to the Union, contests respecting power must arise. Were it even otherwise, the measures taken by the respective governments to execute their acknowledged powers, would often be of the same description, and might sometimes interfere. This however does not prove that the one is exercising, or has a right to exercise the powers of the other." *

NOTE 4.—Article 1, section 8, of the constitution of the United States, which grants to congress authority to regulate commerce with foreign nations and among the several states, is not so exclusive as to prohibit the states from legislating upon the subject of pilots, if congress has not seen fit to legislate upon that same subject. Stilwell v. Raynor, 1 Daley, 47; 12 How. U. S. R. 299. And in absence of federal legislation, the states have a right to protect their commerce, by exercising on the neighboring seas, the power accorded for that purpose to every maritime people. Cisco v. Roberts, 36 N. Y. 292, and cases cited. The regulations of port pilotage, stand substantially upon the same footing with our quarantine laws. It is the right, and duty of the state, by appropriate legislation to guard the public health, and the security of general commerce, and to provide

But this is bordering upon the line of the conflict of laws, which it is no purpose of this work to enter upon. The cases cited in the note, will be found in their reasoning to have been quite exhaustive of the subject, and are full of learning on the question of the extent of the police power of the states. It is more our object to exhibit the existence of the police power in the state, as a necessary and useful power, and to defend it against the charge often made as to its despotic, oppressive and unconstitutional character, than to attempt to enumerate the multiplied subjects which are included within the power.

Among the subjects included in this police power, is that of requiring the observance of the first day of the week as the christian Sabbath, as to which the statutes of the state have provided penalties for their violation. It neither interferes with the religious belief of any citizen, nor with any doctrine of religious faith or practice. It is no violation of the constitution which allows the free enjoyment of free profession and worship, without discrimi-

against the dangers to which every maritime people are exposed by intercepting and averting them on the sea, without the bounds of exclusive territorial dominion. Gilmore v. Philadelphia, 3 Wall. 730. The states have always exercised this power, and from the nature and objects of the two systems of government, they must always continue to exercise it, subject however in all cases, to the paramount authority of congress, whenever the power of the states shall be exerted within the sphere of the commercial power which belongs to the nation.

The stat s may exercise concurrent or independent power in all cases but three. 1st. Where the power is lodged exclusively in the federal constitution. 2d. Where it is given to the United States, and prohibited to the states. 3d. Where from the nature and subjects of the power, it must necessarily be exercised by the national government exclusively. Houston v. Moore, 5 Wheat. 49. It is no objection to distinct substantive powers, that they may be exercised on the same subject. It is not possible to fix definitely their respective boundaries. In some instances their action becomes blended; in some the action of the state limits or displaces the action of the nation; in others the action of the state is void, because it seeks to reach objects beyond the limits of state authority. Gilmore v. Philadelphia, 3 Wall. 730. So, an act of the legislature of New York providing for the appointment of harbor masters in the city of New York, and their fees, &c., does not conflict with the provisions of the United States constitution giving power to congress to collect duties and regulate commerce. Benedict v. Vanderbilt, 25 How. Pr. R. 209. But, an act of the same state imposing a special tax on every sale made by public auction, &c., of merchandize imported from any place beyond the Cape of Good Hope, is unconstitutional and void. People v. Moring, 47 Barb. 642.

nation, or preference, to all mankind. It creates no legal religion in the state. The christian religion is recognized as a part of the common law of this state. The observance of this day, does not interfere with any natural right, or with the equal right of any citizen to entertain any other belief. a It merely restrains the people from secular pursuits and practices which the legislature deem hurtful to the morals and good order of society. This is within the legislative power. So is the right to declare void all contracts made on that day. It does not touch private property, or impair its value.

The christian religion, as a part of the common law of England, can be traced back by positive legislation, (if legislation it may be called,) to the day of the Saxon Kings. The code of King Alfred commences with an enactment of the ten commandments; it recites the advent and passion of our Savior; the founding of the church; the mission of the Apostles, and the letter issued from the church at Jerusalem, recorded in the fifteenth chapter of Acts, verse twenty-three &c. To this summary was added the following remarkable words: " From this, our doom, a man may remember, that he judge every one righteously ; he need no other doom book." These edicts, like most of what are called the early statutes of England, became in time the common law, and continued to be such, down to the time of our American colonization, and we borrowed it from thence, and made it, the ground work of our own ; and afterwards adopted the English common law by our written constitutions, although we rejected all union between church and state, as a part of the fundamental organization.

Though in the political organization of the national and state governments, there was a complete severance between the organized church, and the organized state, there was no intended negative of the doctrines or precepts of the christian religion; or an intended or implied adoption therein, to an equality, of Atheism, Paganism, or any kind of infidelity with the christian religion ; on the contrary, not only in the Declaration of Independence, which was the basis of our fundamentals, but in the whole administration of the law, there is recognized an immortality of the soul, and the retribution of a conscious hereafter, an all powerful, just, and holy

a Lindenmuller v. The People, 33 Barb. 573.

God who will punish evil doers in this life, and in a life to come, with the penalties for sin.   This is also recognized by its adding its sanction of oaths in the administration of justice, and in the administration of governmental affairs.   Such oaths assume the retributions of an hereafter by the God of our holy religion, for a violation of the sacred obligations of them.   In the taking of such oaths by one whose condition requires it, there is placed before him, and he takes upon himself, to deal with the dread realities of a future and unseen world; it commits him to an acknowledgment that God is, that He sees, hears and knows the secret thoughts and intents of his heart; "and that He, will by no means clear the guilty."

In the state of Ohio, under their constitution, it is denied that the christian religion more than any other, is a part of the common law of the state, though they have a statute prohibiting labor on the Sabbath day.   The courts hold this statute to be a mere municipal or *police* regulation, *a* and in Pennsylvania and South Carolina, their Sabbath laws seem to be sustained on the same ground, *b* but, by the courts in New York all secular transactions are held to be violations of statute and void as against public policy. *c*

While therefore, we find that though nearly every state have enacted statutes against the desecration of, and for the quiet observance of what is called the "Lords Day," they do not all agree upon the basis of their enactment.   Those states that deny that these laws were passed out of respect to the christian religion, are disposed to charge that idea as puritanical, or what is more odious, as the offspring of the fanatical persecutions which gave the holy inquisition such horrid force, "and placed the civil and religious liberty, and the lives of nations and men, at the mercy of the bloodiest power that ever inflicted misery upon the human race." *d* Whatever may be the declared policy of the states through its courts, as to these enactments, it can hardly be denied, that the recognition by the legislatures of states of one of the essential features of our religion, to "Remember the Sabbath day to keep it

a Bloom v. Richards, 22 Ohio, 387.

b Specht v. Commonwealth, 8 Barr. 312; Charleston v. Benjamin, 2 Strob. Law, R. 508.

c Watts v. Van Ness, 1 Hill, 76; Smith v. Wilcox, 19 Barb. 581.

d Specht v. Commonwealth, Supra, Penn. R. 1848.

holy; six days shalt thou labor and do all thy work, but the seventh day is the Sabbath of the Lord thy God ; in it thou shalt not do any work;" has had its influence in securing the enactment of such statutes. Nor does the policy of those states stop at that point. The existence of a God; of a hereafter, and a retribution,—pervades the whole administration of the law. These Sunday laws, the state in its administration of justice calling to its aid the solemn sanctions of religion in the use of oaths, still stamps this religion as an integral part of its policy. It is believed that no state would be willing to see these restraints removed from its policy. The social fabric could not endure without them.

So too under this power is the construction of highways by the state, or by others under their authority, with proper police provisions for their regulation and the government of persons using them ; —as to the rate of speed with which they may be traveled, and which way passengers meeting or passing each other shall turn; to prohibit nuisances thereon; to prevent cattle and other animals from runing at large thereon; to regulate the navigation and use of public waters,—to prevent the sale of poisonous drugs,—to require dogs to be muzzled at certain periods,—to prevent the keeping and sale of unwholsome provisions; to regulate markets, and standards of weights and measures; to prohibit the keeping, exhibition, and sale of indecent books and pictures, and the universally acknowledged power to pass laws to punish crimes and misdemeanors.

This enumeration may suffice, though it is but a portion of the instances in which this police power may be and has been exerted. nor can it be deemed necessary to cite authority to sustain the principle upon this enumeration of powers.

CHAPTER XV.

OF CONSTITUTIONAL PROTECTION TO PERSONAL PROPERTY.

In the three preceding chapters, we have examined, under the right of eminent domain, of the taxing power, and the police power of the government, how the superior rights of the government to property, may be called into exercise, to the deprivation of the individuals of their private estates,—and the theory, by which, it is supposed, the individual receives his compensation. We have but incidentally discussed the constitutional provisions, state and national, that private property shall not be taken without *due process of law.* Our examination, in that respect, has been limited to such taking, and what was regarded as due process of law under the right of eminent domain.

We have already shown (in a former chapter) from the provisions of the various state constitutions, that the same constitutional intent of protection is secured to the citizen by language so nearly identical, as not to change the interpretation, viz: "by due process of law," "by due course of law," "by the law of the land," &c. So the definitions in reported cases, though they differ in phraseology, and are more extended or limited, according to the views of jurists who have given expression to them, do not really effect any conflict on the question of intent.

It was held in this state, in the Supreme Court,*a* "that to work a change of property from one private person to another, by due process of law, some proceeding must be had in a court of justice or before magistrates. At least that the legislature should have no power to deprive one of his property, and transfer it to another, by enacting a bargain between them, unless it be in the hands of the latter, as a trust for public use." The meaning of these words was equally well expressed by Mr. Webster in his argument before the Supreme Court of the United States,*b* in which he said: "By the law

a In the Matter of John and Cherry St., 19 Wend. 676–7.
b Dartmouth College v. Woodward, 4 Wheat. 581, 582.

of the land is most clearly intended the general law;—a law which hears before it condemns; which proceeds upon inquiry, and renders judgment only after trial." The meaning is, that every citizen shall hold his life, liberty, property and immunities under the protection of the general rules which govern society. Everything which may pass under a form of enactment, is not, therefore, to be considered the law of the land. If this were so, acts of attainder, bills of pains and penalties, acts of confiscation, acts reversing judgments, and acts directly transferring one man's property to another, legislative judgments, decrees and forfeitures in all possible forms, would be the law of the land.

Such a strange construction, would render constitutional provisions of the highest importance completely inoperative and void. It would tend directly to establish the union of all powers in the legislature. There would be no general permanent law for courts to administer, or for men to live under. The administration of justice would be an empty form, an idle ceremony. Judges would sit to execute legislative judgments and decrees; not to declare the law or to administer the justice of the country.

So in the exposition of the same words in the national constitution, Mr. Justice Curtis said, a "The article is a restraint on the legislative, as well as on the executive, and judicial powers of the government, and cannot be so construed as to leave congress free to make any process, 'due process of law,' by its mere will." These words are found in *Magna Charta*, and have been copied into our national and state constitutions. As in the original royal charter, so in our own, they were intended to secure the individual from the arbitrary exercise of the powers of government, unrestrained by the establishment of the principles of private rights and distributive justice. b This seems to have settled down to be the good sense of mankind.

It has been claimed that this power is universal, not only in its application, but that the citizen under it is entitled to claim a trial by jury in all cases. But the cases of the right of trial by jury, being otherwise expressly provided for in the same constitution, it is not to be deemed as implied in this provision of *due process of law*.

a Murray's Lessees v. Hoboken Land Imp. Co., 18 How. 276.
b Bank of Columbia v. Okely, 4 Wheat. 144.

By the constitution of the United States, a speedy trial by an impartial jury, is secured in all criminal cases, *a* and by the constitution of this state, the trial by jury in all cases in which it had theretofore been used, is secured to remain inviolate forever; but a jury trial may be waived by the parties in all *civil* cases, in the manner to be prescribed by law. *b*

But there are exceptions to the general rule laid down in the cases we have referred to, that to pass title to property from one person to another, there must be the intervention of judicial proceedings so called. The cases of the taxing and police power, and perhaps the right of eminent domain, may be regarded as exceptions, and perhaps there are many other special cases. The general rule to which we have referred, and its general necessity, as a rule, does not preclude the legislature from establishing special rules, for a special or particular class of cases, which range themselves under some general and acknowledged head of legislative power, nor does the requirement of what is technically so called judicial action demand, in every case, a hearing in court. *c*

These cases, which are exceptions to the general rule, are, and should be looked upon with great jealousy by the courts, for fear of establishing a precedent that should look like encroaching upon constitutional securities. They generally relate to legislation as to interests or property to be acquired in future, and seldom or never as to existing interests. Sometimes they relate to the forms of administering justice by courts, or by officers specially appointed by statute to perform certain duties; powers which are incident to the exercise of this branch of the sovereign will, and which must ever be subject to the legislative will.

The line which distinguishes what are called the excepted cases from others, is so nice, and is so bordering upon those that are brought under the heads of right of eminent domain, the taxing and police powers, or under the acknowledged legislative power to change the form of remedies, that the ablest jurists, have been disposed to doubt the existence of even an exception at all. *d* For instance, a statute making it unlawful to sell intoxicating

a Art. 6.   *b* Art. 1. § 2.
c Cooley on Const. Lim. 355.
d Wynchamer v. The People, Per. Comstock, J. 13 N. Y. R. 386-387.

liquors or to keep them for sale, declaring them a nuisance, and authorizing public officers to abate the nuisance by its destruction, has been held to be unconstitutional as applicable to such liquors as were owned or kept at the time of the passage of the law. But it was intimated, *a* that it was competent for the legislature to pass an act containing like provisions to annihilate and destroy such property that might be acquired or created at any time after the passage of such an act. This, it is said, would be however, by virtue of the police power.

So too, the taking of wild lands of an individual for a public highway by the state, and by commissioners appointed by an act of the legislature, without giving compensation to the proprietor, has been held to be within the constitutional power of the legislature. But this is said, also, to come under the taxing power, and based upon the principle, that the owner receives an equivalent by the increased value of the adjoining lands.

"Nevertheless, in many cases and ways, remedial legislation may affect and control the disposition of property, and, in some cases, may change rights, give remedies, where none existed before, and even devest titles, in case the legal and equitable rights do not concur in the same person." *b* But it is believed that no reason of public policy will be sufficient to effect such changes or transfers of property where they operate on vested rights. *c*

It cannot be denied, that the legislature have power to pass an act, which, without acting directly upon its terms, destroys the remedy which a party may have at the time of its passage, or so embarrasses it, that the rights of the creditor under such legal remedies are substantially defeated. *d* It may frequently be difficult to draw the line, between acts affecting the remedy only, and those that are within the legitimate province of the state legislature, and such, as overstepping those bounds, substantially impair the obligation of antecedent contracts; and it is perhaps impracticable to lay down in language, a rule by which all such questions may be tried and determined.

But it is well established law, that the individual citizen with

a Id. 459.
b Cooley on Const. Limits, 357. *c* Id.
d Morse v. Gould, 11 N. Y. 287-291.

all his rights to protection, has no vested right in what is known in the law as, remedies, nor in any particular existing remedy. He has no such vested interest in the existing laws of the state, as precludes their amendment or repeal by the legislature; nor is there any implied obligation on the part of the state—to protect its citizens against incidental injury occasioned by changes in the law. Whatever belongs merely to the remedy, may be altered according to the will of the state, always provided, the alteration does not impair the obligation of the contract; but if a statute so changes the nature and extent of an existing remedy as materially to impair the rights and interests of the owner of property, it is just as much a violation of the constitutional provision, as if it directly overturned his rights and interests. *a* If the remedy does not impair the right or property itself, if it still leaves the party a substantial remedy according to the course of justice, as the right existed at the time of the passage of the statute, it does not impair the obligation of the contract, *b* nor will it be held to do so, merely because the new remedy is less efficient, less speedy, or less convenient than the old one. *c*

Among the class of statutes which have been held not to have impaired the contract, is that of the abolition of imprisonment for debt in this state, upon existing contracts. The power of confinement of the debtor, as a means of inducing him to perform, and punishment for nonperformance, was an efficient power, but the courts have held that imprisonment was no part of the contract; and to release the debtor from the liability to imprisonment did not impair the obligation. *d* A good remedy is still left, and the contract still remains in full force. So another statute of this state abolishing the right of distress for rent in arrear. Though this statute took away a part of the remedy existing at the time of making the leases, it was held to be no violation of this constitutional provision; and an express stipulation between the parties contained in the lease, that the lessor should have this remedy, did not prevent the legislature from abolishing it, because this was

a Brunson v. Kinzie, 1 How, U. S. R. 316; Green v. Biddle, 8 Wheat. 75-76
b Story v. Furman, 25 N. Y. 233; Van Rensselaer v. Snyder, 12 N. Y. 299-305
c Morse v. Gould, 11 N. Y. 281.
d Sturges v. Crowninshield, 4 Wheat. 200, 201.

a subject concerning which, it was not competent for the parties to contract in such a manner as to prohibit the exercise of legislative powers. *a* The court said, " this act provided a new remedy in the cases where the right of re-entry was reserved to enforce the collection of the debt due the landlord. This was an ordinary and proper exercise of legislative power, unless individuals by contract can perpetuate a legal remedy in spite of the legislature, which is absurd." And in another case, they said, " If this is a subject on which parties can contract, and if their contracts when made, become, by virtue of the constitution of the United States, superior to the power of the legislature, then it follows, that whatever at any time exists, as part of the machinery for the administration of justice, may be perpetrated, if the parties choose so to agree. That this can scarcely have been within the contemplation of the makers of the constitution, and that if it prevail as law, it will give rise to grave inconveniences, is quite obvious. Every such stipulation is in its own nature conditional upon the lawful continuance of the process. The state is no party to the contract. It is bound to afford adequate process for the enforcement of rights; but it has not tied its own hands as to the modes by which it will administer justice. Those, from necessity, belong to the supreme power to prescribe, and their continuance, is not the subject of contract between private parties."

So too, a statute of this state, which exempts a portion of a debtors property from liability to execution for debts, even existing debts, and further acts modifiing and increasing such exemptions, are not violations of the constitution, although they seem to diminish the security of the creditor. Chief Justice Taney in relation to that class of cases, said, *b* " Undoubtedly, a state may regulate at pleasure the modes of proceeding in its courts in relation to past contracts as well as future. It may for example, shorten the period of time within which claims shall be barred by the statute of limitations. It may, if it thinks proper, direct that the necessary implements of agriculture, or the tools of the mechanic, or articles of necessity in household furniture, shall, like wearing apparel, not be liable to execution or judgments. Regulations of this

a Van Rensselaer v. Snyder, 13 N. Y. 299; Conkey v. Hart, 14 N. Y. 22.
b Bronson v. Kenzie, 1 How. 315.

description have always been considered, in every civilized community, as properly belonging to the remedy, to be exercised
or not by every sovereignty, according to its own views of policy
and humanity. ,It must reside in every state, to enable it to
secure its citizens from unjust and harrassing litigation, and to
protect them in those pursuits which are necessary to the existence
and well being of every community."

There is no doubt, however, that a statute which should deprive
a party of all legal remedy, would necessarily be void. The
legislature by such statute, intending it to have effect upon legal
contracts lawfully made and binding upon the parties, would
exceed their legitimate powers. Such an act must necessarily
impair the obligation of the contract within the meaning of the
constitution. This has been adjudged. a "And where a statute
does not leave a party a substantial remedy according to the course
of justice, as it existed at the time the contract was made, but
shows upon its face an intention to clog, hamper or embarrass the
proceedings to enforce the remedy, so as to destroy it entirely,
and thus impair the contract, so far as it is in the power of the
legislature to do it, such statute cannot be regarded as a regulation
of the remedy, and is void." b But a lawful repeal of a statute
cannot constitutionally be made to destroy contracts made under it.

We have intended to dwell no longer upon this branch of the
law, than was necessary to lay down the principles which govern
it, and cite to the support of such principles, undoubted authority
of the courts. As we do not intend this to be a work of practice,
we shall not extend the reference to the multitude of cases which
illustrate the principles stated.

The question as to the effect of a state to pass insolvent or
bankrupt laws, and the classes of cases to which they extend, or
can be made to apply, may be considered under this head. The
fourth subdivision of section eight article first of the constitution
of the United States provides, " that congress shall have power
to establish laws on the subject of bankruptcies throughout the
United States." This, it has been supposed, amounted to an
exclusion of the state legislatures, to enact insolvent or bankrupt

a Call v. Hagger, 8 Mass. 429.
b Cooley on Lim. 289; Oatman v. Bond, 15 Wis. 28.

laws, and for a time, legal controversies were frequent which involved the constitutional effect, and operation of state insolvent laws. More recently, the subject has received the consideration of the federal courts, and certain propositions relating to that question may be regarded as having been finally settled. The unquestioned conclusions of that tribunal may be stated as follows: That there are only three cases, in which the states are excluded from the exercise of any power antecedently possessed by them. 1. When a power is granted to congress in exclusive terms. 2. When the states are expressly prohibited from exercising it in a specific form. 3. When a power is granted to congress, the cotemporaneous exercise of which by the states would be incompatible. *a*

It had been previously established, that any state in the union has a right to pass a bankrupt law, provided such law does not impair the obligation of the contracts, and, provided there be no act of congress in force to establish a uniform system of bankruptcy conflicting with such law. That although some of the powers of congress are exclusive, from their nature. without any express prohibition of the exercise of the same powers by the states, the power of establishing bankruptcy laws is not of this description. *b*

More recently it was held, 1. That the power given to the United States to pass bankruptcy laws is not exclusive. 2. That the fair and ordinary exercise of that power by the states, does not necessarily involve a violation of the obligation of contracts, *multo fortiori*, of posterior contracts. *c* And still more recently it was repeated, that a bankrupt or insolvent law of any state, which discharges both the person of the debtor and his future acquisitions of property, was not a law impairing the obligation of contracts so far as respects debts contracted subsequent to the passage of such law. But, it was further settled in the same case, that when in the exercise of that power, the states pass beyond their own limits, and the rights of their own citizens, and act upon the rights of citizens of other states, there arises a conflict of sovereign power, and a collision with the judicial powers granted to the United

a Ogden v. Sanders, 12 Wheat. 229
b Sturgis v. Crowninshield, 4 Wheat. 192.   *c* Cook v. Moffat, 5 How. 310.

States, which renders the exercise of such a power incompatible with the rights of other states, and with the constitution of the United States, a so that, insolvent laws of our state, cannot discharge the contracts of citizens of other states, because they have no extra territorial operation, and consequently the tribunal sitting under them, unless in cases where a citizen of such other state becomes a party to the proceeding, has no jurisdiction in the case.

But though the constitution of the United States does not, in terms, grant to the states the power of passing bankrupt laws, nor prohibit them, they may, in the absence of a law of congress, lawfully pass such acts. So too, it is held, that congress, finding a state in possession of such an act, may by an act of their own, prohibit its future exercise entirely, or restrain it, so far, as national policy may require. The constitution itself has restrained it, so far, as to prohibit the passage of any law impairing the obligation of contracts. And though they may, until the power of congress shall be exercised, so to prohibit or restrain the state law, to pass laws concerning bankrupts, yet they cannot, constitutionally introduce into such laws, a clause which discharges the obligations the bankrupt has already entered into. b

The case in which this was held, was the construction of the terms of an act of the legislature of the state of New York entitled, "An act for the benefit of insolvent debtors and their creditors," passed in April, 1811, which contained a provision discharging the debtor from all liability upon debts contracted previous to his discharge, and including such as were contracted previous to the passage of the act, upon his surrendering his property in the manner prescribed by the act. The defendant had obtained a discharge under this act, and was sued upon obligations made before, though payable after the taking effect of the act. He set up this discharge, as a defence to the suit upon the notes. The case received great consideration, and Chief Justice Marshall, expressing the opinion of the court, held the New York statute, so far as it attempted to discharge contracts made prior to the taking effect of the act, to be unconstitutional, because, impairing the obligation of contracts.

a Baldwin v. Hale, 1 Black. 231.
b Sturgis v. Crowninshield, 4 Wheat. 199.

It cannot be doubted, that the true meaning of this clause in the constitution is, that the body upon which the prohibition rests, and which is restrained thereby, is the legislative department. The subject, upon which the prohibition takes effect, is contracts. In this is included every contract relating to property, or some object of value, which confers rights, and which may be asserted in a court of justice. It is immaterial whether the contract be between a state and an individual, or between individuals only. The contracting parties whoever they may be, stand in this respect upon the same ground. The obligations imposed, and the rights acquired by virtue of the contract, cannot be impaired by a legislative act. A law which discharges these obligations, or abrogates these rights, *impairs* them.

A constitutional act of legislation, which is equivalent to a contract, and is perfected, requiring nothing further to be done in order to its entire completion and perfection, is a contract *executed*. Whatever rights are thereby created, a subsequent legislature cannot impair. Nor can an obligation created by a constitutional law which is in the nature of an *executory* contract, and which is supported by a sufficient consideration, be annulled at the pleasure of the legislature. But a statute, though passed by a legislature having constitutional authority to enact it, which implies a contract executory depending upon the further action of the legislature or its agents for its execution, and which is without consideration in fact or in law, may, before its execution, and the existence of any consideration, be repealed. Such a contract does not create rights or duties, which, in legal contemplation, can be impaired. Such has been adjudged to be the true meaning of this clause of the constitution. *a*

It is obvious therefore, that in every case, where the prohibition is attempted to be applied, the first inquiry is, whether the case be one in which the subject matter is a contract relating to property, or some object of value, and which imposes an obligation capable, in legal contemplation, of being impaired? If it be such a contract, the remaining inquiry is, whether the act of the legislature impairs that obligation? Hence it is a proper subject of

a People v. Platt, 17 John 214, 215 ; Dartmouth College v. Woodward, 4 Wheat. 518; Sturges v. Crowninshield, 4 Wheat. 204.

examination whether the contract be executed, or only executory
If the latter, whether it be upon sufficient consideration, proved,
or presumed, if it be an act of the legislature which constitutes
the contract, it is executed. Has the object of the contract been
performed ? or, is it a mere executory contract requiring the
further action of the legislature, or its agents, to complete its
execution? And if the latter, is it voluntary, or upon sufficient
consideration ? If the contract be one which the legislature has
the constitutional power to make, and it be executed, and no
further act remains to be done, by the state or its agents, as if a
grant of money be made, and the money be delivered, or if it be
a grant of land, and the legislative act is, itself, the conveyance,
not requiring the execution and delivery of a deed or other instrument, nor any other to be done to complete it, the contract has
passed to the form of a grant ; it has become a contract executed ;
and the law in which it originates, cannot be repealed. But if
the contract be executory, as if it be a gift of money or land un-
executed, requiring some further act to its completion, as the
delivery of the money, or the execution of an instrument of conveyance, and is without consideration in fact, or to be presumed,
then, before its completion, and the existence of any consideration,
it may be repudiated ; the gift may be withheld, and the party
who made the promise may revoke it. In this respect, the state
and an individual are subject to the same rule. a

Another distinction is found in the particular character of the
property, between that which may be affected by legislative action,
and that which may not, and more especially between such statutes as are of a retrospective character, and such as are called remedial and prospective. It is hardly questioned, that a retrospective
statute which affects and changes *vested* rights, is founded upon unconstitutional principles, and is consequently inoperative and void.b

Judge Cooley, in his valuable work on constitutional limitations
has well said, "Every man holds all he possesses, and looks forward to, all he hopes for, through the aid and protection of the

a Smith's, com. 384. The Derby Turnpike Co. v. Parks, 10 Conn. 540,
Atwater v. Woodbridge, 6 Conn. 230. Osborne v. Humphrey, 7 Id., 340,
State of New Jersey v. Wilson, 7 Cranch. 165. Fletcher v Peck, .e Cranch. 13
to 138.
b 1   Kent. Com. 455.

laws; but as changes of circumstances, and of public opinion, as well as other reasons of public policy, are all the time calling for changes in the laws, and these changes must more or less affect the value and stability of private possessions, and strengthen or destroy well founded hopes; and, as the power to make very many of them must be conceded, it is apparent that many rights, privileges and exemptions, which usually pertain to ownership under a particular state of the law, and many reasonable expectations, cannot be regarded as *vested rights*, in any legal sense. In many cases, the courts, in the exercise of their ordinary jurisdiction, cause the property *vested* in one person to be transferred to another, either through a statutory power, or by the force of their judgments, or decrees, or by compulsory conveyances. If in these cases the court has jurisdiction, they proceed in accordance with the law of the land, and the right of one man is divested by way of enforcing a higher and better right in another." *a*

But the question, what constitutes *due process of law*, can be, and frequently is raised in the courts and in judicial proceedings, as frequently as elsewhere, and the final decision of the court, when jurisdiction is had of the subject and the person, is conclusive in that particular case. It is the conflict of adjudications in the courts on this question, and upon words of nearly similar import, that has seemed to create conflict of opinion, as to the true interpretation of these words.

This constitutional security to the citizen, that his property cannot be taken but by due process of law, or, by the law of the land, extends even to actions at law in the courts. He cannot even be deprived of it by courts, except they obtain jurisdiction of the subject, and of the person of the proprietor. An adjudication by a court, where jurisdiction is not obtained, is void as to property which its judgments assume to affect, and its owner may repudiate their action, defy their powers, and avail himself of his objection at any stage of their proceedings under the judgment, or decree, as well collaterally as otherwise. In such case the proceeding is not by due process of law, nor by the law of the land, and all persons interfering with individual property under such assumed authority render themselves liable as trespassers.

a Cooley on Const. Lim. 358.

The question of jurisdiction of parties and property, is sometimes determined by the common law, and sometimes by a statute constitutionally enacted. Such statutes affect only the remedy and form of proceeding; but it must be admitted, that the method of acquiring jurisdiction, often seriously affects or impairs the value of this constitutional protection, and the question of jurisdiction is sometimes one of law, and sometimes of fact.

By the statute of this state *a* jurisdiction over the person and property of a party may be obtained without actual personal service upon him of the process or proceeding by which an action may be commenced against him in the courts, by which, proceedings to judgment may be had, and his property taken under its judgments; and similar statutes are found in most of the other states.

In this state such jurisdiction may be obtained, when the party cannot, after due diligence, be found within the state; in a class of cases enumerated, to wit, when a cause of action exists against him, or, when he is a proper party to an action relating to real property in the state. Then, by an order duly obtained according to the directions of the same statute, a judge of the court may direct the service of the process by a publication of it, in specified public newspapers, for a required period, in the following cases: 1. Where the defendant is a foreign corporation, has property within the state, and the cause of action arose therein. 2. Where the defendant, being a resident of this state, has departed therefrom with the intent to defraud his creditors, or to avoid the service of a summons, or keeps himself concealed therein with like intent. 3. Where he is not a resident of this state, but has property therein, and the court has jurisdiction of the subject of the action. 4. Where the subject of the action is real or personal property in this state, and the defendant has, or claims a lien, or interest, actual or contingent therein, or the relief demanded consists wholly, or partly, in excluding the defendant from any interest or lien therein. 5. Where the action is for divorce, in the cases prescribed by law.

The right of the legislature to prescribe such substituted notice by publication, and to give to it the effect of personal service of

a Code, § 135.

process in the enumerated class of cases, is within the legislative power. They may thus, by a remedial and enabling statute, provide a substituted method of service, basing it upon the necessity of the case. This power has long been acted upon, and recognized as being authorized and justified by the courts, and, as being due process of law. *a* Common justice requires that a party in cases provided for in the New York statute, should have some mode of giving notice to his adversary. It cannot be admitted, that a party may defeat the ends of justice as against himself, by so removing himself from the power to make personal service, that not even the legislative power is sufficient to provide the means of reaching his property. The practice of service by publication, is free from reasonable objection under the protection of the courts, and has long been held sufficient. *b*

Under jurisdiction thus acquired, there is no doubt, the private property of one person may, through the instrumentality of the court, and by its judgment or decree, be transferred to another, and this will be held to be due process of law.

No subject, on the question of jurisdiction, obtained under such statutes, has been more prolific of litigation, than that relating to cases of divorce from the bonds of matrimony; raising the question of *fact*, whether the party applying to have the process of the court issued under such a statute, and served only by publication, is, himself or herself, a *bona fide* resident within the state in which such process is issued. This question being one of jurisdiction, is always open to the party affected thereby, even in a collatteral action, to dispute it. So that if a party goes to a jurisdiction other than that of his domicile, for the purpose of procuring a divorce, and has residence there for that purpose only, such residence is not *bona fide*, and does not confer upon the courts of that state or country, jurisdiction over the marriage relation, and any decree they may assume to make, would be void as to the other party.[1]

a Matter of Empire City Bank, 18 N. Y. 200-215; Rockwell v. Nearing, 35 N. Y. 314.

b Nations v. Johnson, 24 How. U. S. R. 206.

NOTE 1.—A valuable note is found in the work of Judge Cooley on constitutional limitations, page 401, which contains a reference to the adjudications of various states, upon the effect of the service of process in the commencement of

This rule of law, that jurisdiction may be thus obtained of a party without personal service of process, is not in conflict with the principle, that a statute which should authorize any debt or damages to be adjudged against a person upon a purely *ex parte*

actions of divorce, by publication and otherwise, where the question of *bon1 fide* residence has been considered by the courts. "These questions," he says in his work, "have frequently demanded the thoughtful attention of the courts, who have sought to establish a rule, at once, sound in principle, and that shall protect as far as possible, the rights of the parties, one or the other of whom, unfortunately, under the operation of any rule which can be established, it will frequently be found, has been the victim of gross injustice." In the case of the "inhabitants of Hanover v. Turner, 14 Mass. 227," instructions to a jury were sustained, that if they were satisfied, the husband, who had been a citizen of Massachusetts, removed to Vermont merely for the purpose of procuring a divorce, and that the pretended cause for divorce, arose, if ever it did arise, in Massachusetts, and that the wife was never within the jurisdiction of the court of Vermont, then, and in such case, the decree of divorce which the husband had obtained in Vermont, must be considered as fraudulently obtained, and that it could not so operate as to dissolve the marriage between the parties. See also Vischer v. Vischer, 12 Barb. 640, and McGiffert v. McGiffert, 31 Barb. 69. In Chase v. Chase, 6 Gray, the same ruling was had to a foreign divorce, notwithstanding the wife appeared in, and defended the foreign suit.• In Clark v. Clark, 8 N. H. R. 21, the court refused a divorce on the ground that the alleged cause of divorce, (adultery,) though committed within the state, was so committed while the parties had their domicile abroad. This decision was followed by Greenlaw v. Greenlaw, 12 N. H., 200. The court say: if the defendant never had any domicile in this state, the libellant could not come here, bringing with her a cause of divorce, over which this court had jurisdiction. If at the time (of the alleged offence) the domicile of the parties was in Maine, and the facts furnished no cause for divorce there, she could not come here and allege those matters which had already occurred, as a ground of divorce under the laws of this state. Should she, under such circumstances, obtain a decree of divorce here, it must be regarded as a mere nullity elsewhere. In Frary v. Frary, 10 N.H 61, importance was attached to the fact, that the marriage took place in New Hampshire‡ and it was held that the court had jurisdiction of the wife's application for a divorce, notwithstanding the offence was committed in Vermont, but during the time of the wife's residence in New Hampshire, see also Kimball v. Kimball, 13 N. H. 225 ; Bachelder v. Bachelder, 14 N. H. 380 ; Payson v. Payson, 34 N. H. 518 ; Hopkins v. Hopkins, 35 N. H. 474. In Wilcox v. Wilcox, 10 Ind. 436, it was held that the residence of the libellant, at the time of the application for divorce, was sufficient to confer jurisdiction, and a decree dismissing the bill because the cause of divorce arose out of the state, was reversed, and see Tolen v. Tolen, 2 Blachf. 407 ; see also Jackson v. Jackson, 1 John 424 ; Barber v. Root, 10 Mass. 263 : Borden v. Fitch, 15 John 121 ; Bradshaw v. Heath, 13 Wend. 407. In any of these cases, the question of actual residence will be open to inquiry wherever it becomes important, notwithstanding the record of

proceeding, without notice of any provision to him for defending, would be a violation of the constitution, and void; for in the case we have discussed, the legislature has afforded a kind of notice, the best suggested, and by which it is reasonably probable, that the party proceeded against will be apprised of what is going on against him, and opportunity is afforded him to defend. *a*

In a variety of other cases, known as proceedings *in rem*,

a Matter of Empire City Bank, 18 N. Y. 215.

proceedings is in due form, and contains the affidavit of residence required by the practice. Leith v. Leith. 39 N. H. 20, and McGiffert v. McGiffert, 31 Barb. 69 ; Todd v. Kerr, 42 Barb. 317. The Pennsylvania cases agree with those of New Hampshire, in holding that a divorce should not be granted unless the cause alleged, occurred while the complainant had domicile within the state. Dorsey v. Dorsey, 7 Walls R. 349 ; Hollister v. Hollister, 6 Penn. St. 449; McDermott's Appeal 8 W. and S. 251. For supporting, to a greater or less extent, the doctrine stated in the text, See Harding v. Alden, 9 Green 140 ; Ditson v. Ditson, 4 R. I. 87; Paroling v. Bird's executors, 13 John, 192; Harrison v. Harrison, 19 Ala. 499 ; Thompson v. State, 28 Ala. 12 ; Cooper v. Cooper, 7 Ohio 594 ; Mansfield v. McIntyre, 10 Ohio 28 ; Smith v. Smith, 4 Greene, (Iowa) 266 ; Yates v. Yates, 2 Beasely 280 ; McGuire v. McGuire, 7 Dana 181 ; Waltz v. Waltz, 18 Ind. 449 ; Hull v. Hull, 2 Strob., Eq., 174; Manly v. Manly, 4 Chand 97; Hubbell v. Hubbell, 3 Wis. 662 ; Gleason v. Gleason, 4 Wis. 64 ; Hare v. Hare, 15 Texas 365, and see Story's Confl. of Laws § 230, and Bishop on Mar. and Div., 727 et seq. Vol. 2, 4th Ed., § 155 et seq. A number of cases cited, hold, that a wife may have a domicile separate from the husband, and may therefore be entitled to a divorce, though the husband never resided in the state. These cases proceed upon the theory, that although in general, the domicile of the husband is the domicile of the wife, yet if he be guilty of such act or dereliction of duty in the relation, as entitles her to have it partially, or wholly dissolved, she is at liberty to establish a separate jurisdictional domicile of her own. Ditson v. Ditson, 4 R. I. 87 ; Harding v. Alden, 9 Green, 140 ; Maguire v. Maguire, 7 Dana 181 ; Hollister v. Hollister, 6 Penn. St. 449. The doctrine in New York seems to be, that a divorce obtained in another state without personal service of process or appearance of the defendant, is absolutely void. Vischer v. Vischer, 12 Barb. 640 ; McGiffert v. McGiffert, 31 Barb. 69 ; Todd v. Kerr, 42 Barb. 317.

Upon the whole subject of jurisdiction in divorce suits, no case in the books is more full and satisfactory than that of Ditson v. Ditson supra, which reviews and comments upon a number of the cases cited, and particularly upon the Massachusetts cases of Barber v. Root, 10 Mass. 265; Inhabitants of Hanover v. Turner, 14 Mass. 227 ; Hartean v. Hartean, 14 Pick 181 ; Lyon v. Lyon, 2 Gray 367. The divorce of one party divorces both, Cooper v. Cooper, 7 Ohio 594, and will leave both at liberty to enter into new marriage relations unless the local statute expressly forbids the guilty party from contracting a second marriage.

because they take notice rather of the thing in controversy, than of the persons concerned, the process is served upon that which is the subject of the action, without specially noticing the interested parties.   Some cases also partake of the nature of both proceedings *in rem*, and of personal actions, since, although they proceed by seizing property, they also contemplate the service of process on the defendant in the action.   Of this class, are the proceedings by foreign attachment, in which the property of a non-resident or concealed debtor is seized and retained by the officer as security for the satisfaction of any judgment that may be recovered against him, but at the same time process is issued to be served upon the defendant, and which must be served, either personally or by such substituted service. *a*

Thus too, attachments are allowed against parties other than corporations, represented to be absent, absconding or concealed debtors ; and the proceeding results in the sale of their property, and the appropriation of its avails, to the benefit of the alleged creditors, and the only notice required is a publication in certain newspapers. *b*   So in justices courts, attachments are authorized against persons who have departed, or are about to depart from the county, or keep concealed with certain intent ; and the notice required is the leaving the attachment at the last place of residence of the party, if such place exists, or, if not, with the person in whose possession the goods may be found. *c*

There are many other examples of the same kind, such as foreclosing mortgages by advertisement; discharging an insolvent debtor upon the petition of a portion of his creditors, those not petitioning being notified of the proceedings only by advertisment in the newspapers.   Various prudential regulations are made with respect to their remedies ; but it may possibly happen, notwithstanding all these precautions, that a citizen who owes nothing and has done none of the acts mentioned in the statutes, may be deprived of his estate, without any actual knowledge of the process by which it has been taken from him. *d*

It was said by the Court of Appeals, *e* " If we hold, as we must,

---

a Cooley on Lim. 403.   *b* 2 Rev. Stat. 3, §§ 1, 28.
c 2 Rev. Stat. 230, 2, §§ 26-31
d Matter of Empire City Bank, Supra.   *e* Id.

in order to sustain this legislation, that the constitution does not positively require personal notice, in order to constitute a legal proceeding *due process of law*, it then belongs to the legislature to determine in the particular instance, whether the case calls for this kind of exceptional legislation, and what manner of constructive notice shall be sufficient to reasonably apprise the party proceeded against, of the legal steps which are taken against him.

A case may be supposed, where the reason for departing from the more safe rule of the common law is so plainly frivolous, or the provision for notice so clearly colorable and illusory, that the courts would be called upon to declare the enactment a fraud upon the constitution."

But it is still, the doctrine of the courts that this substituted service is restricted in its legal effect, and cannot be made available for all purposes. *a* "It will enable the court to give effect to the proceeding, so far as it is one *in rem*, but when the *res* is disposed of, the authority of the court ceases. The statute may give it effect so far as the subject matter of the proceeding is within the limits, and therefore under the control of the state, but the notice cannot be made to stand in the place of process, so as to subject the defendant to a valid judgment against him personally." *b*

"In attachment proceedings, the published notice may be sufficient to enable the plaintiff to obtain a judgment which he can enforce by sale of the property attached, but for any other purpose, such judgment would be ineffectual. The defendant could not be followed into another state or country, and there have recovery against him upon the judgment so obtained, as an established demand. The fact that process was not personally served, is a conclusive objection to the judgment as a personal claim, unless the defendant caused his appearance to be entered in the attachment proceedings." *c* "Where a party has property in a state, and resides elsewhere, his property is justly subject to all valid claims which may exist against him there; but beyond this, *due*

a Pawling v. Bird's Executors, 13 John. 206-207.

b Cooley on Const. 404.

c Cooley on Const. Lim. 404; Pawling v. Wilson, 13 John. 206-7; Kilburn v Woodworth, 5 John. 37; Robison v. Executors of Ward, 8 John. 86; Fenton v Garlock, Id. 194; Bates v. Delavan, 5 Paige, 299.

process of law, would require appearance or personal service, before the defendant could be personally bound by any judgment rendered." This cannot be done by the legislature directly. *a*

We have shown that our statutes includes divorce cases. The courts of the state where the complaining party resides, have jurisdiction of the subject matter by this substituted service of process; and if the other party is a non-resident, they must be authorized to proceed without personal service of process. "The publication which is permitted by the statute, is sufficient to justify a decree in these cases, changing the *status* of the complaining party, and thereby terminating the marriage; and it might be sufficient also to empower the court to pass upon the question of the custody and control of the children of the marriage, if they were within its jurisdiction. But a decree on this subject could only be absolutely binding on the parties, while the children remained within the jurisdiction; if they acquire a domicile in another state or country, the judicial tribunals of that state or country would have authority to determine the question of their guardianship there. *b*

" But in divorce cases, no more than in any other, can the court make a decree for the payment of money by a defendant not personally served with process, and not appearing in the case, which shall be binding upon him personally. It must follow in such a case, that the wife when complainant, cannot obtain a valid decree for alimony nor a valid judgment for costs. If the defendant had property within the state, it would be competent to provide by law for the seizure and appropriation of such property under the decree of the court, to the use of the complainant, but the legal tribunals elsewhere, would not recognize a decree for alimony or for costs, not based on personal service or appearance. The remedy for the complainant must generally, in these cases, be confined to a dissolution of the marriage, with the incidental benefits springing therefrom, and to an order for the custody of the children, if within the state." *c*

---

a Same authorities and Todd v. Kerr, 42 Barb. 317; Ditson v. Ditson, 4 R. I. 87; Mansfield v. McIntyre, 10 Ohio, 28.

b Cooley on Const. 405. Morrell v. Dickey, 1 John. Ch. 156; Woodworth v. Spring, 4 Allen, 321; Potter v. Hiscox, 30 Conn. 508-9.

c Cooley 404.

Other methods of taking the private property of persons without their consent, are the statutes authorizing the taking of the property of lunatics, idiots, and habitual drunkards, to be secured for their future support, or for the payment of their debts; also statutes authorizing the taking of the property of infants to provide the means of their nurture, education or support, and, for more profitable investment of the proceeds, and also, for the partition or sale of the estates of tenants in common, and for a distribution of such estates. All these matters are made subjects of judicial investigation, and courts are the most appropriate departments with which to entrust the administration of the power. In all such cases there will arise disputes of fact, and the judiciary are the most appropriate power to inquire and judge as to what is just and proper in the premises. In the cases of lunatics, idiots, and infants especially, the parties in interest are regarded in theory, as being incompetent to act in their own behalf, and courts are therefore the most competent and impartial forum and body to inquire into, and to guard these interests. As to the power of the legislature to grant it, and of the courts to exercise its administration, it has been adjudged by the court of dernier resort in this state. a "It is clearly (says Chancellor Walworth,) within the powers of the legislature, as the *parens patria*, to prescribe such rules and regulations as it may deem proper, for the superintendence, disposition and management of the property and effects of infants, lunatics, and other persons who are incapable of managing their own affairs."

But it has been held, that an act of the legislature entitled "An act for the better regulation and discipline of the New York State Inebriate Asylum" was void, which authorized a Judge of the Supreme Court, or county judge of the county in which an inebriate might reside, to commit such inebriate to said asylum upon the affidavits of two respectable practicing physicians, and two respectable citizens freeholders of such county, to the effect, that such inebriate is lost to self control; unable from such inebriation, to attend to business, or is thereby dangerous to remain at large; such commitment to be until the examination provided by law shall be had, in no case for a longer period than one year. This

a Cochran v. Van Surlay, 20 Wend. 373.

act authorized an *ex parte* proceeding, which deprived a man of his liberty ; it might be for one year, without an opportunity of being heard in his defence; without his day in court. This was not regarded as due process of law, and was an act repugnant to the constitution of this state and of the United States. *a*

While it seems to be generally conceded, that *general* statutes may be enacted to exercise these powers in all cases, it has been greatly controverted, whether the legislature may enact a special law that shall apply to control and direct in a single or individual case, on the ground, that such an act would be the exercise of a power, that in its nature partakes of the judicial, not legislative authority; or more properly, is a mingling of legislative and judicial power. A jealousy of the legislature, in the disposition to exercise of such a power, seems to have prevailed to such an extent in some of the states, as to have called for constitutional protection against it. In the states of Virginia, Maryland, Kentucky, Indiana, Michigan, New Jersey, Missouri, Oregon, and Nevada, are found provisions forbidding *special* laws, authorizing the sales of the estates of minors and other persons of legal disability. In the constitution of some of the other states, there is a prohibition against all *special* laws, where general laws can be made applicable. But in the state of Massachusetts, it has been held *b* by its courts, that notwithstanding there was a general statute on the subject by the legislature, the legislature could, by the use of a parental or tutorial power for purposes of kindness, without interfering with the rights of other persons, legislate to exercise this power by a special act. And to the same effect, has been the judicial view of the courts in the state of Ohio; *c* and such, was there said, to be the power of the English parliament ; and it seems, that the rule in this state is, that while the legislature cannot generally, constitutionally enact a law which shall transfer an estate or the beneficial use of property of one person to another, there exists an exception in that class of cases, where the rights of third persons are not concerned, as in cases of infants, lunatics, and others, where it can be legally presumed, that the owner of the

a Matter of Jones, 30 How. Pr. R. 446.

b Rice v. Parkman, 16 Mass. 331.

c Carroll v. Olmstead, 16 Ohio, 260

property himself, would have given his consent to the beneficial act, and so to use his property, if he had been in a situation to act for himself; and in cases where the act goes no further than to exercise that paternal or tutorial power over the persons and papers of infants and others, incompetent to act for themselves. This power existed at common law; it was the inherent right of the sovereign power; and it may be therefore exercised by general laws, or, under peculiar circumstances, by a special act of legislation.a In New Hampshire, a different interpretation has been had as to the effect of special legislation on such subjects, where general laws exist; and under the provisions of the constitution of that state. b

This species of legislation, says Judge Cooley, in his work on constitutional limitations, c may perhaps be properly called *prerogative remedial* legislation. It hears and determines no rights; it deprives no one of his property; it simply authorizes one's real estate to be turned into personal, on the application of the person representing his interest, and under such circumstances, that the consent of the owner, if capable of giving it, would be presumed. It is in the nature of the grant of a privilege to one person, which at the same time, affects the rights of no other person injuriously

It was laid down as doctrine in the Supreme Court of this state by Bronson J.,d (affirmed in the court of errors) as follows: "In consequence of the imperfection which pervades all things appertaining to man; cases will sometimes arise which have not been provided for by general laws, and which call for the exercise of a higher power than that possessed by courts of justice ; and if individual interest can, under no possible circumstances, be changed or affected by private acts of the legislature, made without consent, it may happen, that an infant, with a large estate in expectancy, will be utterly destitute of the means of education and support. Although the legislature ought not to interfere upon light considerations, I cannot think that there is any constitutional impediment in the way of enacting private laws affecting individual

a Cochran v. Van Surlay, 20 Wend. 380; Wilkinson v. Leland 2 Pet. 657 Ervine's Appeal, 16 Penn. St. R. 256.
b Opinion of Judges, 4 N. H. 572. c P. 10 3.
d Cochran v. Van Surlay, 15 Wend. 441.

interests, where proper care is taken to preserve the substantial rights of the parties."

But the rule is clearly otherwise in cases where the legislature assumes to exercise the power of inquiry into facts, and to determine rights by legislation between parties adversely claiming interests, as between debtor and creditor, or as to claims to real estate, or to authorize a sale of real estate to satisfy demands in favor of a party that have not been judicially determined. This is clearly attempting to exercise judicial power, and is adjudging and directing the application of one person's property to another. It is so clearly the exercise of a power which has never been conferred upon the legislature, that their act in such or similar cases, would be void. *a*

And so it was held in the Court of Appeals in this state, in a case where lands had been devised to trustees for the use of the testator's daughter for life, with remainders in fee to her issue living at the time of her decease, and for want of such issue, to all the grand-children of the testator then living. During the life of the daughter, (she having children living,) a statute was passed by the legislature, authorizing the trustees with the approbation of a Judge of the Supreme Court, to sell the lands, and out of the proceeds to pay their commissions, costs, and expenses, and all assessments and liens on the lands, and to invest the surplus in securities to be held in trust, the same as if the lands were held under the will. It was held by the court, that no necessity for the act of the legislature having appeared, either in the statute or aside from it, on account of the infancy or other incapacity of the persons living who had vested or contingent interests in the estate, that the act was not within the powers delegated to the legislature, and that the trustees could give no title to the lands sold in pursuance of it. *b* It will doubtless often happen, in a government like our's, where the separate powers of the several departments are not expressly defined and marked out, that even the legislative department may pass acts of this character without that due consideration of the proper boundaries which marks the separation of legislative, from judicial functions. This is also the established rule in the state of Pennsylvania. *c*

a Lane v. Dorman, 3 Scam., Ill , R. 242, 6 Mich. R. 193.
b Powers v. Bergen, 6 N. Y. 358.   *c* Ervine's Appeal, 16 Penn. St. R. 256.

The courts of Pennsylvania have spoken in most emphatic terms against special acts of legislation that affect individual rights,*a* they say : " When in the exercise of proper legislative powers *general* laws are enacted which bear, or may bear, upon the whole community, if they are unjust, and against the spirit of the constitution, the whole community will be interested to procure their repeal, in a voice potential, and that is the great security against unjust and unfair legislation. But when individuals are selected from the mass, and laws are enacted affecting their property, without summons or notice at the instigation of an interested party; who is to stand up for them, thus isolated from the mass, in injury and injustice ? Where are they to seek relief, from such acts of despotic power? They have no refuge but in the courts, the only secure place for determining conflicting rights by due course of law. But if the judiciary give way, and confesses itself too weak to stand against the antagonism of the legislature, and the bar ; one independent, co-ordinate branch of the government, will become the subservient handmaid of another ; and a quiet insidious revolution will be effected in the administration of the government, while its form on paper remains the same."

Our constitutions were established for the protection of personal safety, and private property. They address themselves to the common sense of the people, and ought not to be filed away by legal subtleties. They have their foundations in natural justice; and, without their pervading efficacy, other rights would be useless. If the legislature possessed an irresponsible power over every man's private estate, whether acquired by will, by deed, or by inheritance, all inducement to acquisition, to industry and economy would be removed. The principal object of government is the administration of justice and the promotion of morals. But if property is subject to the caprice of an annual assemblage of legislators, acting tumultuously, and without rule or precedent ; and without hearing the party, stability in property will cease, and justice be at an end. When the the constitution has interdicted the government from taking private property for *public* use without compensation, how can the legislature take it and dispose of it according to their will?

a Id. 268.

Under our system, as has been already said, the legislature can perform no judicial functions; it is their province to enact laws; that of the judiciary to expound them; and that of the executive to enforce them. The judicial power of the state is its whole judicial power; the legislature cannot exercise any part of it there is no such thing under the constitution as a mixed power, partly judicial, partly legislative; were it so, it must be exercised in common; in a joint body, for the judiciary possess as much power to legislate, as the legislature to adjudicate. a

The framers of the constitution, wisely sought to distribute the different powers of government, and to keep them separate and distinct, and each within its own limits. In practice however, it is sometimes difficult, if not impossible, to lay down rules which in all cases, shall determine the precise limits of constitutional restraint, so that in the exercise of the duties of one of the branches, it may not overstep its limits, and infringe upon the peculiar and appropriate functions of another department. These errors, perhaps, are more liable to occur on the part of the legislative department than any other, because their powers are less particularly defined; but with a firm and independent judiciary to correct them, no great evils are likely to occur in that way. b

a Greenough v. Greenough, 11 Penn. St. R. 194.
b Denny v. Mattoon, 2 Allen 361.

CHAPTER XVI.

OF THE CONSTITUTIONAL PROTECTIONS TO PERSONAL LIBERTY.

THE constitutional protections provided for the personal liberty of the citizen, are to be found in both the national and state constitutions, and are expressed in similar language. "The privilege of the writ of *habeas corpus* shall not be suspended, unless, when, in cases of rebellion or invasion, the public safety require it." Const. U. S., Art. 1, § 9; Const. of N. Y. of 1846, Art. 1, § 4. "The citizens of each state shall be entitled to all privileges and immunities of citizens of the several states." Const. U. S., Art. 4, § 2. "No soldier, shall in time of peace be quartered in any house, without the consent of the owner, nor in time of war but in a manner to be prescribed by law." Id., Art. 3 of the Amendments of the Const. of U. S. "The right of the people to be secure in their persons, houses, papers and effects, against unreasonable searches and seizures, shall not be violated, and no warrants shall issue but upon probable cause, supported by oath or affirmation, and particularly describing the place to be searched, and the person or thing to be seized." Id., Art. 4 of Amendments. "No person shall be held to answer for a capital or otherwise infamous crime, unless upon presentment or indictment of a grand jury, except in cases arising in the land or naval forces, or in the militia when in actual service in time of war, or public danger, nor shall any person be subject for the same offence to be twice put in jeopardy of life or limb; nor shall be compelled in any criminal case to be a witness against himself, nor be deprived of life, liberty or property without due process of law, &c." Id., Art. 5.

"In all criminal prosecutions, the accused shall enjoy the right to a speedy and public trial by an impartial jury of the state and district wherein the crime shall have been committed, which district, shall have been previously ascertained by law; and to be informed of the nature and cause of the accusation; to be confronted with the witnesses against him; to have compulsory process for obtaining witnesses in his favor ; and to have the assistance of counsel for his defence." Id., Art. 6. "Excessive bail shall not be required, nor excessive fines imposed, nor cruel and unusual punishments inflicted." Id., Art. 8. "Neither slavery nor involuntary servitude, except as a punishment for crime whereof the party shall have been duly convicted, shall exist within the United States, or any place subject to their jurisdiction." Id., Art. 13.

" All persons born or naturalized in the United States, and subject to the jurisdiction thereof, are citizens of the United States, and of the state wherein they reside. No state shall make or enforce any law which shall abridge the privileges or immunities of citizens of the United States, nor shall any state deprive any person of life, liberty or property without due process of law, nor deny any person within its jurisdiction an equal protection of the laws." Id., Art. 14. By the constitution of this state adopted in 1846, it is provided, "that no member of this state shall be disfranchised, or deprived of any of the rights or privileges secured to any of the citizens thereof, unless by the law of the land, or the judgment of his peers." Art. 1, § 1. The privilege of the writ of *habeas corpus*, and the prohibition against excessive bail, excessive fines, and cruel and unusual punishments, are the same as in the United States constitution, and to which is added, the provision that witnesses shall not be unreasonably detained. Id., §§ 4 and 5. " No person shall be held to answer for a capital, or otherwise infamous crime, (except in cases of impeachment, and in cases of militia when in actual service ; and the land and naval forces in time of war, or which this state may keep with the consent of congress in time of peace ; and in cases of petit larceny under the regulation of the legislature,) unless on presentment or indictment of a grand jury. And in any trial in any court whatever, the party accused shall be allowed to appear and defend in person, and with counsel as in civil actions. No person shall be subject to be twice put in jeopardy for the same offence, nor shall he be compelled in any criminal case to be a witness against himself, nor be deprived of life, liberty or property without due process of law," &c. Id., § 6.

Perhaps, in no government in the world, does the citizen find such full, liberal and ample protection, and so large a share of civil and political liberty, as a citizen of the United States, who is such, by reason of being a citizen of any one of the sovereign states that compose the Union, as also, those who are citizens of the particular states wherein they reside; and all persons are such citizens, and entitled to these protections and privileges, who have either been born, or who have been naturalized in the United States, or in any of the states, or who are subject to the jurisdiction of the United States.

At what time the right to personal liberty first became a subject of political concern in England, belongs to history. The manner in which it was finally secured by constitutional enactments; the spirit and success with which it was defended when assailed by arbitrary princes; the elevating effects upon personal character obtained by its enjoyment to the citizen; are among the influences which controlled the American statesmen in giving it to the citizen of the American republics, secured by the fundamental law.

We do not propose to enter upon the history of the agitations, strifes, and struggles of the masses, with the ruling powers of government, either in our own country, or in that from which we derived many of our laws; and which resulted in obtaining for the citizen the constitutional securities and rights to civil and political liberty, which we have above copied from the fundamental law of these governments. Nor shall we attempt in this work, to give the explanations of causes, by which one portion of a people, created by a just and impartial Creator to an equality of rights with every other portion, and endowed by Him with the unalienable rights of life, liberty and the pursuit of happiness, became, in the process of time, reduced to the unhappy condition of serfs, villeins, menials and slaves; the many submitting themselves to servitude for the few, called the governing classes. These matters belong to the historian, rather than the law writer. It will be our duty to assume, that every citizen is now, in regard to these sacred rights and privileges, entitled to an equal protection; that these rights are just and natural;—and, that the constitution as we find it, is to have a favorable interpretation, as to all its provisions, in favor of the liberty of the citizen.

Although we have chosen, not to enter into the history of the manner of securing this right to personal liberty to the citizen, we cannot well discuss it as a natural right, without a slight reference to its value. It is a right, as has been well declared, unalienable in its nature; inherent in every man, woman, and child; and of inestimable value in giving character and dignity to the citizen.

"Man," says Montesquieu, "is born in society, and there he remains." But as a member of society, in the exercise of his right of liberty, as well as his other absolute rights, he becomes subject to such limitations, and to such penalties for the violations of the rights of others, as the common welfare of all, and the just ends of government may require.

Government, is essential to the preservation of individual rights, including that of liberty, and is the necessity of every society. So, that, properly to enjoy the privileges of liberty, the citizen needs the protection of government. It cannot be otherwise than flattering to the pride of every intelligent American citizen as he reads the history of the nations of the earth, and estimates their condition, to mark the progress, and estimate the advantages of the liberalizing and elevating influence exerted upon the character of a people where the rights of personal liberty, and the equality of all men before the law, is fundamentally secured. It is seen to impart not only vital energy to the government itself, but it adds a stimulus that invites the citizen into enterprises upon the confidence of governmental protection; stimulates his ambition to act upon a sense of individual independence, which a knowledge of his high nature, and noble destiny alone can inspire; and induces him to pursue happiness in all the unobstructed paths which either pleasure or profit may tempt him to follow; and employ all his powers in the exercise of that liberty which secures the highest enjoyments of life.

The limitations to the right to personal liberty, are either of a public, or of a private nature. Among those which are public, is that of individual punishment for the commission of crime, and this punishment, is effected through the instrumentality of the courts. "A court of justice, it has been well said, represents the judicial majesty of the people. Through the forms of law, it utters its mighty voice in judgment. Property, character, liberty, and life itself, are involved in the issues that are brought before it, and it needs all the aid which composure can lend to reason, to enable ıt to discharge wisely, and impartially, its manifold and momentous duties." a   Under this general term, or class of crime, is intended to be included all public offences, down to the lowest grade of misdemeanors, including also contempts committed against courts, and other public bodies who are invested with authority to preserve order.

It follows, from the submission of the individual to the government of the state for his protection, that these rights to the enjoyment of personal liberty, are not so absolute, that they may not be lost or forfeited, and it is entrusted to the exercise of governmental authority to determine, for what causes these rights and privileges shall cease to be enjoyed by the citizen.   These rights and privileges can be properly held only, to aid in the maintenance and administration of governmental authority, for the safety and well-being of society.   When however, it shall happen that the citizen, or a class of citizens, banding themselves together, shall so act as to subvert and destroy society, there can be no question as to the right and duty of those charged with the exercise of the prerogative powers of sovereignty, to disarm the guilty citizen, by disfranchising him of those privileges. b

When the citizens of a state repudiate the charter or constitution under which they have been created a political corporation, and under which they have been entitled to all the natural and inherent political rights which it allows and protects ; and renounce their political connection with, and allegiance to, the authority which has so protected them, and levy war upon it, that they may overthrow and destroy it, and establish themselves in a new organization upon its ruins ; there can be no question that their political franchises are forfeited, and that they, as citizens, are left to be dealt with at the mercy of that sovereignty which they attempted to destroy.

This position is well illustrated in the recent rebellion, in which the citizens of certain states of the Union, attempted, and assumed by a new organization, by their states, to renounce their political connection with, and allegiance to the people and government of the United States ; recalled their senators and representatives from

a Hurd on Personal Liberty, 7.

b Tiffany's Government and Const. 315.

the congress of the Union; threw up their constitutions, or char-ters under which they existed and exercised political rights in respect to state and national interests; adopted other constitu-tions upon their own assumed authority; expelled by force from their limits, all those who attempted to exercise the authority of the United States therein; tore down the flag of the Union; hoisted the flag of rebellion in its place; made war upon the na-tion; and exerted their utmost power to destroy it; claimed and were recognized as having belligerent rights; carried on the war for years, and until overcome and subdued by the power of the nation they renounced and warred against; and only laid down their arms, because they were conquered and utterly subdued. These acts, committed by them against the authority of the nation, is, in its nature, treason; and a forfeiture of all their political rights to governmental protection. The right to protection as a citizen, cannot co-exist with such acts of rebellion in the same individual. The commission of an act of rebellion against the government, ex-tinguishes, and forfeits the right of protection. a

Of the various statutes which authorize, direct, or limit the amount of punishment for offences; and the right of the state to inflict it; presents a subject that belongs to works of practice, or to elementary commentaries upon the philosophy of law and govern-ment. We are treating of constitutional rights as they exist under our system, and to that end, shall assume that system to be the best.

The rights and duties existing between the state under consti-tutional government, and the citizen of the same government, are correlative. While it is the duty of the state to protect the citizen in all his rights, including that of personal liberty, it is equally the duty of the citizen to support the state, by yielding to all its rea-sonable demands, not only of his means, but whenever in the judgment of the state, the public emergency requires it, it is within the power of the state to compel, and the duty of the citizen to yield obedience to the demands of the state; to enter into her ser-vice, to defend or protect and aid the state with his personal service. This is but a reasonable limitation upon his personal liberty, and is but a fulfilment of the duty due from him for governmental pro-tection.

a Id. 316.

CONTEMPTS.

There are various other conditions, which limit the enjoyment of the personal liberty of the citizen, arising out of the duties he owes to the society of which he is a member. Among these, is that of obedience to a subpœna to appear and testify as a witness in court, especially in criminal cases, in which he may be compelled to enter into a recognizance to appear at a future day to give evidence in behalf of the state, and in case of his refusal, he may be committed to prison. *a* So too in civil cases, a refusal to obey, subjects the citizen to liability to punishment for contempt, which may extend to imprisonment; *b* such power, harsh as it may seem, is necessary for the good order of the government. Blackstone says: " Laws without competent authority to secure their administration from disobedience and contempt, would be vain and nugatory. A power therefore in the supreme courts of justice to suppress such contempts by an immediate attachment of the offender, results from the first principles of judicial establishments, and must be an inseparable attendant upon every superior tribunal." *c*

A writer well observes, " The judiciary would hold but a barren scepter, if their powers ceased with declaring the law. They are invested with a power to enforce, as well as to pronounce their judgments. In many cases of contumacious conduct, they secure obedience to their orders by attachment, and commitment of the delinquent party. Imprisonment in such cases, is not regarded merely as a punishment for contempt, but as a necessary means of enforcing compliance with the decision of the court." *d* The power to punish, by the courts for contempts, existed not only at common law, but is expressly conferred by statute. *e* "Every court of record shall have power to punish as for criminal contempt, persons guilty of either of the following acts, and no others. 1. Disorderly, contemptuous or insolent behavior committed during its sitting, in its immediate view and presence, and directly tending to interrupt its proceedings, or to impair the respect due to

a 2 Rev. Stat., 709 § 25. *b* Id. 278, § 10.
c 4 Black Com. 286.
d Hurd on Personal Liberty. 9.
e 2 Rev. Stat. 278, §§ 8 to 13.

its authority. 2. Any breach of the peace, noise or other disturbance directly tending to interrupt its proceedings. 3. Wilful disobedience of any process or order, lawfully issued or made by it. 4. Resistance wilfully offered by any person to the lawful order or process of the court. 5. The contumacious and unlawful refusal of any person to be sworn as a witness, and when so sworn, the like refusal to answer any legal and proper interrogatory. 6. The publication of a false, or grossly inaccurate report of its proceedings; but no court can punish as a contempt, the publication of true, full and fair reports of any trial, argument, proceeding, or decision had in such court.

§ 9. Punishment for contempts may be by fine or by imprisonment in the jail of the county where the court may be sitting, or both, in the discretion of the court, but the fine shall in no case exceed the sum of $250, nor the imprisonment thirty days; and when any person shall be committed to prison for the nonpayment of any such fine, he shall be discharged at the end of thirty days.

§ 10. Contempts committed in the immediate view and presence of the court, may be punished summarily; in other cases, the party charged shall be notified of the accusation, and have a reasonable time to make his defence.

§ 11. Whenever any person shall be committed for any contempt specified in this article, the particular circumstances of his offence shall be set forth in the order or warrant of commitment.

§ 12. Nothing contained in the preceeding sections shall be construed to extend to any proceeding against parties or officers as for a contempt for the purpose of enforcing any civil right or remedy.

§ 13. Persons punished for contempt under the preceeding provisions, shall, notwithstanding, be liable to indictment for such contempt if the same be an indictable offence, but the court before which a conviction shall be had on such indictment, shall, in forming its sentence, take into consideration the punishment before inflicted. By another provision of the Revised Statutes, a every person who shall be guilty of any criminal contempt, (above enumerated) shall be liable to indictment therefor as a misdemeanor, and punished with the same punishment as other misdemeanors.

This power to punish for contempts, is also extended by statute

a Rev. Stat. 692, § 14.

to referees and other officers exercising judicial duties.   Legislative bodies, like judicial tribunals, are also authorized to punish persons, whether members of their body or others, who are guilty of any contempt towards it, by disorderly or contumacious behavior in its presence, or by any wilful disobedience to its orders, and it may be observed, that the contempts punishable by a legislative assembly, are not confined to proceedings in its judicial capacity, but may arise in the course of its legislative, or other functions. *a*

The criminal jurisdiction of a legislative assembly, is much more extensive than the civil courts, or than that of the courts, embracing the misconduct or disorderly behavior of its own members, as well as misdemeanors, breaches of privilege, and other offences committed by other persons.   In both cases, the offence may be committed either against the assembly itself, or against its members individually.   But unlike the powers of a court, which are limited by the letter and control of the statute or common law, the powers of legislative assemblies, seems to be subject to no control or restraint from any appellate power; and within the sphere of this power, it depends solely upon their own absolute will and pleasure. No other tribunal can control their action, set aside their judgment, or revise their proceedings.

This power, as a general rule, will not be greatly abused, inasmuch, as by the theory of our government, the legislative power should be, and doubtless generally is, confided to men eminent for talents, character, experience and virtue, and are selected by the people themselves.   If the conduct of any particular body shall be found an exception to the rule based upon this theory, the evil is temporary, and its correction lies with the people themselves.   The power it is true, if exercised by corrupt or incompetent members, is dangerous in its action, and the injured party is, in degree, remediless.

This concludes all we propose to say on the subject of contempts of courts, which subject, is one of the constitutional qualifications, or limitations of the right of personal liberty of the citizen, except as to contempts committed against legislative bodies, which will be treated of in a separate chapter, by itself.

a Cushing's Legislative Assemblies, § 655.

HABEAS CORPUS.

The privilege of the writ of *habeas corpus*, is the birthright of every citizen, fundamentally secured by the national, as well as the state constitutions. "Personal liberty," says Blackstone, "consists in the power of locomotion, of changing situation, or of moving one's person to whatsoever place one's own inclination may direct, without imprisonment or restraint, unless by due course of law." It is a right strictly natural, which the laws have never abridged without sufficient cause, and in this constitutional government, it cannot be abridged at the mere discretion of the magistrate. The writ of *habeas corpus* is defined by Hurd, *a* "to be that legal process, which is employed for the summary vindication of the right of personal liberty when illegally restrained." It takes its name from the emphatic words which it contained when it was written in latin. It was borrowed by us in our constitutions and statutes from the English statute of 31 Charles II, ch. 2, which provided the great remedy for the violation of personal liberty, by the writ of *habeas corpus ad subjiciendum* and which was often denominated another Magna Charta of the kingdom.

Employed, as this writ ever has been, to vindicate the right of personal liberty, by whatever power infringed, it became inseparably associated with that right; and, in proportion as the right has been valued, so has been the writ by which it has been defended. It was its grateful office, which commended this writ to the favorable regard of the people, and finally dignified it by its name, the writ of *habeas corpus. b*

This writ and its privileges, is not only secured by the national and state constitutions, but in this state also, by the statute which prescribes its form, and which also provides that a penalty of one thousand dollars, shall be forfeited to the party aggrieved, against the court or officers severally, who shall refuse to grant such writ when legally applied for. *c* The forms of proceeding, and the variations in practice applicable to different conditions of the applicant, are also provided by statute, but these belong rather to the practice than to the discussion of the question of constitutional privilege.

a Hurd on Habeas Corpus, 143.   *b* Id. 144.
c 2 Rev. Stat. 565, § 46.

This provision was introduced into the constitution, as one greatly essential to the personal liberty of the citizen. The necessity and importance of such a writ was well appreciated under the British system, and an English author says, " to bereave a man of life, or by violence to confiscate his estate, without accusation or trial, would be so gross and notorious an act of despotism, as must at once convey the alarm of tyrany throughout the kingdom." But confinement of the person, by secretly hurrying him to the jail, where his sufferings are unknown and forgotten, is a less public, a less striking, and therefore a more dangerous engine of arbitrary force. The writ which it was the design of this clause to secure, is that known to the common law as the writ of *habeas corpus ad subjiciendum*, which is directed to one, detaining another, commanding the production of the person detained, and the cause of such capture and detention, *adficiendum, subjiciendum, et recipiendum*, to do, submit, and receive, whatever the court or officer awarding such writ should consider in that behalf. *a*

But even this natural and constitutional right of personal liberty, with all its securities and protections, like all other rights and privileges of the *citizen*, is subject to qualification and limitation for good of the society, and the protection of that government, of which he has submitted himself to become a member, for causes of both a public, and those of a private nature.

Government, like every other contrivance of human invention, has a specific end; but political government, or the government established by society, does not preclude that government that existed by nature before the organization of society; nor that which is based on the rights of nature, the right of government by the parent of his offspring; nor of those kindred, though perhaps delegated rights, which are substitutes for the parental relation, that of instructor and pupil, master and servant. Therefore the theoretic surrender, or resignation by each citizen of a portion of natural rights to society to confer the needful powers of government, for the benefit of all; does not include the patriarchal or parental power of government. These are rights which cannot with any propriety be yielded up, without doing violence to nature.

Those limitations of this right which are of a public nature,

a Smith's Com. 365.

Judge Cooley, in his treatise, a divides into five sub-classes. 1. Those imposed to prevent the commission of crime which is threatened. · 2. Those in punishment of crime committed. 3. Those in punishment of contempts of courts, or of legislative bodies, or, to render their jurisdiction effectual. (This class we have already considered.) 4. Those necessary to enforce the duty citizens owe in defence of the state. 5. Those which may become important to protect community against the acts of those who, by reason of mental infirmity, are incapable of self-control.

All these limitations, are well recognized and understood; but their particular discussion does not belong to our subject; especially those under the second class; that of the liability to arrest and imprisonment on the charge of, or conviction for crime, for which the books of practice must be consulted. Under this 5th class are included, some, who are unable by reason of their mental condition, to render to the state in return, any aid as a compensation for the protection they receive, such as lunatics, idiots and helpless paupers. These, no less than the responsible citizen; have a claim upon the fostering care of the state. As has been well said, "the irresponsible lunatic must not be allowed a *liberty* fraught with danger to himself and others, nor must he, or the idiot, be left exposed to the cupidity and rapacity of designing and heartless relatives. Neither must the invalid pauper, be suffered to starve, in a land overflowing with plenty." b

All civilized governments recognize the obligation of providing for these classes of citizens; and just in proportion to the progress of society; the advance of civilization; and the ameliorating influences of christianity; do we behold the gratifying evidence of that just sense of this public duty, by the erection by government, of asylums and work-houses for these unfortunate classes. These humane institutions, are taking the place of the old barbarous system of chains, and shackles, and whipping for the lunatic, and of a sale of the pauper to the lowest bidder, to any unfeeling keeper, for his support.

"The restrictions of personal liberty in these cases, are designed for the benefit of the unfortunate subjects, and for the safety of

a Cooley on Const. Limitations 339.

b Hurd on Personal Liberty, 10.

the community; and cease when the cause which calls for them, is removed; as when the lunatic recovers his reason, or the pauper becomes possessed of property adequate for his maintenance, by gift or otherwise, or gains sufficient health and strength to earn a support."

These obligations of government, are recognized by statutes, in this and other states, the extensive provisions whereof, it is not a part of the design of this work to copy.

Those limitations which are of a private nature, are divided by him into eight sub-classes, but which are, in this state, really reduced to six, and they are those which spring from the helpless or dependent condition of individuals in the various relations of life. We cannot present these better than in the language of that learned author.

1. " The husband, at common law, is recognized as having legal custody of, and power of control over the wife, with the right to direct as to her labor, and insist upon its performance. The precise nature of the restraints which may be imposed by the husband upon the wife's actions, it is not easy, from the nature of the case, to point out and define; but they can only be such gentle restraints upon her liberty, as her improper conduct may seem to require. a The general tendency of public sentiment, as well as modern decisions, has been to do away with the arbitrary power which the husband was formerly supposed to possess, and to place the two sexes in the married state, more upon a footing of equality. b It is believed that the right of the husband to chastise his wife, under any circumstances, would not be recognized in this country, and in any case, his right to control would be gone, if he should conduct himself towards the wife in a way not warranted by the relation, and which should render it improper for her to cohabit with him, or if he should be guilty of such conduct as would entitle her under the laws of the state to a divorce. His right to control is also gone, when the parties live apart under articles of separation."

There is no relation in life, in which we can find so little of reliable, uniform, settled law, controlling the rights of parties, as

a 2 Kent Com. 181.
b Statutes of 1848, 1849 and 1862, as to rights of married women.

64

this. It was the first relation formed by man, it is the first in the order of nature; it is the most intimate, the most tender, and should possess the nearest possible equality of powers and natural rights. Reasoning from the order of creation, and from nature, we find the man endowed with superior physical power, and perhaps for this reason, he has assumed, what in all countries has been recognized as his right, and would seem to be demanded as his duty, the protection of woman; and it is perhaps also for this reason, that it has been conceded to him, the right of private restraint over the wife. The right to exercise this restraint, and to what extent, are questions which remain almost as much unsettled by the municipal, as by the moral law. This refers, doubtless, to the exercise of physical restraint; but this by no means settles the moral question, that the *necessity* of restraint, does not as often apply to the husband as to wife; and yet in that case, the law recognizes the authority of no one to exercise it. Perhaps the long recognition of this right, as being in the husband, by the adjudications of courts, and the necessity for the existence of an acknowledged head of authority in this relation, is a sufficient ground to concede the law to be, that the power resides in the husband. It is argued, in favor of the right, that it should so reside, that in case the wife inclines to extravagant living, he may protect his estate, and prevent her squandering it. That if she forsakes her duties to her family, and gads about to scandalize her neighbors, or to reform the race, he may bring her home and keep her there. That if she burns with "free love," he may protect his honor, and exclude her from all associations by which it is endangered. These extreme cases, do seem to require the correcting, the restraining power, to exist somewhere. But suppose the other case, which as frequently happens, of an extravagant, intemperate, licentious and spendthrift husband who is squandering the living which ought to be preserved for wife and children, who may possess like "free love" associations and affinities; who then, should possess the power of restraint; who then, will protect the honor of a wife and children? The moral argument upon which the right is based, is insufficient and selfish, until it is demonstrated, that husbands, as a rule, are morally, more pure and perfect than their wives.

What precise amount of force a husband may exert in restraint of the personal liberty of his wife in this country, has not been settled, so as to be adopted as law. Different judges in the same, and in different states, have given us dicta of their views arising under circumstances peculiar to the case in hand, but failing to come up to any general rule; being governed in a greater or less degree, it would seem, by the common law of England, from which country, much of our common law was borrowed. Even Blackstone speaks with doubt as to the modern authorities on this subject; but he informs us, *a* that by the "old law," the husband might give his wife moderate correction, for, as he is to answer for her misbehavior, the law thought it reasonable to entrust him with the power of restraining her by domestic chastisement, in the same moderation that a man is allowed to correct his apprentices or children, for whom the master or parent is also liable in some cases to answer. But this power of correction, was confined within reasonable bounds. The civil law, he informs us, gave the husband the same or larger authority, over his wife. But with us, he says, in the politer reign of Charles the second, this power of correction began to be doubted; and a wife may now have security of the peace against her husband; or in return, the husband against the wife. Yet the lower rank of people (he says) who were always fond of the old common law, still claim and exert their ancient privilege; and the courts of law will still permit a husband to restrain a wife of her liberty in a case of any gross misbehavior.

Bishop, in his work on marriage and divorce, *b* says that the right to chastise a wife is repudiated by the law of Ireland and Scotland, and has met with but little favor in the United States. In New Jersey, Chief Justice Green said, *c* "There was a time in the history of the common law, in which a man was allowed to beat his wife with a rod no larger than his thumb; and at a time still earlier than that, when he was allowed to beat his wife at discretion, and turn her out of doors." This decision, so referred to as to the size of the rod, is said to have been made by a celebrated English Judge. In his defence, called for by public opinion, it was found that he referred to authority found in the day of Brac-

a 1 Com. 444. *b* Sec. 485.

c State v. Barnhard, 2 West. Law Jour. 301.

ton, and as to that ancient case, tradition reports, that the women who lived in the neighborhood of the Judge who pronounced it, raised a meeting, and in mass, for his disregard of the proprieties of their characters and conditions, seized him by force, and plunged him into a horse pond. ."But in this enlightened christian age and country, no man has a right to strike his wife at all. If she interferes with a proper discipline in his domestic relations, he may restrain her; but the law will not justify him in striking a blow." In this state, Judge Walworth, at *nisi prius*, held, that " a husband had no right to beat his wife, or to inflict punishment upon her. He may defend himself against her; he may restrain her from acts of violence towards himself or others, for he is accountable for her acts which injure others." This is a more sensible basis than that of a moral one. Chancellor Kent laid down the rule thus, *a* "The husband may be bound to keep the peace as against his wife; and for any unreasonable and improper confinement, by him she may be entitled to relief upon *habeas corpus*. But as the husband is the guardian of the wife, and bound to protect and maintain her, the law has given him a reasonable superiority and control over her person, and he may even put gentle restraint upon her liberty, if her conduct be such as to require it, unless he renounces that control by articles of separation, or it be taken from him by a qualified divorce."

" But in exercising whatever rights the husband may have by way of restraint of the liberty of the wife, he may not lock her up as a close prisoner; he may not deprive her of the benefit of light and air and exercise; nor of the society of himself, or the family; nor may he exclude her entirely from all intercourse with her neighbors, where there is no ground to apprehend any injurious consequences." *b* Should the wife elope, or be forcibly carried away, he doubtless might retake her, provided the act of recaption was not done riotously, or in a manner to occasion a breach of the peace. " Cruelty or other conduct on the part of the husband, constituting a ground for divorce, gives authority to the wife to leave the husband, and he cannot retake her, whether she applies for a divorce or not. And it has been held, that he cannot retake her

a 2 Com. 181.
b Hurd on Limitation of Liberty, 34.

if she leaves him to obtain a divorce, honestly believing that his treatment afforded sufficient ground for divorce, although it should appear that the facts did not warrant the belief.

2. " The father of an infant, being obliged by law to support his child, has a corresponding right to control his actions, and employ his services during continuance of legal infancy. The child may be emancipated from this control before coming of age, either by the express assent of the father, or by being turned away from his father's home, and left to care for himself; though in neither case, would the father be released from an obligation which rests upon him to prevent the child becoming a public charge; and which the state may enforce whenever necessary. The mother, during the father's life, has a power of control subordinate to his; but on his death, or conviction and sentence to imprisonment for felony, she succeeds to the relative rights which the father before possessed." *a*

" It is in consequence of the obligation of the father to provide for the maintenance, and in some qualified degree, for the education of his infant children," says Chancellor Kent, *b* " that he is entitled to the *custody of their persons*, and to the value of their labor and services. There can be no doubt that this right in the father is perfect while the child is under the age of fourteen years. But as the father's guardianship continues until the child has arrived to full age, and as he is entitled by statute to constitute a testamentary guardian of the person and estate of his children until the age of twenty-one, the inference would seem to be that he was in contemplation of law, entitled to the custody of the *persons*, and to the services and labor of his children during their minority." But in this state, it has been held, that this right of the father, is not an absolute and unalienable right. As a general rule he has the natural right. Like other rights, it may be forfeited by his misconduct, and under circumstances requiring it, the courts, will control this exercise of parental power, and may award the care and custody of minor children to the mother, or others. *c* The father may obtain the custody of his children by the writ of

a People v. Humphries. 24 Barb. 521.　　*b* 2 Com. 193.
c People v. Chegary, 18 Wend. 637; People v. —, 19 Wend. 16; People v. Mercer, 3 Hill. 399; People v. Olmstead, 27 Barb. 9.

hab-as corpus, when they are improperly detained from him; but
the courts, both of law and equity, will investigate the circumstances, and act according to sound discretion, and will not always of
course, interfere upon *habeas corpus,* and take a child, though under
fourteen years of age from the possession of a third person, and
deliver it over to the father against the will of the child. They
will consult the inclination of the child, even if an infant, if it be
of a sufficiently mature age to judge for itself, and even control
the right of the father to the possession and education of his child,
when the nature of the case appears to warrant it."

"This power over the person of the child ceases on its arrival
at the age of majority, which in this state is the age of twenty-one.
This right results from the corresponding duty, to maintain and
educate the child, and in the necessary support of that authority,
he should possess the right to the exercise of such discipline, as
may be requisite for the discharge of that sacred trust. This is
the true foundation of the parental power. On the death of the
father, as a general rule, the mother is entitled to the custody of
the infant children, inasmuch as they are their natural protectors
for maintenance and education." *a* These rights are conferred for
important ends, chiefly affecting the welfare of the child. When
neccessary to the proper discharge of parental duty, the parent
may resort to corporal discipline. He may, and should, in proper
cases, inflict moderate chastisement. "Correct thy son and he
shall give thee rest; yea, he shall give delight to thy soul." *b*
"Foolishness is bound up in the heart of a child, but the rod of
correction shall drive it from him." "Chastise thy son while there
is hope, and let not thy soul spare for his crying." This was the
language of the wise man. "The parent may impose such temporary confinement as may be necessary to secure obedience to
his reasonable commands, so that it is not prejudicial to the life,
limb or health of the child." *c*

"The Roman law anciently gave the father the power over the
life and death of his children, upon the principle, that he who gave
had also the power of taking away; but the rigor of the law was
softened by later constitutions. The power of a parent by the

a 2 Kent Com. 203.   b Proverbs, 29-17; Id. 22-15; Id. 19-18.
c Hurd on Personal Liberty, 43.

law of England is much more moderate ; but still sufficient to keep the child in order and obedience. He may lawfully correct his child being under age in a reasonable manner ; for this is for the benefit of his education." *a* Our own common law has not been materially held to be different from this. The law prescribes no form of parental discipline. It merely designates the purpose for which it may be employed, and confers adequate power for its administration, yet while it authorizes chastisement or confinement, it exacts moderation, and punishes any excess amounting to cruelty, as a crime.

The exercise of this power must be in a great measure discretionary. He may so chastise his child as to be liable in an action by the child against him for the battery. The child has rights which the law will protect him in against the brutality of a barbarous parent. It is a point sometimes of great difficulty to determine with exact precision, when a parent has exceeded the bounds of moderation. Minds will differ ; correction which by some will be considered as unreasonable, will be viewed by others as perfectly reasonable. What may be considered by one as a trifling folly, and for which none, or very trifling correction should be applied, will, by another, be considered as an offence that requires very severe treatment. The parent is bound to correct the child so as to prevent him from becoming the victim of vicious habits, and thereby proving a nuisance to the community.

The true ground upon which this ought to be placed, is, that the parent ought to be considered as acting in a judicial capacity when he corrects ; and of course not liable for errors of opinion. And although the punishment should appear to be unreasonably severe, and in no measure proportioned to the offence ; yet if it should also appear, that the parent acted conscientiously, and from motives of duty, no judgment should be given against him.

But when the punishment is thus unreasonable, and it appears that the parent acted *malo animo* from wicked motives, under the influence of an unsocial heart, he ought to be liable to damages. For error of opinion, he ought to be excused ; but for malice of heart, he should not be shielded from the just claims of the child. Whether there was malice may be collected from the circumstan-

a Black, Com. 452.

ces attending the punishment. The instrument used, the time when, the place where, and the temper of heart exhibited at the time, may all unite in demonstrating what the motives were, which influenced the parent. *a*

Among the methods of inflicting chastisement, to enforce obedience, to reasonable commands, is, doubtless, that of confinement of the child, but this like the other, must be exercised in moderation. The life of the child must not be endangered, nor its health sacrificed or unreasonably exposed; nor its limbs paralyzed or injured; nor can it be imposed upon the child to its prejudice, from sheer malice of heart.

This right of custody and control, as has been said, ceases at the arrival of the child at majority, except perhaps in the case of idiocy or other grievous disability of the child to take care of itself. In such cases it becomes the duty of the state authorities to provide. *b*

This relation may be severed before the child arrives at majority by the express consent of the parent, which is called emancipation, or by the cruel conduct of the parent, in sending it away, or in omitting to provide for it the necessaries of life by repeated acts of barbarity and violence, *c* or other treatment which would render a residence with the parent intolerable. *d* But even such conduct, by no means absolves a parent from his obligation to maintain or support his child; he is still liable at common law for the necessary support furnished to his child, even by a stranger. "This relation may also be severed by the courts of justice, when, in their discretion the morals, or safety, or the interests of the child strongly requires it, and may give their custody elsewhere. *e*

Mothers, during coverture, also exercise authority over their children; but in a legal point of view, it is said, they are considered in this respect as only agents for their husbands, and have no legal authority of their own : *f* howsoever this may be, technically, where both parents reside together, the general custody of

a Reeves' Domestic Relations, 288.

b Upton v. Northbridge, 15 Mass. 237; Orford v. Ramsey, 3 N. H. R. 331.

c 2 Kent. Com. 193.

d Sternburg v. Bution, 7 Watts & Searg. 364.

e 2 Kent. Com. 205.

f Reeves on Domestic Relations, 295.

the children is doubtless, considered to be in him as the head and governor of the family; but by the universal law of implication, and by the implied consent of both, the mother, has a share in that custody and control; if not independently, and of equal extent with the father; yet if he does not absolutely forbid it, she is entitled to an active part in the discipline and correction of the children, and in his absence, to exercise absolute control, to the same extent as the father. She is entitled to the exercise of it to this extent, to secure to her that reverence and respect, that is due from children to a parent.

On the death of the father, the mother remaining at the head of the family, succeeds to the custody, discipline and government of the children, and to all the rights possessed by the father in his lifetime, and doubtless to the same succession of power in case of the civil death of the father, as where he is convicted of felony and confined in the state prison.

3. "The guardian has a power of control over his ward, corresponding in the main, with that which the father has over his child, though in some respects more restricted, while in others it is broader. The appointment of guardian when made by the courts, is of local force only, being confined to the state in which it is made, and the guardian would have no power to change the domicile of the ward to another state or country. But the appointment commonly has some reference to the possession of the property by the ward, and over this property the guardian possesses a power of control which is not possessed by the father over the property owned by the child.

As our discussion of this relation, in this work, is confined to the power of restraint of personal liberty, we shall only examine it in that view. Chancellor Kent informs us, that the relation of guardian and ward, is nearly allied to that of parent and child, a but throughout his whole lecture, he says not a word on the subject of the guardians right to discipline, control, to administer corporal correction, or to exercise any power of restraint over the personal liberty of the ward. In the state of New Hampshire it was expressly said by Woodbury J., b speaking of the rights of a

a 2 Com. 218.
b Hancock v. Hamstead, 1 N. H. 265.

guardian appointed upon the death of parents, "True he had a guardian, but a guardian though *in loco parentis*, as to a few purposes, has no absolute control *over the person*, or services of the ward, unless the ward be a lunatic." Mr. Reeves, who has treated this subject somewhat at large, and speaks of the various kinds of guardians and wards; guardians of the power, as well as guardians of the estate, is entirely silent on the subject of the power of any kind of guardian over the personal liberty of the ward. Blackstone, who has written a full chapter on the several divisions and classes of persons constituting this relation, omits any allusion to the control of the guardian over the personal liberty of the ward, unless it may be implied 'from this : " The power and . reciprocal duty of a guardian and ward are the same *pro tempore* as that of father and child, and therefore I shall not repeat them." *a* In Massachusetts it was held that the guardian had no power to bind the person of his ward. *b*

The absence of expression of opinion by elementary writers on the subject of this power of restraint of the guardian over the person and liberty of his ward, and the remarkable absence of cases in which this question has been passed upon by the courts under the writ of *habeas corpus* or otherwise, makes it hazardous to express an opinion, as to the power of the guardian in this respect; or, if he possesses the power, to say where, and to what extent, and under what circumstances he may exert it. The relation of guardian, has not the same basis to support the power of restraint and discipline, as that of the parent. The parent has first, the natural law of power. By begetting the child, he has entered into an implied and voluntary obligation to endeavor, as far as in him lies, that the life he has bestowed shall be supported and preserved, and thus the child has a perfect and natural right to receive maintenance and support from the parent. *c* This gives to the parent the right to such authority, and to exercise such discipline, as may be requisite for the discharge of the sacred trust. This is the true foundation of parental power. *d* The guardian has no such natural relation ; and he is under no legal obligation whatever, to maintain the ward from his own funds, nor at common

a 1 Black. Com. 462.
c 4 Black. Com. 447.
b Foster v. Fuller, 6 Mass. 58.
d 2 Kent. Com. 203.

law, can he bind him out to service. He can only do this by some express statutory provision. Our statutes define the powers of the several kinds of guardians known to our law, but by none of them is conferred the power of the personal restraint of liberty. If it exists, it exists only at common law. Blackstone indeed does say, that in England, the guardian performs the office, both of *tutor* and *curator* of the Roman law; the former of which, had the charge of the maintenance and education of the minor, the latter the care of his fortune; or, (as he says,) according to the language of the Court of Chancery, the *tutor* was the committee of the person, the curator the committee of the estate; but this office, he says, is always united in our law, in regard to minors. *a* In looking at the civil law, we find the tutor, defined to be, a guardian who has the charge of persons who are under the age of puberty. *Tutores*, latin, from *tueri* to protect; as the law hath it, "to protect, or defend him during the age, in which he cannot protect himself." *b* Though in the civil law, this guardianship *to protect* and *defend* until the age of puberty, and in the English law, a combination of duties till majority; both systems are silent on the subject of the power of restraint of liberty. To protect and defend the person, is not identical with the power to control, to discipline, and restrain.

Mr. Hurd, a modern writer on the laws of the right of personal liberty, however, lays it down thus: *c* "When the ward is within the age of discretion," (which he assumes to be the age, when by law, they may choose their own guardians,) "it is plain enough, that the guardian possesses the right, and that it is clearly his duty, on proper occasions, in a reasonable manner, to correct his ward for misbehavior, with the rod, if in his judgment that mode of correction be necessary. And especially is this true, where the ward resides in the family of his guardian. In such a case, it is important to allow the guardian to employ the usual means of discipline, not only for the benefit of the ward, but to enable him to execute his reasonable plan of family government. For no man fit to be entrusted with the training up of a child, would take the infant stranger under his roof to educate, with any privi-

a 1 Black. Com. 379. *b* Inst. 1, 13, 1.
c Hurd on Personal Liberty, 51-52.

lege to misbehave, or to escape the punishment usually inflicted on his own children for misconduct. It would not be safe perhaps, to deny that in a case of flagrant misbehavior, the guardian possesses the right to chastise his ward, when of somewhat riper years. But when by reason of the advanced age of the ward, this mode of correction becomes deeply humiliating, as well as painful, it is safe, perhaps, to say, that the right cannot be lawfully exercised unless it appears that there was probable cause for it, and that all the other means of correction, less severe were inadequate." These views, though no authority is cited to sustain them, stand on a basis of reason and good practical common sense ; and they are, no doubt, the practice to some extent in the relation of guardian and ward.

4. "The relation of master and apprentice is founded on a contract between the two generally, with the consent of the parent, or party standing *in loco parentis,* to the latter, by which the master is to teach the apprentice some specified trade or means of living. This relation is also statutory and local, and for power to control or punish against the opposition of the apprentice, the statute must be examined."

This relation is a matter of civil contract, and is generally in its forms and creation regulated by the local statutes of the several states, as to the age, time of service, the employment, trade or occupation, to be pursued, and the persons who are authorized to bind the child apprentice to the service of a master. All these being matters of civil contract, do not come within the scope of this work. "The relation of master and apprentice, says Chancellor Kent, *a* "was in its original spirit and policy and an intimate interesting connection, calculated to give the apprentice a thorough trade, education, and, to advance the mechanic arts in skill, neatness and fidelity of workmanship, as well as in the facility and utility of their application. The relationship, if duly cultivated under a just sense of the responsibility attached to it, and with the moral teachings which belong to it, will produce parental care, vigilance, and kindness on the part of the master, and a steady, diligent, faithful and reverential disposition and conduct on the part of the apprentice."

a 2 Com. 265.

The temptations to imposition and abuse to which this contract is liable, have rendered legislative interposition especially necessary. While these regulations upon the one hand protect the master from the interference of other persons with the duty the apprentice owes to him, it also protects the apprentice against misconduct and abuse from his master; by a forfeiture of the claim of the master upon his services, to be adjudged by two justices of the peace upon complaint. *a* So on the other hand, if the apprentice misbehave, by refusing to serve according to the terms of his indenture, and the law in that regard, he may, upon the complaint of the master to certain officers named in the statute, and if he persists in such refusal to obey, &c., be committed to a house of correction, bridewell, or common jail of the city or county, there to remain until he will consent to serve according to law ; *b* and in case he shall wilfully absent himself from such service without leave of the master, he may be compelled in like manner to serve double the time of such absence, even after his majority, not exceeding three years after the end of the original term. *c* Blackstone says, *d* that a master may correct his apprentice for negligence or other misbehavior, so it be done with moderation. And so it seems it was laid down by Hawkins ; *e* and in the reign of Charles I, it was declared of an apprentice, " if he misbehave himself, the master may correct him in his service, or complain to a justice of the peace to have him punished according to the statute ;" *f* but in the thirty-fifth year of the reign of Charles II, Lord Saunders, before whom a trial was had against one Keller for immoderate beating of Brotherwaite, an apprentice; said the apprentice might be discharged by justices of the peace ; but upon the authority of Lord Hale, he still held the defendant responsible, and he was convicted. *g* This right of moderate correction by the master, in case of an offending apprentice, seems to be adopted as common law in this country, though this power does not arise out of the statute provisions. *h*

a 2 Rev. Stat. 159, § 30.

b Id. § 29.

c Id. § 28.   *d* 1 Com. 428.

e 1 Hawk. P. C. 130.   *f* Cro. Car. 179, Gilbert v. Fletcher.

g Dominas, Rex v. Keller, 2 Show. 289.

h 2 Kent Com. 264; Commonwealth v. Baird, 1 Ashmead Penn. R. 267.

5. The power of the master over the servant he employs. As I do not see in this relation, any power that the master can rightfully exert over the personal liberty of the servant, I have not copied the views of the author, or discussed at much length, this relation.

A few unsupported dicta may be found in the old English books apparently justifying moderate chastisement of a hired servant by the master or employer, for dereliction of duty, *a* but no respectable modern authority can be found, bold enough to assert that such a power exists even in England. And in America, where equality of rights of its citizens is announced as the basis of sovereign authority, such an assertion would be too much in conflict with the genius and spirit of our system of government, and with the acknowledged rights of equality of citizenship and freedom, to exist for a single moment as law. It may be that there is an exceptional case; as for instance, where a parent should contract with a master, the service of a minor child, and expressly delegate to the master the parental power of chastisement, or confinement by way of correction for dereliction of duty; but where the servant has arrived at his majority, he has become an emancipated citizen of the government; with unalienable rights to freedom, to liberty, and to an equality of rights before the law, and in which, he has no superior; and over him, no master can exert the humiliating and tyranous power of chastisement and correction.

6. "The relation of teacher and scholar places the former more nearly in the place of the parent than either of the two preceeding relations places the master. While the pupil is under his care, he has the right to enforce obedience to his commands, lawfully given in his capacity as teacher, even to the extent of bodily chastisement or confinement. And in deciding questions of discipline, he acts judicially, and is not to be made liable either civilly or criminally, unless he has acted with express malice, or been guilty of such excess in punishment that malice must be implied. All presumptions are in favor of the correctness of his action."

Technically, where there is no special understanding between parent and teacher, this is the implied legal relation between tea-

---

a 3 Salk. 47 ; 1 Hawk P. c. c. 29, § 5 ; 4 Burns Inst. 119 : Bac. Abr. N. Master and Servant.

cher and scholar. Modern theories do not accord to this rule all the force of law, as thus laid down. Our duty, however, is not to discuss the wisdom of the different theories.

It is doubtless the law, and should be, that in the public school, for the time being, that is, during school hours, the schoolmaster is invested with all the authority of a parent; he ought to be possessed of the power to make rules for the regulation of the conduct; to direct the studies; to order the application; as to the manner of recitations, reading, writing or other exercises; and to keep order and silence; prevent disturbances; and require obedience to all his reasonable rules; obedience to all such proper rules, and known requirements; may be enforced by reasonable and moderate correction, as an established and necessary resort, to this end; and this correction, may doubtless be, by temporary confinement, if, in the judgment of the teacher, that kind of chastisement is most effective in producing obedience to rules, or, in securing diligence and application to studies, or as a punishment for delinquencies. This power of the teacher for the time, is analogous to that which belongs to parents; and the authority of the teacher is regarded as a delegation of parental authority. Indeed the authority is supposed to proceed from a delegation of the parent; it is implied from the very necessity of the case, and need not be conveyed by express agreement. Blackstone says, " that by such delegation to the tutor or schoolmaster of the child, the tutor or schoolmaster is then *in loco parentis*, and has such a portion of the power of the parent committed to his charge, viz., that of restraint and correction, as may be necessary to answer the purposes for which he is employed." *a* And Chancellor Kent was of the same opinion, *b* that he may inflict moderate and reasonable chastisement, and he refers with approbation to a case decided in North Carolina, *c* in which the Supreme Court of that state held the same rule. On a reference to that case, we find the Supreme Court, among other things said: " One of the most sacred duties of parents is, to train up and qualify the children for becoming useful and virtuous members of society. This duty cannot be effectually performed, without the ability to command obedience; to control stubbornness; to

a 1 Black. Com. 453.   *b* 2 Kent. Com. 205. Note.
c State v. Pendergrass, 2 Dev. and Batah.

quicken diligence; to reform bad habits; and to enable him
to exercise this salutary sway, he is armed with the power to administer moderate correction when he shall believe it to be just
and necessary. The teacher is the substitute of the parent; is
charged in part with the performance of his duties, and in the exercise of these delegated duties, is invested with his power. The
law has not undertaken to prescribe stated punishments for particular offences, but has contented itself with the general grant of
the power of moderate correction, and has confided the graduation
of punishments within the limits of this grant, to the discretion of
the teacher."

"The line which separates moderate correction from immoderate
punishment, can only be ascertained from general principles. The
welfare of the child is the main purpose for which the pain is permitted to be inflicted. Any punishment therefore which may
seriously endanger life, limb or health, or shall disfigure the child,
or cause any other permanent injury, may be pronounced in itself
immoderate, as not only being unnecessary for, but inconsistent
with the purpose for which correction is authorized. But any correction however severe, which produces temporary pain only, and
no permanent ill, cannot be so pronounced, since it may have been
necessary for the reformation of the child, and does not affect injuriously its future welfare."

We hold, therefore, that it may be laid down as a general rule,
that teachers exceed the limits of their authority, when they cause
lasting mischief; but act within the limits of it, when they inflict
temporary pain only. When the correction administered is not
in itself immoderate, and therefore beyond the authority of the
teacher, its legality or illegality must depend entirely, we think,
on the *quo animo*, with which it was administered. Within the
sphere of his authority, the master is the judge, where correction
is required, and the degree of correction necessary; and like others,
entrusted with a discretion, he cannot be made penally responsible
for error of judgment, but only for wickedness of purpose. The
best and wisest of mortals are weak and erring creatures; and in
the exercise of functions in which their judgment is to be the guide,
cannot be rightfully required to engage for more than honesty of
purpose, and diligence of execution. His judgment must be *pre-*

sumed to be correct, *because he is the judge*, and also because of the difficulty of proving of the offence, or the accumulation of offences that called for the correction; and of showing the peculiar temperament, disposition and habits of the individual corrected; and of exhibiting the various milder means, that may have been ineffectually used before correction was resorted to.

But the master may be punishable when he does not transcend the powers granted, if he grossly abuse them. If he use his authority as a cover for malice, and, under the pretence of administering correction, gratify his own bad passions, the mask of the judge shall be taken off; and he will stand amenable to justice as an individual not invested with judicial power.

It is perhaps a questionable and unsettled question in the law upon this relation, as to the precise point of time when the parental authority ceases, and that of the master begins; that is, whose authority actually exists when the scholar is on his way to, and on his return from school; that of the parent, or that of the master. Naturally, it is to be presumed, it is that of the parent; the masters dominion is the school-room, and its appurtenances, during school hours. But if there be special regulations understood by the parent to be the rules of the *school;* regulating the deportment of the scholar while on his way to, and from school; then the implication of law would be, that the parent consents, to the masters authority to correct for violations of such rules. So too, doubtless, under the authority of the master to discipline, correct and compel obedience to duty and diligence in study; he may detain a delinquent scholar after the school generally is dismissed, to compel him to complete a lesson or duty which might have been accomplished with due application in the regular hours of school, provided the time of such detention extend only to such reasonable time as is sufficient to perform the task, or had been spent by the scholar in play or idleness, which caused the delinquencies. But in the absence of all school rules regulating the conduct of the scholar on the way, and known to the parent, the legal presumption is, that as parents desire the services of their children at home, except the usual school hours, that they surrender their authority over the child, only, during the regular school hours, and that as the parent and not the teacher is somewhat responsible for the

66

conduct of their children except while in school, the parent is also responsible for the conduct of the child on the way.

7. "Where parties bail another in legal proceedings, they are regarded in law as his jailors, selected by himself, and with the right to his legal custody for the purpose of seizing and delivering him up to the officers of the law, at any time before the liability of the bail has become fixed by a forfeiture being judicially declared, on his failure to comply with the condition of the bond. *a* This is a right they may exercise in person, or by agent, and without resort to judicial process." *b*

This relation of principal and bail in civil cases, commonly called special bail, is a thing of the past. It existed when the debtor was liable to be arrested, as he could be, upon demands arising upon contract, and when so arrested, to avoid further imprisonment, gave bail to the sheriff, conditioned that he would give special bail to the plaintiff in the action within twenty days after the return of the writ, so that the plaintiff might have his body to imprison, in satisfaction of the judgment to be obtained in the action. His special bail became in law the jailors of his own choosing, and he was thus immersed in a living prison, or his body subject to the actual custody of his special bail, and liable at any time, and at all places, to be taken by his bail, and cast into the common gaol upon a copy of the bail piece, by his special bail, or by a person authorized by them. Thanks to the progressive spirit of the age, this barbarous excrescence upon the laws of the past, no longer obscures the jurisprudence of the free citizens of this state. The law to abolish imprisonment for debt, in this and other states, has to that extent, emancipated the honest citizen from this odious penalty arising from his inability to pay his debts. Though he is still liable to be restrained of his personal liberty in what are called actions sounding in tort.

8. "The control of the creditor over the person of his debtor through legal process to enforce payment of his demand, is now nearly abolished, thanks to the humane provisions of the recent statutory and constitutional provisions. In cases of torts, and where debts were fraudulently contracted, or where there is an

a Harp v. Osgood, 2 Hill, 216.
b Parker v. Bidwell, 3 Conn. 84.

attempt at a fraudulent disposition of property with the intent to deprive the creditor of payment, the body of the debtor may be seized and confined ; but the reader is referred to the constitution and statutes of his state for information on this subject."

The causes which in this state give the creditor power over the personal liberty of the debtor, are limited to five, by express provisions of the statute. *a* 1. In an action for the recovery of damages, on a cause of action not arising out of contract, where the defendant is not a resident of the state, or is about to remove therefrom, or where the action is for an injury to the person or character, or for injuring, or wrongfully taking, detaining, or converting property. 2. In an action for a fine or penalty, or on a promise to marry, or for money received, or property embezzled or fraudulently misapplied by a public officer or attorney, solicitor or counsellor, or by an officer or agent of a corporation, or banking association, in the course of his employment as such, or by any factor, agent, broker, or other person in a fiduciary capacity, or for the misconduct or neglect in office, or in a professional employment. 3. In an action to recover the possession of personal property unjustly detained, where the property or any part thereof has been concealed, removed, or disposed of so that it cannot be found or taken by the sheriff, and with the intent that it should not be found or taken, or with the intent to deprive the plaintiff of the benefit thereof. 4. When the defendant has been guilty of a fraud, in contracting the debt, or incurring the obligation for which the action is brought, or in concealing or disposing of the property, for the taking, detention or conversion of which the action is brought, or when the action is brought to recover damages for fraud or deceit. 5. When the defendant has removed or disposed of his property, or is about to do so, with intent to defraud his creditors. But no female can be arrested in any action, except for wilful injury to person, character, or property. Even arrest for these causes cannot be made, until it has been judicially determined by a judge of some court upon proper application, and upon satisfactory evidence to him, that a cause of action exists, and that the case comes within one of the five subdivisions of causes above enumerated, and a sufficient bond or undertaking, satisfac-

a Code, § 179.

tory to, and approved by said judge, shall be given by the plaintiff to pay to the defendant all costs and damages he may recover in such action. The statute further provides the manner in which the defendant arrested for these causes, can be discharged from such arrest. All these matters are subjects that belong to practice, not connected with the question of power of restraint.

These then, are the legal restraints upon, and qualifications to the right of personal liberty. For any other restraint, or for the legal abuse of the legal rights which have been above specified, the party restrained, is entitled to immediate process from the courts, by *habeas corpus*, and to speedy relief thereon.

CHAPTER XVII.

OF CONSTITUTIONAL PROTECTION TO THE PERSON OF THE CITIZEN — OTHER THAN PERSONAL LIBERTY.

RIGHTS AND IMMUNITIES OF THE CITIZEN.

THE leading idea put forth in the declaration of our independence, as well as in the preamble and body of our national constitution, is the equality of rights of all mankind. Not only was it the object of these instruments, to secure them the blessings of liberty and equality, but also to secure alike to each and every citizen, all the benefits which is conferred upon each and every other citizen of the states or of the nation. To secure this end, the federal constitution speaks in an authoritative tone: "The citizens of each state shall be entitled to all the privileges and immunities of citizens of the several states."

It is no part of our purpose to make this work the history of our political organizations, nor to point out the reasons therefrom, that lead to the insertion of this provision in the constitution; but only to treat it as a sacred right secured to every citizen, because we find it so secured by the fundamental law of the government. It is an invaluable privilege; it becomes the birthright of every natural born citizen; and the lawfully acquired right of every naturalized citizen. By this constitutional provision, every citizen of a state, is likewise a citizen of the United States; and as a national citizen, he is in theory, politically and potentially present, and has the right to be actually and personally present, in every part of the national domain. He possesses the right to be personally present in any state or territory of the government, and to enjoy there, the right and freedom to speak his opinions; to do and perform all lawful acts; and to enjoy all the privileges and immunities that any other citizen of that, or any other state or territory, in which it is his pleasure to be, may enjoy; and any state regulation, that interferes with these rights of a national citizen, in manner or effect, different from that which its own citizens enjoy, does an act which directly conflicts with his constitutional rights, whatever may be the pretence for adopting such regulations. Cotemporaneous experience has taught us, that the violation of this sacred right, was one of the leading reasons of bringing on the late national disruption.

QUARTERING SOLDIERS IN PRIVATE HOUSES.

This provision speaks for itself. The experience of all nations, has shown, that a large standing army in time of peace, should be avoided as dangerous to liberty, and that the quartering of soldiers upon the citizens of the state, had been a very common resort of arbitrary princes, and was full of inconvenience and peril to the citizens. It has been well said by Judge Cooley, a that, "It is difficult to imagine a more terrible engine of oppression than the power in an executive, to fill the house of an obnoxious person with a company of soldiers, who are to be fed and warmed at his expense, under the direction of an officer accustomed to the exercise of arbitrary power, and in whose presence the ordinary laws of courtesy, not less than the civil restraints which protect person and property, must give way to unbridled will, of one who is sent as an instrument of punishment; and with whom, insult and outrage may appear quite in the line of duty." The clause, as we find it in the national constitution, has come down to us through the petition of rights; the Bill of Rights of 1688, and the Declaration of Independence; and is carried out in the national constitution; securing the principle to the nation, and to the citizen, that the military shall, in time of peace, be in strict subordination to the civil power. b

UNREASONABLE SEARCHES AND SEIZURES.

This constitutional sanction, and adoption of what had become a feature of the common law, and the test which it affords for trying the legality of any warrant by which a man may be deprived of his liberty, or disturbed in the enjoyment of his property; cannot be too highly valued by the citizens of a free government. This principle had been secured before the adoption of our constitution,

a Cooley on Const. Lim. 308.
b Story on Const § 1900

even in England, and grew out of an arbitrary abuse of power in that country, in issuing, under a statute authorizing it, what was called writs of assistance, by the courts, to revenue, and other officers, empowering them *at their discretion*, to search suspected places for smuggled goods. This, was in that day, pronounced " the worst instrument of arbitrary power ; the most destructive of English liberty, and of the fundamental principles of law, that ever was found in an English law book ; since they placed the liberty of every man in the hands of every petty officer." " This constitutional provision, seems indispensable to the full enjoyment of the rights of personal security, personal liberty, and private property." a Its introduction into the amendments to the constitution, was doubtless, occasioned by the great sensation excited in England, as well as in this country, down to the time of the revolution, upon acts of arbitrary power, exercised under this pretence of law based upon this statute, enacted under the pretence of regulating the press, which authorized the issuing of warrants, to take up, without naming any person in particular, the authors, publishers, and printers of such obscene, or seditious libels, as were particularly mentioned in the warrant. Though this statute was limited in its time of duration ; the practice afterwards continued for a period of seventy years, and down to the year 1763 ; and was followed in practice even in this country. Its legality was then tested in England in the Courts of King's Bench, where it was solemnly declared, that such warrants were void for uncertainty. b It may now be regarded as settled common law, that a warrant, and the complaint upon which it is founded, to be legal, must not only state the name of the party, but also, the time and place, and the nature of the offence, with reasonable certainty, and in New York it is regulated by statutes. c

In the administration of preventive justice, even at common law, it is believed, that in this country, the following rules are of universal adoption, as law, and are held to be the right of every citizen to have kept sacred, viz : That some probable ground of suspicion must be presented to a magistrate possessing judicial authority,

a 2 Story on Const. § 1902.
b Money v. Leach, 3 Burr. 1767.
c 1 Rev. Stat. 93, § 11; Id. 125, § 66, (54); 3 Rev. Stat. 746, §§ 32 to 36.

to issue the writ; that it be supported by oath or affirmation'; that
the party charged be allowed to find reasonable, and not oppressive bail to answer, to avoid being thrown into prison; that he
have the benefit of the writ of *habeas corpus*, and thus obtain his
release if wrongfully confined; and that he may be restored to his
former liberty and rights, in order to prepare for a judicial examination of his case by a day in court.

"A statute which should permit the breaking and entering of a
man's house, and the examination of books and papers with a view
to discover the evidence of crime, might possibly not be void, on constitutional grounds in some cases, as for instance, books and
papers of a public character, retained from their lawful custody ;
for females, supposed to be confined in houses of ill fame ; for
children, enticed or kept away from parents and guardians; and
for counterfeit money, forged bills and the like ; but the power of
the legislature to authorize a resort to this process, is one that
can be properly exercised only in extreme cases, and it is sometimes better, even that crime should go unpunished, than that the
citizen should be liable to have his premises invaded; his trunks
broken open ; his private books, letters and papers exposed to the
prying curiosity, and the misconstructions of ignorant and suspic-
ious persons, and this, under the direction of a mere ministerial
officer who brings with him such assistants as he pleases, and who
will be more likely to select them with reference to physical
strength and courage, than to their sensitive regard to the rights
and feelings of others.   To *incline* against such laws, is to incline
on the side of safety." *a*

"Instances sometimes occur, in which ministerial officers take
such liberties in endeavoring to discover and punish offenders, as
are even more criminal, than the offences they seek to punish. The
employment of spies and decoys to lead men on to the commission
of crime, on the pretence of bringing criminals to justice, cannot
be too often or too strongly condemned ; and the prying into private correspondence, by officers, which has sometimes been permitted by postmasters, is directly in the face of the law, and utterly
unjustifiable.   The importance of public confidence in the inviolability of correspondence through the post office, cannot well be

a Cooley on Const. Limitations, 306.

overrated; and the proposition to permit letters to be opened at the discretion of a ministerial officer, would be met with general indignation. The same may be said of private correspondence by telegraph; the public are not entitled to it for any purpose; and a man's servants, with the same propriety, may be subpœned to bring into court his private letters and journals, or a telegraph operator to bring in his private correspondence. In either case, it would be equivalent to an unlawful and unjustifiable seizure of his papers—such an "unreasonable seizure" as is directly condemned by the constitution." a

"They are obnoxious in *principle*, necessarily odious in the method of execution; and tend to invite abuse and to cover the commission of crime. We think it would generally be safe for the legislature to regard all those "searches and seizures unreasonable" which have hitherto been known to the law, and on that ground to abstain from authorizing them, leaving the parties and the public to the accustomed remedies."

While we regard these views of the learned author as worthy of the highest consideration, and in the main sound and judicious, as well as happily expressed; we are compelled to admit, that there are two sides to this question. In these modern days, when villainy is calling to its aid the highest and chiefest experts in science; when intellect and skill can receive the highest reward in criminal employments; the sound old maxim *salus populi suprema lex*, must be called into application, to defend the public, and aid to secure its safety. There is the known, and generally well understood implied assent on the part of every member of society, that his own individual welfare, his property, liberty, and even his life, shall, under circumstances of emergency, or extreme necessity, be yielded to the public safety, or the public good; that private inconvenience and even mischief, shall be endured rather than great public inconvenience. This is based on the very nature of the social compact, and upon which all municipal law is founded, that even individual liberty is given up to insure the safety and well being of the public.

a Id. 307.

Little need be said upon this constitutional security to the citizen, other than to refer to the provision in both national and state constitutions, in relation to it. No person shall be held to answer for a capital or otherwise infamous crime, unless upon the presentment or indictment of a grand jury. The statutes of the state have regulated the mode of their selection, and have secured to the citizen, the benefit of a high class and character of citizens to compose this body, who, before they enter upon the performance of their duties, are required to be sworn and charged in relation to their duties, by the judge who presides at the court to which they are summoned. There is a minor class of offences called misdemeanors, which the statutes provide may be tried in the inferior cou ts without indictment. The only other exceptions are those mentioned in the constitution, when the citizen belongs to the land or naval forces, or in the militia in time of war, when in actual service or in time of danger. He is secured a speedy trial, or, in a case less than capital, if necessity require it, to be bailed out, by reasonable, and not oppressive bail, to enable him within reasonable time to prepare for his defence; he is allowed a public trial, surrounded by the safeguard of a judge to pronounce the law; he shall previously, be fully, publicly informed of the nature of his offence or accusation; he shall have the assistance of counsel to aid him in his defence; he is entitled to compulsory process to compel the attendance of witnesses; he is entitled to challenge his jurors, and have them tried as to their peculiarities or prejudices, and in this state, is entitled to peremptory challenge of twenty jurors, on the trial of a capital offence, or for an offence punishable in the state prison for ten years or longer; and for lower offences, to a peremptory challenge of five jurors; a he is entitled to be confronted with his witnesses, in the presence of the jury and the court, and he is not compelled to be a witness to testify against himself.

In no other country, and under no other government in the world, is the citizen, who is charged with an offence, so surrounded with substantial safeguards and securities. These are the outlines; the details, which belong to the subject of practice, are equally protective and liberal towards the accused. But beyond these is the still

a 2 Rev. Stat. 734, §§ 9, 10.

further security that he shall not be twice put in jeopardy by a trial, for the same offence.

The right, as well as the mode of traverse by a jury of twelve men, is an essential and inestimable security to the accused. This is what is called a common law jury; and he cannot be deprived of that number to sit in his case; even a consent by him to be tried by a less number, would be mistrial and void, a because it would be a tribunal unknown to the law and constitution, one created by the parties. He is also entitled by the constitution to have his trial not among strangers, or in a distant or strange neighborhood, but in his own vicinage in the district in which the offence is charged to have been committed, and in a district previously fixed by law. Thus, he is secured a trial where he is known; where he has the benefit of his own character and standing among his neighbors; with witnesses near home;. and by jurors who may know not only his character, but that of the witnesses who testify on the trial. He has the benefit of the varieties of opinions of twelve independent men, each entitled to his own way of weighing and appreciating facts as well as witnesses, and he cannot be convicted, except by the unanimous verdict of the twelve jurors.

This is an advantage which can only be appreciated by those who are familliar with the practical workings of the system of jury trials in criminal cases. Jurors of equal intelligence, of equal integrity and conscientiousness, draw different conclusions from the same case. This idea was well expressed by Sir John Vaughn, Kt., Chief Justice of the Common Pleas of England, in a case where there was an attempt to punish a jury for corruptly disagreeing in a case submitted to them. b "I would like to know," said the Chief Justice, "whether anything be more common, than for two men, students, barristers, or judges, to deduce contrary and opposite conclusions out of the same case in law? And is there any difference that two men should infer distinct conclusions from the same testimony? Is anything more known, than that the same author, and place in that author, is forcibly urged to maintain contrary conclusions, and the decisions held, which is in the right? Is anything more frequent, in the controversies of religion, than to

a Cancemi v. The People, 18 N. Y. 128.

b Vaughn R. 141; Bushnell's Case.

press the same text to opposite tenets? How then comes it to pass, that two persons may not apprehend, with reason and honesty, what a witness, or many, say, to prove in the understanding of one, plainly one thing, but in the apprehension of the other, clearly the contrary thing? Must therefore one of these merit fine and imprisonment, because he doth that which he cannot otherwise do, preserving his oath and integrity? And this often is the case of the judge and jury."

Another, and perhaps one of the most important privileges of the accused, and not only a privilege but a right, a constitutional right, is, that he shall be allowed a defence by counsel on the trial, when so accused. When we compare the humanity of this right, with the barbarity of the ancient criminal law of England, which denied to persons accused of the crimes of treason or felony, the aid of counsel, it should inspire a feeling of pride in the American citizen, that he lives under the protection of such a government.

"When an ignorant person, unaccustomed to public assemblies, and perhaps feeble in body or in intellect, was put on trial on a charge of which, whether true or false, might speedily consign him to an ignominious death ; with able counsel on the part of the government, arrayed against him ; and all the machinery of the law ready to be employed to produce the evidence of circumstances indicating guilt, it is painful to contemplate the barbarity which could deny him professional aid ; especially, when in most cases he would be imprisoned immediately on being apprehended, and would thereby be prevented from making even the feeble preparations for defence, that otherwise might have been within his power." *a*

This horrible practice continued in England until the year 1695, the seventh of William III, when a statute was passed allowing counsel to persons indicted for treason. A notable case, (in this day it would be called infamously barbarous), is reported in the sixth volume of the English state trials, which occurred on the day before this statute took effect, but after its passage, William Parkins was indicted for treason. On his arraignment and pleading not guilty, he asked permission "To speak a word ; if your lordship pleases." Lord Chief Justice. "Aye sir, what say you." Parkins. "My lord, I

a Cooley on Const. Lim. 331. Note.

have been kept in hard prison ever since I was committed; nobody has been permitted to come to see me till Friday last—then my counsel came to me; and being charged with many facts as I see in this indictment, it will be necessary to have divers witnesses to clear myself of these particulars; they are dispersed up and down, and I have had no time to look after them, and therefore, I beg your lordship to put off my trial till another day."

Lord Ch. J. "When had you first notice of your trial?"

Parkins. "The first notice of my trial was on Wednesday last, in the afternoon."

Lord Ch. J. "That is a sufficient time of notice; sure you might have provided your witnesses and prepared for it by this time?"

Parkins. "But, my Lord, being kept so close prisoner, I had no opportunity for it, for it was not possible for me to get any body to come to me, till Friday noon, not so much as my counsel, and then, there was but two days, Saturday and Monday, (for Sunday is no day of business,) and it is impossible for me to be ready in the manner that I ought to be. It is a perfect distress and hardship upon me to be put so soon upon my trial without my witnesses, and, what should enable me to make my defence; therefore, I humbly intreat your lordship, to put it off till another day."

After various other interlocutions, immaterial.

Lord Ch. J. "Truly, we do not see any reason to put off the trial upon these suggestions."

Parkins. "My Lord, it is very hard; then I humbly beg that I may have the favor; that I may have counsel allowed me; I have no skill in indictments."

Lord Ch. J. "We cannot allow counsel."

Parkins. "My Lord, if I have no counsel, I do not understand these matters, nor what advantage it may be proper for me to take in these cases."

Lord Ch. J. "You are not ignorant, that counsel has always been refused when desired."

Parkins. "My Lord there is a new act of parliament that is lately made, that allows counsel."

Lord Ch. J. "But that does not commence yet sir."

Parkins. "My Lord, it wants but one day."

Lord Ch. J. "That is as much as if it were for a much longer time. We are to proceed according to what the law is, and not what it will be."

Sufficient of the temper and spirit of English judges of that day, appears in the report of this case, where it is shown, that they were removed from all sympathy with the people, and unrestrained by constitution or statute. The want of common humanity in a judge, manifest by his refusal to postpone this case for even one day, when the law would have allowed counsel to the prisoner; deprived of power to defend himself: needs only the history of the sequel to complete the tyranny of the act of which we have given the prelude. Parkins was of course convicted, and executed the following day, but the *sentence* of his lordship, should be appended to make the tragedy complete, which was as follows:

"That you go back to the place from whence you came, and from thence be drawn on a hurdle to the place of execution, where you shall be hanged up by the neck, and cut down alive; your body shall be ript open; your privy member be cut off; your bowels taken out, and burnt before your face; your hands shall be severed from your body, to be divided into four quarters and your head and quarters to be at the disposal of the King."

The mind that could utter this sentence, surely needed some relief at its close, &c. This was doubtless obtained by his most devout and pious conclusion; "and may the Lord have mercy upon your soul."

We have given this extract from the trial of a case under another government, and another system of administering the criminal law, to show the striking contrast between it, and the system under a constitutionally free government; and while, even in England, now, more liberal views and practice obtains, the same humanity in this respect does not exist, as with us. A liberal view of construction given to our own constitution, is, that the prisoner is not only allowed counsel, but when he is poor and unable to provide counsel for himself, it is the duty of the court to designate appropriate counsel for him, to be paid by the government. Such counsel are not at liberty to decline the duty, but are bound to put forth their best exertions of professional skill to that end, and are bound by all the obligations of duty to their clients, as is required in any other case.

This provision, in general and undefined terms, leaves the amount of punishment, much the subject of discretion by the courts; but statutes, enacted under the spirit of these provisions are to be found, not only passed by the national legislature, but also by the legislatures of the states, which fix and limit the amount of punishment that may be inflicted, for nearly each and every offence known to the law to be offences. These provisions would hardly seem to be necessary in a free government, since it is scarcely possible, that any department of such a government should authorize or justify conduct of judges whose action should be ranked as worthy such terms as we have applied to the English judges. They were doubtless adopted by us as an admonition, as well as caution to all departments of government, against such violent proceedings as had taken place in England in the arbitrary reigns of some of the Stuarts. a "In those times, demand of excessive bail was often made against persons who were odious to the court, and its favorites; and on failing to procure it, were committed to prison. Enormous fines and amercements were also sometimes imposed, and cruel and vindictive punishments inflicted." b Blackstone also informs us, "that sanguinary laws are a bad symptom of the distemper of any state, or at least of its weak constitution. The laws of the Roman kings, and the twelve tables of the Decemviri, were full of cruel punishments. The Porcian law, which exempted all citizens from sentence of death, silently abrogated them all. In this period the republic flourished. Under the Emperor's, severe laws were revived, and then the empire fell." c

While even some of the states of the union, to their disgrace be it said, still continue those disgraceful institutions, the whipping post, the pillory and the stocks; the progress of public sentiment, and the advancing and more gentle and benign influences of the christian religion, are rapidly creating and working out a more humane spirit, in regard to public punishments; and these instruments are now viewed, not only as "cruel and unusual," but as absolutely barbarous.

a 2 Lloyd's Debate, 345.
b 2 Story on Const. § 1903.
c 4 Black. Com. 17.

The right of the people peaceably to assemble and to petition the government for a redress of grievances, is a necessary result of the right of being a free citizen. It is a simple, primitive and natural right. *a* "It is a right, (says Judge Story) which would seem unnecessary to be expressly provided for in a republican government, since it results from the very nature of its structure and institutions." *b* It is impossible that it should be practically denied, until the spirit of liberty had wholly disappeared; and the people had become so servile and debased, as to be unfit to exercise any of the privileges of freemen. "But it has not been thought unimportant to protect this right by statutory enactments, even in England, and indeed it will be remembered, that one of the most memorable attempts to crush out the liberty of the subject, in that country, made the right of petition the point of attack; and collected for its contemplated victims, the chief officers in the Episcopal hierarchy. The trial and acquittal of the seven bishops under James II, constituted one of the decisive battles in English constitutional history; and the right which was then vindicated, is a ' sacred right,' which, in difficult times, shows itself in its full magnitude; frequently serves as a safety valve, if judiciously treated by the recipients; and may give to the representatives, or other bodies, the most valuable information. It may right many a wrong, and the deprivation of it, would at once be felt by every freeman as a degradation." *c*

But despotism is the same in all human governments or institutions, where power is unrestrained. This right of petition was resisted even in our own republican form of government in the congress of the United States, when offered by the friends of freedom on the subject of the slave trade; of the fugitive slave law and of slavery; and to the struggles in that body upon these subjects, we may indirectly trace one of the leading causes of the late rebellion, by that portion of the states, with whom the institution of slavery was a favored institution. *d* The history of this strug-gle belongs not to this work. It is only referred to, as being illus-

a Cooley on Const. Limits, 349.

b Story on Const. § 1894.

c Cooley, 349.

d Benton's Abr of Debates, Vol. 2, 57-60, 182-188, 436-444; Vol. 12, 660-679, 705-743; Vol. 13, 5-28, 266-280, 557-562.

trative of the power of self-interest, upon the one hand, against the declared inalienable rights of all men, to life, liberty, and the pursuit of happiness, upon the other.

THE FREEDOM OF SPEECH AND OF THE PRESS.

It being one of the great fundamental privileges of American governments, that the people are the sovereigns, and that those who administer the government are their agents and servants and not their masters; it would have been a political solicism, to have permitted the smallest restraint of the right of the people, to enquire into, censure, approve, punish or reward their agents, according to their merit or demerit. The constitution, therefore, secures to them the unlimited right to do this, either by speaking, writing, printing, or by any other mode of publishing which they may think proper. This being the only mode by which the responsibility of the agents of the public can be secured, and practically enforced, the smallest infringement of the rights guaranteed by this article, must threaten the total subversion of the government. For a representative democracy ceases to exist, the moment that the public functionaries are by any means absolved from their responsibility to their constituents; and this happens, whenever the constituent can be restrained in any manner, from speaking, writing, or publishing his opinions, upon any public measure, or upon the conduct of those who may advise or execute it. a

Though this amendment to the constitution is in general and unqualified language, yet it is plain, that it imports no more than that every man shall have a right to speak, write, print, or publish his opinions upon any subject whatsoever, without any prior restraint, so always, that he does not injure any other person in his rights, person, property or reputation; and so always, that he does not thereby disturb the public peace, or attempt to subvert the government. b   Chancellor Kent says, c that, "though the law be solicitous to protect every man in his fair fame and character, it is equally careful that the liberty of speech and of the press should be duly preserved. The liberal communication of sentiment, and entire freedom of discussion, in respect to the character and

a Tuckers Black. Vol. 1 297.

b 2 Story on Const. § 1880.   c 2 Vol. Com. 17.

conduct of public men, and of candidates for public favor, is deemed essential to the judicious exercise of the right of suffrage, and of that control over their rulers, which resides in the free people of the United States. It has accordingly become a constitutional principle in this country, that every citizen may freely speak, write, and publish his sentiments, on all subjects, being responsible for the abuse of that right, and that no law can rightfully be passed to restrain or abridge the freedom of speech or the press."

It is neither more nor less than an expansion of the great doctrine brought into operation in the law of libel, that every man shall be at liberty to publish what is true, with good motives, and for justifiable ends. And with this reasonable limitation, it is not only right in itself, but it is an inestimable privilege in a free government. Without such a limitation, it might become the scourge of the republic, first denouncing the principles of liberty, and thereby rendering the most virtuous patriots odious, through the terrors of the press, introducing despotism in its worst form. *a*

That this amendment was intended to secure to every citizen the right to speak, or write, or print, whatever he might please, without any responsibility, public or private therefor, is a supposition too wild to be indulged in by any rational man. This would be to allow to every citizen a right to destroy at his pleasure, the reputation, the peace, the property, and even the personal safety, of every other citizen. A man might, out of mere malice and revenge, accuse another of the most infamous crimes, might excite against him the indignation of all his fellow citizens by the most attrocious calumnies; might disturb, nay overturn all his domestic peace, and embitter his parental affections; might inflict the most distressing punishments upon the weak, the timid, and the innocent; might prejudice all a man's civil, and political, and private rights; might stir up sedition, rebellion, and treason even against the government itself, in the wantonness of his passions, or the corruption of his heart. Civil society could not go on, under such circumstances. Men would then be obliged to resort to private vengeance, to make up for the deficiencies of the law; and assassinations, and savage cruelties would be perpetuated with all the frequency belonging to barbarous and brutal communities. *b*

a 2 Story, § 1880.   *b* Id.

There is no other reasonable construction to be given to this clause in the amended constitution, than to hold it to mean a freedom of speech, and of the press, as broad as existed at common law, when the constitution, which guaranteed it, was adopted. It was such freedom, that was intended to be secured; and it was not intended that the legislature should possess the power to restrict it, except in those cases of publications injurious to private character, or to public morals or safety, which come strictly within the reasons of civil or criminal liability as then existed also at common law, but where, nevertheless, the common law as we had adopted it, failed to provide a remedy, as for instance, at the time of the adoption of this provision. At common law, it was not actionable, (nor indeed, in this state, is it now,) to impute the want of chastity to a female, without proof of special damage. It certainly would not be held to be a constitutional abridgment of the freedom of speech, if the legislature should enact a law creating liability to an action and to damage, for the utterance of such a charge. It is the charge of a grievous wrong, of all others, most destructive to the female character; and no reason can be found in public policy, for protecting the utterance of such a wrong. Many other analagous cases may be stated. The constitutional provisions do not prevent the modifications of the common law rules of liability for libels and slanders, but they would not permit the bringing of new cases within those rules, when they do not rest upon the same reasons. *a*

It is extremely difficult to draw a line which may be adopted as a rule, which shall distinguish between protection or liberty, upon the one hand, and licentiousness upon the other. These two extremes, of liberty and licentiousness, must not be confounded. They are not identical, nor intended to be alike secured in the constitution. "It is a well understood commentary on this provision for the liberty of the press, that it was intended to prevent such *previous restraints* upon publications as had been practiced by other governments; and in early times *here*, to stifle the efforts of patriots towards enlightening their fellow subjects upon the rights and duties of rulers. The liberty of the press was to be unrestrained, but he who used it, was to be responsible in the case of

a Cooley on Const, 430.

its abuse; like the right to bear arms, or to keep fire arms; which does not protect him who uses them from annoyance or destruction." *a*

" The common law is, therefore, left unimpaired by the constitution ; * * and yet there are some exceptions to this as a general rule. The exceptions are all founded in a regard to certain public interests, which are of more importance than the character or tranquility of any individual. All proceedings in legislative assemblies, whether by speech, written documents or otherwise, are protected from scrutiny elsewhere than in those bodies themselves, because it is essential to the maintenance of public liberty, that in such assemblies, the tongue and the press, should be wholly unshackled."

" So proceedings in courts of justice, in which the reputation of individuals may be involved, are to be free from future animadversions, because the investigation of right, demands the utmost latitude of inquiry, and men ought not to be deterred from prosecuting or defending them by fear of punishment or damages. Yet in *these* instances, if this necessary indulgence is abused for malicious purposes, a pretence only being made of the forms of judicial process, the party so conducting himself is amenable to the law."

" The right also of complaining to any public constituted body of the malversation or oppressive conduct of any of its officers or agents, with a view to redress for actual wrong, or the removal of an unfaithful officer, may be justified, because the case will show that the proceeding does not arise from malicious motives, or if it does, because the common interest requires that such representations should be free."

" And there are cases of mere *private* import, such as an honest, though mistaken character of a servant, which, when requested by any one having an interest, the law considers innocent, or privileged. These cases are all provided for by the common law, and they go far to render harmless the much decried rule, that truth is no defence in a prosecution for a libel."

So too, "if a minister of the gospel should be guilty of gross immoralities, and one of his parish should complain to the church in order that an inquiry might be instituted; or, if a candidate for

a Commonwealth v. Blanding 3 Pick. R. 313-314.

the ministry should from vicious habits be unfit for the station he seeks; since all are interested in the purity of the ministerial character, information to those whose duty it is to determine his qualifications, would not be libelous, if communicated in a spirit of truth and candor. *a*

These are the exceptions, " but no state of society could be more deplorable than that which would admit an indiscriminate right in every citizen to arraign the conduct of every other, before the public, in newspapers, in hand-bills or other modes of publication, not only for crimes, but for faults, foibles, deformities of mind, or of person. Even admitting all such allegations to be true; when the accusation is made by public bodies or officers whose duty it is by law to detect and prosecute offences; the charge and investiga-tion are submitted to, and no spirit of revenge is produced; but, if private intermeddlers, assuming the character of reformers, should have the right to become public accusors, and when called to account, to defend themselves by breaking into the circle of friends, families, children, and domestics, to prove the existence of errors or faults which may have been overlooked or forgiven where they were most injurious. The man who is thus accused without lawful process, might be expected to avenge himself by unlawful means; and duels and assassinations, would be the com-mon occurrences of the times. Instances are reccollected where violence and even death has ensued from such proceedings. It was a wise regard to these evils, that the common law has put a check upon the *licentiousness* of the press, and the expression of opinion by writing, painting &c., when the effect and object is to blacken the character of any one, or to disturb his comfort; the public good not being the end and purpose of such publication, or if that is professed, the public peace requiring a different mode of accusation." *b*

" The constitutional liberty of speech, and of the press, as we understand it, in general terms, implies, a right to freely utter and publish whatsoever the citizen may please, and to be protected against any responsibility for the publication, except so far as such publications from their blasphemy, obscenity, or scandalous char-acter, may be a public offence; or, as by their falsehood and malice,

they may injuriously affect the private character of individuals. *a*
The exceptions and qualifications of this rule, beyond those given
above, partake of the character of questions of practice, and are
not within the general scope of this work.

The common law offence of libels against the government or
the constitution, on the ground of their criminality in the excitement of tumult and disaffection, or a revolutionary spirit, have
fallen into disfavor. The general spirit of freedom and independence, is in favor of allowing the right to every citizen to give to the
acts and measures of public men, and measures of public policy,
the most full and free discussions; and great allowance is to
be made in times of political excitements for the criticisms of
what are called the " outs," in the review of the policy measures,
and administrations of the " ins." Sharp criticisms, ridicule, and
exhibitions of deep feeling, such as a sense of injustice for supposed
wrongs engenders, are tolerated, and submitted to, as being wiser
than a resort to a more vindictive measure of prosecution, on the
ground that a conservative public sentiment is always ready to do
justice, and is sufficient to correct the abuse. It is regarded as
far more magnanimous, equally certain, and is more satisfactory
to the injured party, than the vexatious resort to the vengeance of
the law. Indeed the occasions are not infrequent, when criticisms
upon public officers, upon their actions, character, and motives, are
recognized as legitimate, and large latitude, and great freedom
of expression is not only permitted, but is to be desired, so
long as good faith dictates the communication. There are cases,
where it is clearly the duty of every one, to speak with boldness
and freedom, what he feels it his duty to say, concerning not only
public officers, but concerning those who are presented for public
positions. Through the ballot box the electors approve or condemn those who ask for their suffrages, and though this is often
a very erring standard, yet it is our own chosen system; and however emphatic this voice may speak in condemnation or approval
of the condemnation uttered by the press, no action lies for the
publication. *b*

a Cooley on Const. Lim. 422.

b Howard v. Thompson, 21 Wend· 319 &c.   VanWick v. Aspinwall, 17 N. Y. 191;
Thorn v. Blanchard, 5 John, 528-530; Hunt v. Bennett, 19 N. Y. 178; Root v. King,
4 Wend. 113.

Perhaps there is no question of law, more unsettled by general and definite rules, than that of the law of libel in our courts; and some confusion in practice has grown out of the difference in the administration of the law between libels in civil, and libels in criminal actions. In trials of the latter class, as will be seen by the constitution of New York, the jury have a right to determine the law and the fact, *a* but it cannot be denied that the cases lack uniformity in more than one particular, and that they are not quite satisfactory to political public journalists who claim the greatest latitude and most liberal construction of the clause in this respect in the federal constitution.

Judge Cooley, in his work on Constitutional Limitations complains of a peculiarity of views of the New York courts. He says, " The narrowness of any such rule, (especially the rule in Root v. King). consists in its assumption, that the private character of a public officer is something aside from, and not entering into or influencing, his public conduct, and that a thoroughly dishonest man may be a just minister, and that a judge who is corrupt and debauched in private life, may be pure and upright in his judgments; in other words, that an evil tree is as likely as any other to bring forth good fruits." Any such assumption, he says, is false to human nature, and the public have a right to assume that a corrupt life will influence public conduct, however plausibly it may be glossed over. They are therefore interested in knowing what the character of their public servants is, as well as that of persons, offering themselves for their suffrages. If so, it would seem that there should be some privilege of comment; that, that privilege could only be limited by good faith and just intention, and of these, a jury might judge, taking into account the nature of the charges made; and the reasons which existed for making them. *b*

We have given the above views of an able writer upon this point rather to illustrate, the statement above made; that in different states, under different statutes, and with difference of judicial views of latitude of this constitutional protection, there is not an entire uniformity of rule, among the states. To attempt to show the variations of this rule in the several states, and the settled

a Constitution of N. Y; Art 1 § 8. and cases supra.
b Cooley on Const. 440

rule in each, would swell this volume into a digest, or work of practice, and is hardly called for; therefore, our own views as above expressed, is intended to be those only of the settled law in this state, and which may be gathered from the cases cited in the notes.

But to these rules, there will also be found exceptions in a class of cases, where, from reasons of public policy, certain utterances are so absolutely protected, that no inquiry as to motives, is tolerated in actions for libel or slander. A single case may be referred to, to prove the exception. No action for slander or libel can be maintained against a party, called as a witness in a judicial proceeding, for testimony given as such witness which may reflect upon the character of a party, and which might otherwise be regarded as slanderous, even though malice be charged in the utterance; though false accusations made voluntarily, in the papers, affidavits and other proceedings, preliminary to the commencement of an action, or to other judicial proceedings for the accusation of crime, are not absolutely protected. *Prima facie*, they are protected, but *actual* malice may be averred and proved; and if proved, the privilege does not protect. *a* Wanton abuse is not protected by law; the privity is not to be abused on the part of the witness, nor is a party to be permitted to utter slanderous words against the witness by way of insult, and not in the legitimate course of his defence.

Not materially different from these privileges and this protection, and coming under this same constitutional provision that "every citizen may freely speak," &c.; is the right of counsel who represent parties in judicial proceedings. The value of this right to the counsel, and to the party whom he represents, depends nearly altogether upon the freedom with which he is allowed to act, to speak, to comment upon facts, circumstances, character and conduct of witnesses and parties whose action or motives may be traced or deduced from the evidence, or from the surroundings and circumstances connected directly, or remotely with the subject of

a Burlingame v. Burlingame, 8 Cowen 141; Jarvis v. Hathaway, 3 John· 180; Gilbert v. The People, 1 Denio 41; McGlaughy v. Wetmore, 6 John. 82; Rector v. Smith, 11 Iowa, 362 ; Bradley v. Heath, 12 Pick. 163 ; Kean v. McLanglen, 2 Searg. & Maule, 471; Hosmer v. Loveland, 19 Barb. 111; State v. Burnham, 9 N. H. 34.

the judicial inquiry in which he is called to act. The law justly and necessarily, in view of the importance of the privilege, allows very great liberty in such cases to counsel, and surrounds them with a protection that is a complete shield in all cases, except in those, where the counsel has abused his legal privilege, by using the occasion to gratify his private malice, and unnecessarily heaping slander upon some one connected with the proceeding. a

"The question therefore in such cases, is not whether the words spoken are true; not whether they are actionable in themselves; but whether they were spoken in the course of judicial proceedings; and whether they are relative and pertinent to the cause or subject of the inquiry. And in determining what is pertinent, much latitude must be allowed to the judgment and discretion of those who are intrusted with the conduct of a cause in court; and a much larger allowance made for the ardent and excited feelings, with which a party or counsel, (who naturally, and almost necessarily identifies himself with his client,) may become animated, by constantly regarding one side only of an interesting controversy, in which the dearest rights of such party may become involved. And if these feelings sometimes manifest themselves in strong invectives, or exaggerated expressions beyond what the occasion would strictly justify, it is to be recollected, that this is said to or in the presence of a judge who hears both sides; in whose mind the exaggerated statement may be at once controlled, and met by evidence and argument of a contrary tendency from the other party; and who, from the impartiality of his position, will naturally give to an exaggerated assertion, not warranted by the occasion, no more weight than it deserves. Still this privilege must be restrained by some limit, and we consider that limit to be this : that a party or counsel shall not avail himself of his situation to gratify private malice by uttering slanderous expressions, either against a party, witness or third person, which have no relation to the cause or subject matter of the inquiry. Subject to this restriction, it is on the whole for the public interest, and best calculated to subserve the purposes of justice, to allow counsel full freedom of speech in conducting their cases, and in advocating the rights of their constituents ; and this freedom of discussion ought

a Hoar v. Wood, 3 Met. 197; McMillan v. Burch, 1 Binney, 186.

69

not to be impaired by numerous and refined distinctions. *a* In the Court of Errors in this state, it was held that this privilege of *counsel* in advocating the rights of his client, and of the *party* himself when he manages his own cause in a judicial proceeding, is as broad as that of a legislative body, however false and malicious may be a charge made by the counsel, or the party upon such an occasion affecting the reputation of another ; and an action of slander will not lie, *provided* that what is said, be pertinent to the question under discussion. *b* But it was also held, that proving the defendant knew the charge to be false, would unquestionably be evidence of *express malice*, and would destroy the defence in this class of cases; and that the plaintiff in such case, has a right to prove express malice.

The privileges of a legislator, are expressly protected by both national and state constitutions. It would seem, that something beyond the common right of freedom of speech was intended. While counsel, and parties, and other citizens may be held to account for an abuse of this privilege, the protection to the legislator, would seem from the terms employed, to be an absolute freedom from liability under all circumstances. " For any speech or debate in either house of the legislature, the members shall not be questioned in any other place." This is a broader and more complete immunity than is given to others. Doubtless for an abuse of this privilege, he is amenable to the body of which he is a member, and can be expelled therefrom, but to no other punishment, for freedom of debate.

" The privilege secured by this constitutional provision, though of a personal nature, is not so much intended to protect the members against prosecution, for their own individual advantage, as to support the rights of the people, by enabling their representatives to execute the functions of their office without fear, either of civil or criminal prosecutions ; and therefore it ought not to be construed strictly, or confined strictly within the literal meaning of the words in which it is expressed ; but to receive a liberal and broad construction, commensurate with the design for which it was established." *c* It is accordingly held, that this privilege secures every

a Opinion of Shaw, Ch. J., in Hoar v. Wood, 3 Metcalf, 197.
b Hastings v. Lush, 22 Wend. 410.   *c* Coffin v. Coffin, 4 Mass. 1.

member an immunity from prosecutions for anything said or done by him as a representative of the people in the exercise of the functions of that office ; whether such exercise is regular according to the rules of the assembly, or irregular and against their rules ; whether the member be within his place, within the house delivering an opinion; uttering a speech ; engaging in debate ; giving his vote ; making a written report; communicating information, either to the house or to a member; or whether he is out of the house sitting in committee, and engaged in debating or voting therein, or in drawing up a report to be submitted to the assembly ; in short, the privilege in question secures the members, of a legislative assembly against all prosecutions, whether civil or criminal, on account of anything said or done by them, during the session, resulting from the nature, and in the execution of their office. It is hardly necessary to add, that as a legislative assembly has no existence or authority, as such, except when regularly in session, the members cannot claim this privilege for anything said or done at any other time. It is to be observed, however, that the mere temporary adjournments, for the convenience of the members, and not for the purpose of putting an end to the session, are in fact continuations of and not terminations of it." *a*

"But, though a member, in the exercise of the functions of his office may speak, write, or vote in any manner that he deems proper, and may consequently give utterances with impunity, with what would subject a private person to a prosecution for libel or slander ; yet he will not therefore be justified in printing and publishing what he has spoken, if it contains matter injurious to the character of an individual ; not even if the publication is intended to correct a misrepresentation contained in the report of his speech previously published without his authority or sanction." *b*

The representative is not indebted to the will or pleasure of the house for this privilege ; he derives it not from them, but from the highest source of power, the will of the people expressed in the constitution, which is paramount to the will of either, or of both branches of the legislature.

While these protections are secured to citizens, parties, counsel,

a Curtis Law and Pr. of Assemblies, § 603.
b Id. § 604.

and legislators, from motives of high public policy upon the one hand, neither the constitution, the law, or public policy, will tolerate the destruction of private character upon the other, by a public publication of the proceedings of the body of the assembly, or courts, to the injury of the character of the citizen. It does not at all follow, that because counsel may speak freely what he believes, or what he is instructed to say, in court, that he may publish his speech containing slanderous imputations out of court. The first was allowed in order to discharge a high duty to a client; but with the ending of the suit, that duty was at an end ; the subsequent publicity must be at his individual peril, if it be unfair, unjust, or injurious to another; and this rule applies equally to the publication of judicial proceedings. Though a fair and impartial account of them is justifiable, and favored in law; an unfair or injurious report reflecting upon the character of the citizen, to his prejudice, is not privileged as against the injured party. The publisher must find his justification not in the *privilege*, but in the truth of the publication. *a* It is even libelous to publish a correct account of judicial proceedings, if accompanied with comments and insinuations tending to asperse a man's character. *b* The report must be confined to the actual proceeding in court, and must contain no defamatory observations or comments from any quarter whatever, in addition to what forms strictly and properly the legal proceedings. *c* The case was of privilege of a member of the House of Commons in England, and was p'ead to an action for l bel y a private citizen. *d* It was the report published by order of the house for the members of the body, and also for sale, which report contained reflections upon the character of the plaintiff. Lord Denman said, "Most willingly would I decline to enter upon an in uiry which may lead to my differing from that great and powerful assembly. But when one of my fellow subjects, presents himself before me in this court demanding justice for an injury, it is not at my option to grant or withhold redress. I am bound to afford it, if the law declares him entitled to it. The decision of the court was unanimous that the privilege did not exist in regard to those copies of the report sold

a Stanley v. Webb. 4 Sand. 21.

b Thomas v. Croswell, 7 John 264; Commonwealth v. Blanding, 3 Pick. 304.

c Kirg v. Carlisle, 3 B. & A. 167.

d Stockdale v. Hemsard, 9 Adol & Ellis, 1; Rex v. Creevy, 1 Maule & Selwin, 273.

to others." " The protection of the character of the citizen, triumphed over a *privilege*, claimed to have existed for a period so
long, that it had become hoary with age." *a* The editor of a newspaper has a right to publish the fact that an individual has been
arrested, and upon what charge, but he has no right while the
charge is in the course of investigation before the magistrate, to
assume that the person accused is guilty, or to hold him out to the
world as such. *b* Nor is such publication, often, less a public
offence. If the nature of the case is such, as to make it improper
that the proceedings should be spread before the public because
of their immoral tendency, or of the blasphemous or indecent
character of the evidence exhibited, the publication, though impartial and full, will be a public offence and punishable accordingly. *c*

So *ex parte* proceedings, or mere preliminary examinations,
though they may perhaps be called judicial, are not privileged, and
when they reflect injuriously upon individuals, the publisher derives
no protection from their having been already delivered in court. *d*
Their tendency is to prejudge those whom the law still presumes
to be innocent, and to poison the sources of justice. It is of infinite importance to all, that whatever has a tendency to prevent a
fair trial, should be guarded against. Every one is liable to be
questioned in a court of law, and called upon to defend his life and
character. We would then wish to meet a court or a jury of our
country with unbiassed minds.

If anything is more important than another in the administration of justice, it is, that jurymen should come to the trial of those
persons on whose guilt or innocence they are to decide, with minds
pure and unprejudiced. Is it possible they should do so, after
having read for weeks, and months before, *ex parte* statements of
the evidence against the accused, which the latter had no opportunity to disprove or controvert? By their own public declarations,
we know that the minds of jurymen are often preoccupied by such
statements, and that they proceed with terror to the discharge of

a Campbell' Lives of Chancellors, 293; King v. Abingdon, 1 Espurass R. 226.
b Usher v. Severance, 2 Appleton, 9.
c Rex v. Carlisle, 3 B. & A. 167; Rex v. Creevy, 1 M & S. 273.
d Stanley v. Webb, 4 Sand. 21; Huff v. Bennett, Id. 120; Matthews v. Beach, 5
Id. 256.

their duty, from the apprehension that an antecedent bias may influence their verdict. These publications tend alike to the conviction of the innocent, and the acquittal of the guilty.

The publication of proceedings in courts of justice where both sides are heard, and matters are *finally* determined, is salutary, and therefore permitted. The publication of these preliminary proceedings has a tendency to pervert the public mind, and to disturb the course of justice ; and it is therefore illegal. What is injurious to individuals and to the community, the law considers criminal. *a*

A distinction has been attempted to have settled as law, between editors of public newspapers and other persons, making the former an exception to the general rule, on account of the peculiarity of their occupation. It was claimed, that it was their business to disseminate useful knowledge among the people ;—to publish such matters relating to correct events of the day, happening at home or abroad as fell within the sphere of their observation, and as the public curiosity demanded ;—and that it was impracticable for for them at all times, to ascertain the truth or falsehood of the various statements contained in other journals, and it was argued, that if the law were not thus indulgent, some legislative relief might become necessary for the protection of this class of citizens.

The Supreme Court of this state, in a case where this argument was presented, said, *b* "Undoubtedly if it be necessary to pamper a depraved appetite or taste, (if there be any such) by a republication of all the falsehoods and calumnies upon private character that may find their way into the press—to give encouragement to the widest circulation of these vile and defamatory publications by protecting the retailers of them—some legislative interferance will be necessary ; for no countenance can be found for the irresponsibility claimed in the common law. That, reprobates the libeller, whether author or publisher, and subjects him to both civil and criminal responsibility. His offence is then ranked with that of the receiver of stolen goods, the perjurer and suborner of perjury,

---

a Rex v. Fisher, 2 Camp. 563–570, Per. Lord Ellenborough.

b Hotchkiss v. Oliphant, 2 Hill. 513; King v. Root, 4 Wend. 138; Cooper v. Stone, 24 Wend. 434; Same v. Barber, Id. 105; Same v. Greely 1 Denio, 347; Stone v. Cooper, 2 Denio, 293; Fry v. Bennett, 28 N. Y. 324.

the disturber of the public peace, the conspirator, and other offenders of a like character."

In another case the editor of a paper attempted to justify the libel, by showing that the article published, was published in good faith, having the name of the author attached to it.   Chief Justice Kent held, that the attempted defence was properly rejected, and said, a " The same principles which are applied to public libels, are applicable to private calumny, and renders all equally liable who are in anywise concerned in the publication of it.   Individual character must be protected, or social happiness and domestic peace are destroyed.   It is not sufficient that the printer by naming the author, gives the party agrieved an action against him. This remedy may afford no consolation, and no relief to the injured party.   The author may be some vagrant individual who may easily elude process, and if found he may be without property to remunerate in damages.   It would be no check on the libelous printer who can spread the calumny with ease, and with rapidity throughout the community.   The calumny of the author would fall harmless to the ground without the aid of the printer.   The injury is inflicted by the press, which, like other powerful engines, is mighty for mischief as well as for good.   I am satisfied that the proposition contended for on the part of the defendant, is as destitute of foundation, as it is repugnant to principles of public policy."

The act of publication, is an adoption of the original calumny, which must be defended in the same way as if invented by the defendant.   The republication assumes and endorses the truth of the charge, and when called on by the aggrieved party, the publisher should be held strictly to the proof.   If he chooses to become the endorser and retailer of private scandal, without taking the trouble of enquiring into the truth of what he publishes, there is no ground for complaint, if the law, which is studious to protect the character as the property of the citizen, holds him to this responsibility.   The rule is not only just and wise in itself, but if steadily and inflexibly adhered to and applied by courts and juries, will greatly tend to the promotion of truth, good morals and common decency on the part of the press, by inculcating caution and inquiry into

a Dole v. Lyon, 10 John. 450.

the truth of charges against private character before they are published and circulated throughout the community. a

The legislature of the state of New York in the year 1854 enacted a statute in some degree modifying the common law as above laid down in regard to newspaper publications, b as follows : "No reporter, editor or proprietor of any newspaper, shall be liable to any action or prosecution, civil or criminal, for a fair and true report in such newspaper, of any judicial, legislative, or other public official proceedings of any statement, speech, argument, or debate in the course of the same, except upon actual proof of malice in making such reports, which shall in no case be implied from the fact of the publication. § 2. Nothing in the preceding section contained shall be so construed as to protect any such reporter, editor or proprietor from an action or indictment for any libellous comments or remarks superadded to, and interspersed or connected with such report."

Some very sensible reasons for a modification of the common law as it regards the publishers of newspapers, may be found in the views of Judge Cooley in his work under the head of "Liberty of Speech and of the Press." c He says, "Among the inventions of modern times by which the world has been powerfully influenced, and civilization advanced with wonderful celerity, must be classed the newspaper. Beginning with a small sheet, insignificant alike in manner and appearance, published at considerable intervals, and including but few in its visits, it has become the daily vehicle to almost every family in the land, of information from all quarters of the globe, and upon every subject. Through it, and by means of the electric telegraph, the public proceedings of every civilized country, the debates of the leading legislative bodies, the events of war, the triumphs of peace, the storms in the physical world, and the agitation of the moral and mental, are brought home to the knowledge of every reading person, and, to a very large extent, before the day is over on which the events have taken place. And not public events merely are discussed and described, but the actions and words of public men are made public

a Mapes v. Weeks, 4 Wend 659; Inman v. Foster, 8 Wend. 602.
b Sess. Laws 1854, Ch. 130.
c Cooley, pp. 451-2.

property; and any person sufficiently notorious to become the object of public interest, will find his movements chronicled in this index of the times."

" Every party has its newspaper organs; every shade of opinion on political, religious, literary, moral, industrial, or financial questions has its representative; every locality has its press to advocate its claims, and advance its interests, and even the days regarded as sacred, have their special papers to furnish reading suitable for the time. The newspaper is also the medium by means of which all classes of the people communicate with each other concerning their wants and desires, and through which they offer their wares, and seek bargains. As it has gradually increased in value, and in the extent and variety of its contents, so the exactions of the community upon its conductors have also increased, until it is demanded of the newspaper publisher, that he shall daily spread before its readers, a complete summary of the events transpiring in the world, public or private, so far as those readers can reasonably be supposed to take an interest in them; and he who does not comply with this demand must give way to him who will."

The newspaper is one of the chief means for the education of the people. The highest and the lowest in the scale of intelligence resort to its columns for information; it is read by those who read nothing else, and the best minds of the age make it the medium of communication with each other on the highest and most abstruse subjects. Upon politics it may be said to be the chief educator of the people; its influence is potent in every legislative body; it gives tone and direction to public sentiment on each important subject as it arises; and no administration in any free country ventures to overlook or disregard an element as pervading in its influence, and withal so powerful.

And yet it may be doubted if the newspaper, as such, has ever influenced at all the current of the common law in any particular, important to the interests of the publishers. The railway has become the successor of the king's highway, and the plastic rules of the common law have accommodated themselves to the new condition of things; but the changes accomplished by the public press, seem to have passed unnoticed in the law, and save only, where modifications have been made by constitution or statute, the publisher of the daily paper occupies to-day the position in the courts that the village gossip and retailer of scandal occupied two hundred years ago; with no more privilege and no more protection.

The rule as to the privilege of publication does not seem to be changed when the publication is that of legislative proceedings. Doubtless a member of congress or of the state legislature has a right to publish his speech, but it is upon his own responsibility, and at his own peril if he makes that speech and its publication a vehicle of slander, or a libel against an individual. *a* To speak in the legislative body, he is protected by the constitution, privileged to say what he will, but he must stop then, if the speech contains libellous matter. If he chooses to publish it abroad, other than for the use of the body of which he is a member, his constitutional privilege has ceased, and he may for that be convicted and fined, for the libel, and be held amenable to the citizen whose character has been traduced. *b* Whether the publicity given to speeches made in congress by publishing them by order of that body in the *Globe*, is privileged, has not yet, it seems, been tested by judicial decision. It is exceedingly doubtful whether or not a libel so published would be privileged.

FREE EXERCISE OF RELIGIOUS OPINION.

Upon no subject which calls for the exercise of the human mind is man found to be so incapable of exercising an unprejudiced judgment, as in that of his religious opinions. Prejudices is always incapable of perceiving or of estimating truth. The history of the persecutions in bigoted governments of other days, was a sufficient ground for providing this constitutional security. Neither force or violence, but reason and conviction, should dictate to us the religion, or duty, we owe to our Creator, as well as the manner of discharging it. In vain therefore may the civil magistrate interpose the authority of human laws, to prescribe that belief, or produce that conviction, which human reason rejects ; in vain may the secular arm be extended, the rack stretched, and the flames kindled,

a King v. Abingdon, 1 Eshmasse, 226.
b Rex v. Creevy, 1 M. & S. 278.

to realize the tortures denounced against unbelievers by all the various sects of the various denominations of fanatics and enthusiasts throughout the earth. The martyr at the stake, glories in his tortures, and proves that though human laws can punish, they cannot convince. The pretext of religion, and the pretences of sanctity and humility, have been employed throughout the world as the most direct means of gaining influence and power, and have all failed to accomplish that end. Hence, as we learn from history, the numberless martyrdoms, and massacres that have drenched the whole earth with blood, from the first moment that civil and religious institutions were blended together. To separate these institutions by constitutional barriers that can never be overcome, is the only means by which our duty to God; the peace of mankind; and the genuine fruits of charity and paternal love, can be preserved, or properly discharged. This constitutional prohibition, therefore, may be regarded, as the most powerful cement of the federal government. Those who prize the union of the states, will never attempt to touch this fundamental article with unhallowed hands. " The ministry of the unsanctified sons of Aaron, in their unhallowed doing, scarcely produced a flame more sudden and more destructive, than such an attempt would inevitably excite." *a*

Nor can it be charged that this article, was the result of a feeling of infidelity, or want of respect to the sanctions of religion, on the part of the patriot fathers who prepared it. " Indeed, in a republic, there would seem to be a peculiar propriety in viewing the christian religion, as the great basis on which it must rest for its support and permanence. It may be regarded as above all others, the religion of liberty." *b* Montesquieu has remarked, that the christian religion is a stranger to mere despotic power. The mildness so frequently recommended in the gospel, is incompatible with the despotic rage with which a prince punishes his subjects and exercises himself in cruelty. *c* It is the christian religion, that in spite of the extent of the empire, and the influence of the climate, has hindered despotic power from being established in Ethiopia, and has carried into the heart of Africa the manners and laws of Europe. *d* Citizens professing to believe in the christian religion,

a Id.   *b* 2 Story on Const. § 1783.

c Montesquieu's Spirit of Laws, B. 24 Ch. 3.   *d* Id.

are infinitely more enlightened as to the various duties of life; having the warmest zeal to fulfill them. The more they believe themselves indebted to religion, the more they recognize the duties they owe to their country. The principles of christianity when deeply engraven on the heart, are far more powerful than the influ- ence of the false honor of monarchy, the human virtues of a republic, or the servile fear of a despotism. "The rights of con- science, however," says Judge Story, *a* "are, indeed beyond the just reach of any human power. They are given by God, and cannot be encroached upon by human authority, without a crim- inal disobedience to the precepts of natural, as well as revealed religion."

"This amendment," he says, "cut off the means of religious persecution (the vice and pest of former ages,) and of the subver- sion of the rights of conscience in matters of religion, which had been trampled upon, almost from the days of the Apostles, to the present age. The history of the parent country, had afforded the most solemn warnings and melancholy instructions on this head ; and even New England, the land of persecuted puritans as well as other colonies where the Church of England had maintained its superiority, would furnish out a chapter as full of the darkest bigotry and intolerance, as any which could be found to disgrace the pages of foreign annals. Apostacy, heresy, and nonconformity, had been standard crimes for public appeals, to kindle the flames of persecution, and to apologize for the most attrocious triumphs over innocence and virtue." *b*

"It was under a solemn consciousness of the danger from eccle- siasticle ambition, the bigotry of the spiritual pride, and the intol- erance of sects, thus exemplified in our domestic, as well as foreign annals, that it was deemed advisable to exclude from the national government, all power to act upon the subject. The situation too, of the different states, equally proclaimed the policy, as well as the necessity, of such an exclusion:" *c*

Perhaps the constitutional provision of the state of New York on this subject, is, as an epitome, as sound a commentary as can

a 2 Story on Const. § 1876.
b Id. § 1877, Vol. 1 §§ 53, 72, 73; 4 Black. Com. 43-59.
c 2 Story on Const. § 1789; Elliot's Debates. 195-197.

be given of religious freedom, and restriction. "The free exercise and enjoyment of religious profession and worship, without discrimination or preference, shall forever be allowed in this state to all mankind; and no person shall be rendered incompetent to be a witness on account of his opinions on matters of religious belief; but the liberty of conscience hereby secured, shall not be so construed as to excuse acts of licentiousness, or justify practices inconsistent with the peace or safety of the state."

A fair commentary upon this provision, in general terms, is, that no law shall be passed creating preferences in favor of one religious sect or denomination, or as to their mode of worship over another; there shall be no established religion by the state; whatever establishes a *distinction* for or against one sect, as against another, is not equal toleration; is not religious equality; but has its tendency towards religious persecution. Whether laws passed authorizing the raising of money by general taxation, to be appropriated to the education of children of one particular religious faith or sect, are not violations of this fundamental law, is yet to be determined. Whether under color of appropriations for secular education, moneys can be so raised and applied to those of one particular religious faith, is a question for the future. It is clearly against the spirit and intent of the constitution.

"This provision, excludes the right to enact laws compulsory of attendance upon religious instruction. The citizen must be led by his own choice and sense of duty, to attend the ordinances of religion. The duties he owes to his Maker, can only be enforced by the admonitions of his conscience; human laws cannot enforce this by penalties; nor can they impose any restraints upon the free exercise of religion according to the dictates of each individual conscience. No state or civil authority can come between the finite being and the Infinite, when the former is seeking to render that homage which is due, and in a mode which commends itself to his belief, as suitable for him to render, and as is acceptable to its object. a Nor can any restraints be imposed upon a reasonable expression of religious belief. If the believer regards it his duty to propogate his opinions, the freedom of speech under the other provision of the constitution, secures him the right to do so, subject

a Cooley on Limitations, 470.

to the restraints therein imposed. Nearly every state constitution in the Union, in similar provisions, confers this privilege. It was the intention, that the citizen be left to adopt his own creed to his own convictions, and both, to such light and understanding as a free inquiry into his own nature, needs, duty and relation to God, and man will give him.

While this freedom of opinion is thus secured and conceded, it will be denied by few, "that the promulgation of the great doctrines of religion; the being, and attributes, and providence of one Almighty God; the responsibility to Him for all our actions founded upon moral freedom and accountability; a future state of rewards and punishments; the cultivation of all the personal, social, and benevolent virtues; can never be a matter of indifference in any well ordered community. It is, indeed, difficult to conceive how any civilized society can well exist without them. And at all events, it is impossible for those who believe in the truth of christianity as a divine revelation, to doubt, that it is the especial duty of government to foster and encourage it among all the citizens and subjects. This is a point wholly distinct from that of the right of private judgment in matters of religion, and of the freedom of public worship according to the dictates of one's conscience." a

"Whatever may be the shades of religious belief, all must acknowledge the fitness of recognizing in important human affairs, the superintending care and control of the Great Governor of the universe, and of acknowledging with thanksgiving, His boundless favors, at the same time that we bow in contrition, when visited with the penalties of his broken laws. No principle of constitutional law is violated when Thanksgiving, or Fast days are appointed ; when chaplains are designated for the army or navy, when legislative sessions are opened with prayer, or the reading of the scriptures ; or when religious teaching is encouraged by exempting houses of religious worship from taxation for the support of state government. Undoubtedly, the spirit of the constitution will require, in all these cases, that care be taken to avoid all discrimination in favor of any one denomination or sect; but the power to do any of these things will not be unconstitutional,

a Story on Const. § 1871.

simply because of being susceptible of abuse. This public recognition of religious worship, however, is not based entirely, perhaps even mainly, upon a sense of what is due to the Supreme Being himself, as the author of all good, and of all law; but the same reasons of state policy which induce the government to aid institutions of charity, and seminaries of instruction, will also incline it to foster religious worship and religious institutions, as conservators of the public morals, and valuable, if not indispensable assistants to the preservation of the public order." *a*

"Nor while recognizing a superintending Providence, are we always precluded from recognizing also, in the rules prescribed for the conduct of citizens, the patent fact, that the prevailing religion of the states is Christian. Some acts would be offensive to public sentiment in a christian community, and would tend to public disorder, which, in a Mahomedan, or in a Pagan country, might be passed without notice, or even be regarded as meritorious. The criminal laws of every country have reference in a great degree to prevailing public sentiment; and punish those acts as crimes, which disturb the peace and order, or tend to shock the moral sense of the community. The moral sense, is measurably regulated and controlled by the religious belief; and therefore it is, that those things which, estimated by a christian standard, are profane and blasphemous, are properly punished as offences, since they are offensive in the highest degree to the general public sense, and have a direct tendency to undermine the moral support of the laws, and corrupt the community." *b*

Christianity has also been recognized in our judicial decisions, and is so far carried out in our criminal jurisprudence, as that the law will not permit the essential truths of revealed religion to be ridiculed and reviled. In other words, that blasphemy is an indictable offence at common law. *c*

Blasphemy has been defined as the speaking evil of the Deity, with an impious purpose to derogate from the Divine Majesty, and to alienate the minds of others from the love and reverence of God. It is purposely using words concerning God, calculated and

a Cooley on Religious Liberty, 471.   *b* Id.

c Vidal v. Girard, 2 How. U. S. R. 198; Updegraph v. The Commonwealth, 11 Searg. & R. 394.

designed to impair and destroy the reverence, respect, and confidence due to Him, as the intelligent Creator, Governor and Judge of the world. It embraces the idea of detraction, when used towards the Supreme Being, and as "calumny," and usually carries the same idea, when applied to an individual. It is a wilful and malicious attempt to lessen men's reverence of God, by denying his existence, or his attributes as an intelligent Creator, Governor and Judge of men, and to prevent their having confidence in Him. a Blasphemy against God, and contumatious reproaches, and profane ridicule of Christ, or of the Holy Scriptures, are offences punishable at the common law. b "Such offences have always been considered independent of any religious establishment, or the rights of an established church. They are treated as affecting the essential interests of civil society. There is nothing in our manners or institutions which has prevented the application, or the necessity of this part of the common law. We stand in need of all that moral discipline, and of those principles of virtue, which help to bind society together. The people of this nation, and of this state, profess the general doctrines of christianity as the rule of their faith and practice; and to scandalize the Author of these doctrines, is not only, in a religious point of view, extremely impious, but a gross violation of decency and good order. Nothing could be more offensive to the virtuous part of community, or more injurious to the tender morals of the young, than to declare such profanity lawful. It would go to confound all distinction between things sacred and profane; for, to use the words of one of the greatest oracles of human wisdom: Lord Bacon, "Profane scoffing doth, by little and little deface the reverence for religion." Things which corrupt moral sentiment, as obscene actions, prints, and writings, and even gross instances of seduction, have upon the same principle been held indictable; and shall we form an exception in these particulars, to the rest of the civilized world? No government among the polished nations of antiquity; and none of the institutions of modern Europe, ever hazarded such a bold experiment upon the solidity of the public morals, as to permit with impunity, and under

a Commonwealth v. Kneeland, 20 Pick. 213.
b People v. Ruggles, 8 John. 290.

the sanction of their tribunals, the general religion of the community to be openly insulted and defamed. *a*

But it does not follow, because blasphemy is punishable as a crime, that therefore one is not at liberty to dispute and argue against the truth of the christian religion, or of any accepted dogma. Its "divine origin and truth" are not so far admitted in the law, as to preclude their being controverted. To forbid discussion upon this subject, except by the various sects of believers, would be to abridge the liberty of speech and of the press in a point which with many, would be regarded as most important of all. Blasphemy, implies something more than a denial of any of the truths of religion, even of the highest and most vital. A bad motive must exist; there must be a wilful and malicious attempt to lessen men's reverence for the Deity, or for the accepted religion. But outside of such wilful and malicious attempt, there is a broad field for candid investigation and discussion, which is as much open to the Jew and the Mahomedan, as to the professors of the Christian faith. No author or printer who fairly and honestly promulgates the opinions with whose truths he is impressed with, for the benefit of others, is answerable as a criminal. A malicious and mischievous intention in such case, is the broad boundary between right and wrong. It is to be collected from the offensive levity, scurrillous and approbrious language, and other circumstances, whether the act of the party was malicious. *b*

Nor is the constitutional provision of this state, that no person shall be rendered incompetent to be a witness on account of his opinions on matters of religious belief, to be interpreted as a repudiation of the doctrine that the christian religion shall remain the common law of the state. The legislative and practicable interpretation of this provision, is in harmony with the common law. By the Revised Statutes of this state, *c* it is provided, that every person who shall be elected or appointed to any civil office or public office, or public trust, before he shall enter on the duties of such trust, shall take the following oath or affirmation: "I do solemnly swear" or "affirm," as the case may be, "that I will sup-

a Id. 294, per Kent, Ch. J.

b Updegraph v. Commonwealth, 11 Searg. & R. 394.

c 1 Rev. St. 119.

71

port the constitution of the United States, and the constitution of the state of New York, and that I will faithfully discharge the duties of the office of —— to the best of my ability." This oath is required of all executive, legislative, judicial and civil officers of the state. By another statute provision, *a* it is further provided, that the usual mode of administering oaths, now practiced by the person who swears, by laying his hands upon and kissing the gospels, shall be observed in all cases, in which an oath may be administered, except if a person desire it, it shall be : "You do swear in the presence of the everliving God," he holding up his hand or not, at his discretion; or to a person having conscientious scruples against taking an oath, he may be permitted to make a solemn declaration in the following form : "You do solemnly, sincerely and truly declare and affirm." And the courts are thereby authorized, where they are satisfied that a person has some peculiar mode of swearing, connected with or in addition to the laying his hand upon the gospel, and kissing the same, which is more solemn and obligatory upon such person, in their discretion, to allow him to be sworn in such other way. And it also provides, that persons believing in another than the christian religion, may be sworn according to the ceremonies of his religion, instead of the above prescribed modes. So too, every person believing in the existence of a Supreme Being, who will punish false swearing, may be sworn if otherwise competent. Thus, it is seen, that the gospels, that is, the doctrine of the New Testament, is by the strongest implication, adopted as the religion of the state by its statutes; and the oath, which is a solemn appeal to God, with an implied invocation of His curse upon him who makes it, in the event of its violation, is a further acknowledgment of the moral government of God. And under whatever religion, or by whatever form of oath the person may choose to be sworn, is made equally subject to all the pains and penalties of perjury; thus holding all persons equally liable to the crime against God, against morals, religion and law.

In all this, while it is seen, that in the forms and practice, the statute has fully carried out that other constitutional right, that no person shall be rendered incompetent to be a witness on account

a 2 Rev. Stat. 407–408.

ot his opinions on matters of religious belief; yet the constitution itself has given the qualifying caution, that this liberty of conscience, so secured, shall not be so construed as to excuse acts of licentiousness, or justify practices inconsistent with the peace or safety of the state. Montesquieu informs us, "that such was the influence of an oath among the Romans, in binding them to the laws, that they did more for its observance, than they would have done for the thirst of glory, or the love of their country; that Rome was for a long period of time, held by two anchors, religion and morality, in the midst of a furious tempest." a

To this extent, then, do the laws of this christian government give toleration. All religions are recognized by law, to the extent of allowing all persons to be sworn and to give their evidence, who believe in a Supreme superintending Providence who rewards and punishes; and that an oath is binding upon their consciences. Wherever the common law remains unchanged, it must be held no violation of religious liberty to recognize and enforce its distinctions. The infidelity, or unbelief of a witness, will ever go to his credibility; though competent to be sworn, it is for a Christian jury to say, what credibility they will allow to evidence, which is given, without a regard to a Christian's responsibility to his Maker for its truth.

It is upon this principle of liberty of speech, and of conscience, that our statutes to prevent the desecration of the christian Sabbath, excepts the Jew, and all other persons who regard the seventh day of the week as the Sabbath, from liability to the violation of the law making the first day of the week the Christian Sabbath. The law intends not to intermeddle with the natural and indefeasible right of all men to worship Almighty God, according to the dictates of their own consciences; it compels no one to attend to, erect, or support any place of worship; or to maintain any ministry against his consent; it pretends not to control or interfere with the rights of conscience; and it establishes no preference for any religious establishment or mode of worship. It treats no religious doctrine as paramount in the state; it enforces no unwilling attendance upon the celebration of Divine worship. It says not to the Jew or Sabbatarian, "you shall desecrate the day you esteem

a B. 8, Ch. 13.

holy and keep sacred to religion, that *we* deem to be so." It enters upon no discussion of rival claims of the first and seventh days
of the week; nor pretends to bind upon the conscience of any man
any conclusion upon a subject which each must decide for himself.
It intrudes not into the domestic circle to dictate, when, where, or
to what God its inmates shall address their orisons, nor does it
presume to enter the synagogue of the Isrealite, or the church
of the seventh day Christian, to command, or even persuade
their attendance in the temples of those who especially approach the altar on Sunday. It does not in the slightest degree
infringe upon the Sabbath of any sect, or curtail their freedom of
worship. It detracts not one hour from any period of time they
may feel bound to devote to this object. Nor does it add a moment beyond what they may choose to employ. Its sole mission
is to inculcate a temporary weekly cessation from labor, but it
adds not to this requirement any religious obligation. *a*

Unquestioned history has taught us, that in all Pagan countries
where the Sabbath is unknown;—where the true God is never
adored, the soul of man is debased; the man prostrates himself
before the sun, the moon, monsters, reptiles, blocks of wood, and
even to demons. In France, where the Sabbath was for a time
abolished, an impious phantom, called the Goddess of Reason,
was substituted in the room of the Omnipotent and Eternal God;
the Bible was held up to ridicule, and committed to the flames;
man was degraded, and his mind assimilated to the level of the
brutes; and the cheering prospects of immortality, were trans-
formed into the shades of an eternal night. Atheism, Scepticism,
Fatalism, almost universally prevailed; the laws of morality were
trampled under foot; and anarchy, and plots, and assassinations,
massacres and legalized plunder, became the order of the day.
With the abolition of the Sabbath, followed the loss of the knowledge of God as the Governor of the universe, with all impressions
of the Divine presence, and all sense of accountability for human
actions. The restraints of religion, and the prospect of a future
judgment, no longer deterred from the commission of crimes; and
nothing was left but the dread of the dungeon, the gibbet or the
rack, to restrain the people from deeds of cruelty, injustice and

a Specht v. Commonwealth, 8 Penn. St. R. 312.

violence. We are thus taught by history and experience, in confirmation of the Divine Revelation, that the Sabbath was originally instituted as a sacred memorial of the finishing of the work of creation; and in accordance with the law of the Decalogue, it is a day for the contemplation of the perfections and holiness of its Almighty Author. It was a day made for man, as a wise and merciful appointment for a day of rest, repose and reflection.

CHAPTER XVIII.

OF PARLIAMENTARY LAW; AND OF THE PRIVILEGES AND INCIDENTAL POWERS OF LEGISLATIVE ASSEMBLIES.

THE legislative department of the government, is one of the three depositories of the sovereign power of the state. It is co-ordinate to the other two departments, the executive and judicial; and within its sphere, is independent of the others. To enable it to perform its appropriate duties, and to exercise its proper functions, it is necessary and essential, that they should possess all needful powers, and all necessary rights and privileges, for the free and independent exercise of their separate action.

It would seem to be the natural result of the establishment of such a department, under a constitution recognizing the existence and force of the common law in regard to their powers and privileges; and in the absence of words of restriction, or negative words prohibiting the power or right; that by necessary implication, (which is equivalent to an express grant,) there is conferred upon each branch of the legislative department, all the powers and privileges necessarily incident to a legislative assembly.

If the *powers* are expressed, and enumerated in the constitution, and no negative or restrictive words are employed as to their *privileges*, the latter may be implied to be such as are necessarily incident to such a body, and such as exist by the common law.

These rights and immunities, as well of members individually, as of the body in its collective capacity, are known by the general name of *privileges ;* and when they are disregarded by any individual, or authority, whose duty it is to take notice of them, or when they are directly attacked in any way; or in general, when any impediment or obstruction is interposed to the free action of the legislative assembly or its members, the offence is denominated a *breach of privilege.*

" The privileges of a legislative assembly would be entirely ineffectual to enable it to perform its legitimate functions, if it had no power to punish offenders, to impose disciplinary regulations upon its members, or to enforce obedience to its commands. These powers are so essential to the authority of a legislative assembly, that it cannot well exist without them; and they are consequently to be regarded as belonging to every such assembly as a necessary incident. The *privileges* and *powers* of a legislative assembly, are therefore so far connected together, that the latter are the necessary complement of the former. *a*

At an early day, in England, the House of Commons, under the claim of privilege, had so far arrogated to themselves power, as to exercise *exclusive* jurisdiction in all cases coming directly before them; and even in cases in which they were only incidentally concerned, they denied to all other tribunals, the right to question their power, not only, but they claimed the right to determine for themselves, what the law of privilege actually was, and, to declare it from time to time to be, whatever their will and pleasure, and their claimed prerogative, dictated it to be. But this arrogant pretence was carried to such an extent, and the usurpation became so odious, that both the judicial, and legislative authorities, were called in, to correct, restrain, modify, and limit this unauthorized abuse of assumed power. So that, since the statutes of 13 William III, and 10 George III, which abridged the powers and privileges of parliament, the courts have taken notice of, declare, and decide, the extent of these powers and privileges, whenever they arise in court; though without prejudice to the right of the house itself to decide upon the question in an equally conclusive manner, if the case comes within their jurisdiction.

In this country, so far as privileges of legislative bodies, or of the individual members thereof are concerned, they are believed to be substantially the same, as now modified they exist in England; but the *powers* of legislative bodies, and in some of the states their *privileges*, rest upon constitutional, or statute provisions. Therefore, though a legislative assembly may be said to judge exclusively of its privileges, it is only so to certain intents and purposes. *b*

In England, since the year 1700, and statute of 10 George III, in 1770, the powers and privileges of the two houses, have been so well

a Cushing on Legislative Assemblies, § 533.   *b* Coffin v. Coffin, 4 Mass. 32.

defined, regulated and limited by statute direction, and judicial construction, that they are now as well defined, established and known, as any portions of the common law; and this common law, before the American revolution, was adopted and admitted in this country, as controlling and applicable to the colonial and provincial legislatures. Since the revolution, portions óf this common law has been adopted into the national; and also into some of the state constitutions; in other states, it is regulated and limited in their statutes; with such omissions and restrictions, additions and modifications, as the new and changed circumstances, and more free and liberal institutions have made necessary to a new and improved order of things.

In some of these constitutions and statutes, certain powers and privileges are enumerated in affirmative language; sometimes accompanied by a general provision covering all other necessary powers and privileges; in some, negative words are used in reference to particular powers; in some, and especially in the state of New York, there is an *express* provision in the statute, giving certain privileges to members of the legislature, which, by legal construction, excludes all other privileges, so far as regards third persons, and as to all persons except individual members of the body themselves, and to the collective body of the assembly; and as to their powers, if not expressed, they are such well known principles of parliamentary law as are known to themselves, to the courts, and to all other persons. An uncontrolled power in a legislative assembly, equally here, as in England, would be dangerous to the liberties of the citizen.

Cases can well be supposed, perhaps may have existed, where an uncontrolled power in a legislative assembly may work great injustice. Such cases, however, ought to be the exceptions. Justice Story, in his work on the constitution, *a* in regard to this point, has wisely said, that "Public bodies, like private persons, are occasionally under the dominion of strong passions and excitements; impatient, irritable and impetuous. The habit of acting together, produces a strong tendency to what, for the want of a better word, may be called the corporation spirit, or what is so happily expressed in a foreign phrase, *l'esprit du corps.* Certain popular leaders

a Story on Const. § 550.

often acquire an extraordinary ascendancy over the body, by their talents, their eloquence, their intrigues, or their cunning. Measures are often introduced in a hurry, and debated with little care, and examined with less caution. The very restlessness of many minds, produces an impossibility of debating with much deliberation, when a measure has a plausible aspect, and enjoys a momentary favor. Nor is it infrequent, to overlook well founded objections to a measure, not only because the advocates of it have little desire to bring them in review, but because the opponents are often seduced into a credulous silence. A legislative body, is not ordinarily apt to mistrust its own powers, and far less the temperate exercise of those powers. As it prescribes its own rules for its own deliberations, it easily relaxes them whenever any pressure is made for an immediate decision. If it feels no check but its own will, it rarely has the firmness to insist upon holding a question long enough under its own view, to see and mark it in all its bearings and relations, &c."

Among the subjects or offences which a legislative assembly may adjudge to be a contempt, and for which they may inflict punishment, and thus interfere with personal liberty of the citizen, is that of a breach of privilege of the house, or of one of its members. It is highly important for preservation of order, and for the protection of legislative bodies in the due and proper discharge of their duties for the state, that they, and each of its component members, should possess freedom of action, and be fully protected in their persons; that they should not be withdrawn or prevented from attendance by causes of a less important character; but, that for a certain time, at least, they should be excused from obeying any other call, not so immediately necessary for the services of the state; and hence it has always been admitted, that the members of a legislative assembly, during their service and attendance as such, are entitled to be exempted from several duties, and not considered as liable to some legal processes to which other citizens are by law obliged to pay obedience. a

They are entitled by acknowledged parliamentary law, not only to the right of free attendance, but to be protected in the free enjoyment of the right of speech, debate, and determination in refer-

a Cushing's Legislative Assembly, § 529.

72

ence to all subjects, upon which they may rightfully be called upon to deliberate and act; and it is established as a general principle of parliamentary law, that no member of a legislative body can be questioned or punished by any other court or authority, but only by the assembly itself of which he is a member, for anything said or done by him in that capacity. These rights and immunities, belong not only to the member himself directly, but also indirectly to the assembly itself. But since the day of the English statutes above referred to, neither house of the British parliament have ever gone the length of claiming an exemption from the operation of *criminal* laws; or of attempting to protect themselves from any prosecution for treason, felony, or breach of peace; and down as late as 1831, Lord Brougham declared, a "That the true ground to use in regard to the law of privilege, is, that it never extends to protect from punishment, though it may extend to protect from *civil* process, and that it never extends to protect from civil process when the object of the process is the delivery up of a person wrongfully detained from a party, and that it is upon this ground, that the jurisdiction of the courts can safely and securely rest."

It can hardly be warranted in this work, to trace the various discrepancies and differences existing in constitutional provisions and statutes relating to parliamentary law in the several states of the Union. To do it justice, it would alone fill a volume.

In this country, though the same general principles of parliamentary law prevail as in England from whence we derived it, yet what are called the law of *privileges* of legislative assemblies, varies in different states of the Union, and is different between the assemblies of the several states, and that of the national assembly. There is no such thing, in this country, as a settled and uniform law of privilege of members to legislative assemblies. In the national legislature, the law of privilege is secured, and defined, by the express provisions of the national constitution. In some of the independent states it is secured and defined in their state constitutions; in others only by statute. Among these, the law of privilege is not expressed in language entirely uniform. In the state of New York the privilege of members is conferred

a Mr. Long, Wellesley's case, 2 Rals. & 3 Mylne 673.

by statute in the following words: *a* "Every member of the legislature shall be privileged from arrest on *civil* process, during his attendance at the session of the house to which he shall belong, except on process issued in any suit brought against him for any forfeiture, misdemeanor, or breach of trust in any office or place of public trust held by him. He shall enjoy the like privilege for the space of fourteen days previous to such session, and also while going and returning from such session, provided such time do not exceed fourteen days; and also during any adjournments that do not exceed fourteen days; and also while absent from the session by leave of the house. These privileges, also extend to officers of the house while in actual attendance, and each house has the power to punish as a *contempt*, and by imprisonment, a breach of its privileges, or of the privileges of its members, the arresting of a member, and for other disorderly conduct against its rules or orders therein specified."

This power of judging, and of inflicting punishment for an adjudged contempt, or breach of privilege committed against themselves, and judged of by themselves, however dangerous in theory, inasmuch as these bodies, thus become their own accusers, witnesses and judges, is found by experience, to have been subject to very little abuse. Their own self-respect, and a due respect to public opinion, public censure, and public criticism to which they are amenable, it is believed, will generally restrain them from unreasonable acts of injustice to the individual citizen. Perhaps the only danger to be apprehended, is, in times of high political excitement, when bodies of this kind, controlled by popular and unprincipled leaders, excite a spirit, which Judge Story calls, *l'esprit du corps*, against some supposed violator of privileges or dignity of the body.

A more real and serious danger to the integrity of the government, and to a co-ordinate branch of the sovereignty of the government, is when the legislative assembly, in either body of it, shall attempt to exercise this seemingly unlimited power of punishment for contempts, upon the representatives of another co-ordinate and coextensive department of the sovereign power of the state.

a 1 Rev. Stat. 154.

In the whole history of this government, and of the general harmonious workings of its system in the division of its sovereignty into the three distinct and co-ordinate departments of its power,—the executive, the legislative, and the judicial,—each being independent of the other within its proper sphere of action, and each, by our theory of government, having no higher tribunal to call them to account for their independent action; only a single case has occurred, in the nation or in any state, in which a conflict has arisen between them, by which, one of these co-ordinate departments has attempted to coerce another, to wit: one branch of the legislative body, the assembly of the state of New York, attempting to hold the judicial department of the same state, responsible for a claimed breach of privilege of the assembly, in issuing process of arrest by attachment against a member of assembly, for contempt, in the disobedience to a subpœna issued out of a criminal court of original jurisdiction of the said state.

The case was novel, and unprecedented. It was the occasion of excitement and interest. It was discussed on the part of the assembly by a labored report by a committee of the house of assembly, in behalf of that department of the government in which the breach of privilege was claimed, and the right to inflict punishment asserted, as against the member of the court whose action was complained of. The judge appeared on the day appointed, and argued the question in defence of his co-ordinate department of the government. The result, settled no parliamentary law, or question of breach of privilege; its discussion, nevertheless presented the different views of these co-ordinate departments of the government, as to their respective powers and privileges, in such a manner as to make the report of the assembly and the argument of the judge in defence of the judiciary, a matter sufficiently important to be presented to the profession, and to the co-ordinate departments of the government for consideration, whenever it is brought in question there.

IN THE MATTER OF HON. PLATT POTTER, ARRAIGNED AT THE BAR OF
THE ASSEMBLY, FOR ALLEGED BREACH OF PRIVILEGE.

On the 21st day of January, 1870, a subpœna, requiring one
Henry Ray to appear and testify as a witness in a certain criminal
proceeding pending before the grand jury, at the Saratoga Oyer
and Terminer, was issued under the authority of the court, the
Hon. Platt Potter, a justice of the Supreme Court, presiding, and
was duly served on Mr. Ray, at the city of Albany. He declined
to obey its mandate, on the ground of his privilege as a member
of the assembly of the state of New York. Winsor B. French, the
district attorney of Saratoga county, thereupon applied to the
court for, and procured, an attachment against Mr. Ray for such
disobedience, upon which the latter was arrested, taken before the
grand jury, and required to testify on such proceeding. The arrest
of Mr. Ray created some excitement in the assembly, of which he
was a member, as it was claimed to be a flagrant violation of the
privilege of that body. A committee was thereupon appointed,
to investigate the matter of the arrest. Subsequently the committee made a report, in which, after setting forth the facts of the
arrest, and of the examination before them of Justice Potter and
others, relative thereto, they proceeded as follows:

"The question therefore arises, and the only question which
your committee is called upon to consider is, whether or not Mr.
Ray was exempt from arrest under the process issued in this case.

The privilege of legislative bodies is as old as the common law,
from which we have gathered our liberties, and by which the rights
of the people have been and are to be protected. It is older than
Magna Charta, older than the writ of *habeas corpus*, older than the
courts either of law or equity, and from the parliament of a nation
and legislatures of the states have come those laws and rules of
practice which are calculated to secure to the citizen all the benefits and privileges conferred by the government under which he
may live. Your committee, in the examination of the question,
have found that, in this country, the violations of parliamentary
privilege, either of members of congress or of members of state
legislatures, have been rare. In the earlier history of the British
parliament, when the house of commons, for long years, struggled
against the prerogative of the crown, against the overbearing aris-

tocracy of the lords, and against the assumption of power on the part of the courts, which were for centuries the mere servants and tools of the crown, we find many instances where the commons secured and maintained the privileges of members of that body.

In the case of Shirley v. Fagg, as far back as 1675, Mr. Fagg, a member of the house of commons, was summoned on a process, issuing from the court of chancery, to appear before the bar of the house of lords and plead to an appeal. The house of commons held this to be an unquestioned violation of its privilege, and passed, on the 18th of May, 1675, the following resolution :

' *Resolved*, That it is the undoubtful right of this house that none of their members be summoned to attend the house of lords during the session or privileges of the parliament.' (3 Grey, 170.)

On the 20th of May, 1675, Sir Thomas Leigh, from a committee appointed by the house of commons, gave the following, among other reasons, why a member of the commons was not compelled to appear before the bar of the house of lords, and this, it will be borne in mind, was when the house of lords was sitting as a court of appeals of the British realm : ' The privilege of a member is the privilege of the house, and is a restraint to the proceedings of inferior courts, but not to the house itself ;' thus implying that the house whose privilege has been violated is the only body possessing the right to pass upon the question whether such privilege has or has not been violated. (2 Grey, 399.) It is laid down as a principle in parliamentary law, in England, that the privilege of parliament extends to all cases except three—treason, felony and breach of the peace. (4 Inst. 25 ; Lex Parl. 381.)

Sir William Blackstone lays down the following as the privileges of parliament : ' 1st. They are at all times exempted from question elsewhere for anything said in their own house during the time of privilege. 2d. Neither a member himself, his wife or servants, for any matter of their own, may be arrested on mesne process, in any civil suit. 3d. Nor be detained under execution, though levied before the time of privilege. 4th. Nor impleaded, cited or *subpœnaed* in any court. 5th. Nor summoned as a witness or juror. 6th. Nor may their lands or goods be distrained. 7th. Nor their persons assaulted or character traduced.' (1 Blackstone, 163, 164.)

Mr. Thomas Jefferson, in his note upon this quotation of Blackstone, says: 'The constitution of the United States has only privileged senators and representatives themselves from the single act of arrest in all cases except treason, felony and breach of the peace, during their attendance at the session of their respective houses, and in going to and returning from the same, and from being questioned in any other place for any speech or debate in either house.'

'Under the general authority to make all laws necessary and proper for carrying into execution the powers given them, they may provide by law the details which may be necessary for giving full effect to the enjoyment of this privilege.' He goes on and says further: 'The act of arrest is void *ab initio*. (2 Strange, 989.) The member arrested may be discharged on motion. The arrest, being unlawful, is a trespass, for which the officer and others concerned are liable to action or indictment in the ordinary courts of justice, as in other cases of unauthorized arrest. The court before which the process is returnable is bound to act as in other cases of unauthorized proceeding, and liable also, as in other similar cases, to have its proceedings stayed or corrected.' He says further: 'This privilege from arrest, privileges of course against all process, the disobedience to which is punishable by an attachment of the person, *(the very case in point,)* as a subpœna *ad respondendum* or *testificandum* or a summons on a jury; and with reason, because a member has superior duties to perform in another place.' He goes on to say: 'When a representative is withdrawn from his seat by summons, the people whom he represents lose their voice in the debate and vote, as they do in his voluntary absence. When a senator is withdrawn by summons, his state loses half its voice in debate and vote, as it does in his voluntary absence. The enormous disparity of evil admits of no comparison.'

In December, 1795, the house of representatives of the United States committed two persons, of the names of Randall and Whitney, for attempting to corrupt the integrity of certain members, which they considered as a contempt and breach of the privilege of the house; and the facts being proved, Whitney was detained in confinement a fortnight and Randall three weeks, and was reprimanded by the speaker. The editor of the *Aurora*, of Philadelphia, William Duane, was, for defamatory articles, declared to be guilty of breach of the privilege of the senate.

In the debate in the Duane case, Mr. Senator Pinckney, who opposed the proceedings, after citing the privileges of congress, says that each house has power to enforce complete order and decorum within their own chamber; to clear the galleries if an audience is unruly, and to punish their own members; to take care that no arrests except for treason, felony or breach of the peace, shall keep their members from their duty.

There can be no doubt but that the legislature of the state of New York has as extensive, if not more extensive, privileges than the congress of the United States. It is the successor of the colonial legislature, which derived its privileges from the parliamentary law of England, and is not restricted in its privileges by the constitution of the state. Mr. Pinckney, in the speech quoted above, seemed to intimate that the privileges of state legislatures were more in their discretion than those of congress.

The constitution of this state, of 1777, declares that the assembly should enjoy the same privileges, and do business in like manner as the assembly of the colony of New York of right formerly did.

It is admitted that the parliament of England, and the courts of law, have cognizance of contempts, and are authorized to punish for such contempts. It is also admitted that the state legislatures have equal authority, because their powers are plenary; they represent their constituents completely, and possess all their powers, except such as their constitutions have expressly denied them; that congress has no natural or necessary power, nor any powers but such as are given to it by the constitution. Therefore, the constitution expressly and directly exempts members of congress from personal arrest, and, therefore, with congress no further law is necessary, the constitution itself being the law; still, under the provision of the constitution, which confers upon congress the right to make all laws necessary and proper for carrying into execution the powers vested by the constitution in them, it would be within their power to establish any regulation of law in regard to the breach of their privilege, which they might desire. It is laid down by parliamentary writers that, 'even in cases of treason, felony and breach of the peace, to which privilege does not extend, as to substance, yet in parliament a member is privileged as to the mode of proceeding. The case is first to be laid before the house, that it may judge of the fact and of the grounds of the accusation, and how far forth the manner of the trial may concern their privilege. Otherwise it would be in the power of other branches of the government, and even of every private person, under a pretense of a charge of treason, felony and breach of the peace, to take any man from his service in the house, and so as many, one after another, as would make the house what he desired it should be.'

The rule in this country has not been carried to this extent, but the ruling is well established that, where any body desires the appearance of a member of the legislature, or of congress, as a witness, or in any other manner, first the permission of the house of which he is a member is asked, and then the question is before the house, whether they will or will not grant permission to the member to attend before any court or other house of parliament. The senate of the state of New York has no right to summon within its presence, or before any committee of that body, any member of the assembly, without first, in due and courteous form, asking permission of the assembly that such member may be summoned. If, then, the senate of the state has no such power, can it in reason be contended that a court, an inferior body, and, to a great extent, under the direction and control of the legislature, shall have the power to subpœna, at its will, a member of either house of the legislature, and take him from his duties as a representative of the people? Your committee are of the opinion that no such doctrine can be maintained, upon any well settled and grounded principles of parliamentary law, as applicable either to the parliament of England, or to any legislative bodies in this country, and your committee can readily see the great danger to which such assumption of power on the part of the courts would inevitably lead.

Your committee have examined, with great care, the instances of breaches of privilege of the congress of the United States, the first parliamentary body in this country, and they find but few instances where the privileges of either house of congress have been violated. On the 22d of June, 1822, it seems that an assistant doorkeeper of the senate of the United States had been subpœnaed before a committee of the house of representatives, when Mr. Senator Holmes, from the state of Maine, offered a resolution that said assistant doorkeeper be permitted to attend as such witness. During the debate on the resolution, Mr. Foote, a senator from Connecticut, used the following language: 'That as the officers of the senate were not subject to be taken from their duties by the process of any court, so neither could a doorkeeper, by any process from the other house, be taken from his duties.' It was conceded that the doorkeeper was only required to attend before the committee during the recess of the senate, and therefore the discussion ceased. This statement by Senator Foote seems to show the fact to be, that up to that time there was no question but what members of congress, and the officers thereof, were exempt from obeying any writ of subpœna, whether issued by a court or by either house of congress.

Your committee have found but two English cases in their researches, which would in the least question the principles they believe govern questions of this character. The one is the case reported in 1 Salkeld, 279, (Dominus Rex v. Dominus Preston.) There Lord Preston had been committed by the court of quarter sessions for refusing to appear and testify before the grand jury in a case of high treason. He was brought before the court of king's bench on a writ of habeas corpus, when Lord Holt used the dictum that it was a great outrage, and had he been present at the committal he would have imposed a fine. It does not appear that Lord Preston was even a member of parliament, or that parliament was in session at the time; nor does it appear that he pleaded his privilege, either as member of parliament or as a peer of the realm. And under the English rule, as your committee understands it, had parliament not been in session, and had the time of exemption after the session of parliament expired, then Lord Preston would not have been exempt from testifying before the grand jury in a case of high treason. The next is the case of Lord Ferrers, which occurred in 1757. An attachment issued against Lord Ferrers out of the court of Westminster Hall for refusing to obey a writ of habeas corpus which had been issued, requiring him to produce in the court of Westminster Hall the body of Lady Ferrers, she alleging, by prayer addressed to the chief justice, that the conduct of her husband was so harsh, tyrannical and abusive, and so en langered her peace of mind and her life, that she required to be .present at the court to present her petition, and ask its protection. In that case it was a refusal to obey a writ of habeas corpus, where the party who was required to obey such writ had, as appeared to the court, been guilty of a breach of the peace, to wit: physical abuse to Lady Ferrers. Under these circumstances the house of lords passed the following resolution: 'It is hereby ordered and declared that no peer or lord of parliament hath privilege against being compelled, by process of the courts of Westminster Hall, to pay obedience to a writ of habeas corpus directed to him.'

The writ of habeas corpus requires not the presence of the member himself, but the production of some person alleged to be in his custody or under his control, and therefore can be complied with without the necessity of the member being absent from his duties in the house of which he may be a member, and is very different from arrest under a process issued out of court, which actually takes the body of the member, and therefore takes him from his duties in the house to which he has been elected.

The people of the state of New York very early took into consideration this question of privilege; and the legislature, as far back as the 20th of February, 1788, passed the following statute:

'Every member of the legislature shall be privileged from arrest on civil process during his attendance at the session of the house to which he shall belong, except on process issued in any suit brought against him for any forfeiture, misdemeanor or breach of trust in any office or place of public trust held by him.' (Laws of 1788; 1st ed. of Revised Statutes, vol. 1, p. 154.)

This qualification would indicate that in all other cases the member was absolutely exempt from arrest.

The gentlemen who appeared before the committee seemed to press very strongly the idea that an attachment was not a civil process. There can be no question but what the subpœna issued in this case was a civil process, and, under the authorities above cited, void *ab initio*. Therefore your committee cannot see by what force of reasoning an attachment issued against a person for non-compliance with a summons of subpœna can be tortured into a criminal process. In other words, your committee are of the opinion that the proceedings are void from the beginning, and that no legal process can be founded upon one which was void of itself. If a member was privileged from attending on the summons of a grand jury in the first place, his refusal was no contempt of the court out of which such process issued, for he had committed no offense. He had simply availed himself of a right which the statute of the state and parliamentary law gave him; and your committee is of opinion that it is a novel doctrine, dangerous in itself, that a person availing himself of the privilege granted to him by the laws and constitution of the land, becomes guilty of a crime and is liable to arrest for the exercise of the privilege thus conferred upon him. The distinguished judge himself admitted the danger to which the construction of the statute, which he seemed to desire to press upon the committee, would lead, and it needs no argument to show how dangerous it would be if such a course were allowed to be pursued. There are sixty-two counties in this state. There are sixty-two grand juries sitting, many of them during the session of the legislature. Suppose it established that a member is liable to arrest for disobeying a summons to appear before a grand jury. How easy would it be for designing men to thus deprive the house of members to an extent sufficient to embarrass its business; or again, for designing persons to change the political complexion of the house from one party to another, by getting up fictitious charges before a grand jury and issuing subpœnas to members, and on their non-compliance, issuing attachments, and causing their arrest and transportation to the different shire towns of the counties. Your committee deem it not necessary to follow this line of argument. The mere statement of it is sufficient to show how dangerous such a rule would be.

Finally, your committee, in full view of the facts, and after a full consideration of the law and precedent governing cases of this kind, have come to the conclusion that the arrest on January 21, 1870, of the Hon. Henry Ray, a member of the assembly from the first district of the county of Ontario, on an attachment issuing out of the court of oyer and terminer, then being held in the county of Saratoga, of which the Hon. Platt Potter was presiding justice, was a high breach of the privileges of this house by said Potter, and deserves the censure of this house. And your committee are further of the opinion, that W. B. French, in causing the issuing of such attachment, was guilty of a high breach of the privileges of this house; and that the said Windsor B. French, district attorney as aforesaid, deserves the censure of this house. Your committee are also of the opinion, that the arrest of Henry Ray, in the city and county of Albany, by Mr. Elisha D. Benedict, a deputy sheriff of the county of Saratoga, was a high breach of the privileges of this house, and that said officer deserves the censure of this house."

On the 14th day of February, 1870, the Hon. Platt Potter had served upon him, by the sergeant-at-arms of the assembly, the following notice and resolutions:

STATE OF NEW YORK, IN ASSEMBLY, }
ALBANY, Feb. 11, 1870. }

HON. PLATT POTTER:

SIR—This day the assembly of the state of New York, passed the following resolutions:

Resolved, That the Hon. Platt Potter, Justice of the Supreme Court of the fourth judicial district, be summoned and required to appear before the bar of this House, for a high breach of its privilege in issuing an attachment for the arrest of the Hon. Henry Ray, a member of the Assembly of the state of New York, from the first district of the county of Ontario; that the House will then take such action as the House in its judgment may see fit.

Resolved, That Hon. Platt Potter, residing in the city of Schenectady, in the state of New York, be and he is hereby ordered to attend at the bar of this House, on the 16th day of February, inst., at 12 M., at which time he will have opportunity to make explanation of his conduct in issuing the attachment for the arrest of Hon. Henry Ray, a member of this House; and this Assembly will then proceed to take further order on the subject.

By order of the Assembly,

C. W. ARMSTRONG, Clerk.

At 12 o'clock at noon of the 16th day of February, Judge Potter appeared at the bar of the assembly chamber, when the speaker addressed him as follows:

Mr. Platt Potter,—You have been summoned to the bar of the assembly of the state of New York, for a high breach of its privileges, in issuing the attachment under which the Hon. Henry Ray, a member of this house from the first district of Ontario county, was arrested and taken from his duties as a member of this house, and conducted to Ballston Spa, in the county of Saratoga, there to testify before a grand jury of the court of oyer and terminer, of which court you were the presiding justice. What have you to say in excuse for your conduct in the premises?

Mr. Potter inquired if the presence of his counsel would be permitted. [Mr. W. A. Beach.]

Mr. Fields stated that the presence of counsel is unusual.

The speaker declined to accede to the request.

Judge Potter: Then I will speak for myself; and proceeded as follows:

Mr. Speaker: I appear in obedience to the resolution and order of this honorable body, to give such explanations as I am permitted, in relation to what is assumed to be a high breach of privilege in causing the arrest of an honorable member of this house.

In thus appearing, sir, I do not acknowledge the power of this house—I do not acknowledge the authority of this house to call me to any account whatever; and coming here by courtesy—only out of respect to this house, I proceed to make such statements as I am permitted to make by this honorable house, without waiving the objection, which, by counsel, I am advised I might make, and decline to appear here at all by any authority that this house may have over me.

And while I stand here, thus giving all respect to this high department of the state government, I also stand here to protest against the legal right—against the legal authority of this body, to call in question my judicial acts performed within the sphere of the judicial department of this same government, in which I have the honor to hold a place.

I claim, sir, that the judicial department of this government is entrusted with an equal portion of the sovereign power of the state; that it is possessed of equal dignity with any other; that it is a department whose powers are co-ordinate and co-extensive with, and entirely independent of, the legislative power. That, to be sovereign and independent, when acting within its proper sphere, there must exist no other or higher tribunal to call them to account for their independent action. I protest, and claim, sir, that there is no way known to the constitution or laws of this state by which a judge can be called to account, be tried, degraded, or the dignity of the judicial office impaired, except by the only method known to the constitution, by way of impeachment for corruption in office. Of this there is no pretence here.

I am not called here, sir, as an individual, to answer for an individual offence. No, sir, this case assumes vastly greater proportions and magnitude than that. Sir, I come as a justice of the Supreme Court of New York; as one representing the judicial department of the state, to defend my *judicial* action. In speaking in their defence, common propriety demands that I should speak with all respect to this honorable body; duty to my department equally demands that I, as their representative, should speak with boldness of defence as if that whole body were here speaking to an equal. Sir, with all respect, I deny the power; I deny the legal, the constitutional power of this house to call my judicial acts in question.

I protest in the name, and as the representative, of the judicial department, to the exercise or to the attempted exercise of such a power by this house. I protest in the name of the sovereign people of this state; I protest in behalf of the constitutional independence of the judicial department, against the power of this house to punish by censure or otherwise, the individual, for acts performed while exercising the functions of a magistrate of the highest court of original jurisdiction of this state.

Sir, I should be a traitor to the interests, to the dignity, to the sacred character of the judicial department, to its independence, to the right to protection, if by any act of mine, or by passive submission, I should consent to the aggressive assumption of power which proposes to strike so deadly a blow at their independence; nay, if I did not with boldness, with fearlessness of consequences to myself, protest, solemnly, earnestly protest, against a proceeding so calculated, in its effects, to overawe them in the exercise of their duties, and thus to destroy their independence.

Sir, if this measure shall be carried out upon the assumed powers of this house, what is left of character or of independence to the judicial department? If one department of this government possess the power to command obedience of another of co-extensive and equal power; if the legislative can usurp the authority to hold in awe, or punish, the judicial, then indeed have we a despotism, and not a government of freedom. If for an official, if for a judicial act of a Judge, this house possess the power to punish, even for mistaken judgment, where is the boasted protection to an independent judiciary? Where will there be found a spirit craven enough to accept a place on the judicial bench?

Sir, allow me to say, that in my opinion, it will be a sad day for this republic; a sad day for the liberties of this people, when such a doctrine shall be established.

With what offence, then, am I charged? Not with having acted corruptly; but that, as a judge, acting officially, acting in the discharge of a high and solemn duty imposed by the constitution and laws of this state, which I have sworn to support and obey, I had the independence, nay, if you please, the daring to pronounce the law, as I understood it then, and as I understand it now; yea, more, I feel bound to say here, before this high tribunal, now, in full view of all the terrors of its threatened power, with all the power which it may deem in its power to exert, that as I *still* understand the law of privilege in this state, were I called upon to-morrow to act again as I acted in this case, as I feel responsible to God only for its conscientious performance, I should repeat the act for which I am now called upon to explain, regardless of any action this house shall take in this matter.

My offence, then, is that in so pronouncing the law, I have differed in opinion with the honorable committee; perhaps with the whole house. A high offence, indeed! But, sir, I have committed no contempt. No contempt has been committed. As a judicial officer so acting, I could commit no contempt for which I could be held responsible. It is not the individual who is before you, whose acts you propose to punish by censure or otherwise, that has committed any act whatever. It is a high court of this state that performed the act; yes, sir, it is a high court that has committed the sin; and the theory of this proceeding is, that the individual who at the time was clothed by the constitution and laws with the power to execute the sovereign will; he who was the mere minister of justice, acting according to his solemn sworn convictions; executing not his own, but the peoples will, that is

to be humiliated, threatened, overawed, for daring to do his constitutional duty.

Sir, a case like this is unheard of. It is an anomaly in this; it
is an anomaly in any and every civilized government upon the
earth. Yes, sir, it was reserved for this honorable house, in the
year 1870, to initiate such a proceeding. It is an anomaly in every
step of its progress. First, in its progress, the judge was sub-
poenaed to appear before an honorable committee of this house, to
give evidence of the facts upon which one of its honorable members
had been arrested. To this step no possible objection could be
urged. None was urged. He appeared in obedience to that summons. Knowing his legal protection, little did he imagine that he
was called there to be made informer against himself for an offence;
to be used as his own accuser.

A becoming respect to, and confidence in the body before whom
he appeared, forbid such an idea. He was not summoned there
for trial. Had he been, he would have put himself there. as he
does here, upon his defence. He relied upon a reciprocal confidence, upon comity, upon the magnanimity of an honorable
committee that no such object was in view as a trial. The legitimate duty of that committee, as he supposed, was, to inquire as to
facts, and by what law an honorable member had been arrested;
whether there had been a breach of privilege; whether the law
was sufficiently protective, and if not to recommend one that
should be. He knew that he had acted in the conscientious convictions of duty, and that he was not amenable. What had he to
fear at the hands of honorable men? He knew that if he had acted
corruptly then only could he be dealt with. He supposed, too,
that if any doubt existed as to his rightful exercise of power, that
some committee, like that of the judiciary, would be selected, and
who would dare to place their legal opinion, for which they would
be willing to be held responsible before the legal world, upon the
records of the legislative department; that before such a committee,
(not now intending disrespect to this,) an opportunity would be
given to discuss so grave a question.

But, sir, with no avowal of such an object; without a trial, I
am charged by that honorable committee, that as a judge of the
Supreme Court, I have committed a high breach of privilege of

74

this house; that as such judge, I have struck a blow at the independence of this co-ordinate branch of the government; and the theory of your honorable committee is, that this house possess the power to punish by censure or otherwise, without a trial; not the body who committed the act, but the minister of that department who executed its power. This is an assumption of the pre-eminence of power of this house, an assumption of authority over the judicial department, which has no foundation in this government. It is an assumption that the legislative power, or that one branch of its body, is superior in authority to the judicial department. This is an assumption that no lawyer of any standing dare assert; and one that this house will not stultify its understanding by asserting. If this proposition as to its power is untrue, how can they exercise the power of punishment? How then is it proposed to heal this supposed deadly wound upon their dignity of privilege? They cannot punish the court; that is physically impossible. How then can they punish its minister? It is proposed, sir, to heal this wound by the *lex talionis;* the law of the right of retaliation; the right of inflicting a like injury upon a co-ordinate department; that is, to commit a breach of privilege in return upon the judicial department, in satisfaction of the offence. Sir, I stand here protesting against the right to commit such a breach. I stand here claiming the privilege also of the judicial department. I assert that you have no right to bring these two departments into conflict; that you would thereby endanger the stability, the perpetuity, the independence of the government, whose trusts you have in part taken in charge.

Believe not, sir, that I say these things through any fear of consequences personal to myself. I well know that as you cannot punish the court with material or physical punishment; that you cannot punish its members without a trial; that you cannot try its Judges but by impeachment; that you cannot impeach but for corruption, and that in the constitutional form. True, you can resolve, you can send forth your resolve in the language of degradation, and though there may be degradation, it will not degrade him against whom it is issued. It is not such degradation that I fear; if such resolution shall be issued, it will fall harmless upon him against whom it is issued. Nay, sir, were I ambitious, I would invite it. I would court its favor. But, sir, I have no such ambition; no ambition, but that in the sight of that God, in whom I trust, to do my judicial duty fearlessly; to the best of my ability; unawed, unterrified, uninfluenced by caprice or favor—the will of assumed rulers, or the more fearful influence of passion, of popular applause, or of popular excitement and prejudice.

But, before I proceed further upon this view of the case, I propose, candidly for a moment, to look at the law of privilege to members of the legislature of this state, and, with all intended respect to the argument of your honorable committee, I deny, I solemnly deny, that the law of privilege of the British parliament, as claimed by them, is the law of privilege of the state of New York, and I shall show it to be otherwise. I deny that the privilege of the house of congress, is the same law of privilege as that of the legislature of the state of New York; and while I accord to that committee credit for much research into the law of privilege of Great Britain, I shall show that they did not search far enough to find it; and it will be seen that their report is entirely deficient in the examination of the law of privilege of this state. The law of privilege of members of congress, is not the same law as that of the British parliament; but is secured to them in the constitution of the United States, which limits and restricts the common law of England, as cited in that report. The laws of the several states, differ from each other, and differ from that of congress. The law of privilege of the state of New York is peculiar to itself. It is not, as is that of congress, in the constitution, but is regulated by a statute. It is so brief in its provisions, that I shall be excused for repeating it. It is all embraced in two lines, to wit: "Every member of the legislature shall be privileged from arrest on civil process." No lawyer of any standing or credit will deny the rule of construction to be given to this language by a maxim as old as the common law, which applied to this case, is, "the expression of one privilege is the exclusion of every other." Members of the legislature of this state, by this rule, are *only* privileged from arrest on *civil process*.

Would any honorable member of this house; would any free citizen of this government, like to see the legislature of this state possess the uncontrollable power of the British parliament, as cited by your committee? Why, sir, Blackstone says, "that parliament possesses sovereign and uncontrollable authority. The whole sovereign power of the kingdom is vested in it—legislative and judicial." The English writers say, "That with parliament the sovereign power is despotic; it runs without limit and rises above all control." Is it the law of privilege of such a government, that seems to have charmed your honorable committee? It is the privilege of the law of Great Britain, which your honorable committee claims to be in force in this state. Sir, with all due respect to that honorable committee, I deny it; and shall show it otherwise. It is the law of privilege of the state of New York only, which this house can assert, and which is now before them for their consideration.

I shall be able to demonstrate, that by that law, no breach of privilege has been committed. It is only from civil process that there is privilege.

The honorable member has not been arrested on civil process. It is impossible in the nature of things that he should have been. The process in question was issued out of the court of Oyer and Terminer. That court is a criminal court only. It has no jurisdiction in civil cases. It cannot issue civil processes. That court possesses the power like other courts, to compel obedience to its process. All the forms of law were complied with. Disobedience to its process was proved by the proper forms of evidence. The court, composed of three persons, not of one individual, solemnly adjudged that there had been a contempt of its authority. It issued its process to arrest for this contempt. This, sir, is the high breach of privilege complained of.

Was this *civil* process? Without intending disrespect to any member of this body, I assert it to be little less than an absurdity so to claim. The judiciary of this state I apprehend would be startled at this novel assertion, that this was civil process. The elementary books of authority which influence courts in their opinions, say otherwise. They define "attachment" to be a process in the nature of a criminal proceeding, issuing out of a court of record against a person who has committed some contempt of court; enumerating among other things, "the disregarding of its process," or "omitting to do anything that shows his disre-

gard of the authority of the court." Burrill's Dictionary, title
"Attachment." 4 Black. Com., 284. 4 Stephens Com., 19. People v. Nevins, 1 Hill, 154. Baily, J., in King v. Clement, 4 Barn.
and Ald., 231. Jac. Law Dict. Attachment.

So, too, in like authority, is found the definition of criminal
proceedings as follows : " Civil proceedings are distinguished from
criminal in this—the former are for a civil injury, or for a right
due from one citizen to another; the latter is for a breach of violation of some public duty in which the state or community, in its
aggregate capacity, are interested." In this state, criminal proceedings are cases in behalf of the people. In the highest court
of this state, in the case of Spaulding v. The People, 7 Hill, 303.,
the character of this process upon which the honorable member
was arrested, was expressly passed upon by the court. Chief
Justice Nelson, delivering the opinion, (and which case was afterwards affirmed by the Supreme Court of the United States,) said,
among other things, " that *criminal contempts* was where one unlawfully interfered with the process or proceedings in an action,
or by the refusal of a witness to attend or be sworn," &c. " All
these," says the learned Judge, " are strictly cases of criminal
contempts, which have nothing to do with the collection of debts
or the enforcement of civil remedies." Enough perhaps upon this
head of *civil process.* Except to say, that I concur in the opinion of
the Court of Errors of this state ; and this learned committee must
excuse me, when I am compelled to say, that, as a Judge, I shall
in future act upon that opinion, in preference to theirs, at page 9,
of their report, in which they hold the contrary rule.

They must further excuse me from differing with them in the
opinion that a member of the legislature is privileged from the
service of a summons or subpœna to give evidence before a grand
jury, or that the service of such subpœna or summons is void. In
the recent case of Wooley and others against Benjamin F. Butler,
decided in the state of Maryland, the defendant was a member of
congress ; in passing through that state, he was served with process,
commencing a civil action against him. He applied to the court
to set it aside on the ground of privilege. The court held the
service of process, which did not arrest the defendant, to be good,
and not void. Either that court was in error, or this honorable

committee must be; and, if between such conflicting opinions, a Judge should happen to be mistaken in his selection of authority, is he to be punished for contempt? But, sir, our statute has defined what are *criminal* and what are *civil* proceedings.

By the "Code of Procedure," *criminal* and *civil* actions are defined as follows:

§ 2. An action is an ordinary proceeding in a court of justice by which a party prosecutes another party for the enforcement or protection of a right, the redress of a wrong, *or the punishment of a public offence.*

§ 3. Every other remedy is a special proceeding.

§ 4. Actions are of two kinds.

    1. Civil.

    2. Criminal.

§ 5. A criminal action is prosecuted by the people of the state as a party against a party charged with a public offence for the punishment thereof.

§ 6. Every other is a civil action.

The proceeding pending in the Court of Oyer and Terminer, before the grand jury, was a "*criminal* action prosecuted by the people of the state as a party against a party charged with a public offence for the punishment thereof."

The same definition in substance is given by Burrill of a *civil* action. He says, "it is an action brought to recover some civil right, or to obtain redress for some wrong, *not being a crime or misdemeanor.* In this latter respect it is distinguished from a criminal action or prosecution."—Burrill's Law Dic., Civil Action.

And the same author defines "Civil Right," to be "the right of a citizen; the right of an individual as a citizen, to sue for a right due from one citizen to another, the privation of which is a civil injury, for which redress may be sought in a *civil action.*"—Id. Tit. Civil Rights.

And the word "civil" is defined to be something "belonging or relating to, or affecting a person as a *citizen,* relating to or affecting the rights and duties of a *citizen,* particularly as between one citizen and another."—Id. Tit. "Civil."

From all these authorities it conclusively appears that "*civil process*" must necessarily, *ex-vi-termini,* include only such process, as one citizen is by law entitled to have issued by the courts to enforce or aid in enforcing some civil right in his favor against another citizen or party ; and that criminal process, on the other hand, is such as issues on behalf of the people as a party, to enforce or aid in enforcing the *criminal* law against an offender and for the punishment of a public offence. Nor so far as the definition of the term " *civil process*" is concerned, are we without authority from our highest court. In the People v. Campbell (40 N. Y. 137) the Court of Appeals, Mason, Justice, giving the opinion said, " It has never been questioned but such a process as this, to enforce a *civil* remedy, by the collection of a specified sum of money is to be regarded as '*civil process.*' "

But, sir, it is still alleged that the Court of Oyer and Terminer, whose jurisdiction is *exclusively criminal,* and which has no civil jurisdiction whatever, can yet issue a *civil process,* and that the the subpœna served on Mr. Ray to appear before the grand jury, was such " *civil process.*" If this was true, still the statute does not " *privilege*" him from such *service.* A member of assembly is *only* exempted from " *arrest*" on " *civil process,*" and not from its *service,* where it may be served without an *arrest* being made. Not being *privileged* from the *service* of the subpœna therefore, then the statute imposed the duty on him to obey its mandate.

But it is further absurdly said, that the subpœna being civil process, nothing can be built upon it, or can grow out of it, that makes the party subpœnaed liable to arrest. Sir, no *lawyer* will make such an argument. By a provision of the Revised Statutes, vol. 2, page 278, § 10, it is provided that " Every Court of Record shall have power to punish, as for a *criminal contempt*, persons guilty of the following acts." Among the enumerated acts is, " that of willful disobedience of any process issued by it." And, sir, must not the court issue *criminal* process in order to punish this disobedience? This, however, is said to be a forced construction ; that it is not, after all, criminal process ; that under such pretence the *dignity* of this honorable body would be assailed, and its members withdrawn from the state interests ; it is claimed that the true meaning of this statute of privilege is, that it must be a process that would arrest the member for a criminal charge against himself. Sir, a refusal to obey the process of the court is *criminal.*

It is made so by statute, 2 Rev. Stat. 692., It is an indictable offence. If, instead of the criminal process by attachment, the
honorable member had been indicted by the grand jury for his
disobedience; would the bench warrant issued by the district
attorney be *civil process?* And would not a *criminal bench war-
·ant*, equally with a *criminal* attachment, have taken the honorable
member from this house? The question of *policy* has nothing to
do with the law. Sir, the idea of arraigning a Judge before this
honorable house, for enforcing the law made by your predecessors,
which you, as well as he, are bound to obey, is a new idea in the
workings of our system of government never attempted till now.

But, Mr. Speaker, I have spent too much time in showing that
I have acted right. So far as your power over me, or over the
department of government in which I hold place is·concerned, it
is immaterial whether I acted right or wrong. Your honorable
body have no more power over me in the one case than in the
other; that is, no power at all.

Sir, your honorable committee, by their report, in which they
have regarded me as an offender, but with which they did not favor
me with a copy (but for the favor of which I am indebted to the
honorable representative of my own county,) have stated supposed
cases of almost infinite mischief, if the privilege of members is not
made as absolute as they claim. I am not here to discuss such a
question. I, too, can suppose cases of monstrous public injustice,
if their claimed law of privilege was the law of the land. If a case
of murder or felony is committed in the presence or within the
knowledge of a member of the legislature; and if, without his testimony before a grand jury or a court, the felon would escape
public justice, should there be no power in this government to compel his attendance to testify? Is the dignity of a member of the
legislature paramount to the public security? Do not felons and
outlaws now sufficiently abound in community? Shall new devices
be presented beyond the present intricacies of law, by which their
escape from punishment shall be secured? But, sir, my duty was
to inquire what is the law; not what is policy.

It is my duty to say, however, in regard to the particular case
before us, in justice to the case of the honorable member whose
arrest is complained of here, I neither knew his name, the name

of the accused, nor the crime with which he was charged. All I now know about it is, upon the statement of the public prosecutor, that upon the testimony alone of that honorable member before the grand jury, the accused was indicted and is now held for trial. That the accused had been perpetrating enormous frauds upon that community, claiming that he was acting as the agent of that honorable member. It appears to me, that it should have been the pleasure of that honorable member to do cheerfully, what he did of compulsion; to give the lie to the foul charge, and bring the culprit, who was assailing his fame, to justice. It is justice to him for me to say, that I do not think his refusal to appear and testify was any indisposition to have crime punished; but based soely on a mistaken opinion of his privilege as a member.

I do not further propose to discuss the question of policy presented in the report of your honorable body; nor would it become a judge to discuss with that committee the policy of the law. Judges, when acting as such, must decide what the law is; not what it should be, nor what policy dictates. If the law is wrong, it is the province of the legislature, not of the Judge, to alter it. If the law is obscure or doubtful, it is equally the duty of the legislature to declare it and make it plain. If its obscurity or uncertainty is such as to make the judiciary doubt, still *they* must act upon their best and most conscientious convictions; and if they mistake in this—if, in the view taken by this honorable house, which is but another, and only an equal department of the government—an error has been committed, is the latter clothed with power to punish for a mistake of judgment? Is this the independance of the judicial department of the government? Even if the decision of the judge happens to be upon the question of *privilege*, must he not still decide upon that question also, when it comes before him? Sir, no civilized government on earth, and, above all, no free government, ever placed their judiciary in circumstances so hazardous, so despotic, as this theory proposes; subject not only to accusation, but subject to have their accusors the judges, who shall try them for the offence of a mistaken opinion; and those judges, too, a body easily moved to anger by anything that looks like an indignity offered to their own order.

Mr. Speaker, I crave the privilege of a single word upon the

75

accusation made in the report by your honorable committee. It is not of material facts omitted in their report, which would, if stated, give a more favorable view of the facts of the case, that I complain, although I might complain of that, but for the great injustice (unintentional, no doubt,) of the statement in one short paragraph of the report, not of the evidence, but of the conclusions of the committee ; as follows : They say :

" His Honor, Judge Potter, before the committee, in the first place attempted to extenuate or excuse his conduct by a statement that the attachment was issued inadvertently, and that his attention was not called to ·the fact that Mr. Ray was a member of the assembly, although it subsequently appeared by the statements of Judge Potter, of the district attorney, and of Mr. Waldron, the surrogate of Saratoga county, that prior to the issuing of the attachment, the fact that Mr. Ray was a member of the assembly, was brought to the knowledge of the judge. It will thus appear that the subpœna was issued to Mr. Ray, and the attachment issued upon return of the service of said subpœna notwithstanding such knowledge."

This statement, in its effect, is not only calculated to create prejudice against me before this house, by whom it is claimed I am to be tried ; but to degrade me in public estimation. *I did not attempt to extenuate or excuse my conduct ; but on the contrary, justified the act then as I do now ; nor was the act done by inadvertance.* That honorable committee will now do me the justice to remember, that though I did state the fact, that at the time I signed the attachment, I did not know that Mr. Ray, against whom it was moved, was a member of assembly ; that I signed many on that day, and this among the number ; that it was not stated at the time in my hearing, that Mr. Ray was a member of the legislature. This I stated as fact ; but I did declare to that committee that I had previously given the public prosecutor, and also to the surrogate whom he sent, the opinion that a member was not privileged ; and I also declared to that committee, that had I known at the time that Mr. Ray was a member, I should have deemed it my duty, to have issued the attachment all the same. I declared it then ; I declare it now to this house, and to the world. Such was, indeed, my opinion. I stated the fact that I did not know of his being a representative at the time the process was issued. I stated this *as a fact*, because it was true; and because the honorable chairman called upon me first to state the facts. But, sir, I deny that I claimed to be excused, or attempted to extenuate my conduct, for that reason, further than the fact itself should have that effect. Sir, the conclusion that I attempted to excuse or extenuate, is inconsistent with avowals before that committee, that I previously advised the public prosecutor of my opinion of the law, on being asked; it is inconsistent with my avowal that had I known the fact of membership at the time, with my opinions of duty, I should have issued it all the same. The honorable member from Oswego will remember that he replied to me, that, with my opinion of the law, he did not see how I could do otherwise. In this, sir, that honorable committee (unintentionally, no doubt,) has done me great injustice. I thrust back such a charge with indignation and contempt, as being against all my convictions. I stand here to defend myself upon the broad ground of duty conscientiously performed, admitting that I had given the opinion stated, but still repeating the fact that when I signed the process, I did not know the name of Henry Ray was that of a member.

Mr. Speaker, the fear of being tedious, compels me to omit the discussion of many points vital to the subject now pending before this honorable body; more vital, perhaps, than a mere superficial view would suggest. A conflict between two equal departments of the same government, possessing co-extensive powers, each being sovereign within its own sphere, is fraught with dangers too serious for contemplation—too serious to be disposed of under an an excitement of the moment by the complaining party, who are to sit also in judgment upon their own supposed grievances. For one department, by their action, to attempt thus to reduce another to a state of servile obedience, or to destroy their independence; to bring the judiciary into a state of servile dependence upon the legislative will; would leave the former at the mercy of the latter, and the institution of an independent judiciary, would perish by its own imbecility, or want of power.

Permit me to say, Mr. Speaker, with all due courtesy, in all kindness of feeling, it is my deliberate conviction, that your honorable committee, unintentionally, and without the reflection that their resolutions were to involve the consideration of such a fearful precedent, would now, in view of its solemn importance, prefer either to withdraw them for further considerotion,—refer them to the judiciary committee, or to the attorney general of the state, for a *legal*, a *responsible* opinion upon the great questions of the conflict of power which I have discussed, which are here for action under a state of excitement by those who are to act as judges; and which questions, that committee have not at all considered.

Thus far, Mr. Speaker, I have argued this solemn question upon my individual views ; perhaps the argument would carry more profound respect, should I cite to its support the opinions of some of the sages of the law, who, with prophetic vision, did consider, and who have given opinions upon this very case.

I have thus far intended to utter no word of disrespect to this honorable body, and I shall hope to receive from them in return, that respect to my department, which the theory of our government has established as its right. In this defence, I intend to utter no language of my own, equal in its severity to that of the profoundest expounders of the rights of the judiciary, under our constitutional system.

Mr. Justice Story, that distinguished jurist and expounder of the constitution, whom all so much respect, said, "Every government must, in its essence, be unsafe and unfit for a free people, where such a department as the judiciary does not exist with powers co-extensive with those of the *legislative* department. Where there is no *judicial* department to interpret, pronounce and execute the law, to decide controversies, and to enforce rights, the government must either perish by its own imbecility, or the other departments of government must usurp powers, for the purpose of commanding obedience to the destruction of liberty. The will of those who govern, will become under such circumstances, absolute and despotic ; and it is wholly immaterial whether power is vested in a single tyrant, or in *an assembly of tyrants*." He cites the remarks of Montesquieu with approbation, "that it is found in human experience, that there is no liberty, if the judiciary power be not separated from the legislative and executive ;" and he adds "that it is no less true, that personal security and private property rest entirely upon the wisdom, the stability, and the integrity of the courts of justice." " That government can be truly said to be despotic and intolerable, and will be rendered more oppressive and more mischievous, when the actual administration of justice is dependent upon caprice or favor upon the will of rulers, or the influence of popularity." *When power becomes right*, it is of little consequence whether decisions rest upon corruption or weakness, upon the accident of chance, or upon deliberate wrong.

In every well organized government, therefore, with reference to the security both of public rights and private rights, it is indispensable that there should be a judicial department to ascertain and decide rights, *to punish crimes*, to administer justice, and to protect the innocent from injury and usurpation.

But, perhaps, this honorable body would better like an opinion still nearer home. That distinguished jurist, whose name every citizen of New York repeats with veneration, Chancellor Kent, said : " In monarchial governments the independence of the judiciary is essential to guard the rights of the subject from injustice of the crown ; but in republics, it is equally salutary in protecting the constitution and laws from the encroachments and the tyranny of faction. Laws, however wholesome or necessary, are frequently the object of temporary aversion, and sometimes of popular resistance. It is requisite that courts of justice should be able at all times to present a determined countenance against all licentious acts, *and to deal impartially and truly according to law*, between suitors of every description or whether the cause, the question, or the party be popular or unpopular. To give the courage and the firmness to do it, the judges ought to be confident of the security of their station. Nor is an independent judiciary less useful, *as a check upon the legislative power*, which is sometimes disposed *from the force of party*, or the temptations of interest, to make a sacrifice of constitutional rights."

But Judge Story, was so imbued with the fear of legislative encroachments upon the judicial, that in another place he says, " that there is a great absurdity in subjecting the decisions of men, selected for the knowledge of the laws, acquired by long and laborious study, to the revision and control of men, who for want of the same advantage, cannot but be deficient in that knowledge. *The members of the legislature will rarely be chosen with a view to*

those qualifications which fit men for the stations of judges, and on
this account t er will be great reason to apprehend all the ill conse-
quences of defective information; so on account of the natural pro-
pensity of such bodies *to party divisions,* there will be no less
reason to fear that the pestilential breath of faction, *may poison
the fountains of justice."* "These considerations," he says, "teach
us to applaud the wisdom of those states who have committed the
judicial power, not to a part of the legislature, *but to distinct and
independent bodies of men."*

This may, perhaps, suffice upon this point. But I approach
another point, which is, to ask what is the duty of a judge, even
if the question of *privilege* is before him for decision? Upon this
question I demand such an unprejudiced, patriotic, sensible response, that this honorable body will dare to stand upon it before
an impartial constituency, and before the intelligence of the world.
This is, perhaps, one of the most important points in the case.
Perhaps the opinion of Chief Justice Marshall might not be inappropriate to cite on this question. Surely no intelligent lawyer,
no patriotic legislator, would hesitate to look up to such a source,
for advice.

In looking back upon my conduct as a judge in this matter, it is
a source of sincere pride, that I may call him, this profoundest of
American jurists, and noble patriot, to my aid. In Cohen v. Vir
ginia, reported in 4 Wheaton, 404, that illustrious jurist said
"The judiciary cannot, as the legislature may, avoid a measure
because it approaches to the confines of the constitution. *W
cannot* pass by a question because it is doubtful. With whateve:
doubt, with whatever difficulties, a case may be attended, *we mus*
decide it if it be brought before us. We have no more right to de ·
cline the exercise of deciding, than we have to usurp a power that
is not given. The one or the other would be treason to the constitution. Questions may occur which we would gladly avoid, but
we cannot avoid them. All we can do is to exercise our best
judgment, *and conscientiously to perform our duty."*

In another case this great judge said, "The legislative, executive
and judicial powers of every well constructed government (9.
Wheat., 818), are co-extensive with each other." If this is sound,
where is the power of the one to call the other to account? I

still another case, (1 Peters, 814), Justice Johnson said, "In conflicts of power and opinion, inseparable from our very peculiar
relations, cases may occur in which the maintenance of principle
and the administration of justice may require different courses;
and when such cases do come, our courts *must do their duty*."

Mr. Speaker, I do not stand here to deny the power and authority of this house to punish, as for contempt, one who commits an
act amounting to a breach of privilege of one of its members; but
I stand here denying that as an individual I have committed any
such act, or intended to commit any. The act was that of court,
of which I was but one of its ministers, and that as such minister,
I boldly assert, that I am protected by the sanctity of the position—by the fact that it was judicial action; that my decision was
one in which duty called upon me to act, and I was bound to render such a judgment in the matter as a conscientious conviction
of duty demanded. It is human to err. If I have mistaken the
law, it is such an error as every other judge who has ever sat upon
a bench has committed; and this is the first instance in the history
of American jurisprudence in which a judge has been arraigned
for having mistaken the law. Yes, sir, and I may predict, *it will
be the last.*

But, sir, have I even made a mistake? No court has ever adjudged it to be such. I trust none ever will. Suppose that in the
opinion of your honorable committee it is a mistake; yet my convictions are otherwise; and since the passage of your resolutions
I have the voluntarily offered opinions of distinguished jurists and
lawyers, more in number than compose that honorable committee,
who assure me I am right. The question, then, still remains undecided, which is right, with no high judicial court to pass upon
it. Suppose I am right, after all; and this honorable house shall
decide that I am wrong? It will not, therefore, be wrong. No,
sir. Nor can any resolve that you shall pass make it wrong.
Your resolve will establish no law; and no independent judge will
ever pay it the least regard, if he deems it wrong. My opinion
here, may be disregarded. I cannot vote here on the question, or
if I could, for aught I know, one hundred and twenty-eight, or a
majority of that number, men, perhaps, my superiors in legal
knowledge, can outvote me. I have said this was an anomalous

proceeding. It is so. My accusers, who have already adjudged that I have committed an indignity upon their high privileges, are to be my judges. Under such circumstances, I have been told, there is no hope of the act being justified. It may be so. It would be so, it is true, if only the party, feeling and acting in the spirit of wounded dignity is to control—feeling that the exercise of their power is beyond control of any other power; and knowing that there is no power of appeal. But, sir, if you shall believe I am conscientious, would it not be a higher magnanimity—would it not be a better spirit of patriotism; nay, would it not be elevating, to divest the case of feeling and prejudice, and to look upon the case as a high court of law, uninfluenced by personal considerations, would look upon it? Sir, this spirit of magnanimity gives me hope, even against the spirit of supposed wounded dignity.

I have already said there are high governmental reasons why the precedent now to be established should be a good one; that if the law is in doubt, you have the power to remove that doubt by legislation. The courts have no power to do so, because it has not been before them. If the theory of your honorable committee is wrong, conscientious judges who differ from them, will repeat the error, regardless of your action. Thus then they will stand, with the terror of legislative precedent suspended over them upon the one side, but with a more awful terror, that of Almighty vengeance, if they violate their consciences, upon the other. Call you, sir, such a position as this, that of an independent judiciary? Sir, with all respect, this would be solemn mockery.

One word more, Mr. Speaker. Your committee inform you that they have based their resolutions upon parliamentary law, and have given you its antiquity and its evidence of wisdom. They have assumed that this law of privilege is uniform. I have demonstrated by the statutes and constitutions that it is not, and that their conclusions in this particular were in error. I have shown that the national legislature have their privileges secured by the national constitution—that some of the independent states have their law of privilege secured by constitutions, and some by statutes; that the law of privilege of this state is qualified, and limited by the statute, and differs from that of the nation, of other states, and of Great Britain. If this honorable committee, as I insist, have been led into unintentional error in this; if they are equally in error as to the law of privilege in Great Britain, may not the resolutions based upon such opinions be also error? Can you rely upon such a mistaken view of the law as a safe basis of action?

Sir, I have read the cases referred to in that report upon the English law of privilege, and what will be found as most remarkable, is the fact, that not one of those cases was determined within the last century, nor since the year 1700. If that learned committee had extended their research to that year, which was the thirteenth year of the reign of William III, they would have found an English statute *limiting* the privileges of members of parliament, which is entitled: "An act for preventing any inconveniences that may happen by privilege of parliament." In that act, sir, the privilege was so limited that members of parliament, including peers of the realm, were made liable to the service of any *civil* process which did not arrest their persons; and service of such process upon them was not void, as your honorable committee say of the subpoena, and as has lately been held in the case cited in the state of Maryland.

If that learned committee had extended their research still further, down to the year 1770, just one hundred years ago, to the thirteenth year of the reign of George III, they would have found another statute, still further abridging the privileges of members of parliament; setting forth in its preamble that it was to obviate the inconvenience and delay, by reason of *privilege* to the king, and his subjects in prosecuting their suits, &c. What suits had the king but suits in his name, which in this country are suits in the name and in behalf of the people?

In fact, sir, for the *last one hundred years*, the privilege of parliament has not been such as your honorable committee report it to be—but has been, as it has been here, limited and restricted by statute, and confined to arrest *in civil cases*—and the English law of privilege now, is not materially different from that of the state of New York. Your learned committee have as much mistaken the law of privilege of Great Britain as they have the law of privilege of the state of New York.

When this last bill to limit privilege was before parliament, that

76

great light of English jurisprudence, Lord Mansfield, advocated its passage, and I quote the following most significant remarks from his speech, which may be regarded as judicial construction of that law. He says : "It may not be popular to take away any of the privileges of parliament, for I very well remember, and many of your lordships may remember, that not long ago the popular cry was for an extension of privileges, and so far did they carry it at that time, that it was said that privilege protected members from *criminal actions*, and such was the power of popular prejudice *over weak minds*, that the very decisions of some of the courts were tinctured with that doctrine. * * * It was, said he, undoubtedly an abominable doctrine. The laws of this country allow no *place* or *employment* as a sanctuary for crime, *and where I have the honor to sit as judge, neither royal favor nor popular applause shall ever protect the guilty*." * * Noble patriot! In another part of his speech, he said, "that members of both houses should be free in their persons, *in cases of civil suits*, for there may come a time when the safety and welfare of this whole empire may depend upon their attendance in parliament. God forbid that I should advise any measure that would in future endanger the state. But this bill has no such tendency. It expressly secures the persons of members from arrest *in all civil suits*. I am sure were the noble lords as well acquainted as I am with but half the difficulties and delays that are every day occasioned in the courts of justice under pretense of privilege, they would not, they could not oppose this bill." The bill, sir, passed ; and for one hundred years that is the law of privilege in Great Britain, and is *not* now, as your honorable committee have reported it to be.

No cases can be found like those cited by your honorable committee since the passage of that bill, even in the English courts. The cases cited by your honorable committee are before that time, and, as that noble man declared, *they contained a tincture of that abominable doctrine.*

Mr. Speaker, have I not shown errors enough, in the basis, upon which your honorable committee have proposed action, to show that the law of privilege is not in this state, what is claimed for it? There is not now even an approach to it, as laid down by your committee, in England. Why, sir, ten years before the passage of this last English statute, Lord Preston, a peer of the realm, was committed by an inferior court of that realm, a court of quarter sessions, for refusing to give evidence before a grand jury on an indictment for high treason. He obtained a habeas corpus before a higher court—the king's bench, for his discharge. When Holt, Lord Chief Justice, said: " He had committed a great contempt, and had I been there I would have fined him, and committed him till he paid the fine."

But, sir, I have done with English authority.

Now, sir, it only remains to give construction to the words *civil process* in our statute. If an attachment issuing out of a criminal court is *civil process*, then have I been misled by books of authority; then have I mistakenly erred in deciding the law. If it is not *civil process*, then my decision is law, and must stand approved by the courts, whatever this house may do. Oh! the peril to an independent judiciary! Would to God, that a Marshall, or a Kent, or Mansfield had the decision of this great question! That is, if they would stop one moment to entertain such question. But, sir, I am not called upon to establish that the subpoena issued by the district attorney was *criminal process*, that burthen is *not* legally put on me. No lawyer will say it was *civil process*. I did not issue that, the statute makes it the duty of the district attorney to do that,—and yet, in theory, it issues out of the court of oyer and terminer; and disobedience to its commands is regarded as contempt of that court. But the question is not that. If regularly issued, its service was good, and not void. It was in the eye of the law a contempt to disobey it. And all the question that remains is if this honorable body have the power, and could entertain it all, was the process issued upon that contempt a *civil process?* This honorable body is called upon to vote distinctly upon the meaning of those words. I am not unwilling to see that record of names. I have no indisposition to see the lawyers of this house put their names to such a record. If with the light of intelligence of this day—if with a sacred regard for judicial independence—if with a patriotic desire to avoid conflicts between the co-ordinate and co-extensive departments of the sovereign power —if you shall act with freedom from all spirit of wounded dignity— if with jealous care you feel that you are sitting both as accusers and judges, and that the sovereign people will hold you responsible for your action—if you shall place yourselves upon that lofty plane of devotion to the constitution and the best interests of this noble state; if it shall be your just pride to guard and protect the rights of an independent judiciary from the terrors of aggression of a co-ordinate power; then, sir, I have no fears of the result.

I invoke these noble and elevating considerations to your honorable body. But, Mr. Speaker, I desire to say again, that my appearing here to-day is out of respect to this high department of the government—not waiving my right to protest against being brought here at all. Nay, sir, by the advice of my counsel I should not have appeared at all, and should have put in defiance the power of this body,—should have allowed your officer to execute the process of this house upon my person and held you responsible for the act. But my own judgment has dictated to me to come here out of courtesy—without waiving my right of protest or acknowledging myself in your custody. Although I have appeared here and offered this defence, I do not say that I submit this case to you, though probably that will be the effect of your action; but, sir, I stand here PROTESTING, earnestly PROTESTING, that I am not here in obedience to your power, but here out of courtesy to an independent department of this government.

At the close of this argument, Mr. Fields made a motion that Judge Potter now withdraw from the house until his case be disposed of.

The speaker then informed the honorable judge that he could now withdraw to the library room until his case was decided.

Judge Potter—I prefer to stay, and unless driven from the house by its power, shall remain.

The Speaker—The request of the honorable judge will be granted.

Judge Potter—I have made no request—and took his seat.

A long and exciting debate followed.

Mr. Fields offered the following resolution:

"*Resolved*, That the Hon. Platt Potter, in issuing the attachment for the arrest of Hon. Henry Ray, a member of assembly from the first district of the county of Ontario, was guilty of a high breach of the privileges of this house, and censurable therefor, and that he be reprimanded by the speaker in the presence of this house."

This resolution received no support, and was withdrawn.

Mr. Alvord offered the following amendment to Mr. Field's resolution :

" *Resolved*, That the Hon. Platt Potter was mistaken as to the privileges of this house in the action taken by him in the arrest of Hon. Henry Ray, and did commit a breach of its privilege in so doing; but this house do not believe that any intention or desire to interfere with the independence or dignity of the house actuated him in the performance of that which he deemed his official duty."

Mr. W. D. Murphy offered the following as a substitute :

" *Resolved*, That the Hon. Platt Potter, a justice of the Supreme Court of this state, be discharged from the custody of this house until the hour of twelve o'clock on the first day of March, and that in the meantime the opinion of the attorney general be communicated to this house as to the construction of the term " civil process," in the statute exempting members of the legislature from arrest." Lost.

The question was then taken upon the resolution of Mr. Alvord, and was adopted by a vote of 92 to 15, and the case was discharged.

But as we have seen, that the legislature of the state of New York, have not consented to the view of the limitation and restriction of the law of privilege as it is claimed to be under our statutes, and have insisted in their report, that they possess more extended powers of the ancient common law though they have settled no law by their action, it may be well to enter upon a discussion of that common law.

If it then be true, that notwithstanding our statute, which would seem to create a limitation, and specifies its extent, that there is still a *common law* privilege, adopted into our system, from the common law of England, it may be well to give a little attention to the ancient parliamentary law of England ; with its privileges, and see what it really was ; how and by what law it has been construed, and practised ; and how far its power extends. This will present many grave, and vexed questions upon the very threshhold of the inquiries. The subject is one of great delicacy, and of still greater importance, and requires to be treated with integrity and freedom, and at the same time, with decorum and respect.

It is in England called the law of parliament. This law, and what it was, what it is, and how it has been changed and modified by common law and statute to conform to the spirit of progress, the due appreciation of the advancing spirit of liberty, and the independence of the citizen, we shall briefly attempt to show. It can be found by any one, and by all who desires its attainment, by diligent seeking. It is like all other knowledge, the reward of search. It certainly will not be obtained by intuition. There is no light imparted by inspiration to a mere legislator, unacquainted with its history, whatever may have been his experience; it is acquired only by application, research, and industry; by examining the records of parliament, consisting of unwritten customs, and maxims as they existed from period to period, with its changes wrought by statute and the adjudications of the judges of the several courts of law; from experience and study, and familiarity with the judicial decisions of present jurists, and their predecessors.

"The law of parliament, says Hallam, a as determined by regular custom, is incorporated into our (English) constitution; but not so far as to warrant an indefinite, uncontrollable assumption of power in any case, least of all, in judicial proceedings, where the form and essence of justice are inseperable from each other." Junius, an English writer of great notoriety, says, b that, "to establish a claim of privilege in either house, and to distinguish original right from usurpation, it must appear, 1st, that it is indispensably necessary for the performance of the duty they are employed in; and 2ndly, that the privilege claimed, has been uniformly allowed, so as to establish it as law."

Dwarris, in his work, on the subject of parliamentary privilege, has collected, in a condensed form, more of the customs and claims of members of parliament on the question of their privilege; and may be regarded as more reliable authority, than perhaps, any other English writer. Many of his most judicious citations and comments, may with advantage and profit be transcribed into an American work, as the law of privilege in this country, even though

a Hist. of Middle Ages, Vol. 2.   b Letter 44.

it may here be. limited, and perhaps regulated, by constitutions and statutes..

This parliamentary law and the law of privilege has been but little discussed in this country, and the want of uniformity in the law of legislative privilege, in the different states, has left this law peculiar indefinite, undefined, uncertain, complex and obscure, or, in the language of Lord Coke, a "*ab omnibus quaerenda, a multis iquorata, a paucis coquita;*" "to be sought by all, unknown to many, and known to few." Which Lord Holt says, b is "because they will not apply themselves to understand it."

This sober and warranted claim of a peculiar law, (says Dwarris), c determined by regular custom, never has been, and is never likely to be, disputed by the courts of common law, which are by no means wanting in deference for the legislature, or disinclined to support their "ancient and just privileges." A class peculiarly instructed in the history of our institutions, will always best know, how far the real essential privileges of parliament have been in the past, and may again become in the future, the safeguards of the rights and liberties of the people. Any privilege truly essential to the dignity, and to the proper exercise of the authority of the legislature, will be as safely guarded by the judges of the present times, as by the most popular senator, or member of the house. No doubt the constitutional lawyer will be ever vigilant to detect, and firm to oppose, the encroachments of arbitrary power, in however specious forms, and under however venerable names, it may appear. Tyranny, he will say, is not privilege. Privilege, when the term is not improperly used and confounded with power, (which may be abused;) implies protection. Privilege is, or ought to be, protection—against the tyranny of the one, the few, or the many. Such an inquirer will temperately call for —the record of regular custom; the palpable evidence of enjoyment;—the sanction, the recognition of allowance; the admitted precedents and authorities, the series of which establishes the right;—and if he find the claim unaccompanied with, and unsupported by, these, he will plainly repudiate the "tyrant plea of necessity" for advanced powers.

a 1 Inst. 11.   b 2 Ld. Hayn, 1114.
c Vol. 1, 105.

By this customary law, which if it be not anywhere prescribed in clear and explicit terms, or expounded in particular stated maxims, is yet ascertainable, as being determined by regular custom, and subject to certain prescriptive limitations, are all questions of parliamentary privilege to be tried. And such law is to be expounded by that house, to which any matter that arises properly relates, and no where else; *exceptis excipiendis.*

Blackstone seems to suppose that " the dignity and independence of the two houses are in a great measure preserved by keeping their privileges undefined."

It is the unrestricted use of these and similar expressions, " nowhere ascertained," " indefinite," and "undefined," which has probably led to so many crude conceptions, and even vague speculations, upon the true nature of this customary law. Because the *lex parliamenti* has not been dogmatically treated in an institutional method; because it has not been defined, distinguished, codified, classified, expounded and commented upon ; (simplified, like other branches of English law, till it became complex, and elucidated, till it was made obscure) ; it has been often erroneously supposed that it must be unsettled in its doctrines, indeterminate and arbitrary. But then it was forgotten that the very name and nature of this special law and particular system of customs, *ex vi termini*, imports something permanent, uniform and universal. A legal or parliamentary *custom* must be certain, known, fixed and invariable. And if not set out in stated maxims in any institute or commentary, yet, when it can be ascertained by learned lucubrations from the *"præteritorum memoria eventorum ;"* then, in the contemplation of law, *id certum est quod certum reddi potest.* And maxims of a peculiar law, which can be found in precedents, traced in parliamentary history, and verified by the records of both houses of parliament, do really acquire, from the authentic nature of their evidence, a character of fixity and stability, which more than levels them in point of certainty, with any other traditionary branch of our municipal jurisprudence.

But who, it will be inquired, are to be the judges of this law, and how is it to be expounded? The two houses of parliament respectively, claim to be the proper and sole judges of their own peculiar privileges. In what sense is this claim to be understood?

As a claim of exclusive jurisdiction (and not of uncontrollable power;) it is intelligible and (rightly considered,) not ill founded; though subject to some qualification, and to an exception which does not destroy the rule. Where a privilege is undeniable, and only its observance is in question, the house to which the matter relates, is alone competent to try the issue of its respect or violation. And the courts of common law, which will ever readily support and give effect to all the rightful privileges of parliament which can be unequivocally ascertained, will also cautiously abstain from interfering with the punishments of either house for a contempt, which is certainly "proper to the jurisdiction against which the contempt is."

But it is obvious that cases may arise, where a privilege may be claimed by either house of parliament, and regarded as essentially necessary to the due discharge of its legislative functions, which is not so much supported by direct proof, as drawn from analogies, more or less just; in which event reasonable doubts as to the existence or extent of the privilege, may be entertained, both in the courts and in the country. In all such cases, where the privilege is imperfectly evidenced, obscure or doubtful, the fittest and most desirable course would ever seem to be, with a view to quiet the public mind and to avoid all unseemly collisions, to settle the question by a declaratory act. The claim of privilege was originally the claim of the high court of parliament; not of either house separately, but of both houses conjointly; and where the privilege is real, and essentially just and necessary, there can be no doubt but that both houses would concur, to support and declare it.

The right then, in either house of parliament, of exclusively determining upon any violation of their acknowledged privileges, is unquestioned, when acting within the sphere of their authority. In this primary sense, and subject to this limitation, the two houses respectively, are with propriety said, to be the sole judges of their own privileges; that is, whether the privileges in question are notorious, and have been infringed in the particular instance; and in what manner they shall be vindicated and their infraction punished.

They are also, singularly, the persons to judge of their own peculiar forms and manner of proceeding. The house is con-

77

fessedly the sole judge of its own privileges, where the subject-
matter falls properly within its jurisdiction; as, for any matter that
occurs within the walls of parliament; so, upon whatever is necessary to the transaction of business there, or for the protection of
individual members, to enable them to discharge their parliamentary functions; or for the punishment of persons guilty of contempts to the house, or of obstructing its proceedings.   When the
subject-matter falls within the jurisdiction of the house, its adjudication is final, and a court of law cannot question its judgment;
for, in such case, the power of the house, or the due exercise of its
power, is the original and primary matter propounded to the
court, and arises directly.

The judges will however take conusance of the privileges of parliament, where questions concerning those privileges, are brought
collaterally or incidentally before them for judgment, in the way
of suit or action, when the court is obliged to determine the question raised, to prevent a failure of justice.   They will not themselves raise the question, or suffer it to be raised by others, when
it has been properly decided by competent authority.   They will
not entertain the point so disposed of, when it comes before them,
as it is then held to do, directly; because cognizance of it belongs
ad aliud examen; but will entertain it only when, as Sir Thomas
Jones said in Lord Shaftesbury's case, *a* " It is an incident to the
cause before them, of which they are already possessed."   And
then, it should never be forgotten, that the rule by which the
question will be tried,—the law upon which the decision of the
judges will proceed, is that same peculiar law, the identical *lex et
consuetudo parliamenti,* truly said to be a part of the *lex terræ,* of
which the judges are bound to inform themselves, and by which
the determination of such matters is held to be properly governed.

To draw the line between the question of privilege coming
directly before the court and the cases in which it comes incidentally, would be a rash undertaking in a text writer.   The rule is
certainly difficult of application; but it is quite sufficient for his
province, to demonstrate, that it *is* the rule, according to the de-

a 2 State Trials, 615; 1 Mod. 144.   This was a case of contempt, committed by
a member of the house of lords, within their own body while in session—an act
within their exclusive jurisdiction, and the court of king's bench for this reason
held that they had no jurisdiction to grant relief.

cisions of the most learned judges, ancient and modern. Where the interests of third persons involved in litigation, come to be decided upon in a court of law, the direct question before the court is the right of parties who are strangers to the houses of parlianent; and if a collateral issue be raised in the course of the ileadings on any question of parliamentary privilege, *that* comes in incidentally. Where either house of parliament has adjudicated upon the particular case between the same parties, and that question of privilege is afterwards brought before a court of law, it arises directly.

But two things must concur, to make the decision of the house final. They must have decided the precise question ;—the contested matter must have passed *in rem judicatam ;* and they must possess jurisdiction to decide it; and then no court ought to inquire whether the house has adjudicated properly or not. But where the house has clearly no jurisdiction, at all, over the subject-matter ; as, if the house of commons assumed the exercise of a general criminal jurisdiction,—or the lords, that of original jurisdiction over suits,—accompanied in both cases by resolutions that they respectively possessed the power to put men to death for offences, and to entertain original suits,—notwithstanding any adjudications made by them, and also, that the question would arise directly upon the act of either house, the court would still undoubtedly interfere. This shows that the test afforded, though a known and settled distinction, is quite unsatisfactory, without also considering the question of jurisdiction in the adjudicating *forum.* Where either house has expressly decided upon a question of privilege, the only question any longer open, is whether the subject-matter does properly fall within its jurisdiction, or whether the claim set up, exceeds the legal limits of privilege, and the house has usurped a power it does not possess.

But, (as if it were designed to prop up a defective authority, which it could not supply) ; the house has sometimes declared by votes or resolutions, that it does possess the privilege in question ; and in addition to being party and judge, claims to be a witness ;—and that, an interested witness, giving testimony in his own favor ! What is the due effect of such resolutions ?

When privileges claimed by the house of commons have been

of necessity, submitted to the examination of the courts of common
law, and have been found unsupported by usage and evidence of
enjoyment, (upon which they confessedly depend), such claims
have, (whatever votes may have passed in either house upon the
subject), always been disallowed.   As, when a joint privilege was
claimed by members of the house of commons "not to be imprisoned or impleaded during the time of parliament," the barons
of the exchequer, a while they recognized the former claim of
privilege, decided that there was no such privilege as the latter,
" *quin quod implacitari debent ;*" deciding one claim in favor of the
house of commons, and one, against them.   So, in the great case
of b Burdett and Abbott, the house of commons of that day, be-
comingly submitted the existence, as well as the exercise, of the
privilege then disputed, to the decision of a court of justice.   The
question was, (as it must be), entertained by the court of queen's
bench,—was most elaborately argued and comprehensively considered.   The court unanimously upheld the arrest of the defendant as legal, and their judgment was unanimously affirmed in the
exchequer chamber, and afterwards in the house of lords.   The
courts of law, original and appellant, supported the house of com
mons and affirmed the privilege ; as they always will be found to
do, when the claim is proper.   But the proceeding of the house of
commons, relied upon in that case as a defence, was upheld, not
because it was claimed as a privilege by the house, or declared or
resolved by them to be their privilege, but because it was a privilege, well known to, and always recognized by law.   "There can
be no privilege," says Lord Clarendon, " of which the law doth
not take notice, and which is not pleadable, by, and at, law."

"Thus," as was most ably urged in the excellent argument in
Burdett and Abbott, "is it rendered apparent, that one branch of
the legislature cannot, by any votes, create a new privilege; because in several of the cases, the commons had claimed privileges,
which were questioned in the courts of law and disallowed by the
parliament."   *No resolution of either house of parliament can make
that a legal and constitutional privilege which was not so before.   A
court cannot give itself jurisdiction by adjudging that it enjoys it.*

To create a new privilege would in effect, be making a new law,

a Donne and Walsh, 4 Register, 752.   b 14 East, 140.

which one house singly, cannot do.   This leads to the necessary qualification of the stated rule.   The law of parliament may be expounded by themselves, from time to time, but cannot be extended, without the authority of the whole legislature.   Members of either house of parliament, constituting *per se*, only a *part* of the sovereign power in the state (which alone can make new laws), have not an unlimited right of creating and extending exceptions in their own favor.   When Fortescue says *a* of parliament :—"It is so high and mighty in its nature, that it may make law, and that which is law it may make no law." he is enlarging upon the transcendent power of parliament in its collective and legislative capacity.   And what is obviously true of the whole, becomes monstrous when applied to a part.   And this is not only sound legal doctrine, but it is also admitted parliamentary "law and custom."   In 1704, the lords communicated a resolution to the commons, at a conference : " That neither house of parliament have power, by any vote or declaration, to create to themselves new privileges, not warranted by the known law and custom of parliament ; which was assented to by the commons;" and, indeed, is not now contested on their behalf.   And yet, who will logically deny, that if they could give themselves jurisdiction to decide in favor of doubtful powers, they would create new privileges ? [1]

The result is, that the determination and knowledge of privilege of parliament, belongs to the members of the two houses respectively, with the limitation before stated ; but in declaring the law, they act judicially, and are under a solemn obligation *jus dicere* and not *jus dare ;* and they must not extend their jurisdiction, or the determination will be *coram non judice*, and void.   Their's is, at the very utmost, indisputably, a special jurisdiction, exercised in expounding a peculiar law within circumscribed bounds, which must not be exceeded.   And if they should in any case decide mistakingly, *(et multi et boni homines idem fecerunt,)* and pronounce a judgment in favor of a privilege new in principle, and not merely

a Thorpe's Case, 32 Hen. 6; 5 Rot. Parl. 239.

NOTE 1.—This resolution, it may be borne in mind, was four years subsequent to the act of parliament of 13 Geo. III, abridging and defining the privilege of members of parliament, and was but a modest and public manifestation of willing obedience to law, and to the demands of public sentiment

in terms, and never before claimed or allowed in the history of parliament; such their new, unfounded, parliamentary law,—like any erroneous decision of the judges in the common law courts;—must be declared not to be parliamentary law according to the *lex et consuetudo parliamenti;* it must be pronounced, that there exists no such privilege!

To be as explicit as possible upon so delicate a subject, it is apprehended that the decisions of the two houses of parliament, in cases, of which, (when within their jurisdiction,) they are admitted to be the sole competent judges, are fitly governed by usage and controlled by precedents. "They are," says Lord Clarendon, "the only judges of their own privileges; but that their being judges of their own privileges, should qualifiy them to make new privileges, or that their judgment should create them such, was a doctrine never before now, heard of." *a*

And if,—when they suppose themselves, to be only recognizing an old privilege, they are in reality, creating a new one, is it not too much to contend that their not ill intentioned mistake, may not be corrected; that their eroneous judgment, when brought before the sworn judges of the land sitting to administer justice according to law, in all cases brought judicially before them; neither seeking—nor declining,—but only conscientiously deciding questions which must be decided,—that a judgment, of which they, the recognized interpreters of the law, discover the unsoundness, must be received as valid,—allowed,—adopted and enforced by the judges sworn to do the right—and, all the while perceiving this to le the wrong! Is not this absurd and most unreasonable? Is it not monstrous?

It is, also, impracticable. The attempt to withdraw the ultimate determination of questions of privileges, coming in question in cases within the jurisdiction of the respective courts, from the courts of common law;—from those courts, in which the prerogatives of the crown are subject to be questioned and overruled,—will never succeed. Parties and their witnesses, judges, officers, sheriffs, counsel and attorneys, may all be, again and again, committed; but fresh actions will be brought, and succeeding judges, officers, and professional men will do, what they deem, their duty.

Is it not better then, to acquiesce, in the known, settled, and single exception to the rule, that the members of the two houses respectively, are the sole judges of their own privileges ; *except when they come in question incidentally and collaterally before the courts of law in the way of suit or action ;*—or when the house has no jurisdiction over the subject matter ;—in both of which cases the appointed constitutional expositors of the law, must inquire into and determine the question, to prevent a failure of justice ?

And if such be the reason and justice of the case, how stands it upon the foot of precedent and authority ?

The counsel for the house of lords in Lord Shaftsbury's case, *a* the attorney general (Jones,) himself admitted, " that, if an action be brought where privilege is pleaded, the court ought to judge of it ; as an incident to the suit, whereof the court is possessed."

The same rule was laid down by Lord Chief Justice Holt, in the case of the Aylesbury men. *b*

The same doctrine was recognized by Lord Chief Justice De Gray in Brass Crosby's case. *c* " The counsel at the bar," my lord said, " have not cited one case, where any court of this hall, ever determined a matter of privilege, which did not come incidentally before them."

And this result of the case was referred to with commendation, by Grose, J., in R. v. Flower. *d*

All these eminent authorities, agree in the right and the duty of the judges, to take conusance of the privileges of parliament, when questions concerning those privileges are brought incidentally in judgment before the court in actions by parties complaining of injuries within the jurisdiction of the court. " When in a common action, the privilege of parliament does come to be part of the plea or justification, it is of necessity." says Sir Orlando Bridgman, " that the privilege set up to defeat the action, whether there be such, and what the extent of it, come also into consideration." *e*

This the sworn duty of the judges of the land, is confined however, to cases of privilege brought judicially before them. The

a 2 State Trials, 605. 1 Mod. 144.   b 8 State Trials, 162.
c 3 Wills. 202.   d 8 T. R. 345.
e Benyon and Everlyn, T. 14, Car. 2, Rot. 2558.

judges will decline to pronounce an opinion upon privilege of parliament, except where the question comes before them in a legal way;—as they did in Thorpe's case; and *then*, (when it is in such manner, forced upon them;) the highest authorities concur in holding, that they are bound to take cognizance of the existence and extent of the privilege, and to decide upon it. "If a question arise, determinable in the King's Bench, the King's Bench must decide it;" said Lord Holt in R. v. Knollys. *a*

And even Mr. Justice Powell, whose opinions were ever strong and decided in favor of parliamentary privilege, recognized in R. v. Paty, *b* this single exception to the doctrine of exclusive jurisdiction in parliament. "This court," he said, "judges the privilege, only incidentally; for when an action is brought in this court, *it must be given one way or the other.*"

Mr. Justice Patterson made the same remark in Stockdale and Hansard; with the addition that the judgment he was compelled to give, should be the conclusion of his own mind, and not the dictation of others. To the same effect are the judgments of the other judges in the modern cases.

Such is believed to be the sound doctrine upon this delicate and difficult subject, and it will be found to admit all the claims of the two houses to the determination of questions of privilege, which can be supported upon a temperate consideration of the subject; and to reject such views alone, as are not only not consonant to reason, or agreeable to law, but are also repugnant to the spirit of the constitution.

It will have been collected from the preceeding pages, that the two houses of parliament respectively, are empowered to try questions relating to their own privileges, (in which they are consequently parties,) by a peculiar law of their own. That they are ordinarily, the sole judges and interpreters of that law; and it will be seen subsequently, that they themselves, execute their own decrees, by officers of their own. This anomalous and most extensive authority, they indisputably possess, and it may be essentially necessary to the free and independent exercise of their high, constitutional functions, that they should be invested with such extraordinary powers.

a 2 Salk. 509.   *b* 2 Lord Raym. 1105.

" But this is not all. The peculiar law, by which these cases are governed, is not enunciated; is unascertained *a priori;* which necessarily subjects Englishmen, (in this one particular instance) to the dominion of the *jus vagum et incognitum,* said to be ever, the worst species of tyranny. And the law being thus kept undivulged in the breasts of the judges, is, (as is avowed by the indiscreet advocates of indefinate privilege,) extendible, at their pleasure, to all other cases, *pro re nata.* How desirable is it; that such an authority, should have some circumscription! the limitation of usage; the control of precedents.

And these extraordinary powers, are not deemed sufficiently transcendent, but it has been unadvisedly contended, that every decision of parliamentary privilege in either house, however erroneous it may, by possibility, be, shall be, final and conclusive. And every rextravagant excess of jurisdiction; every assumption of power, however arbitrary and unfounded, shall be withdrawn from the control of the common law!

The true doctrine;—that the law of parliament is determined by regular custom;—the rule, that the determination of privilege belongs to the two houses respectively;—the qualification; that, although they may generally expound, they must not extend it; with the exception,—of cases not within the jurisdiction of the house ;* or where privilege is brought before the judges incidentally, as matter of excuse or justification imported into a cause, and absolutely requiring their judgment;—the general doctrine, the rule and the exception, are believed to have been all, before correctly stated.

Happy will be the result, if a dispassionate consideration of the principles and authorities; the law and practice; shall tend to settle the distressing doubts which have long existed, shall contribute to terminate those fraternal conflicts between the legislature and the judicature, which the best and wisest men, will see the most reason to deplore. And are not some traces perceptible of

---

* As, *e. g.* if the house of commons were to claim to determine questions of property without a jury; or to inflict punishments for not taking an oath, which they have no power to administer; cases not likely to occur now, but used for illustration.

an approximation to this desirable end; —this legislative and judicial unanimity?* Cannot future collisions be prevented.

As regards the past, no slight errors have been committed on
both sides; but when questions come to be calmly considered,
when the voice of reason is attended to, juster views will gradually
obtain, and sounder principles become established.

The claim on the part of parliament to be governed by a peculiar
law, has been sometimes too lightly questioned. The *lex parlia-*
mentaria, has been said to be merely a part of the *lex terræ*; like
the ecclesiastical, military, or maritime laws; *leges* indeed; but
sub graviori lege: to be construed at all times by the common law
courts in the ordinary way.

But such is *not* the case with the *lex parliamentaria*, which is
1st, a peculiar law of a special nature, and 2ndly, is confessedly to
be construed by the parliament itself; and only determined by the
judges in extraordinary cases, when they cannot escape from deciding it. And then, whatever the court, superior or inferior, the
case is always to be tried by the law of parliament. In this respect then, some *scintillæ* of doctrine have been advanced, which
cannot, it is apprehended, in strictness be supported.

On the part of the house of commons, extravagant claims of
privilege,—unwarrantable extensions of jurisdiction, and unfounded
assumptions of power, have been at various times preferred and
abandoned; *a* but it was never denied that the wish and intention
of the house, was still to act fairly and equitably, while maintaining its own dignity and authority, with sometimes a little undue
jealousy and precipitancy,—and an excess of animation.

On the other hand, the great anti-privilege champion, Lord
Holt, who made so glorious and successful a stand, though almost
unsupported, in Ashby and White, *b* when a most valued right of

a See the case of Floyd, *post;* Admiral Griffin's Fishpond case, 9 Ad. and El.
14, *et al. ibid.*

b 17 L. J. 714.—App. 3, Hatsell.

* *Quære tamen:* the result of the best intentioned endeavor to reconcile these
big and little endians, may be *that* described in Alma:

"Dear Dick, if we could reconcile
"Old Aristotle with Gassendus;
"How many would admire our toil,
"And yet, how few would comprehend us!"—*Prior.*

the subject was in danger to be defeated by privilege, (as the house of commons were pleased to claim it; resting their case on that untenable ground, rather than on a plausible hypothesis of judicature); who most luminously laid down the great general principles of the law, and based it upon grounds from which his successors are not likely to depart; who reasoned irresistibly, that, as parliament had only circumscribed powers, if it exceeded those, it must, like every one else, that has exceeded his powers, be corrected.

" When Paty was brought up on *habeas corpus*, and the cause shown, was commitment for a certain act which the house voted a contempt, the chief justice stood alone and dissented from all the other judges, who held that the prisoner must be remanded; *a* thus resisting the authority of Shaftesbury's case, who was committed "for high contempts" of the house of lords, without showing when,—where,—or how, committed; *b* an authority to which Lord Chief Justice De Grey, Lord Ellenborough, and Lord Denman himself, with all the judges of our times, have (it may be with reluctance in some instances), conformed. For the power of commitment for a contempt, must belong to every legislative and judicial body. And when it appears that the house has adjudged the offence to be a contempt, the court, it is said, is bound to give credence to that determination. If the house professes to commit for a contempt, and the commitment is in a general form, the contempt cannot be inquired into: " the adjudication is a conviction, and the commitment in consequence an execution." To prevent a conflict of jurisdictions, no court can discharge a person in execution by the judgment of another court of competent jurisdiction. A court, which is not a court of error or appeal, cannot entertain the question whether the authority has been properly exercised in another court. *c* Lord Holt, indeed, did not question the power of commitment in the house of commons in Paty's case; but he thought the warrant itself, in that case, showed an excess of jurisdiction; and so, left his opinion not irreconcileable with Shaftesbury's case, which has always been supported and followed, where the commitment was in a general form.

a Lord Ray, 1105, 3 Wils. 205.
b 6 Howell's St. Trials, 1269.
c 5 Dow. 199.

But if, instead of a commitment in a general form, a return were to shew a cause which could not by any possibility be construed, agreeably to sound reason and natural justice, to amount to a breach of privilege ; * if there were on the face of the warrant itself evidence of an abscence of contempt, Lord Ellenborough plainly intimated in Burdett v. Abbott, that in such case the court would " do its duty." *a* He had before, in the same case, repudiated the doctrine that where a contempt was charged, the court would not look at a warrant and judge of its formal sufficiency ; though he certainly gave full effect to the doctrine in Shaftsbury's case.

It will not be denied that whatever the strict law may be, (and that cannot be questioned after the decision of Burdett v. Abbott, in the house of lords *b* ;) yet, agreeably to natural justice, the imputed offence should always appear on the face of the warrant sent with the prisoner, in order that, as well expressed by Chief Justice Vaughan, in Bushell's case, " the cause of commitment should appear as plainly to the court before which the commitment is returned, as to the court who made the commitment." *c* When the Lord Chancellor for the time being, committed a member of the house of commons, (Mr. Lechmere Charlton,) for a contempt, the committee appointed by the house to inquire into that case, called for the particulars of his contempt; and rightly so, to enable them to judge whether they were really such as to warrant his commitment. *d* But after the house of commons had imprisoned the sheriff of Middlesex, for executing the process of the court of which W. E. and J. W. were the officers, the house was persuaded to make a return to a writ of *habeas corpus*, not shewing " the particulars of the contempt," to enable the court of law to judge of its sufficiency." *e*

a 14 East, 1.   *d* Parl. Rep. 1837, No. 45.
b 5 Dow, 199.   *e* 11 Ad. and El. 273.
e Vaughan, 137.

* See 1 Hargrave's Juridcial Arguments, as to " reconsidering this doctrine of the unappealable and unexaminable nature of commitment for contempt." He puts the case of the lords sentencing a person to work in Bridewell for his life, as was actually done by the lords in 1684 ; and supposes it to be for suing out a writ of habeas corpus to examine the legality of a former commitment by the lords. But does not say how that is to appear !

Now this was not " doing as they had been done unto ;" it was
not agreeable to morals or religion, according to Tully or Saint
Paul; but the attorney general was just able to say, that it was
" according to law." For, where care is taken to make the commitment general, Lord Shaftsbury's case stands unimpeached;
and men to whom the bare necessity to stand sheltered under a
technicality, would of itself, in private life, excite suspicion that
they were not following the pure and high line of conduct; who
would feel that there was something abhorrent from a frank and
loyal nature, in withholding any part of the truth from judicial
inquiry; and most of all *that* part which might rescue a prisoner
from confinement; yet acting as a body and influenced by an *esprit
de corps*, the same men are carried away by a desire of victory,
and do not sufficiently weigh the means for attaining the end.
Others little comprehend what they are doing, and would, if competent to judge of it, be very much ashamed of the dexterity by
which they succeed. " It would be unseemly," says Lord Denman,
": to suspect that a body acting under such sanctions as a house
of parliament, would, in making a warrant suppress facts, which
(if disclosed,) might entitle the prisoner committed to his liberty.
If they ever did so act, I am persuaded that on further consideration they would repudiate such a proceeding. What injustice
might not have been committed in past times if such a course had
been recognized; as for instance, if the recorder of London, in
Bushell's case, had in the warrant of commitment suppressed the
fact, that the jury were imprisoned for returning a verdict of acquittal. I am certain that such will never become the practice of
any body of men amenable to public opinion. In Brass Crosby,
Burdett's and Hobhouse's cases, words were used shewing the
nature of the contempt." *a*

"Nevertheless, though the judges in this case perceived and re-
gretted the *suppressio veri*, and fully appreciated the motive, they
did not swerve from their line of duty. In this, the strongest possible case, where it was notorious that the prisoners were their own
officers, committed whilst acting in the lawful execution of the
process of the court, the judges of the court of queen's bench,
finding the warrant general in form, acted upon the doctrine of

a 11 Adolphus and Ellis, p. 292.

Shaftsbury's case, and remanded the prisoners.   The same *a* course had been taken by the judges of each of the other courts, in similar cases.   And as the courts of law, have thus been conspicuously, and most creditably seen, in the case of their own officers arrested while acting in obedience to the rules of the court, to lay aside all personal feelings, (prejudice and passion enter not into the elements of justice) ; and to act only upon the circumscribed views of the law ; so may the parliament, before a long time has elapsed, not only be found to repose full confidence in the integrity of the judges, submitting their privileges fearlessly to their upright decision; but will probably also be seen vieing with the courts of law in forbearance and self-control.   Then may they be found to magnanimously renounce, to spontaneously divest themselves of, so frightful a power, (amounting to a virtual repeal of the *habeas corpus* act);* as the use of commitments in a general form.

General warrants they will not permit to the crown, even in cases of high treason and rebellion ; and in calmer times they may renounce them, when they are themselves engaged in a squabble with a bookseller or an attorney.   They may become themselves desirous, (as they will never wish to posess any privileges which are not just in themselves, essentially necessary to the discharge of their important functions, and really beneficial to the community) ; that their claims of privilege may stand the test of forensic inquiry, and receive the added sanction of the highest judicial authority.   This would, at least, be a recommendation of their exclustve privileges to the people, and might conduce to a better feeling, both as regards the use of privilege and the interference with the administration of justice, than at present exists."

When the course of justice is allowed to flow unimpeded, decisions are seldom unsatisfactory.   Whenever the parliament has stopped, or tried to stop, actions at law, menaced suitors and witnesses, and in-

---

a C. P. in Crosby's case, 3 Wils. 203; Exchequer in Oliver's case; cases of Murray, Burdett, and Hobhouse, in K. B.

* In 1704, the lords resolved that " every Englishman, who is imprisoned by any authority whatever, has an undoubted right to a writ of *habeas corpus*, in order to procure his liberty by due course of law."   The law of commitment for contempt, says, according to Hargrave : " You shall have a *habeas corpus* ; but it shall answer no purpose to you ; for, however illegal the commitment, the judges shall not be permitted to set you at liberty."—*Juridical Arguments*, p. 14.

*terrupted the regular administration of justice in the due course of
law, it has never been with advantage to the character, or authority,
or dignity of parliament.* It has always been viewed by the country in the light in which it is placed by the resolution of the lords
in Paty's case; " That the deterring parties from prosecuting actions in the ordinary course of law, and terrifying attorneys, solici-
tors, counsellors and serjeants-at-law from soliciting, prosecuting,
and pleading in such cases, by voting their so doing to be a breach
of the privileges of the house of commons, is a manifest assuming
a power to control the law, to hinder the course of justice, and
subject the property of Englishmen to the arbitrary votes of the
house of commons." *a*

" In vain has the house of commons attempted to place its privileges on the foot of unquestionable and unlimited power. " The
court of queen's bench decided in Stockdale and Hansard, *b* that
thsre was no power in this country above being questioned by
law; and I abide by that judgment," said Lord Denman. *c*

May exact boundaries be ascertained and solid principles established; may the parliament and the law flourish irrespective of
each other; yet each lending to the other its separate support and
sanction! In the unavoidable conflict of laws and jurisdictions,
may the general law of the whole empire, the superintending, controlling common law, prevail in the first instance, but subject to
revision in ascending courts of error; ever remembering that the
real, ultimate, last resort of judicature is, in the whole legislature
of kings, lords, and commons, to correct all mistakes, and to repair
every possible wrong!"

Privilege, at first, was the claim generally of members of the
high court of parliament. But the two houses, now distinct
branches of the legislature, must be taken to be invested with all
the essential privileges which antecedently to their separation belonged to the aggregate body of the parliament, so far at least as
they have been subsequently evidenced by enjoyment. Supposing the separate existence of the house of commons to have begun
only in the 49 Hen. 3, or at some other period within the time of
legal memory; yet if the parliament itself, in any anterior form of

a In 1702.   *b* 9 Adol. & El. 14.
c Case of the Sheriff of Middlesex, 11 Adol and Ellis, 286.

its existence, be of prescriptive antiquity, (about which no reasonable doubt can be entertained); the same privileges then enjoyed by it, may be prescribed for by parliament, in the form into
which it has since resolved itself, and now subsists. *a*   It will follow that privileges claimed by the house of commons, if evidenced
by enjoyment, need not strictly be prescribed for.

Since the 10 Geo. 3, c. 50, all claim of protection for member's
lands and goods, *b* and all privileges of domestics, being by that
statute taken away, and all other privileges which obstruct the
ordinary course of justice being abolished, the privileges of speech
and of person are the most familiar of those which remain to be
considered. The principle on which these privileges have formerly been claimed and allowed, is thus broadly, and somewhat
diffusely stated :—" As it is an essential part of the constitution of
every court of judicature, and absolutely necessary for the due
execution of its powers, that persons resorting to such courts,
whether as judges or as parties, should be entitled to certain privileges to secure them rom molestation during their attendance ;
it is more peculiarly essential to the court of parliament, the first
and highest court in this kingdom, that the members who compose it should not be prevented by trifling interruptions from their
attendance on this important duty, but should, for a certain time,
be excused from obeying any other call, not so immediately necessary for the great services of the nation." *c*

" But this privilege, so essential to the very existence of a free
council, so freely exercised under Edward III and Henry IV, and
so constantly demanded as of right, by every successive speaker
posterior to 33 Hen. 8, was frequently cavilled at by the courtiers
of the reigns of Queen Mary and Queen Elizabeth, as intrenching
upon the royal prerogative, and the house, it must be owned, in
part, perhaps, from gallantry towards queens, acquiesced in general too easily in these doctrines. " It was reserved," (so Mr.
Hatsell *d* excellently expresses a generous sentiment) "for a more
enlightened age, and for times when the true spirit of liberty
should be better understood, to ascertain and establish this privi-

a Lord Ellenborough, Burdett and Abbott. 14 East 140.

b 2 Hats. 217; 5 T. R. 686.

c 1 Hats. 1, 2.   *d* 1 Hats. 126.

lege in its utmost extent, consistently with the language of good-breeding, and the behavior of men of liberal education."

Nevertheless, this alarming power of committing members for a supposed breach of the prerogative by their speeches in the house of commons, continued to be exercised by the ministers of the crown in the succeeding reigns. *a*

Of the several instances that follow, the case of Sir Edwyn Sandys, in 1621, is on many accounts the most memorable; but chiefly so, because it produced the famous "PROTESTATION" in vindication of the rights and privileges of the house, which occasioned the immediate dissolution of that parliament. *b*

The king having written to the house of commons, " We cannot allow of your style—calling it ' your ancient and undoubted right and inheritance,'—but could rather have wished that you had said that your privileges were derived from the grace and permission of our ancestors and us ;" a committee of the whole house was appointed to meet the next morning, "to consider all things incident to, or concerning, the privileges of the house ;" and having met, with the assistance of Sir Edward Coke, Mr. Noy, and Mr. Glanville, prepared the celebrated protest :

" That the liberties, franchises, privileges and jurisdictions of parliament, are the ancient and undoubted birthright and inheritance of the subjects of England; and that the arduous and urgent affairs concerning the king, the state, and the defence of the realm, and of the Church of England, and the making and maintenance of laws, and redress of mischiefs and grievances which daily happen within this realm, are proper subjects and matters of counsel and debate in parliament ; and that in the handling and proceedings of those businesses, every member of the house hath, and of right ought to have, freedom of speech to propound, treat, reason, and bring to conclusion the same ;" which having been read several times, was allowed and ordered to be entered of record in the journal of the house ; and which (though the king, by ' sending for the journal, and striking out the entry with his own hand," was in hopes to have obliterated all traces of), is still pre-

a D'Ewes, 410; Cases of Cope, Wentworth, and others.
b 1 Hats. Prec. 137.

served, and will *a* for ever remain, a memorial of the true spirit and firmness, the temper, moderation, and wisdom, of the great men who *b* directed the councils of that parliament, and of whom several of the principal, will be found to have belonged to the liberal as well as learned profession of the law.

Indeed, it is to the sagacity, research, prudence, skill, and above all, to the courage of the lawyers of that period, that this country is almost entirely indebted for possessing its present perfection of civil liberty. Whitelocke truly said, that "those in power had most occasion to be displeased with this profession, as a bridle to their power." When Wolsey went with state and pomp to the house of commons, to overawe the house into the grant of a parliamentary aid, who was it that had the firmness to tell him, "that his manner of coming thither was neither expedient, nor agreeable to the ancient liberties of that house?" *c*—who framed the petition of rights?—to whom are we principally indebted for the bill of rights?—who unavailingly advised proper terms and conditions, with due limitations, upon the power of the crown at the restoration?—to whom do we chiefly owe the principles established at the revolution? *d*—Fortescue, Sir Thomas Moore, Coke, Selden, Hale, Somers, Whitelocke, are all names gloriously distinguished for services to the national freedom. Other bright names have a different praise,—Bacon, Clarendon, &c.

It is observable, that in all these cases it was pretended by the ministers, that such commitments were not for any liberties taken in speeches, but for offences of another sort committed out of parliament; "well knowing," says Hatsell, "that if the parliament could be deluded by these pretences, their end would be equally attained. If this claim, set up by James I, and Charles I, to imprison the members of either house, at any time, and under any pretence, could have been established, it would have made no inconsiderable part of that system of prerogative government, which they were so desirous of erecting."

The great case of Sir John Elliott, Holles and Valentine, in which the judgment proceeded upon the mistaken ground that the

---

a 1 Hats. 138.   *c* 3 Hats. 1; Sir Thomas Moore, Speaker.
b Parl. Hist. Vol. 5.   *d* See Amos's Fortescue, *passim.*

act in Strode's case, was a private act, was a prosecution of those members for their conduct in parliament; a when the house of commons asserted "their indubitable and essential right of freedom of speech, and personal freedom of their members," and refused to proceed to any business till their members were restored to them.

"The last violent and fatal step taken by that misguided monarch (!) (Charles I), which was subversive of every idea of privilege in the house of commons, and precluded all hope of reconciliation with his parliament and people, was the going in person and endeavoring to seize the members whose freedom of speech had displeased him." b

The judgment against Elliott, Holles, &c., was reversed by the house of lords, in April 1668, after the restoration; and Strode's Act was resolved by both houses of parliament to be a general law.

By the Bill of Rights, it was expressly and legislatively declared, at the revolution, as one of the fundamental liberties of the people; "that the freedom of speech and debates and proceedings in parliament, ought not to be impeached or questioned in any court or place out of parliament." c

"The instances of serious invasion of this indispensible privilege principally occur where they were chiefly to be apprehended, from the power of the crown. Interference on the part of the executive would naturally be regarded with greater jealousy than any stupid contempt or perverse obstructions from other quarters. Still there can be no reasonable doubt that any attack or reflection from any other quarter, either upon the house collectively, or upon the members who compose it, as individuals; for any motion, debate, question, resolution, statement made, or decision come to, in the regular course of parliamentary proceedings, would be visited with censure and punishment, as involving an undoubted breach of useful privilege. Accordingly, in an d instance (not perhaps a very discreet one,) in 1559, Frower, a servant of the master of the rolls, was ordered to attend to answer to certain evil words spoken

a See 9 Com. J. 25; 12 L. J. 166, that this was an illegal judgment and against the freedom and privilege of parliament.
b 1 Hats. ad fin.　　　　　c 1 Wm. and Mary, s. 2, c. 2,
d 1 Hats. 194.

by him against the house, saying, "That if a bill were brought in for womens' wyers in their pastes, they would dispute it, and go to the question." for which offence, though he be denied the words, he was committed to the serjeant's keeping.

27 Eliz. 1584, John Bland, a currier, for making dishonorable reflections on the house of commons was brought to the bar, and pardoned on his submission; paying twenty shillings fee to the serjeant, and taking the oath of supremacy.

Reflections on the speeches and conduct of members, assaults upon, or menaces to members, on account of their behavior in parliament, have been frequently resented as indignities to the house itself.

12 Feb. 18. Jac. 1. Mr. Lovel, a member of the house, informed it, "That one Darryel threatened his person that for a speech spoken by him in the house, he should be sent to the tower during the parliament, or immediately after." Darryel was committed to the serjeant till the Saturday following, and then to acknowledge his fault, or be committed to the tower."

But though a member of parliament has privilege of speech in parliament, and may speak in his place in either house what he thinks material or useful, whether in praise or in censure of the conduct of others, without being questioned in any place or court out of parliament, he is not therefore justified in publishing what he has spoken, if it contain matter injurious to the character of an individual. In the former case, in his character of a a member of parliament, he is protected; but if, unauthorized by the house, he choses to publish his speech, it then becomes a subject of common law jurisdiction. And the circumstances, in the latter case, b of its being accurate, and intended to correct a misrepresentation, will not make him less amenable to the common law, in respect of the publication.

As regards reports, resolutions, parliamentary proceedings and papers printed, (and now sold,) by the authority of either house of parliament, considerable doubt was hitherto entertained by the most competent persons, what should be the proper rule.

It seems unquestioned that the courts of law will take judicial

a R. v. Lord Abingdon, 1 Esp. N. P. C. 226.
b R. v. Creevy, 1 M. & S. 273.

notice of the order of proceeding in parliament and in committees. *a* Of parliamentary papers, what is printed for the use of the members, had been long established to be undoubtedly privileged.

The first case that occurs as to the publishing parliamentary papers of a defamatory nature, was that of Lake v. King, *b* where certain parliamentary papers had been printed, which aspersed the character of Sir Edward Lake. The defendant justified the libel he had printed, by pleading that it was only printed for the use of members. On demurrer, the court held the plea good, because it was the order and course of proceeding in parliament, to print and deliver copies for the use of members, whereof the judges ought to take judicial notice. Lord Hale and the court sustained the defence ; because being necessary to their functions, it was the course to print parliamentary papers for the use of members. And the judges in the case of Stockdale v. Hansard, *c* considered the line drawn in this case, to be correct in law.

A criminal information was refused for publishing the report of a committee of the house of commons, which contained a paragraph charging an individual with having views hostile to the government ; after he had been tried for treason and acquitted ; on the ground, that a proceeding in parliament could not be deemed libelous. *d* In a latter case, *e* Lord Ellenborough expressed an inclination to lay down the doctrine with somewhat more of limitation, than was to be found in that case.

The recent and leading case of Stockdale v. Hansard, was an action brought against the printer of the house of commons for a libel contained in a parliamentary publication. The defendant justified his publication by the supposed privileges of the house to publish for sale such papers, though containing defamatory matter. The house resolved that it actually possessed the power. The judges of the court of queen's bench admitted that if such a privilege did exist, it would protect the printer, but held that such privilege did not exist, and that the resolution of the house would not create it. There were, and still are, lawyers, who hold opin-

a R. v. Wright, 8 T. R. 283.   *b* 1 Saund, 131.
c 9 Adol. & Ellis, 1.   *d* 8 Term Rep. 298.
e R. v. Creevy, 1 M. & S. 276.

ions favorable to the privilege claimed in this case, and they may have been founded in such doctrine ; but that the judges uprightly discharged their duty in entertaining the inquiry,—arriving at, and acting upon a conviction of their own,—instead of yielding to a resolution of the house of commons, cannot admit of a reasonable doubt. And, as no writ of error was brought upon the judgment, it must now be taken, that the privilege did not exist.* It is unnecessary to enter more fully into Stockdale's case in this place, because by statute 3 Vict. c. 9, s. 3, "An act to give summary protection to persons employed in the publication of parliamentary papers"—it is provided that proceedings, criminal or civil, against persons for publication of reports, papers, proceedings, &c., printed by order of parliament, may be stayed upon delivery of a certificate under the hands of the chancellor or deputy speaker of the lords, or speaker or clerk of the house of commons, to the effect that such publication was by order of either house of parliament."

Although the act passed in Strode's case, 4 Henry 8, provides for the personal immunity and protection of the members themselves, for speeches made or acts done, in parliament or concerning the same ; this does not regard what Lord Ellenborough termed the vindictive privileges of the house for offences done against the body of the house generally, in breach of the rights and privilege of the whole house. a   Whilst a member may not be questioned out of parliament for any expressions he may have used in debate, he is liable to censure and punishment by the house itself, of which he is a member. And instances have occurred, of members having been imprisoned and even expelled, for offensive language and indignities to the house, and disobedience to its orders.

Thus in 1580, Arthur Hall, a member of the house of commons, b was punished for a libel on the dignity of the house, by being committed and expelled. In c more recent cases, the judges of the court of king's bench were unanimously of opinion that the house of commons has the power of commitment of a member for a breach of their privileges. In Hobhouse's case, the house of commons having voted the defendant guilty of a breach of their privi-

a R. v. Flower. 8 T. R. 314.   b D'Ewes Journal, 291.
c Burdett v. Abbott, 14 East, 1.

* This case was cited as the law of legislative privilege by **Senator Sumner**, in **his great** speech on that subject 27th May, 1871.

leges for publishing a libel upon the house, and having ordered him
to be committed to Newgate during their pleasure, and the speaker's warrant being returned into the court of king's bench upon a
habeas corpus sued out by the defendant, the court refused to discharge him out of custody. *a* "It was necessary," says Lord
Ellenborough, in the former of the cases referred to, *b* "that
members (of the high court of parliament generally) should have
the most complete personal security to enable them freely to meet
for the purpose of discharging their important functions, and also
that they should have the right of *self-protection,* I do not mean
merely against acts of individual wrong; for poor and impotent
indeed would be the privileges of parliament, if they could not also
protect themselves against injuries and affronts offered to the aggregate body, which might prevent or impede the full and effectual
exercise of their parliamentary functions. This is a right essentially inherent in the supreme legislature of the kingdom. Can
the high court of parliament, or either of the two houses of which
it consists, be deemed not to possess intrinsically that authority of
prosecuting summarily for contempts, which is acknowledged as
belonging to every superior court of law of less dignity, undoubtedly, than itself? And is not the degradation and disparagement
of the two houses in the estimation of the public, by contemptuous libels, as much an impediment to their efficient acting with
regard to the public, as the actual obstruction of an individual
member by bodily force, in his endeavour to resort to the place
where parliament is holden?

And not only is every member subject to the censure of the
house, for whatever is spoken in the house, but for every other
part of his conduct. *c* In 1626, Mr. Moor was sent to the tower
for speaking out of season.

Sir William Widdrington *d* and Sir Herbert Price sent to the
tower for bringing in candles, against the desire of the house.

Mr. Hugh Benson, *e* a member of the house, having granted
many protections for money, taking for some sixteen, seventeen,
forty shillings; resolved upon the question, that Mr. Hugh Benson

a R. v. Hobhouse, 2 Chitty, 207.   *b* Burdett v. Abbott, 14 East, 1.
c Nalson's Introd. 61.
d 2 Nalson, 272.   *e* Ibid, 596.

is unworthy and unfit to be a member of this house, and shall sit
no longer as a member of this house.

18 Eliz. 1575, Edward Smalley was, upon the question, adjudged
by the house to be guilty of contempt and of abusing the house
by the fraudulent practice of procuring himself to be arrested upon
execution of his own assent, and with intention to be discharged
as well as of his imprisonment as of his said execution. Smalley,
and a conspirator with him, were both ordered to the tower ; and
the said Smalley to remain there for a month, and after ; till he
gave sufficient assurance for payment of a hundred pounds to the
creditor, and forty shillings for the serjeant's fees. a

The next petition affecting individual members, was for freedom
from arrest. This claim also was never made until of late years ;
yet "this privilege," says Elsynge, "did ever belong to the lords
and commons, and to their servants also coming to the parliament,
staying there, and returning home." b   So Hakewill observes, c " the
petition for privilege from arrests is of later days ;" but notices
that Sir J. Cheny, 1 Hen. 4, made a general request for all privileges, which might include it.   And in Atwyll's case, 17 Ed. 4, the
preamble to the commons' petition confidently asserts the " pryv
ylege, that eny of theym shuld not be empleded in any action per-
sonell, nor be attached by their persone or goods, in their conıying
to any such parliament, there abydyng, nor fro thence to their
propre home resortyng ; which liberties and franchises your high-
ness, by your auctorite roiall, at commencement of this parliament,
graciously have ratified and confirmed to us, your said comens ;"
which ratification could only have been in his majesty's answer to
the speaker's petition.

The privilege itself, of freedom from arrest in civil suits, at
whatever time first formally claimed, was certainly always exercised,
and must have been coeval with the existence of parliaments. The
exemption from arrests was considered the privilege, generally, of
a member of the high court of parliament ; and the reason given for
it by the judges, applies equally to the members of both houses,
viz.   "That they may have their freedom and liberty freely, to
intende upon the parliament." Accordingly, Hakewill speaks d

a Petyt's Miscel. Parl. 16. 18.   b Elsynge, 184.
c Hakewill, 213.   d Hakewill, 62.

of it as established parliamentary law, that " every knight, citizen, burgess, baron of the five ports, or others, called in the parliament of the king, shall have privilege of parliament during the session of parliament; so that he, that doth arrest any of them during that time, shall be imprisoned in the tower, by the nether house, of which he is, and shall be put to his fine; a and the keeper also, if he will not deliver him when the serjeant-at-arms doth come for him, &c. And all the privileges which do belong to those of the commons house of parliament, a fortiori do appertain to all the lords of the upper house. Their persons are not only free from arrest during the parliament, but during their lives; nevertheless the original cause, is by reason they have voice and place in parliament." Freedom from arrest of peers, however, with great deference to Mr. Hakewill, (to whom I am greatly indebted,) but whom I cannot implicitly follow in this instance; being the privilege of peerage, and not of parliament, b extends to peers not members of the legislature; viz., Scotch and Irish, (and formerly to Roman Catholic peers.) The person of a peer (by the privilege of peerage) is ever sacred and inviolable. c This immunity rests upon ancient custom, and is recognized by statutes, 12 and 13 Wm. 3, c. 3, and 2 and 3 Anne, c. 18.*

The principle, that attendance in parliament ought not to be interrupted by the process of an inferior court in matters of civil jurisdiction, being admitted in the earliest times, (an instance will be shewn in 9 Ed. 2,) a practice founded upon it, will appear universally to have prevailed. Possessing a power that was never disputed, for the prevention of arrest or the enlargement of their members by writ of privilege, or *habeas corpus*, the course of the house of commons seems to have been, to provide in each instance for the particular case, without procuring any general law upon the subject. There occur, indeed, in the parliamentary records, and in the documents brought to light by the indefatigable industry of Prynne, several instances of petitions presented by the commons, praying the king to have their claims in this respect (and they are stated as appertaining to the whole parliament, peers as well as commons) allowed and enforced by the sanction of a law; but the answer was, that they already possessed a sufficient remedy.

a Dyer, 60.   b 2 Strange. 985.   c 1 Bl. Comm. 165.

* It is to be observed these cases arose prior to the stat. 13 Wm. III & 13 Geo. III

The present inquiry will be understood to be of necessity, almost entirely confined to the privileges claimed in the speaker's prayer. And thus narrowed, it will be rendering a more acceptable service, to present the reader with the brief result of the cases, than to enter into any more labored exposition of the doctrine.

In the great case of Lord Arundel, who had been imprisoned by the king, in 1625, the lords resolved *nem con*, "That the privilege of this house is, that no lord of parliament, sitting the parliament, or within the usual time of privilege of parliament, is to be imprisoned or restrained, without sentence or order of the house, unless it be for treason, felony, or for refusing to give surety for the peace." *a*

In the house of commons, the cases of Bogo de Clare, 18 Ed. 1, relating to the service of a citation in a privileged place and exempt jurisdiction; and of John de Thoresby, 10 Ed. 3, founded on the service of ecclesiastical process in the court of chancery; usually first cited, because furnished by Sir Edward Coke *b* in his fourth institute, were thought by Prynne, *c* and are declared by Sir Orlando Bridgeman in his judgment in Benyon v. Evelyn, and by Lord Ellenborough in Burdett v. Abbott, to have no reference to the privilege of parliament.

The first case which *does d* apply is the prior of Malton's case, 9 Ed. 2, and it seems quite conclusive of the claim; but upon that case no judgment has been found. The original *e* writ recites the privilege as follows: "*Prelatos, comites, barones et alios, tam clericos quam laicos, in veniendo ad eadem parliamenta, ibidem morando et exinde redeundo, ab omni-modis injuriis, oppressionibus et gravaminibus, nos oportet protegere et tueri,*" &c.

In the parliament, *f* 5 Hen. 4, was a petition from the commons to the king, in which asserting that "*ne devoient per ascum dette, accompt, trespas ou autre contrat qconque estre arester ou en ascun manere emprisonez en le meme temps ;*" they pray the king "to make any breach of such privilege punishable by fine and ransom to

a And see. in the same year, Feb. 9, 1625; a stay of proceedings in the star chamber, granted to the Lord Vaux, on the ground of privilege, 3 L. J. 496.

b 4 Inst. p. 24.

c Prynne's Animadv. on 4 Inst. 20 Reg. 386.

d Elsynge, 186.   *e* 1 Hats. 13.

f Parliament Roll. Vol. 3, p. 541, No. 71.

himself, and treble damages to the party." The king answers them, " *Y ad sufficient remede en le cas.*" That sufficient remedy was, says Prynne, their enlargement by writ of privilege or habeas corpus, which the law allowed them, in such cases, if not in execution ; whereby the plaintiff lost the benefit of his arrest, and was put to the charge of new process, &c. But in Lark's case, 8 Hen. 6, *a* where the commons prayed not only a special redress in the particular case in the discharge of their member, but a general recognition *b* by a declaratory law, that "no lords nor knights, citizens, burgesses or others, may be arrested or detained during the time of parliament, except for treason, felony, or surety of the peace ;" the king *c* refused them, giving a parliamentary negative : " *Le Roy s'avisera.*" The house of lords, in their answer to this case, when cited by the attorney general in Lord Arundel's case, suppose the ground of this negative to have been, that the latter part of the bill comprehended more than it was at that time thought fit, the royal assent should be given to. " There is no doubt but that any of the house of commons being *detained* in prison upon an *execution* served upon them before the time of privilege of parliament, or being in execution in any ordinary course of justice before that time, ought to be *detained* still, as is practised at this day." They then supposed that a prisoner, by being chosen a member, could not claim to be discharged ; now a different doctrine prevails.

There was, however, in the case of Lark, *d* an enactment, by the consent of the plaintiff's counsel, for the discharge of Lark out of custody ; but there was also a saving to the plaintiff of his execution, after the end of the parliament, and of the fine to the king for the trespass. As Sir O. Bridgeman pithily states it : " There was a special act of parliament for a new execution and by a new way against Lark, but the king refused to make a general law in it." In point of fact, it was then, and long after, considered doubtful whether privilege of parliament extended only to arrests on mesne process, or to executions also. And accordingly in the next case, we find a fourth limitation added to the former exceptions ; " if a member be arrested in such cases as be not for treason,

a Rot. Parl. 8 Hen. 6, No. 57.
b Elsynge, 217.
c 1 Hats. 20.
d Moor, 340; 5 T. R. 362.

felony, surety of the peace, or for a *condempnation had before the parliament*, it is used that such persons be released of such arrests, and make an attorney," being the instances excepted by the judges in Thorpe's case, 31 Hen. 6. This perso'n, who was a baron of the exchequer as well as speaker of the house of commons, and moreover a Lancasterian, had been imprisoned during a prorogation, on an execution at the suit of the Duke of York. The commons, as in Lark's case, where they did not act upon the claim themselves, but submitted it to the rest of the parliament, as a matter of general concern, sent some of their members to complain of a violation of privilege to the king and lords in parliament, and to demand Thorpe's release. The lords referred the question to the judges, who, *inter alia*, stated the law of privilege as cited above. Notwithstanding this answer of the judges, the lords determined that Thorpe should remain in prison and directed the commons to proceed with all goodly haste and speed to the election of a new speaker, which they did immediately.

That, after the formal declaration of the judges upon this occasion, and their exact enumeration of all the cases excepted out of parliamentary privilege, the lords should have immediately adjudged that Thorpe, who appeared to come within none *a* of these descriptions, should according to law, remain still in prison, while the commons cheerfully acquiesced in this decision, and immediately proceeded to the choice of a new speaker, has created great and reasonable surprise and well-founded suspicion, and occasioned it to be repeatedly *b* mentioned, as " a case begot from the iniquity of the times." A solution of the difficulty is furnished in the case of Hodges * v. Moore, 1 Car. 1, as reported by Latch. *c*

a Prynne, 4 Reg. 810.   c Latch. 15, 48, 150, Noy. 83.

b First by Sir N. Rich, on its being cited in debate, March 1620.

* In this case, Moore, having privilege of parliament, procured the speaker, Sir. H Finch, to write his letter in the name of the parliament, to the court of king's bench to stay judgment. The court was greatly offended at this proceeding, (which had been the practice for a century,) and it is said, would have returned a sharp answer to the parliament, (if it had not been dissolved): "because it is against the oaths of the judges," &c.; but "the way is to procure a supersedeas." They also referred to what the judges said in Thorpe's case, that "there is no general *supersedeas* brought to surcease all process; for if there were, then this high court of parliament should let the process of the common law, and so should put the party complainant without a remedie."

Thorpe, it seems, had only a *general supersedeas* for all actions, and the opinion of the judges being taken, *that* was held ill; he should have had a *particular writ of supersedeas* for each action. Thus a technical ground, however narrow, was laid for this tyranical proceeding. This explanation, moreover, is not inconsistent with the account afforded by Hakewill, *a* who says that Thorpe was arrested in vacation, and lays it down as the doctrine of his time, that parliament doth not give privilege *tempore vacationis sed sedente curia* only. So Elsynge *b* is reduced to the supposition that the judgment proceeded on the ground that the expression " condempnation had before the parliament,ᵢ" is to be understood of such arrests as happen in the interval between the adjournment and the access. These considerations, if they do not remove all the suspicion that attaches to that case, will in some degree serve to explain the proceedings on it, and the judgment eventually given by the parliament. The lords, adopting the advice of the judges, disallow the privilege claimed, because Thorpe had only a general *supersedeas*, and not a particular *supersedeas* in that suit; and because the condemnation was " be.)re the parliament began," being during a prorogation, not an adjournment. *

Clarke's case, 39 Hen. 6, and Hyde's case, 14 Ed. 4, resemble Lark's case in many particulars, all three members being taken in execution, and it being thought necessary, in each case respectively, to have an act of parliament to save to the plaintiff a new execution after the time of privilege: and they vary only, in its having been thought necessary or expedient in the latter cases to have the chancellor, sheriffs, and warden of the fleet indemnified; " Which," says Hatsell, " induces me to suspect that the right such persons had by law to writs of privilege and *habeas corpus* for their delivery, did not extend to cases of persons imprisoned under a writ of execution."

Two years previous to the last mentioned case of Hyde, occurred the case of Donne v. Walsh, *c* copied by Prynne from the records in the court of exchequer. It was a demurrer to a plea of writ of privilege. The writ recited an entire privilege of the lords

a Hakewill, 63.		b Elsynge, 247.
c 4 Register, 752.
* It appears by the rolls of parliament, that it was then *prorogued.*

and commons not to be imprisoned or *impleaded* during the time of parliament. The barons, with the advice of the judges of both the other courts, formally declare their opinion that persons entitled to privilege, "*ratione alicujus transgressionis, debiti, computi, conventionis, contractus conjuscunque, dum sic in parliamento Regis morentur, cadi aut arrestari non debent ; sed nullum hujusmodi consuetudinem fore, quod quin implacitari debent, prout in brevi illo suponitur.*"

There is a similar decision of the same court of exchequer in Ryver v. Cosins, the same year, in which the barons repeated *verbatim* their opinion in Walsh v. Donne ; yet, in Hyde's case *a* the king's bench remanded Mr. Hyde to Newgate, though arrested in a civil action ; and the house of commons, in a subsequent case, renewed their claim to exemption from being impleaded. This was in Atwyll's case, 17 Ed. 4, *b* in which, however, the plaintiff's execution was expressly saved to him after the end of the parliament ; which negatives in effect, this claim of exemption; " The inference *c* is strong. The act of parliament did allow the foundation, and proceeding, and judgment against Atwyll a member of parliament, during the parliament, though it discharged the execution."

The next claim, in Sadcliff's case, 1 Hen. 7, omits the privilege of not being impleaded in personal actions, which had been so often disallowed.

The last case which relates to a claim of privilege " not to be impleaded," is of much later date, 14 Car. 2, and is only stated here by anticipation, to prevent the necessity of a recurrence to the subject. In the case of Benyon v. Evelyn, 14 Car. 2, Sir Orlando Bridegman decided that the privilege of parliament which exempted members from arrest, did not prevent an original being sued out or prosecuted against a member during the sitting of parliament. This is the case in which Lord C. J. Bridgeman gave so learned and elaborate a judgment, worthy of his common law reputation; obscured, not extinguished, in chancery. It was an action of assumpsit for goods sold and delivered to a member of parliament ; the defendant pleaded the statute of limitations ; the

---

a 12 Ed. 4, Rot. 7.   *b* 17 Ed. 4, No. 35.

c Sir O. Bridgeman's judgment in Benyon v. Evelyn.

plaintiff replied that he could not sue the defendant sooner, because he was a member of parliament and privileged from suits, the defendant denied that position, and said that though members of parliament cannot be arrested, they may be sued. The learned judge considered himself bound to decide the question of privilege thus brought before him, lamenting the necessity. He says, " When in a common action, the privilege of parliament doth come to be part of the plea or justification, it is of necessity that the privilege, whether there be such, and what the extent of it is, come also into consideration. For as in the register it is said of the ecclesiastical court, which is inferior to the common law, if a common law point come in question there, *non est consonum rationi, quod cognitio accessarii in cousa christianitatis impediatur, ubi cognitio causæ principalis ad forum ecclesiasticum noscitur pertinere ;* so I may say here, the privilege of parliament coming incidentally as part of the case, as a consequent, must, in this particular case, be also debated here." The decision was against the privilege claimed : that is, that a member had no exemption from being sued ; though such a privilege had been frequently claimed.

Hitherto it has been seen, that when a member or his servant has been imprisoned, the house of commons have never proceeded to deliver such person out of custody by virtue of their own authority ; but if the member has been in execution, have applied for an act of parliament to enable the chancellor to issue his writ for his release ; or, if the party was confined only on mesne process, he has been delivered by his writ of privilege, which he was entitled to at common law. The truth was, *a* says Hallam, that with a right pretty clearly recognized, as is admitted by the judges in Thorpe's case, the house of commons had no regular compulsory process at their command.

In 34 Hen. 8, Ferrer's case introduced a new mode of proceeding in this particular. Though in custody in execution for " a condemnation had before the parliament," the member arrested was delivered, " not in this case, by virtue of an act of parliament —not by any writ of privilege, but by the serjeant at-arms, without any other warrant than his mace ;" "Albeit the lord chancellor offered them to grant a writ." Secondly, the parties who opposed

a Middle Ages, vol. 2, c. 8.

his delivery in this novel and extraordinary manner, (as it then was,) were imprisoned by the house of commons, some in the tower, some in Newgate. Thirdly, the creditor himself, who procured the arrest, was also committed for his contempt of the privilege of parliament. As the matter is condensed in a sentence of Sir O. Bridgeman's judgment, "This case doth not only determine the law for the privilege against the execution, but also that the party ought to be discharged without writ, when the serjeant-at-arms comes for him." There was however, no slight aggravation in this case, in the violent and contemptuous manner in which the sheriffs and their officers treated the serjeant-at-arms bearing the ensign of his official authority, the mace ; and there was another fact which may, at least in Hatsell's opinion, serve to explain the measure here adopted, and the doctrines now for the first time laid down, as to the extent of the privileges of the house of commons. Ferrers was an immediate servant of the king; so that the allowance of the privilege in this case was as well in respect of the claim of the king for his servant, as of the claim of the house for its members. Add to this, he was only a surety, and was arrested on his way to attend the parliament. An inferior court would liberate a person arrested under similar circumstances in his progress to attend the court in obedience to a lawful summons. When the vehement displeasure of the house had at length subsided, they acted equitably as usual, saving the plaintiff's execution against the principal debtor, (who would have been discharged if the taking of Ferrers were lawful,) and discharging Ferrers himself by a majority of only fourteen, and after a long debate of nine or ten days.

Lawyers, it is to be expected, would scarcely admit such innovations without finding room for difficulty and scruples. They would naturally feel some hesitation in saying that the sheriffs ought to have discharged the prisoner on their own responsibility, on the mere order of the serjeant bearing his mace. They would consider that if that should not be deemed a good authority at law for the discharge, the sheriffs would have made themselves liable for the debt. They might retain, too, for a time, their former opinion, that privilege did not extend to arrest in execution on a judgment had before the time of privilege. Accordingly, we find that afterwards, in 6 Queen Eliz., *a* Dyer, when chief justice, said, "That if a man is condemned in debt, or trespass, and is elected a member of parliament, and then is taken in execution, he cannot have the privilege of parliament; and so it was held by the sages of the law in the case of Ferrers, in the time of Hen. 8, "*Et coment que le privelege a ceo temps fuit a luy allow, ceo fuit minus just.*" Dyer *b* himself reports a case which occurred within two or three years after Ferrer's case, in 36 and 37 Hen. 8, *videlicet :*

Trewynnard's case, who *c* being a burgess of parliament, and taken in execution, and in custody at the commencement of the session on a judgment entered up during a very long prorogation, was freed, not by the mace or serjeant-at-arms, but by a writ of *supersedeas* of privilege; which writ was a security to the sheriffs against an action for an escape, whether the privilege were allowable or not. Such an action *was* brought, but no judgment given. There is also a peculiarity in the writ in this (Trewynnard's) case, that the claim of privilege is for the first time extended, in point of duration, beyond the time of members going to parliament, residing there, or returning home—to persons *venientes seu venire intendentes.*

From Ferrer's case to 1575, for above thirty years, the house or commons, instead of adopting the mode of delivery by the mace, ordered writs of privilege to be issued in almost every instance. It appears from Hogan's case, in 1601, that it was still later before the house of lords exerted this privilege, and Hogan was a servant of the queen; as Ferrers, in whose case it was first adopted, has been seen to have been of the king. In Smalley's case, however, (the next that occurs,) the house proceeded with great deliberation, and adopted the course, after a long debate and consultation; and it was not till long after, that the practice became established.

Sir Thomas Shirley's *d* case, in 1603, in which the warden of the fleet, refusing to release the prisoner when demanded by the serjeant-at-arms, was committed to the tower, and there persisting in his obstinacy, to the *dungeon of little ease,* (a dismal hole in the tower,) seems at last to have rendered it apparent, that neither the law of parliament, nor any statute, had satisfactorily pointed

a Moore's Reports, 57.   *b* Dyer, 61.
c Prynne's Fourth Register, 784.   *d* Parl. Hist. Vol. 5, p. 118.

out a mode by which the member in custody in execution, should be delivered; or had taken care to secure the goaler from an action, or to ensure to the creditor his right to a new writ of execution. To effect the two latter objects it was always thought necessary or prudent, to make a particular law; though this opinion is controverted by Elsynge, *a* who considers the arrest as " merely void, and an act to deliver him that is arrested, or to save the plaintiff's execution, *ex abundanti* and needless."

In order to avoid all difficulty for the future, it was thought expedient to pass the general law, 1 Jac. 1, *b* "for new executions to be issued against any which shall hereafter be delivered out of execution by privilege of parliament, and for discharge of them out of whose custody such persons shall be delivered;" with this proviso, " Provided always, that this act, or anything therein contained, shall not extend to the diminishing of any punishment to be hereafter by censure in parliament inflicted, upon any person which shall hereafter make, or procure to be made, any such arrest as aforesaid;" which was then a direct parliamentary recognition of the right in the two houses of parliament, not only to liberate persons entitled to privilege, but to inflict punishment by censure in parliament, in the particular case of arrests.

After the act of 1 Jac. 1, c. 13, some formal step and process at law seems to have been at first always thought necessary to give that act its full operation, no privileged person in custody in execution, having been for sometime, delivered by any other method, than by virtue of a writ of privilege, or by a writ of *habeas corpus*, issued in obedience to a warrant under the speaker's hand, made by order of the house. *c* But in 1625, the commons declared that " the house hath power, when they see cause, to send the serjeant immediately, to deliver a prisoner."

Colonel Pitt's case, reported in Strange, *d* determines by what means the courts of law, can discharge a privileged person from custody. The arrest of a member since the statute 10 Geo. 3, in civil cases, is held in that case, to be void *ab initio*, and it is thenceforth established, that he may be discharged immediately upon motion

---

a Manner of holding parliaments in England.

b 1 Jac. 1, c. 13.   *c* 1 Hats. 165.

d 2 Strange, 985.

in the court from which the process issued. But this determination was, of course, confined to the methods of releasing a member, which can be pursued in Westminster Hall. There was then no parliament in existence.

When parliament was sitting, before the last named statute, the house of commons had not abandoned their claim to the power of releasing their members arrested under civil process, by their own officers and *proprio vigore*. In 1677, Sir Robert Holt was discharged, though he had been taken in execution "out of the privilege of parliament." In 1707, Asgill, *a* a member in execution, was discharged; the serjeant being sent with the mace to the warden of the fleet. In many other cases during the seventeenth century, peers and members arrested in execution, were released without writ of privilege or *habeas corpus*. And in cases of arrest on mesne process, the practice prevailed of releasing the prisoners by a warrant, or sending the black rod in the name of the house to demand them. It is now settled that members may be discharged immediately by warrant; and this does not obtain, only where the privilege existed anterior to the arrest; but is enforced where a person has been arrested on mesne process and is in custody,—but is afterwards elected a member. So it is now enforced where he has been in custody in execution before his election. *b*

The parties effecting an arrest, were not lightly dealt with in former times. In 1621, Sir J. Whitelocke's man being arrested, the parties were called to the bar and heard on their knees. They acknowledged their fault and craved forgiveness of the house and of Sir J. Whitelocke; but it was ordered upon the question, "That they shall both ride upon one horse bare-backed, from Westminster to the exchange, with papers on their breasts, with this inscription,—'For arresting a servant to a member of the commons house of parliament.'"

To return to the subject of the freedom of a member's person, (from which, the consideration of the means and process employed to deliver him when in custody, has led to this digression); the law is now, at all events, settled upon a rational basis. A peer or mem-

a 15 Com. J. 471.

b Mill's case, 1807; Christie Burton's case, 1819.

ber of parliament may be sued, but cannot be arrested or detained in custody. His person shall not be subjected to any imprisonment upon process in civil suits; but the pretended privilege of lands and goods being taken away, (if it ever existed); a peer's or member's property may be sequestered for non-performance of an order or a decree of a court of equity,—or levied upon under a *distringas* issued by a court of law. *a*

By the 10 Geo. 3, "Any person may commence and prosecute any action in any court of record, or court of equity, or of admiralty, (or in causes matrimonial and testamentary, in any court having cognizance of such cause,) against any peer or member of the house of commons, or any of their menial or other servants, or any other person entitled to privilege of parliament; and no proceedings thereupon shall be delayed under color of such privilege. But this shall not subject the person of any member of the house of commons to be arrested or imprisoned, on any such suit or proceedings. And to remedy the dilatoriness by process of *distringas*, the court out of which the writ proceeds, may order the issues levied from time to time, to be sold, and the money arising thereby, to be applied to pay such costs to the plaintiff, as the court shall think just, and the surplus to be detained till the defendant shall have appeared, or other purpose of the writ to be answered. And obedience may be enforced to any rule of the court of king's bench, common pleas, or exchequer, against any person entitled to privilege, by distress infinite, if the person entitled to the benefit of such rule, shall choose to proceed in that way."

The privilege of freedom from arrest in civil suits, extends to protect members of either house from attachment for non-payment of money, or for non-performance of an award. *b* So likewise against informations, and as well in the king's suit as a subject's.

But there is no such exemption in criminal cases and breaches of the peace. To proceedings on these, privilege of parliament is not considered applicable. The case of writing and publishing seditious libels was, in 1763, resolved by both houses not to be entitled to privilege upon reasons which extended equally to every indictable offence. The only privilege of parliament in such cases, of crimes

a 10 Geo. 3, c. 50.
b Walker v. Earl Grosvenor. Catimer v, Sir E. Knatchbull, 7 T. R. 171-448.

and misdemeanors, seems to be the right of receiving immediate information of the imprisonment or detention of any member, with the reason for which he is detained; a practice that is daily used upon the slightest military accusations, preparatory to a trial by court martial, and which is recognized by the several temporary statutes for suspending the *habeas corpus* act; whereby it is provided that no member of either house shall be detained, till the matter of which he stands suspected, be first communicated to the house of which he is a member, and the consent of the said house obtained for his commitment or detaining. But yet the usage has uniformly been, *a* ever since the revolution, that the communication has been subsequent to the arrest.

Neither, in matters of this nature, are peers or members protected against the process of the courts, to punish disobedience to their orders. To this effect is the following entry b; " *It is ordered and declared, that no peer or lord of parliament hath privilege against being compelled, by process of the courts of Westminster Hall, to pay obedience to a writ of habeas corpus directed to him."   Accordingly, an attachment may be granted, if the peer refuses obedience to the writ; for being a contempt, a peer has no privilege.* c

In 1831, *Mr. Long Wellesley was committed by Lord Brougham for a contempt of the high court of chancery, and a committee of privileges in the house of commons, held that Mr. Wellesley's claim to be discharged from imprisonment, by reason of privilege of parliament, ought not to be admitted.*

In 1837, *Mr. Lechmere Charlton was committed by Lord Cottenham for contempt in writing an improper letter to a master in chancery.   The house of commons inquired fully into the nature and particulars of the contempt, and then declined to interfere for the member's liberation by virtue of the privilege.*

As, since the 10 Geo. 3, c. 50, a person having privilege of parliament may be sued without protection, *d* so may he, be made bankrupt in the following manner. If any person within the description of the acts relating to bankrupts, having protection of parliament, does not within one calendar month after personal

---

a 1 Black. Com. 167.   *b* L. J. 7th Feb. 1757.

c R. v· Earl Ferrers, 1 Burr.

d 4 Geo. 3, c. 33, s. 4.   45 Geo. 3, c. 24, s. 1.   6 Geo, 4, c. 16.

service of a summons, (an affidavit of debt having been filed by the creditor,) pay or secure, or compound for such debt, to the creditor's satisfaction, or enter into a bond in such sum, and with two such sufficient sureties, as any of the judges of the court out of which the summons issued shall approve, or does not within one calendar month next after personal service of such summons, cause an appearance to be entered to such action or actions in the proper court, every such trader is to be adjudged *d* a bankrupt from the service of such summons. And by section 11, if any such trader disobeys any decree pronounced in any cause depending in any court of equity, or any order made in bankruptcy or lunacy against any such trader for the payment of money, the same having been duly served upon him, and a peremptory day fixed for such payment, such trader is to be deemed a bankrupt from the service of such order for peremptory payment.

If a bankrupt be a member of parliament, the commissioners cannot commit him for not attending, or not answering; he can only be imprisoned in such cases as are made felony by the acts relating to bankrupts. But a member of parliament, who is become a bankrupt, vacates his seat, *a* unless the commission is superseded within twelve months from its being issued, or the creditors are paid their debts in full within the same period ; and is disqualified for sitting in the interim.[1]

It is a sufficient objection *a* to bail, that he hath privilege of parliament, whereby the plaintiff may be delayed in obtaining payment from him.

The extent, then, of the privilege last under consideration, may now be regarded as sufficiently ascertained and fixed. It may be generally laid down, that no member of either house can be arrested and taken into custody, or detained in custody, unless for some indictable offence. In a civil suit, a peer or member cannot be arrested, or imprisoned, without a breach of the privileges of parliament, which either house, upon the report of the committee, will upon good reason punish by commitment. But how, it is material to learn, is a party to be delivered out of custody when arrested

a 6 Geo. 4, c. 16, s. 11.   *b* 52 Geo. 3, c. 144.
c 4 Taunt. 249.

NOTE 1.—Quære. What might be the effect upon a New York legislature if this is the common law of that state?

ın a civil suit, supposing the parliament not to be sitting, or to be dissolved? In what manner can courts of justice take cognizance of privilege of parliament? For it has been seen, *a* that when a letter was written by the speaker to the judges, to stay proceedings against a privileged person, they rejected it as contrary to their oath of office. These objects were formally affected in two ways; 1st, the discharge of such privileged *b* person might be procured by writ of privilege, in a nature of a *supersedeas*; 2d, such arrest being irregular *ab initio, c* the party can be discharged upon motion; *d* he may move the court from which the process issued, that he may be discharged immediately.

Writs of privilege are now discontinued. When the house is sitting, members are discharged directly by warrant. In 1819, Mr. Christie Burton had been elected member for Bɜverly, but being in custody in execution and on mesne process, was unable to attend his service in parliament. The house determined that he was entitled to privilege, and ordered him to be discharged out of the custody of the warden of the fleet. An action was brought against the warden by the assignees of the creditors of Mr. Burton, on his escape. The assignees were declared guilty of a breach of privilege, and ordered to attend the house. They acknowledged their offence and the matter was dropped.

The extent of this privilege of parliament, and the mode of procuring the liberation of parties improperly arrested —points which were found so embarrassing in the greater part of the cases referred to—being thus established, the next question affecting this privilege is its duration. In the case of peers, the privilege is perpetual; but as to members,—where the privilege is that of parliament,—its duration, the reader will be surprised to learn, is no where precisely *e* determined. It certainly is the received opinion, that it extends to forty days after every prorogation, and forty days before the next appointed meeting; and, after a dissolution, to a reasonable time to return home.'

Privilege of parliament cannot be waived, "because it is said, the privilege is not so much that of the person *f* as of the house."

---

a Hodges v. Moore, *ante.*   *b* Latch. 150. Dyer 60. *a*   *c* Fort. 342.
d Pitt's case, 2 Stra. 985.   *e* Strange, 985.   *f* D'Ew. Jaurn. 436. Scobell, 95.

Note 2.—In this particular, New York differs from England, in having a statute fixing the limit of privilege.

The speaker charges a person brought to the bar for an offence, with breach of the privilege, " of the house."

The privileges enjoyed by individual members, and which are essential to their regular attendance on parliament and to the independent discharge of their duties in the house, were, on that account, brought prominently forward in the speaker's prayer; but it will now be proper to treat generally of the collective privileges of the two houses, or rather of the high court of parliament. These can be best, and indeed only, ascertained, by examining what have been, on various occasions, declared breaches of the privileges of either house.

Such are among others, indignities to the character, or obstructions to the proceedings of either house; assaulting, obstructing, insulting or menacing any member in his coming to or going from the house; so, the endeavor to compel members by force, to declare themselves in favor of or against, any proposition.

Challenging a member for his conduct in the house or in a committee. Libellous reflections against the honor and dignity of the house in general, or any member thereof. These, and similar offences, have been voted breaches of privilege and punished accordingly, whether committed by members or strangers. *a*

And first in the case of members : In 1675, Lord Shaftesbury, who had been committed by the house of lords for high contempt against the house, was brought before the court of queen's bench by *habeas corpus,* and the commitment for a contempt generally, being returned, the prisoner was remanded. In 1586, Arthur Hall, a member of the House of Commons, was imprisoned, expelled and fined; the latter a power not acknowledged, and which the house has not since been in the habit of exercising. *a* Hall's offence was having published a libel, " containing matter of infamy, of sundry particular members and of the whole state of the house, and also of the power and authority of the house." In 1810, Sir Francis Burdett, was sent to the tower for publishing " a libelous and scandalous paper reflecting upon the just privileges of the house." In Hobhouse's case, in the year 1819, the house of commons having voted the defendant

---

a See cases cited in the appendix to the second report on Sir F. Burdett, in 1810 ; and the head of " Complaints" in the several Journal Indexes.

guilty of a breach of their privileges, for publishing a libel upon the house, and having ordered him to be committed to Newgate during their pleasure, and the speaker's warrant being returned into the court of King's bench upon a *habeas corpus* sued out by the defendant, the court refused to discharge him out of custody.

In the case of defendants, not members of either house, the following are selected instances : In 1779, Flower was fined and committed for a libel on the bishop of Llandaff. In 1798, Messrs. Lambert and Perry were fined £50 each, and committed to Newgate for three months, for a newspaper paragraph, highly reflecting on the honor of the house of lords. *b* On the 22d June, 1781, complaint was made that Sir J. Wrottesley had received a challenge for his conduct as a member of an election committee; and Swift, the person complained of, was committed to the custody of the serjeant-at-arms. *c*

Besides insults and obstructions to the house and its proceedings, disobedience to the rules and orders of either house is treated as a breach of privilege. The house will punish those who refuse compliance with their orders, or obstruct their execution. And that, whether the orders be general; as that *d* "no printer or publisher of any printed newspaper do presume to insert in any newspaper, any debates or other proceedings of the house ;" or particular; such as orders relating to " attendance before committees ;" " the production of papers and records, &c."

Another offence against the collective privileges of the house, is the corruption or hindrance of witnesses summoned to attend or appear before it. *e*

Anciently no person was to be taken into the custody of the serjeant-at-arms, upon any complaint of a breach of privilege, until the matter of the complaint had been examined by the committee of privileges, and reported to the house. *f* Now, although the committee of privileges is still formally appointed at the commencement of each session, no members are nominated. If, therefore, any special circumstances arise out of a complaint of breach

a p. 137, ante. *b* Lords J. 506.
c Com. J. 535-537. *d* 20 Com. J. 99.
e See Synthetical Table of the proceedings of the house of commons, framed by Lord Colchester, and prefixed to the Index of the Commons' Journal.
f Resolution, 1701.

of privilege, it is usual to appoint a select committee to inquire into them. In ordinary cases the party complained of is " ordered to attend the house," and is examined at the bar.

Both houses proceed in the same manner to declare the party guilty of a breach of privilege, amounting to a contempt of the high court of parliament, for which they deal with him by censure or commitment; to which the lords can add a fine.

For there is a difference in the punishments inflicted by the lords and commons. The house of lords claim to be a court of record, because it is such unquestionably, when it acts in its judicial capacity. It therefore not only imprisons, but also imposes fines; and formerly in cases of libel, (when disgracefully severe punishments used to be awarded); often added the pillory.

The lords have also power to commit offenders to prison for a specified time, beyond the duration of the session ; and to order security for good behavior.

The house of commons, which is not a court of record, has tacitly abandoned the imposition of fines, but imposes the condition of the payment of fees before an offender is discharged, which is equally part of his punishment, and virtually amounts to a fine No period of imprisonment is named by the commons, and the confinement terminates with the session.

In Floyd's case, who had spoken offensive words of the king's daughter and the Elector Palatine, temp. Jac. I., the house of commons set up an unfounded claim to criminal jurisdiction ; for it was impossible to make such mere indecencies of language, amount to a breach of privilege. Acting as a court of judicature, they pronounce sentence that Floyd, a gentleman by birth and station, and a country magistrate, should pay a fine of £1000, stand twice in the pillory, and ride backward on a horse with the horse's tail in his hand. a They, however afterwards discovered their error, and changed the course of proceeding b into an impeachment of Floyd before the lords; with an ambiguous and unmeaning protestation as to the rights and privileges of the com mons remaining in the same plight as before. The lords, it is said equally disgraced themselves in this case. e

a 1 Com. J. 609. 5 Parl. Hist.   b Ib. 619.
c 3 Lords J, 134,

Instead of "kneeling at the bar," to receive his sentence which was formally required, but not always complied with ; the judgment of the house is now received by a prisoner standing at the bar. *a*

Having treated of the punishments inflicted by either house of parliament, for obstructions or contempts, or disobedience to orders, it remains to speak of the protection afforded to their own officers, to parties, witnesses and others.

The officers of either house, are supported by the house in the execution of their orders. As the officers of the courts of justice, charged with the execution of the process of the courts, may break open doors, if necessary, in order to execute it ; so, Lord Ellenborough said, it cannot be contended that the houses of the legislature, are less strongly armed in point of protection and remedy against contempts toward them, than the courts of justice are. *b*

But by a recent case, the serjeant-at-arms, though he has a right to enter the house of the person against whom a warrant has been issued by the speaker and to search for the party, had no right to remain in the house, if the defendant be from home, in order to await his return ; for that is an excess of jurisdiction. *c*

Another action was subsequently brought by the same plaintiff against the same defendant, and a messenger of his, for another trespass in executing a warrant of the speaker. The warrant was so drawn as to make it legally doubtful, and three of the judges felt themselves compelled to pronounce it illegal. All the judges agreed that they were bound to examine into its sufficiency ; one held that it was sufficient. The house of commons in this case directed a discussion of this point in a court of error, but the point involved is of secondary importance.

We have already said that we have not with us in America as there is in England, one uniform common law of parliament and of privilege applicable alike to the congress of the United States, and to the several states of the Union ; but, that great diversity exists between the privileges of members of congress, and that of the several states ; and that parliamentary law and the law of legislative privileges of the several states, differ from each other ;

a 33 Com. J. 594.   *b* 14 East, 1.

c Carrington and M. 382. 11 Adol. & El. 209.

that the law of privilege of the state of New York which is regulated and limited by statute, is, in its features; in its length and breadth; in what it allows and what it prohibits; in nearly every particular, identical with the law of privilege of parliament of England, which, like ours, is now regulated by statute, and in almost identity of language.

In compiling this chapter from the English common law, believed to be in force here, there has been the endeavor, to present the American readers, in this brief review, with as much of the legal powers and privileges of parliament, as shall direct their minds, and the minds of members who shall compose our legislative assemblies, to the authorities cited, and, to more elaborate sources of knowledge of the science of parliamentary law. Few men should be regarded as fit for legislators, who require to be informed, that nearly all the privileges of civil liberty, of which the American citizen now so proudly boasts, first had their introduction, if not their origin, in the house of commons of the British parliament. It is as equally untrue now in England, as it is in the state of New York, that parliamentary law is vague, unsettled, and uncertain. It is not true, that either the law of the parliament of England, or that of either, or both the houses of the legislature of the state of New York, is just what those bodies see fit to declare it. It is a branch of the common law, as easily traced and determined as any other, and if we have succeeded in nothing else, we hope to have succeeded in exciting such a spirit of inquiry into a knowledge and of the science, of parliamentary law, as shall save experienced legislators in future, from the assumption of a knowledge of and an attempt to exercise powers inconsistent with established law and of constitutional right; aggressive upon the sacred rights of a co-equal, and co-ordinate department of the government; unbecoming to the character of intelligent legislators; and evincing the want of comity and respect due to an equal.

In this compilation of English parliamentary law, the authorities, before the thirteenth year of Wm. III, have also been given. We have done this to show what was the law before, as well as since that day: so that by reference, to either period, it will be seen how little knowledge of English parliamentary law is sometimes found in legislative bodies. We have also cited the changes wrought in the common law by the statute of William III as well as that of 13 Geo. 111, which entirely abrogated the arbitrary and unlimited powers claimed by Sir Edward Coke (when speaker of the house of commons, in one of the parliaments in the reign of Queen Elizabeth,) who declared, "that the high court of parliament subsists by its own laws and customs; that it is the law and custom of parliament, that all weighty matters therein concerning the peers of the realm or commons, ought to be determined, adjudged and discussed according to the course of parliament, and not by the civil law, nor yet by the common law used in the more inferior courts." But the modern writers since the statutes above referred to such as Dwarris, Cobbitt, in his Parliamentary Debates, May's Treatise, Hatsell, and the judicial decisions cited, present a uniform body of parliamentary law, which is now as well understood in England to be the settled law, as is any other branch of the common law.

The remaining privileges of parliament not herein discussed, however essential and useful, they might be, are too remote from the subject of the present inquiry, and too wide and extensive in their consequences, to be comprehended in the present treatise.

CHAPTER XIX.

OF CONSTITUTIONAL INTERPRETATION.

IN some of the preceding chapters, the rules of interpretation of statutes compiled from the distinguished authors whose names and works are therein given, have extended their rules in some respects, beyond the mere interpretation and construction of *statutes;* they include in part, the construction of what are called constitutions, but not in the American sense, that of written constitutions established by the people themselves. While treating of the subject of interpretation, therefore, in a work which treats of constitutional powers, we should fail in duty, should we omit to present an outline of the best American views of construction of American constitutions, so necessarily connected with the construction of statutes, which depend for their force upon, and are enacted in subordination to, constitutional power.

There is a striking analogy, and generally, an entire harmony between the rules of interpretation of constitutions, and those of statutes; but inasmuch as the former are superior in power and authority to the latter, and as in cases of conflict here, the latter must give way, and yield to the former, (by rules of construction peculiar to our system, for which, other governments furnish no precedent), and that construction must necessarily be adopted, which is more especially applicable to our somewhat complex theory of laws, enacted in subordination to the written, but limited constitutions.

First, of the constitution of the United States. It is the constitution of a government ordained and established by the people of the United States for themselves and their posterity; and they have declared it to be the supreme law of the land; *a* but it is still a limited government. The people who made it, have defined its powers. They have limited it to the exercise of certain powers, and have reserved all other powers to the states or to the people. *b* "It is a popular government. Those who administer it, are responsible

---

a Constitution U. S., Art. 6.   *b* Story on Constitution, § 397.

to the people. It is as popular, and just as much emanating from the people, as the state governments. It is created for one purpose; the state governments for another. In short, it was made by the people, made for the people, and is responsible to the people." *a*

Mr. Justice Story says, that much of the difficulty of interpretation of this instrument, has arisen from the want of uniform rules; and he then proceeds in the endeavor to ascertain, and lay down true rules of interpretation applicable to this constitution, so that we may have some fixed standard by which to measure its powers, limit its prohibitions, guard its obligations, and enforce its securities of our rights and liberties. *b*

He says "that the first and fundamental rule in relation to the interpretation of all instruments, applies to the constitution; that is, to construe them according to the sense of the terms, and the intention of the parties; and he adopts Blackstone's remark, that the intention of a law is to be gathered from the words,—the context, the subject matter, the effects and consequences, or the reason and spirit of the law, *c* and that words are generally to be understood in their usual and most known signification, not so much regarding the propriety of the grammar, as their general and popular use; that if words happen to be dubious, their meaning may be established by the context, or by comparing them with other words and sentences in the same instrument; that illustrations may be further derived from the subject matter, with reference to which the expressions are used; that the effect and consequence of a particular construction is to be examined, because if a literal meaning would involve a manifest absurdity, it ought not to be adopted; and that, the reason and spirit of the law, or the causes which led to its enactment, are often the best exponents of the words, and limit their application." *d*

"Where the words are plain and clear, and the sense distinct and perfect arising on them, there is generally no necessity to have recourse to other means of interpretation. It is only where there is some ambiguity or doubt arising from other sources, that interpretation has its proper office. There may be obscurity as

a Webster's Speeches, 410 to 419.　　　*c* 1 Com. 59.
b Story on Constitution, § 399.　　　*d* See Vattels Rules, Ch. 5.

to the meaning, from the doubtful character of the words used, —from other clauses in the same instrument or from an incongruity or repugnancy between the words, and the apparent intention derived from the whole structure of the instrument or its avowed object. In such cases, interpretation bécomes indispensible." a

This learned commentator adopted the rules of interpretation laid down by Rutherford, which will be found in a preceding chapter, b as applicable to constitutional interpretation. We do not therefore propose to repeat them here. These, which he calls elementary explanations, he says, will aid in making a closer practical application when we arrive at more definite rules.

In construing the constitution of the United States, it must be remembered, that it is the fundamental law of the land ;—that it was ordained and established by the people of the nation for the purpose of instituting a national government to be invested with supreme authority to provide for their common defence ;—to promote their general welfare, and to secure to themselves and their posterity the blessings of civil liberty.

We are also to consider first, what is its nature, its objects, scope and design, as apparent from the structure of the instrument itself viewed as a whole, and also as viewed in its component parts.

Where its words are plain, clear and determinate, they require no interpretation, as a general rule. If in such case interpretation is ever admitted, it is only in some case of actual necessity to escape an absurd consequence, or to guard against some fatal evil. c

Where words admit of two senses, each of which is conformable to common usage, that sense is to be adopted, which, without departing from the literal import of the words, best harmonizes with the nature and objects, the scope and design of the instrument. Where the words are unambiguous, but the provisions may cover more or less ground according to the intention, which is yet subject to conjecture ; or, where it may include in its general terms more or less than might seem dictated by the general design, as that may be gathered from other parts of the instrument, there is much more room for controversy.

a Story on Constitution, § 401.   c Story on Constitution, § 404.
b Chapter 5.

It is regarded as appropriate for the courts, and, as a matter entitled to their most careful consideration, in giving construction to the constitution; to look back at the situation of the country at the time, and antecedent to the time of its adoption; to look at its then existing institutions, at the existence and operations of the then state governments, at the powers and workings of the old confederation, and at all other circumstances which had a tendency to produce or obstruct its formation and ratification; *a* and it is also held, that contemporary history and contemporary interpretation may be called in to aid in arriving at just conclusions. *b*

"The safest rule of interpretation, will be found to be, to look into the nature and object of the particular powers, duties and rights, with all the lights and aids of contemporary history, and to give to the words of each, just such operation and force consistent with their legitimate meaning, as may fairly secure, and attain the ends proposed. *c* It will indeed, probably be found, when we look into the character of the constitution itself, the objects which it seeks to obtain, the powers which it confers, the duties which it enjoins, and the rights which it secures, as well as the known historical fact that many of its provisions were matters of compromise of opposing interests and opinions, that no uniform rule of interpretation can be applied to it which may not allow, if it does not positively demand, many modifications in its actual application to particular clauses."

While these aids of contemporary history and construction may be resorted to to illustrate and confirm the text, to explain a doubtful phrase, or to expound an obscure clause, they must be resorted to with great reserve and much qualification. They cannot abrogate the text; they can never fritter away the obvious sense; they can never narrow down its true limitations; they can never enlarge its natural boundaries. *d* The private interpretation of any particular man, must manifestly be open to much objection. The constitution was adopted by the whole people; the whole of which, was submitted as it stood in the text to the whole people who are to be presumed to have adopted it upon a just examina-

a Story, § 405.			*b* Stuart v. Laird, 2 Cranch. 309.

c Bigg v. Commonwealth of Penn. 16 Pet. R. 610; Cohens v. Virginia, 6 Wheat. 418, per Marshall, Ch. J.			*d* Story on Constitution, §§ 406-407.

tion of its provisions.   Doubtless, in different states, different objections were raised, and different opinions may have prevailed as
a reason for its adoption ; and there is no certainty that different
states, or conventions, gave the same uniform interpretation to its
language ; or that the same reasoning prevailed with a majority
of any one state who supported and adopted it.   Therefore the
difficulty, not to say dangers, of attempting to resort to opinions
of those who either assisted in forming or adopting it.   Some may
have implied limitations and objects, which others would have
rejected, and the latter may have favored its ratification by implying entirely, limitations and powers, from the same language of
the text.

Some may have taken a cursory view of its enactments, and
others have studied them with profound attention ; some may have
been governed by a temporary interest or excitement, and have
acted upon that exposition which most favored their present views ;
others may have seen lurking beneath its text, what commended it
to their judgment against even present interests.   Some may have
interpreted its language strictly and closely, others from a different habit of thinking, have given to it a large and liberal meaning.
It is not to be presumed, that even the convention that framed
it, that every sentence and expression was always understood in
precisely the same sense.   Every member necessarily judged for
himself, and the judgment of no one could, or ought to be conclusive upon that of others.   Nothing but the text itself was adopted
by the people. *a*

The first general rule of interpretation laid down by Story, to
be drawn from the nature of the instrument, is, " It is to be construed as a *frame*, or *fundamental law* of government, established
by the *people* of the United States, according to their own free
pleasure and sovereign will.   In this respect it is in no wise distinguishable from the constitutions of the state governments.

Each of these are established by the people for their own purposes, and each is founded on their supreme authority.   The
powers which are conferred, the restrictions which are imposed, the
authorities which are exercised, the organization and distribution
thereof which are provided, are, in each case for the same object,

a Story on Const., § 406.

the common benefit of the governed, and not for the profit or dignity of the rulers." a

When it is said, that the constitution of the United States should be construed *strictly*, viewed as a social compact whenever it touches the rights of property, or of personal security, or liberty; he rule is equally applicable to the state constitutions in like cases. The principle upon which this interpretation rests, if it has any foundation, must be, that the people ought not to be presumed to yield up their rights of property or liberty beyond what is the clear sense of the language and the objects of the constitution.

All governments are founded upon a surrender of some natural rights; and they impose some restrictions. Therefore—in construing a constitution of government, framed by the *people* for their own benefit and protection, for the preservation of their rights, and property, and liberty, where the delegated powers are not, and cannot be used for the benefit of their rulers who are but their temporary servants and agents, but are intended solely for the benefit of the people, no presumption arises of an intention to use the words of the constitution in the most restricted sense. The *strict*, or most *extended* sense, being equally within the letter, may be fairly held to be within their intention, as either shall best promote the very objects of the people in the grant, and as either shall best promote or secure their rights, property or liberty. b

" The words, are not, indeed, to be stretched beyond their fair sense; but within that range, the rule of interpretation must be taken which best follows out the apparent intention." c This is the mode (it is believed), universally adopted in construing the state constitutions. It has its origin in common sense. And it can never be an object of just jealousy, because the rulers can have no permanent interest in a free government distinct from that of the people, of whom they are a part, and to whom they are responsible.

This view, is in no danger of producing a conflict between the ederal and the state governments, for if the powers of the general government are of paramount and supreme obligation; if they constitute the supreme law of the land; no conflict as to obedience can be found. Whenever the question arises, as to whom obedience is due, it is to be judicially settled; and being settled, it regulates at once, the rights and duties of all the citizens.

Thus adopting a uniform rule of interpretation for national and state constitutions, neither is to be construed alone, or without reference to the other. Each belongs to the same system of government; each is limited in its power; and within the scope of its powers, each is supreme. Each by the theory of our government is essential to the existence and due preservation of the powers and obligations of the other. The destruction of either would be equally calamitous, since it would involve the ruin of that beautiful fabric of balanced government which has been reared with so much care and wisdom, and in which the people have reposed their confidence, as the truest safeguard of their civil, religious and political liberties. a

In McCulloch v. Maryland, b Chief Justice Marshall said, "The government of the Union is emphatically a government of the people. In form and substance it emanates from them. Its powers are granted by them, and are to be exercised directly on them and for their benefit." "But the question respecting the extent of the powers, actually granted, is perpetually arising, and probably will continue to arise as long as our system shall exist." "In discussing these questions, the conflicting powers of the general and state governments must be brought into view, and the supremacy of their respective laws, when they are in opposition, must be settled." "If any one proposition could command the universal assent of mankind, we might expect it would be this—that the government of the Union, though limited in its powers, is supreme within its sphere of action. This would seem to result from its nature. It is the government of all; its powers are delegated by all; it represents all; and acts for all."

Judge Story, in Martin v. Hunter's Lessee, c says, "the constitution of the United States was ordained and established, not by the states in their sovereign capacities, but emphatically as its preamble declares, by the people of the United States. There can be no doubt that it was competent for the people to invest

---

a Story on Constitution, § 416, Federalist, No. 37.

b 4 Wheat. 404-5.   c 1 Wheat. 324.

the general government with all the powers which they might deem proper and necessary; to extend or restrain these powers according to their own good pleasure, and to give them a paramount and supreme authority. As little doubt can there be, that the people had the right to prohibit to the states the exercise of any powers which were in their judgment incompatible with the objects of the general compact; to make the power of the state governments, in given cases, subordinate to those of the nation, or to reserve to themselves those sovereign authorities which they might not choose to delegate to either. The constitution was not therefore necessarily carved out of the existing state sovereignties, nor a surrender of powers already existing in the state institutions, for the powers of the states depend upon their own constitutions; and the people of every state had the right to modify and restrain them according to their own views of policy or principle. On the other hand it is perfectly clear, that the sovereign powers vested in the state governments, by their respective constitutions, remained unaltered and unimpaired, except so far as they were granted to the government of the United States."

The government of the United States then, it is seen, is limited in its powers. It can exercise no power not conferred by the constitution, either in express terms, or by necessary implication. Like every other grant, this instrument is to have reasonable construction according to the import of its terms, and words are to be taken in their natural sense, not unreasonably restricted or enlarged.

The severest struggles, and most earnest controversies that have arisen, and which the courts have been called upon to settle, are such as have arisen between the advocates of the different theories of construction; between the two extremes; the advocates of a narrow and strict construction, and those of a more enlarged and liberal one. Each extreme perhaps equally dangerous and impracticable. Such as contend for the narrowest construction, that of confining the government to such powers as the express letter of its language imports, would cripple its powers and render it unequal to the objects for which it was instituted; the other extreme would by construction, so enlarge and extend the meaning of words beyond their natural and obvious import, as to destroy the force of the instrument, and destroy it as a protective charter for individual rights, individual security, and personal liberty.

Chief Justice Marshall doubtless laid down the true rule, when he said, a "this instrument contains an enumeration of powers expressly granted by the people to their government." "We know of no rule for construing the extent of such powers other than is given by the language of the instrument which confers them, taken in connection with the purposes for which they were conferred." In another case he said, b "the *intention* of the instrument must prevail; this intention must be collected from its words; and its words are to be understood in that sense in which they are generally used by those for whom the instrument was intended; its provisions are neither to be restricted into insignificance, nor extended to objects not comprehended in them, nor contemplated by its framers."

By reasonable interpretation, is meant, by way of illustration, that in a case where words are, by reason of the imperfection of human language, susceptible of two different senses, the one strict, the other more enlarged; that should be adopted which is most consonant with the apparent objects of the constitution; that which will give it efficacy, and force as a government, rather than that which will impair its operations and render it useless; so as on the one hand to avoid obvious mischief, and on the other hand to promote the public welfare. This for the reason, that this constitution, which was founded by the people for themselves and their posterity, and for objects of the most momentous nature; for the perpetual Union; for the establishment of justice; for the general welfare; and for the perpetuation of the blessings of liberty; requires that every interpretation of its powers should have a constant reference to these objects. c

That such were its objects appears from the language of the instrument itself; and we have the extrinsic evidence in the history and spirit of its adoption, which appears from the address of its framers to the people on submitting it for their approval. They said, "In all our deliberations, we kept steadily in view that which appears to us the greatest interest of every true American—the

a Gibbons v. Ogden. 9 Wheat. 1.   b Ogden v. Saunders, 12 Wheat. 332.
c Story on Const., § 422.

consolidation of our Union; in which is involved our prosperity, felicity, safety, perhaps, our national existence. The constitution which we now present, is the result of a spirit of amity, and of that mutual deference and concession which the peculiarity of our political situation renders indispensable." In this spirit it was adopted by the people.

It will be seen, as was remarked by Justice Story, a "that the constitution unavoidably deals in general language. It did not suit the purposes of the people, in framing this great charter of our liberties, to provide for minute specifications of its powers, or to declare the means by which those powers should be carried into execution. It was foreseen that this would be a perilous and difficult, if not impracticable task. The instrument was not intended merely for the exigencies of a few years, but was to endure through a long lapse of ages, the events of which were locked up in the inscrutable purposes of Providence. It could not be foreseen what new changes and modifications of power might be indispensable to effectuate the general objects of the charter, and restrictions and specifications which at the present might seem salutary, might in the end prove the overthrow of the system itself. Hence its powers are expressed in general terms, leaving to the legislature from time to time to adopt its own means to effectuate legitimate objects, and to mould and model the exercise of its powers, as its own wisdom and the public interests should require."

The wisdom of the framers of this constitution and this early exposition of its true spirit and meaning, was demonstrated in the necessities of the government in the time of the recent rebellion, in the enactment by congress, on the 25th of February, 1862, of an act entitled, "An act to authorize the issue of United States notes, and for the redemption or funding thereof, and for funding the floating debt of the United States." This act authorized the secretary of the treasury to issue on the credit of the United States one hundred and fifty millions of the United States notes, and declared that the same should be receivable in payment of all taxes, internal duties, excises, debts and demands against the United States of every kind whatsoever, except for interest upon bonds and notes which shall be paid in coin, and shall also be lawful

a Martin v. Hunter, 1 Wheat. 304.

money, and a legal tender in payment of all debts, public and private, within the United States, except duties on imports and interest, as aforesaid."

There is in the constitution no express grant of power to enact such a law. The two theories of construction, to which we have referred, were never brought to bear upon this great charter, with greater force of learning and power of argument at the bar or upon the bench, than upon the constitutional power of the national legislature to enact this statute. There was a crisis in the affairs of the national government. The very existence of the nation, it was believed, by those who claimed the existence of the power, depended upon this question of constitutional construction; and it may be, the fearful hazard of a different interpretation, may unwillingly have influenced, if it did not determine its decision, on the ground that such an interpretation was not only authorized by the implied powers contained in the instrument itself, but that an emergency had arisen which demanded the exercise of the power as indispensable to effectuate the great objects of the creation of the government itself. *

It is not within the scope of this work, and it is not therefore intended to argue as to the right of this question, or the effect of this statute, upon prospective or retrospective demands, but to present it, as one of the great national questions of this government, which depended entirely upon the interpretation of constitutional power. But it may be asserted here, that whenever the power has been judicially established, as an existing power, it is equally potent, if it exists by implication, as if granted in express terms.

Mr. Justice Story was of opinion, that every form of government unavoidably includes a grant of some discretionary powers, and that it would be wholly imbecile without them; that if they could be foreseen it would be impossible *ab ante* to provide for them. He says, "the means must be subject to perpetual modification and change; they must be adapted to the existing manners, habits, and institutions of society which are never stationary; to the pressure of dangers or necessities; to the ends in view; to general

* Since the preparation of this chapter it has been judicially settled by the highest federal court that the power to pass such an act existed under the implied powers of the constitution.

and permanent operations, as well as to fugitive and extraordinary emergencies." "In short, (he says) if the whole society is not to be revolutionized at every critical period, and remodeled in every generation, there must be left to those who administer the government; a very large mass of discretionary powers, capable of greater or less actual expansion, according to circumstances, and sufficiently flexible, not to involve the nation in utter destruction from the rigid limitations imposed upon it by an improvident jealousy." *a*

With great diffidence, and with all our veneration for this most learned and profound commentator, we protest that we are unable to see how this doctrine can be applied to a limited constitutional government, of different co-equal departments, in which, the people have constructed the charter containing positive restrictions applicable as well to the executive department of the government, as to each and every other department. If the learned commentator means, that laws will be required to be enacted from time to time to meet the suggested emergencies, and to be remoddled in each generation to conform them to the habits and manners and institutions of society, to the advance and progress of the age; to the march of intelligence; and the development of the arts and sciences, we concur. But he is writing upon constitutional interpretation. Who then is the *government*, under our American system, that should be entrusted with this *flexible and discretionary power* to do all these things? It seems to assume that there must exist a power to control, against the restrictions of the constitution, in certain emergencies, by those who administer the government. But we are taught by the constitution itself that those who administer this government are divided into three co-ordinate departments; each of these can only act within his own limited sphere, and they respectively, are the servants of the sovereign power, the people. There is no power above the people. There is no discretionary power, granted in the constitution, for either of these departments, nor for all of them united, to exercise a discretionary expansion and flexible power against its rigid limitations, even though such limitations were imposed by improvident jealousy. If abuse exist by reason of defects in the constitution,

a Story on Const., § 425.

present or prospective, the true source of authority, the people, have the power, and doubtless, the wisdom and patriotism to correct them; and this, in the American idea, is the safe and only depository.

In a chapter on constitutional interpretation, we have deemed it a duty to call attention to this view, of this distinguished author in this particular, in order to protest not only against the error, but also against what seems to be the better and sounder views of the same author, which are found contained in another part of the same work, to which we have largely given credit.

The other extreme of these theories, that of too enlarged a construction of constitutional power; of going beyond the fair scope of its terms, or necessary implications, is equally mischievous and dangerous. Restrictions may be regarded as inconvenient, and as interfering with favorite policies, but in this respect also, the remedy lies in the power of amendment, rather than by a hazardous extention of power by construction, which would be in effect, the making of a constitution, the people have not made. Such an act of construction by a court, would be a usurpation of functions, not committed to them. "The sound principle is to declare, *ita lex scripta est;* to follow and to obey." a "It should be, so far at least as human infirmity will allow, not dependent upon the prejudices and excitements growing out of particular policies, nor · upon the passions of parties of particular times, but the same yesterday, to day and forever." b

Another division of advocates is found upon constitutional construction, viz., such as claim to adhere to the strict letter, and such as claim that its spirit is to be regarded, as sometimes differing from its letter. But this, really, resolves itself into the same question, as that of strict and liberal interpretation. It is true, the spirit, is to be respected and taken as the sound construction, but the spirit is to be collected chiefly from the letter. No construction of a given power is to be allowed which plainly defeats or impairs its avowed objects. If words are found which are fairly susceptible of two interpretations according to their common sense and use, the one of which would defeat the objects for which the constitution was obviously made, and the other would

a Story on Constitution, § 426.   b Ibid.

OF CONSTITUTIONAL INTERPRETATION.

preserve and promote those objects, the latter would be held to be the true interpretation. Such a rule is the plainest dictate of common sense, as well as an established rule of construction. a

In the interpretation of what are called the implied powers of the constitution, all the ordinary and appropriate means to execute it, are deemed a part of the power itself. "This results from the very nature and design of a constitution. In giving the power, it does not intend to limit it to any one mode of exercising it, exclusive of all others. It must be obvious that the means of carrying into effect the objects of a power, may, nay, must be varied, in order to adapt themselves to the exigencies of the nation at different times." b

It was this view of interpretation of the implied powers of the constitution, that was adopted by the Court of Appeals of this state c in giving construction to the act of congress of February 25th 1862, called the legal tender act.

Chief Justice Marshall, whose views of constitutional interpretation are seldom doubted as to their soundness, has said, d "it may with great reason be contended that a government entrusted with such ample powers, on the due execution of which, the happiness and prosperity of the nation so vitally depends; must be entrusted with ample means for their execution. The power being given, it is the interest of the nation to facilitate its execution. It can never be their interest, and cannot be presumed to have been their intention, to clog and embarrass its execution by withholding the most appropriate means." "But the constitution itself does not profess to enumerate the means by which the powers it confers may be executed." "The government which has the right to do an act, and has imposed on it the duty of performing that act, must, according to the dictates of reason, be allowed to select the means." "But the constitution has not left the right of congress to employ the necessary means for the execution of the powers conferred on the government, to general reasoning." To its enumerated powers is added that of making, "all laws which shall be necessary and proper for carrying into execution

a Vattel, B. 2, Ch. 17, §§ 279-302.   b Story on Const., 430.
c Metropolitan Bank v. Vandyck, 27 N. Y. R. 400,
d McCulloch v. Maryland, 4 Wheat. 408-415.

the foregoing powers, and all other powers vested by this constitution in the government of the United States or in any department thereof."

"The subject, (which he was then considering) is the execution of those great powers on which the welfare of a nation especially depends. It must have been the *intention* of those who gave these powers, to insure, as far as human prudence could insure, their beneficial execution. This could not be done by confiding the choice of means to such narrow limits as not to leave it in the power of congress to adopt any which might be appropriate, and which were conducive to the end.   This provision is made in a constitution intended to endure for ages to come, and, consequently to be adopted to the *crisis* of human affairs.   To have prescribed the means by which the government should, in all future times, execute its powers, would have been to change, entirely, the character of the instrument, and give it the properties of a legal code.   It would have been an unwise attempt to provide by immutable rules, for exigencies which, if foreseen at all, must have been seen dimly ; and which can best be provided for as they occur.   To have declared that the best means shall not be used, but those alone without which the power given would be nugatory, would have been to deprive the legislature of the capacity to avail itself of experience, to exercise its reason—and to accommodate its legislation to circumstances.   If we apply this principle of construction to any of the powers of the government we shall find it so pernicious in its operation, that we shall be compelled to discard it."

.   Should there be any error committed by congress, in the enactment of laws that overstep the boundaries of power, there remains the judiciary whose province it is to declare it, and to afford the proper relief; and behind this remains the last resort of the correcting power, the people, who may redress all such excesses by the legitimate methods of exercising their authority.

Another question which affects the interpretation of certain portions of the federal constitution is, its connection, and possible conflict of powers with the several state constitutions, which in certain respects, and over certain subjects, possess exclusive jurisdiction, and over certain other subjects, possess concurrent jurisdiction, with the government of the United States. This involves some of the most delicate questions which grow out of our peculiar system of government. We do not here propose to review or discuss the almost endless cases that have been disposed of, in which these questions have been raised, nor has such a period of time elapsed, as to incline us to suppose that we approach as yet, the end of these controversies. A few general principles, may appropriately be referred to.

Justice Story in an opinion *a* given in the federal court has said, "The sovereignty of a state in the exercise of its legislation, is not to be impaired unless it be clear that it has transcended its legitimate authority, nor ought any power to be sought, much less to be adjudged, in favor of the United States, unless it be clearly within the reach of its constitutional charter." The constitution, of the United States containing a grant of powers, in many instances similar to those already existing in the state governments, and some of these being of vital importance also to state authority and state legislation; it is not to be admitted that a mere grant of such powers in affirmative terms to congress, does, *per se*, transfer an exclusive sovereignty on such subjects to the latter. On the contrary, a reasonable interpretation of that instrument necessarily leads to the conclusion, that the powers so granted are never exclusive of similar powers existing in the state, unless, where the constitution has expressly, in terms given, an exclusive power to congress, or the exercise of a like power is prohibited to the states, or there is a direct repugnancy, or incompatibility in the exercise of it by the states. "In all other cases not falling within the classes above mentioned, it seems unquestionable that the states; retain concurrent authority with congress, not only upon the letter and spirit of the eleventh amendment of the constitution, but upon the soundest principles of general reasoning. There is this reserve, however, that in cases of concurrent authority, where the laws of the states, and of the union are in direct and manifest collision on the same subject; those of the union, being "the supreme law of the land," are of paramount authority, and the state laws, so far, and so far only, as such incompatibility exists, must necessarily yield."

a Houston v. Moore, 5 Wheat. 48.

An attempt to illustrate these principles by the almost number-less cases to be found in the books of reports, would divert this work from a treatise, to a digest, which is not intended. A few instances will suffice. This subject it will be seen, affords an ample field for discussion, and is susceptible of being renewed and elaborated by the various changes and modifications which arise in practice. The system as a whole, is complex; it presents the rare, novel and difficult scheme of one general government whose action extends over the whole, but which still possesses only enu-merated powers; and also, now, of at least thirty-six different state governments, which retain and exercise many powers not delegated to the union. Of course contests respecting power must arise. a

"All experience shows that the same measures, or measures scarcely distinguishable from each other, may flow from distinct powers; but this does not prove that the powers themselves are identical. Although the means used in their execution may some-times approach each other so nearly as to be confounded, there are other situations in which they are sufficiently distinct to es-tablish their individuality." b

Thus, an *affirmative* power in congress to lay taxes, &c., is not necessarily incompatible with a like power in the states. Both may exist without interference; and if any interference should arise in a particular case, the question of supremacy would turn, not upon the nature of the power, but upon supremacy of right in the exercise of power in that case. Unless from the nature of the power, or from the obvious results of its operations, a repugnancy must exist, so as to lead to a necessary conclusion that the power was intended to be exclusive, the true rule of interpretation is, that the power is merely concurrent. It would seem that the convention which formed the federal constitution, thought, that concurrent jurisdiction was preferable to subordination; and it is evident that it has at least the merit, of reconciling an indefinite constitutional power of taxation in the federal government, with an adequate and independent power in the states to provide for their own necessities. c

The chances of conflict between the laws of the Union and

a Gibbons v. Ogden. 9 Wheat. 205.   b Id.

c Federalist No. 32, by Hamilton.

those of the states, was doubtless foreseen by the framers of the constitution, and its possibility, nay even its probability, wisely and expressly provided against in the declaration, that its laws, &c. "shall be the supreme law of the land;" so that if a state pass a law inconsistent with the constitution of the United States, it is a mere nullity. Even if a state pass a law clearly within its own apparent constitutional powers, if it conflict with the exercise of a power given to congress, to the extent of the interference, its operation is suspended; for, in a conflict of laws, the superior must govern, and it is the same, if the conflict be with a treaty. a

This is an axiom as well in law as in logic, that the controlling power cannot be controlled by its inferior or subordinate. So also of these propositions, 1st, That if power is given to create a thing, it implies a power to preserve it. Secondly, that a power to destroy, if wielded by a different hand, is hostile to and incompatible with the power to create and preserve. Thirdly, where this repugnancy exists, the authority which is supreme, must control, and not yield to that over which it is supreme; consequently the inferior power becomes a nullity. b

Another question naturally arises out of the exercise of a concurrent power, by both the federal and the state governments. In that case, does the actual legislation by congress, after legislation by the state on the same subject, supersede, or does it only suspend the operation of the state law over the same subject matter? It is believed that no answer can be given to this interrogatory which shall be of universal application. In a case in the federal court, c it was equally divided on this question. That was a case, where congress under the power to provide for "organizing, arming and disciplining the militia," had passed an act for that purpose, and afterwards the state of Pennsylvania passed an act upon the same subject. The state law was held not to be repugnant to the constitution and laws of the United States. Justice Washington delivering an able opinion to the contrary.

Another similar question arose under the power of congress to establish uniform laws on the subject of bankruptcies. Was this

a Gibbons v. Ogden, 9 Wheat, 210; Story on Constitution, § 439.
b McCulloch v. Maryland, 4 Wheat. 426.
c Houston v. Moore, 5 Wheat. 1.

OF CONSTITUTIONAL INTERPRETATION.

power exclusive, or concurrent with the states? a It was held, that the states have authority to pass bankrupt laws, provided such law does not impair the obligation of contracts, and provided there be no act of congress in force to establish a uniform system of bankruptcy conflicting with such law. And that whenever the terms in which a power is granted by the constitution to congress, or whenever the nature of the power itself requires that it should be exercised exclusively by congress, the subject is as completely taken away from the state legislatures as if they had been expressly forbidden to act on it. They also held, that the power granted to congress of establishing uniform laws on the subject of bankruptcies, is not of that description; and that the power of the states to pass bankrupt laws is not extinguished by the enactment of a uniform bankrupt law throughout the union by congress. It is only suspended so far as the two laws conflict.

This power of congress may be exercised or declined, as the wisdom of that body shall decide. It is not the existence of the power, but its exercise, which is incompatible with the exercise of the same power by the states. It seems, at this day, to be conceded, that the power of taxation given to congress, is not exclusive. So too, as to the power of congress to organize, discipline, and arm the militia, it is held is not exclusive; and is held not to be incompatible with the exercise of the like power by the states, and especially it is held, that the states possess this power in the absence of congressional legislation. It would then be indispensable to the defence and security of the states. b Again, congress have power to call forth the militia to execute the laws of the Union, to suppress insurrections, and repel invasions; and it is not incompatible that the states should possess the same power, for the same purposes, to call out their own militia. c

Upon this subject it will be found that the exceptions to, and modifications to general rules, become a subject too prolific and exhaustless, to be followed up in this work.

Justice Story, in his work on the constitution, has laid down a few general rules of interpretation of constitutional powers, d

a Sturgis v. Crowninshield, 4 Wheat. 192–196, &c.

b Houston v. Moore, 5 Wheat 50, 51, 52.

c Id.   d Story on Const., § 447.

which we cannot omit to transcribe, as deductions from what precedes them in his work:

"1st. Whenever the power given to the general government requires, that, to be efficacious and adequate to its end, it should be exclusive, there arises a just implication for deeming it exclusive. Whether exercised or not, in such case, it makes no difference.

"2d. Whenever the power in its own nature is not incompatible with a concurrent power in the states, either in its nature, or exercise, there the power belongs to the states.

"3d. But in such case, the concurrence of the power, may admit of restrictions or qualifications in its nature or exercise. In its nature, when it is capable from its general character of being applied to objects or purposes which would control, defeat or destroy the powers of the general government. In its exercise, when there arises a conflict in the actual laws and regulations made in pursuance of the power by the general and state governments. In the former case, there is a qualification engrafted upon the generality of the power excluding its application to such objects and purposes. In the latter, there is, (at least generally,) a qualification, not upon the power itself, but only upon its exercise, to the extent of the actual conflict in the operations of each.

"4th. In cases of implied limitations or prohibitions of power, it is not sufficient to show a possible, or potential inconvenience. There must be a plain incompatibility, a direct repugnancy, or an extreme practical inconvenience, leading irresistibly to the same conclusion.

"5th. If such incompatibility, repugnancy, or extreme inconvenience would result, it is no answer that in the actual exercise of power, each party may, if it chooses, avoid a positive interference with the other. The objection lies to the power itself, and not to the exercise of it. If it exist, it may be applied to extent of controlling, defeating or destroying the other. It can never be presumed that the framers of the constitution, declared to be supreme, could intend to put its powers at hazard, upon the good wishes, or good intentions or discretion of the states in the exercise of their acknowledged powers.

"6th. Where no such repugnancy, incompatibility, or extreme

85

inconvenience would result, then the power in the states is restrained, not in its nature, but in its operations; and then, only to
the extent of the actual interference.   In fact it is obvious, that
the same means may often be applied to carry into operation
different powers.   And a state may use the same means to effectuate an acknowledged power in itself, which congress may apply
for another purpose in the acknowledged exercise of a very different power.   Congress may make that a regulation of commerce,
which a state may employ as a guard for its internal policy, or to
preserve the public health or peace, or to promote its own peculiar interests.   These rules seem clearly deducible from the nature
of the instrument; and they are confirmed by the positive injunctions of the tenth amendment of the constitution."

Certain maxims and rules of construction adopted or discussed
by Judge Story, are deserving of consideration in this chapter,—
among which are, "that a specification of particulars in an instrument, is the exclusion of generals;" or in other words, "the expression of one thing, is the exclusion of another."   And Lord Bacon's
remark is cited with approbation, viz: "that as exception
strengthens the force of a law in cases not excepted; so enumeration weakens it, in cases not enumerated."   Safe as such maxims
are, as a general rule, it still requires skill to see that they are not
applied to the subversion of the intent and object of the instrument.   They are, in particular cases, susceptible of being so improperly applied, by the ingenious devices of legal advocates.
Thus, Judge Story says, a "it has been suggested, that an affirmative proposition in a particular case, excludes the existence of
the same thing in every other case; and a negative provision in a
particular case, admits the existence of the same thing in every
other case."   But these are not found in practice to be universal rules.   Chief Justice Marshall said, in a case b in the United
States Court, that these principles, though generally correct, are
too broad for universal rules.   It was claimed, that the constitution having provided for the trial by jury in criminal cases, there
was an implied exclusion of it in civil cases.   This rule could not
be allowed to apply in such case.   Judge Story says, c "One

a Story on Const., § 448.   c § 448, Supra.
b Cohens v. Virginia, 6 Wheat. 401, and Federalist, No. 83.

might with just as much propriety hold, that because congress has power to declare war," but no express power to make peace, that the latter is excluded; or, that because it is declared that no bill of attainder or *ex post facto* shall be passed by congress, therefore congress possess the power and right in all other cases, to pass laws. The true rule is, in order to ascertain how far our affirmative or negative provision, includes or implies others, that we must look to the nature of the provision, the subject matter, the objects, and the scope of the instrument. These, and these only, can properly determine the rule of construction. There can be no doubt that an affirmative grant of powers in many cases, will imply an exclusion of all others. As for instance, the constitution declares that the powers of congress shall extend to certain enumerated cases. This specification of particulars, evidently excludes all pretentions to a general legislative authority. Why? Because an affirmative grant of special powers would be absurd, as well as useless, if a general authority were intended. In relation then to such a subject as a constitution, the natural and obvious sense of its provisions, apart from any technical or artificial rules, is the true criterion of construction."

"Another rule of interpretation of the constitution suggested by the foregoing, is, that the natural import of a single clause, is not to be narrowed so as to exclude implied powers resulting from its character, simply because there is another clause which enumerates certain powers, which might otherwise be deemed implied powers within its scope; for in such cases, we are not, as a matter of course, to assume that the affirmative specification, excludes all other implications." *a*

We cannot do better in laying down rules that belong to verbal criticisms upon the interpretation of words employed in the constitution, than to adopt those laid down by Judge Story

"In the first place, then, every word employed in the constitution, is to be expounded in its plain, obvious, and common sense meaning, unless the context furnishes some ground to control, qualify or enlarge it. Constitutions are not designed for metaphysical or logical subtleties; for niceties of expression; for critical propriety; for elaborate shades of meaning; or for the exercise of

a Story on Const., § 449.

philosophical acuteness, or judicial research. They are instruments of a practical nature, founded on the common business of life, adopted to common wants, designed for common use, and fitted for common understandings. The people make them; the people adopt them; the people must be supposed to read them with the help of common sense; and cannot be presumed to admit in them, any recondite meaning, or any extraordinary gloss." a

"But in the next place, words, from the necessary imperfection of all human language, acquire different shades of meaning, each of which is equally appropriate, and equally legitimate; each of which recedes in a wider or narrower degree from the others, according to circumstances; and each of which, receives from its general use, some such indefiniteness and obscurity as to its exact boundary and extent. b We are, indeed, often driven to multiply commentaries, from the vagueness of words in themselves; and perhaps still more often, from the different manner in which different minds are accustomed to employ them. They expand or contract, not only from the conventional modifications introduced by the changes of society, but also from the more loose, or more exact uses to which men of different talents, acquirements, and tastes, from choice, or necessity, apply them. No person can fail to remark the gradual deflections in meaning of words, from one age to another; and so constantly is this process going on, that the daily language of life in one generation, sometimes requires the aid of a glossary in another. It has been justly remarked, that no language is so copious, as to supply words and phrases for every complex idea; or so correct, as not to include many equivocally denoting different ideas. Hence it must happen, that however accurately objects may be discriminated in themselves, and however accurately the discrimination may be considered, the definition of them may be rendered inaccurate, by the inaccuracy of the terms in which it is delivered. We must resort then to the context, and shape the particular meaning, so as to make it fit that of the connecting words, and agree with the subject matter." c

"In the next place, where technical words are used, the technical meaning is to be applied to them, unless it is repelled by the con-

a Story on Const. § 451.   c Story on Const., § 452.
b Vattel, B., 2 Ch. 17, §§ 262, 299.

text. But the same word often possesses a technical, and also a
common sense meaning. In such a case, the latter is to be preferred, unless some attendant circumstance points clearly to the
former. No one would doubt, where the constitution has declared
"that the privilege of the writ of *habeas corpus* shall not be suspended unless under peculiar circumstances, that it referred, not
to every sort of writ which has acquired that name ; but to that,
which has been emphatically so called, on account of its remedial
power to free a party from arbitrary imprisonment. *a* So again,
where it declares that in suits *at common law*, &c., the right of trial
by jury shall be preserved, though the phrase *common law* admits
of different meanings, no one can doubt, that it is used in a technical sense. When, again, it declares that congress shall have
power to provide a navy, we readily comprehend, that authority
is given to construct, prepare, or in any other manner to obtain a
navy. But when congress is further authorized to provide for
calling forth the militia, we perceive at once, that the word "*provide*," is used in a somewhat different sense." *b*

" And this leads us to remark in the next place, that it is by no
means a correct rule of interpretation, to construe the same word
in the same sense wherever it occurs in the same instrument. It
does not follow, either logically or grammatically, that because a
word is found in one connection in the constitution, with a definite
sense, therefore the same sense is to be adopted in every other
connection in which it occurs. *c* This would be to suppose, that
the framers weighed only the force of single words, as philologists
or critics, and not the whole clauses and objects, as statesmen
and practical reasoners. And yet nothing has been more common,
than to subject the constitution to this narrow and mischievous
criticism. Men of ingenious and subtle minds, who seek for sym-
metry and harmony in language, having formed in the constitution
a word used in some sense which falls in their favorite theory of
interpreting it, have made that the standard, by which to measure
its use in every other part of the instrument. They have thus
stretched it, as it were, on the bed of Procrustes, lopping off its
meaning when it seemed too large for their purposes, and extend-

a Ex Parte, Bolman, 4 Cranch. 100.   *c* Vattel, B. 2, Ch. 17, § 281.
b Story on Const., § 453.

ing it when it seemed too short. They have thus distorted it to the most unnatural shapes, and crippled, where they have sought only to adjust its proportions according to their own opinions.

It was very justly observed by Mr. Chief Justice Marshall in the case of Cherokee Nation v. Georgia, *a* that "it has been said, that the same words have not necessarily the same meaning attached to them, when found in different parts of the same instrument. Their meaning is controlled by the context. This is undoubtedly true. In common language, the same word has different and various meanings, and the peculiar sense, in which it is used in any sentence, is to be determined by the context. A very easy example of this sort will be found in the use of the word " establish," which is found in various places in the constitution. Thus, in the preamble ; one object of the constitution is avowed to be " to establish justice ;" which seems here to mean, to settle firmly, to fix unalterably, or rather, perhaps, as justice, abstractedly considered, must be considered as forever fixed and unalterable,—to dispense or administer justice. Again, the constitution declares, that congress shall have power, " to establish a uniform rule of naturalization, and uniform laws on the subject of bankruptcies," where it is manifestly used as equivalent to *make or reform*, and not *to fix or settle*, unalterably and forever. Again, " congress shall have power to establish post-offices and post-roads," where the appropriate sense would seem to be, " to create," to found, and to regulate ; not so much with a view to permanence of form, as to convenience of action. Again, it is declared, " that congress shall make no law respecting an establishment of religion ;" which seems to prohibit any law, which shall recognize, found, confirm, or patronize any particular religion, or form of religion ; whether permanent or temporary ; whether already existing, or to arise in future. In this clause, " establishment," seems equivalent in meaning to settlement, recognition, or support. And again, in the preamble, it is said, " We the people, &c., do ordain and establish this constitution, &c.," where the most appropriate sense seems to be to create, to ratify and confirm. So the word "*state*" will be found used in the constitution, in all the various senses to which we have before alluded. It sometimes means, the separate sections of territory occupied by the political societies within each; sometimes the particular governments established by these societies; sometimes these societies as organized into these particular governments; and lastly, sometimes the people composing these political societies in their highest sovereign capacity.

"But the most important rule in cases of this nature, is, that a constitution of government does not, and cannot from its nature, depend in any great degree upon mere verbal criticism, or upon the import of single words. Such criticism may not be wholly without use; it may sometimes illustrate, or unfold the appropriate sense; but unless it stands well with the context, and subject matter, it must yield to the latter. While then, we may well resort to the meaning of single words to assist our enquiries, we should never forget, that it is an instrument of government we are to construe; and, as has already been stated, that must be the truest exposition, which best harmonizes with its design, its objects, and its general structure." a

The remark of Mr. Burke, may, with a very slight change of phrase, be addressed as an admonition to all those, who are called upon to frame, or interpret a constitution. "Government, is a practical thing, made for the happiness of mankind, and not to furnish out a spectacle of uniformity to gratify the schemes of visionary politicians. The business of those who are called to administer it, is to rule, and not to wrangle. It would be a poor compensation, that one had triumphed in a dispute, while we had lost an empire; that we had frittered down a power, and at the same time had destroyed the republic."

a Vattel, B. 2, Ch. 17, §§ 285-286.

INDEX.

86

F

G

H

I

J

JUDICIAL power, when necessary, for what purpose exercised, **65, 66.**
    department, its value and protection, 65, 66, 67.
JUDICIARY, their functions and value, duties, 65, 66, 67.
    power to declare statutes void, 65–67.
    their duty to do so, when, 365–368.
JURISPRUDENCE, history of, English, French, American, 296–330.
    how developed, 298·
    and legislation, distinction between, 299.
    power of, 317–319.
JURISDICTION, between national and state governments, boundary line, &c., **361.**
    over parties, how obtained, 480–489.
    how in divorce cases, 481–483.
JURY trial, 469, 470.
    what cases are excepted from this right, 470, 471.

K

KING of England, his authority in making laws, 39, 40.
            his name in caption of statutes, **41.**

L

LAW, its origin and necessity, 34.
    the result of society, 35.
    the act of government, 35.
    its supremacy, 35.
    statute, what, its definition, 35.
            void, if it conflict with the constitution, **46.**
            respect due to it, 37.
            its definition, 37.
            its elements, 38.
    municipal, its origin, 36.
            includes statute law, 37.
    human, why imperfect, 36.
            cannot abrogate the Divine, 37.
            is composed of two elements, 38.
            its effect upon a nation, 38.
    common, what it is, 42, 43.
            Enghlish, adopted by the colonies, 43.
                    adopted by New York constitutions, **43.**
    of domicile and of contrast, 97, 98.
    who has power to make it, in civilized governments, 330–334.
    different theories as to source of power, 330–334.
    American theory, 330–334.

www.ingramcontent.com/pod-product-compliance
Lightning Source LLC
Chambersburg PA
CBHW020446270326
41926CB00008B/503